Quantitative Decision Making

Quantitative Decision Making

Guisseppi A. Forgionne
Bucknell University

Wadsworth Publishing Company
Belmont, California
A Division of Wadsworth, Inc.

Economics Editor: Stephanie Surfus
Editorial Assistant: Holly Allen
Production Editor: Sandra Craig
Print Buyer: Ruth Cole
Cover and Interior Designer: Andrew H. Ogus
Cover Illustrator: Philip Li
Copy Editor: Janet Greenblatt
Technical Illustrator: Art by Ayxa
Compositor: Composition House Limited

The symbol used on the cover and part and chapter opening pages was adapted from Peter S. Stevens, *Handbook of Regular Patterns: An Introduction to Symmetry in Two Dimensions*, copyright 1981 by Peter S. Stevens, published by The MIT Press. Used by permission.

Printed in the United States of America

1 2 3 4 5 6 7 8 9 10---90 89 88 87 86

ISBN 0-534-05364-5

Library of Congress Cataloging in Publication Data
Forgionne, Guisseppi A., 1945–
   Quantitative decision making.
   Includes bibliographies and index.
   1. Management science. I. Title.
HD30.23.F69   1986   658.4′03   85-13920

To my mother, Mary, and to Jesus

Contents

Chapter 11   Network Topics   538

Preface

This book gives an introductory survey of management science/operations research. The text provides complete coverage of today's major quantitative models and shows how they are applied to managerial problems in public and private organizations. Much effort has been spent in making each topic interesting and easy to read. The purpose is to provide the user with a sound conceptual understanding of the role of quantitative analysis in the decision-making process.

FOCUS The focus is on the practical and applied. The text explains how to formulate decision problems, how to solve them with an appropriate quantitative analysis, and how to apply the recommended solution. However, there is an emphasis on concepts rather than mechanical manipulation. Hence, a significant part of the discussion is devoted to problem formulation, technique assumptions, potentials, limitations, and interpretation of the results of the analysis from the perspective of the decision maker.

There is a simplified, logical presentation of quantitative tools with extensive use of examples, graphs, tables, and other illustrative devices. Furthermore, each chapter has technique summaries incorporated at appropriate points within the discussion. In addition, the discussion highlights the connection between management science/operations research and computer information systems. Appropriate batch and interactive computer programs are identified. Computer data and models are presented, solution procedures are discussed, and the results are interpreted. There are also end-of-chapter glossaries for easy reference.

Quantitative decision making, like athletics and music, is best learned by doing. Beginners can facilitate their understanding by practicing the concepts in the types of situations actually encountered by decision makers. Therefore, there is an abundance of realistic examples that are scaled-down versions of problems encountered in public and private organizations. Each chapter contains several examples in the body of the text and numerous exercises and a case at the end.

End-of-chapter exercises are divided into thought exercises (extension of basic concepts), technique exercises (practice of procedures), and applications exercises (selection of concepts and techniques, and development of solution). Each chapter concludes with a modified version of an actual private- or public-sector case. Cases require an integration and extension of text concepts, quantitative analysis, formulation of a decision recommendation, and presentation of results in a form understandable to management.

Mathematics is kept at an accessible level for the beginning user of quantitative decision making. The only prerequisites are college algebra, elementary probability, and basic statistics. Other relevant mathematics is developed as needed. The orientation should put the material within reach of a junior, senior, or beginning MBA student.

ORGANIZATION

The book is organized in a way that leads to a coherent treatment of the subject. First, major topics are divided into modules, or parts. Part I provides the foundations. It defines the nature of management science, discusses its role in the decision-making process, and identifies the steps necessary for successful implementation. The second part presents a general decision-making framework and shows how strategies can be formed in various decision environments. Part III addresses linear and other mathematical (integer, goal, heuristic, and nonlinear) programming problems and methods. The next part provides a comprehensive review of general network flow problems, including transportation, transshipment, assignment, minimal spanning trees, cycles and routes, maximal flows, and PERT/CPM. Part V considers some standard situations involving sequential decisions, queuing, and inventory problems. Simulation is the topic of the final module.

Although each module after Part I is essentially independent, the modules are arranged in a logical progression. Part II deals mainly with decisions made in an uncertain or risky environment. The mathematical programming module, Part III, extends the analysis to constrained optimization problems that involve primarily certain circumstances. In Part IV, the mathematical programming concepts are applied to network flow problems. Part V considers some standard analytical models that build on the concepts developed in preceding modules. In many cases, available analytical models are of little value because of the complex or unstructured nature of the problem. The final module presents an approach designed for these situations.

Each module, or part, is also designed to eliminate the effect of variability in student capabilities and motivation. Starting at the simplest level, there is a gradual development of ideas and applications. Eventually, the student progresses to near the state of the art in the field. Similar independent modularity is provided within the chapters. Each chapter starts with elementary concepts, progresses through increasingly complex material, and ends with the most advanced topics.

With this arrangement, students can be assigned a continuous sequence of pages within a module. Then, when the level within the module exceeds the course objectives, students can be directed to another part of the book. In this way, the instructor can easily control the level for any particular topic. Furthermore, by directing the sequence of modules, the instructor can readily satisfy different course plans. These features provide the topical flexibility necessary for matching content with course objectives and student profiles.

The selection of topics reflects the introductory nature of the text. The book emphasizes the most popular quantitative approaches used today by public and private organizations. Unfortunately, some techniques, like nonlinear programming, require a preparatory background in management science/operations research. In these instances, the topic is merely identified and illustrated, and text notations and a bibliography refer the user to appropriate advanced treatments. However, the book provides the essential, relevant material covered in almost all one-semester/two-quarter introductory survey courses in quantitative decision making.

SUPPLEMENTARY MATERIAL The Instructor's Manual contains fully worked-out solutions, hints in selecting problems for student assignments, and a bank of potential examination problems complete with solutions. The hints include a brief description of the problems, an assessment of their level of difficulty, and the relationships between the concepts and problems. In addition, the Manual provides sample course outlines and chapter-by-chapter ideas for presenting the material.

ACKNOWLEDGMENTS I wish to thank the staff of Wadsworth Publishing Company for their helpful suggestions. In particular, Jon Thompson and Stephanie Surfus, my acquisition editors, did an excellent job. I also appreciated the work of the designer, Andrew H. Ogus, and the production editor, Sandra Craig. I would like to express my appreciation to my colleagues, students, and family, who have contributed greatly to the project. Also, I am indebted to the administration of California State Polytechnic University, Pomona, for their support, especially Gerry White and the rest of the staff of the School of Business Administration Steno Pool. Pamela Scroggs, a student assistant, deserves special commendation for her help in assembling the final draft of the manuscript. Finally, I'd like to thank the reviewers of the manuscript: Bruce Bowerman, Miami University of Ohio; Harrison S. Carter, Georgia Southern College; Lawrence Ettkin, University of Tennessee at Chattanooga; John A. Lawrence, California State University at Fullerton; Michael Middleton, University of San Francisco; Alan Neebe, University of North Carolina at Chapel Hill; Paul Rackow, Fordham University; Harold J. Schleef, University of Oregon; Michael Sklar, University of Georgia; Willbann Terpenning, University of Notre Dame; Frederick P. Williams, North Texas State University.

Guisseppi A. Forgionne

Quantitative Decision Making

Part I
Foundations

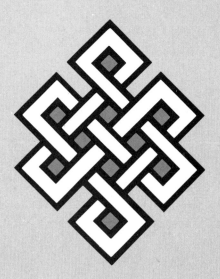

Part I will provide you with the necessary foundations to effectively comprehend and successfully utilize the concepts of quantitative decision making.

Chapter 1 is an introduction. It begins with a historical perspective, then outlines the characteristics of the approach, and concludes with a discussion of the areas of application. After reading this chapter, you should understand the nature, purpose, and relevance of the discipline.

In chapter 2, you will learn about the management science process and its role in modern decision making. This chapter presents the steps involved in quantitative decision making and model construction and analysis, as well as the role of management information and decision support systems. It concludes with a discussion of implementation problems and strategies.

Chapter 1
Introduction

CHAPTER OUTLINE

- ◆ Evolution of Quantitative Decision Making
  Origins
  Early Development
  Maturity
- ◆ Characteristics
  Focus on Problems
  Systems Approach
  Scientific Method
  Team Approach
  Mathematics and Computers
- ◆ Applications
- ◆ **Case:** The Cookbook Conspiracy

CONCEPTS

- ◆ The nature of management science/ operations research
- ◆ Stages of historical development of management science/operations research
- ◆ Characteristics of management science/ operations research
- ◆ Areas of application
- ◆ The future of quantitative decision making

APPLICATIONS

- ◆ Forecasting military battles
- ◆ Inventory management
- ◆ Advertising media selection
- ◆ Deploying fire-fighting equipment
- ◆ Vehicle routing
- ◆ Profit planning
- ◆ Fleet management
- ◆ Fuel management
- ◆ Tar sands mining
- ◆ Managing a sales force

Contemporary organizations exist in a dynamic world of increased population, rapid social and political change, energy shortages, inflation, and economic stagnation. Hence, the resulting decision problems are more challenging, significant, and complex than ever before. In this environment, today's manager can make proper decisions only by using systematic, rational approaches based on information and scientific analysis. Such methods are referred to as **management science**. Depending on the focus of the academician or practitioner, the discipline may also be called operations research, decision science, or systems analysis, among other names. Since successful implementation generally relies on numerical information, we prefer the alternative title of quantitative decision making.

The past three decades have seen a steady—and, at times, spectacular —growth in the development and application of quantitative approaches to decision making. As a result, there has been a continually increasing demand on managers to participate in the design of, provide data for, and use the output from these methods. Of particular significance has been the phenomenal impact of the electronic computer on the traditional tasks of management. Our first section traces this historical development.

EVOLUTION OF QUANTITATIVE DECISION MAKING

Prior to the twentieth century, enterprises functioned in a relatively simple, stable, and predictable environment. As a result, managers were able to make effective decisions based on intuition or by repeating procedures successfully used by other executives. Such approaches often did not attack the problem in a systematic manner and did little to improve or advance the managerial decision process.

Nevertheless, we can find some early examples of systematic approaches to decision making. In the fifteenth century, for example, Venetian shipbuilders used an assembly line of sorts in outfitting their vessels. And based on his analysis of straight pin manufacturing, Adam Smith suggested a division of labor in 1776. In 1832, Charles Babbage presented a number of concepts of industrial engineering, including a skill differential in wages. However, a true progressive movement did not originate until the late nineteenth century.

ORIGINS   In the late 1800s, an American engineer named Frederick Taylor formally advocated a scientific approach to the problems of manufacturing. According to Taylor, there was one "best" or most efficient way to accomplish a given task. He used time studies to analyze work methods, establish standards, and evaluate worker performance. A contemporary, Henry L. Gantt, extended these concepts by including human behavioral factors. He also espoused the importance of the personnel department to the scientific approach to management. Perhaps Gantt's greatest contribution, however, was his scheduling system for loading jobs on machines. Basically a recording device that showed work planned and completed over time, Gantt's chart minimized job completion delays by permitting machine loadings to be scheduled months in advance.

These early scientific approaches were limited mainly to establishing or improving efficient performances for specific tasks in the lower levels of organizations. In the early twentieth century, however, several pioneers applied a number of mathematical techniques to a variety of problems at various organizational levels. Table 1.1 gives a summary of these ap-

Table 1.1 Early Scientific Approaches to Management

Date	Originator	Method	Application
1914	F. W. Lanchester	Mathematical equation	Forecasting outcomes of military battles
1915	F. W. Harris	Lot size formula	Economic order quantity for inventory control
1917	A. K. Erlang	Queuing theory	Prediction of waiting time for callers using an automatic telephone exchange
1924	W. Shewhart	Theory of probability and statistical inference	Production quality control charts
1927–28	H. Dodge and H. Romig	Theory of probability and statistical inference	Production sampling inspection
1930s	H. C. Levinson	Mathematical expressions	Study of marketing relationships

proaches. Still, despite such advances in the scientific approach to management, quantitative decision making did not emerge as a field until World War II.

EARLY DEVELOPMENT World War II created unprecedented problems in resource allocation, production planning and scheduling, inventory and quality control, transportation and logistics, and other areas. No one was experienced in dealing with these new, unique, and enormously complex problems. Thus, decision makers did not have much success by repeating previously used procedures. Also, the problems were much too important to justify solution by the haphazard approaches of intuition and guesswork. Leaders recognized the need for an innovative approach based on analytical reasoning. Therefore, teams of physical scientists, engineers, mathematicians, and military leaders were formed to study these problems and recommend solutions. They were called operations analysis or operations research groups, and their multidisciplinary, or team, approach became a characteristic of such studies.

Mathematics is the language of the scientific disciplines. Thus, it was natural for operations research groups to formulate the problems mathematically. In addition, the advent of computer technology provided the means to analyze certain mathematical formulations of the operational problems.

After World War II, many of the former participants in military operations research applied the same concepts to related industrial problems. However, few universities had formal academic programs in operations research. The few professionals in the field usually had backgrounds in engineering, mathematics, or the physical sciences. Professional societies were formed in the late 1940s and early 1950s, and their journals communicated the latest developments in the field.

Industrial applications spread in the 1950s when computer technology was developed further and made commercially available. However, the technology was not sufficient to handle large-scale, sophisticated mathematical models. Hence, operations research focused on the development of techniques to solve practical, well-defined, well-structured, small-scale operational problems.

Formal academic programs in operations research/management science became well established in the 1960s, and trained graduates eventually attained managerial positions. These people made their organizations aware of the innovative methods of the new discipline, which in turn encouraged further development of the field.

Academic growth encouraged a focus of interest and research on the tools and techniques of operations research/management science. New solution techniques were developed and others refined. Advances in computer technology provided the means to solve the more sophisticated mathematical models. In addition, "canned" computer programs were developed for various standard techniques, and the advent of computer-based management information systems helped supply some of the data required by the procedures.

Unfortunately, some researchers forgot that the original motivation for developing the field was to aid the process of decision making. Application and implementation received little emphasis in the 1960s, and this neglect created certain difficulties. According to W. J. Duncan [3] and J. H. Huysmans [7], the most serious problems involved behavioral and monetary factors. Many managers with limited technical background and experience did not fully understand the nature of and potential benefits from management science. Yet, operations research analysts frequently did not have enough organizational training, patience, or diplomatic skill to effectively explain, interpret, and justify their methods and recommendations. In other cases, managers perceived the new procedures as a threat to their job security and decision-making power. Also, managers were skeptical about the ability of management scientists to deliver timely and profitable results. When attempting to "sell" the quantitative disciplines, most analysts did not consider these political and monetary factors, nor the personalities of the managers. In addition, decision makers accused management scientists of being more interested in finding a problem that fit the techniques than in starting with a managerial problem and deciding how best to analyze it. Predictably, some organizations had unsuccessful initial experiences with the field. However, professionals gained a more realistic view of the potentials and limitations of operations research/management science.

MATURITY The field matured in the 1970s. Operations research/management science again concentrated on providing assistance to decision makers. New techniques were developed, but there was also an emphasis on solving managerial problems. M. Radnor and R. Neal [11] discovered that implementation problems still persisted in the 1970s but were less severe than in the sixties. Furthermore, G. N. Powell [10] found that there was more interest in strategies for implementing decision science concepts within the organizational framework.

Advances in computer-based management information systems also enhanced implementation by providing better data for the management science techniques. Concurrently, the development of time-sharing computer systems made it possible for decision makers to interact directly with the quantitative formulations. In addition, **SHARE**, a library of computer programs for management science, was developed and made available commercially on a national basis at a nominal cost to users. Such systems made the power of large-scale computers available to small organizations at a reasonable price. These factors promoted a rapid expansion in the range of quantitative decision-making applications.

CHARACTERISTICS

Management science has evolved into a unique approach to decision making, encompassing the following characteristics:

1. A primary focus on managerial problems
2. The examination of the decision situation from a broad, overall perspective
3. The application of the scientific approach to decision making
4. The use of methods and knowledge from several disciplines
5. A reliance on formal mathematical techniques
6. A dependence on a high-speed electronic computer

FOCUS ON PROBLEMS

Frequently, managers are faced with extremely complex problems that do not have obvious solutions. Some situations involve problems for which the decision maker has no past experience. In addition, the problem may have very significant financial and organizational impacts. Consequently, management may want to conduct a thorough analysis before attempting a decision. Also, there are repetitive problems that, once formulated and standardized, do not require the manager's continuous attention.

Under these circumstances, the decision maker may recognize the need for some assistance in formulating and analyzing the problem. A management scientist could be asked to study the problem, develop appropriate quantitative techniques, and recommend a solution. This primary focus on managerial problems is a central theme in operations research/management science.

SYSTEMS APPROACH

We should recognize that the organization is a collection of interrelated parts (divisions, departments, machinery, people, and so on) intended to accomplish specific objectives. As such, it constitutes a **system**. Furthermore, a decision made in one part of the organization may significantly affect the operations of other segments. An inventory problem within a firm's production department, for example, may disrupt marketing, finance, accounting, and personnel functions. Therefore, when possible, the problem should be examined from the overall organizational point of view. Such a viewpoint is called the **systems approach**. This systems perspective is a key characteristic of management science/operations research.

It is also important to realize that the organization itself is merely a component of the environment in which it operates. The firm's actions may affect market, social, and political conditions. Similarly, actions by unions, consumers, competing firms, and government can affect the firm's operations. Incorporating these environmental factors into the analysis, where applicable, should be part of the systems approach.

SCIENTIFIC METHOD Another fundamental characteristic of management science/operations research is its scientific approach to decision making. This approach, which involves the process shown in Figure 1.1, is also known as the **scientific method**.

In this method, the analyst first examines the decision situation. Suppose, for instance, that the marketing manager of a consumer goods firm has noticed a significant decrease in the sale of its major soap product. This observation suggests the existence of a problem. Based on the examination, the decision maker must now define the precise nature of the problem. In the soap illustration, suppose further observation indicates that the firm's price has recently been raised much higher than that charged by competitors. The marketing executive believes that the problem is to determine a new price policy that will increase sales. The decision maker must now propose a hypothesis, or tentative explanation, for the observed phenomenon. The hypothesis may also represent a tentative solution to the problem. Sales of similar products, for example, may suggest that soap demand varies inversely with the "competitive price ratio." That is, as the firm's relative (to competitors) price increases, soap sales decrease. Based on these data, the marketing manager may hypothesize that a price decrease will lead to more sales.

Experiments are designed and performed to test whether the hypothesis accurately describes the situation. For instance, the marketing manager can try a range of lower prices in selected markets for a trial period and then observe the effect on soap sales. Observations of the resulting sales will either confirm or disprove the initial hypothesis. In addition, the verification process can be used to refine the initial hypothesis or develop alternative explanations. Hence, the soap executive may identify a precise price reduction policy on the basis of the test market results. Valid hypotheses can help predict the future behavior of the system and implement appropriate decision recommendations.

Unfortunately, organizations operate in a constantly changing, complex environment. Furthermore, many of the relevant factors are beyond the firm's control. In the soap illustration, for example, there is no guarantee that competitors' actions will be stable in the test market during the trial period. Also, the test markets may not be truly representative of the general consuming public. Consequently, complete verification is not

Figure 1.1 Scientific Method

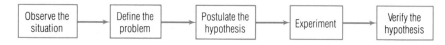

always possible. However, that does not preclude the use of a scientific approach to decision making. It simply means that there is usually some degree of uncertainty about the final results. In general, the manager can be far more confident in a scientific decision than in one based on hunches and guesses.

TEAM APPROACH Many managerial problems have behavioral, social, political, economic, statistical, mathematical, physical, biological, engineering, and business aspects. By assembling a group with a variety of backgrounds, managers often can obtain innovative approaches to problems. The scientific minds from each discipline extract the essential elements of the situation and then relate the structure to similar problems encountered in their own fields. After drawing such analogies, the researcher may determine whether the problem can be solved with methods traditionally successful in his or her field. When scientists from several disciplines collectively follow this process, the pool of possible approaches is large enough to reinforce the individual disciplines. As a result, management science/operations research is frequently characterized by this **team, or multidisciplinary, approach**.

However, some problems are simple enough to be handled by a single qualified researcher, especially one with multidisciplinary training. Also, relevant information about other disciplines can often be retrieved quickly, easily, and at nominal cost. In that case, a person with minimal training in several fields may be able to employ (and benefit from) a team approach.

MATHEMATICS AND COMPUTERS Mathematics is the language of science. In addition, it is often the most useful way to express the complex interrelationships involved in many managerial problems. Where applicable, mathematical analysis is usually less expensive, less cumbersome, quicker, and more flexible than other methods. Consequently, most management science/operations research projects rely on at least some formal mathematical techniques.

Even when the analyst uses sophisticated mathematical techniques, the search for and evaluation of alternative solutions may involve a gigantic computational effort. In such circumstances, it may take a lifetime to solve the problem with a manual, or hand, calculator. On the other hand, computers provide a relatively inexpensive means for rapid calculation. These high-speed electronic devices also possess the accuracy and flexibility needed to experiment with and solve complex managerial problem formulations. Thus, the use of computers has been closely associated with management science/operations research.

As the availability of computers increases and data-processing and manipulation costs decrease, there will be even more use of this equipment in management science. Indeed, the development of management science closely parallels the advance in computer technology.

APPLICATIONS Currently, management science/operations research is an international discipline with professional societies in North America, Europe, and Asia. Table 1.2 lists the major societies and their principal publications. At least ten other journals, including *Interfaces*, the *Journal of Operational Research*, and the *European Journal of Operational Research*, publish articles dealing with management science/operations research. Also, there are thousands of teachers, researchers, and practitioners throughout the world.

Table 1.2 Major Professional Societies

Society	Founded	Journal
Operational Research Society of the United Kingdom	1948	*Operational Research Quarterly*
Operations Research Society of America (ORSA)	1952	*Operations Research*
The Institute of Management Science (TIMS)	1953	*Management Science*
The American Institute for Decision Sciences (AIDS)	1969	*Decision Sciences*

Most large firms, many smaller companies, and various government agencies practice some form of quantitative decision making or consult management scientists. Table 1.3 gives a partial list of the applications. Furthermore, studies by N. Gaither [4], W. Ledbetter and J. Cox [8], and E. Turban [14] report increases in the breadth and depth of management science activities. Most organizations receive substantial benefits from these applications, as Table 1.4 illustrates.

As you can see from Tables 1.3 and 1.4, management science has been applied by a wide range of organizations to a wide range of problems.

Table 1.3 Applications of Quantitative Decision Making*

Private Institutions	Public Institutions
Finance	Health
Capital budgeting	Ambulance depot location
Corporate financial planning	Diet planning
Dividend policy determination	Evaluation of health care delivery
Equipment replacement analysis	systems
Portfolio management	Hospital staffing
Marketing	Inventory control of human blood
Advertising media selection	Military
Analysis of packaging effectiveness	Missile allocation for national defense
Assessment of competitive marketing	Reliability analysis of military equipment
strategies	Search and rescue effort
Assignment of sales personnel	War games simulation
Location of distribution facilities	Weapon systems analysis
Marketing budget mix determination	Social and Environmental
Sales forecasting	Courtroom scheduling
Production	Deploying fire fighting and police
Allocation of production resources	facilities
Inventory control	Educational planning and scheduling
Maintenance policy formulation	Highway and air traffic control
Plant layout analysis	Mass transit systems analysis
Production planning and scheduling	Political redistricting analysis
Product quality control	Public utilities regulation
Others	Refuse collection scheduling and routing
Airline scheduling and routing	Urban planning
Agricultural feedmix planning and	Water and air pollution control
control	Others
Auditing policy formulation	Forecasting general economic conditions
Professional sports draft selection	Queuing analysis of toll facilities
analysis	Regional and international economic
Telephone circuit switching policies	development
Utilization of banking facilities	Reliability analysis of space vehicles

* Private-sector applications are taken from D. A. Aaker [1] and recent issues of *Interfaces*. E. J. Beltrami [2], W. Helly [6], C. K. McKenna [9], L. J. Schuman et al. [12], and recent issues of *Interfaces* discuss public-sector applications.

Included are regional, national, and international enterprises of all sizes in both private and public sectors. There have been applications to general management, the functional areas of production, finance, marketing, and logistics, and the staff areas of accounting, personnel, and auxiliary services. Benefits typically have been in the magnitude of several million dollars.

Table 1.4 Benefits from Management Science*

Company	Application	Benefits
Public Sector		
British Airways	Profit planning and analysis	Increased profits by more than $25 million per year.
DuPage County, Illinois	Land use planning	Reduced use of "high-cost" acreage by 50%.
New York City	Deploying fire-fighting companies	Maintained safe level of service with six fewer fire companies for a cost savings of $5 million per year.
U.S. Postal Service	Vehicle routing	Reduced travel time per truck by 2 hours per day and distance traveled by 25%.
Private Sector		
Booth Fisheries	Materials management	Reduced inventories by 55%, transport costs by 9%, and production expenses by 8%; increased order fill rate by 8%.
Cahill May Roberts	Facilities and resource planning	Reduced delivery costs by 23% and transportation expenses by 20%.
Cerro de Pasco	Production planning	Increased profits by several million dollars.
Flying Tiger Line	Flight crew scheduling	Saved $300,000 per year.
Getty Oil Company	Financial planning and analysis	Increased earnings by several million dollars.
Hertz Rent-a-Car	Fleet management	Increased productivity by 10%.
National Airlines	Fuel management	Saved millions of dollars.
RCA	Establishing a satellite communication system	Established least-cost state-of-the-art system.
Scott Paper Company	Resource allocation	Increased productivity by two million cases per year.
Syncrude of Canada Ltd.	Tar sands mining	Established least-cost state-of-the-art mining system.
Union Carbide	Distribution planning	Saved several million dollars.
United Airlines	Sales force management	Increased sales productivity by 8%.
Whirlpool Corporation	Distribution management	Saved several million dollars per year.

* Public-sector illustrations are taken from recent issues of *Interfaces*. A. M. Geoffrion and R. F. Powers [5] and recent issues of *Interfaces* report the private-sector applications.

Regardless of the organization or position, then, there is a strong possibility that a decision maker will be involved with management science. For this reason, private and public organizations are more attracted to current or prospective employees with training in quantitative decision making. Universities are responding by offering degrees in the field and requiring courses in the subject for most professional academic programs.

Future organizations will exist in a world even more complex and dynamic than today's. Decision makers will need to rely further on rational means for developing and justifying various courses of action. Consequently, management science will be more widely practiced in all types of institutions. In particular, we can expect a continuation of the recent trend toward public applications, especially in nonprofit organizations such as museums, theater companies, and private foundations. According to H. Simon [13] and others, management scientists also will develop new approaches to ill-defined, ill-structured, complex problems. These new approaches will include the psychological aspect of the human decision-making process, a science of data measurement and collection, and interactive computer systems. The purpose of these new tools will be to enhance the intuitive powers of managers.

SUMMARY This chapter has been an introduction to quantitative decision making. The subject originated with the scientific approach to management in the late 1800s. It grew into a recognized discipline between 1940 and 1970 and matured into a significant aid to public and private decision makers during the 1970s.

Depending on the focus of the practitioner or academician, the discipline is also called management science, operations research, decision science, and systems analysis. It is characterized by a managerial problem orientation, a systems and team approach, the application of the scientific method, and a reliance on mathematics and the computer.

Quantitative decision making has become an international discipline with thousands of teachers, researchers, and practitioners. The concepts have been successfully applied by a wide range of private- and public-sector organizations to a broad scope of problems. As the world becomes even more complex and dynamic, the need for management science approaches will be even greater.

Glossary *management science* All systematic and rational approaches to decision making that are based on information and scientific analysis.

scientific method The process of observing the situation, defining the problem, postulating a hypothesis, experimenting, and verifying the hypothesis.

SHARE A library of computer programs for management science commercially available on a national basis at a nominal cost to users.

system A collection of inter-related parts intended to accomplish specific objectives.

systems approach Method of examining a problem from a systems perspective.

team, or multidisciplinary, approach Approach in which a group of people from several disciplines analyzes a problem.

References

1. Aaker, D. A. "Management Science in Marketing: The State of the Art." *Interfaces* (August 1973):17.

2. Beltrami, E. J. *Models for Public Systems Analysis.* New York: Academic Press, 1977.

3. Duncan, W. J. "The Researcher and the Manager: A Comparative View of the Need for Mutual Understanding." *Management Science* (April 1974):1157.

4. Gaither, N. "The Adoption of Operations Research Techniques by Manufacturing Organizations." *Decision Sciences* (October 1975):797.

5. Geoffrion, A. M., and R. F. Powers. *Management Support Systems.* Western Management Science Institute Working Paper No. 287, UCLA, March 1979.

6. Helly, W. *Urban Systems Models.* New York: Academic Press, 1975.

7. Huysmans, J. H. *The Implementation of Operations Research.* New York: Wiley, 1970.

8. Ledbetter, W., and J. Cox. "Are OR Techniques Being Used?" *Industrial Engineering* (September 1977):19.

9. McKenna, C. K. *Quantitative Methods for Public Decision Making.* New York: McGraw-Hill, 1980.

10. Powell, G. N. "Implementation of OR/MS in Government and Industry: A Behavioral Science Perspective." *Interfaces* (August 1976):83.

11. Radnor, M., and R. Neal. "The Progress of Management Science Activities in Large U.S. Industrial Corporations." *Operations Research* (March–April 1973):427.

12. Schuman, L. J., et al. "The Role of Operations Research in Regional Health Planning." *Operations Research* (March–April 1974):234.

13. Simon, H. *The New Science of Management Decisions.* Rev. ed. Englewood Cliffs, N.J.: Prentice-Hall, 1977.

14. Turban, E. "A Sample Survey of Operations Research Activities at the Corporate Level." *Operations Research* (May–June 1972):708.

Thought Exercises

1. It has been said that quantitative decision making originated in the early systematic and scientific approaches to decision making. What elements of these approaches are characteristic of management science/operations research? How did the early scientific approaches to decision making differ from management science?

2. Do you think that an operations research discipline would have emerged in the 1940s if there had not been a world war? Explain.

3. Why did the early development of management science/operations research take as long as twenty years? What were the crucial factors leading to a maturity in the discipline?

4. For each of the following situations, identify whether management science can be used to assist the manager in formulating and analyzing the problem. Explain.
   a. Marketing a new product
   b. Making a plant location decision
   c. Establishing an inventory control policy
   d. Engaging in nuclear warfare

5. Identify the appropriate system in each of the following decision situations. Explain.
   a. Buying a new house
   b. Installing pollution control equipment
   c. Manufacturing cement
   d. Regulating electricity rates

6. Briefly discuss how the scientific method can be applied to each of the following problems:
   a. Establishing railway schedules
   b. Introducing a new educational program
   c. Establishing a government budget
   d. Growing oranges

7. Identify whether a team approach is desirable in each of the following situations. Explain.
   a. A merger decision
   b. A student project
   c. Writing a sports article
   d. Developing advertising strategy

8. Explain why you agree or disagree with each of the following statements:
   a. Scientific management is the same thing as management science.
   b. Management science will eventually replace the manager.
   c. Some problems can be solved by intuition, hunches, and guesses.
   d. Management science consists of a group of techniques in search of problems.

Technique Exercises

1. Go to your library and compile a list of sources on management science, operations research, decision science, systems analysis, and quantitative decision making. Using these sources, obtain a definition for each of these terms. How do the definitions differ? How are they similar? Use this information to develop a consensus definition.

2. Compile a list of journals from your library that publish articles on management science/operations research.

3. Some of the applications in Table 1.3 are taken from recent issues of *Interfaces*. Using the volumes of this journal in your library, compile a list of references that deal with these applications.

4. Some of the illustrations in Table 1.4 are taken from recent issues of *Interfaces*. Using the volumes of this journal in your library, compile a list of references that deal with these illustrations.

5. Use the management science/operations research journals to compile a list of the most recent applications in the following areas:
   a. Health care administration
   b. Banking
   c. Government
   d. Education
   e. Retail and wholesale companies
   f. Hotel, travel, and restaurant management

6. Use the management science/operations research journals to compile a list of the most recent applications in your area of interest.

7. The text mentions the studies by Gaither, Ledbetter and Cox, and Turban. Using these studies, report the managerial problem areas in which management science has been most frequently used.

Applications Exercises

1. The production manager for Eronoco Enterprises, Inc., is concerned about the quality of the company's plastic containers. Recently, Eronoco has received many consumer complaints about the product's durability. The manager wants to design and develop a new quality control program to alleviate the problem. Eronoco's general manager, however, first wants a preliminary study that will identify the overall impact of such a program. The study should identify the relevant objective, affected departments, and appropriate market influences. Assume that you are the production manager and prepare the report.

2. The Federal Drug Administration (FDA) has been commissioned to certify whether the latest cold remedy, Cold Gone, is fit for use by the general public. Suppose you were put in charge of this project. Describe how you would scientifically conduct Cold Gone's certification process.

3. Jalestown University's athletic department has been given a grant to develop an Olympic training program for gymnasts. The program will include nutrition, physical and psychological development, gymnastic exercises, and social behavior. O. M. Swell, the university's athletic director, will administer the program. Who should Director Swell include on the training staff? Explain.

4. Howard Humphrey is chief commissioner on the state's Public Utility Board (PUB). Recently, a major natural gas company serving the southeastern portion of the state has petitioned for a rate hike to offset its latest cost increases. The company claims that the hike is necessary to maintain the "fair" return on investment previously granted by the PUB. Describe how Humphrey could employ a scientific, multidisciplinary, systems approach to make the rate decision.

CASE: The Cookbook Conspiracy

There was once a kingdom called Usalium, a peaceful, contented place. The functioning of Usalium was highly dependent on the efficient operation of its kitchens, because gastric delights were of prime importance to the populace. All was well for many years. The School of Chefs was staffed by a competent group of gastric scientists skilled in the preparation of proper diet, in pleasurable menus, and in the principles and methodology of basic constructs of gastric delight. The school always produced skilled chefs who were immediately equipped to apply their knowledge in the kitchens of Usalium. Graduate chefs were able to adopt the methodology of the School of Chefs to please the specific tastes of even the most fastidious Usalii.

But alas, even kingdoms change. The Usalii began to multiply. Alien recipes were brought home by Usalium's foreign merchants and armed forces. The Usalii's interest slowly shifted to specific recipes, and the king decreed that the School of Cookery be established to meet this demand.

The School of Cookery began to flourish, and cookery pervaded the entire kingdom. The School of Cookery offered such delightful curricula as the principles of baked beans, the placement of knives and forks, the preparation of french fries, and other gastric delights imported from various foreign Schools of Cookery. Cookbooks soon proliferated throughout Usalium, containing recipes of unimaginable variety and peculiarity. In time, the School of Chefs was phased out, and eventually nearly all the chefs disappeared. Usalii thought that the techniques and specific details of various recipes were more important than the ideas and methodological foundations of these gastric pleasures. It was a gourmet's delight! Soon, the

entire curriculum of the School of Cookery was aimed at "how to do it" recipes. The cooks of the kingdom thought they were too sophisticated to be concerned with the curriculum of the old School of Chefs.

But things were not going well in the kingdom. Stomach irritation became prevalent, the populace began to develop various forms of peculiar maladies, and, most important, the king frequently had indigestion. The maladies caused a slowing of the operations of the kingdom, and there were enormous inefficiencies in its main activities. Because of bulging midriffs, basking in the sunshine was no longer a favorite occupation, hospital time was interfering with work activities (such as sowing wild oats and basket weaving), and the king's armies were no longer able to function effectively (overweight horses, men, and the like). Even the king's efficiency expert (the queen) was beginning to show the signs of excess.

What's more, young cooks graduating from the School of Cookery were failing to adjust to the real-life kitchens of Usalium. It seems that the recipes that they had learned were not always applicable to the specific gastric pleasures of their various placements. Also, the young cooks were unaware of the whys and wherefores of the recipes, nor did they understand the principles and methodologies of gastric delight. Reference to the many cookbooks in the kingdom did not seem to help, for these books contained more specific recipes.

The queen took action. As efficiency expert, she demanded a formal investigation of the problem. The king responded in the usual way: He had the chief cook of the School of Cookery guillotined. However, nothing seemed to work. New chief cooks were appointed, but all seemed to fail. Meanwhile, the kingdom was on the verge of collapse.

Just when things looked worst, there was some encouraging news from Calpolot, a remote province of Usalium. It seems that Calpolot had none of the maladies of Usalium. The prince (under threat of the guillotine) was commissioned to examine the situation and isolate the source of gastric contentment. And here is what the prince discovered: One of the few remaining graduates from the old School of Chefs had moved to Calpolot. Therefore, the cookery revolution had not materialized there. Instead, the principles of the School of Chefs were still being practiced.

The king immediately summoned the retired chef of Calpolot to save Usalium. The chef was able to restore the curriculum of the old School of Chefs, the School of Cookery was disbanded, the cooks were sent back to school for retraining, cookbooks were outlawed, and the chef was made a wizard in arms. Amazingly, the kingdom gradually returned to its former peaceful, contented state. In the end, Usalium became, once again, a happy place.

1. What moral does the fable have for businesses? For business schools? For students?

2. Do you see any analogy between the cookbook approach depicted in the fable and developments in the academic phase in the history of decision sciences? Explain.

3. There are other analogies in the fable. Explain those relating to each of the following:
   a. The maturation phase in the history of decision sciences
   b. The implementation problem in decision sciences
   c. The potential applications of decision sciences
   d. The role of quantitative analysis in the decision-making process

Chapter 2
The Management Science Process

CHAPTER OUTLINE

- ◆ Quantitative Formulation
  Defining the Problem
  Formulating a Quantitative Model
  Types of Models
  Mathematical Models
  Gathering Relevant Quantitative Data

- ◆ Analysis and Solution
  MIS Process
  Preparing Summary Reports
  Processing Inquiries
  Solving the Quantitative Model
  Decision Support Systems

- ◆ Implementation
  Barriers to Implementation
  Implementation Strategies

- ◆ **Case**: Jane Allen's Career Choice

CONCEPTS

- ◆ The nature of decision making

- ◆ The role of quantitative methods

- ◆ The steps involved in quantitative analysis

- ◆ Model construction and analysis

- ◆ Management information systems

- ◆ Decision support systems

- ◆ Implementation problems and strategies

APPLICATIONS

- ◆ Food purchasing

- ◆ A typing service

- ◆ Production planning

- ◆ Commuting

- ◆ Advertising

- ◆ Career selection

Everyone makes decisions. People choose their friends, entertainment, work, food, clothes, home, car, life-style, and other personal matters. Consumers select brands of merchandise, the stores they will shop, and their method of payment. Political organizations and politicians identify the groups they will represent, funding techniques, and campaign strategies. Doctors, lawyers, teachers, and other professionals choose their area of expertise, clientele, and schedules. Managers formulate plans and strategies, establish an organization, hire employees, allocate resources, and control activities.

Some decisions, such as buying toothpaste, are relatively simple and insignificant. Others, like building a factory or engaging in war, are complex and very important. Yet all involve the same basic process.

This chapter examines decision making and the role of quantitative analysis in this process. First we will discuss the essential elements in defining the problem and show how to develop a quantitative formulation. Then we will examine the methods for gathering, processing, and analyzing relevant data, as well as review the most popular solution techniques. We will conclude with a discussion of implementation problems and strategies.

QUANTITATIVE FORMULATION

Although most people do not stop to think about it, decision making involves the basic process shown in Figure 2.1. The decision maker observes a real situation and becomes dissatisfied with its current state. He or she recognizes a problem and identifies alternative courses of action. Qualitative and quantitative information is gathered and used to evaluate the alternatives. Next, the decision maker selects the alternative that is most preferable in terms of his or her evaluation criteria. Then the decision maker implements the choice. Example 2.1 illustrates a routine decision.

Jack's relatively simple problem is to decide which brand of salt to buy. Brand prices are quantitative facts, while brand quality is qualitative information.

Figure 2.1 Decision-Making Process

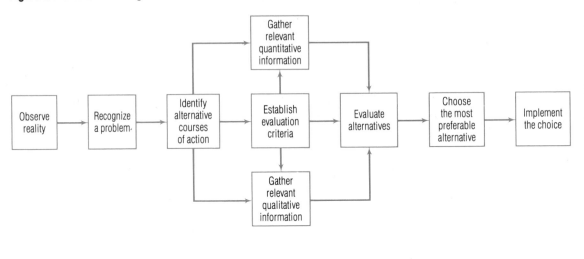

EXAMPLE 2.1 Food Purchasing

Jack Johnson needs salt. Four brands are available: Min at 18 cents, Sed at 15 cents, Tug at 16 cents, and Doe at 17 cents per package. All brands are available at the store closest to Jack's home.

Jack is interested in home economics, and his knowledge and experience indicate that all brands are similar in quality. Thus, he typically buys the lowest-cost salt.

Managers in public and private organizations go through the same decision-making process. However, their decisions are usually more complex. The problem is more significant in scope and impact, and alternatives are more numerous and often difficult to define. Qualitative knowledge may be available, but it is more difficult to obtain reliable, relevant quantitative information. There are many evaluation criteria, which are often difficult to measure. Evaluation of alternatives is usually more sophisticated than a simple numerical comparison of outcomes. Also, the decision maker must act as an agent of change if he or she hopes to implement the selected alternative in the organization.

Judgment is required at all stages of this decision-making process. Management science/operations research aids such judgment by providing relevant quantitative information. However, to effectively utilize the information, the decision maker must have some knowledge about the quantitative analysis process. Since it is unlikely that he or she will ever have to formulate and solve sophisticated mathematical expressions,

Figure 2.2 Management Science Process

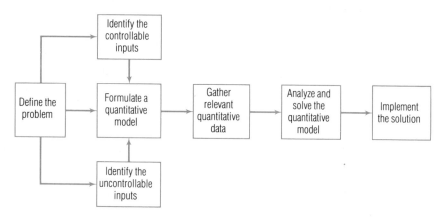

professional expertise is not necessary. On the other hand, the manager should be able to recognize situations in which management science may be appropriate. In addition, the manager should have some skill in formulating problems and selecting relevant techniques. To be confident about implementing the results, management must also understand the assumptions, limitations, and benefits from the analysis.

In short, quantitative decision making is not a substitute for competent management. Rather, it is a methodology that can significantly improve the executive's ability to make effective decisions. To see how, let us examine the management science process shown in Figure 2.2.

DEFINING THE PROBLEM Quantitative decision making is problem oriented, so the first step is to define the managerial problem clearly and concisely. The goal should be specified and relevant restrictions identified. Since this step affects the outcome of the entire process, it is extremely important and deserves careful consideration. Many operations research studies fail simply because the problem is poorly defined.

The problem must be stated precisely to be suitable for analysis. We start with a broad, or general, description and refine to a specific, well-defined statement. For example, an organization may translate the broad problem of declining production into a specific objective of maximizing output subject to an available resource constraint.

Many people should be involved in defining the problem. Top management can provide input on the nature of the problem, overall objectives and constraints, policies, and guidelines. Middle and first-line managers have firsthand knowledge about their operations and the corresponding constraints. Specialists in computer programming, accounting, personnel services, and other areas can offer their own unique insights. In addition, all these groups or individuals may eventually be affected by the project. By encouraging their active participation, the decision scientist will have a better chance of gaining support and acceptance of the project.

The problem may also have an impact on several parts of the organization and be significantly influenced by the environment in which the firm operates. Consequently, the systems approach should be used to define the problem.

FORMULATING A QUANTITATIVE MODEL

A **model** is a simplified representation of a real object or situation. The representation includes only essential, relevant features. For example, a scale model railroad is a physical replica of the general appearance and operating characteristics of the real thing. However, the model excludes some important elements of a real railroad, such as personnel, that are usually irrelevant to most railway modelers.

Building and studying a model facilitate our understanding of the real situation or object. Hobbyists, for instance, can gain an insight into railroading by constructing, operating, and maintaining a scale model. Railway officials might use a similar procedure to more fully comprehend the implications of organizational objectives, policies, constraints, and operating assumptions. Much as a physical scientist uses a laboratory, the decision analyst can use the model to perform experiments and test hypotheses. Hence, railway officials may use a model railroad to study various real operating problems and experiment with prospective decisions. Such decisions may involve train length, schedule, route, types of cargo, equipment, and facilities. An analysis of the model then enables the decision maker to draw conclusions about the real object or situation.

Experimenting with models is generally less expensive, less time-consuming, and less risky than experimenting with the real thing. Certainly, a model railroad is quicker and less expensive to build and study than a real railroad. In addition, a bad decision that causes the model railroad to operate inefficiently might then be avoided in the real situation.

However, we should realize that a model is not an exact representation. Many assumptions and simplifications are embodied in the model, often without ever being made explicit. Hence, the validity of the conclusions and decisions will depend on how accurately the model represents the real situation. For instance, the more closely the model railroad represents the real railroad, the more accurate will be the predictions and conclusions about railway operations.

Management and operating personnel are the people most closely involved with the decision situation. Thus, they are in the best position to determine whether the assumptions are good approximations of reality. Indeed, wise managers will probe for these assumptions and question their validity and reasonableness. Also, management and operating personnel can provide the information necessary for constructing an accurate model. Consequently, these individuals should be encouraged to participate actively in the model-building process.

When formulating a model, we also must consider data and solution requirements. Although it is important to develop an accurate representation of the real situation, implementation should be the primary concern. A model will be of limited practical use unless the decision maker is able to gather relevant data and identify a solution to the problem.

Remember, a model is an abstraction of reality and, as such, cannot capture all aspects of the problem. In fact, if decision makers attempt to incorporate all elements, they may have a model too large and complex to implement. It would be better to formulate a simpler and more easily understood model that *can* be implemented.

Of course, the model's usefulness can be severely limited if the simplifications produce a grossly distorted representation of the problem's important and relevant characteristics. Such distortions could (and should) be avoided by encouraging management and operating personnel to participate in the model-building process.

TYPES OF MODELS

Models can be presented in various forms. A physical replica, such as the scale model railroad, is called an **iconic model**. Other examples include toys, photographs, aircraft and space vehicle training simulators, mannequins, and scale models of production plant and retail store interior layouts.

Other situations or objects deal with more abstract concepts like speed, temperature, time, space, processes, and ideas. These concepts are usually represented with **analog models**, which are in a physical form but do not look like the real thing. Figure 2.1 is an analog model of the decision-making process. In this diagram, boxes, lines, and arrows represent our chain of thoughts in reaching a decision. A mercury thermometer is an analog model representing temperature. The position of the mercury in the thermometer represents the degree of heat. Other examples include an automobile speedometer, a watch, an oil dipstick, blueprints, maps, sales charts, organizational charts, and tables and graphs.

Some situations are so complex that they cannot be represented physically. Or a physical representation may be too cumbersome, time-consuming, or expensive to construct and manipulate. **Mathematical models** are typically used for these circumstances. Such models represent

Figure 2.3 Structure of a Mathematical Model

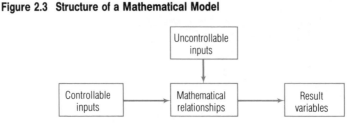

the real situation with a system of symbols and mathematical expressions. As P. Rivett [9] demonstrates, the approach forces the model builder to explicitly state his or her assumptions about the important elements and cause-and-effect relationships of the real situation. Mathematical models also facilitate scientific experimentation and analysis. Such representations are an essential part of any quantitative approach to decision making. Since this text deals primarily with mathematical models, let us look more closely at the structure of these representations.

MATHEMATICAL MODELS All mathematical models have the general structure illustrated in Figure 2.3. When initially considering a problem, the analyst specifies one or more measures that will be used to evaluate the performance or effectiveness of the system. Such measures are called **result variables**. Examples include profit, rate of return, cost, market share, and customer satisfaction.

Inputs are the other elements of a mathematical model. **Controllable inputs**, or **decision variables**, are the factors that influence the model's outcome and are controlled or determined by the decision maker. That is, the decision maker can change and manipulate these variables at will. Examples might include the level of output, the number of sales personnel assigned to a territory, and the timing of investment. **Uncontrollable inputs,** or **environmental variables**, are factors that must be considered but are beyond the decision maker's control. Interest rates, building codes, tax regulations, and import prices are possible illustrations. However, it is important to recognize that an uncontrollable input in one circumstance may be a controllable input in another, and vice versa. For example, available capacity may be limited today and hence uncontrollable. Yet, in time, a firm could build additional facilities and effectively make capacity a decision variable.

Result, decision, and environmental variables are tied together by sets of mathematical expressions. The expressions include a statement of the objective and possibly one or more restrictions or limitations. Example 2.2 illustrates.

EXAMPLE 2.2 A Typing Service

Leslie Jackson is a college student who earns money typing letters and manuscripts in her spare time. She has a given amount of spare time available in a given period, and each page of a project utilizes a specified amount of that time. Leslie earns a given profit per page. There is practically an unlimited demand for her work. Leslie wants to earn as much money as possible.

Since Leslie wants to earn as much money as possible, her objective is to maximize profit. Total earnings are determined by multiplying the profit per page times the number of pages. By letting

P = total profit

p = profit per page

and

Q = quantity of pages

Leslie's objective can be stated as follows:

(2.1)   maximize $P = pQ$

This type of mathematical expression, which describes the goal of the problem, is called an **objective function**.

Total profit is restricted by Leslie's available time. The demand for her work will equal the time utilized per page multiplied by the quantity of pages. This demand must not exceed her available time. Letting

t = the time utilized per page

and

T = Leslie's available time per period

the relationship can be described with the following mathematical expression:

(2.2) $tQ \leq T$

The symbol $\leq$ indicates that the total time required (tQ) must be less than or equal to the available time T. This type of expression is referred to as a **constraint**. Another restriction is that Leslie cannot type a negative number of pages. That is,

(2.3) $Q \geq 0$

which states that the quantity of pages must be greater than or equal to zero.

Figure 2.4 Structure of Leslie's Model

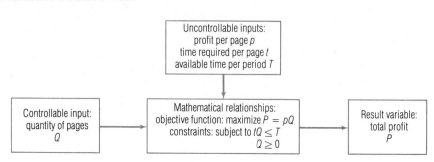

Leslie's problem is to determine the quantity of pages Q that will maximize her profit P per period from the typing service. Also, the recommended quantity must not require more than her available time. Expressions (2.1)–(2.3), or

maximize $P = pQ$

subject to $tQ \leq T$

$Q \geq 0$

provide a complete mathematical model for her problem.

In this model, the quantity of pages Q is Leslie Jackson's only controllable input. Profit p per unit, the time t required per page, and the available time T per period are all uncontrollable inputs. Cost of materials and equipment and the demand for typing might influence profit per page, but Leslie has little, if any, control over these factors. Similarly, academic and social activities are factors that make available time and time required per page uncontrollable. The only result variable or measure of performance is total profit P. Consequently, the structure of Leslie's mathematical model would appear as in Figure 2.4.

Depending on the information available, the values of the uncontrollable inputs may be exactly known or uncertain and subject to variation. For example, Leslie may know her exact schedule in the coming week and the precise form of the manuscripts to be typed. Based on this information, she may be able to forecast the values of p, t, and T with certainty. In this case, Leslie knows the exact values of the uncontrollable inputs, and her model is said to be **deterministic**. On the other hand, unforeseen examinations, dates, and other activities may create uncertainty about her available time for typing in the coming month. Depending on the nature of these activities, T could be any one of several values in a given range. In this situation, the value of an uncontrollable input is uncertain and subject to variation, and Leslie's model is said to be **stochastic**. In fact, profit p and the time t required per page may also be uncertain. Then there may be several alternative stochastic models.

GATHERING RELEVANT QUANTITATIVE DATA

Models require data on the values of the uncontrollable inputs. Since we cannot perform a thorough analysis or recommend a solution without this information, data collection is a critical part of the management science process. Leslie Jackson, for example, must know the values of unit profit (p), typing time per page (t), and available time (T) before she can determine the most profitable quantity of work.

In Leslie's case, the necessary information might be available from her experience, records on past jobs, published social and academic schedules, and recorded commitments. Organizations could gather data from past accounting, sales, financial, inventory, production, and engineering records and reports. Published documents, such as research studies and government statistical summaries, are other sources. Managers and operating personnel can provide information about markets, financial conditions, productivity, and other factors that are unavailable elsewhere.

ANALYSIS AND SOLUTION

In most cases, there is a tremendous volume of data available, and a considerable amount of time is required to collect and organize this information. Furthermore, the data are usually not in a form suitable for decision-making purposes. More effort, then, is necessary for processing and analyzing the data. As a result, many organizations have designed and implemented formal systems for collecting, analyzing, and reporting relevant and timely information. Such a structure is referred to as a **management information system (MIS)**.

MIS PROCESS

The essential role of an MIS is to transform available data into information that is useful for decision making. This transformation involves the general process shown in Figure 2.5.

First, the data must be collected from the available sources. In simple cases, like Leslie Jackson's typing problem, the data may simply be recorded in accounting ledgers or other report journals. On the other hand, most organizations have a very large volume of factual information available. Hence, they usually store the data in a computer. As J. A. Senn [10] demonstrates, the data may be recorded initially on punched cards or tapes and then electronically transmitted to the computer. Alternatively, the data may be fed by telephone or cable directly to the computer from a console or other electronic transmitting device.

Figure 2.5 MIS Process

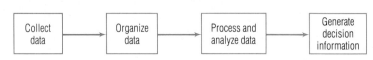

Once collected, the data are organized into general files, subfiles, and components. For example, Leslie Jackson may have a work file that gives complete information on all past and current typing jobs. A subfile might contain all data related to a specific job, with the components consisting of the customer name, mailing address, telephone number, type of manuscript, date submitted, and so on. Organizations may have several files. There may be a sales file consisting of all sales records. A subfile might contain information relevant to a specific sale, and components might include the product type, purchase price, and salesperson. Similarly, a personnel file would consist of all employee records. A subfile might contain data on a single employee and include the person's name, mailing address, and social security number as components. Other typical data files reflect production and inventory status, accounts receivable and payable, purchases, financial transactions, and customer service records. The collection of these organized files is called a **data base**.

Raw data from the data base is processed, analyzed, and transformed into information useful for decision-making purposes. The bulk of work in all management information systems is routine, primarily involving the definition of new files and processing of transactions through existing files. Leslie Jackson's work file, for instance, must be updated each time she accepts a new job or progresses on a current one. Similarly, an organization will update its inventory status file whenever a new product is manufactured or existing items are sold. These routine tasks are necessary to maintain an accurate data base. As T. Dock and others [3] demonstrate, however, all management information systems do not have the same data processing and analysis capabilities. Furthermore, each MIS class will generate a different type of decision information.

PREPARING SUMMARY REPORTS

The simplest type of MIS is a system that transforms the data base into historical and current status reports on business activities. Such a system is referred to as a **report-generating MIS**. Basically, this system consists of several procedures, each designed to access the data base and create a specific report. Leslie Jackson, for example, may have a set of instructions designed to generate a list of past customers from her work file. To use the system, she merely selects and follows the designated instructions. Figure 2.6 illustrates the concept.

Figure 2.6 Report-Generating MIS

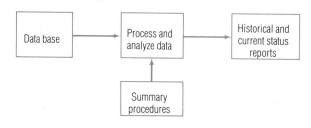

Table 2.1 Examples of MIS-Generated Reports

Periodic Administrative Reports	Deviation Control Reports
Absenteeism	Budget overruns
Balance sheets	Defective products
Current customer billings	Delinquent accounts payable
Current inventory status	Delinquent accounts receivable
Income statements	Inventory depletion
Payments to suppliers	Production delays
Payroll checks	Reservation overbooking
Production efficiency	Sales projection lags

Most organizations use an automated system in which the procedures are translated into computer programs. The decision maker gets the computer to produce a specific report by requesting the desired program. The reports (information) generated by these systems essentially attempt to describe the results of the organization's past and present operations. Table 2.1 gives some examples of MIS-generated reports. Many of these systems also incorporate safeguards and auditing capabilities designed to detect (and protect against) transaction errors and fraud.

Advanced systems frequently allow the user to select specific information and then define how it will be organized and presented in the report. Suppose a manufacturer is offering a special discount on all televisions ordered in the coming month. The purchasing manager for a department store might want to take advantage of this discount by ordering those brands of televisions that have good sales records. To identify this equipment, the manager could request a special report showing the past history of television sales categorized by manufacturer, brand, and style name.

Airline reservations systems offer another illustration. A reservations clerk can determine a listing of available seats on specific flights categorized by reservation status and travel class. If space is available, the clerk can then reserve a seat that meets customer preferences and enter the information into the data base. Later, this information can be accessed for purposes of issuing a ticket, canceling the reservation, informing the passenger of a delay, and so on.

A similar system is the computer-controlled, twenty-four-hour machine tellers now used by many banks. In this system, the customer can insert a bank card into the machine and obtain information on the status of his or her personal accounts. It is even possible to change the status by withdrawing or transferring funds.

Hopefully, the decision maker can utilize the information generated by these reports to make better decisions. To evaluate possible strategies, however, decision makers need a system that does more than just organize and summarize data. There must be some additional capability to directly identify the potential consequences of future conditions and decisions. Unfortunately, the typical report-generating MIS does not produce such information. As a result, other types of systems have been developed to provide this analytical capability.

PROCESSING INQUIRIES Management frequently must determine the effects of various conditions and decisions on business activities. Here are some typical questions that may be asked:

1. What will be the effect on profits if product prices are changed?
2. How will the production rate be affected by a wage increase?
3. What will be the effect on the corporate debt structure if there is an increase in interest rates?
4. How will the inflation rate affect the state budget?
5. What will be the effect on regional employment patterns if the eastern warehouse is closed?

Management information systems have been developed that input such "what if" questions into the data base and create reports summarizing the projected consequences. This type of system is called an **inquiry-processing MIS**.

In its basic form, this system consists of several procedures or computer programs. Some are designed to access the data base and generate historical and current status statements similar to a report-generating MIS. Others are structured to take the decision maker's "what if" questions, perform the necessary data analysis, and create reports summarizing the projected results. Figure 2.7 illustrates this inquiry-processing MIS concept.

Figure 2.7 Inquiry-Processing MIS

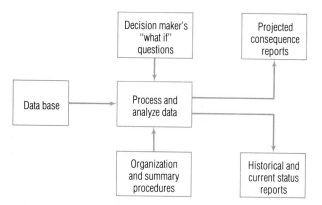

To answer the "what if" questions, the system must contain data analysis procedures. The most common are statistical routines that forecast the future levels of interest rates, inflation, and so on. In addition, the system should include mathematical expressions for projecting the corporate debt structure, the state budget, and so on, from forecasted conditions and decisions. Such statistical routines and mathematical expressions are critical elements in this type of system. They provide the information that enables the MIS to progress from a simple report-generating device to an evaluative tool.

Example 2.3 provides an illustration.

EXAMPLE 2.3 A Small-Scale MIS

Leslie Jackson has the same problem discussed in Example 2.2. She wants to determine the quantity of pages Q that will:

maximize $P = pQ$

subject to $tQ \leq T$

   $Q \geq 0$

Leslie knows her schedule and the type of manuscripts she will be typing during the coming week. Using a simple forecasting formula and her work file (data base), she estimates that these manuscripts will require exactly 6 minutes

(.1 hour) per page. Leslie also predicts that she will have exactly 20 hours of spare time available in the coming week. Her estimated earnings are 80 cents per page.

Leslie has used a simple forecasting routine to generate exact values for the uncontrollable inputs (p, t, and T) from her work file (data base). In this case, $p = \$.80$, $t = .1$ hour, and $T = 20$ hours. Hence, Leslie's problem can be expressed as follows:

$$\text{maximize} \quad P = \$.80Q$$
$$\text{subject to} \quad .1Q \leq 20 \text{ hours}$$
$$Q \geq 0$$

Since all values of the uncontrollable inputs are exactly known, this model is deterministic.

At this stage, Leslie can use the mathematical model to evaluate the effects of various trial quantities on the resource constraint ($.1Q \leq 20$ hours) and total profit ($P = \$.80Q$). For instance, what if she typed $Q = 100$ pages during the coming week? Since each page requires $t = .1$ hour, this quantity would use

$$t \times Q = .1(100) = 10 \text{ hours}$$

and hence be within her time constraint ($T = 20$ hours). Such a policy would also yield a projected profit of

$$P = p \times Q = \$.80(100) = \$80$$

Leslie can use this simple inquiry-processing MIS in a similar manner to evaluate other potential strategies. Table 2.2 presents a possible projected-consequences report for this system.

In addition, Leslie might want to see how changes in the uncontrollable inputs will affect time utilization and profits. By inputting trial changes for p, t, and T into her inquiry-processing MIS, she can obtain revised time utilization and total profit information. In this way, Leslie can evaluate the consequences of future conditions and test prospective strategies before making a final decision.

To provide user flexibility and fast response capability, advanced versions of the MIS often are operated on an interactive basis. In this approach, there is a central MIS that is accessed by many different users from various remote locations. The communication device is usually a computer terminal in the decision maker's office or work station. Since the central facility is being apportioned among several users, this method of operation is referred to as **time sharing**.

Using the remote computer terminals, the decision maker inputs "what if" questions into the MIS and immediately obtains the projected results. A system with this immediate processing capability is said to operate on a **real-time** mode. Management then uses the results to modify the "what if" questions and continue interactive communication with the system until the desired information is obtained. Such direct interaction is said to put the user **on line** with the computer. As R. H. Bonczek and others [2] demonstrate, the feedback (interactive) process enables the decision maker to deal with problems as they arise. It also makes it possible to refine information needs while actually using the system.

Table 2.2 Summary Report from Leslie Jackson's Inquiry-Processing MIS

Quantity of Pages (Q)	Projected Profit (P = $.80Q)	Total Time Required (T = .1Q)	Is Total Time Required ≤ Available Time? (.1Q ≤ 20 hours)
0	0	0	Yes
50	40	5	Yes
100	80	10	Yes
150	120	15	Yes
200	160	20	Yes
250	200	25	No
300	240	30	No

SOLVING THE QUANTITATIVE MODEL After formulating the model and collecting, processing, and analyzing the data, the manager is ready to develop a solution to the decision problem. A solution is an input of the model, projecting what would happen if particular values of the controllable and uncontrollable inputs occurred in the real situation.

Trial and error is one method of obtaining a solution. In this approach, the model is used to test and evaluate alternative values for the controllable inputs. The actual analysis, in practice, may be performed by an inquiry-processing MIS. Leslie Jackson used such a system to evaluate the impact of selected trial quantities on her resource constraints ($.1Q \leq 20$ hours, $Q \geq 0$) and total profit ($P = \$.80Q$). From the projected results in Table 2.2, you can see that the trial quantity of $Q = 300$ pages leads to the largest profit $P = \$240$. Unfortunately, the 30 hours required to type this quantity is more than Leslie's available time (20 hours) for the week. Hence, this solution is not feasible. Among the feasible alternatives, $Q = 200$ pages is the quantity leading to the largest profit $P = \$160$. According to this trial and error, then, Leslie should type 200 pages during the coming week.

Of course, Leslie has not tested all possible quantities. As a result, this trial and error recommendation ($Q = 200$ pages) may not represent the optimal solution to the problem. In fact, trial and error can seldom guarantee an optimal solution. Also, the approach is cumbersome and inefficient, especially for large-scale problems. For these and other reasons, management scientists have developed special solution techniques for various classes of problems. In a recent study, G. Thomas and J. DaCosta [12] found that the most popular techniques among large U.S. corporations are those presented in Table 2.3.

Table 2.3 Popular Management Science Techniques

Technique	Information on Uncontrollable Inputs	Typical Problem Area	Percentage of Firms Using Technique
Statistical analysis	Stochastic	Forecasting and experimentation	93
Simulation	Deterministic and stochastic	Studying ill-structured, complex decision problems	84
Linear programming	Deterministic	Allocating scarce resources	79
PERT/CPM	Deterministic and stochastic	Planning, scheduling, and controlling projects	70
Inventory theory	Deterministic and stochastic	Maintaining and controlling inventories	57
Queuing theory	Stochastic	Analyzing service systems	45
Nonlinear programming	Deterministic	Interdependent activities	36
Heuristic programming	Deterministic and stochastic	Planning large-scale, complex systems	34
Bayesian decision analysis	Stochastic	Risky decisions	32
Dynamic programming	Deterministic and stochastic	Sequential decisions	27
Integer programming	Deterministic	Indivisible activities	2

Statistical analysis includes probability theory, statistical sampling, hypothesis testing, correlation and regression, and time series methods, including exponential smoothing. Since most students take a separate course in statistics, this text will not include these topics. The text does, however, include an introductory coverage of all the other techniques listed in Table 2.3. In particular, there is an emphasis on such frequently used approaches as simulation, linear programming, and PERT/CPM.

The text also discusses some important extensions to the basic management science techniques. Utility and game theory, for example, are tools for decision making under special types of risky circumstances. Goal programming deals with mathematical (primarily linear and integer) programming problems that involve multiple, and sometimes conflicting, objectives. Transportation, assignment, routing, and PERT/CPM are all different forms of network flow problems. Markov analysis is another variety of sequential decision making. In fact, many organizations actually use these extensions but report them in surveys under more general titles like decision analysis, linear programming, and so on.

Some of the techniques, such as linear programming and much of inventory theory, are designed to provide the optimal solution to the problem. Heuristic programming, on the other hand, involves logical search procedures that attempt to identify a good (approximate) problem solution. Other approaches, like most of simulation, queuing theory, and

Markov analysis, merely describe and predict the behavior of the relevant system.

DECISION SUPPORT SYSTEMS

Many of the popular management science techniques will generate a recommended decision. Furthermore, there are computer packages available that will provide a recommendation from data inputted by the decision maker. A few organizations have even incorporated such packages into their management information systems. In such cases, the MIS has the capability of ultimately translating "what if" questions into recommended decisions. Such an MIS is referred to as a **decision support system (DSS)**.

As P. G. W. Keen and S. S. Morton [5] and R. H. Sprague and H. J. Watson [11] demonstrate, a DSS is an integration of MIS and management science concepts. A decision support system, like a report-generating MIS, contains several procedures or computer programs that retrieve relevant decision information from the data base and produce status reports. As in the inquiry-processing MIS, a DSS also takes the manager's "what if" questions, performs the necessary data analysis, and creates projected consequence reports. In addition, there is a decision models component that takes processed data and "what if" information, utilizes an appropriate solution procedure, and generates recommended courses of action.

The decision models component may take a variety of forms. It can involve popular techniques, such as linear programming and PERT/CPM, that are used, as needed, for predefined, relatively well structured problems like fuel blending and project scheduling. Alternatively, there may be specific models and procedures developed for specialized purposes like facilities location or plant layout.

On the other hand, many problems are too poorly structured and too complex to be completely solved by a straightforward application of any particular model. As T. H. Naylor [8] demonstrates, corporate planning is such a problem. In this situation, the decision maker must establish overall company objectives and develop corresponding policies that will affect marketing, production, and financial operations in complex, dynamic, and often uncertain ways. To deal with such problems, the decision component of a DSS should include routines designed to provide the manager with a model-building capability. Typically, these routines involve groups of management science models that can be assembled, as desired, by the decision maker to develop a complete formulation of the problem. A corporate-planning model, for example, may involve a financial cash flow simulation built from a specialized representation of marketing revenues and a linear programming formulation for production costs.

The decision maker's insights and judgments are needed at all stages of

Figure 2.8   Decision Support System (DSS)

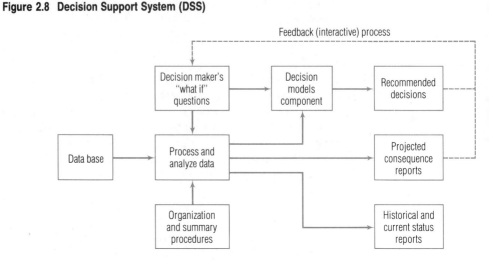

problem solving, from formulation and data selection to solution evaluation and implementation. To achieve maximum effectiveness, then, a DSS should provide managers with the capability to interact quickly with all components of the system. User-friendly, English-like languages have been developed to facilitate this interaction on line without the intermediary of a computer programmer. As S. L. Alter [1] shows, these DSS languages enable the decision maker to conduct a "what if" dialogue with the system. Using these languages, the manager can store, retrieve, display, and manipulate data, select and build models, and evaluate recommendations. In addition, the manager can add or delete assumptions, change the desired accuracy level of the analysis, and establish aspiration levels for the results. Furthermore, the dialogue can be done in real time on a computer terminal screen with results displayed immediately in the form of executive reports, tables, graphs, and so on. Figure 2.8 illustrates this decision support system concept. You can see that a decision support system is a kind of MIS with decision models.

In effect, a DSS provides the technology to support the process of exploring and structuring decision situations, evaluating and interpreting alternative solutions, and implementing the recommendations. A. Vazsonyi [13] predicts that this technology will extend the manager's range and capability for dealing with problems and decrease the cost and time required to perform the various phases of decision making. It is important to understand that a DSS does not attempt to automate the decision process, predefine the problem, or impose solutions. Rather, under the manager's control, it creates specialized tools that support (not replace) the decision maker's judgment. By encouraging such management participation, a DSS enhances the collaboration between the decision maker, the management scientist, and the information systems analyst. It also facilitates the implementation of results and takes us one step closer to the embodiment of a true systems approach in decision making.

IMPLEMENTATION

The quantitative analysis process is not complete until the model's solution information is reported to the decision maker and the results are implemented. Such data constitute only one of the inputs considered by the manager when a final decision is being made. Therefore, it is essential to present the quantitative information in a managerial report that will be easily understood by the decision maker. The report should include the recommended decision and a concise summary of other pertinent information about the model results that may be helpful to the decision maker. Relevant information might include the model's assumptions, alternative solutions, and qualitative considerations.

The process does not end, however, with the delivery of the running model and report to management. Even the most carefully developed and tested model may not work as planned. Management scientists must get feedback from the decision maker regarding the validity of the model and, if necessary, make appropriate adjustments or modifications. Moreover, there may be other problems in implementing management science concepts within the organizational framework.

BARRIERS TO IMPLEMENTATION

According to a recent study by H. J. Watson and P. C. Marett [14], the most serious classes of implementation problems are those shown in Table 2.4. Clearly, there are several types of barriers to successful implementation. Some deal with particular aspects of the project, such as problem definition, the time needed for analysis, and the relative benefit from the approach (items 6, 4, and 7). Other barriers deal with the implementation climate. In this respect, there are organizational problems, such as management's educational background, the lack of adequate data, and the shortage of personnel (items 2, 3, and 8). There are also behavioral factors, including the fear of change, communication difficulties in selling quantitative techniques to managers, insufficient user understanding, and the poor reputation of management scientists (items 10, 1, 5, and 9).

IMPLEMENTATION STRATEGIES

Several steps have been suggested for alleviating various problems and promoting more successful implementation. As M. J. Ginzberg [4] points out, perhaps the most important action is to obtain management participation in, and support of, the entire quantitative analysis process. Man-

Table 2.4 Management Science Implementation Problems

Problem	Percent of Respondents*
1. Difficulty selling management science methods to managers	35
2. Top and middle managers lacking educational background to appreciate management science	34
3. Lack of adequate data	32
4. Insufficient time to analyze a real problem with a sophisticated approach	23
5. Inability of users to understand methods and results	22
6. Difficulty defining problems for application	19
7. Sufficient benefits from using unsophisticated methods	16
8. Shortage of personnel	12
9. Poor reputation of management scientists as problem solvers	11
10. Individuals feeling threatened by management science	10

* Since several respondents had more than one problem, the total percentage sums to more than 100.

agement science projects often affect a variety of departments, groups, and individuals within the enterprise. Top management specifies organizational objectives and constraints, translates them into policies and guidelines, and communicates the information to appropriate personnel. Thus, these managers are in the best position to assess potential program contributions, guide project formulation, provide relevant input, evaluate results, and encourage organizational support. Similarly, middle management has a firsthand comprehensive understanding of operations and the corresponding limitations and constraints. Such input is necessary to any management science project. Moreover, operating management's support may be transmitted to the people directly affected by the proposed changes.

According to A. G. Lockett and E. Polding [6], another important step is to improve communication and cooperation between management scientists and managers. Through education, training, and dialogue with executives, management scientists can gain a better understanding of managers' information needs, schedule needs, and cost constraints. To further facilitate mutual understanding, the initial stages of quantitative projects should begin with small, tentative formulations and be characterized by end user involvement. Later, when the need is clearly justified, the initial statement can evolve into a more comprehensive formulation. At the same time, executive development programs and intensive project involvement will give managers a better understanding of the resource requirements in quantitative analysis.

Advances in computer-based MIS and DSS also will enhance implementation. As W. T. Morris [7] indicates, these systems provide better data for the quantitative decision-making techniques, encourage management participation in the process, and provide results on line in real time.

SUMMARY In this chapter we examined decision making and the role of management science in this process. We saw how management scientists provide quantitative information to help the manager reach a final decision.

The first step in the process is to define the managerial problem clearly and concisely. Next, we represent the essential features of the situation with a model. Several types of models were discussed, including physical replicas, analogs, and mathematical representations.

Models require information; therefore, data collection, processing, and analysis are a critical part of the management science process. A management information system (MIS) can aid this process by providing accurate, relevant, and timely information to decision makers. Several management information systems were presented, including the report-generating and inquiry-processing MIS.

After formulating a model and collecting and analyzing data, the manager is ready to develop a solution to the problem. Trial and error is one method of obtaining a solution. However, it is too cumbersome and time-consuming for most realistic management problems. For these and other reasons, management scientists have developed special solution techniques for various classes of problems. Table 2.3 summarized the popular approaches.

We also saw how decision support systems integrate MIS and management science concepts. Using a DSS, management is able to store, retrieve, display, and manipulate data, select and build models, and evaluate recommendations. In effect, these systems provide the technology to support the process of exploring and structuring decision situations, evaluating and interpreting alternative solutions, and implementing recommendations in real time.

Implementation is the final step in the management science process. It begins with the delivery of a formal report and running model to the decision maker. In addition, management scientists must get feedback from the decision maker regarding the validity of the model and, if necessary, make appropriate adjustments and modifications. Even then, there may be barriers to implementing management science concepts within the organizational framework. The most significant problems were summarized in Table 2.4.

Several steps were suggested for alleviating problems and promoting more successful implementation. Perhaps the most important action is to obtain management participation in, and support of, the entire quantitative analysis process. Another useful step is to improve communication and cooperation between management scientists and managers. Advances in MIS and DSS are also expected to enhance implementation by providing better data and directly involving management in the quantitative analysis process.

In spite of the implementation barriers, management science is readily accepted by executives in public and private enterprises because the methodology can significantly improve their ability to make effective decisions. In subsequent chapters, we will show you how to effectively utilize this methodology. We will consider managerial problems, examine the appropriate quantitative approaches, and develop recommended solutions. The objective is not to train you for work as a management scientist, but to show how you can become a more effective decision maker by using quantitative analysis to augment your other managerial skills.

Glossary

analog model   A physical form that does not look like the real object or situation.

constraint   A mathematical expression that describes restrictions, or limitations, involved in the problem.

controllable inputs, or decision variables   Factors that influence the model's outcome and are controlled or determined by the decision maker.

data base   An organized collection of data, usually in an MIS and frequently dealing with a firm's past and present operations.

decision support system (DSS)   An MIS that transforms "what if" questions into recommended decisions.

deterministic model   A model in which the values of the uncontrollable inputs are known exactly.

iconic model   A physical replica of the real situation or object.

inquiry-processing MIS   An MIS that inputs "what if" questions into the data base and creates reports summarizing the projected consequences of possible conditions and decisions.

management information system (MIS)   A system designed to collect, analyze, and report relevant and timely information needed by management to make effective decisions.

mathematical model   A system of symbols and mathematical expressions that represent the real situation.

model   A simplified representation of a real object or situation.

objective function   A mathematical expression that describes the objective of a problem.

on line   Interacting directly with a computer system.

real time   Providing processing results to the user in sufficient time to affect the decision process.

report-generating MIS An MIS that creates historical and current status reports on business activities.

result variables Measures used to evaluate the performance or effectiveness of a system.

stochastic model A model in which the values of the uncontrollable inputs are uncertain and subject to variation.

time sharing The utilization of a computer system by many different users, typically through a series of remote terminals.

uncontrollable inputs, or environmental variables Factors that must be considered but are beyond the decision maker's control.

References

1. Alter, S. L. *Decision Support Systems: Current Practice and Continuing Challenges.* Reading, Mass.: Addison-Wesley, 1980.
2. Bonczek, R. H., et al. "Computer-Based Support of Organizational Decision Making." *Decision Sciences* (April 1979):268.
3. Dock, T., et al. *MIS—A Managerial Perspective.* Chicago: Science Research Associates, 1977.
4. Ginzberg, M. J. "Steps Toward More Effective Implementation of MS and MIS." *Interfaces* (May 1978):57.
5. Keen, P. G. W., and S. S. Morton. *Decision Support Systems: An Organizational Perspective.* Reading, Mass.: Addison-Wesley, 1978.
6. Lockett, A. G., and E. Polding. "OR/MS Implementation—A Variety of Processes." *Interfaces* (November 1978):45.
7. Morris, W. T. *Implementation Strategies for Industrial Engineers.* Columbus: Grid Publishing, 1979.
8. Naylor, T. H. "Why Corporate Planning Models?" *Interfaces* (November 1977):87.
9. Rivett, P. *Model Building for Decision Analysis.* New York: Wiley, 1980.
10. Senn, J. A. *Information Systems in Management.* Belmont, Calif.: Wadsworth, 1978.
11. Sprague, R. H., and H. J. Watson. "A Decision Support System for Banks." *OMEGA, The International Journal of Management Science* 4 (1976):657.
12. Thomas, G., and J. DaCosta. "A Sample Survey of Corporate Operations Research." *Interfaces* (August 1979):102.
13. Vazsonyi, A. "Decision Support Systems: The New Technology of Decision Making?" *Interfaces* (November 1978):72.
14. Watson, H. J., and P. C. Marett. "A Survey of Management Science Implementation Problems." *Interfaces* (August 1979):129.

1. Use Figure 2.1 to outline your decision-making process for the following personal decisions:

    a. Choice of life-style
    b. Choice of an automobile
    c. Selection of a brand of toothpaste
    d. Selection of a holiday vacation
    e. Choice of movie

2. Explain how quantitative analysis can help you to make each of the personal decisions listed in thought exercise 1.

3. Illustrate the potential value of management science to each of the following decision makers:

    a. A hospital administrator
    b. The production manager of a large petroleum company
    c. The marketing director of a medium-sized grocery chain
    d. The vice president in charge of loans for a small credit union
    e. Your present or potential position

4. Explain how a management information system can benefit each of the following decision makers:

    a. A marketing manager who needs a sales history in selected territories for each of the firm's products
    b. A government analyst who needs a forecast for selected components of the economy's gross national product
    c. A financial executive who wants a forecast of interest rates in the next quarter
    d. A production manager who wants to determine which of several specified output levels results in least cost

5. Refer to Figure 2.7. Suppose the inquiry-processing MIS was made interactive with the decision maker using projected consequence feedback to refine "what if" questions. Illustrate how you would modify Figure 2.7 to account for this interaction.

6. Observe how customers are served at a checkout facility (for example, a grocery store checkout register, a theater box office, or a restaurant checkout stand). Develop iconic, analog, and mathematical models of the process. Explain how your models would be affected by rush hour traffic.

7. Explain how a decision support system could benefit each of the following managers:

    a. A U.S. president's evaluation of alternative economic policies
    b. A military commander's evaluation of alternative retirement programs
    c. An executive's evaluation of alternative management compensation plans
    d. A public utility commissioner's evaluation of a telephone company's request for a rate increase

8. Do you agree or disagree with the following statements? Explain.
   a. There is no need for managers to study quantitative decision making; if they need that type of information, they can have a quantitative specialist perform the analysis.
   b. Quantitative specialists are the true agents of change in modern organizations.
   c. The best practice for an aspiring quantitative analyst is to search for decision problems that fit available tools and techniques.
   d. Quantitative models are invalid because they do not incorporate all the factors in a decision problem.
   e. Decision makers can eliminate their responsibility to make decisions by employing quantitative models.
   f. Since we cannot unconditionally determine the optimal solution to a stochastic model, this formulation is more difficult to solve than a deterministic representation.

Technique Exercises

1. A company uses the following equation to forecast sales for a particular product:

$$Q = 20{,}000 - 300P + 5A + 2Y$$

where Q = annual number of units sold, P = price (in dollars), A = advertising expenditures, and Y = average household income. Suppose the price is $120, advertising expenditures are $50,000, and household income averages $20,000 this year. What is the sales forecast?

2. The marketing analyst for a company has determined that revenue for their product is given by the following mathematical expression:

$$R = 30{,}000P - 60P^2$$

where R = total revenue (in dollars) and P = price (in dollars).
   a. If the price is $20, what will be the corresponding revenue?
   b. Use trial and error to find the price that maximizes revenue. Restrict the search to prices between $200 and $300. Also, search only in increments of $10 ($200, $210, $220, and so on).

3. A government economist has developed the following simple model to forecast national income:

$$Y_t = C_t + I_t + G_t$$
$$C_t = .4Y_{t-1} + 100$$
$$I_t = 2(Y_{t-1} - C_{t-1} - G_{t-1})$$
$$G_t = .3(C_t + I_t)$$

where Y = national income (in billions of dollars), C = consumption (in billions of dollars), I = investment (in billions of dollars), G =

government expenditures (in billions of dollars), t = current time period, and $t - 1$ = immediately preceding period. Suppose preceding income was $600 billion. Of this amount, $300 billion was consumption and $200 billion was government expenditures. What will be the forecast for national income this year?

4. Consider the following mathematical model of production:

maximize $Q = 20L$

subject to $L \leq 400$ hours

$L \geq 0$

where Q = total output in a given time period and L = total number of labor hours employed in a given time period.
   a. What is the objective? What are the controllable and uncontrollable inputs?
   b. What is the maximum output?
   c. Suppose each hour of labor generates only 10 units of output; what is the maximum output? What is the maximum output if each labor hour generates 30 units of output?
   d. Assume there are 200 labor hours available; what is the maximum output? What is the maximum output if there are 500 available labor hours?

5. Refer to Examples 2.2 and 2.3. Leslie Jackson wanted to determine the quantity of pages Q that would

maximize $P = \$.80Q$

subject to $.1Q \leq 20$ hours

$Q \geq 0$

Trial and error indicated that the optimal solution was to type $Q = 200$ pages per week for a maximum profit of $P = \$160$. Use mathematics to determine the optimal solution. (*Hint*: Start with the available time constraint expression.) Does your answer agree or disagree with the trial and error solution? Explain.

6. Table 2.3 lists popular management science techniques. Make a list of the computer packages available at your institution that deal with these techniques.

7. Use the management science/operations research journals (for example, *Management Science*, *Operations Research*, *Decision Sciences*, and *Interfaces*) to compile a list of the most recent applications of decision support systems.

8. Again refer to Examples 2.2 and 2.3. Suppose Leslie Jackson is now typing manuscripts that require 9 minutes per page and that earn $1.20 per page. However, Leslie is uncertain about how much spare time she will have available in the coming month. Depending on her academic and social activities, it could be 60, 90, or 120 hours.

   a. Formulate the appropriate model for this situation. How does it differ from the model given in Examples 2.2 and 2.3? Explain.

   b. Determine the optimal solution for the new problem.

   c. Suppose Leslie could hire an assistant. How would this affect the new situation? Explain.

9. Ace Products, Inc., originally had the following problem:

$$\text{maximize} \quad \pi = \$.60Q$$

$$\text{subject to} \quad Q \le 2000 \text{ hours of productive capacity per month}$$

$$Q \ge 0$$

where Q = number of jars of Ace Cream sold per month and π = total dollar profit. Now the company adds another product, Ace Lotion, which sells for 20 cents a bottle. Both lotion and cream require 2 hours of productive capacity. Capacity has recently been expanded to 10,000 hours per month. All other conditions remain the same.

   a. Assuming that the objective is still to maximize profit, formulate Ace's new problem. Let B represent the number of bottles of Ace Lotion.

   b. What are the controllable and uncontrollable inputs?

   c. How many bottles of lotion and how many jars of cream should Ace produce to maximize total monthly profit?

   d. Solve Ace's original problem. Interpret the difference between the solution to Ace's original problem and the solution to Ace's new problem.

Applications Exercises

1. A commuter is concerned about the energy crisis and wishes to minimize his monthly fuel purchases. He knows that the cost of fuel will depend on the number of miles that he drives. He also knows that he drives at least a given number of miles per month to and from work. Other known facts are the cost per gallon of fuel and his car's number of miles per gallon.

   a. Develop a mathematical model for the commuter's problem using the symbols Q for number of miles, C for total cost, c for cost per gallon of fuel, M for minimum total monthly miles, and m for miles per gallon.

   b. What is the objective? What are the controllable and uncontrollable inputs?

   c. Use your own experience to gather data on the uncontrollable inputs. Is your model deterministic or stochastic? Explain.

   d. Assume that you are the commuter. Use the data you gathered and the model you developed to determine the minimum monthly fuel cost.

2. A small newsstand orders a specific number of Sunday newspapers from a distributing agent. It costs $1 to place an order. The exact number of orders depends on demand, which has been steady at 10 purchases per Sunday. In addition, each newspaper costs the newsstand 10 cents for display and other inventory expenses. The newsstand wants to order the number of Sunday papers that will minimize the total cost of ordering plus display.

   a. Formulate a mathematical model of the newsstand's problem. Use Q to represent the quantity of Sunday newspapers ordered.

   b. Enumerate the costs associated with quantities ranging from 0 to 12.

   c. Which quantity results in minimum total cost? What are the ordering and display costs at this quantity?

3. A local automobile dealership wants to attract more customers to its showroom. Ads are placed in local newspapers and on local radio broadcasts. A radio spot costs a given amount C_r and is expected to generate a given amount a_r of new shoppers, while a newspaper ad costs C_n and is expected to generate a_n new shoppers. The dealership wants to spend no more than D dollars for a given time period, and it wants to obtain a maximum of A new shoppers.

   a. Formulate a mathematical model of this decision problem, specifying the objective and the controllable and uncontrollable inputs.

   b. Gather data on the uncontrollable inputs from a local automobile dealership and from local newspapers and radio stations. Is your model stochastic or deterministic?

   c. Determine the dealership's maximum number of new shoppers for a given month.

4. Bright University publishes texts written by its faculty for use in courses offered on campus. These texts are sold to the students through the university bookstore. Jonathan Smart has just completed a text for his introductory accounting course. The university is trying to decide whether or not to publish and sell the text. Publishing the text will involve production and marketing costs. These costs can be recovered only if there are sufficient book sales. The relevant financial data are as follows:

Fixed costs	
Printing setup	$1000
Shelf display and promotion material	500
Total	$1500
Variable costs	
Material per book	$5
Labor per book	5
Total	$10
Selling price per book	$15

a. Formulate a profit model for this problem.
b. What sales volume will the university need to break even (earn zero profit)?
c. How many books must be sold to earn a 20% return on fixed costs?
d. Suppose approximately 400 students take the course each year. Should the university publish the text? Explain.

CASE: Jane Allen's Career Choice

Jane Allen has recently graduated from college cum laude with a major in accounting. She is trying to plan a career. There are many choices available. She could become an accountant, but is undecided about the specific field or type of employer. Jane also enjoys the academic atmosphere, so she is considering graduate study and a subsequent career in university teaching. Also, Jane and her boyfriend have talked about marriage. Her boyfriend has a good job, and Jane would have the option of being primarily a housewife and mother. She is attracted to a family environment. In addition, several companies have offered her positions in sales and office management.

Jane has some quantitative facts: graduate aptitude test scores, graduate study expenses, available fellowships and other financial aid, her boyfriend's estimates of his salary and potential earning power, published general salaries in various positions, and general living costs in different geographical areas. Friends, family, professors, and other personal advisors have also provided qualitative information: job duties and responsibilities for different career choices, opinions on her aptitude for various positions, opinions about life-styles, and opinions about the degree of personal satisfaction she can expect in various career choices.

Jane's career goals are to achieve personal happiness and financial security. She defines financial security as a positive net financial worth for the career: earnings plus fringe benefits less employment and living costs for the life of the career. One career has greater financial security than another if it has a higher net financial worth. Jane admits that it is difficult to devise an objective measure of personal happiness. However, she believes that it is possible to use the available qualitative information to subjectively evaluate each identified career choice.

1. What is Jane's problem? What are her alternative courses of action? What are her criteria of evaluation?

2. If you were Jane, how would you outline your decision-making process for this problem?

3. Construct a tabular net financial worth model for each identified alternative.

4. Gather relevant data for your quantitative model and evaluate each alternative's net financial worth.

5. Gather relevant qualitative information on your personal happiness in each career. Use the information to subjectively rank the alternatives.

6. On the basis of your analysis, what career would you advise Jane to choose?

Part II
Decision Analysis

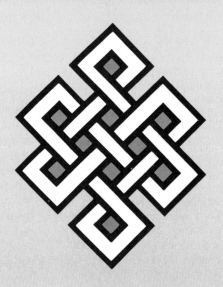

Part I presented the foundations of quantitative decision making. It defined the nature of management science, discussed its role in the decision-making process, and identified the steps necessary for successful implementation. We showed that management science involves an explicit formulation, systematic analysis, and solution of decision problems. This next part of the text develops a general structure or framework within which managers can conceptualize these problems. It also presents rational ways to perform the systematic analysis and develop a recommended solution.

Chapter 3 introduces the decision theory approach. It shows how to structure a problem, identify the nature of the decision environment, and develop appropriate strategies for various situations. Often, the situation involves a series of interrelated decisions. This third chapter also presents a model specifically designed for such problems.

You will see that formulating an appropriate decision strategy depends on adequate information. If little information is available, a strategy may be extremely risky. Chapter 4 explores ways in which managers can reduce the risk involved in decision making. It shows how to incorporate additional information from sampling and experimentation into the analysis, measure its value, and evaluate the effects on the decision.

In chapter 5, we consider several extensions to the basic decision theory concepts. We see how to develop strategies in terms of the manager's perceived (rather than the actual monetary or physical) value for the decision outcomes. In addition, this chapter covers methods of decision making for problems with multiple (often conflicting) objectives. There is also a discussion of conflict situations.

After reading this part of the text, you should be able to:

◆ recognize the various types of decision-making situations

◆ measure the value of decision-making information

◆ develop decision strategies for various types of situations

This background will also facilitate your understanding of the concepts in subsequent chapters.

Chapter 3
Decision Theory

CHAPTER OUTLINE

- Structure of the Problem
  Elements
  Decision Tables

- Decision Criteria
  Types of Situations
  Dominance
  Decision Making Under Uncertainty
  Decision Making Under Risk
  Decision Making Under Certainty

- Sequential Decisions
  Decision Trees
  Finding the Solution
  Applications

- **Case**: The Healthy Food Store

CONCEPTS

- Structuring a decision problem

- Identifying the nature of the decision-making situation

- Developing appropriate decision strategies

- Dealing with problems involving a series of interrelated decisions

APPLICATIONS

- Plant construction

- Pest control

- Investment analysis

- Buying or renting equipment

- Car pools

- Product pricing

- University staffing

- Vendor selection

- Television programming

- Insurance coverage

- Product testing

- New product strategy

- Health system design

- Food preparation

In chapter 2, we saw that decision making involves a relatively well defined process. First, the manager precisely states the problem and its objectives. Next, he or she identifies the available alternatives and collects relevant information. This information is then used to evaluate the alternatives, develop a recommended solution, and implement the choice.

In many of these problems, the manager has only limited, or partial, information about the decision environment. Management scientists have developed a rational methodology for conceptualizing, analyzing, and solving such problems. The approach is referred to as **decision analysis** or **decision theory**.

This chapter begins with a section on how to structure a problem in decision theory format. It identifies the essential components and formulates an appropriate decision model, or framework, for analysis. As you will see, the appropriate decision strategy depends on the nature of the decision environment. We then go on to identify the various types of environments and examine rational methods for making decisions in each of these situations. All these approaches focus on one-time decisions. In many situations, however, the manager must make a series of interrelated decisions. The final section presents a model specifically designed for such problems.

STRUCTURE OF THE PROBLEM

Every decision problem involves the same basic components illustrated in Example 3.1.

EXAMPLE 3.1 Plant Construction

Naddol Toy Company, Inc., is introducing a revolutionary new children's toy—the Star Cruiser. The company will have to build a new plant to produce this product. Four different-sized plants are under consideration— small, moderate, large, and very large. The appropriate size will depend on the level of product demand. However, the level of demand is uncertain. It can be low, medium, or high.

Naddol has used the best information available to estimate the profits associated with each plant size alternative. If the company builds a small plant, it forecasts a $250,000 profit with low demand, a

$40,000 loss with medium demand, and $0 profit with high demand. A moderate plant is expected to result in a $50,000 loss with low demand, a $350,000 profit with medium demand, and a $60,000 profit with high demand. The large plant gets an estimated $100,000 loss with low demand, an $80,000 profit with medium

demand, and a $400,000 profit with high demand. If the company builds a very large plant, management predicts a $120,000 loss with low demand, a $75,000 profit with medium demand, and a $400,000 profit with high demand.

Management wants to determine the most profitable plant size.

ELEMENTS Every decision has one or more objectives. It may be to select the most fuel-efficient and comfortable automobile, to choose the least costly transportation route, or to find the most profitable and least risky investment. Some objectives, like cost and profit, can be measured in monetary terms. Other physical measures include quantity, distance, time, and market share. Goals such as comfort and risk, on the other hand, involve the perceptions and attitudes of the decision maker. As a result, these objectives are usually expressed in psychological terms.

The first step in decision theory is to define the problem and identify the objectives. In Example 3.1, Naddol's problem is to determine the most profitable plant size. The single goal, profit maximization, is expressed in monetary (dollar) terms.

The next step in the process is to identify the choices available for the decision maker. Since the choices typically are controlled by the manager, they are equivalent to the controllable inputs of the mathematical model from chapter 2. In decision theory, these controllable inputs are referred to as **courses of action** or **decision alternatives**.

In many cases, the problem may involve an unlimited number of decision alternatives. For example, when blending fuel, a petroleum manager could choose among an infinite number of mixes. Often, however, current knowledge, past experience, and the nature of the problem will limit the number of available actions. The "rules of good blending," for instance, may limit the manager's alternatives to a very narrow range of fuel mixtures. Similarly, there may be only four investment alternatives currently available to a particular investor.

Sometimes, the decision alternatives are expressed in qualitative terms. Thus, a car buyer may describe each alternative by the automobile make and model, and an airline may designate route options by origin and destination codings. In other situations, the alternatives are described quantitatively. Each course of action in a manufacturing problem, for example, may be a specific production quantity. In a similar manner, research and development alternatives could be represented by the various dollar amounts spent on a particular project.

In Naddol's case, management can select among four distinct plant sizes: small, moderate, large, or very large. Hence, there is a finite number of decision alternatives, and each choice is described in qualitative terms. The case at the end of this chapter presents a situation in which a finite number of choices is expressed quantitatively. J. M. Jones [14], J. W. Newman [15], and D. J. White [23] discuss problems with a very large number of choices.

The effectiveness of each decision alternative will depend on future circumstances. Hence, the next step in the process is to identify the conditions that are expected to occur. Since such events are usually beyond the manager's control, they are equivalent to the uncontrollable inputs of the mathematical model from chapter 2. In decision theory, these uncontrollable inputs are called **events**, **possible futures**, or **states of nature**.

States of nature may result from many economic, social, political, and physical forces pushing in various directions. In a car purchase decision, for example, future laws and regulations will affect each automobile model's fuel efficiency and comfort and thus influence the buyer's choice. Yet, these laws and regulations are beyond the buyer's control. Frequently, the uncontrollable future conditions result from actions taken by competing decision makers. For example, the effectiveness of a firm's advertising will depend on the competitor's promotional strategy.

In many situations, there is an unlimited number of possible futures, particularly when these conditions are expressed in quantitative terms. A firm's profit, for instance, may depend on total industry sales, and theoretically, there could be an infinite variety of potential demands. In other cases, experience or the problem form will limit the number of events to a very narrow, finite range of values. Furthermore, the decision maker may prefer to describe the range with a few qualitative categories. For example, potential economic conditions could be classified simply as poor, fair, or good. Similarly, an electric utility's nuclear plant construction decision could face a political climate that might be described as favorable, indifferent, or unfavorable.

It is advisable to define the states of nature in a way that precludes any two (or more) events from occurring simultaneously. The occurrence of one state will then exclude all others. Such events are said to be **mutually exclusive**. Also, in defining the events, the decision maker should include all possible future situations. The group of events is then said to be **collectively exhaustive**.

In Naddol's problem, management's plant construction choice will depend on future market demand conditions. The possibilities are the mutually exclusive and collectively exhaustive events of low, medium, or high demand. Thus, there is a finite number of three states of nature, and each is expressed in qualitative terms. R. V. Brown and colleagues [3], C. A. Holloway [12], and V. M. R. Tummala [20] extend the analysis to problems involving a very large number of states expressed in quantitative terms.

To evaluate the choices, management must measure the outcome that will result from each possible combination of decision alternative and state of nature. These outcomes are equivalent to the result variables of the mathematical model from chapter 2. In decision theory, these result variables are referred to as **payoffs** or **decision outcomes**.

The payoffs must be measured in terms relevant to the decision objective. In selecting the least costly transportation route, for instance, a shipping agent will want to express the decision outcomes in terms of appropriate operating and financial expenses. Frequently, it is also important to specify an appropriate time frame. When using present value to evaluate long-term investments, for example, the decision maker must selectively discount returns and costs over the relevant planning period.

In Naddol's problem, the decision outcomes are the profits associated with each combination of plant size and demand condition. For instance, when the company builds a moderate plant and there is medium demand, it will earn a $350,000 profit. On the other hand, this same alternative will result in only a $60,000 profit if there is high demand. As you can see, there will be a different outcome for each alternative and event combination.

DECISION TABLES

By denoting Naddol's decision alternatives as

a_1 = build a small plant

a_2 = build a moderate plant

a_3 = build a large plant

a_4 = build a very large plant

and the states of nature as

s_1 = low demand

s_2 = medium demand

s_3 = high demand

we can conveniently organize and summarize Naddol's problem elements as shown in Table 3.1. This kind of format is referred to as a **payoff table** or **decision table**. Each row in a decision table represents a course of action, and each column depicts a state of nature. Entries in the squares (cells)

Table 3.1 Naddol's Decision Table

Decision Alternatives	States of Nature		
	s_1 = low demand	s_2 = medium demand	s_3 = high demand
a_1 = build a small plant	$250,000	− $40,000	$0
a_2 = build a moderate plant	− $50,000	$350,000	$60,000
a_3 = build a large plant	− $100,000	$80,000	$400,000
a_4 = build a very large plant	− $120,000	$75,000	$400,000

Loss   Profit

give the corresponding decision outcomes. In this way, the decision table provides a framework for structuring relatively simple, one-time decision problems. Later we will discuss a graphic representation designed for more complex problems.

DECISION CRITERIA The next step in the decision theory approach is to select the alternative that best meets the decision objectives. Several logical methods, called **decision criteria**, can be used to make this selection. The choice of a criterion will be based on the manager's knowledge about the decision situation.

TYPES OF SITUATIONS In structuring a decision problem, the manager should be able to identify the courses of action, states of nature, and outcomes. Yet, each situation will involve different degrees of knowledge about the states of nature. It is customary to divide this knowledge into three segments, or zones.

At one extreme is the situation in which the decision maker can identify the possible future conditions. However, this individual does not have enough information to assess the likelihood for each state of nature. Such a situation is referred to as **uncertainty**. This circumstance is undesirable but occasionally unavoidable. As E. Turban and N. P. Loomba [21] demonstrate, it may arise when there is a completely new phenomenon, like the 1973 energy crisis or the space shuttle program. Innovative circumstances, such as the introduction of a completely novel product or the development of new technology, can also create uncertainty. F. H. Barron [1] and G. A. Whitmore [24] provide additional examples.

Usually, however, there is some information available that can be used to at least quantify the uncertainty. One source of this information is the decision maker. Managers possess intuition and, during their careers, have accumulated much individual and collective knowledge and experience. As R. K. Sarin [17] and C. S. Spetzler and C. A. Stael von Holstein [18] demonstrate, decision makers can use this information to subjectively assign probabilities for each state of nature. Such personal beliefs or judgments about the likelihood of future events are called **subjective probabilities**.

Subjective quantification of uncertainty is most useful for problems like product line expansion, plant relocation, and educational program development. In these circumstances, the future conditions are familiar to the decision maker, but observed data are unobtainable, insufficient, or an unreliable indicator of the future. Subjective input is also one way to incorporate intangible factors into the analysis. Chapter 5 will present additional methods. As D. W. Conrath [4] and A. R. Oxenfelt [16] show, the major problem is that each manager may assign a different probability to the same state of nature. Moreover, peer pressure, emotion, and learning can cause the decision maker to change his or her assessment. Consequently, it may be difficult in practice to arrive at a consistent or consensus subjective probability.

Often, it is not necessary to rely solely on subjective assessments. In many situations, the underlying process is relatively stable, and future conditions will follow the same pattern as past events. Examples include airline travel, insurance, department store sales, and quality control. Under these circumstances, the decision maker can observe past events or conduct laboratory, statistical, or market experiments. The data can then be used to calculate the proportion of times that each state of nature was actually observed in the past or in the experiment. Such a proportion is referred to as an **objective probability**. Managers can use objective probabilities as the likelihoods for various states of nature and as additional inputs to update subjective assessments.

When the decision maker has information sufficient to assess only the probability of occurrence for each state of nature, the situation is referred to as **risk**. As R. DeNeufville and R. L. Keeney [6] and B. E. Fries [10] demonstrate, this type of situation is very common in planning, operating, and control problems.

At the other extreme is the situation where the manager has acquired enough information to know exactly which state of nature will occur. Such a circumstance is referred to as **certainty**. Although this situation is not as prevalent as risk, it nevertheless occurs. Standardized and routine operat-

Figure 3.1 Decision Situations

ing systems, such as highly automated production lines or a series of mechanized electricity transmission stations, tend to create an environment of certainty. It may also arise in contractual situations, like the commodity and currency "futures" markets, in problems involving budgets or quotas, and in situations when the planning horizon is relatively short.

Figure 3.1 illustrates the range of decision situations. Certainty is equivalent to the deterministic model of chapter 2, while risk and uncertainty are stochastic representations. As Figure 3.1 indicates, you can move from uncertainty toward certainty, and thus make more informed choices, by increasing your knowledge about the decision environment. Subjects like marketing research, statistics, and research and development provide such knowledge. And that is precisely why they are so important in modern decision making.

DOMINANCE At this stage, the decision maker can perform an initial screening to determine if some alternatives can be eliminated from consideration. To illustrate, let us compare alternatives a_3 and a_4 in Table 3.1. When there is low demand (s_1), the large plant (a_3) leads to a smaller loss than the very large plant (a_4). Similarly, in a medium-demand situation (s_2), the $80,000 profit from the large plant is better than the $75,000 gain with a very large plant. If the demand is high (s_3), the profits are identical from both the large and very large plants. Regardless of the demand, then, a_3 provides outcomes equal to (when s_3 occurs) or better than (for s_1 and s_2) the payoffs for a_4. In such a case, we say that a_3 **dominates** a_4.

Dominated actions are inferior to other alternatives and thus can be disregarded. Since a_4 is a dominated alternative in Naddol's problem, management should eliminate from further consideration the possibility of building a very large plant, obtaining Table 3.2.

The decision maker should continue to screen the alternatives until all dominated actions have been eliminated. Occasionally, a single alternative will dominate all others and thus represent a solution to the problem. A

Table 3.2 Naddol's Relevant Decision Table

Decision Alternatives	States of Nature		
	s_1 = low demand	s_2 = medium demand	s_3 = high demand
a_1 = build a small plant	$250,000	−$40,000	$0
a_2 = build a moderate plant	−$50,000	$350,000	$60,000
a_3 = build a large plant	−$100,000	$80,000	$400,000

Loss   Profit

check of Table 3.2, however, will show that there is no additional dominance in Naddol's problem. Consequently, company management still must develop some method for selecting among the three remaining relevant plant sizes.

DECISION MAKING UNDER UNCERTAINTY In its present form, Naddol's plant construction decision (Example 3.1) involves uncertainty. The company has been able to identify the courses of action, states of nature, and outcomes and then structure the problem with a decision table (Table 3.1 and then Table 3.2). Apparently, however, the Star Cruiser toy is so revolutionary that management does not have enough information to even assign probabilities for the possible demand conditions. Yet, like most problems involving uncertainty, the decision will substantially affect operations for some time and have a significant financial impact on the firm. Several criteria have been proposed for making decisions in this type of environment.

Optimism In one approach, the decision maker assumes that each alternative will result in the most favorable possible outcome. Then he or she selects the alternative that leads to the best of these most favorable outcomes. This selection procedure is known as the **optimistic criterion**. When the objective is to select the smallest outcome, as with costs or time, such an approach is also labeled the **minimin criterion**. If the decision maker wants to select the largest outcome, as with profits or output, the optimistic procedure is often called the **maximax criterion**.

In applying this criterion to Naddol's problem, management first determines the largest profit (most favorable outcome) associated with each plant size (decision alternative). From Table 3.2, you can see that the

Table 3.3 Naddol's Most Favorable Outcomes

Decision Alternative	Largest Profit
a_1 = build a small plant	$250,000
a_2 = build a moderate plant	$350,000
a_3 = build a large plant	$400,000 ← —— Maximum of the largest profits

decision to build a small plant (a_1) could result in three possible outcomes. There will be a $250,000 profit if demand is low (s_1), a $40,000 loss with medium demand (s_2), and no net change if there is a high demand (s_3). Clearly, the most favorable outcome for alternative a_1 would be the $250,000 profit. Similarly, $350,000 is the largest profit associated with a_2, and a $400,000 profit is the most favorable outcome for alternative a_3. Table 3.3 summarizes this information.

Naddol's management then selects the decision alternative that results in the maximum of these largest profits. As Table 3.3 indicates, that alternative is a_3. Hence, the recommended decision with the optimistic criterion is to build a large plant.

Although the optimistic criterion provides the opportunity for the largest possible profit ($400,000), it also exposes Naddol to the possibility of the maximum ($100,000) loss. In using this criterion, the decision maker, in effect, is acting like a gambler who disregards the dangers and looks foward only to the rewards. A company should not use such an approach unless it can afford the potential loss and unless this loss is small compared to the possible gain.

Pessimism   Another approach is to assume that each alternative will result in the worst possible outcome. Then the decision maker selects the alternative that leads to the best of these worst outcomes. Such a selection procedure is referred to as the **Wald** or **pessimistic criterion**. If the objective is to select the smallest outcome, this approach frequently is labeled the **minimax criterion**. When the decision maker seeks the largest outcome, the pessimistic approach is often called the **maximin criterion**.

In applying this criterion to Naddol's problem, management first determines the largest loss (or smallest profit) associated with each plant size. Table 3.2 shows that the decision to build a small plant (a_1) could result in a loss of as much as $40,000. This worst possible outcome would occur if there is medium demand (s_1). Similarly, $50,000 is the largest loss associated with a_2, and a $100,000 loss is the worst outcome associated with alternative a_3. The information is summarized in Table 3.4.

Naddol's management then selects the decision alternative that results

Table 3.4 Naddol's Worst Possible Outcomes

Decision Alternative	Largest Loss (Negative Profit)
a_1 = build a small plant	− $40,000
a_2 = build a moderate plant	− $50,000
a_3 = build a large plant	− $100,000

− $40,000 ← Minimum of the largest losses

in the minimum of these largest losses. As Table 3.4 indicates, that alternative is a_1. Thus, the recommended decision with the pessimistic criterion is to build a small plant.

By using this criterion, management avoids the possibility of extremely unfavorable outcomes. Naddol, for instance, can do no worse than a $40,000 loss. However, it also neglects potentially rewarding opportunities. Decision makers are inclined to have such an ultraconservative outlook when potential losses may be unacceptable and even ruinous for the organization. Military or defense decisions often involve this criterion.

Weighted Extremes   In practice, most decision makers are neither perfect optimists nor pure pessimists. Rather, their outlook tends to be somewhere in between. This observation led to a compromise criterion in which the manager first identifies both the best and worst outcomes associated with each decision alternative. Next, a scale of 0 to 1 is used to measure the decision maker's degree of optimism concerning the attainment of the most favorable outcomes. On such a scale, 0 represents complete pessimism and 1 signifies total optimism. The actual measurement, labeled alpha (α), is known as the **coefficient of optimism**. Each best outcome is weighted by this coefficient α, and the corresponding worst outcome is multiplied by the index of pessimism $(1 - \alpha)$. The resulting value

(3.1) $\alpha(\text{best outcome}) + (1 - \alpha)(\text{worst outcome})$

gives a weighted outcome for each decision alternative. Then the decision maker selects the alternative that provides the best of these weighted outcomes. Such a procedure is referred to as the **Hurwicz** or **coefficient of optimism criterion**.

In applying this criterion to Naddol's problem, let us assume that management is 40% confident that the company will always get the best possible outcome. Hence, $\alpha = .4$, and Naddol expects the worst to happen $1 - \alpha = 1 - .4 = .6$, or 60%, of the time. Using these weights, the best and

Table 3.5 Naddol's Weighted Outcomes with $\alpha = .4$

Decision Alternative	Largest Profit	Largest Loss (Negative Profit)	Weighted Profit = α(Largest Profit) + $(1 - \alpha)$(Largest Loss)
a_1 = build a small plant	$250,000	−$40,000	(.4)($250,000) + (.6)(−$40,000) = $76,000
a_2 = build a moderate plant	$350,000	−$50,000	(.4)($350,000) + (.6)(−$50,000) = $110,000
a_3 = build a large plant	$400,000	−$100,000	(.4)($400,000) + (.6)(−$100,000) = $100,000

Largest weighted
profit

worst outcome data from Tables 3.3 and 3.4, respectively, and expression (3.1), management would obtain the results shown in Table 3.5. As the table indicates, decision alternative a_2 leads to the largest weighted profit ($110,000). Therefore, the recommended decision with the coefficient of optimism criterion is to build a moderate plant.

This coefficient of optimism procedure is a more general approach than either the optimistic or pessimistic criterion. In fact, the optimistic and pessimistic criteria are merely special cases of the Hurwicz method. When $\alpha = 1$, for instance, all the weight is given to the best outcome. In that case, the coefficient of optimism criterion leads to the same recommendation as the optimistic criterion. Alternatively, if $\alpha = 0$, then all the weight is given to the worst outcome. In this case, the decision with the coefficient of optimism criterion is identical to the decision with the pessimistic criterion.

However, there are difficulties with the coefficient of optimism approach. The main problem is how to measure the value of α. Since α is a personal index of optimism, it should be based on the decision maker's subjective assessments. In practice, however, it is difficult to make such assessments in a consistent manner or arrive at a consensus. G. P. Huber [13] discusses several proposed methods. Unfortunately, none has been found entirely satisfactory.

Another concern involves the amount of data utilized in the approach. In computing weighted payoffs, the coefficient of optimism criterion considers only the best and worst outcomes. As a result, this approach ignores other outcomes that may be relevant to the decision. The optimistic and pessimistic criteria have a similar shortcoming.

Lost Opportunity   Other approaches consider more than just the two extreme outcomes. In one of these procedures, the evaluation is based on the remorse that the manager might experience after selecting a decision alternative. To see what is involved let us again examine Table 3.2.

Suppose that Naddol builds a small plant (a_1) and then learns that there is a high demand (s_3) for Star Cruisers. Table 3.2 indicates that the resulting profit will be $0. But if management knew beforehand that demand was going to be high, then the company would have built a large plant (a_3) and earned $400,000 profit. The difference between the best possible payoff ($400,000) and the outcome actually received ($0) is known as the **regret** or **opportunity loss** from the decision. Hence, when state of nature s_3 occurs, Naddol will incur an opportunity loss of

$400,000 - $0 = $400,000

if they selected alternative a_1.

Regrets can be calculated in a similar manner for each combination of decision alternative and state of nature. Table 3.2 indicates that $350,000 is the largest profit possible when there is medium demand (s_2). But if Naddol builds a small plant (a_1), then the company will *not* earn the $350,000 under the s_2 condition and in fact will lose $40,000. In other words, Naddol will have a regret of

$350,000 - (-$40,000) = $390,000

On the other hand, if the company builds a moderate plant (a_2) and then state of nature s_2 occurs, it will earn the largest possible profit ($350,000). Thus, the company will have a

$350,000 - $350,000 = $0

opportunity loss, or no regret.

Table 3.6 summarizes the opportunity loss information for Naddol's problem. Such a representation is called a **regret table** or **opportunity loss table**. Note that by its nature, the value of regret can never be negative.

Poor decisions will result in high opportunity losses. Hence, it has been argued that managers should avoid alternatives associated with large regrets. There are several ways to do so. One suggested approach is to first identify the largest possible opportunity loss for each decision alternative. Then the decision maker selects the alternative that leads to the smallest of these largest opportunity losses. Such a procedure is known as the **Savage** or **regret criterion**. Since this criterion is equivalent to selecting the best of the worsts, it, like the Wald approach, is pessimistic in nature.

Naddol's management can apply the Savage criterion by first using the opportunity loss data from Table 3.6 to determine the largest possible regret for each plant size. Table 3.7 reports the results.

Then the decision maker selects the plant size that results in the minimum of these largest opportunity losses. As Table 3.7 indicates, that alternative would be a_2. Therefore, the recommended decision with the regret criterion is to build a moderate plant.

By using this criterion, management will avoid extremely regretful

Table 3.6 Naddol's Regret Table

Decision Alternatives	States of Nature		
	s_1 = low demand	s_2 = medium demand	s_3 = high demand
a_1 = build a small plant	$0	$390,000	$400,000
a_2 = build a moderate plant	$300,000	$0	$340,000
a_3 = build a large plant	$350,000	$270,000	$0

Regret or opportunity loss

Table 3.7 Naddol's Largest Possible Regrets

Decision Alternative	Largest Regret
a_1 = build a small plant	$400,000
a_2 = build a moderate plant	$340,000 ← Smallest of the
a_3 = build a large plant	$350,000 largest regrets

decisions. Naddol, for instance, will limit its opportunity loss to $340,000. On the other hand, it also forgoes the potential benefits from exceptionally good decisions. In this respect, the Savage criterion is similar to hedging, that is, settling for an intermediate outcome rather than engaging in speculative ventures. The practice is prevalent in international and domestic commodity and currency trade.

Unfortunately, there is a technical flaw with the regret criterion. Remember, the opportunity losses from a particular state of nature are determined by comparing the outcomes for all available decision alternatives. Thus, when management adds or drops some alternatives, there are corresponding changes in the opportunity losses. If these added or dropped actions are not the best choices, they should have no effect on the selection of the remaining alternatives. But the opportunity loss changes could alter the ranking of alternatives and result in a revised recommendation. In addition, although all outcomes are considered in computing opportunity losses, the regret criterion utilizes only a portion of this information (the largest losses) to reach a decision.

Table 3.8 Naddol's Simple Average Outcomes

Decision Alternative	Simple Average of Profits
a_1 = build a small plant a_2 = build a moderate plant a_3 = build a large plant	($250,000 − $40,000 + $0)/3 = $70,000 (−$50,000 + $350,000 + $60,000)/3 = $120,000 (−$100,000 + $80,000 + $400,000)/3 = $126,666.67

Best of the
average profits

Average Outcome   It is possible to incorporate all outcome information in the evaluation process. A suggested approach is to first find the simple average of the outcomes associated with each decision alternative. Then the decision maker selects the alternative that results in the best of these average outcomes. This method is known as the **Laplace** or **rationality criterion**.

Table 3.2, for example, indicates that when Naddol builds a small plant (a_1), the company earns $250,000 profit if demand is low (s_1). On the other hand, it loses $40,000 when there is medium demand (s_2) and breaks even (earns $0 profit) in a high-demand situation (s_3). Consequently, this a_1 alternative will result in a

$$\frac{\$250,000 - \$40,000 + \$0}{3} = \frac{\$210,000}{3} = \$70,000$$

average profit. The simple average for each decision alternative is reported in Table 3.8. As the table indicates, decision alternative a_3 leads to the largest of the simple average profits ($126,666.67). Therefore, the recommended decision with the rationality criterion is to build a large plant.

By using the rationality criterion, the decision maker implicitly assumes that each state of nature is equally likely. This assumption is based on the **principle of insufficient reason**. According to this principle, if there is no basis for claiming that one event has a higher probability than another, each should be assigned an equal likelihood. In many practical situations, however, it would be difficult to accept the equal likelihood assumption. Why would a government budget analyst, for instance, believe that prosperity and depression are equally likely to follow a period of economic stagnation? Similarly, it seems unreasonable for a maintenance manager to assume that the probability of a breakdown will be the same on old and new equipment.

There is another problem with the rationality criterion. Suppose that a decision problem originally has three states of nature. Management subsequently separates one of them into two distinct events, each with the

Table 3.9 Decision Making Under Uncertainty

Optimism	Pessimism	Coefficient of Optimism	Regret	Rationality
1. Identify the most favorable outcome associated with each decision alternative. 2. Select the alternative that leads to the best of the most favorable outcomes.	1. Identify the worst outcome associated with each decision alternative. 2. Select the alternative that leads to the best of the worst outcomes.	1. Identify both the best and worst outcomes associated with each decision alternative. 2. Identify the decision maker's coefficient of optimism (α). The coefficient has a value between 0 and 1. 3. Calculate the following weighted outcome for each decision alternative: α (best outcome) + $(1 - \alpha)$ (worst outcome) 4. Select the alternative that leads to the best weighted outcome.	1. Calculate the regret associated with each state of nature. Regret is the difference between the best possible payoff and the outcome actually received from selecting a decision alternative. 2. Identify the largest regret associated with each decision alternative. 3. Select the alternative that leads to the smallest of largest regrets.	1. Compute the simple average outcome for each decision alternative. The simple average is the sum of outcomes divided by the number of events. 2. Select the decision alternative that leads to the best of these simple average outcomes.

same outcomes as the original state of nature. Although there are now four (instead of three) events, the basic structure of the problem remains the same. Consequently, the separation should not affect the selection of a decision alternative. Remember, however, that the simple average is found by summing the outcomes for a particular alternative and dividing the result by the number of events. When management creates the additional states of nature, it implicitly assigns a weight of $\frac{1}{4} + \frac{1}{4} = \frac{1}{2}$ rather than $\frac{1}{3}$ to the outcomes for the original event. In effect, then, the separation changes the original simple average. Unfortunately, such changes could alter the ranking of alternatives and lead to a revised decision.

Comparison of Criteria Table 3.9 summarizes the criteria for decision making under uncertainty. In applying these criteria to Naddol's problem, we have arrived at the following conclusions:

1. The pessimistic recommendation is to build a small plant (a_1).

2. The coefficient of optimism and regret decisions are to build a moderate plant (a_2).

3. The optimistic and rationality choices are to build a large plant (a_3).

Hence, even for this simple situation, there is lack of agreement among the criteria about the selection of a decision alternative. Such a result should not be surprising. Each manager has a unique attitude, outlook, and philosophy. Ultimately, this person will select a decision criterion that, according to his or her judgment, is consistent with these personal characteristics and is most appropriate for the situation. Our five criteria merely reflect what some decision makers might do. You may do something else and thus devise your own personal decision criterion.

Unfortunately, the ambiguous nature of decision making under uncertainty can cause problems. In practice, many decisions are made by committees. As E. F. Harrison [11] demonstrates, when these committees consist of individuals with conflicting philosophies, it may be difficult to arrive at a consensus. J. S. Dyer and R. F. Miles [8] discuss a method for resolving the conflicts, but even if such methods are successful, there may be a significant delay in the decision process. Sometimes, a committee may even be unable to make a decision.

In addition, each of the proposed criteria has a deficiency that can cause the manager to make a disastrous decision. These inadequacies can be traced to the same cause: None of the criteria utilize all the information generally available to the decision maker.

In effect, then, uncertainty about the states of nature limits our ability to analyze the decision situation. Increasing our knowledge about the environment will enable us to make more informed decisions. That is why most companies will not make a final decision until enough information is acquired to at least measure the uncertainty with probabilities.

DECISION MAKING UNDER RISK

Let us consider Example 3.2.

EXAMPLE 3.2 Toy Demand

This problem is a modified version of Example 3.1. Naddol's board chairperson thinks that the plant construction decision is too important to make under such uncertain conditions.

Consequently, she polls a group of company executives, industry officials, and consumer panels about the potential marketability of the Star Cruiser toy. Based on this information, she believes that

there is a 30% chance of low, 60% chance of medium, and 10% chance of high demand.

The chairperson wants to use this information for selecting the most profitable plant size.

In Example 3.2, Naddol's board chairperson has used executive and consumer opinions, as well as her own judgment, to subjectively assign probabilities for the states of nature. Specifically, if

$P(s_1) = $ probability of low demand

$P(s_2) = $ probability of medium demand

$P(s_3) = $ probability of high demand

she believes that

$P(s_1) = .3$

$P(s_2) = .6$

$P(s_3) = .1$

Each state of nature, then, has some likelihood of occurrence, and since the demand levels are collectively exhaustive, the sum of the probabilities is .3 + .6 + .1 = 1. As a result, Naddol's situation now involves risk rather than uncertainty.

In a risk situation, any one of the events is possible. Thus, decision criteria should, in some way, consider the outcomes associated with each state of nature. The criteria that best utilize all available information are based on expected outcomes.

Expected Value One approach usually suggested for decision making under risk is to first compute a weighted average outcome for each alternative. This average, which is called an **expected value**, is found by multiplying each outcome by its probability of occurrence and then summing the results. The decision maker then selects the alternative that leads to the best expected value. For obvious reasons, such a procedure is referred to as the **expected value (EV) criterion**. When the outcomes are measured in monetary terms, such as dollar profit or cost, this approach is also called the **expected monetary value (EMV) criterion**.

In applying this criterion to Naddol's problem, management must first determine the expected profit from each plant size. To do so, it will need the profit data from Table 3.2 and the chairperson's subjective probability assessments. This information indicates that the decision to build a small plant (a_1) will earn \$250,000 during $P(s_1) = .3$ proportion of the time (when there is low demand). In addition, alternative a_1 will provide a \$40,000 loss during $P(s_2) = .6$ proportion of the time (medium-demand occasions) and \$0 during $P(s_3) = .1$ proportion of the time (high-demand situations). Therefore, Naddol's weighted average or expected profit will be

$$\$250,000(.3) - \$40,000(.6) + \$0(.1) = \$51,000$$

if the company builds a small plant.

You can see that the more likely outcomes are given more weight than less probable payoffs. Furthermore, the probability of occurrence for an outcome is equivalent to the likelihood of the corresponding state of nature. In general, the expected monetary value for decision alternative a_i is given by the expression

$$(3.2) \quad \text{EMV}(a_i) = \sum_{j=1}^{n} [P(s_j)O_{ij}]$$

where O_{ij} = monetary outcome resulting from alternative a_i when state of nature s_j occurs, $P(s_j)$ = probability that state of nature s_j will occur, n = number of states of nature, and $\text{EMV}(a_i)$ = expected monetary value from alternative a_i. By using expression (3.2) to calculate the expected profit for each plant size, Naddol's management will get the results shown in Table 3.10.

The company should then select the plant size that leads to the largest expected profit. According to Table 3.10, that would be alternative a_2. Thus, the recommended decision with the expected monetary value criterion is to build a moderate plant.

It is important to realize that the expected value is not the outcome that the decision maker will get when he or she selects the recommended alternative. If Naddol builds a moderate plant, for instance, the company should not expect to receive a $201,000 profit. Indeed, as Table 3.2 shows, depending on the level of demand, actual profits will be $-$50,000$, $350,000, or $60,000. Rather, the expected value represents the average outcome that results over the long run from continually repeating the decision alternative. Suppose, for example, that Naddol plans to build a large number of moderate toy plants. Then the expected value of $201,000 will provide a good estimate of the average profit from such ventures.

An expected value approach can also be appropriate and valuable for one-time, nonrepetitive decision situations. A company may have to make several one-time decisions that each involve the same relative magnitude and structure. Such a situation resembles a single decision that will be repeated many times. By consistently using an expected value approach for each one-time decision, management will obtain an average outcome similar to that for the repetitive situation.

Expected Opportunity Loss   A related approach is to base the evaluation on the regret that the manager could expect from selecting each alternative. In this method, the decision maker first redefines the outcomes in terms of opportunity losses. Next, he or she calculates the expected value of the opportunity losses associated with each decision alternative. Then the manager selects the alternative that leads to the smallest of these expected opportunity losses. Such a procedure is referred to as the **expected opportunity loss (EOL) criterion**.

Table 3.10 Naddol's Expected Profits

a_1 = Build a Small Plant			
State of Nature s_j	Probability $P(s_j)$	Profit O_{ij}	Probability × Profit $P(s_j)O_{ij}$
s_1	.3	$250,000	$75,000
s_2	.6	−$40,000	−$24,000
s_3	.1	$0	$0

Expected Profit EMV(a_1) = $51,000

a_2 = Build a Moderate Plant			
State of Nature s_j	Probability $P(s_j)$	Profit O_{ij}	Probability × Profit $P(s_j)O_{ij}$
s_1	.3	−$50,000	−$15,000
s_2	.6	$350,000	$210,000
s_3	.1	$60,000	$6,000

Expected Profit EMV(a_2) = $201,000

a_3 = Build a Large Plant			
State of Nature s_j	Probability $P(s_j)$	Profit O_{ij}	Probability × Profit $P(s_j)O_{ij}$
s_1	.3	−$100,000	−$30,000
s_2	.6	$80,000	$48,000
s_3	.1	$400,000	$40,000

Expected Profit EMV(a_3) = $58,000

Table 3.6 gives Naddol's opportunity losses. These data and the chairperson's subjective probabilities indicate that alternative a_1 will involve no ($0) regret 30% of the time (occasions of low demand). However, this alternative will generate a $390,000 opportunity loss 60% of the time (occasions of medium demand) and a $400,000 regret 10% of the time (occasions of high demand). Therefore, Naddol's expected opportunity loss from building a small plant will be

$$\text{EOL}(a_1) = \$0(.3) + \$390,000(.6) + \$400,000(.1) = \$274,000$$

Similarly, if the company builds a moderate plant, there will be an expected opportunity loss of

$$\text{EOL}(a_2) = \$300,000(.3) + \$0(.6) + \$340,000(.1) = \$124,000$$

and if the company constructs a large plant, the expected opportunity loss will be

$$\text{EOL}(a_3) = \$350,000(.3) + \$270,000(.6) + \$0(.1) = \$267,000$$

These results indicate that alternative a_2 leads to the smallest expected opportunity loss. Consequently, the recommended decision with the EOL criterion is to build a moderate plant.

Recall that the expected monetary value criterion also recommended alternative a_2. This is not a coincidence. *The decision alternative with the best expected monetary value will always be the action that leads to the smallest expected opportunity loss.* Indeed, the EMV and EOL approaches are merely different sides of the same coin. Each offers a different philosophical explanation of why people make particular choices. Chapter 4 will show how this relationship between the EMV and EOL can be used to measure the value of information.

Most Probable Event   Sometimes, a decision maker assumes that the most likely state of nature is the event that will actually occur. The individual then selects the decision alternative that leads to the best outcome associated with this event. Such a procedure is known as the **maximum likelihood (ML) criterion**.

In applying this criterion to Naddol's problem, recall that the probabilities for the states of nature are .3 for s_1, .6 for s_2, and .1 for s_3. Hence, medium demand (s_2) is the most likely event. According to Table 3.2, when s_2 occurs, the company will incur a \$40,000 loss if a small plant was built (a_1). On the other hand, there will be a \$350,000 profit from a moderate plant (a_2) and an \$80,000 gain from a large plant (a_3). As you can see, a_2 is the most profitable alternative associated with the most likely event (s_2). Therefore, the recommended decision with the maximum likelihood criterion is to build a moderate plant.

Some nonrepetitive decisions are based on this criterion. A new venture, for instance, may have a high (.9 or more) likelihood for success. Although there is a chance of failure, the decision often will be based only on what happens when the venture succeeds (the most likely event).

There are some serious shortcomings in the maximum likelihood criterion. The major deficiency is that the approach ignores all but the most likely state of nature and thus uses only a small portion of the available information. In addition, suppose there is a large number of events and each has a small, nearly equal probability of occurrence. Under these circumstances, it may be difficult (if not impossible) to make a decision with this criterion.

Evaluation of Criteria   Table 3.11 summarizes the criteria for decision making under risk. Note that the expected value (EV) and expected

Table 3.11 Decision Making Under Risk

Expected Value (EV)	Expected Opportunity Loss (EOL)	Maximum Likelihood (ML)
1. Calculate the expected value for each decision alternative. 2. Select the alternative that leads to the best expected value.	1. Calculate the regret associated with each state of nature. 2. Compute the expected opportunity loss for each decision alternative. 3. Select the alternative that leads to the smallest expected opportunity loss.	1. Identify the state of nature that has the largest probability of occurrence. 2. Select the decision alternative that leads to the best outcome associated with the most likely state of nature.

opportunity loss (EOL) criteria always lead to the same decision recommendation and hence are interchangeable. These approaches are best suited for repetitive decisions or a group of one-time, nonrepetitive situations that involve a similar structure and magnitude of outcomes. Since the EV and EOL approaches both utilize all available problem information, they are the preferred criteria for decision making under risk.

An expected value measure, however, may be meaningless or inappropriate for a few rare nonrepetitive decisions. In such cases, the decision maker can resort to the maximum likelihood criterion. By doing so, the manager will, in effect, change the situation from risk to certainty.

DECISION MAKING UNDER CERTAINTY Suppose Naddol introduces the Star Cruiser in a wide variety of test markets and then measures sales over a period of several months. The company also continues to use the product in its consumer panels. Based on the test performance, panel data, and collective staff opinion, management is certain that there will be a medium demand for the toy. In effect, then, the decision maker can assign a probability of 1 to state of nature s_2. As a result, Naddol is now in a situation of certainty.

When there is certainty, the situation can be mapped as a decision table with a single column. In particular, Naddol's decision table would look like Table 3.12.

In this environment, the decision maker compares all the outcomes associated with the single state of nature and then selects the alternative that best meets the decision objective.

Table 3.12 supplies the relevant data for Naddol's problem. According to the table, when there is medium demand, the company will lose $40,000 with a small plant (a_1), will gain $350,000 with a moderate plant (a_2), and will gain $80,000 with a large plant (a_3). Since management wants to maximize profits, the best decision alternative under certainty is to build a moderate plant.

Table 3.12 Naddol's Decision Table Under Certainty

	State of Nature
Decision Alternatives	s_2 = medium demand
a_1 = build a small plant	$-$\$40,000
a_2 = build a moderate plant	\$350,000
a_3 = build a large plant	\$80,000

At first glance, it may appear that problems under certainty are quite simple, even trivial, to solve. In reality, decision making under certainty can be very difficult. The major obstacle arises from the large number of alternatives that the decision maker usually has to consider. In cases involving a finite number of options, it might be possible to examine each alternative with the aid of a computer. Typically, however, the decision maker has neither the time nor the resources to expend such an effort. And when there are an infinite number of alternatives, it is physically impossible to examine each possibility.

To some extent, these same computational difficulties exist for problems involving risk and uncertainty. That is why management scientists have developed mathematical models specifically designed for large-scale decision-making problems. Many of these models, including mathematical programming, network flows, sequential formulations, queuing and inventory theory, and simulation, will be discussed later in the text.

Figure 3.2 summarizes the decision theory process considered so far.

SEQUENTIAL DECISIONS

So far, we have considered only problems that involve a single, one-time decision. In these situations, the decision maker, at an isolated point in time, selects from among several independent alternatives. Furthermore, the resulting outcome is a direct consequence of the single alternative selected. Such circumstances are conveniently portrayed in a decision table.

Frequently, however, the problem involves a series of interrelated decisions. Under some of these circumstances, such as production scheduling, actions are required at specific times. For other situations, like product research and development, there is a natural order for the relevant tasks, but the dates might not be so important. In both cases, the manager must progressively select from among several separate but related alterna-

Figure 3.2 Decision Theory Process

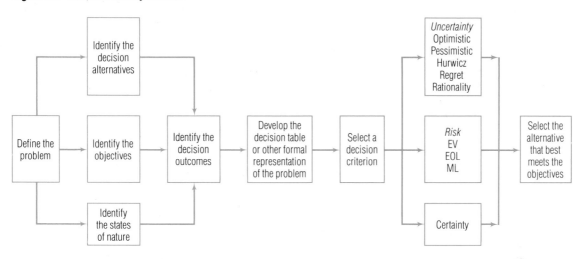

tives. Additionally, the outcome will depend on the entire sequence of actions taken. This type of situation is referred to as a **sequential decision**. It is also called a **multiperiod decision** when the required actions are represented by time or a **multistage decision** if there is a natural order of tasks. Example 3.3 provides an illustration of a sequential decision problem.

EXAMPLE 3.3 Pest Control

An infestation by the Adriatic fruit fly (adfly) is threatening the state's agricultural economy. In response to this threat, the governor has assembled a panel of pest control specialists and asked them to study the problem and develop some methods for attacking the adfly. After careful deliberations, the panel has identified three possible approaches. One method is to spray the infested areas from the air with an insecticide called malathion.

Although such a program is expected to be 100% effective, it will cost $10 million and result in "environmental damages" totaling an additional $5 million.

A second proposal calls for a multiple-step eradication program. In the first stage, a special scent will be used to lure male adflies into mechanical traps. It will cost $2 million to place and collect the traps. Next, argriculture personnel will conduct tests on the

scent/trap results to determine the number of fertile males remaining in the native population. Previous experience indicates that these traps have a 60% chance of reducing the fertile male population to a small number. There is also a 40% likelihood that the remaining number will be large. After studying the test results, the state will choose either one of two actions. One alternative is to sterilize the trapped males in a laboratory and then release them in the native population. Although sterilization has an estimated $3 million cost, it would, if successful, eradicate the adfly in a relatively short time and limit crop damage to $4 million. Otherwise, the damage is expected to reach $12 million. Previous studies indicate that if the traps leave a small number of fertile males, sterilization will succeed 70% of the time and fail 30% of the time. When the remaining number is large, however, there is only a 20% chance of success and an 80% likelihood of failure. A second alternative after testing the trap results is to spray the infested areas on the ground with malathion. Ground spraying will cost $6 million and result in another $4 million worth of "environmental damage," but it will completely eradicate the adfly.

The third proposal is to spray the infested areas from the air with a juvenile hormone that prevents the larvae from maturing into adult adflies. This program will cost $7 million but create no environmental damage. If it works, the adfly will become extinct in a short time, and crop damage will be limited to $3.5 million. Otherwise, the damage is expected to total $20 million. Previous experience indicates that the hormone has worked 50% of the time and failed on 50% of its applications.

The governor wants to use the least costly pest control program.

The pest control problem is different from our previous examples in two important ways. For one thing, the situation involves two separate but related decisions. The state government must first choose from among aerial malathion spraying, a scent/trap program, and the juvenile hormone approach. If it sets traps, officials must conduct tests, analyze the results, and then either release sterile male flies or ground-spray with malathion. Also, the same events do not apply to each decision alternative. Aerial malathion spraying has a certain known outcome, while the two other alternatives each involve a unique risk.

It would be difficult and cumbersome to depict such a problem with a decision table. That is why management scientists developed a tool designed specifically for these complex sequential decision problems.

DECISION TREES The decision maker can use a graph to conveniently organize and summarize the elements of the state's pest control problem. The decision maker starts by depicting the initial choice that must be made. The choice to be made is usually designated by a square with the alternatives shown as lines branching out to the right. In this graphic approach, such a square is referred to as a **decision point**.

Figure 3.3 portrays the initial decision point in the pest control problem. It shows that the government initially has three decision alternatives: to air-spray malathion, place scent traps, or air-spray the juvenile hormone.

The next step is to identify the immediate consequences of selecting each of the initial alternatives. Aerial spraying, for instance, has only one effect: It will completely eradicate the adfly. Scent traps, however, are another matter. The immediate result of this program is to leave either a small or a

Figure 3.3 The Government's Initial Decision Point

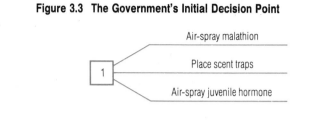

Air-spray malathion

Place scent traps

Air-spray juvenile hormone

Figure 3.4 The Government's Initial Chance Points

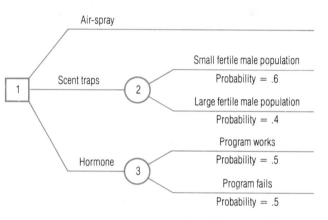

large number of fertile male flies in the native population. There is a 60% chance that the remaining number will be small and a 40% likelihood of it being large. Similarly, the juvenile hormone will either work (50% of the time) or fail (50% of the time).

Such stochastic events are typically shown as circles with lines branching to the right. In this graphic approach, these circles are called **event points** or **chance points**. The government's initial chance points are illustrated in Figure 3.4. Notice that on a chance point branch, the state of nature appears above the line and the probability below the line.

Management must continue this process of branching from left to right until it has identified all possible decision and chance points involved in the problem. At this stage (Figure 3.4), the scent trap program is the only initial alternative that involves further branching. After collecting traps, conducting tests, and studying the results, the government must make another choice. It will either sterilize the trapped male flies in a laboratory and then release them in the native population, or it will spray the infested areas on the ground with malathion. The choice must be made whether there is a small number or large number of remaining fertile males. The second decision points are shown in Figure 3.5.

Figure 3.5 The Government's Second Decision Points

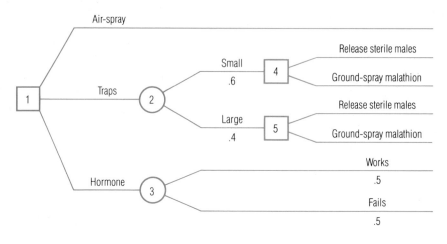

The government is certain that ground spraying will eradicate the adfly. Hence, this action will create no further branching. On the other hand, if the traps leave a small number of fertile males, sterilization will succeed 70% of the time and fail 30% of the time. When the remaining number is large, there is only a 20% chance of success and an 80% likelihood of failure with sterilization. As a result, the problem involves the additional chance points shown in Figure 3.6.

After constructing all the branches, the decision maker must then identify the corresponding outcomes. For example, aerial malathion spraying will cost $10 million and result in "environmental damages" totaling an additional $5 million. Thus, there will be a $15 million cost associated with the air-spray branch in Figure 3.6. Similarly, the scent traps cost $2 million and sterilization another $3 million. In addition, when this scent/sterilization program is successful, crop damage for the adfly will be limited to $4 million. Consequently, the traps/small/sterilize/success (or traps/large/sterilize/success) branch in Figure 3.6 results in a $9 million cost. However, when scent/sterilization is a failure, crop damage will reach $12 million, Thus, the traps/small/sterilize/failure (or traps/large/sterilize/failure) branch has a cost of $17 million.

The outcomes associated with each branch in the government's pest control problem are shown at the right of Figure 3.7. This type of graphic representation is referred to as a **decision tree**. It shows at a glance the order in which decisions are expected to be made, the consequences of these actions, and the resulting outcomes. As such, the decision tree serves as an excellent management communication device.

Although decision trees are best suited for complex sequential managerial problems, they are also applicable to simpler single-stage situations. In

Figure 3.6 The Government's Second Chance Points

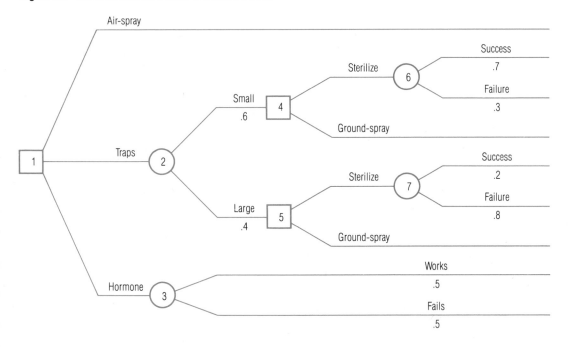

other words, the decision tree can be an effective substitute for a payoff table.

FINDING THE SOLUTION The government is now in a position to evaluate the three pest control plans. To do so, it first must identify the outcomes that can be expected from each decision alternative. In the case of aerial malathion spraying, the identification process is easy. The government is certain that this spraying will cost $15 million. However, the two other alternatives involve risk, and one of these also requires a sequence of decisions. As a result, it will be more difficult to determine the expected costs of the scent/trap and juvenile hormone programs.

Consider the scent/trap program. As Figure 3.7 indicates, if the traps leave a large number of fertile males and the government subsequently ground-sprays the infested areas, the cost will total $12 million. On the other hand, the government can release sterile males in the native population rather than ground spraying the infested areas. If successful, sterilization in this situation will result in a cost of only $9 million. Thus, the cost of the scent/trap program will depend on the events that occur and the resulting actions taken after the government sets the traps.

Figure 3.7 The Government's Decision Tree

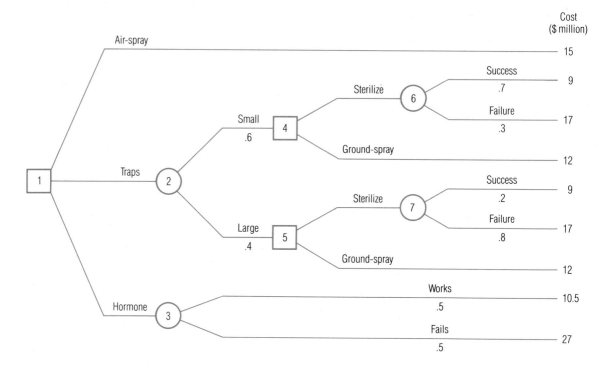

Consequently, to determine this cost, the decision maker must start at the right of the decision tree and work backward to the initial decision point.

For example, let us examine the action required if the traps leave a small number of fertile male flies in the native population. Figure 3.8 shows the relevant portion of the government's decision tree. As you can see, the action involves decision point 4.

If the government decides to sterilize, it will be faced with the risk depicted by chance point 6. That is, there will be a .7 probability of incurring a $9 million expense and a .3 chance that the cost will be $17 million. In this situation, then, sterilization has an expected cost of

$9(.7) + $17(.3) = $11.4 million

For convenience, this value is placed above the applicable chance point inside a rectangle.

The decision to ground-spray at decision point 4 will lead to a certain cost of $12 million. Since the expected cost ($11.4 million) for sterilization is less than $12 million, the government should disregard ground spraying at decision point 4. That is, if the traps leave only a small number of fertile males, the decision maker should release sterile flies in the native popula-

Figure 3.8 Small Portion of the Government's Decision Tree

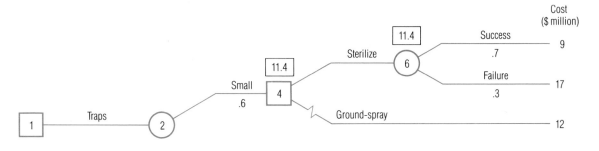

Figure 3.9 Large Portion of the Government's Decision Tree

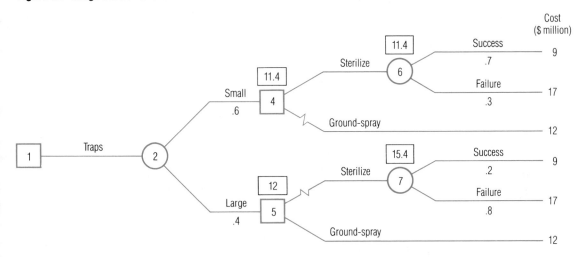

tion. This choice, of course, assumes that expected monetary value is an appropriate decision criterion for the government officials.

For convenience, the branch of the disregarded alternative in Figure 3.8 is marked with a jagged line. Also, the best outcome ($11.4 million) is placed inside a rectangle above the applicable decision point (4).

Government officials can handle decision point 5 in a similar manner, as Figure 3.9 illustrates. In this situation, the $12 million cost of ground spraying is less than the

$$\$9(.2) + \$17(.8) = \$15.4 \text{ million}$$

expected cost for sterilization. Thus, if the traps leave a large number of fertile males, the government should ground-spray the infested areas with

Figure 3.10 The Government's Backward Induction Analysis

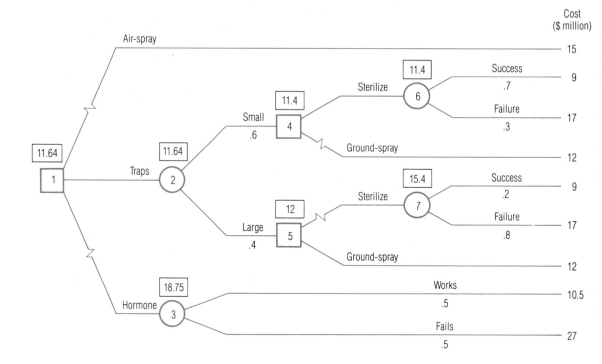

malathion. Also, note that the $12 million cost for decision point 5 becomes the outcome associated with the branch emerging from chance point 2, for a large number of fertile males. Furthermore, there is a 40% chance of incurring this cost. Similarly, the $11.4 million expected cost for decision point 4 becomes the outcome associated with the branch emerging from chance point 2 for a small number of fertile males. There is a 60% likelihood of incurring this expense.

Management must continue to "prune" branches in a similar manner by successively working from right to left through the decision tree. The right-to-left movement will end when the decision maker has evaluated each alternative at the initial decision point. Management scientists refer to this process as **backward induction**.

Figure 3.10 completes the process for the government's pest control problem. As the figure indicates, the trap program's expected cost ($11.4 million) is less than the known expense ($15 million) for aerial malathion spraying. The scent/trap approach also has a lower expected cost than the $18.75 million juvenile hormone program. Thus, at decision point 1, the government should select the scent/trap program and disregard the aerial malathion spraying and juvenile hormone program. We indicate this choice in Figure 3.10 by marking the air-spray and hormone branches with a jagged line. Also, the lowest expected cost ($11.64 million) is placed inside a rectangle above decision point 1.

According to the backward induction analysis, the government should institute the scent/trap program. If the traps leave a small number of fertile males, the government should then release sterile flies in the native population. However, if there is a large number of remaining fertile males, the government is advised to ground-spray the infested areas with malathion. This decision plan, illustrated by the "unpruned" branches that remain on the decision tree in Figure 3.10, provides the minimum expected cost ($11.64 million) of adfly control.

APPLICATIONS Decision trees have been applied to a wide variety of managerial problems. J. D. Braverman [2], L. A. Digman [7], and F. E. Williams [25] each report a different marketing application. D. O. Cooper and colleagues [5] and S. C. Wheelwright [22] show how the decision tree approach can be used in financial analysis. A plant expansion application is presented by W. G. Sullivan and W. W. Claycombe [19], while R. A. Flinn and E. Turban [9] examine the role of the decision tree in the analysis of an industrial research and development project.

SUMMARY This chapter introduced the subject of decision theory. We begin by identifying the essential elements of a decision problem. These elements consist of one or more objectives, at least two decision alternatives, several states of nature, and various resulting outcomes. The elements are then organized and summarized in a decision table. This formal structure, or model, provides a framework for analyzing simple, single-stage decision problems. It also makes it easier to perform an initial screening and eliminate any dominated strategies from further consideration.

The next step in the decision theory approach is to select the alternative that best meets the objectives. Several criteria can be used to make this selection. The choice of a criterion is based on the manager's degree of knowledge about the states of nature. In this respect, there are situations of uncertainty, risk, and certainty.

In a situation of uncertainty, the decision maker knows the possible states of nature but is unable to assign probabilities to the events. Under these circumstances, the manager can use the optimistic, pessimistic, Hurwicz, regret, or rationality criterion to select a decision alternative. (Table 3.9 summarized these criteria.) Unfortunately, each of the criteria has a deficiency that can cause the manager to make a disastrous decision. These inadequacies exist because none of the criteria utilize all the information generally available to the decision maker.

Since uncertainty severely limits the analysis, most decision makers acquire additional information before making a final decision. If the knowledge enables the manager to assess state of nature probabilities, the situation is called risk. In this situation, management can use the expected value (EV), expected opportunity loss (EOL), or maximum likelihood (ML) criterion to select an alternative. (Table 3.11 summarized these criteria.) The expected monetary value and expected opportunity loss criteria are interchangeable. Each is best suited for repetitive decisions or a group of one-time, nonrepetitive situations that involve similar structures and magnitudes of outcomes. The maximum likelihood approach is appropriate for the few rare nonrepetitive situations in which an expected value measure would be meaningless.

When the decision maker knows exactly which state of nature will occur, the situation is called certainty. In this environment, management compares all outcomes associated with the single event and then selects the alternative that best meets the objectives. The major obstacle is the large number of alternatives that usually must be considered.

Figure 3.2 summarized the decision theory process. Then the analysis was extended to problems involving a series of interrelated decisions. In such cases, the problem is best portrayed as a decision tree consisting of decision points, branches, and event or chance points. Management selects the best sequence of actions with a backward induction analysis of the decision tree.

Glossary

backward induction   The process of evaluating alternatives by successively working from right to left through the decision tree.

certainty   A situation where the decision maker knows exactly which state of nature will occur.

coefficient of optimism   A value between 0 and 1 that measures the decision maker's degree of optimism concerning the attainment of the most favorable outcomes in a decision problem.

collectively exhaustive events   A group of events that includes all possible future situations.

courses of action (decision alternatives)   The controllable inputs, or the options available to and controlled by the decision maker.

decision analysis (decision theory)   A rational way to conceptualize, analyze, and solve problems in situations involving limited, or partial, information about the decision environment.

decision criteria   Logical, or rational, methods for choosing the alternative that best meets the decision objectives.

decision point A square on a graph indicating that a choice must be made between two or more alternatives.

decision tree A graphic representation of the courses of action, states of nature, and outcomes involved in a decision problem.

dominance The situation where one alternative provides outcomes that are, for some events, equal to and, in one or more states, better than the payoffs from another action.

event (chance) point A circle on a graph indicating that two or more states of nature will follow.

events, possible futures, or states of nature The uncontrollable inputs or future events that affect the outcome of a decision.

expected monetary value (EMV) criterion An expected value criterion in which the outcomes are measured in monetary terms.

expected opportunity loss (EOL) criterion Selecting the decision alternative that leads to the smallest expected opportunity loss.

expected value An average found by multiplying each outcome by its probability of occurrence and then summing the results.

expected value (EV) criterion Selecting the decision alternative that leads to the best expected value.

Hurwicz (coefficient of optimism) criterion Weighting each best outcome by α and the corresponding worst payoff by $(1 - \alpha)$, summing the result, and then selecting the decision alternative that leads to the best weighted sum.

Laplace (rationality) criterion Selecting the decision alternative that leads to the best simple average outcome.

maximax criterion An optimistic criterion in which the objective is to find the largest outcome.

maximin criterion A pessimistic criterion in which the objective is to find the largest outcome.

maximum likelihood (ML) criterion Selecting the decision alternative that leads to the best outcome associated with the most probable state of nature.

minimax criterion A pessimistic criterion in which the objective is to find the smallest outcome.

minimin criterion An optimistic criterion in which the objective is to find the smallest outcome.

multiperiod decision A sequential decision in which the alternatives are selected at several points in time.

multistage decision A sequential decision in which tasks are arranged in a natural order.

mutually exclusive events Events that cannot occur simultaneously.

objective probability The proportion of times that an event was actually observed in the past or in an experiment.

optimistic criterion Selecting the decision alternative that leads to the best of the most favorable outcomes.

payoff (decision outcome) The outcome that will result from the combination of a decision alternative and a state of nature.

payoff table (decision table) A tabular representation of the elements (courses of action, states of nature, and outcomes) in a decision-making problem.

principle of insufficient reason The principle that if there is no basis for claiming that one event has a higher probability than another, each should be assigned an equal likelihood.

regret (opportunity loss) The difference between the best possible payoff for a state of nature and the outcome actually received from selecting a decision alternative.

regret table (opportunity loss table) A tabular representation of the decision alternatives, states of nature, and opportunity losses associated with a decision problem.

risk A situation in which the decision maker can assess only the probability of occurrence for each state of nature.

Savage (regret) criterion Selecting the decision alternative that leads to the smallest of the largest possible regrets.

sequential decision A problem that involves a series of inter-related decisions.

subjective probability The decision maker's personal belief or judgment about the likelihood of a future event.

uncertainty A situation in which the decision maker can identify the states of nature but is unable to assess their likelihood of occurrence.

Wald (pessimistic) criterion Selecting the decision alternative that leads to the best of the worst possible outcomes.

References

1. Barron, F. H. "Behavioral Decision Theory: A Topical Bibliography for Management Scientists." *Interfaces* (November 1974):56.

2. Braverman, J. D. "A Decision Theoretic Approach to Pricing." *Decision Sciences* (January 1971):1.

3. Brown, R. V., et al. *Decision Analysis for the Manager*. New York: Holt, Rinehart & Winston, 1974.

4. Conrath, D. W. "From Statistical Decision Theory to Practice: Some Problems with the Transition." *Management Science* (April 1973):873.

5. Cooper, D. O., et al. "A Tool for More Effective Financial Analysis." *Interfaces* (February 1975):91.

6. DeNeufville, R., and R. L. Keeney. "Use of Decision Analysis in Airport Development for Mexico City," in *Analysis of Public Systems*, edited by A. W. Drake. Cambridge: M.I.T. Press, 1970.

7. Digman, L. A. "A Decision Analysis of the Airline Coupon Strategy." *Interfaces* (April 1980):97.

8. Dyer, J. S., and R. F. Miles. "An Actual Application of Collective Choice Theory to the Selection of Trajectories for the Mariner Jupiter Saturn 1977 Project." *Operations Research* (March–April 1976):220.

9. Flinn, R. A., and E. Turban. "Decision Tree Analysis for

Industrial Research." *Research Management* (January 1970):27.

10. Fries, B. E. "Bibliography of Operations Research in Health-Care Systems." *Operations Research* (September–October 1976):801.

11. Harrison, E. F. *The Managerial Decision Making Process.* Boston: Houghton Mifflin, 1975.

12. Holloway, C. A. *Decision Making Under Uncertainty.* Englewood Cliffs, N.J.: Prentice-Hall, 1979.

13. Huber, G. P. *Managerial Decision Making.* Dallas: Scott, Foresman, 1980.

14. Jones, J. M. *Introduction to Decision Theory.* Homewood, Ill.: Irwin, 1977.

15. Newman, J. W. *Management Applications of Decision Analysis.* New York: Harper & Row, 1971.

16. Oxenfelt, A. R. *A Basic Approach to Executive Decision Making.* New York: AMACOM, 1978.

17. Sarin, R. K. "Elicitation of Subjective Probabilities in the Context of Decision Making." *Decision Sciences* (January 1978):37.

18. Spetzler, C. S., and C. A. Stael von Holstein. "Probability

Encoding in Decision Analysis." *Management Science* (November 1975):340.

19. Sullivan, W. G., and W. W. Claycombe. "The Use of Decision Trees in Planning Plant Expansion." *Advanced Management Journal* (Winter 1975):29.

20. Tummala, V. M. R. *Decision Analysis with Business Applications.* New York: Intext Educational Publishers, 1973.

21. Turban, E., and N. P. Loomba. *Readings in Management Science.* Dallas: Business Publications, 1976. Chap. 2.

22. Wheelwright, S. C. "Applying Decision Theory to Improve Corporate Management of Currency-Exchange Risks." *California Management Review* (Summer 1975):48.

23. White, D. J. *Decision Methodology.* New York: Wiley, 1975.

24. Whitmore, G. A. "A Simple Proof That Dollar Averaging Is a Maximin Investment Strategy." *Decision Sciences* (July 1978):510.

25. Williams, F. E. "Decision Theory and the Innkeeper: An Approach for Setting Hotel Reservation Policy." *Interfaces* (August 1977):18.

Thought Exercises

1. Identify the courses of action and states of nature in each of the following situations. Explain.

   a. The proprietor of a newspaper stand must decide how many copies of tomorrow's edition to order. He does not know how many copies will be purchased.

    b. Jane Tompkins is trying to decide on the amount of the deductible for the collision insurance on her automobile. Her decision will be influenced by the potential damage that may occur in an accident.

    c. Mammoth Enterprises can invest its excess cash in blue-chip growth stocks. The potential profits depend on stock market trends. There can be continued growth, stability, or a gradual decline.

2. Consider the following statements:

    a. If I buy a T plus account, the savings and loan association will pay me the prevailing treasury bill rate plus $\frac{1}{4}\%$.

    b. These 3 gallons of gasoline will allow me to drive 90 miles.

    c. Depending on weather conditions, our boat will sail 10, 20, or 30 miles today.

    d. We can build three homes on each acre of land.

Identify the decision environment described by each statement. Explain.

3. For each of the following situations, indicate whether the decision maker should use a subjective or objective method to assign probability. Explain.

    a. A real estate agent wants to know the probability that interest rates will rise next month.

    b. A product shipment is known to contain one defective part. The purchasing manager wants to determine the probability that a randomly chosen part will turn out to be defective.

    c. NASA has just launched a unique rocket mission to Venus. Its director is asked to estimate the mission's chance for success.

    d. The manager of a large department store wants to know the probability that a randomly chosen person who enters the store will make a purchase.

    e. A movie producer wants to estimate the chance that her new picture will earn a profit.

4. A television executive is attempting to assign probability values to the possible viewing audience for a new program. Relying on knowledge, experience, and intuitive judgment, the executive subjectively assigns the following probabilities:

    $P(\text{under two million viewers}) = .20$

    $P(\text{two to five million viewers}) = .45$

    $P(\text{over five million viewers}) = .25$

Before the executive uses these estimates to perform further probability calculations, what advice would you offer?

5. To save on gasoline expenses, Janet and Joe agree to form a car pool for traveling to and from school. After limiting the travel routes to two alternatives, the students cannot agree on the best way to get to school. The situation is represented by the following payoff table, where entries represent travel time.

	States of Nature	
Decision Alternatives	$s_1 =$ light freeway traffic	$s_2 =$ heavy freeway traffic
$a_1 =$ take freeway	10 minutes	40 minutes
$a_2 =$ take Walnut Avenue	20 minutes	20 minutes

The students do not know the condition of the freeway ahead of time. If Janet is an optimist, which route do you think she prefers? Explain. If Joe is a pessimist, which route do you think he prefers? Explain.

6. A marketing manager has the product-pricing problem represented by the following payoff table, where entries represent the percentage change in demand for the product. Research indicates that $P(s_1) = .1$, $P(s_2) = .7$, and $P(s_3) = .2$.

	States of Nature		
Courses of Action	$s_1 =$ low brand loyalty	$s_2 =$ moderate brand loyalty	$s_3 =$ high brand loyalty
$a_1 =$ no change in price	0%	2%	10%
$a_2 =$ lower the price	1%	3%	5%

This manager always treats the most likely event as if it were certain to occur. Then he selects the course of action that will lead to the best payoff for that state. Can you predict what price policy this manager will select? Explain.

7. Two university presidents have the same staffing problem. It is represented by the following payoff table, where entries represent the change in net revenue for the university. At these universities, each enrollment state is equally likely.

	States of Nature		
Courses of Action	$s_1 =$ increase in enrollement	$s_2 =$ no change in enrollment	$s_3 =$ decrease in enrollment
$a_1 =$ hire more faculty	$200,000	$0	−$100,000
$a_2 =$ keep the same number of faculty	$150,000	$50,000	−$20,000
$a_3 =$ fire some faculty	$10,000	$30,000	$50,000

One university president selects the course of action that leads to the most preferred expected payoff. The other simply adds the payoffs for each action (row) and selects the alternative with the most preferred total payoff. Yet each arrives at the same decision. Can you explain this result?

8. U. N. Able has the investment problem represented by the following payoff table, where entries represent return on investment. Historical data indicate that the probabilities of the economic conditions are $P(s_1) = .3$, $P(s_2) = .5$, and $P(s_3) = .2$.

Courses of Action	States of Nature		
	s_1 = recession	s_2 = stability	s_3 = expansion
a_1 = invest in savings	$10,000	$10,000	$10,000
a_2 = invest in bonds	$5,000	$20,000	$25,000
a_3 = invest in stocks	$-$10,000	$15,000	$50,000

According to Able's investment counselor, the bond investment will lead to the smallest possible regret. On that basis, the counselor recommends a_2. How did the counselor reach this conclusion? What would you recommend? Explain.

9. Refer back to Examples 3.1 and 3.2 in the text. Suppose Naddol's board chairperson has continued the consultation process with marketing and sales personnel, industry officials, and consumer groups. Through this additional consultation, she learns that toys like the Star Cruiser have life spans of approximately two years. The information also reveals that her subjective probabilities of $P(s_1) = .3$, $P(s_2) = .6$, and $P(s_3) = .1$ are appropriate for market conditions mainly during the first half of the product life cycle. Industry experience reveals that sales could rise, remain the same, or fall during the second year. According to available data, there is a 20% chance for a sales increase and a 30% likelihood that they will remain stable.

Based on this information, the chairperson instructs company management to adopt a wait and see approach. At the beginning of the two-year cycle, Naddol will build a small, moderate, or large plant. One year later, management will compare plant output to market demand. At that time, they must decide whether or not to expand capacity. Expansion will be considered only if the first-year demand is sufficient to warrant additional capacity. Hence, Naddol might want to expand when the original plant is small and first-year sales are medium or large. Similarly, there could be expansion if sales are high but the plant is moderate in size.

The experts believe that Table 3.2 represents only the first-year profits and losses. If Naddol expands, they could obtain an additional $50,000 profit when the initial plant is small, first-year

demand is medium, capacity expands, and second-year sales
increase. Other possibilities are summarized in the following table.

Initial Plant Size	First-Year Demand	Second Action	Second-Year Sales	Additional Profit ($ thousand)
Small	Medium	Expand	Rise	50
Small	Medium	Expand	Same	−10
Small	Medium	Expand	Fall	−30
Small	Medium	Do not expand	Rise	0
Small	Medium	Do not expand	Same	0
Small	Medium	Do not expand	Fall	−5
Small	High	Expand	Rise	85
Small	High	Expand	Same	−10
Small	High	Expand	Fall	−30
Small	High	Do not expand	Rise	0
Small	High	Do not expand	Same	0
Small	High	Do not expand	Fall	−5
Moderate	High	Expand	Rise	125
Moderate	High	Expand	Same	110
Moderate	High	Expand	Fall	75
Moderate	High	Do not expand	Rise	0
Moderate	High	Do not expand	Same	0
Moderate	High	Do not expand	Fall	0

a. How does this problem differ from Examples 3.1 and 3.2?
b. How would you structure this decision problem? Develop such a structure.
c. What decision plan should Naddol's management follow in this new situation? Explain.
d. How does your recommendation compare to the solution for Example 3.2? Explain.

10. Explain why you agree or disagree with each of the following statements:
   a. Courses of action are independent of the states of nature.
   b. States of nature are mutually exclusive and collectively exhaustive events.
   c. Decision trees are most useful when the problem involves a sequence of decisions.
   d. In one sense, management science can be thought of as an attempt to move the decision maker from a state of uncertainty toward a state of certainty.
   e. Since the criteria for decision making under uncertainty can lead to different recommendations, these approaches are too ambiguous to use in practice.
   f. The best decision is always the one that leads to the minimum expected opportunity loss.
   g. The criteria for decision making under uncertainty are also appropriate for risk situations.

1. You are given the following decision table. Develop the corresponding decision tree.

	States of Nature	
Courses of Action	s_1	s_2
a_1	20	50
a_2	30	10
a_3	80	60

2. Develop the decision table that corresponds to the following decision tree.

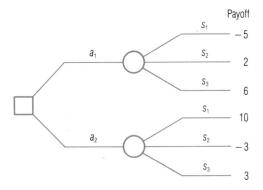

3. You are given the following decision table, where entries represent profits in millions of dollars.

Decision Alternatives	**States of Nature**		
	s_1	s_2	s_3
a_1	-2	2	6
a_2	-1	0	5
a_3	2	3	1

What is the recommended decision under each of the following criteria?

a. Optimistic
b. Pessimistic
c. Hurwicz with $\alpha = .3$, then $\alpha = .8$
d. Regret
e. Rationality

4. Consider the following decision tree. What is the recommended decision under each of the following criteria?
   a. Optimistic
   b. Pessimistic
   c. Hurwicz with $\alpha = .5$
   d. Regret
   e. Rationality

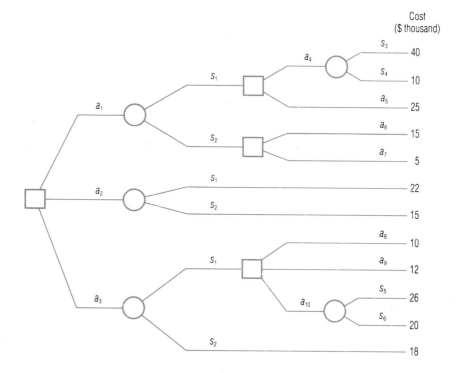

5. Consider the following decision table for a particular investment problem. The payoffs represent profits in millions of dollars.

Courses of Action	State of Nature		
	s_1 = prices go up	s_2 = prices remain stable	s_3 = prices go down
a_1 = invest in project A	2	1	−.5
a_2 = invest in project B	4.5	.2	−.3
a_3 = do not invest	0	0	0

a. Develop the corresponding decision tree.
b. What is the recommended optimistic decision?
c. What is the recommended pessimistic decision?
d. If the investor knows that prices will remain stable, what is the recommended decision?

6. Icetown Ski Resort is considering the addition of equipment that would create artificial snow. The situation is represented by the following decision table, where the entries in the cells are weekly profits or losses.

Decision Alternatives	States of Nature		
	s_1 = light snowfall	s_2 = moderate snowfall	s_3 = heavy snowfall
a_1 = buy a machine	$15,000	$10,000	− $5,000
a_2 = modify equipment	$ 12,000	$8,000	− $1,000
a_3 = do not invest	− $6,000	$0	$4,000

a. What is the recommended regret decision?
b. Assume that the resort manager has a coefficient of optimism of $\alpha = .6$. Using the Hurwicz criterion, what is the recommended decision?

7. You are given the following decision table, where entries represent monetary returns. Also, $P(s_1) = .3$, $P(s_2) = .5$, and $P(s_3) = .2$.

Courses of Action	States of Nature		
	s_1	s_2	s_3
a_1	$50,000	$100,000	$150,000
a_2	$100,000	$20,000	$0
a_3	− $30,000	$0	$200,000

a. What is the recommended EMV decision?
b. What is the recommended EOL decision?
c. Compare the results from parts (a) and (b).
d. What is the recommended ML decision?

8. Consider the following payoff table, where entries represent costs in millions of dollars. Also, $P(s_1) = .2$, $P(s_2) = .4$, $P(s_3) = .3$, and $P(s_4) = .1$.

Decision Alternatives	States of Nature			
	s_1	s_2	s_3	s_4
a_1	5	2	1	-4
a_2	-3	0	2	4

a. What is the recommended EMV decision?
b. What is the recommended EOL decision?
c. Compare the results from parts (a) and (b).
d. What is the recommended ML decision?

9. Refer to technique exercise 5. Assume that $P(s_1) = .2$, $P(s_2) = .5$, and $P(s_3) = .3$.
   a. What is the recommended EOL decision?
   b. What is the expected profit from the EOL decision in part (a)?
   c. Determine the expected profit for each of the recommended decisions in technique exercise 5.
   d. Compare the results of parts (b) and (c).

10. Refer to Icetown's equipment decision (technique exercise 6). Assume that $P(s_1) = .3$, $P(s_2) = .4$, and $P(s_3) = .3$.
    a. What is the recommended EOL decision?
    b. What is the expected profit from the EOL decision in part (a)?
    c. Determine the expected profit for each of the recommended decisions in technique exercise 6.
    d. Compare the results of parts (b) and (c). What does the comparison indicate?

11. Consider Naddol's plant construction problem (Example 3.1). It is represented by the following decision table.

Courses of Action	States of Nature		
	s_1 = low demand	s_2 = medium demand	s_3 = high demand
a_1 = build a small plant	$250,000	$-$40,000	$0
a_2 = build a moderate plant	$-$50,000	$350,000	$60,000 ← Profit
a_3 = build a large plant	$100,000	$80,000	$400,000

Loss

Assume that $P(s_1) = .2$, $P(s_2) = .6$, and $P(s_3) = .2$. What is the recommended EMV decision? Compare this decision to those recommended by the criteria for decision making under certainty and uncertainty. Comment.

12. A local government agency is planning its paper supply needs for the coming month. The situation is represented by the following payoff table, where the entries in the cells give the annual purchase costs.

Decision Alternatives	States of Nature		
	s_1 = low usage	s_2 = moderate usage	s_3 = high usage
a_1 = order from supplier A	$100,000	$200,000	$400,000
a_2 = order from supplier B	$50,000	$150,000	$500,000

a. Assume that the agency's director has a coefficient of optimism of $\alpha = .9$. Using the Hurwicz criterion, what is the recommended decision?

b. Develop the opportunity loss table.

c. Develop the corresponding decision tree (in terms of opportunity losses).

d. Use the decision tree to determine the recommended regret decision.

e. Assume that $P(s_1) = .1$, $P(s_2) = .4$, and $P(s_3) = .5$. What is the recommended EOL decision? Show the backward induction involved in the decision tree.

f. Compare the EOL for the results in parts (d) and (e). Comment.

13. You are given the following decision tree. What decision plan do you recommend? What will the expected revenue be from your plan?

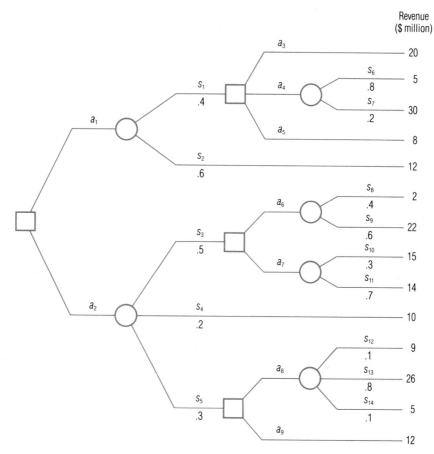

14. A personnel manager has the following decision tree. The numbers to the right of the decision tree represent the change in an employee's monthly output. What testing/promotion policy would you recommend? What will be the expected change in monthly output from your plan?

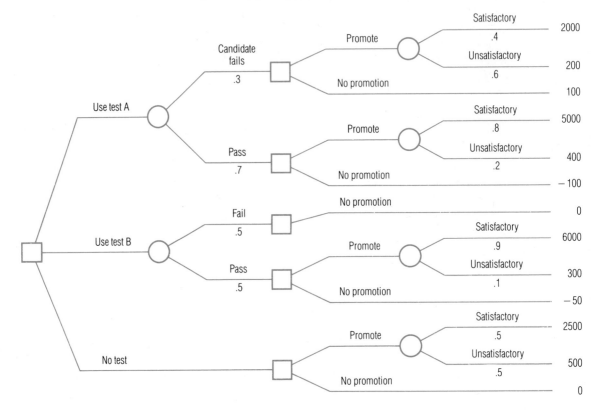

Applications
Exercises 1. The public-service television network has been receiving low ratings for its 5–7 P.M time slot. Currently, management is considering three alternatives for this slot: a sports show, travel films, or a political discussion program. The percent of viewing audience estimates depend on the demographic characteristics of the viewers. Audiences are demographically classified as "family oriented" or "sensation oriented." Market research indicates that the network can expect 10% of a "family-oriented" audience to view the sports show telecast. Five percent (5%) of a "family-oriented" audience can be expected to view travel films, and 40% of this audience will watch the political discussion program. Among the "sensation-oriented" viewers, the network can expect 20% to watch the sports show, 25% to view travel films, and 5% to watch the political discussion program.

   a. The network public relations executive is completely optimistic and wants to select the program that leads to the best possible percentage of the viewing audience. Which program should this executive select?

   b. The program manager points out the risk involved and believes that the network should try to minimize the largest possible regrets. Which program should this executive select?

   c. Which program would you select? Explain.

2. The state treasurer is considering the purchase of a fire insurance policy for the new governor's mansion. A nondeductible policy provides complete coverage for an annual cost of $5000. The deductible plan only costs $2000 a year, but the state must absorb the first $28,000 of damage. If minor fire damage occurs to the mansion, the state anticipates a refurbishing cost of $20,000. It would cost $200,000 to replace the structure if there was major damage or total destruction.

   The treasurer wants to make the most realistic decision. She is reasonably optimistic and believes there is a 5% chance that the worst will happen. Which policy, if any, should she buy? Explain.

3. A consumer products testing agency is currently experiencing an increased demand for its services. It is considering hiring more testing personnel to meet the additional demand. The agency could hire a small, moderate, or large number of testers. The staffing decision depends on whether the uncertain additional demand will be low, medium, or high.

   Preliminary research indicates the following profit possibilities. If the company hires a small number of additional testers, the incremental profit will be $100,000 for any additional demand. If they hire a moderate number, the incremental profit will be $200,000 if the additional demand is either medium or high. However, profit increases by only $50,000 if they hire a moderate number and additional demand is low. If the company hires a large number of additional testers, profit will decrease by $100,000 when additional demand is low. Profit will not change if they hire a large number and additional demand is moderate. Yet a large additional staff will increase profit by $300,000 when there is a high additional demand.

The staffing decision will be made by an executive committee consisting of J. Lemon, T. Grape, and O. Right. Lemon is a pessimist, while Grape is an optimist. Right always selects the action that results in the smallest of the largest possible regrets. What will be Lemon's, Grape's, and Right's recommended decisions? What decision do you recommend? Why?

4. An investment analyst believes that there is a 40% chance of an upturn in the steel industry during the third quarter of the year. Also, there is about an equal likelihood of no change and a downturn. A client is considering the investment of $50,000 either in a mutual fund specializing in steel industry common stocks or in corporate AAA bonds yielding 10% per year. If the steel industry experiences an upturn during the third quarter, the value of the mutual fund shares will increase a net 20% during the next twelve months. The value will increase by a net 6% when there is no change. If there is a downturn, the value will decrease by 15%. What investment should the client make? What is the resulting dollar return?

5. Samson Enterprises manufactures athletic equipment. The company is considering the introduction of a new universal exerciser, the Body Builder. Profit potential depends on whether demand is low, moderate, or high. If the company markets the Body Builder, profit will be −$100,000 with low sales, $20,000 with moderate sales, and $200,000 with high sales. Market research indicates that there is a 30% chance of high sales. Low and moderate sales are equally likely. Should Samson introduce the Body Builder? If so, what is the expected profit?

6. The federal government is considering two national health plans. One would provide complete funding from general tax revenues. The alternative would make it mandatory for every citizen to purchase some form of health insurance from privately owned companies. Mandatory health insurance would be subsidized by the federal government, so that the cost would be within everyone's reach. The cost of the various plans depends on the social and economic conditions that give rise to various diseases. These conditions are classified as low, moderate, or high illness states.

In a low illness state, it would cost $2 billion to finance the general revenue plan and $1 billion for the mandatory insurance program. In a moderate illness state, it would cost $5 billion for the general revenue program and $7 billion for the mandatory plan. A high illness state would cost the federal government $15 billion under the general revenue program and $8 billion under the mandatory plan.

The third alternative is to continue with existing health care systems. Currently, these systems cost the federal govenment $3 billion in indirect expenses (Medicare, Medicaid, and other related welfare) in a low or moderate illness state. The cost is $5 billion in a high illness state.

Government health officials estimate that there is a 60% chance of a moderate illness state. Also, they believe that low and high illness states are equally likely. The government wants to select the system that leads to the smallest expected cost. Which system should the government select?

7. Mammoth Enterprises (ME) is a major producer and distributor of natural gas. Currently, they must decide whether to develop a particular exploration site or sell the rights to independent companies. Development will be desirable, of course, if there are substantial deposits of natural gas beneath the surface. Before making the decision, ME has the option of taking seismographic readings. These readings will provide geological and geophysical information that would enable them to determine if the subsurface structures are conducive to natural gas formation. However, natural gas has sometimes been found where no suitable subsurface structure was detected, and vice versa. Thus, there will still be some uncertainty remaining after the seismic testing.

It will cost Mammoth $3 million to develop the site, but it will yield an expected $8 million in revenues. Each seismic test costs $150,000. On the other hand, ME could sell the rights, before development or testing, for $500,000. If Mammoth takes seismographic readings and no subsurface structure is detected, the site will be considered almost worthless by other companies. In this case, ME will barely be able to sell the rights for $50,000. When a substructure is indicated, however, Mammoth can sell the rights for $2 million. If no natural gas is found, there will be no value attached to the exploration site.

There is a .25 probability of finding natural gas without any test. Previous experience indicates that 35% of all seismographic tests detect a suitable subsurface structure. If there is a suitable substructure, Mammoth will have a 75% chance of finding natural gas. If the substructure is unsuitable, there will be an 80% likelihood of finding no deposits.

What should Mammoth do? Explain.

CASE: The Healthy Food Store

The Healthy Food Store sells health foods in a beach community. Oliver Healthy, the manager, is filling out the orders for the next supply of fortified yeast. He has a contract with a major supplier that calls for orders of either one, two, or three batches every six days. Each batch contains 100 pounds.

It costs Oliver $2 to prepare a pound of yeast for sale, and the product sells for $4 per pound. Since it takes two days to prepare the product, Healthy must order in advance. The exact demand is unknown, but Oliver can list the possible demands as 100, 200, or 300 pounds. If the customers order more than Healthy has prepared, Oliver must purchase a higher-quality substitute yeast. The substitute is already prepared, but it costs $6 per pound. Since the new yeast cannot be stored more than four days without spoilage, Healthy cannot inventory excess production until the next six-day order. Therefore, if the customers order less than Oliver has prepared, the excess production must be reprocessed. The reprocessed yeast has a value of only $1 per pound.

1. Oliver wants to prepare the quantity that will lead to the smallest of the largest possible regrets. How many batches will he want to order?

2. Oliver's wife, Marissa, is concerned about the risk involved in this ordering decision. She wants to order the most realistic quantity. Marissa is only 30 % confident that the best outcome will always occur. How many batches will she want to order?

3. Compare the recommended decisions in parts (1) and (2). What does this comparison indicate?

4. The supplier's research indicates that there is a 50 % likelihood of a two-batch demand and a 30 % chance of a three-batch demand. Based on this information, how many batches do you think Oliver should order?

5. Compare your recommendation to Marissa's and Oliver's. What does this comparison indicate?

6. Suppose that Oliver could purchase the original yeast from another health food store in the next town for $3.50 rather than ordering the prepared higher-quality substitute for $6. Furthermore, there is a 60 % chance that the other store would have up to 100 pounds already in stock and available to Healthy Food Store. In addition, there is a 20 % chance that the other store would have up to 200 pounds available and a .2 probability for a maximum availability of 300 pounds. How would this situation affect Oliver's decision?

Chapter 4
Bayesian Analysis

CONCEPTS

♦ Identifying the nature of risk in a
 decision problem
♦ Measuring the value of perfect
 information
♦ Incorporating additional information
 into the decision analysis
♦ Measuring the value of the additional
 information
♦ Using the additional information to
 develop a decision strategy

APPLICATIONS

♦ New product marketing
♦ A make or buy decision
♦ Flight routing
♦ Sanitation disposal
♦ Recreation planning
♦ Market research
♦ College admissions
♦ Public transportation

As chapter 3 demonstrated, a key element in decision analysis is the manager's degree of knowledge about the states of nature. In most cases, decision makers have enough prior experience to make an initial assessment of the probabilities of uncertain events. Consequently, these decisions will be made under risk, usually with the expected value criterion.

The expected value calculations are affected by the probabilities assigned to the states of nature. Indeed, the recommended decision often may be altered by slight changes in these probabilities. Hence, the probability assessments play a crucial role in the decision analysis. As a result, management may be willing to expend additional effort in refining these probability assessments before making a final decision.

One approach is to gather additional information about the states of nature. Potential sources include experiments, such as raw material sampling, product testing, and test marketing; surveys, such as attitude and opinion polls; and statistical reports. Then the additional information can be used to revise or update the initial assessment of the event probabilities. Such an approach is referred to as **Bayesian analysis**.

The additional information should at least reduce the risk involved in decision making. Occasionally, this knowledge may even remove the risk completely and provide a situation of certainty. Such information, of course, is usually costly to obtain. An important aspect of Bayesian analysis is to compare these costs with the resulting benefits.

This chapter examines the Bayesian approach to decision analysis. In the opening section, we discuss the relevance of and potential benefits from knowledge about event probabilities. We begin by considering a methodology for determining the sensitivity of the recommended decision to changes in these probabilities. Then we see how to identify and measure the resulting risk. Such an analysis may indicate that the decision maker should seek additional information about the states of nature. The second section shows how this additional information can be used to revise or update the initial assessment of the event probabilities.

The availability of additional information, however, creates a sequential decision problem. First, management must decide whether or not to obtain the extra knowledge. Depending on the results of this first action, it will then select the decision alternative that best meets the original objectives. The final section shows how the revised probabilities can be used to develop an optimal decision plan under these circumstances.

VALUE OF INFORMATION

Let us consider Example 4.1.

EXAMPLE 4.1 New Product Marketing

Pucter and Simple (PS) is a consumer household goods manufacturer that wants to consider the introduction of a new toothpaste. The new product, which will be labeled Brite, could replace a relatively low-profit existing brand called Kist. Product profits would depend on sales volume, which could be low or high. The situation is depicted by Table 4.1, where entries represent potential profits. Based on available current data and experience with similar products, management believes there is a 45% chance of low sales. The company wants to select the alternative that results in the maximum expected profit.

Table 4.1 Pucter and Simple's Decision Table

	States of Nature	
Decision Alternatives	s_1 = low sales	s_2 = high sales
a_1 = market Brite	−$500,000	$1,000,000
a_2 = modify Kist	$100,000	$400,000

In this marketing situation, the probability of low sales is $P(s_1) = .45$. Assuming that the states of nature are mutually exclusive and collectively exhaustive, the probability of high sales must therefore be

$$P(s_2) = 1 - P(s_1) = 1 - .45 = .55$$

Since these likelihoods are based on prior experience and existing information, they could be thought of as preliminary, or initial, assessments of the state of nature probabilities. Such initial assignments are referred to as **prior probabilities**.

By using these prior probabilities and the profit data from Table 4.1, PS management will find that alternative a_1 has an expected profit of

$$-\$500,000\,(.45) + \$1,000,000\,(.55) = \$325,000$$

while the expected profit from a_2 is

$$\$100,000\,(.45) + \$400,000\,(.55) = \$265,000$$

The available current information, then, indicates that PS can maximize expected profit at \$325,000 by marketing Brite (a_1). Since the selection is based on the initial probability assessments, this action may be referred to as the **prior decision**.

SENSITIVITY OF THE DECISION From Table 4.1, you can see that the prior decision (a_1) may potentially lead to severe consequences (a \$500,000 loss) if there are low sales (s_1). Furthermore, PS management may not be completely confident in the prior probability assessments. Consequently, the company might be unwilling to accept the risk of marketing Brite without further reassurance.

As a first step, management could measure the sensitivity of the prior decision to changes in the probabilities for the states of nature. Such an approach is referred to as **sensitivity analysis**. If the sensitivity analysis reveals that very large errors are necessary to change the prior decision, then management can be reasonably confident with the prior decision. On the other hand, when small changes in the event probabilities alter the decision recommendation, then management will have little confidence in the prior action.

In Pucter and Simple's case, management knows that marketing Brite (a_1) will yield an expected profit of

(4.1) $-\$500,000\ P(s_1) + \$1,000,000\ P(s_2)$

Similarly, the expected profit from modifying Kist (a_2) is given by the following expression:

(4.2) $\$100,000\ P(s_1) + \$400,000\ P(s_2)$

A pictorial representation of expressions (4.1) and (4.2) is given in Figure 4.1.

As the figure indicates, when the probability of low sales, $P(s_1)$, is relatively small, the expected profit from marketing Brite (a_1) exceeds the corresponding return from modifying Kist (a_2). Hence, in these circumstances, PS management would prefer alternative a_1 rather than a_2. As

Figure 4.1 Pucter and Simple's Expected Profits

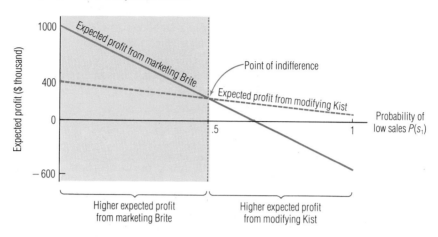

$P(s_1)$ increases, however, marketing Brite becomes a less attractive alternative. In fact, at some probability value, each alternative will have an identical expected outcome. At this point, the decision maker will be indifferent between (equally attracted to) marketing Brite and modifying Kist.

From expressions (4.1) and (4.2), you can see that the expected profits from a_1 and a_2 are equal when

$$-\$500,000\ P(s_1) + \$1,000,000\ P(s_2)$$
$$= \$100,000\ P(s_1) + \$400,000\ P(s_2)$$

or

$$\$600,000\ P(s_2) = \$600,000\ P(s_1)$$

Since $P(s_2) = 1 - P(s_1)$, PS management will be indifferent between marketing Brite (a_1) and modifying Kist (a_2) if there is a

$$\$600,000[1 - P(s_1)] = \$600,000\ P(s_1)$$

or

$$P(s_1) = .5$$

probability of low sales. Such a likelihood is known as an **indifference probability**.

Figure 4.1 also shows that when $P(s_1)$ is greater than the indifference probability (.5), the expected profit from modifying Kist exceeds the corresponding return from marketing Brite. Therefore, under these circumstances, PS management would prefer alternative a_2 rather than a_1.

Notice that the indifference probability (.5) is very close to PS management's initial assessment of the likelihood for low sales (.45). Hence, it would take only a small error in this initial assessment to completely alter the prior decision recommendation. Given the relatively high degree of sensitivity in this situation, the company may want to identify and measure the resulting risk. Based on this analysis, the decision maker may then decide to reduce the risk by collecting additional information before making a final decision.

PERFECT INFORMATION Pucter and Simple's prior decision to market Brite (a_1) is based on imprecise knowledge about the states of nature. Let us see what would happen if management knew exactly when each market condition would occur. Table 4.1 will be useful in this analysis.

Suppose that Pucter and Simple is certain when there will be low sales (s_1). According to the data in Table 4.1, the company should then modify Kist (a_2) and earn $100,000 profit rather than marketing Brite (a_1) and incurring a $500,000 loss. Since s_1 occurs only 45% of the time, management can expect to earn

$100,000 × .45 = $45,000

from this choice. Similarly, if the company is certain that there will be high sales (s_2), it should select a_1 (instead of a_2) and earn a $1 million profit (rather than a $400,000 profit). The $P(s_2) = .55$, and thus management can expect to earn

$1,000,000 × .55 = $550,000

from this selection.

Table 4.2 summarizes these calculations. As this table demonstrates, if PS knew exactly when each market condition would occur, the company could expect to earn as much as $595,000 profit. Such a total is known as the **expected value under certainty (EVC)**.

Table 4.3 outlines the procedure for finding EVC when there is a finite number of decision alternatives and states of nature. SRI Decision Analysis Group [13] and R. L. Winkler [18] extend the analysis to more complex situations.

From Table 4.2, you can see that Pucter and Simple obtains the EVC by mixing the decision alternatives. The company selects a_2 when s_1 occurs and a_1 when s_2 occurs. Such a strategy is possible if the decision maker has exact knowledge (knows exactly when each state of nature will occur). Initially, however, PS knows only the probability (rather than the exact timing) of each market condition. The imprecise nature of this information leads management to select the single alternative of marketing Brite (a_1), regardless of the environment. As a result, the company does not obtain

Table 4.2 Pucter and Simple's Expected Profit with Exact Knowledge

State of Nature	Proba- bility	Best Decision Alternative	Profit	Profit × Probability
s_1	.45	a_2	$100,000	$100,000 × .45 = $45,000
s_2	.55	a_1	$1,000,000	$1,000,000 × .55 = $550,000
				Total expected profit = $595,000

Table 4.3 Calculating the Expected Value Under Certainty

1. List each state of nature.
2. Identify the probability for each state of nature.
3. Identify the best decision alternative associated with each event.
4. Identify the outcome that is associated with each best decision alternative.
5. Multiply each best outcome by the corresponding probability and sum the results. The sum is the expected value under certainty (EVC).

EVC = $595,000, but instead must settle for the $325,000 maximum expected profit from the prior decision.

In effect, then, the lack of precise information results in a regret, or opportunity loss, of

$595,000 − $325,000 = $270,000

Such a penalty is referred to as the **expected value of perfect information (EVPI)**. Symbolically,

(4.3)   EVPI = |EVC − EVP*|

where EVP* stands for best expected value with prior knowledge, and | | is a symbol indicating that the value of EVC − EVP* should always be expressed as a positive number.

EXPECTED OPPORTUNITY LOSS There is another way to look at the problem. Remember, if Pucter and Simple had exact knowledge about the states of nature, management could always select the best decision alternative for each known market condition. Such a strategy would enable the company to earn a profit equal to the expected value under certainty (EVC). In the initial analysis, however, Pucter and Simple knows only the probability (rather than the exact

Table 4.4 Pucter and Simple's Opportunity Loss Table

	States of Nature	
Decision Alternatives	s_1 = low sales	s_2 = high sales
a_1 = market Brite	$600,000	$0
a_2 = modify Kist	$0	$600,000

timing) of each market condition. The imprecise nature of this information leads management to select a single alternative regardless of the decision environment and results in some regret (lost expected profit).

To see what is involved, let us again consider Pucter and Simple's decision table (Table 4.1). Suppose that management decides to market Brite (a_1) and afterward learns that there are low sales (s_1). According to the data in Table 4.1, the resulting outcome is a negative profit (financial loss) of $500,000. On the other hand, in this s_1 situation, if the company had modified Kist (a_2), it could have obtained a $100,000 profit. Hence, under these circumstances, there is a

$$\$100,000 - (-\$500,000) = \$600,000$$

regret, or opportunity loss, associated with alternative a_1 when s_1 occurs. Similarly, Pucter and Simple will incur a

$$\$1,000,000 - \$400,000 = \$600,000$$

opportunity loss if the company selects alternative a_2 when s_2 occurs.

Table 4.4 presents the opportunity losses associated with each decision alternative and state of nature combination in Pucter and Simple's problem. Notice that there is no opportunity loss when management selects the best alternative for a particular state of nature. We have just noted, for instance, that when there are low sales (s_1), the best alternative is to modify Kist (a_2). Thus, as Table 4.4 indicates, if PS selects a_2 when s_1 occurs, there will be a $0 regret.

By using the opportunity loss data from Table 4.4 and prior probabilities $P(s_1) = .45$ and $P(s_2) = .55$, PS management will find that marketing Brite (a_1) involves an expected opportunity loss of

$$\$600,000(.45) + \$0(.55) = \$270,000$$

Similarly, if the company modifies Kist (a_2), there will be a

$$\$0(.45) + \$600,000(.55) = \$330,000$$

expected opportunity loss.

Table 4.5 Pucter and Simple's Expected Profits and Opportunity Losses

Decision Alternative	Expected Profit	Expected Opportunity Loss	Expected Profit + Expected Opportunity Loss = EVC
a_1	$325,000	$270,000	$595,000
a_2	$265,000	$330,000	$595,000

Recall that alternative a_1 has an expected profit of $325,000 and a_2 an expected profit of $265,000. Also, in this problem, the expected value under certainty (EVC) is $595,000. Table 4.5 compares these expected profits with the corresponding opportunity losses and relates them to EVC.

As Table 4.5 demonstrates, the expected profit plus expected opportunity loss from each decision alternative will always equal the expected value under certainty. We can express this relationship as

(4.4) $\text{EVC} = \text{EV}(a_i) + \text{EOL}(a_i)$

where $\text{EV}(a_i)$ = expected value from decision alternative a_i and $\text{EOL}(a_i)$ = expected opportunity loss from decision alternative a_i. In view of this relationship, it is also apparent that the alternative (a_1) with the largest expected profit ($325,000) must necessarily have the smallest expected opportunity loss ($270,000).

If Pucter and Simple had perfect information, they could earn the

$$\text{EVC} = \text{EV}(a_1) + \text{EOL}(a_1) = \$325,000 + \$270,000 = \$595,000$$

The lack of such precise knowledge, however, limits profit to $\text{EV}(a_1) = \$325,000$ and results in an

$$\text{EVPI} = \text{EVC} - \text{EV}(a_1) = \text{EV}(a_1) + \text{EOL}(a_1) - \text{EV}(a_1)$$

or

$$\text{EVPI} = \text{EOL}(a_1) = \$270,000$$

from the prior decision to market Brite.

In effect, then, the minimum expected opportunity loss from the prior decision also represents the expected value of perfect information. That is,

(4.5) $\text{EVPI} = \text{EOL}^*$

where EOL^* is the smallest expected opportunity loss from the prior decision. Table 4.6 summarizes this opportunity loss procedure for finding the EVPI and compares it with the EVC approach. These procedures assume that there is a finite number of decision alternatives and states of

Table 4.6   Finding the Expected Value of Perfect Information (EVPI)

Outcome Approach [Equation (4.3)]	Opportunity Loss Approach [Equation (4.5)]
1. Develop the decision table.	1. Develop the opportunity loss table.
2. Identify the prior probabilities for the states of nature.	2. Identify the prior probabilities for the states of nature.
3. Calculate the expected values for each decision alternative.	3. Calculate the expected opportunity losses for each decision alternative.
4. Identify the decision alternative that leads to the best expected value. This action is the prior decision.	4. Identify the decision alternative that leads to the smallest expected opportunity loss.
5. Determine the expected value under certainty (EVC).	5. The expected value of perfect information (EVPI) is equal to the smallest expected opportunity loss.
6. Take the difference between EVC and the expected value of the prior decision. The result is the expected value of perfect information (EVPI).	

nature. SRI [13] and Winkler [18] extend the analysis to more complex situations.

MEASURING THE BENEFIT OF ADDITIONAL KNOWLEDGE

The imprecise nature of Pucter and Simple's initial knowledge about market conditions leads management to select a single alternative (a_1) regardless of the decision environment. Such an action limits the expected profit to $325,000 and results in a regret (lost expected profit) equal to the EVPI of $270,000. If the company had more accurate market condition information, it could increase the initial $325,000 expected profit by as much as $270,000.

In effect, then, the EVPI measures the maximum potential value that can be obtained by collecting additional information about the states of nature. As a result, it also identifies the upper limit on the price that management should be willing to pay for such knowledge.

By collecting more accurate market condition information, for example, Pucter and Simple could expect a maximum additional profit of EVPI = $270,000. If the cost of obtaining the additional knowledge is less than this EVPI, then the company may benefit from a further market study. But management should not pay more than $270,000 for such a study.

UPDATING PROBABILITIES

In a risk situation, the state-of-nature probabilities have a significant influence on the decision recommendation. When the decision is based only on the initial, or prior, probability assessments, there may be considerable opportunity loss. For that reason, surveys, experiments, and simulations are used to gather additional information about the states of nature. Such knowledge enables management to sharpen and refine the initial probability assessments. It may even identify precisely which event will actually occur. Then the decision maker can select the best alternative for each potential event and avoid any opportunity loss.

This section shows how the additional information is used to revise, or update, the initial probability assessments. In the next section, we will consider a method for evaluating the potential benefits from such knowledge and discuss the effects of this information on the decision-making process. Example 4.2 will illustrate the analysis.

EXAMPLE 4.2 Marketing Research

This problem is an extension of Example 4.1. Pucter and Simple's management is concerned about the relatively high expected opportunity loss associated with the prior decision to market Brite. Consequently, the company will consider hiring Research Corporation (RC) to do a test market study of the potential product demand.

Research Corporation's study is expected to report either a favorable or an unfavorable market for the new product, Brite. Furthermore, according to RC's past record on similar studies:

1. When there have been low sales, the test study indicated a favorable market 14% of the time.

2. When there have been high sales, the test indicated an unfavorable market 6% of the time.

RC charges a $20,000 fee for its market indicator service.

SAMPLE DATA Recall that Pucter and Simple initially assigns a probability of $P(s_1) = .45$ to low sales and $P(s_2) = .55$ to high sales. The RC test market study will provide additional knowledge about these demand conditions. Specifically, the test will indicate whether there is a favorable or unfavorable market for Brite. Let us denote these test outcomes as follows:

I_1 = favorable market for Brite

I_2 = unfavorable market for Brite

Such additional knowledge is usually referred to as **sample** or **indicator information**.

There are several important probability relationships between Research Corporation's indicator information and Pucter and Simple's states of nature. Some are specified in the problem, while others must be derived from the available data.

According to the data in Example 4.2, there is a 14% chance that the test will indicate a favorable market (I_1) when there actually have been low sales (s_1). Using shorthand notation, this likelihood of I_1 given the condition that s_1 has occurred is written as

$$P(I_1|s_1) = .14$$

where the vertical bar stands for "given the condition that." Such a likelihood is referred to as a **conditional probability**.

There are two mutually exclusive and collectively exhaustive indicators (I_1 and I_2). Hence, given a specific state of nature, the sum of the conditional probabilities for the indicators must equal 1. In the case of low sales (s_1), for instance,

$$P(I_1|s_1) + P(I_2|s_1) = 1$$

Consequently,

$$P(I_2|s_1) = 1 - P(I_1|s_1) = 1 - .14 = .86$$

In other words, there is an 86% chance that the test will indicate an unfavorable demand condition (I_2) when there have been low sales (s_1).

Also, according to the data in Example 4.2, there is a 6% likelihood that the test will indicate an unfavorable market (I_2) when sales actually have been high (s_2). That is,

$$P(I_2|s_2) = .06$$

Since

$$P(I_1|s_2) + P(I_2|s_2) = 1$$

there is a probability of

$$P(I_1|s_2) = 1 - P(I_2|s_2) = 1 - .06 = .94$$

that the test will indicate a favorable market (I_1) when sales have been high (s_2).

Figure 4.2 organizes the prior and conditional indicator probabilities in a convenient format. This type of diagram is called a **probability tree**. As chance point 1 at the left of the figure indicates, Pucter and Simple's sales can be either low (s_1) or high (s_2). The initial probability assessments, $P(s_1) = .45$ and $P(s_2) = .55$, are written below the corresponding sales branches emerging from this point. These initial assessments will be revised by Research Corporation's study results. However, the test is not infallible. Favorable or unfavorable test results can be obtained regardless of the true market conditions. For example, as chance point 2 in Figure 4.2 demonstrates, when sales are actually low (s_1), the test result could either be favorable ($I_1|s_1$) or unfavorable ($I_2|s_1$). The corresponding probabilities, $P(I_1|s_1) = .14$ and $P(I_2|s_1) = .86$, appear below the appropriate

Figure 4.2 Pucter and Simple's Probability Data

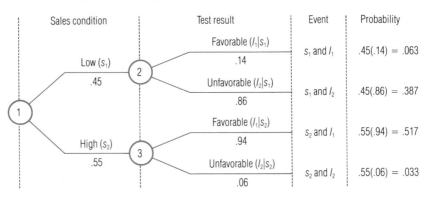

branches emerging from this point. Similarly, chance point 3 identifies the relevant test results when sales are high (s_2). Branches emerging from this point show that when s_2 occurs, the test has a $P(I_1|s_2) = .94$ chance of reporting favorable conditions and a $P(I_2|s_2) = .06$ likelihood of suggesting an unfavorable market.

Notice that there are now four distinct events:

1. Low sales and a favorable test (s_1 and I_1)
2. Low sales and an unfavorable test (s_1 and I_2)
3. High sales and a favorable test (s_2 and I_1)
4. High sales and an unfavorable test (s_2 and I_2)

As Figure 4.2 illustrates, each of these events is depicted as a separate path through the probability tree. For instance, the path along the s_1 and $I_1|s_1$ branches identifies the s_1 and I_1 event. In a similar manner, the s_1 and I_2 event corresponds to the path along the s_1 and $I_2|s_1$ branches of the tree.

The likelihood of such an event is given by the product of the probabilities along the branches of the corresponding path through the tree. Consider, for example, the s_1 and I_1 event. Figure 4.2 shows that there is a $P(s_1) = .45$ chance of low sales and, given this market condition, a $P(I_1|s_1) = .14$ likelihood of a favorable test. Thus, the probability of both low sales and a favorable test is

$$P(s_1 \text{ and } I_1) = P(s_1) \times P(I_1|s_1) = .45(.14) = .063$$

Also, since $P(I_2|s_1) = .86$, there is a

$$P(s_1 \text{ and } I_2) = P(s_1) \times P(I_2|s_1) = .45(.86) = .387$$

chance of both low sales and an unfavorable test. These likelihoods are referred to as **joint probabilities**.

In general, then, the joint probability for state of nature j and indicator i can be found with the following expression:

$$(4.6) \quad P(s_j \text{ and } I_i) = P(s_j) \times P(I_i|s_j)$$

where $P(s_j) = $ prior probability for state of nature j and $P(I_i|s_j) = $ conditional probability of indicator i given the condition that state j has occurred. By using this expression for each state and indicator combination, PS management will obtain the joint probabilities presented at the right of the corresponding sales/test paths (events) in Figure 4.2. Since the events are mutually exclusive and collectively exhaustive, these joint probabilities must (and do) add up to 1.

The event information is also useful in computing the probability of each indicator. Consider, for example, the favorable market situation (I_1). As Figure 4.2 demonstrates, there are exactly two events that involve a favorable indicator:

1. Low sales and a favorable test (s_1 and I_1)
2. High sales and a favorable test (s_2 and I_1)

Since

$$P(s_1 \text{ and } I_1) = .063$$

and

$$P(s_2 \text{ and } I_1) = .517$$

there must be a

$$P(I_1) = P(s_1 \text{ and } I_1) + P(s_2 \text{ and } I_1) = .063 + .517 = .58$$

likelihood of obtaining a favorable indicator.

Similarly, Figure 4.2 shows that there are only two events that lead to an unfavorable (I_2) condition:

1. Low sales and an unfavorable test (s_1 and I_2)
2. High sales and an unfavorable test (s_2 and I_2)

Furthermore,

$$P(s_1 \text{ and } I_2) = .387$$

and

$$P(s_2 \text{ and } I_2) = .033$$

Hence, there is a

$$P(I_2) = P(s_1 \text{ and } I_2) + P(s_2 \text{ and } I_2) = .387 + .033 = .42$$

chance that the test study will indicate an unfavorable market condition. Cumulative likelihoods—such as $P(I_1)$ and $P(I_2)$—are called **marginal probabilities**.

In effect, then, the marginal probability of a particular indicator is simply the sum of the corresponding joint probabilities. By letting $P(I_i) =$ marginal probability of indicator i and $n =$ number of mutually exclusive and collectively exhaustive states of nature, we can express the relationship as follows:

$$P(I_i) = P(s_1 \text{ and } I_i) + P(s_2 \text{ and } I_i) + \cdots + P(s_n \text{ and } I_i)$$

or

$$(4.7) \quad P(I_i) = \sum_{j=1}^{n} P(s_j \text{ and } I_i)$$

In addition, since the indicators are mutually exclusive and collectively exhaustive, their probabilities also must (and do) sum to 1. Put another way, for the case of Pucter and Simple, there is a probability of

$$P(I_1) + P(I_2) = .58 + .42 = 1$$

or a 100% chance that the test will indicate either a favorable or an unfavorable market.

REVISED PROBABILITIES

Pucter and Simple's management can use the test market (indicator) information to update the initial (prior) probability assessments for potential sales. In particular, the company can now determine the likelihood of each sales level, given the results of the test market study.

Suppose, for instance, that the test study indicates a favorable market condition (I_1). Management knows that this condition will occur $P(I_1) = .58$, or 58%, of the time. On these occasions, there is a

$$P(s_1 \text{ and } I_1) = .063$$

likelihood that there will also be low sales (s_1). Consequently, there is only a

$$P(s_1|I_1) = \frac{P(s_1 \text{ and } I_1)}{P(I_1)} = \frac{.063}{.580} = .11$$

probability of obtaining low sales if the test study indicates a favorable market. Similarly, since $P(s_2 \text{ and } I_1) = .517$, Pucter and Simple has a

$$P(s_2|I_1) = \frac{P(s_2 \text{ and } I_1)}{P(I_1)} = \frac{.517}{.580} = .89$$

chance of achieving high sales when the test study indicates a favorable market. These revised or updated likelihoods, $P(s_1|I_1)$ and $P(s_2|I_1)$, are called **posterior probabilities**.

Generally, then, the posterior probability for state of nature j, given indicator i, can be found with the following equation:

Figure 4.3 Updating Probabilities with Bayes's Formula

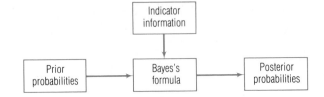

$$(4.8) \quad P(s_j|I_i) = \frac{P(s_j \text{ and } I_i)}{P(I_i)}$$

In other words, a posterior probability is the ratio of a joint probability to a marginal probability. This relationship is also known as **Bayes's formula or Bayes's theorem.** A schematic representation of the Bayesian revision process is presented in Figure 4.3.

According to Bayes's formula (4.8), if the test study indicates an unfavorable market (I_2), Pucter and Simple has a

$$P(s_1|I_2) = \frac{P(s_1 \text{ and } I_2)}{P(I_2)} = \frac{.387}{.420} = .92$$

chance of obtaining low sales (s_1). Also, under these circumstances, there will be a

$$P(s_2|I_2) = \frac{P(s_2 \text{ and } I_2)}{P(I_2)} = \frac{.033}{.420} = .08$$

probability of achieving high sales (s_2).

TABULAR APPROACH It may be cumbersome and complicated to apply equation (4.8) in practice. As a result, decision makers may prefer a tabular approach to Bayesian analysis. In this approach, the decision maker first must list the available states of nature and indicator data. Figure 4.4a presents this information for Pucter and Simple's situation. Notice that each row represents an indicator and each column a state of nature. Entries in the cells give the conditional indicator probabilities. Prior probabilities for the states of nature are presented above the appropriate columns in the diagram.

Next, the decision maker computes the joint probabilities by multiplying each prior probability by the corresponding indicator probability. The calculations are presented as cell entries in Figure 4.4b. Row totals identify the relevant marginal probabilities for the indicators, while column totals again represent the prior probabilities of the states of nature.

Figure 4.4 Tabular Approach to Bayesian Analysis

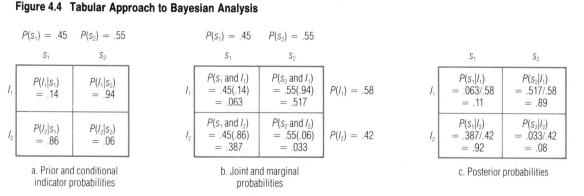

a. Prior and conditional
indicator probabilities

b. Joint and marginal
probabilities

c. Posterior probabilities

Table 4.7 Bayesian Procedure for Updating Probabilities

1. List each possible state of nature.
2. Identify the prior probability for each state of nature.
3. Multiply each prior probability by the corresponding conditional indicator probability. The results are called joint probabilities.
4. Sum the joint probabilities. The results are called marginal probabilities.
5. Divide each joint probability by the corresponding marginal probability. The results are the updated, or posterior, probabilities.

Finally, the posterior probabilities are found by taking the ratios of the joint to marginal probabilities. Figure 4.4c presents these computations. Notice that the sum of the posterior probabilities for each indicator (row in the diagram) is 1.

Table 4.7 summarizes the Bayesian procedure for updating probabilities when there is a finite number of indicators and states of nature. SRI [13] and Winkler [18] extend the analysis to more complex situations.

DECISION MAKING WITH ADDITIONAL INFORMATION

Research Corporation's indicator information is not perfect. After all, there is only a $P(I_2|s_1) = .86$ probability that the test will indicate an unfavorable market when sales actually have been low. Furthermore, if sales have been high, there is just a $P(I_1|s_2) = .94$ likelihood that the test will indicate a favorable market. Yet this sample data has enabled PS management to refine (update) its initial (prior) probability assessments.

Initially, Pucter and Simple's management felt that there was a $P(s_1) =$

.45 chance of low product sales and a $P(s_2) = .55$ likelihood of high sales. Now the company knows that if the test indicates a favorable market (I_1), there is only a $P(s_1|I_1) = .11$ probability of low sales but a $P(s_2|I_1) = .89$ chance of high sales. On the other hand, when the test indicates an unfavorable market (I_2), there is a $P(s_1|I_2) = .92$ likelihood of low sales and a $P(s_2|I_2) = .08$ probability of high sales.

Observe that the prior probability of low sales, $P(s_1)$, is different from each of the corresponding posterior probabilities, $P(s_1|I_1)$ and $P(s_1|I_2)$. In addition, the prior probability of high sales, $P(s_2)$, differs from each corresponding posterior probability, $P(s_2|I_1)$ and $P(s_2|I_2)$. Consequently, the expected profits from actions taken with the prior knowledge will be different from the corresponding returns with the additional indicator information.

The test results are also important. Notice that $P(s_1|I_1)$ is different from $P(s_1|I_2)$, and $P(s_2|I_1)$ does not have the same value as $P(s_2|I_2)$. Hence, the expected profit from marketing Brite (a_1) under favorable test circumstances (I_1) will be different from the corresponding earnings for unfavorable test conditions (I_2). Similarly, the expected profit from modifying Kist (a_2) will differ in the I_1 and I_2 indicator situations.

Pucter and Simple still wants to maximize expected profits, and these earnings again depend on the company's actions (a_1 and a_2). However, such actions will now be influenced by the availability and nature of the RC test market information. As a result, PS management must consider a series of interrelated decisions.

SEQUENCE OF DECISIONS

By letting a_3 denote the alternative of buying RC's indicator service and a_4 the action of not purchasing the service, Pucter and Simple's problem can be depicted by Figure 4.5. Again, decision points are portrayed by squares and chance points by circles.

Management first must decide whether to buy (a_3) or not buy (a_4) the RC indicator service. This initial choice is shown as decision point 1 in Figure 4.5. If PS buys the service (follows the a_3 branch emerging from decision point 1), it must pay a $20,000 fee to Research Corporation. The fee is shown as a negative $20,000 profit at chance point 2. Next, PS must identify the test study outcome.

Branches emerging from chance point 2 show that the test could indicate either a favorable market (I_1) or an unfavorable market (I_2). Decision points 3 and 4 illustrate that in each of these situations, PS management then has the choice to either market Brite (a_1) or modify Kist (a_2). The resulting profits will depend on product sales.

Let us consider the case when there is a favorable indicator (I_1). If PS markets Brite (follows the a_1 branch emerging from decision point 3), chance point 5 shows that the company could obtain either low ($s_1|I_1$) or

Figure 4.5 Pucter and Simple's Decision Tree

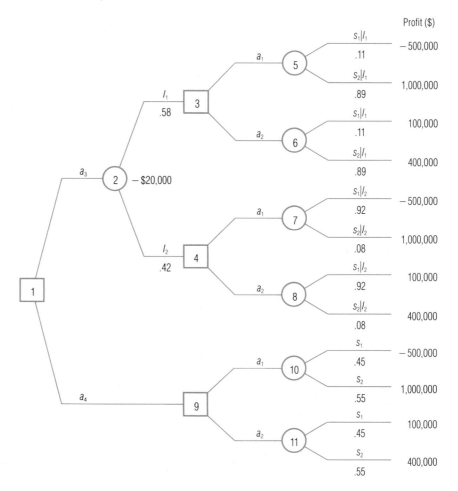

high ($s_2|I_1$) sales. Low demand (the $s_1|I_1$ branch emerging from point 5) results in a $500,000 loss, while high demand (the $s_2|I_1$ branch) leads to a $1 million profit. When PS modifies Kist (follows the a_2 branch emerging from decision point 3), chance point 6 illustrates that the company also could obtain either low ($s_1|I_1$) or high ($s_2|I_1$) sales. In this case, however, low sales (the $s_1|I_1$ branch emerging from point 6) lead to a $100,000 profit; high demand (the $s_2|I_1$ branch) results in a $400,000 profit.

There is a similar sequence when the indicator is unfavorable (I_2). If PS markets Brite (follows the a_1 branch emerging from decision point 4), chance point 7 demonstrates that the company could get either low ($s_1|I_2$) or high ($s_2|I_2$) sales. Low sales (the $s_1|I_2$ branch emerging from point 7) again result in a $500,000 loss, and high demand (the $s_2|I_2$ branch) results in a \$1 million profit. If PS modifies Kist (follows the a_2 branch emerging from decision point 4), chance point 8 shows that the company could obtain either low ($s_1|I_2$) or high ($s_2|I_2$) sales. In this situation, low demand (the $s_1|I_2$ branch emerging from point 8) leads to a \$100,000 profit. High sales (the $s_2|I_2$ branch) result in a \$400,000 profit.

Finally, suppose that PS does not purchase the RC indicator service and hence follows the a_4 branch emerging from decision point 1. In this case, PS will make its new product decision (shown as decision point 9) with only the initial, or prior, information. If the company markets Brite (follows the a_1 branch emerging from decision point 9), chance point 10 illustrates that it could obtain either low (s_1) or high (s_2) sales. Low sales (the s_1 branch emerging from point 10) result in a \$500,000 loss, while high sales (the s_2 branch) lead to a \$1 million profit. If the company modifies Kist (follows the a_2 branch emerging from decision point 9), chance point 11 shows that it also could get either low or high sales. Under these circumstances, however, low sales (the s_1 branch emerging from point 11) lead to a \$100,000 profit; high demand (the s_2 branch) results in a \$400,000 profit.

EVALUATING THE INFORMATION

As Figure 4.5 demonstrates, Pucter and Simple's test market decision (a_3 versus a_4) will depend on the profits achievable from the resulting product actions. To compute these profits, management must start at the right of the tree and progressively work backward through the appropriate chance and decision points. Figure 4.6 illustrates the calculations for the a_4 segment of the decision tree.

As Figure 4.6 shows, marketing Brite (a_1) under these circumstances leads to an expected profit of

$$-\$500,000(.45) + \$1,000,000(.55) = \$325,000$$

This expectation is recorded in a rectangle above chance point 10. On the other hand, by modifying Kist (a_2), PS can obtain an expected profit of only

$$\$100,000(.45) + \$400,000(.55) = \$265,000$$

This value appears in a rectangle above chance point 11.

Thus, if Pucter and Simple does not purchase the indicator service (selects the a_4 alternative), the best product action is to market Brite (a_1). By doing so, the company will maximize expected profit at \$325,000. This recommendation is depicted in Figure 4.6 by "pruning" the a_2 branch and placing the \$325,000 in a rectangle above decision point 9.

By working backward through the a_3 segment of the decision tree in a similar manner, management will obtain the results presented in Figure 4.7. Let us first consider the I_1 segment of Figure 4.7. According to the

Figure 4.6 Evaluating the a_4 Segment of the PS Decision Tree

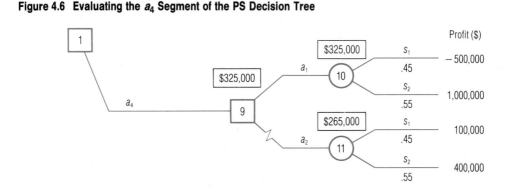

Figure 4.7 Evaluating the a_3 Segment of the PS Decision Tree

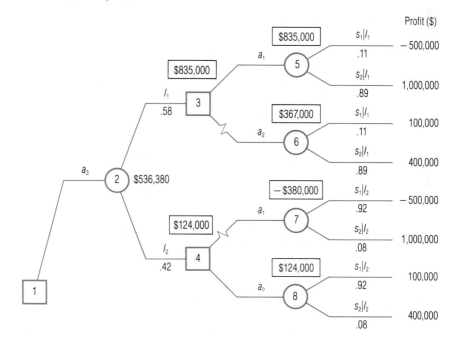

computations in this diagram, Pucter and Simple can obtain an expected profit of

$$-\$500,000(.11) + \$1,000,000(.89) = \$835,000$$

by marketing Brite (a_1) under these I_1 conditions. This expectation appears in a rectangle above chance point 5. Alternatively, if the company modifies Kist (a_2), the expected profit will be only

$100,000(.11) + $400,000(.89) = $367,000

This value is recorded in a rectangle above chance point 6. Hence, if the test study indicates a favorable (I_1) situation, Pucter and Simple should market Brite (a_1) and obtain a maximum expected profit of $835,000. The recommendation is depicted in Figure 4.7 by "pruning" the a_2 branch emerging from decision point 3 and placing the $835,000 in a rectangle above that point.

A similar analysis of the I_2 segment of Figure 4.7 shows that the a_1 alternative leads to an expected profit of

$-$500,000(.92) + $1,000,000(.08) = -$380,000

Under these circumstances, action a_2 results in an expected profit of

$100,000(.92) + $400,000(.08) = $124,000

These expectations are placed in rectangles above chance points 7 and 8, respectively. According to these results, then, if the test indicates an unfavorable (I_2) market, Pucter and Simple can maximize expected profit at $124,000 by modifying Kist (a_2). This recommendation is depicted in Figure 4.7 by "pruning" the a_1 branch emerging from decision point 4 and placing the $124,000 in a rectangle above that point.

Figure 4.7 also shows that there is a $P(I_1) = .58$ probability of a favorable indicator and a $P(I_2) = .42$ likelihood of an unfavorable indicator. Consequently, if Pucter and Simple buys the indicator service (selects alternative a_3), the company will earn a gross expected profit of

$835,000(.58) + $124,000(.42) = $536,380

This expectation is reported next to chance point 2 in the diagram.

Recall that when Pucter and Simple uses only the prior knowledge (selects alternative a_4), the company can expect to earn no more than $325,000 profit. Thus, the additional RC indicator information could increase Pucter and Simple's gross expected profits by a potential

$536,380 − $325,000 = $211,380

This potential outcome is referred to as the **expected value of sample information (EVSI).** Note that the expected value of sample information is simply the difference between the best expected value with indicator information and the best expected value with prior knowledge. By letting EVS* = best expected value with sample, or indicator, information and EVP* = best expected value with prior knowledge, we can express this relationship by the equation

(4.9)   EVSI = |EVS* − EVP*|

Once more, the symbol | | indicates that the difference should be expressed as a positive number.

The EVSI, in effect, measures the maximum potential benefit that can be obtained from the specified sample, or indicator, information. However, such knowledge usually involves some costs. Thus, to properly evaluate the information, management must compare these benefits and costs.

Pucter and Simple, for example, can expect to gross an EVSI = $211,380 by using the indicator information. Therefore, management should never pay more than this amount for such knowledge. Since Research Corporation charges a fee of only $20,000, PS can expect to net

$$\$211{,}380 - \$20{,}000 = \$191{,}380$$

in profits from the test market service. This difference is called the **expected net gain from sampling (ENGS).** That is,

(4.10) $ENGS = EVSI - CS$

where CS denotes the cost of the sample, or indicator, information.

It will be worth gathering the indicator information as long as there is a positive expected net gain from sampling (ENGS > 0). Since the RC indicator information has ENGS = $191,380 (greater than zero), Pucter and Simple should purchase the test market service.

Another useful measure of evaluation can be derived from the EVSI. Recall that perfect knowledge enables the decision maker to identify exactly which state of nature will occur. The economic value of this knowledge is measured by the EVPI. Sample, or indicator, information usually will not be as accurate as perfect knowledge. However, it will provide a gross economic benefit equal to the EVSI. Thus, management can use the equation

(4.11) $E = \dfrac{EVSI}{EVPI} \times 100$

to rate indicator information. The value E is known as the **efficiency rating.**

Sample information will have an efficiency rating somewhere between 0% and 100%. A high (close to 100%) rating indicates that the sample data are almost as good as perfect information. Low (close to 0%) ratings suggest that the indicator information is a poor substitute for perfect knowledge.

In effect, then, E measures the ability of the indicator information to accurately predict the states of nature. As a result, when there is a low efficiency rating, the decision maker may want to consider better and/or additional data sources.

Recall that Pucter and Simple has an EVPI equal to $270,000 and an EVSI equal to $211,380. Hence, besides being worthwhile (having an ENGS > 0), Research Corporation's test market service is

$$E = \frac{\text{EVSI}}{\text{EVPI}} \times 100 = \frac{\$211,380}{\$270,000} \times 100 = .783$$

or 78.3% as efficient as perfect information. Consequently, PS management should feel relatively confident about using the RC sample data to help make the product decision.

The process of evaluating the indicator information (computing and analyzing ENGS and E) is known as **preposterior analysis**.

DEVELOPING A STRATEGY Pucter and Simple can use the preposterior results to develop a complete decision strategy. Figure 4.8 illustrates.

If Pucter and Simple does not purchase the indicator service (selects alternative a_4), then the company must use only the prior knowledge to

Figure 4.8 Working Backward Through the Entire PS Decision Tree

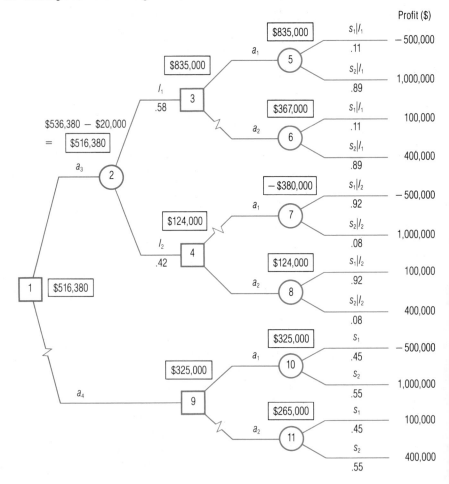

make the product decision. As Figure 4.8 demonstrates, under these circumstances, the company can maximize expected profit at $325,000 by marketing Brite (selecting the a_1 branch emerging from decision point 9).

On the other hand, if PS buys the service (selects a_3), it can use both prior and test information to make the product decision. Figure 4.8 shows that the following strategy is appropriate in this case:

1. Wait for the test results before making the product decision.
2. If the test indicates a favorable condition (I_1), market Brite (a_1).
3. If the test indicates an unfavorable market (I_2), modify Kist (a_2).

By adjusting the decision strategy in this manner, Pucter and Simple can earn a gross expected profit of $536,380. However, Research Corporation charges a $20,000 fee for the test service. Therefore, PS can expect to net only

$$\$536,380 - \$20,000 = \$516,380$$

from alternative a_3. This expectation is recorded in a rectangle above chance point 2.

Since a_3 provides more earnings than a_4, Pucter and Simple should buy the service and use the test results to help make the product decision. This recommendation is depicted in Figure 4.8 by "pruning" the a_4 branch and placing the $516,380 expected profit from the selected alternative (a_3) in a rectangle above decision point 1.

The process of using sample, or indicator, information to develop a decision strategy is referred to as **posterior analysis**.

COMPUTER ANALYSIS Table 4.8 summarizes the procedure for decision making with sample, or indicator, information. In practice, such a procedure could be quite cumbersome and time-consuming, especially when there are many alternatives and events. Fortunately, R. Schlaifer [12] and others have developed computer programs designed to perform the necessary calculations and report the results. One such program, **DECIDE**, is available on the California State University and College (CSUC) computer system.

Figure 4.9 illustrates how DECIDE can be used to solve Pucter and Simple's new product marketing problem. The decision maker executes DECIDE by inputting the probability and outcome data, branch by branch, from the decision tree. The program prompts an input by displaying a question mark. An appropriate response is to provide the following data in the order listed:

1. The decision or chance point (called a node, in this program) from which the branch emerges
2. The destination point for the branch

Table 4.8 Decision Making with Sample, or Indicator, Information

1. Develop a decision tree that accurately describes the sequential nature of the problem.
2. Perform the following preposterior analysis:
   a. Use the prior probability assessments and sample data to determine the indicator and posterior probabilities.
   b. Assign these probabilities to the appropriate branches of the decision tree.
   c. Work backward through the decision tree to determine the expected values of each decision alternative.
   d. Identify the best expected values with the sample/indicator information and prior knowledge.
   e. Take the difference between the expected values found in step d. The result is the expected value of sample information (EVSI).
   f. Subtract the cost of sampling (CS) from EVSI. The result is the expected net gain from sampling (ENGS).
   g. If ENGS > 0, obtain the sample, or indicator, information.
3. Perform the following posterior analysis:
   a. Use the preposterior results to work backward through the entire decision tree.
   b. Select the decision strategy (sequence of actions) that results in the best expected value at each decision point in the tree.

3. The probability associated with the branch
4. The outcome, if any, associated with the branch
5. The year that the outcome is received (appropriate only for multiple time period problems)
6. The interest rate associated with the year (appropriate only when the outcomes must be expressed in terms of present value)

In this program, each branch must have a starting and ending point (node).

For example, consider the a_3 branch in the left portion of Pucter and Simple's decision tree (Figure 4.5). This branch is recorded as the first entry (1,2,0, − 20000,0,0) in the DECIDE program (Figure 4.9). It emerges from decision point 1, ends at chance point 2, involves no probability, results in a − $20,000 profit, and has no year or interest rate. Similarly, the $s_1|I_1$ branch at the top of Figure 4.5 is presented as the fourth entry (5,12,.11, − 500000,0,0) in Figure 4.9. This branch emerges from chance point 5, ends at an artificial point 12, has a probability of .11, results in a − $500,000 profit, and involves no year or interest rate. Artificial point 12 is created merely to have a distinct ending point for this branch in the computer program.

To terminate the data section of the program, the user enters the command (− 1,0,0,0,0,0). DECIDE then sorts the input data, evaluates the decision tree, and identifies the preferred decisions. The sort segment

Figure 4.9 Solving Pucter and Simple's Problem with DECIDE

```
PROGRAM DECIDE FOR FORGIONNE

ENTER   FROM NODE #, TO NODE #, PROBABILITY, VALUE, YEAR, INTEREST RATE
        ALL SEPARATED BY COMMAS.

EXAMPLE    :   2,3,.4,100000,2,5
TO END ENTER :   -1,0,0,0,0,0

? 1,2,0,-20000,0,0
? 2,3,.58,0,0,0
? 3,5,0,0,0,0
? 5,12,.11,-500000,0,0
? 5,13,.89,1000000,0,0
? 3,6,0,0,0,0
? 6,14,.11,100000,0,0
? 6,15,.89,400000,0,0
? 2,4,.42,0,0,0
? 4,7,0,0,0,0
? 7,16,.92,-500000,0,0
? 7,17,.08,1000000,0,0
? 4,8,0,0,0,0
? 8,18,.92,100000,0,0
? 8,19,.08,400000,0,0
? 1,9,0,0,0,0
? 9,10,0,0,0,0
? 10,20,.45,-500000,0,0
? 10,21,.55,1000000,0,0
? 9,11,0,0,0,0
? 11,22,.45,100000,0,0
? 11,23,.55,400000,0,0
? -1,0,0,0,0,0


        ***********SORTED INPUT DATA*************
  FROM    TO             DOLLAR            INTEREST
  NODE   NODE   PROB      VALUE   YEARS     RATE
   1      2    0.000    -20000.    0.      0.000
   1      9    0.000        0.     0.      0.000
   2      3     .580        0.     0.      0.000
   2      4     .420        0.     0.      0.000
   3      5    0.000        0.     0.      0.000
   3      6    0.000        0.     0.      0.000
   4      7    0.000        0.     0.      0.000
   4      8    0.000        0.     0.      0.000
   5     12     .110   -500000.    0.      0.000
   5     13     .890   1000000.    0.      0.000
   6     14     .110    100000.    0.      0.000
   6     15     .890    400000.    0.      0.000
   7     16     .920   -500000.    0.      0.000
   7     17     .080   1000000.    0.      0.000
   8     18     .920    100000.    0.      0.000
   8     19     .080    400000.    0.      0.000
   9     10    0.000        0.     0.      0.000
   9     11    0.000        0.     0.      0.000
  10     20     .450   -500000.    0.      0.000
  10     21     .550   1000000.    0.      0.000
  11     22     .450    100000.    0.      0.000
  11     23     .550    400000.    0.      0.000
```

Figure 4.9 Continued

```
*********EVALUATED DECISION TREE***********
FROM   TO              DOLLAR           INTEREST
NODE   NODE   PROB     VALUE   YEARS    RATE
  1      2   DECIDE   516380.    0.     0.000
  1      9   DECIDE   325000.    0.     0.000
  2      3    .580    484300.    0.     0.000
  2      4    .420     52080.    0.     0.000
  3      5   DECIDE   835000.    0.     0.000
  3      6   DECIDE   367000.    0.     0.000
  4      7   DECIDE  -380000.    0.     0.000
  4      8   DECIDE   124000.    0.     0.000
  5     12    .110    -55000.    0.     0.000
  5     13    .890    890000.    0.     0.000
  6     14    .110     11000.    0.     0.000
  6     15    .890    356000.    0.     0.000
  7     16    .920   -460000.    0.     0.000
  7     17    .080     80000.    0.     0.000
  8     18    .920     92000.    0.     0.000
  8     19    .080     32000.    0.     0.000
  9     10   DECIDE   325000.    0.     0.000
  9     11   DECIDE   265000.    0.     0.000
 10     20    .450   -225000.    0.     0.000
 10     21    .550    550000.    0.     0.000
 11     22    .450     45000.    0.     0.000
 11     23    .550    220000.    0.     0.000


     PREFERRED DECISIONS ARE
 FROM    TO    EXP. VALUE
   1      2     516380.
   3      5     835000.
   4      8     124000.
   9     10     325000.
```

simply presents the decision tree (Figure 4.5) data in a tabular format. In the evaluation section, the program computes all relevant expected values and identifies each branch of the decision tree that involves a decision alternative. Such branches are denoted DECIDE, and their dollar values correspond to the expectations placed in the rectangles above the decision and chance points in Figure 4.8. In Figure 4.8, for instance, the branch emerging from point 1 and ending at point 2 identifies decision alternative a_3. When Pucter and Simple selects this alternative, the company will obtain the $516,380 expected profit appearing in a rectangle above chance point 2. Hence, in the evaluation section of Figure 4.9, the branch from point 1 to point 2 is denoted DECIDE and has a dollar value of $516,380.

The last section of the DECIDE program identifies the preferred alternative at each decision point in the tree and lists the corresponding expected values. As Figure 4.9 shows, Pucter and Simple's preferred strategy is first to go from point 1 to point 2. This action corresponds to the selection of alternative a_3 at decision point 1 in Figure 4.8. Then, if the company encounters point 3 (follows the I_1 branch in Figure 4.8), it should go to point 5. This action corresponds to the selection of alternative a_1 at decision point 3 in Figure 4.8. Alternatively, if PS encounters point 4 (follows the I_2 branch in Figure 4.8), it should go to point 8 (select alternative a_2 emerging from decision point 4). By following such a strategy, the company will obtain the $516,380 expected profit listed alongside the point 1 to point 2 action in the last section of the DECIDE program (Figure 4.9).

Note that the preferred decisions from the DECIDE program correspond to the optimal strategy identified by working backward through Figure 4.8. Furthermore, the results from DECIDE can be used to calculate the expected value of sample information (EVSI).

Figure 4.9 shows that if Pucter and Simple buys the indicator information (selects alternative a_3 or goes from point 1 to point 2), the company can obtain an expected profit of $516,380. On the other hand, if the company does not purchase the service (selects alternative a_4), it will next encounter decision point 9. According to the results from DECIDE (Figure 4.9), the preferred decision would then be to go from point 9 to point 10 and obtain an expected profit of $325,000. Hence, there is a

$516,380 - $325,000 = $191,380

expected net gain from sampling (ENGS = $191,380).

Now, according to equation (4.10),

ENGS = EVSI − CS

Hence,

EVSI = ENGS + CS

Since ENGS = $191,380 and CS = $20,000,

EVSI = $191,380 + $20,000 = $211,380

APPLICATIONS Bayesian analysis has been applied to a wide variety of business and economic problems. Table 4.9 presents a partial list of these applications.

SUMMARY As Chapter 3 demonstrated, the manager's degree of knowledge about the states of nature is a key element in any decision analysis. Usually, the decision maker has enough information to make an initial assessment of the probabilities of the uncertain events. Consequently, these decisions will be made under risk, typically with the expected value criterion.

Often, however, the expected value calculations are very sensitive to changes in the probability values. In such cases, the decision maker may

Table 4.9 Applications of Bayesian Decision Analysis

Area of Application	Reference
Production	
Plant location	T. M. Carroll and R. D. Dean [2]
Manufacturing systems engineering	E. Y. Chang and W. Thompson [3]
	D. V. Mastran [9]
	B. Ronen and J. S. Pliskin [11]
Manufacturing operations	S. J. Grossman et al. [6]
Marketing	
Product pricing	P. E. Green and D. S. Tull [5]
	J. Thomas and P. Chhabra [14]
Consumer behavior	G. L. Lilian et al. [8]
Product planning	J. W. Ulvila et al. [15]
Finance/accounting	
Investments	D. F. Bradford and H. H. Kalejian [1]
Insurance	J. Ferreira [4]
Auditing	J. E. Reinmuth [10]
Financial analysis	J. C. Wiginton [17]
Service sector	
Sports	S. P. Ladany [7]
Government social programs	M. Wang et al. [16]

want to gather additional information and perform a Bayesian analysis before making the final decision. This chapter examined this Bayesian approach.

The first section discussed the relevance of, and potential benefit from, accurate knowledge about the event probabilities. We considered a methodology for determining the sensitivity of the recommended decisions to changes in these probabilities. Then we saw how to identify and measure the resulting risk. We saw that if management knew exactly when each event would occur, it could expect to earn as much as the expected value under certainty (EVC). Table 4.3 summarized the procedure for calculating the EVC. However, since decision makers usually do not have such precise knowledge, they incur a penalty equal to the expected value of perfect information (EVPI). Table 4.6 summarized the procedures for calculating the EVPI.

A relatively large EVPI indicates that there is a substantial opportunity loss associated with the prior decision. In such cases, it is wise for the decision maker to consider collecting additional information before making a final decision. The second section showed how this additional information can be used to revise, or update, the initial probability assessments. Figure 4.3 illustrated the process, and Table 4.7 outlined the procedure. The last section presented a method for evaluating the potential benefits from such knowledge and discussed the effects of this information on the decision making process. Table 4.8 summarized the relevant procedures and concepts. A partial list of applications was presented in Table 4.9.

The last section of the chapter also showed how computers can be used to perform a Bayesian decision analysis.

Glossary

Bayesian analysis The process of using additional information to revise and update the initial assessments of the event probabilities.

Bayes's formula (Bayes's theorem) The relationship that states that a conditional probability is the ratio of a joint probability to a marginal probability. In decision analysis, it is used primarily to find the updated, or posterior, probabilities for the states of nature.

conditional probability The probability of one event, given the condition that some other event has occurred.

DECIDE A computer program designed to solve sequential decision problems.

efficiency rating The ratio of EVSI to EVPI multiplied by 100. It measures the ability of the sample, or indicator, information to accurately predict the states of nature.

expected net gain from sampling (ENGS) The difference between the EVSI and the cost of the sample or indicator information.

expected value of perfect information (EVPI) The difference between the expected value under certainty (EVC) and the best expected value with only prior knowledge. It measures the expected value of information that would tell the decision maker exactly which state of nature will occur.

expected value of sample information (EVSI) The difference between the best expected value with the indicator information and the best expected value with only prior knowledge. It is a measure of the economic benefit that can be obtained from the specified sample, or indicator, information.

expected value under certainty (EVC) The best possible expected value of the objective if the decision maker knows exactly when each state of nature will occur.

indifference probability The event probability that equates the expected outcomes of the decision alternatives.

joint probability The probability that two or more events will jointly occur.

marginal probability The cumulative probability that an event will occur.

posterior analysis The process of using sample, or indicator, information to develop a decision strategy.

posterior probability The revised or updated probability of a state of nature, given the condition that a particular indicator has occurred.

preposterior analysis   The process of evaluating sample, or indicator, information.

prior decision   A decision based on the prior probabilities.

prior probabilities   Preliminary, or initial, assessments of the probabilities for the states of nature.

probability tree   A diagram that organizes the prior and con-

ditional indicator probabilities in a convenient format.

sample (indicator) information
The new or additional knowledge provided through surveys, experiments, or simulations.

sensitivity analysis   Measuring the sensitivity of an optimal decision to changes in the uncontrollable inputs.

References

1. Bradford, D. F., and H. H. Kalejian. "The Value of Information for Crop Forecasting with Bayesian Speculators: Theory and Empirical Results." *Bell Journal of Economics* (Spring 1978):123.

2. Carroll, T. M., and R. D. Dean. "A Bayesian Approach to Plant-Location Decisions." *Decision Sciences* (January 1980):81.

3. Chang, E. Y., and W. Thompson. "Bayes Analysis of Reliability for Complex Systems." *Operations Research* (January–February 1976):156.

4. Ferreira, J. "The Long-Term Effects of Merit-Rating Plans on Individual Motorists." *Operations Research* (September–October 1974):954.

5. Green, P. E., and D. S. Tull. *Research for Marketing Decisions*. 4th ed. Englewood Cliffs, N.J.: Prentice-Hall, 1978. Chap. 2.

6. Grossman, S. J., et al. "A Bayesian Approach to the Production of Information

and Learning by Doing." *Review of Economic Studies* (October 1977):553.

7. Ladany, S. P. "Optimal Starting Height for Pole-Vaulting." *Operations Research* (September–October 1975):968.

8. Lilian, G. L., et al. "Bayesian Estimation and Control of Detailing Effort in a Repeat Purchase Diffusion Environment." *Management Science* (May 1981):493.

9. Mastran, D. V. "Incorporating Component and System Test Data into the Same Assessment: A Bayesian Approach." *Operations Research* (May–June 1976):491.

10. Reinmuth, J. E. "On the Application of Bayesian Statistics in Auditing." *Decision Sciences* (July 1972):139.

11. Ronen, B., and J. S. Pliskin. "Decision Analysis in Microelectronic Reliability: Optimal Design and Packaging of a Diode Array." *Operations Research* (March–April 1981):229.

12. Schlaifer, R. *Computer Programs for Elementary Decision Analysis.* Boston: Harvard Business School, Division of Research, 1971.

13. SRI Decision Analysis Group. *Readings in Decision Analysis.* Menlo Park, Calif.: Stanford Research Institute, 1976.

14. Thomas, J., and P. Chhabra. "Bayesian Models for New Product Pricing." *Decision Sciences* (January 1975):51.

15. Ulvila, J. W., et al. "A Case in On-Line Decision Analysis for Product Planning." *Decision Sciences* (July 1977):598.

16. Wang, M., et al. "A Bayesian Data Analysis System for the Evaluation of Social Programs." *Journal of the American Statistical Association* (December 1977):711.

17. Wiginton, J. C. "A Bayesian Approach to Discrimination Among Economic Models." *Decision Sciences* (April 1974):182.

18. Winkler, R. L. *An Introduction to Bayesian Inference and Decision.* New York: Holt, Rinehart & Winston, 1972.

Thought Exercises

1. Col. Jolley Ender is the logistics officer at Flywell AFB. Currently, she is trying to minimize the expected round-trip flight time for a particular cargo shipment. There are several possible routes. Flight time over these routes depends on uncertain weather conditions. Based on current available data on weather probabilities, the best expected flight time is 2 hours and 20 minutes. If Col. Ender knew when each weather condition was going to occur, she could reduce the time to 1 hour and 50 minutes by rescheduling flights. Each hour of "wasted" time involves a $20,000 opportunity loss to the base.

   How much should Col. Ender be willing to pay for more accurate weather information? Explain.

2. East Western University offers a course in business policy. It is typical for the professor to invite executives as guest lecturers. Recently, the manager of a large financial institution closed his presentation with the following statements. "All decision makers know that time involves money. We in the financial world also know that uncertainty has its price. That's why we constantly seek updated information about market conditions. Few financial analysts would pay for such information if they knew exactly what was going to happen."

   During the next class meeting, the business policy professor noted that the financial manager's comments really were a practical interpretation of the EVPI. As an assignment, the professor asked the class to give an EVPI interpretation of the manager's closing statements. Pretend you are a member of the class and do the assignment.

3. The mayor of Smithfield must decide whether or not to approve a sanitation department project that would expand the city's sewer system. Her action will depend on the projected demand for the facilities. Based on the best current available forecast, the mayor would approve the project. Such an action would maximize expected cash flow. However, the decision involves a $500,000 opportunity loss when there is a low demand and a $2 million penalty if demand is moderate. The best initial estimates indicate a 10% chance of low demand and a 20% likelihood of moderate demand.

   The regional planning commission estimates that it would cost $525,000 to obtain additional information about demand conditions. There is no other way of obtaining the knowledge at a lower cost within the time frame required for decision making. What should the mayor do? Explain.

4. Adam Full, advertising manager of T. J. Mentals Tobacco Company, is considering a media proposal from his assistant, Cynthia Lovelly. Ms. Lovelly suggested spending $300,000 in advertising on a new filter cigar. Full returned the proposal to Cynthia with the following comment: "If you can convince me that there is at least a 75% chance that the product will earn $150,000 more than the media cost, I'll authorize your proposal." After several days of research, Cynthia projected sales as follows:

Sales (Millions)	Probability
1	.05
2	.15
3	.30
4	.40
5	.10

   The company would make 15 cents per cigar. Can Ms. Lovelly convince her boss? Explain.

5. *Management Researcher* is a professional publication that supports itself mainly by subscription fees. The managing editor has calculated that variable costs are $10 per subscription. Fixed costs are $100,000 annually. A subscription is $30 per year. The journal's planning board estimates that total subscriptions will show the following distribution:

Subscriptions (Thousands/Year)	Probability
5	.10
10	.40
15	.30
20	.20

Based on this information, the editor decides to continue publishing *Management Researcher*. However, he is worried about the probability of a financial loss. The editor is considering a poll of past subscribers, professors, business people, and other interested parties in order to get a more accurate estimate of subscriptions. Such a poll would cost $100.

Explain why the editor decided to continue publishing the journal. What is the probability of loss associated with the decision? Should the poll be taken? Explain.

6. Do you think that a Bayesian decision analysis is appropriate in each of the following situations? Explain.

a. A company is trying to decide whether or not to introduce a new cooking appliance. Each unit would contribute a constant amount to cost and would sell for a fixed price. Total profit would depend on the sales volume, and demand would follow a normal distribution.

b. A laundry is trying to decide whether to lease or buy a line of automatic washing machines. The decision will depend on work volume. This volume is normally distributed with a known mean and standard deviation. The lease involves a fixed charge plus a constant variable expense per unit of volume. If the machines are owned, the variable cost is expected to decrease as volume increases.

c. A city's department of education wants to install electronic games in its high school recreation rooms. The department is considering three brands. Each brand has a constant operating cost per hour of use. Profit will depend on the total hours of use. There is a normal distribution of use.

d. The government's printing office is trying to decide whether or not to publish the final statistics of a terminated agency. There is a constant profit per volume. The publication can be sold only in whole unit quantities. However, sales volume can be approximated by a normal distribution.

7. Hamilton Tang is the general manager of Universal Hardware, Inc. He must decide whether his firm should produce a new line of power tools. In his judgment, there is a 70% likelihood that the line will be successful. Based on this assessment and available profit data, the best decision is to introduce the tools. The expected profit from this decision is $300,000. If Universal knew that the product would ultimately be successful, it could expect to make $500,000.

A market survey firm has submitted a bid for doing the fieldwork of interviewing hardware store owners. The company wants $20,000 for a report containing the following data:

◆ If there is a favorable market condition, Universal should introduce the line. The maximum expected profit would then be $400,000. There is a 60% chance of a favorable condition.

◆ If there is an unfavorable market condition, Universal should not introduce the power tools. Then the maximum expected profit would be $350,000.

Should Universal buy the survey? Explain.

8. Do you agree or disagree with each of the following statements? Explain.
   a. In a deterministic model, the expected value of perfect information is zero.
   b. The prior decision and EVC both involve the selection of a single course of action, regardless of the decision environment.
   c. Bayes's formula is not appropriate when there is an infinite number of states of nature.
   d. In Bayes's formula, the sum of all (conditional, indicator, and posterior) probabilities must equal 1.
   e. We should obtain sample information as long as the EVPI is greater than the cost of the additional knowledge.
   f. The EVSI can never be negative.

Technique Exercises

1. You are given the situation represented by the following decision table, where entries in the cells represent millions of dollars of profit. The prior probabilities are $P(s_1) = .6$ and $P(s_2) = .4$.

	States of Nature	
Decision Alternatives	s_1	s_2
a_1	2	−1
a_2	−3	6

   a. Use the prior probabilities to find the optimal decision.
   b. Find the expected value under certainty.
   c. Use the expected value under certainty to find the expected value of perfect information.

2. Consider the cost minimization problem represented by the following decision table, where entries in the cells represent cost. The prior probability of s_1 is .3.

	States of Nature	
Decision Alternatives	s_1	s_2
a_1	$150,000	$85,000
a_2	$90,000	$125,000
a_3	$115,000	$105,000

a. Use the prior probabilities to find the optimal decision.
b. Find the expected value under certainty (EVC).
c. Use the EVC to find the EVPI.
d. Determine the opportunity loss table.
e. Find the course of action that minimizes expected opportunity loss (EOL).
f. Compare the minimum EOL with the EVPI. What do you find?

3. A company is considering the introduction of a new product. The planned selling price is $410 per unit. There is a fixed cost of $200,000 for developing and manufacturing the product, while the variable cost would be $210 per unit. Demand for the product is described by the following distribution:

Demand	Probability
1000	.05
1500	.10
2000	.15
2500	.50
3000	.20

a. Based on the current available data, should the company introduce the product?
b. What is the probability of a loss?
c. What is the EVPI?

4. JM Enterprises, Inc., is going to buy a new machine that could generate significant labor cost savings on a certain operation. The company is considering two brands, X and Y. Brand X involves a fixed charge of $500,000 and a variable operating cost of $250 per hour of operation. Brand Y has a fixed expense of $600,000 and a variable operating cost of $200 per hour. Annual operating hours are distributed as follows:

Operating Hours	Probability
100	.1
200	.2
300	.3
400	.2
500	.2

a. Based on the current available data, which brand should JM Enterprises buy?
b. Develop the operating loss (OL) function.
c. What is the EVPI?

5. You are given $P(s_1) = .3$ and $P(s_3) = .3$. Also, indicator information shows that $P(I_1|s_1) = .4$, $P(I_2|s_2) = .8$, and $P(I_1|s_3) = .2$.
   a. Use Bayes's formula to develop an equation that will give $P(s_2|I_2)$.
   b. Use the equation you developed in part (a) to find $P(s_2|I_2)$.

6. A decision maker has a problem with four states of nature. The prior probabilities are $P(s_1) = .2$, $P(s_2) = .3$, $P(s_3) = .4$, and $P(s_4) = .1$. Additional research is conducted. Indicator probabilities are given as follows:

$P(I_1|s_1) = .1$	$P(I_1|s_2) = .6$	$P(I_1|s_3) = .7$	$P(I_1|s_4) = .9$
$P(I_2|s_1) = .4$	$P(I_2|s_2) = .3$	$P(I_2|s_3) = .2$	$P(I_2|s_4) = .1$
$P(I_3|s_1) = .5$	$P(I_3|s_2) = .1$	$P(I_3|s_3) = .1$	$P(I_3|s_4) = 0$

   a. Show the probability tree for this problem.
   b. Use the tabular method to find the desired posterior probability calculations.

7. Consider the following decision table, where the entries in the cells represent returns. The prior probabilities are $P(s_1) = .8$ and $P(s_2) = .2$.

	States of Nature	
Decision Alternatives	s_1	s_2
a_1	18	13
a_2	11	15
a_3	7	32

   a. Using the prior probabilities, find the course of action that maximizes expected return.
   b. Find the EVPI.
   c. Suppose some indicator information I_1 and I_2 is obtained. It shows that $P(I_1|s_1) = .6$ and $P(I_2|s_2) = .7$. Construct the appropriate decision tree.
   d. Work backward through the tree to develop the optimal decision strategy. Show your work on the tree.

8. Refer back to Pucter and Simple's evaluated decision tree (Figure 4.8). Use the data in this tree to compute the expected value of perfect information (EVPI). Show your work on the decision tree.

9. Consider the following segment of a decision tree representation of a problem with two indicators, two decision alternatives, and two states of nature.

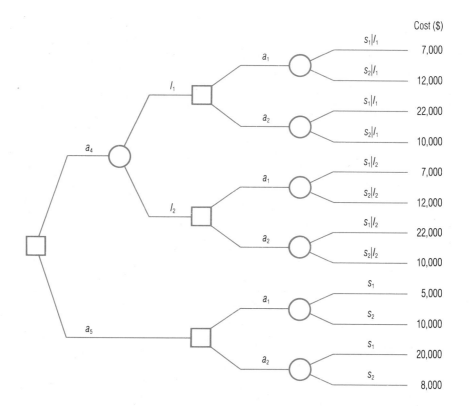

Cost ($)

The values at the end of the tree include the cost of the indicator information. Assume the following conditional probability information: $P(s_1) = .3$, $P(I_2|s_1) = .4$, and $P(I_1|s_2) = .8$.

a. What are the values for $P(I_1)$ and $P(I_2)$?
b. What are the values of $P(s_1|I_1)$, $P(s_2|I_1)$, $P(s_1|I_2)$, and $P(s_2|I_2)$?
c. Work backward through the decision tree to determine the optimal decision strategy.
d. What is the expected value of the optimal decision without the indicator information?
e. What is the expected value of the optimal decision with the indicator information?
f. Find the EVSI, CS, and ENGS.

10. A company's decision situation is represented by the following decision table, where entries represent returns. The prior probabilities are $P(s_1) = .2$, $P(s_2) = .6$, and $P(s_3) = .2$.

	States of Nature		
Decision Alternatives	s_1	s_2	s_3
a_1	−$500,000	$100,000	$1,000,000
a_2	$10,000	$200,000	$400,000

a. Which alternative maximizes expected returns? Show your work.
b. Find the EVC and EVPI.
c. Suppose a market research firm can provide the following indicator information: $P(I_1|s_1) = .1$, $P(I_1|s_2) = .5$, and $P(I_1|s_3) = .8$. The firm charges a $10,000 fee for its service. Find the indicator and posterior probabilities.
d. Construct a decision tree that describes the sequential nature of the problem.
e. Find the EVSI and ENGS.
f. Use the decision tree to develop an appropriate decision strategy.

Applications Exercises

1. The administration of South Southern College feels that four characteristics should be considered when selecting students for admission to its MBA program. These factors are the undergraduate grade point average, the entrance test score, recommendations, and professional experience. Each of the factors is given a standardized score on a 100-point scale. At this time, there are four candidates for the one available position. Student factor scores are given in the following table.

	Factor			
Student	Grade Point Average	Test Score	Recommendations	Professional Experience
Adamson	85	90	95	70
Caine	90	90	85	80
Dante	95	70	95	85
Mueller	90	80	90	95

Based on their knowledge and experience, the admissions board believes that recommendations are twice as important as the undergraduate grade point average. Also, professional experience is three and one half times more important than the undergraduate grade point average. The entrance test score and professional experience are considered of equal importance.

The admissions committee wants to select the student with the highest expected total score. Using the current available data, which student should be admitted to the program?

Suppose that admissions standards are an important determinant of college accreditation. In an attempt to increase the total expected score of accepted students, South Southern will collect additional admission factor information. Such knowledge will enable the admissions committee to more accurately forecast the relative importance of each criterion. What is the maximum number of points that the new information can add to the total expected score for accepted MBA students?

2. Cyanide Chemical Company has a new processing machine on trial and must either return it or buy it this week. The machine costs $150,000, but it saves about $100 per hour in operating expenses. H. T. Oh, the equipment manager, estimates there will be 2000 operating hours annually. However, Oh is only 50% confident in this estimate. She also feels that there is a 30% chance for the actual operation to involve 1500 hours. The other possibility is that the machine will be needed for 3000 hours of annual operation.
   a. Based on current available data, should Cyanide invest in the machine? Explain.
   b. Suppose that Cyanide's industrial engineering department can do a production study that would forecast operating hours almost exactly. What price should Oh be willing to pay for such a study?

3. An office manager will lease a photocopy machine from one of two manufacturers. The Fastpace leases for $10 per week plus a duplication charge of 5 cents per page. Alternatively, the Quietone leases for $25 per week plus a duplication charge of 4 cents per page. Each manufacturer requires a five-year lease. During its useful life, the photocopy machine's volume of work is not expected to change. Based on current available information, the manager believes there is a 40% chance that volume will be 1000 copies per week. He also feels that the actual volume could differ from this estimate by plus or minus 200 copies. Each of these differences is thought to be equally likely.

   The manager wants to lease the machine that will minimize expected total lease cost. Which brand should he lease? Suppose that one of the photocopy machine manufacturers offers to conduct a work study that would forecast the duplication volume more accurately. What is the maximum premium that the office manager should be willing to pay for the study results? Explain.

4. The research and development manager for Slippery Oil Corporation is considering whether the company should commercialize a new lubricant. It is assumed that the product will be a major success, a minor product line expansion, or a failure. If the product is a major success, it will contribute $2 million annually to corporate profit. Since the product will help sell other products in Slippery's line, even a minor commercial expansion will contribute $100,000 profit per year. However, a product failure will cost the company $1.5 million. Based on the opinion of the research team and the manager's own belief, there is a 20% likelihood of a major success and a 10% chance of failure. The manager feels that the decision is too important to base it on this preliminary information. Therefore, the company will delay the decision pending the outcome of a series of experiments by an independent research institute. Do you agree with this assessment? Explain.

   The research institute wants a fee to develop a report that would contain scientific data on the technical aspects of the lubricant. Past records show that on 90% of the occasions when a product has been a major commercial success, its technical report has been sound. When a product has been a minor product line expansion, its technical report has been sound 40% of the time. Also, 80% of the time that a product has been a failure, it had an unsound technical report. What would be Slippery's optimal decision strategy with the additional information? How much should the company be willing to pay for the new knowledge?

5. United Post Services delivers a particular package weekly from Millard to Fillmore. There are three possible routes: northern, central, or southern, and delivery time depends on uncertain weather conditions. It could rain, be overcast, or be clear. Over the northern route, it takes 30 minutes to deliver the package when it rains, 25 minutes when it is overcast, and 15 minutes in clear weather. Delivery over the central route takes 40 minutes in rain, 15 minutes when overcast, and 10 minutes when it is clear. It takes 20 minutes to deliver the package over the southern route no matter what weather conditions prevail.

Preliminary weather information indicates that there is a 20% chance of rain and a 30% likelihood of clear conditions. Based on this preliminary information, what route would result in the minimum expected delivery time? If United had more accurate weather information, how many minutes could they reduce the expected delivery time?

Suppose that the company could subscribe to a satellite-based weather-forecasting service. This service will indicate whether the conditions will be fair or inclement. Past records show that the service has forecasted fair conditions when it has rained 30% of the time. They have forecasted inclement conditions when it has been overcast 40% of the time. Also, on 80% of the clear occasions, the service has predicted fair weather. What would be United's optimal decision strategy with the additional information? How much do you think the company would benefit from the new knowledge? Explain.

6. Management at Bittell Toys, Inc., must decide whether the company should produce a new Christmas toy, the Computerized Chocolate Bar. The executive administrator feels that there is a 60% chance that the toy will be successful. If the product is successful, the firm will earn $600,000. On the other hand, an unsuccessful Chocolate Bar will cost Bittell $400,000.

Two market survey firms have submitted bids for doing the fieldwork of interviewing toy store owners. Delta Research, Inc., is known to conduct highly accurate surveys at rather high cost. Its fee is $40,000 for a report containing data on owners' product impressions. Past studies show the following results:

♦ When a product has been successful, 90% of the interviewed owners have been favorably impressed.

♦ When a product has been unsuccessful, 75% of the interviewees have been unfavorably impressed.

Iota Surveys Corporation has a lower fee, but tends to provide less accurate information. This corporation wants $20,000 for the same basic report as Delta's. Iota's past studies show the following results:

♦ When a product has been a success, 80% of the interviewees have been favorably impressed.

♦ When a product has been a failure, 60% of the interviewees have been unfavorably impressed.

Should Bittell's management buy no survey, buy Delta's survey, or buy Iota's survey?

CASE: Municipal Transit Authority

Municipal Transit Authority provides public transportation for the growing city of Metroville. The Authority must expand facilities to meet the ever-increasing demand for services. Some plan must be developed to finance the expansion. The Authority is considering three possibilities: a fare increase, a subsidy from city general revenues, or an issue of municipal bonds. Net revenues from the expanded facilities will depend on demand for public transportation in the next ten years. The demand may grow at or above the current rate, or it may grow rapidly in the next three years and then stabilize. Also, it may actually decline after the initial growth period. Continued growth would create a demand of more than 2 million passenger-miles in the next ten years. Rapid growth followed by stability would involve between 1 and 2 million passenger-miles. Decline after initial growth means a demand for less than 1 million passenger-miles.

Wade Trinkle, Municipal's rate engineer, believes that the most likely demand is 1.5 million passenger-miles.

He also feels that there is a 95% likelihood that demand will be between 520,000 and 2.48 million passenger-miles.

A fare increase would be the best method of finance if there is natural continued growth. The subsidy would be most economical under conditions of rapid growth followed by stability. Bonds would work best if there is a decline after initial growth. Sada Tontor, Municipal's chief economist, has done a financial analysis of the situation. The results can be summarized as follows:

♦ A fare increase would involve a net loss of $1 million if there is decline after initial growth. On the other hand, this policy would generate a net revenue of $200,000 under rapid growth/stable conditions and $3 million with continued growth.

♦ The subsidy would earn a net revenue of $400,000 under growth/decline conditions and $1.5 million for a rapid growth/stable state. Such a policy would involve a $600,000 loss if there is continued growth.

♦ The bond strategy would earn a net revenue of $1.6 million for a growth/decline state and $100,000 under rapid growth/stable conditions. However, this policy would create a $1.2 million loss if there is continued growth.

Agnes Peron, Municipal's general manager, realizes the economic importance of the decision. Thus, she wants to consider additional demand information before making a final decision. Two state agencies can provide some new knowledge for the cost of their reports. For $100,000, the Office of Planning (OP) can project economic growth in Metroville. From similar studies of public services, OP has been able to relate economic growth to demand. Its report will include the following data:

♦ On those occasions involving a growth/decline demand state, there has been economic decline 70% of the time and stable economic growth 20% of the time.

♦ When there has been a rapid growth/stable demand condition, there has been a 40 % chance of economic decline and a 50 % likelihood of economic stability.

♦ If there has been continued demand growth, there has been a 20 % chance of economic stability and a 60 % likelihood of economic growth.

For $200,000, the state Budget Department (BD) can project price trends in the Metroville area. From similar studies of public services, BD has been able to relate prices to demand. Its report will include the following data:

♦ In a growth/decline demand state, there have been stable prices 80 % of the time.

♦ There has been a 90 % likelihood of stable prices when there has been a growth/stable demand condition.

♦ On the occasions involving continued demand growth, there has been a 70 % chance of rising prices.

Ms. Peron forms an executive analysis committee made up of you, Wade Trinkle, and Sada Tontor. The committee is given the assignment of evaluating the financial policy alternatives and recommending an action. Peron wants the evaluation presented in a concise managerial brief. It should contain the following information:

1. The decision table for the problem

2. The preliminary probabilities for the demand conditions

3. The recommended decision based on the preliminary probabilities

4. The price that Municipal should be willing to pay for more accurate demand information

5. Decision trees for the problem with OP's and BD's additional information

6. Updated demand probabilities from OP's and BD's additional information

7. The optimal decision strategies with OP's and BD's additional information

8. A recommendation on whether Municipal should obtain no additional demand information, buy OP's report, or purchase BD's study

Prepare the assigned management report. (*Hint:* You will have to use normal distribution concepts in developing the prior probabilities. Winkler [18] provides a useful review of these concepts.)

Chapter 5
Utility and Game Theory

CHAPTER OUTLINE

- Utility Analysis
  Measuring Utility
  Using Utility for Decision Making
  Attitudes Toward Risk
  Limitations

- Multiple Criteria
  Priority Systems
  Transformations
  Multiattribute Utility Theory
  Limitations

- Conflict Situations
  Characteristics
  Dominance
  Pessimistic Criterion
  Mixed Strategy
  Extensions

- **Case:** Rural Vehicles, Inc.

CONCEPTS

- Developing nonmonetary measures of performance

- Using these measures for decision making

- Dealing with problems involving multiple criteria

- Developing approaches to decision making in conflict situations

APPLICATIONS

- Real estate investment
- Business expansion
- Fire insurance
- State lottery
- Franchise location
- Technical staffing
- Management training
- Television programming
- Land-use planning
- Automobile marketing
- Treaty negotiation
- Equipment purchasing

C hapters 3 and 4 have presented the fundamental concepts of decision analysis. As these chapters demonstrated, management should always select the alternative that best meets its criteria, or measures of performance. Hence, it is important to develop appropriate and accurate outcome measures.

Most of the decision problems considered in these previous chapters have used monetary values as outcomes. In many situations, however, such values are not appropriate measures of performance. The first section of this chapter considers such situations and then shows how to develop and use more relevant measures.

Our previous decision analysis has also assumed that there is a single objective. Frequently, however, managerial problems involve several (sometimes conflicting) criteria. The second section presents methods designed to deal with these multiple criteria problems and shows how these concepts can be used in decision making.

Finally, many decision problems involve a conflict between competing parties. In such cases, each party's actions will be influenced by the reaction pattern of the competitors. The last section presents a framework for analyzing these situations and shows how the model can be used to develop a decision strategy.

UTILITY ANALYSIS

It may seem natural to express decision outcomes in terms of monetary values (like costs, revenues, and profits) or some other absolute numerical measure (such as quantity, time, and distance). However, many practical real-life situations involve intangible factors that are difficult to express on an absolute numerical scale.

Risk and the decision maker's attitude toward this factor are among the most important intangibles. Investments provide a good illustration. Many savers cannot afford substantial financial losses or have an aversion toward risk. As a result, these people frequently invest in guaranteed rate, federally insured bank time deposits (such as T bills), even though these accounts usually yield lower returns than more risky alternatives. On the other hand, others will gamble on a highly speculative venture (like mineral exploration) in the hope of obtaining very large profits. Such investors may also be attracted to the risk or have significant discretionary funds.

A related intangible deals with the perspective of the decision maker. Consider, for example, an identical lump sum $1200 annual pay raise granted to both a low-paid clerical worker and a high-salaried executive. In all likelihood, the raise will have a more substantial impact on the clerk's spending and savings plans than on the executive's. Hence, the $1200 will be more valuable to the clerk than to the executive.

Enjoyment and satisfaction are other very important intangible factors. For instance, an interstate highway may be the most rapid and shortest route between two cities. However, it could also bypass many beautiful places and gratifying entertainment centers along the way. Consequently, a family on vacation may prefer to travel along a scenic route that includes these attractions rather than take the interstate.

In these situations, an absolute numerical measure (like monetary value, time, or distance) may be inadequate or inappropriate, and management will need a more comprehensive criterion that incorporates relevant intangibles as well as these absolute numerical values. In addition, the criterion must measure the true worth of the outcomes to the decision maker. This type of composite measure is known as **utility**.

MEASURING UTILITY Mathematicians and economists have been trying to develop a precise measure of utility since the eighteenth century. Their efforts generally have not produced a universal or absolute scale of measurement. As P. C. Fishburn [5] and R. L. Keeney and H. Raiffa [10] demonstrate, however, it is possible to infer a specific set of utility values from the observed decision behavior of an individual. The concepts can be illustrated with Example 5.1.

EXAMPLE 5.1 Real Estate Investments

Medfern Associates is a real estate investment firm operating in the southwestern part of the state. A large developer recently offered Medfern the opportunity to invest in two current building projects. One involves a condominium development in an attractive area of Oceanside, and the other deals with a housing tract under construction in Springdale. Profits from the investments would depend on uncertain real estate market conditions.

After considering all relevant information, Medfern management believes that the situation can be represented by Table 5.1. Furthermore, the executives feel that there is a $P(s_1) = .1$ chance that real estate prices will go up, a $P(s_2) = .3$ likelihood that they will remain stable, and a $P(s_3) = .6$ probability of falling real estate prices. At present, the company can afford only one investment.

Initially, Medfern was interested in the most profitable investment. Using the profit data from Table 5.1 and the event probabilities, management found that the expected profit was $320,000 for alternative a_1, $210,000 for a_2, and $0 for a_3. Since alternative a_1 led to the largest expected profit, the company was inclined to invest in condominiums. However, Medfern's current financial position is weak. In fact, management feels that a substantial loss on the next investment could force the company out of business.

To properly evaluate the development opportunity, then, Medfern must consider the risk of financial loss as well as profit. The company will do so by determining the true worth, or utility, of each profit to management. Then it will select the alternative that leads to the largest expected utility.

Table 5.1 Medfern's Decision Table

	States of Nature		
Decision Alternatives	s_1 = prices go up	s_2 = prices remain stable	s_3 = prices go down
a_1 = invest in condominiums	$2,000,000	$1,000,000	− $300,000
a_2 = invest in houses	$4,500,000	$200,000	− $500,000
a_3 = do not invest	$0	$0	$0
	Profit		Loss

Medfern wants to determine a utility value for each profit level in Table 5.1. Management can begin by arbitrarily assigning utility values to both the best and worst outcomes in the problem. Any values will work as long as the best outcome is given a higher utility than the worst payoff.

As the data from Table 5.1 indicate, Medfern's best possible profit is the $4,500,000 associated with alternative a_2 and event s_1. Suppose that management assigns a utility U of 100 to this profit. That is,

$$U(\$4,500,000) = 100$$

Also, Table 5.1 shows that the worst outcome is the $500,000 loss (negative profit) associated with alternative a_2 and event s_3. If Medfern's management assigns a utility of 0 to this outcome, then we have

$$U(-\$500,000) = 0$$

All other payoffs in Table 5.1 are better than the worst (− $500,000) but not as good as the best ($4,500,000) outcome. Hence, these other outcomes should have utility values somewhere between 0 and 100. The proper utility values can be inferred from the decision maker's answers to a series of questions dealing with his or her preferences for various outcomes.

To see what is involved, let us consider the $2,000,000 profit associated with alternative a_1 and event s_1. First, Medfern's management is asked to visualize a hypothetical situation in which it would have the option of investing in either (1) a project that is sure to yield the $2,000,000 profit or (2) a lottery ticket that has a p chance of earning the $4,500,000 best possible profit but a $(1 - p)$ likelihood of obtaining the $-$500,000 worst outcome. This option is similar to the proposition offered to contestants on some popular television game shows.

Clearly, the decision maker's preference will depend on the value of p. Since p is a probability, it will have a value between 0 and 1. If p is very close to 0, the lottery ticket virtually ensures a $500,000 loss. Under these circumstances, most managers would select the project yielding the sure $2,000,000 profit. However, as p increases, the lottery ticket will grow in value and hence become increasingly more attractive. Eventually, at some p value, the executive will have no greater preference for the sure $2,000,000 profit than for the lottery ticket. This p value is called the **lottery indifference probability**. Beyond this point, the preference for the sure project will change into a preference for the lottery. In particular, if p is very close to 1, the lottery ticket practically assures a $4,500,000 profit and thus should be preferable to a project yielding $2,000,000.

Each decision maker, of course, will have his or her own personal lottery indifference probability. Some trial and error questioning may be required to identify the precise value. It begins with the arbitrary assignment of a probability, say $p = .85$, to the $4,500,000 best outcome from the lottery. Next, the decision maker is asked if he or she prefers the sure $2,000,000 profit to the lottery ticket with this $p = .85$ probability. If the decision maker answers yes, then the lottery is made progressively more attractive by slowly increasing p to $p = .86$, $p = .87$, and so on. The adjustment process continues until the executive is indifferent between the sure return and the ticket. If, on the other hand, there is a preference for the lottery, then the value of p should be adjusted downward to the indifference point by a similar trial and error process.

Suppose these queries indicate that Medfern's management would be indifferent between the sure $2,000,000 and the lottery if there is a 90% chance of obtaining the $4,500,000 best outcome. In this case, the lottery indifference probability is $p = .9$. The sure $2,000,000 profit is known as the **certainty equivalent** of this particular lottery.

If Medfern is indifferent between the sure $2,000,000 and the lottery ticket, then these two alternatives must have the same utility to management. That is,

$$\underbrace{U(\$2,000,000)}_{\substack{\text{Utility of} \\ \text{the certainty} \\ \text{equivalent}}} = \underbrace{pU(\$4,500,000) + (1-p)U(-\$500,000)}_{\substack{\text{Expected utility of the} \\ \text{lottery ticket}}}$$

Since $p = .9$, $U(\$4,500,000) = 100$, and $U(-\$500,000) = 0$, the utility of the $\$2,000,000$ profit is

$$U(\$2,000,000) = .9(100) + (1-.9)(0) = 90$$

Table 5.2 The Lottery Ticket Approach to Utility Measurement

1. Identify the best and worst outcomes in the problem.
2. Arbitrarily assign different utility values to both the best and worst outcomes. Any values will work as long as the best outcome is given a higher utility than the worst payoff.
3. Define a hypothetical situation in which the decision maker has the option of investing in either:
   a. a project that is sure to yield a particular outcome between the best and worst payoffs, or
   b. a lottery ticket that has a p chance of earning the best outcome but a $(1-p)$ likelihood of obtaining the worst payoff.
4. Use a series of trial and error questions to determine the value of p that makes the decision maker indifferent between the sure outcome and the lottery ticket. This value of p is called the lottery indifference probability for the sure outcome.
5. Use the formula

$$U(\text{sure outcome}) = pU(\text{best outcome}) + (1-p)U(\text{worst outcome})$$

   to calculate the utility of the sure outcome.

Table 5.3 Medfern's Utility Calculations

Profit	Lottery Indifference Probability (p)	Utility
$4,500,000	Does not apply	100
2,000,000	.9	$.9(100) + (.1)(0) = 90$
1,000,000	.8	$.8(100) + (.2)(0) = 80$
200,000	.6	$.6(100) + (.4)(0) = 60$
0	.5	$.5(100) + (.5)(0) = 50$
−300,000	.2	$.2(100) + (.8)(0) = 20$
−500,000	Does not apply	0

In other words, Medfern's management gets 90 units of utility from a $2,000,000 profit.

Similar hypothetical lotteries can be used to find the utilities for the other outcomes. Table 5.2 summarizes the procedure. Such an approach is designed primarily for problems, like Medfern's, that involve a finite number of decision alternatives and events. Fishburn [5] and Keeney and Raiffa [10] extend the analysis to more complex situations.

Now we can use the procedure to find the utilities for each outcome in Medfern's decision table (Table 5.1). For instance, suppose a series of trial and error questions reveals that when $p = .8$ management is indifferent between a sure $1,000,000 profit and the lottery ticket. In this case, then, management will receive

$$U(\$1,000,000) = pU(\$4,500,000) + (1 - p)U(-\$500,000)$$

or

$$U(1,000,000) = .8(100) + .2(0) = 80$$

units of utility from the $1,000,000 profit. Furthermore, assume that the $200,000 profit involves a lottery indifference probability of $p = .6$, while $0 is associated with $p = .5$, and the $300,000 loss entails a $p = .2$ Then the corresponding utilities would be the values presented in Table 5.3.

USING UTILITY FOR DECISION MAKING By substituting the utility values from Table 5.3 for the corresponding outcomes in Table 5.1, Medfern will obtain the results presented in Table 5.4. Since this table identifies the utility of each decision outcome to management, it is called a **utility table**.

Table 5.4 Medfern's Utility Table

Decision Alternatives	States of Nature		
	s_1 = prices go up	s_2 = prices remain stable	s_3 = prices go down
a_1 = invest in condominiums	90	80	20
a_2 = invest in houses	100	60	0
a_3 = do not invest	50	50	50

Units of utility to management

Remember, there is a $P(s_1) = .1$ chance that prices will go up, a $P(s_2) = .3$ likelihood that they will remain stable, and a $P(s_3) = .6$ probability that they will fall. Using these probabilities and the data in Table 5.4, Medfern will find that the condominium investment (a_1) leads to an expected utility of

$$90(.1) + 80(.3) + 20(.6) = 45$$

On the other hand, there is an expected utility of

$$100(.1) + 60(.3) + 0(.6) = 28$$

from the housing project (a_2) and

$$50(.1) + 50(.3) + 50(.6) = 50$$

from the no investment alternative (a_3).

Management wants to obtain as much total worth, or utility, as possible. Since decision alternative a_3 leads to the largest expected utility (50), Medfern should not invest in either real estate venture.

ATTITUDES TOWARD RISK

Refer back to the data given in Example 5.1. Notice that the expected monetary value (profit) recommendation (a_1) is different from the recommended decision (a_3) from the expected utility analysis. The difference results from the attitude of Medfern's management toward risk.

As Table 5.1 and the event probabilities show, the condominium investment (a_1) involves a $P(s_3) = .6$, or 60%, chance of obtaining a $300,000 loss. Medfern cannot afford such a serious financial setback. Yet the $320,000 expected profit from alternative a_1 may not adequately reflect the seriousness of this risk and the corresponding impact on the firm.

On the other hand, there is no risk of financial loss associated with not investing (a_3). As the data in Example 5.1 demonstrate, however, Medfern receives a $0 expected profit from this alternative. In selecting a_3, then, management will sacrifice $320,000 - $0 = $320,000 in expected profit to avoid risk. This type of attitude is referred to as **risk averse**.

Medfern's attitude can be examined from another perspective. Using the data in Table 5.3, we can develop a graph that shows the relationship between monetary value and utility. The result, presented in Figure 5.1, is called a **utility curve**.

As Figure 5.1 demonstrates, a growth in monetary value leads to an increase in utility. This property is characteristic of all utility curves. In Medfern's case, however, the increase is not proportional. For example, a $300,000 loss involves 20 units of utility, while a $0 profit has a 50-unit

Figure 5.1 Medfern's Utility Curve

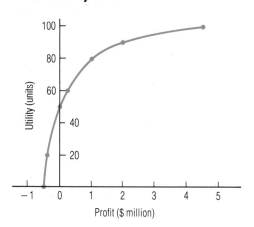

utility to company management. Hence, within this range of monetary values, utility increases at the rate of

$$\frac{\text{increase in utility}}{\text{increase in profit}} = \frac{50 - 20}{\$0 - (-\$300,000)} = \frac{30}{\$300,000} = 0.0001$$

unit per $1 growth in profit. On the other hand, between profit levels of $0 and $200,000, utility increases at the rate of

$$\frac{\text{increase in utility}}{\text{increase in profit}} = \frac{60 - 50}{\$200,000 - \$0} = \frac{10}{\$200,000} = 0.00005$$

unit per $1 growth in monetary value.

A value of 0.00005 is smaller than 0.0001. Thus, the rate of increase in utility declines with the growth in monetary value. In other words, Medfern's utility does not grow as fast as profit. This characteristic, which is known as a diminishing marginal utility for monetary gain, reflects management's desire to avoid the higher risks associated with the larger profits. Namely, it is a consequence of the company's risk aversion.

In effect, then, a risk-averse decision maker will have a diminishing marginal utility for monetary gain. Furthermore, such a manager's utility curve will have the shape shown in Figure 5.1.

But decision makers may have other attitudes toward risk, as Example 5.2 illustrates.

EXAMPLE 5.2 Business Expansion

This problem is an extension of Example 5.1. Suppose that Medfern is now trying to expand by selling stock. Each of the two prospective buyers wants enough stock to take over effective control of the company. One of the potential owners, Speculative Enterprises, has a surplus of cash and a very stable future. The company is looking for investments that may be risky but have a potential for substantial profit. The other prospective purchaser, Conglomerate Incorporated, is a very large international petroleum company. This firm would neither suffer greatly from a $500,000 loss nor increase its wealth significantly with a $4,500,000 profit.

Before offering the stock, Medfern wants to determine both Conglomerate's and Speculative's attitudes toward risk. In this respect, the lottery ticket approach (Table 5.2) is used to poll the executives of each prospective firm concerning their attitudes about Medfern's outcomes (Table 5.1). For comparison purposes, the pollster again arbitrarily assigns 100 utility units to the best ($4,500,000) and 0 units to the worst (−$500,000) outcome. Table 5.5 presents the results.

Table 5.5 Speculative's and Conglomerate's Utility Values

| Profit ($) | Speculative | | Conglomerate | |
	Lottery Indifference Probability (p)	Utility	Lottery Indifference Probability (p)	Utility
4,500,000	Does not apply	100	Does not apply	100
2,000,000	.25	25	.50	50
1,000,000	.10	10	.30	30
200,000	.03	3	.14	14
0	.02	2	.10	10
−300,000	.01	1	.04	4
−500,000	Does not apply	0	Does not apply	0

Table 5.5 shows that Speculative assigns 1 unit of utility to a −$300,000 profit. At this utility value, management is indifferent between the sure $300,000 loss and a lottery ticket. In the lottery, there is a $p = .01$ chance of earning $4,500,000 but a $1 - p = .99$ likelihood for a $500,000 loss. Hence, the company will obtain an expected profit of

$$.01(\$4,500,000) + .99(-\$500,000) = -450,000$$

from the ticket. Yet management would just as soon take this lottery as the sure (and smaller) $300,000 loss.

Also, Speculative assigns 25 units of utility to a $2,000,000 profit. The corresponding lottery ticket involves a 25% likelihood of earning

$4,500,000 but a 75% chance for a $500,000 loss. Even though this lottery has an expected profit of only

$$.25(\$4,500,000) + .75(-\$500,000) = \$750,000$$

management is indifferent between this ticket and the sure $2,000,000.

In either case, Speculative will take a high risk of absorbing a large ($500,000) loss in order to have an opportunity for a substantial ($4,500,000) gain. Such an attitude is called **risk seeking**.

Conglomerate, on the other hand, exhibits a different type of attitude. Table 5.5 shows that this company's management assigns 50 units of utility to a $2,000,000 profit. Furthermore, at this utility, it is indifferent between the sure $2,000,000 and a lottery ticket. In the lottery, there is a 50% chance of earning a $4,500,000 profit but a 50% likelihood for a $500,000 loss. Thus, the company will obtain an expected profit of

$$.50(\$4,500,000) + .50(-\$500,000) = \$2,000,000$$

from the ticket. Management, in effect, is assigning utility in such a way that the expected profit ($2,000,000) from the lottery ticket equals the sure outcome. As a result, Conglomerate is neither seeking nor avoiding risk. In fact, monetary value, not risk, is the main consideration. Decision makers with this attitude are said to be **risk neutral**.

The prospective buyers' utility curves provide another perspective. By using the data from Table 5.5 to develop these curves and then superimposing the results on Figure 5.1, we get the graph shown in Figure 5.2. As the figure illustrates, Speculative's utility grows at a faster rate than profit. Such a property is known as an increasing marginal utility for monetary gain. On the other hand, Conglomerate's rate of increase in utility remains the same as profit increases. A curve with this characteristic is said to have a constant marginal utility for monetary gain.

In effect, then, risk-seeking decision makers, like Speculative, will show an increasing marginal utility for monetary gain. Their utility curve will be shaped like Speculative's curve in Figure 5.2. Also, risk-neutral management, such as Conglomerate, will have a constant marginal utility for monetary gain and a linear, or straight-line, utility curve.

Most people have both a speculative side and a conservative side. Thus, it is possible for a decision maker to display all three risk attitudes toward the range of monetary values in a particular situation. Such a pattern, referred to as a **risk-complex** attitude, might generate the utility curve shown in Figure 5.3.

Large monetary losses usually create a great deal of anxiety and typically motivate a change from the status quo. Many decision makers try to eliminate these losses by engaging in very risky ventures. Such a risk-seeking attitude is depicted as the portion of the utility curve to the left of

DECISION ANALYSIS

Figure 5.2 Medfern's, Conglomerate's, and Speculative's Utility Curves

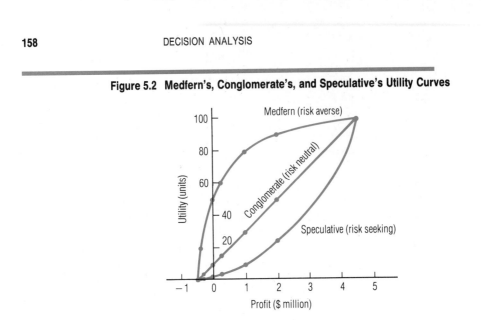

Figure 5.3 Risk-Complex Attitude Toward Risk

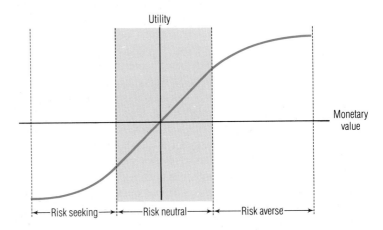

the shaded region in Figure 5.3. As the losses diminish, management may become indifferent toward risk. This risk-neutral attitude, shown as the straight line in the shaded portion of Figure 5.3, may prevail as long as the monetary gains are modest. Continual growth in monetary value, however, generally involves an increase in risk. Eventually, the decision maker may sacrifice some gains to avoid this risk. This risk aversion is represented by the portion of the utility curve to the right of the shaded region. Fishburn [5] and Keeney and Raiffa [10] discuss other forms of risk-complex attitudes.

LIMITATIONS Utility analysis may be troublesome to implement in practice. It is a highly subjective approach that can be time-consuming, costly, and frustrating to apply. In addition, the decision maker may not fully understand, appreciate, or relate to the trial and error questioning involved in the process. As a result, it may be difficult to develop an accurate and reliable assessment of utility.

The concept itself creates additional difficulties. Utility is a reflection of management expectations, attitudes, and perceptions regarding a particular decision situation at a specific point in time. Perspectives, however, can change over time. Hence, a decision maker's previous utility assessment may not be appropriate for current or future conditions. Consequently, management must continually update the assessment prior to each decision.

There is a related limitation. Each person has a unique perspective. Thus, several managers may each describe the same situation with a different utility curve. Then, using these individual curves, each decision maker could arrive at a different solution to the same problem.

In fact, that is exactly what happens in Examples 5.1 and 5.2. Medfern exhibits risk aversion toward the real estate investment. Such an attitude results in the utility data given in Table 5.4. An expected utility analysis of this data leads management to select the noninvestment alternative (a_3).

Speculative, on the other hand, has a risk-seeking attitude toward the venture. By substituting its utility values from Table 5.5 for the corresponding dollar outcomes in Table 5.1, the company will obtain the results presented in Table 5.6.

Since $P(s_1) = .1$, $P(s_2) = .3$, and $P(s_3) = .6$, Speculative obtains an expected utility of

$$25(.1) + 10(.3) + 1(.6) = 6.1$$

from the condominium alternative (a_1),

$$100(.1) + 3(.3) + 0(.6) = 10.9$$

from housing (a_2), and

$$2(.1) + 2(.3) + 2(.6) = 2$$

if it does not invest (a_3). This company's management can therefore maximize its expected utility at 10.9 units by investing in houses.

A similar analysis of Conglomerate's data will show that the condominium alternative (a_1) provides the largest expected utility for this firm's risk-neutral management.

Therefore, to maximize expected utility, Conglomerate would choose a_1, Speculative a_2, and Medfern a_3. In effect, then, the dissimilar risk attitudes would lead each company to select a different investment strategy for the same real estate venture.

Table 5.6 Speculative's Utility Table

	States of Nature		
Decision Alternatives	s_1 = prices go up	s_2 = prices remain stable	s_3 = prices go down
a_1 = invest in condominiums	25	10	1
a_2 = invest in houses	100	3	0
a_3 = do not invest	2	2	2

Many decisions, in practice, are made by committees. When these groups consist of several people with divergent viewpoints, it may be difficult to arrive at a consensus expected utility recommendation.

The limitations often discourage organizations from using utility as an outcome measure. Instead, managers are more inclined to use the more familiar monetary value analysis. If risk is the only other relevant factor and the decision maker has a risk-neutral attitude, this practice will involve little danger. To see why, let us compare Medfern's expected monetary value analysis (in Example 5.1) and Conglomerate's expected utility analysis of the real estate venture. Notice that risk-neutral Conglomerate makes the investment (a_1) recommended by the expected monetary value analysis. This result is not a coincidence. In fact, when management is risk neutral (has a straight-line utility curve), an expected utility analysis and an expected monetary value analysis always lead to the same decision.

However, when management (such as Medfern's) has substantial risk aversion or (like Speculative) seeks risk, an expected utility analysis and an expected monetary value analysis generally result in different decisions. Under these circumstances, it would be wise for the decision maker to consider an expected utility analysis. A utility analysis also may be advisable if the problem involves many goals or several intangibles. These situations are discussed in the next section.

MULTIPLE CRITERIA So far, our discussion has focused on situations that involve a single objective, such as profit maximization or cost minimization. In many situations, however, the decision maker must consider many, often conflicting, criteria. Consider, for example, a college graduate just entering the job market. He or she wants a position with the largest possible salary and fringe benefits, most pleasant work environment, and favorable advancement opportunities. Unfortunately, high-paying jobs frequently involve unpleasant working conditions or unfavorable promotional prospects. In selecting a position, then, the graduate must analyze each alternative in terms of its potential impact on these criteria.

There are several ways to deal with these multiple-criteria decision situations. The concepts can be illustrated with Example 5.3.

EXAMPLE 5.3 Book Publishing

The local university publishes texts written by its faculty for use in courses offered on campus. Then the texts are sold through the bookstore to students.

Jonathan Smart has just completed a manuscript for an introductory accounting course, and the bookstore must now decide how many copies to publish. The production alternatives will be influenced by the estimated demand.

Previous experience with similar projects indicates that the bookstore can sell either 1000, 1200, or 1400 copies per academic year. Furthermore, there is a 30% chance of selling 1000 copies, a 50% likelihood for a 1200-unit demand, and a 20% probability of selling 1400 copies.

Management will evaluate each production alternative on the basis of its impact on anticipated cash requirements and projected profits. An initial investigation suggests that Table 5.7 is a reasonable representation of the bookstore's decision situation.

Table 5.7 University Bookstore's Decision Table

Decision Alternatives	States of Nature		
	s_1 = sell 1000	s_2 = sell 1200	s_3 = sell 1400
a_1 = publish 1000	profit = $3500 cash requirement = $11,500	profit = $3100 cash requirement = $14,900	profit = $3700 cash requirement = $17,300
a_2 = publish 1200	profit = $2800 cash requirement = $14,200	profit = $4500 cash requirement = $13,500	profit = $2900 cash requirement = $16,900
a_3 = publish 1400	profit = $2600 cash requirement = $16,400	profit = $3800 cash requirement = $16,200	profit = $4950 cash requirement = $15,500

Bookstore management will consider both profit and cash requirements before making its publication decision. That is why each cell in the decision table (Table 5.7) has an entry (outcome) for both of these attributes.

Separate criteria can be developed for each decision attribute. For instance, the bookstore may want to publish the quantity of texts that maximizes profit or minimizes cash requirements. However, by separately applying each criterion, the decision maker could arrive at two (or more) different conclusions. To generate a single recommendation, management must evaluate each alternative's simultaneous impact on all criteria.

PRIORITY SYSTEMS In one approach, management first identifies the most important decision criterion. This primary criterion is treated as the single objective of the problem. Next, acceptable or target levels are established for the other criteria and additional relevant attributes. These targets, or goals, become restrictions on the primary criterion. Then the decision maker selects the alternative, among those satisfying all constraints, that best meets the primary objective.

Suppose, for example, that the highest priority of the university bookstore is to maximize expected profit. However, management does not want the expected cash requirements for Smart's manuscript to exceed $15,000. Also, although the bookstore has no explicit sales objective, management feels that demand is another relevant attribute. In this respect, there must be at least a 60% chance of selling the published quantity of texts.

Under these circumstances, the objective of the bookstore is to select the publication quantity that maximizes expected profit. This objective is constrained by the expected cash requirements and demand goals.

We can begin the analysis with the target on the probability of demand. According to Example 5.3, there is a $P(s_1) = .3$ chance of selling 1000 copies of Smart's book. The bookstore also has a $P(s_2) = .5$ likelihood of making 1200 sales and a $P(s_3) = .2$ probability for 1400 sales. Thus, there is a

$$P(s_1) + P(s_2) + P(s_3) = .3 + .5 + .2 = 1$$

or 100% chance of at least 1000, a

$$P(s_2) + P(s_3) = .5 + .2 = .7$$

or 70% likelihood for at least 1200, and a

$$P(s_3) = .2$$

or 20% probability for at least 1400 sales. Since management wants at least a 60% chance of selling the selected production quantity, the university should publish no more than 1200 copies of Smart's text.

Now consider cash requirements. By using the data from Table 5.7 and the probability information, the bookstore will find that the expected cash requirement for publishing 1000 texts (a_1) is

$$\$11,500(.3) + \$14,900(.5) + \$17,300(.2) = \$14,360$$

Similarly, there is an expected cash requirement of

$$\$14,200(.3) + \$13,500(.5) + \$16,900(.2) = \$14,390$$

for publishing 1200 texts (a_2) and

$$\$16,400(.3) + \$16,200(.5) + \$15,500(.2) = \$16,120$$

for publishing 1400 copies (a_3). Since management does not want this requirement to exceed \$15,000, the bookstore should publish no more than 1200 copies.

The university can therefore satisfy both the cash requirements and the demand constraints by publishing either 1000 or 1200 texts. Data from Table 5.7 and the probability information indicate that there is an expected profit of

$$\$3500(.3) + \$3100(.5) + \$3700(.2) = \$3340$$

from publishing 1000 copies (a_1) and

$$\$2800(.3) + \$4500(.5) + 2900(.2) = \$3670$$

from producing 1200 copies (a_2). Therefore, management can achieve its primary objective of maximizing expected profit at \$3670 per academic year by publishing 1200 texts. This quantity will also meet the cash requirements and demand goals.

The decision maker could encounter some difficulties in applying this goal constraint approach. For one thing, it may not be possible to find a decision alternative that satisfies all the constraints. In such cases, management will have to add alternatives, relax the constraints, or alter the objectives. Also, goals are viewed differently by various individuals and groups within the organization. Furthermore, changes in the decision situation, organization, or environment could alter the original goal structure. As a result, the decision maker may be unable to identify a stable preeminent criterion or establish a consensus on the acceptable levels of the other objectives.

Some of these difficulties can be avoided by using a system based on alternative priorities. In this second approach, the decision maker first establishes a priority ranking for the objectives. Next, each decision alternative is rated in terms of the objective with the highest priority. If two or more alternatives receive the same rating, management then uses the second-ranked objective to evaluate these options. The evaluation process continues, in sequence, through lower-priority objectives until management identifies a single best alternative or exhausts the list of objectives.

Suppose, for instance, that the most important objectives of the university bookstore are, in order, to maximize expected profit and minimize expected cash requirements. Previous calculations have already indicated that the store can earn an expected profit of $3340 from alternative a_1 and $3670 from alternative a_2. Also, by using the data from Table 5.7 and the probability information in Example 5.3, management will find that there is an expected profit of

$$\$2600(.3) + \$3800(.5) + \$4950(.2) = \$3670$$

from producing 1400 texts (a_3). Thus, the bookstore can maximize expected profit at $3670 by publishing either 1200 or 1400 copies of Smart's text.

The highest-priority criterion, expected profit maximization, eliminates a_1 but does not provide an unequivocal recommendation regarding the other alternatives $(a_2$ and $a_3)$. Consequently, management must now evaluate the survivors in terms of the second-ranked objective (minimizing expected cash requirements).

In this regard, previous computations have shown that there is an expected cash requirement of $14,390 associated with a_2 and $16,120 associated with a_3. Hence, among these two highest-profit alternatives, a_2 has the smallest expected cash requirement. According to this ranked priority approach, then, the bookstore should publish 1200 copies of Smart's manuscript.

In the university bookstore situation, the goal constraint and ranked priority approaches both lead to the same recommendation. The result is merely a coincidence. However, notice how much easier it is to apply the ranked priority concept. Instead of identifying a preeminent criterion and setting targets for the other objectives, management merely has to rank-order the criteria.

One of the difficulties is that the ranked priority approach may identify a single best alternative without considering all relevant objectives. Under some circumstances, a recommendation could be obtained after evaluating the alternatives in terms of only the highest-priority objective. In such cases, the ranked priority approach effectively becomes a single criterion system and thus considers fewer objectives than the goal constraint method. Also, several participants in the formulation process could develop different assessments of the priorities for the objectives. Furthermore, these assessments can change over time and in different decision situations. Consequently, the decision maker again may be unable to establish a stable consensus hierarchy of objectives. And neither the goal constraint nor ranked priority approach is designed to deal with problems involving several essentially equal criteria.

Table 5.8 University Bookstore's Decision Table in Terms of ROI

Decision Alternatives	States of Nature		
	s_1	s_2	s_3
a_1	$3500/$11,500 = .3043	$3100/$14,900 = .2081	$3700/$17,300 = .2139
a_2	$2800/$14,200 = .1972	$4500/$13,500 = .333	$2900/$16,900 = .1716
a_3	$2600/$16,400 = .1585	$3800/$16,200 = .2346	$4950/$15,500 = .3194

ROI = profit/cash requirement

TRANSFORMATIONS As a result of the theoretical and practical limitations of priority systems, management scientists have developed other approaches to multiple-criteria decision making. In one approach, the decision maker begins by transforming all attributes into a single composite measure. This measure should, in some way, reflect the impact of each alternative on the original attributes. Management next develops a decision criterion from the single composite measure and then selects the alternative that best meets this criterion.

High profits and small cash requirements, for example, are each desirable attributes for the university bookstore. Management also may be happy with the following combinations: (1) high profits and stable cash requirements, (2) stable profits and small cash requirements, or (3) stable profits and stable cash requirements. However, the bookstore would not want small profits and large cash requirements.

The ratio of profit to cash requirements, which could be called the return on investment (ROI), reflects each of these consequences. Hence, it may be useful for management to transform the original two attributes into this composite ROI measure, in which case the bookstore's decision situation would be represented by Table 5.8. An appropriate objective for this situation, then, is to select the alternative that maximizes the expected return on investment (ROI).

By using the data from Table 5.8 and the probability information from Example 5.3, management will find that the expected ROI from alternative a_1 is

$$.3043(.3) + .2081(.5) + .2139(.2) = .2381$$

Similarly, there is an expected return on investment of

$$.1972(.3) + .3333(.5) + .1716(.2) = .2601$$

from a_2 and

$$.1585(.3) + .2346(.5) + .3194(.2) = .2287$$

from a_3. Hence, a_2 yields the largest expected ROI at 26.01%. According to this composite criterion, the bookstore should publish 1200 copies of Smart's text.

Unfortunately, many problems involve intangibles or noncomparable attributes. In these cases, the decision maker may be unable to define a single composite measure. Even when such a measure is available, management usually must make some subjective trade-offs between the component attributes. For instance, falling profit is an undesirable attribute for the university bookstore. Yet its return on investment (ROI) could increase under these circumstances if the corresponding cash requirements fall more rapidly than profit. Thus, by using the composite ROI criterion, bookstore management implicitly is willing to trade off the reduced profit for the more substantial decrease in cash requirements.

C. L. Huang and others [9] and Keeney and Raiffa [10] present other transformation processes designed for situations involving intangibles and noncomparable attributes. However, these processes also require the decision maker to make some implicit trade-offs between the attributes. In an attempt to describe these trade-offs more explicitly, management scientists have developed a multiple-attribute utility system for decision making.

MULTIATTRIBUTE UTILITY THEORY

In this approach, the decision maker first assigns utility values to each multiple-attribute outcome in the problem. The purpose of this step is to transform the original attributes into the single composite measure of utility. Management then selects the alternative that maximizes expected utility.

The multiple-attribute nature of the outcomes, however, complicates the task of assigning utilities. Still, there are several methods available for this purpose. In the traditional method, a separate utility curve is developed for each relevant attribute in the problem. The lottery ticket approach, outlined in Table 5.2, typically is used to construct these curves. Individual curves are then amalgamated into a multiattribute utility assessment.

Suppose, for example, that the university bookstore uses the lottery ticket approach to develop separate utility curves first for the profit attribute and then for the cash requirement attribute. According to Table 5.2, management begins the process by assigning arbitrary utility values to the best and worst outcomes in the problem.

Table 5.7 indicates that the largest profit of $4950 is obtained when the bookstore publishes and sells 1400 copies of Smart's manuscript. The

Table 5.9 The Utility of Profit to Bookstore Management

Profit ($)	Lottery Indifference Probability (p)	Utility
4950	Does not apply	100
4500	.90	90
3800	.75	75
3700	.70	70
3500	.65	65
3100	.55	55
2900	.40	40
2800	.15	15
2600	Does not apply	0

smallest profit of $2600 occurs when the bookstore publishes 1400 copies but sells only 1000. If management assigns a utility of 100 to the $4950 and 0 to the $2600, then

$$U(\$4950) = 100$$

denotes the utility of the best profit and

$$U(\$2600) = 0$$

denotes the utility of the worst profit.

These values can then be used in various hypothetical lottery situations to derive the utilities for the other profit levels in Table 5.7. In one of these situations, for example, bookstore management could be given the option of investing in either (1) a project that is sure to yield the $3500 profit associated with the a_1 and s_1 combination in Table 5.7 or (2) a lottery ticket that has a p chance of earning the best ($4950) profit but a $(1 - p)$ likelihood of yielding the worst ($2600) profit. Next, a series of trial and error questions is employed to determine the value of p that makes management indifferent between the sure $3500 and the lottery. Then the bookstore can use this lottery indifference probability (p) in the formula

$$U(\$3500) = pU(\$4950) + (1 - p)U(\$2600)$$

to find the utility of the $3500 profit.

If the indifference probability for this lottery is $p = .65$, then

$$U(\$3500) = .65U(\$4950) + (1 - .65)U(\$2600)$$

or, since $U(\$4950) = 100$ and $U(\$2600) = 0$,

$$U(\$3500) = .65(100) + .35(0) = 65$$

This lottery ticket process is then repeated for each bookstore profit. Let us assume that such a process provides the results shown in Table 5.9.

Table 5.10 The Utility of Cash Requirements to Bookstore Management

Cash Requirement ($)	Lottery Indifference Probability (p)	Utility
11,500	Does not apply	100
13,500	.80	80
14,200	.60	60
14,900	.50	50
15,500	.35	35
16,200	.25	25
16,400	.20	20
16,900	.10	10
17,300	Does not apply	0

A similar process can be used to find the utility values for the cash requirement attribute. Table 5.7 indicates that the smallest (best) cash requirement of $11,500 is obtained when the bookstore publishes and sells 1000 copies of Smart's book. The largest (worst) cash requirement of $17,300 occurs when the bookstore publishes 1000 copies but sells 1400. Hence, if management assigns a utility of 100 to $11,500 and a utility of 0 to $17,300, then

$$U(\$11,500) = 100$$

and

$$U(\$17,300) = 0$$

These values are then used in various hypothetical lottery situations to derive the utilities of the other cash requirement levels in Table 5.7.

In the situation involving the a_1 and s_2 combination, for instance, bookstore management could be given the option of receiving either (1) an order that is sure to require $14,900 cash or (2) a lottery ticket that has a p chance of generating the best ($11,500) cash requirement but a $(1 - p)$ likelihood for the worst ($17,300) cash requirement. If a series of trial and error questions reveals that $p = .50$ for this lottery, then

$$U(\$14,900) = pU(\$11,500) + (1 - p)U(\$17,300)$$

or

$$U(\$14,900) = .5(100) + .5(0) = 50$$

Again, this lottery ticket approach is then repeated for each cash requirement. Let us assume that such a process provides the results shown in Table 5.10.

Management must now amalgamate the separate utility assessments for the individual profit and cash requirement attributes into a compound

Table 5.11 The University Bookstore's Multiattribute Utility Values

Alternative/Event Combination	Outcomes		Utilities		Multi-attribute Utility Values
	Profit ($)	Cash Requirement ($)	Profit ($)	Cash Requirement ($)	
a_2 and s_2	4500	13,500	90	80	170
a_1 and s_1	3500	11,500	65	100	165
a_3 and s_3	4950	15,500	100	35	135
a_1 and s_2	3100	14,900	55	50	105
a_3 and s_2	3800	16,200	75	25	100
a_2 and s_1	2800	14,200	15	60	75
a_1 and s_3	3700	17,300	70	0	70
a_2 and s_3	2900	16,900	40	10	50
a_3 and s_1	2600	16,400	0	20	20

Table 5.12 The Bookstore's Multiattribute Utility Table

Decision Alternatives	States of Nature		
	s_1	s_2	s_3
a_1	165	105	70
a_2	75	170	50
a_3	20	100	135

Units of multiattribute utility to management

multiattribute utility measure. The simplest approach is to identify the attribute levels for each outcome and then sum the corresponding utility values.

Table 5.7 shows that the bookstore obtains a profit of $3500 and needs $11,500 in cash when it publishes and sells 1000 texts. As Tables 5.9 and 5.10 indicate, management separately assigns 65 units of utility to the $3500 profit and 100 units to the $11,500 cash requirement. Under the additive amalgamation approach, this a_1 and s_1 combination receives a multiattribute utility assessment of $65 + 100 = 165$.

If the bookstore repeats this additive approach for each multiattribute outcome, it will obtain the results presented in Table 5.11. By substituting the utility values from Table 5.11 for the corresponding multiple-attribute outcomes in Table 5.7, the bookstore will obtain Table 5.12.

Remember, there is a $P(s_1) = .3$ chance that the store will sell 1000 texts, a $P(s_2) = .5$ likelihood of 1200 sales, and a $P(s_3) = .2$ probability of selling 1400 copies. Using these probabilities and the data from Table 5.12, management will find that there is an expected utility of

$$165(.3) + 105(.5) + 70(.2) = 116$$

from a_1,

$$75(.3) + 170(.5) + 50(.2) = 117.50$$

from a_2, and

$$20(.3) + 100(.5) + 135(.2) = 83$$

from a_3. Therefore, the bookstore can maximize expected multiattribute utility at 117.50 units by publishing 1200 copies of Smart's book (a_2).

This simple additive amalgamation process assumes that each component attribute is equally important to the decision maker. Yet, in many situations, the attributes may carry different weights and priorities. Huang and others [9] and Keeney and Raiffa [10] discuss methods designed to identify the appropriate weights and incorporate them properly into the analysis. These concepts are applied to facility performance evaluation by J. S. Dyer and others [4], to solar energy project selection by K. Golabi and others [7], and to financial analysis by H. Levy and M. Sarnat [11].

LIMITATIONS Table 5.13 summarizes the approaches to multiple-criteria decision making that have been discussed in this section.

All these approaches, in effect, attempt to create a single objective from the multiple criteria in the problem. Individual criteria are either integrated into a composite measure (as in traditional multiattribute utility theory) or treated as secondary considerations (as in the ranked priority system). However, such approaches do not fully consider the fundamental trade-offs that managers must make between the objectives in a multiple-criteria situation. Also, some of these approaches require the decision maker to supply the essential information. In the acquisition process, it may be necessary to create artificial situations (like lottery tickets) that could seem unrealistic or irrelevant to management. Consequently, management may be unable to accurately and completely furnish the relevant information.

These limitations have led to the recent development of alternative, more sophisticated, multiple-criteria decision-making approaches. One of these approaches, called goal programming, is presented in chapter 9 of this text. M. Zeleny [21] discusses many of the other methods in detail.

Table 5.13 Multiple-Criteria Decision Making Approaches

Priority Systems		Transformations	
Goal Constraints	Ranked Priorities	Single Composite Measure	Traditional Multiattribute Utility Theory
1. Identify the most important decision criterion. 2. Establish target levels or goals for the other criteria and/or additional relevant attributes. 3. Select the decision alternative, among those satisfying all goals, that optimizes the primary criterion.	1. Establish a priority ranking for the objectives. 2. Rate each alternative in terms of the highest-priority objective. 3. Continue the evaluation process, in sequence, through lower-priority objectives until you identify a single best alternative or exhaust the list of criteria.	1. Transform all attributes into a single composite measure that in some way reflects the impact of each alternative on the original attributes. 2. Develop a decision criterion from the composite measure. 3. Select the alternative that best meets the single composite criterion.	1. Develop a separate utility curve for each relevant attribute. 2. Amalgamate the individual curves into a multiattribute utility assessment of each decision alternative. 3. Select the alternative that maximizes expected multiattribute utility.

CONFLICT SITUATIONS

So far, we have discussed situations in which choices are made by only one decision maker or by a group of decision makers in agreement. Yet many problems involve a conflict between competing parties. Examples include athletic competition, collective bargaining, television programming, and military operations. In such cases, the outcomes are determined by the collective actions of several individual decision makers. To make effective decisions under these circumstances, management must consider the opponent's alternatives, anticipate the competitor's actions, and then develop an appropriate strategy.

Within the part forty years, management scientists have developed a framework for analyzing these conflict situations. Because such situations resemble parlor and casino games, this framework has been labeled **game theory**. Its concepts are illustrated in Example 5.4.

EXAMPLE 5.4 Collective Bargaining

Under a new law, state public employees will be represented in pay and benefit negotiations by the union federation CSPT. A committee of government officials will form the personnel board (PB). The PB will be the sole state representative in collective bargaining. After considering its decision alternatives, CSPT has decided to take one or more of the following positions during the negotiations: It will be aggressive, flexible, or submissive. The state PB, meanwhile, has decided to be belligerent, stubborn, flexible, or supportive. Each party has used judgment and the experience in neighboring states to estimate outcomes for the various combinations of actions. The consensus can be summarized as follows:

1. If CSPT is aggressive, state workers will get a 5% increase in the pay/benefit package when PB is belligerent. Also, this policy will result in a 6% increase when PB is stubborn, 8% if PB is flexible, and 12% should PB be supportive.

2. When CSPT is flexible, it can expect a 1% decrease in the pay/benefit package if PB is belligerent. Also, such a policy will yield no increase if PB is stubborn, a 4% increase when PB is flexible, and a 7% increase should the board be supportive.

3. A submissive policy for CSPT will result in a 7% decrease in the package if the board is belligerent and a 2% decrease when PB is stubborn. This action will also get a 1% increase when PB is flexible and a 3% increase if the board is supportive.

The union federation wants to get the largest possible pay/benefit package increase, while the personnel board wants to limit the package as much as possible.

CHARACTERISTICS The collective bargaining problem involves two parties (CSPT and PB) seeking a common interest (pay/benefits). The CSPT will negotiate with PB to increase the pay/benefit package as much as possible. On the other hand, PB will attempt to limit the increase as much as it can. In fact, PB would like to negotiate for no increase, or even for a decrease. Thus, the union federation and the state personnel board are in direct competition.

Although the problem can be examined from the perspective of either party, it seems more realistic to describe the outcomes (pay/benefit changes) from a labor perspective. In this regard, the union federation (CSPT) can select the following three alternative bargaining positions:

a_1 = be aggressive

a_2 = be flexible

a_3 = be submissive

The choice will be influenced by the negotiation stance of the state personnel board (PB). The four possibilities for PB can be denoted as follows:

s_1 = be belligerent

s_2 = be stubborn

s_3 = be flexible

s_4 = be supportive

Unfortunately, CSPT does not know PB's strategy in advance. Both parties, however, know the potential outcomes of the bargaining process.

Table 5.14 Game Table for the Collective Bargaining Problem

Union Federation Alternatives	Personnel Board Alternatives			
	$s_1 =$ be belligerent	$s_2 =$ be stubborn	$s_3 =$ be flexible	$s_4 =$ be supportive
$a_1 =$ be aggressive	5%	6%	8%	12%
$a_2 =$ be flexible	−1%	0%	4%	7%
$a_3 =$ be submissive	−7%	−2%	1%	3%

Annual % decrease in pay/benefits   Annual % increase in pay/benefits

This information is summarized in Table 5.14, where each row represents a decision alternative for one party (CSPT) and each column an action by the competitor (PB). Entries in the cells give the outcomes associated with each combination of alternatives. Typically, these entries are expressed as outcomes to the competitor represented by the rows (CSPT, in this case). Such a representation is referred to as a **game table**.

In our earlier discussion of decision analysis, the states of nature were treated as essentially passive conditions. Now, however, these states represent the alternatives of a competing decision maker. As Table 5.14 demonstrates, the actions taken by the personnel board are the states of nature for the union federation. In a similar manner, if the problem is examined from the board's perspective, then CSPT's alternatives become the states of nature for PB.

Under these circumstances, each party reacts to the competitor's actions. When PB is flexible (s_3), CSPT can maximize the pay/benefit increase at 8% by being aggressive (a_1). But if PB knows that CSPT is going to be aggressive, the board can react by being belligerent (s_1) rather than flexible. In this way, the government can limit employee gains to 5%. Similarly, when the union federation is submissive (a_3), PB can force a 7% decrease in pay/benefits by being belligerent (s_1). On the other hand, if CSPT knows that PB is going to be belligerent, the union will not be submissive; instead, CSPT will be aggressive (a_1) and get a 5% pay/benefit increase.

Each party would like to wait until the competitor acts before reacting. Unfortunately, both opponents are uncertain about the other's bargaining position. The union federation, for instance, does not know when the

Table 5.15 Characteristics of Game Theory Problems

1. There are two or more competing parties.
2. These parties are in a conflict situation, competing for a common attribute.
3. Each competitor can select various decision alternatives.
4. Both parties know the outcomes associated with each combination of alternatives.
5. Each competitor will react to the opponent's actions.
6. Each party is uncertain about the other's actions and reactions.
7. Usually, the situation will be repeated often.
8. Both parties simultaneously must develop a strategy that leads to the best expected outcome for each competitor, regardless of the opponent's actions.

personnel board will be belligerent (s_1), stubborn (s_2), flexible (s_3), or supportive (s_4). In fact, CSPT does not even know the probabilities of PB's actions. Also, PB does not know when CSPT will be aggressive (a_1), flexible (a_2), or submissive (a_3) or even the probabilities of these actions. Yet both parties simultaneously must develop negotiation positions before they begin bargaining.

Since pay/benefit increases must be negotiated from time to time, the collective bargaining process will be repeated often. Hence, each party must develop a complete, predetermined plan for selecting a decision alternative under every possible circumstance. Furthermore, this plan, called a **game strategy**, should lead to the best expected outcome for the decision maker, regardless of the opponent's actions.

Table 5.15 summarizes the characteristics of the collective bargaining situation. Problems with these properties are known as **games**.

DOMINANCE Recall our discussion about dominance in chapter 3. If the outcomes of one alternative are as good as, and in at least one case better than, the corresponding payoffs of another action, the first alternative is said to dominate the second. Furthermore, a rational decision maker should not select a dominated action. As a result, management can eliminate dominated alternatives from further consideration and thus reduce the scope of the problem, perhaps even identifying a solution.

Each competitor may apply the same dominance concept to the collective bargaining situation depicted in Table 5.14. Compare, for example, the union federation's outcomes from the aggressive (a_1) and flexible (a_2) alternatives. When the personnel board is belligerent (s_1), the union would prefer the 5% pay/benefit increase associated with a_1 rather than the 1% decrease associated with a_2. The aggressive action (a_1) also yields a preferable outcome (a 6% instead of 0% pay/benefit increase) for the union when PB is stubborn (s_2). In fact, a_1 always leads to better outcomes for the union than a_2, regardless of the board's bargaining position. That is, a_1 dominates a_2. Consequently, the union federation should never adopt a flexible (a_2) bargaining position.

Now let us compare the union federation's outcomes from the aggressive (a_1) and submissive (a_3) alternatives. As Table 5.14 indicates, the outcomes from a_1 (5%, 6%, 8%, and 12% pay/benefit increases) are all better for CSPT than the corresponding payoffs from a_3 (-7%, -2%, 1%, and 3%). In other words, a_1 also dominates a_3. Hence, the union federation should never be submissive (a_3).

In effect, then, the union federation (CSPT) will always be aggressive (a_1), regardless of the personnel board (PB) strategy. Now, PB has the same information and thus knows that the union will adopt its dominant (a_1) bargaining position. The board can react by being belligerent (s_1), stubborn (s_2), flexible (s_3), or supportive (s_4). According to Table 5.14, s_1 would provide a 5%, s_2 a 6%, s_3 an 8%, and s_4 a 12% pay/benefit increase for state employees. Since the personnel board wants to limit the package as much as possible, it should always be belligerent (s_1) in the negotiations.

Notice that each party in the collective bargaining situation repeatedly selects only one alternative, regardless of the opponent's actions. Specifically, the union federation will be aggressive all the time, while the personnel board will always be belligerent. In such cases, each competitor is said to have a **pure strategy**.

Now refer back to Table 5.14. When each party adopts its pure strategy (CSPT repeatedly being aggressive and PB belligerent), the outcome is a 5% pay/benefit increase for public employees. This payoff, which represents the expected outcome of the conflict when each party repeatedly selects the optimal strategy, is called the **value of the game**.

PESSIMISTIC CRITERION There is another way to look at the collective bargaining situation. In this game, the personnel board (PB) wants to limit expenditures. Consequently, the board should react to each union federation (CSPT) action by adopting the strategy that would provide employees with the minimum (worst) pay/benefit package possible.

For example, Table 5.14 shows that when the union takes an aggressive stance (a_1), public employees will get a 5% pay/benefit increase if the personnel board reacts belligerently (s_1). Yet the increase will be 6% if the board takes a stubborn position (s_2), 8% if PB is flexible (s_3), and 12% if it reacts in a supportive manner (s_4). Under these circumstances, the board's rational reaction is to be belligerent (s_1) and thus grant a 5% pay/benefit increase.

Similarly, when the union takes a flexible position (a_2), the board's rational reaction is to be belligerent (s_1) and force a 1% decrease in pay/benefits. Also, if the union is submissive (a_3), the rational PB reaction is to push for a 7% pay/benefit decrease by taking a belligerent negotiation stance (s_1).

By anticipating these rational personnel board reactions, the union federation can expect:

1. A 5% pay/benefit increase when it negotiates aggressively (a_1)

2. A 1% decrease in the package if it is flexible (a_2)

3. A 7% decrease in pay/benefits when it takes a submissive position (a_3)

Notice that each expected outcome represents the minimum value (worst payoff) in the corresponding row of Table 5.14.

Public employees want the pay/benefit package to be as large as possible. In light of the anticipated personnel board reactions, this objective is best achieved when the union federation always takes an aggressive negotiation position (a_1). Then public employees can be guaranteed a 5% increase in pay/benefits, regardless of the personnel board's actions. Since this 5% increase represents the maximum of the minimum expected outcomes for the employees, alternative a_1 is, in effect, the union's maximin strategy.

Since the union's maximin strategy leads to the best of the worst possible outcomes for public employees, it is an application of the pessimistic criterion discussed in chapter 3. The personnel board can simultaneously develop its optimal strategy by using a variation of this same criterion. To see how, let us examine the collective bargaining situation depicted in Table 5.14 from the government's perspective.

The government knows that the union wants to enlarge the pay/benefit package. Hence, when the board bargains belligerently (s_1), the rational CSPT reaction is to be aggressive (a_1) and strive for a 5% increase in the package. Alternatively, if PB takes a stubborn position (s_2), the union's rational reaction will be to press for a 6% increase by negotiating aggressively (a_1). Also, when the board negotiates in a flexible manner (s_3), the rational federation action is to be aggressive (a_1) and force an 8% increase. Finally, if the government is supportive (s_4), CSPT's rational reaction is to be aggressive (a_1) and push for a 12% pay/benefit increase.

By anticipating these rational union federation reactions, the personnel board can expect to grant:

1. A 5% pay/benefit increase when it bargains belligerently (s_1)

2. A 6% increase when it is stubborn (s_2)

3. An 8% increase if it takes a flexible position (s_3)

4. A 12% increase in the package when it negotiates in a supportive manner (s_4)

Observe that each expected outcome represents the maximum value (worst personnel board payoff) in the corresponding column of Table 5.14.

Government wants the pay/benefit package to be as small as possible. In light of the anticipated union reactions, this objective is best achieved when the personnel board always takes a belligerent (s_1) negotiation position. Then the government will never have to give public employees more than a 5% pay/benefit increase, regardless of the union federation's actions. Since this 5% increase represents the minimum of the maximum expected losses (costs) for the government, alternative s_1 is, in effect, the board's minimax strategy.

As long as the personnel board sticks with this minimax (s_1) strategy, the union federation should adhere to its maximin (a_1) strategy. Otherwise, as Table 5.14 shows, public employees will receive a decrease in pay/benefits rather than the 5% increase guaranteed by this maximin strategy. Similarly, as long as the union adheres to its maximin (a_1) strategy, the board should stick with its minimax (s_1) strategy. As Table 5.14 indicates, any deviation by the board from this minimax strategy will force the government to grant more than the planned maximum 5% increase in pay/benefits.

In effect, then, when CSPT clings to its maximin strategy and PB to its minimax strategy, the opponents create an equilibrium from which neither can advantageously deviate. At the equilibrium, also known as a **saddle point**, each negotiator adopts a pure strategy and public employees receive a 5% increase in pay/benefits. This payoff, which represents the value of the game, is simultaneously the best of the worst expected outcomes for each participant in the game.

Table 5.16 summarizes the procedure for solving pure strategy games. As this summary implies, a game may involve no dominance and yet have

Table 5.16 Solving a Pure Strategy Game

1. Develop the game table.

2. Use the dominance concept to reduce the size of the game. In some cases, this procedure may identify the pure strategy for each opponent and the resulting value of the game.

3. Identify the minimum outcomes in each row of the game table.

4. Identify the decision alternative that leads to the maximum of these row minimums. This alternative is the maximin strategy for the participant represented by the rows in the game table. Furthermore, the maximin is a pure strategy for the row participant.

5. Identify the maximum outcomes in each column of the game table.

6. Identify the decision alternative that leads to the minimum of these column maximums. This alternative is the minimax strategy for the participant represented by the columns in the game table. Furthermore, the minimax is a pure strategy for the column participant.

7. If the maximin and minimax strategies both lead to the same outcome, the game has an equilibrium, or saddle point. This outcome represents the value of the game.

8. To obtain this value, the row participant must always adopt its maximin strategy and the column participant its minimax strategy.

a pure strategy or saddle point solution. On the other hand, if such a solution exists, it can always be found with the pessimistic (maximin/minimax) criterion.

MIXED STRATEGY   Many conflict situations do not involve a pure strategy solution, as Example 5.5 illustrates.

EXAMPLE 5.5 Athletic Competition

Prudence Tech and Swami U have advanced to the final game of the Division 6 National Collegiate Rugby Championship. Lew Cross, Tech's coach, must decide whether to use his "quick" or "strong" team. Amy Allweather, Swami's coach, must make the same decision. In each case, the quick team is composed of different athletes than the strong unit. Also, the rules limit the amount and nature of substitution. Consequently, it will be difficult for each coach to change teams freely during the game.

Using ratings of the athletes' relative abilities and comparative scores against common opponents, the "experts" have estimated Tech's chances of winning the championship. The consensus is summarized in Table 5.17. Entries in this table represent Tech's chances of winning the championship.

Each coach wants to select the strategy that will give his or her team the best chance of winning the game.

Table 5.17 The Rugby Championship Game Table

Tech's Alternatives	Swami's Alternatives	
	s_1 = use the quick team	s_2 = use the strong team
a_1 = use the quick team	40%	80%
a_2 = use the strong team	70%	10%

An examination of Table 5.17 shows that neither opponent has a dominant alternative. Hence, each coach must consider both of his or her available alternatives when developing an optimal game strategy.

The quick team (a_1) will give Tech a minimum 40% chance and the strong team (a_2) a minimum 10% likelihood of winning the game. By adopting a maximin strategy and always selecting the a_1 alternative, Lew

Cross can guarantee that Tech will have at least a 40% chance of capturing the championship. Amy Allweather, on the other hand, can increase her team's likelihood of winning by adopting a strategy that limits Tech's chances as much as possible. In this respect, Table 5.17 shows that her quick team (s_1) will provide Tech with a maximum 70% chance of capturing the championship. When Swami uses the strong team (s_2), Tech has as much as an 80% likelihood of winning the game. Therefore, by adopting a minimax strategy and always selecting alternative s_1, Amy can guarantee that Tech would have no more than a 70% chance of capturing the championship.

Suppose that Amy starts the game with her minimax strategy (s_1) and Lew with his maximin strategy (a_1). As soon as Lew notices that Amy is always using her quick team (s_1), he will switch to a strong team (a_2). Table 5.17 shows that in this way, Tech's chances of capturing the championship will increase from 40% to 70%. However, when Amy notices that Lew is always using his strong team (a_2), she will switch to a strong unit (s_2). As Table 5.17 indicates, Amy will thereby reduce Tech's chances from 70% to 10%. Yet when Lew notices that Swami always has its strong team (s_2) in the game, he will switch back to a quick unit (a_1). Then Tech's chances of capturing the championship will increase from 10% to 80%. To reduce these chances from 80% to 40%, Amy again will counter with her quick team (s_1). At this point in the game, Amy has reverted to her minimax strategy (s_1) and Lew to his maximin strategy (a_1). Consequently, the second guessing will begin all over again.

In effect, then, neither coach has a pure strategy that simultaneously guarantees each team the best of its worst possible outcomes. Put another way, there is no saddle point in the rugby championship. Under these circumstances, each coach must keep the other guessing by changing teams at random during the game. Such random shifting from one decision alternative to another is known as a **mixed strategy**. Therefore, each coach's problem is to find the mixed strategy that gives his or her team the greatest expected chance of capturing the championship, regardless of the opponent's actions.

Suppose, for example, that Lew Cross randomly uses his quick team (a_1) in the proportion $P(a_1)$ and the strong unit (a_2) on $P(a_2)$ occasions during the championship. As Table 5.17 indicates, this mixture of strategies will give Tech an expected outcome of

$.4P(a_1) + .7P(a_2)$

if Swami uses its quick team (s_1) and

$.8P(a_1) + .1P(a_2)$

when Swami employs its strong unit (s_2).

Figure 5.4 Tech's Expected Outcomes

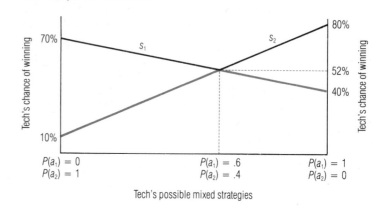

Tech's possible mixed strategies

Figure 5.4 shows how these expected outcomes will vary with each possible combination of $P(a_1)$ and $P(a_2)$. The straight line labeled s_1 represents Tech's expected outcome

$$.4P(a_1) + .7P(a_2)$$

if Swami uses its quick team (s_1). At one extreme, Lew Cross can adopt the pure strategy of always using his strong team (a_2). In this case, $P(a_1) = 0$ and $P(a_2) = 1$, and Tech's expected outcome will be

$$.4(0) + .7(1) = .7$$

Lew's other extreme is to adopt the pure strategy of always using his quick team (a_1). Then $P(a_1) = 1$ and $P(a_2) = 0$, and Tech's expected outcome will be

$$.4(1) + .7(0) = .4$$

Points on the line connecting these extremes give Tech's expected outcomes from every possible combination of $P(a_1)$ and $P(a_2)$ when Swami selects s_1. Such combinations, in effect, provide various mixed strategies.

Similarly, the straight line labeled s_2 represents Tech's expected outcome

$$.8P(a_1) + .1P(a_2)$$

if Swami uses its strong team (s_2). Under these circumstances, the $P(a_1) = 0$ and $P(a_2) = 1$ combination gives Tech a

$$.8(0) + .1(1) = .1$$

chance, while the $P(a_1) = 1$ and $P(a_2) = 0$ combination provides a

$$.8(1) + .1(0) = .8$$

likelihood of winning the game. Points on the line connecting these extremes present Tech's expected outcomes from each possible combination of $P(a_1)$ and $P(a_2)$ when Swami selects s_2.

Observe what happens in Figure 5.4 when Lew uses his quick team (a_1) between $P(a_1) = 0$ and $P(a_1) = .6$. In this situation, Tech will have a larger expected chance of winning the game if Swami counters with its quick (s_1) rather than its strong (s_2) team. Since Amy wants to limit Tech's chances as much as possible, Swami's rational reaction will be to select s_2. But if Lew uses his quick team (a_1) more often than $P(a_1) = .6$, Tech will have a smaller expected outcome when Swami counters with s_1 instead of s_2. Hence, under these circumstances, Swami's rational reaction will be to use its quick team (s_1). By anticipating these rational Swami reactions, Lew Cross can then expect Tech to receive the outcomes indicated by the colored lines in Figure 5.4.

Lew wants Tech's chances of capturing the championship to be as large as possible. In light of Swami's anticipated reactions, this objective is best achieved when Lew adopts the mixed strategy that leads to the maximum of Tech's minimum expected outcomes. Figure 5.4 shows that the maximum occurs at the intersection of the s_1 and s_2 lines. At this point,

$$\underbrace{.4P(a_1) + .7P(a_2)}_{\substack{\text{Expected outcome if} \\ \text{Swami selects } s_1}} = \underbrace{.8P(a_1) + .1P(a_2)}_{\substack{\text{Expected outcome if} \\ \text{Swami selects } s_2}}$$

or

$$.6P(a_2) = .4P(a_1)$$

And since $P(a_2) = 1 - P(a_1)$, we have

$$P(a_1) = .6$$

with

$$P(a_2) = .4$$

Furthermore, by randomly using his quick team (a_1) with a frequency of $P(a_1) = .6$ and the strong unit (a_2) with a frequency of $P(a_2) = .4$, Lew will guarantee Tech the same

$$.4P(a_1) + .7P(a_2) = .8P(a_1) + .1P(a_2)$$

or

$$.4(.6) + .7(.4) = .8(.6) + .1(.4) = .52$$

or 52% expected chance of capturing the championship, regardless of Swami's actions.

To achieve this expectation, however, Lew must be sure to use the a_1

and a_2 actions in a random fashion. There must be no apparent pattern. For example, he should not always use his quick team for a duration of 3 minutes and then bring in the strong squad for the next 4 minutes. Otherwise, Amy will detect this pattern, and Swami will no longer be uncertain about Tech's strategy. In other words, there no longer would be a game.

Amy Allweather can determine her optimal mixed strategy in a similar manner. Suppose that she randomly uses her quick team (s_1) on $P(s_1)$ occasions and the strong unit (s_2) in the proportion $P(s_2)$ during the game. As Table 5.17 indicates, this mixture of strategies will give Swami an expected outcome of

$$.4P(s_1) + .8P(s_2)$$

if Tech uses its quick team (a_1) and

$$.7P(s_1) + .1P(s_2)$$

when Tech employs its strong team (a_2). Figure 5.5 shows how these expected outcomes will vary with each possible combination of $P(s_1)$ and $P(s_2)$. The straight line labeled a_1 represents Swami's expected outcome

$$.4P(s_1) + .8P(s_2)$$

if Tech uses its quick team (a_1). At one extreme, Amy can adopt the pure strategy of always using her strong team (s_2). In this case, $P(s_1) = 0$ and $P(s_2) = 1$, and Swami's expected outcome will be

$$.4(0) + .8(1) = .8$$

Amy's other extreme is to adopt the pure strategy of always using her quick unit (s_1). Then $P(s_1) = 1$ and $P(s_2) = 0$, and Swami's expected outcome will be

$$.4(1) + .8(0) = .4$$

Points on the line connecting these extremes give Swami's expected outcomes for every possible combination of $P(s_1)$ and $P(s_2)$ when Tech selects a_1. Such combinations, in effect, provide various mixed strategies.

Similarly, the straight line labeled a_2 represents Swami's expected outcome

$$.7P(s_1) + .1P(s_2)$$

if Tech uses its strong team (a_2). Under these circumstances, the $P(s_1) = 0$ and $P(s_2) = 1$ combination gives Swami a

$$.7(0) + .1(1) = .1$$

chance, while the $P(s_1) = 1$ and $P(s_2) = 0$ combination provides Swami a

$$.7(1) + .1(0) = .7$$

Figure 5.5 Swami's Expected Outcomes

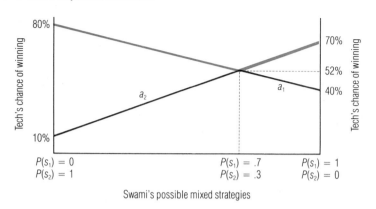

Swami's possible mixed strategies

likelihood of winning the game. Points on the line connecting these extremes present Swami's expected outcomes for each possible combination of $P(s_1)$ and $P(s_2)$ when Tech selects a_2.

Observe what happens in Figure 5.5 when Amy uses her quick team (s_1) between $P(s_1) = 0$ and $P(s_1) = .7$. In this situation, Tech will have a larger expected chance of winning the game if Lew counters with his quick (a_1) rather than his strong (a_2) unit. Since Lew wants Tech's chances to be as great as possible, his rational reaction will be to select a_1. But if Amy uses her quick team (s_1) with a frequency greater than $P(s_1) = .7$, Tech will have a smaller expected outcome when Lew counters with a_1 instead of a_2. Hence, under these circumstances, Tech's rational reaction will be to use its strong team (a_2). By anticipating these rational Tech reactions, Amy can then expect Tech to receive the outcomes indicated by the colored lines in Figure 5.5.

Amy wants Tech's chances of capturing the championship to be as small as possible. In light of Lew's anticipated reactions, this objective is best achieved when Amy adopts the mixed strategy that leads to the minimum of Tech's maximum expected outcomes. Figure 5.5 shows that the minimum occurs at the intersection of the a_1 and a_2 lines. At this point,

$$\underbrace{.4P(s_1) + .8P(s_2)}_{\substack{\text{Expected outcome if} \\ \text{Tech selects } a_1}} = \underbrace{.7P(s_1) + .1P(s_2)}_{\substack{\text{Expected outcome if} \\ \text{Tech selects } a_2}}$$

or

$$.7P(s_2) = .3P(s_1)$$

And since $P(s_2) = 1 - P(s_1)$, we have

$$P(s_1) = .7$$

Table 5.18 Rugby Championship Solution

Tech's Best Strategy	Outcome of the Game	Swami's Best Strategy
Randomly use the quick team (a_1) 60% of the time. Randomly use the strong team (a_2) 40% of the time.	Tech can expect to have a 52% chance of capturing the championship.	Randomly use the quick team (s_1) 70% of the time. Randomly use the strong team (s_2) 30% of the time.

with

$$P(s_2) = .3$$

Furthermore, by randomly using her quick team (s_1) with a frequency of $P(s_1) = .7$ and the strong unit (s_2) with a frequency of $P(s_2) = .3$, Amy will limit Tech to the same

$$.4P(s_1) + .8P(s_2) = .7P(s_1) + .1P(s_2)$$

or

$$.4(.7) + .8(.3) = .7(.7) + .1(.3) = .52$$

or 52% expected chance of capturing the championship, regardless of Lew's actions.

To achieve this expectation, however, Amy also must be sure to use the s_1 and s_2 actions in a random fashion. Otherwise, she will take away Tech's uncertainty and, in effect, eliminate the game.

Table 5.18 summarizes the mixed strategy solution to the rugby championship game.

There are some important characteristics to note about the solution. Recall that when Lew adopts the pure maximin strategy of always using his quick team (a_1), Tech is willing to settle for a 40% likelihood of winning the game. As Table 5.18 demonstrates, however, by using his best mixed strategy to confuse the opponent, he increases Tech's chances from 40% to an expected 52%. There is a similar result for Swami. Remember, when Amy adopts the pure minimax strategy of always using her quick team (s_1), she is willing to concede Tech a 70% likelihood of capturing the championship. But by using her best mixed strategy and thereby keeping the opponent guessing, Amy reduces Tech's chances from 70% to an expected 52%. In this game, then, each coach can obtain a better expected outcome for his or her team from a mixed rather than a pure strategy.

Table 5.19 Solving Mixed Strategy Games

1. Develop the game table.

2. Eliminate all dominated decision alternatives for each participant.

3. Let $P(a_1)$ = proportion of time that the row participant uses the a_1 decision alternative and $P(a_2)$ = proportion of time that the row participant uses the a_2 alternative.

4. Multiply the $P(a_1)$ and $P(a_2)$ values by the corresponding outcomes in the first column of the game table and then sum the results. This expression represents the row participant's expected outcome when the column participant selects decision alternative s_1.

5. Multiply the $P(a_1)$ and $P(a_2)$ values by the corresponding outcomes in the second column of the game table and sum the results. This expression represents the row participant's expected outcome if the column participant selects alternative s_2.

6. Set the expression found in step 4 equal to the expression found in step 5 and then solve the resulting equation for the values of $P(a_1)$ and $P(a_2)$. These values represent the row participant's optimal mixed strategy.

7. Substitute the $P(a_1)$ and $P(a_2)$ values into the expression found either in step 4, 5, or 6. The resulting expected outcome represents the value of the game.

8. Let $P(s_1)$ = proportion of time that the column participant uses the s_1 decision alternative and $P(s_2)$ = proportion of time that the column participant uses the s_2 alternative.

9. Multiply the $P(s_1)$ and $P(s_2)$ values by the corresponding outcomes in the first row of the game table and then sum the results. This expression represents the column participant's expected outcome when the row participant selects a_1.

10. Multiply the $P(s_1)$ and $P(s_2)$ values by the corresponding outcomes in the second row of the game table and then sum the results. This expression represents the column participant's expected outcome when the row participant selects a_2.

11. Set the expression found in step 9 equal to the expression found in step 10 and then solve the resulting equation for the values of $P(s_1)$ and $P(s_2)$. These values represent the column participant's optimal mixed strategy.

In addition, Tech's and Swami's best mixed strategies both lead to the same expected outcome, regardless of the opponent's actions. Hence, each coach should feel very secure with his or her strategy. Furthermore, as Figures 5.4 and 5.5 demonstrate, the resulting outcome is the best that each team can expect in light of the opponent's anticipated reactions. Consequently, neither coach has any incentive to change his or her strategy. In other words, the solution in Table 5.18 creates an equilibrium from which neither Lew nor Amy can advantageously deviate.

Table 5.19 summarizes the procedure for solving mixed strategy games that involve only two participants who each have two decision alternatives. M. Shubik [16] discusses the procedures for solving more complex mixed strategy games. One of the tools used in these procedures, called linear programming, is discussed in Part 3 of this text.

EXTENSIONS There are only two opponents in the rugby game. Hence, Tech's plus Swami's likelihood of capturing the championship must sum to a constant 100%. Put another way, Swami's outcome will equal the difference between Tech's chances and this constant sum. For example, when Lew uses his quick team (a_1) and Amy counters with her strong unit (s_2), Tech will have an 80% chance of winning the game (refer to Table 5.17). Under these circumstances, Swami will have a $100\% - 80\% = 20\%$ likelihood of capturing the championship. Similarly, if each coach adopts his or her best mixed strategy, Tech will have an expected outcome of 52% (Table 5.18). As a result, Swami can expect to have a $100\% - 52\% = 48\%$ probability of winning the game. Such a situation is referred to as a **constant sum game**.

The collective bargaining situation is a special type of constant sum game. In this situation, the employee union federation is negotiating with the government personnel board for a change in the pay/benefit package. Under these circumstances, a gain (more pay/benefits) for public employees is necessarily an equivalent loss (more expense) for the government. For example, when the union is aggressive (a_1) and the board counters with a flexible action (s_3), public employees get an 8% increase in pay/benefits (see Table 5.14). Consequently, government's discretionary funds are reduced by 8%. Similarly, a loss (less pay/benefits) for public employees must necessarily be an equivalent gain (less expense) for the government. For instance, when the union is flexible (a_2) and the board reacts with a belligerent action (s_1), public employees receive a 1% decrease in pay/benefits. As a result, the government's discretionary funds are increased by 1%. In each case, the union's outcome plus the board's payoff sum to zero. Therefore, such a situation is called a **zero sum game**.

In practice, however, taxes, special expenses, and other factors create differences between the gain of one participant and the loss of the opponent. Income taxes, for instance, would reduce the pay/benefit package received by public employees from the personnel board. Also, each opponent may attach a different total worth, or utility, to the outcomes in a game. For example, instead of striving for maximum security, Tech and Swami both may prefer to gamble on winning the rugby championship. Assuming that Amy and Lew have separate risk-taking attitudes, each coach would then make a different utility assessment of the outcomes in Table 5.17. In addition, each opponent could have complementary as well as competing interests. The only two banks in a small rural town, for instance, both may want to encourage community development, even though one might gain more than the other. Finally, each game participant could have a different set of multiple criteria that vary in both form and number over time. One of the rural banks, for example, currently may want to increase deposits and reduce mortgages, while the other might prefer an increase in profits and additional facilities.

In these instances, each combination of the opponents' decision alternatives typically will yield a different outcome sum to the participants. Put another way, the sum of the outcomes will be variable. Hence, such situations are known as **variable sum games**. Behavioral factors play an important role in the solution of these variable sum games, as Example 5.6 illustrates.

EXAMPLE 5.6 Prisoners' Dilemma

Two men suspected of committing a crime together are awaiting trial in separate cells. Each suspect may either confess or remain silent. The possible consequences of their actions are described in Table 5.20. Azon and Bungle each want to receive the smallest possible prison term.

Table 5.20 Prisoners' Possible Sentences

Azon's Alternatives	Bungle's Alternatives	
	s_1 = confess	s_2 = remain silent
a_1 = confess	Azon's prison term = 3 years Bungle's prison term = 3 years	Azon's prison term = 1 year Bungle's prison term = 8 years
a_2 = remain silent	Azon's prison term = 8 years Bungle's prison term = 1 year	Azon's prison term = 2 years Bungle's prison term = 2 years

---

An examination of Table 5.20 will show that Azon can always get a smaller prison term by confessing (a_1) rather than remaining silent (a_2), regardless of Bungle's action. Also, Bungle can always receive a shorter sentence by confessing (s_1) instead of remaining silent (s_2), regardless of Azon's actions. Thus, if each prisoner acts independently and rationally selects his dominant strategy, both will confess and receive 3-year prison terms.

Such a strategy, however, assumes that the prisoners have diametrically opposed interests. In reality, both Azon and Bungle can gain by cooperating and forming an agreement to remain silent. As Table 5.20 demonstrates, in this way, each will receive a 2-year, rather than a 3-year, sentence.

Example 5.6, then, illustrates the importance of communication and

Table 5.21 Applications of Game Theory

Area of Application	Reference
Operations management	
Policy analysis and planning	K. C. Bowen [1]
Television programming	S. J. Brams [3]
Organizational behavior	R. D. McKelvey [13]
Marketing	
Advertising strategy	H. D. Shane [15]
Marketing policy	A. R. Washburn [19]
	G. Wolf and M. Shubik [20]
Marketing Channels	P. Zusman and M. Etgar [22]
Finance	
Offshore petroleum leasing	D. K. Reece [14]
Electricity rate setting	J. R. Sorenson et al. [17]
Public sector	
Military operations	J. Bracken et al. [2]
	Y. Friedman [6]
Collective bargaining	J. C. Harsanyi [8]
Airport operations	S. C. Littlechild and G. F. Thompson [12]

cooperation in a variable sum game. Yet these features create additional complications. Now each participant must consider the personality, psychological status, needs, and relative bargaining strength of the opponent. Moreover, each participant must also evaluate threats, bluffs, and the impact of various collusive agreements. Shubik [16] and R. D. Spinetto [18] discuss these issues in detail and present some recommended solution procedures.

Another important consideration is the number of participants. Although our discussion has focused on two-party situations, practical games typically involve several opponents. When there are three or more participants, the competitors may attempt to form collusive agreements or coalitions for their mutual benefit.

The draft of college athletes by professional football teams is an illustration of a collusive agreement. In the absence of the draft, there would be competitive bidding among the teams for the services of the best athletes. By forming a binding agreement to select players in a predetermined order, each team obtains its share of quality athletes. The draft also reduces the athletes' options and, in effect, limits the overall salary scale.

World War II provides an example of a coalition. Germany, Japan, Italy, France, the Soviet Union, the United States, and the United Kingdom were all participants in this military conflict. France, the United Kingdom, the United States, and later the Soviet Union had similar political interests or economic resources that complemented one another's needs. Consequently, these countries became allies and formed a coalition against their common enemies, Germany, Japan, and Italy. Meanwhile, Germany, Japan, and Italy formed a coalition against the allies.

Unfortunately, a game with several participants can involve a very large number of possible collusive arrangements and coalitions. Furthermore, opponents often can alter existing coalitions or form new ones by making payments to selected participants. In addition, each coalition may form a variety of collusive agreements. Since the formation and alteration processes can go on indefinitely, there may never be a stable group of competing parties or outcomes in the game. Shubik [16] discusses these issues and presents some recommended solution approaches. One of these approaches, called simulation, will be discussed in the final part of this text.

In spite of these complications, game theory concepts have been applied to a variety of public- and private-sector problems. Table 5.21 gives a partial list of the applications.

SUMMARY

Chapters 3 and 4 focused on decision problems that involve a single, absolute measure of performance. The previous discussion also assumed that there was a passive decision environment. This chapter has extended the decision analysis to situations that involve intangibles, multiple criteria, and conflict between competing parties.

In the first section, we saw that many real-life problems involve intangibles such as risk, the decision maker's attitude, and enjoyment. Since these factors are difficult to express on an absolute numerical scale, the more comprehensive measure of utility was proposed as the appropriate criterion for such circumstances. Table 5.2 summarized a method for measuring the utility, or total worth, of an outcome to the decision maker. As the analysis demonstrated, separate decision makers can assign different utility values to the same outcome. Often, the assignment depends on whether management has a risk-averse, risk-neutral, risk-seeking, or risk-complex attitude. This first section, in addition, showed how to use utility for decision making and presented the limitations of such an analysis.

In the second section, we saw that the decision maker also must frequently consider problems with several often conflicting criteria. Several methods were presented to deal with these situations. Some, like the goal constraint and ranked priority approaches, attempt to focus on the most important objectives. Others, such as the transformation and multiattribute utility concepts, integrate the multiple criteria into a single overall objective. Table 5.13 summarized these various methods, but, as was demonstrated, each approach had its limitations.

The final section presented a framework for dealing with problems that involve a conflict situation between competing parties. Such situations, called games, include war, athletic competition, collective bargaining, and television programming. Their characteristics were summarized in Table 5.15. In some games, each decision maker has a single dominant alternative that provides the best outcome, regardless of the opponent's actions. Table 5.16 summarized the procedure for developing such an alternative, called a pure strategy. In other games, each participant's best strategy is to keep the opponent guessing by randomly switching from one decision alternative to another. The procedure for developing this kind of strategy, called a mixed strategy, is summarized in Table 5.19.

These pure and mixed strategy solution procedures assume that the decision maker is faced with a two-party, constant sum game. As we saw, however, practical games typically involve multiple parties and variable sums. We saw how such games include the possibility of communication, cooperation, collusive agreements, and coalitions. Such features add considerable complexity to the analysis.

Glossary

certainty equivalent   The sure outcome that the decision maker considers equivalent to a lottery providing a p chance for the best and a $(1 - p)$ likelihood of the worst outcome in a decision problem.

constant sum game   A game in which the outcomes to each participant sum to a constant value.

games   Problems that involve a conflict situation between two or more competing parties, each of whom knows the decision outcomes but is uncertain about the opponent's actions and reactions.

game strategy   A complete, predetermined plan for selecting a decision alternative for every possible circumstance. This plan should lead to the best expected outcome for the decision maker, regardless of the opponent's actions.

game table   A table showing the outcomes associated with each combination of decision alternatives in a conflict situation.

game theory   A framework for analyzing conflict situations.

lottery indifference probability   The probability that will make the decision maker indifferent to receiving a specified sure outcome or a risky lottery ticket. The lottery provides a p chance of earning the best possible outcome but a $(1 - p)$ likelihood of obtaining the worst payoff in a decision problem.

mixed strategy   The strategy whereby a participant in a game randomly shifts from one decision alternative to another.

pure strategy   The strategy whereby each party repeatedly selects only one decision alternative, regardless of the competitor's strategy.

risk averse Willing to sacrifice some monetary value in order to avoid risk.

risk complex Displaying a combination of risk-averse, risk-neutral, and risk-seeking attitudes toward a range of monetary values.

risk neutral Neither seeking nor avoiding risk, but instead prizing money at its face value.

risk seeking Willing to take a high risk of a large loss in order to have an opportunity for a substantial gain.

saddle point The equilibrium solution formed when each participant in a game adopts a pure strategy.

utility A comprehensive criterion that incorporates absolute numerical measures (like monetary value) and intangible factors (such as attitudes and perceptions). It measures the true worth of the outcomes to the decision maker.

utility curve A graph that shows the relationship between monetary value and utility.

utility table A table that identifies the utility to management of each decision outcome.

value of the game The expected outcome of the conflict when each opponent repeatedly selects its optimal strategy.

variable sum game A game in which each combination of the opponents' decision alternatives typically will yield a different outcome sum to the participants.

zero sum game A game in which the gains of one participant are necessarily the equivalent losses to the opponent. It represents a special type of constant sum game in which the sum of the outcomes is always zero.

References

1. Bowen, K. C. *Research Games: An Approach to the Study of Decision Processes.* New York: Halsted Press, 1978.

2. Bracken, J., et al. "Two Models for Optimal Allocation of Aircraft Sorties." *Operations Research* (September–October 1975): 979.

3. Brams, S. J. "The Network Television Game: There May Be No Best Schedule." *Interfaces* (August 1977): 102.

4. Dyer, J. S., et al. "Utility Functions for Test Performances." *Management Science* (December 1973): 507.

5. Fishburn, P. C. *Utility Theory for Decision Making.* New York: Wiley, 1970.

6. Friedman, Y. "Optimal Strategy for the One-Against-Many Battle." *Operations Research* (September–October 1977): 884.

7. Golabi, K., et al. "Selecting a Portfolio of Solar Energy Projects Using Multiattribute Preference Theory." *Management Science* (February 1981): 174.

8. Harsanyi, J. C. *Rational Behavior and Bargaining Equilibrium in Games and Social Situations*. New York: Cambridge University Press, 1977.

9. Huang, C. L., et al. *Multiple Objective Decision Making, Methods, and Applications: A State of the Art Survey*. New York: Springer-Verlag, 1979.

10. Keeney, R. L., and H. Raiffa. *Decisions with Multiple Objectives*. New York: Wiley, 1976.

11. Levy, H., and M. Sarnat. *Financial Decision Making Under Uncertainty*. New York: Academic Press, 1977.

12. Littlechild, S. C., and G. F. Thompson. "Aircraft Landing Fees: A Game Theory Approach." *Bell Journal of Economics* (Spring 1977): 186.

13. McKelvey, R. D. "A Theory of Optimal Agenda Design." *Management Science* (March 1981): 303.

14. Reece, D. K. "Competitive Bidding for Offshore Petroleum Leases." *Bell Journal of Economics* (Autumn 1978): 369.

15. Shane, H. D. "Mathematical Models for Economic and Political Advertising Campaigns." *Operations Research* (January–February 1977): 1.

16. Shubik, M. *The Uses and Methods of Game Theory*. New York: Elsevier-North Holland Publishing Company, 1975.

17. Sorenson, J. R., et al. "A Game Theoretic Approach to Peak Load Pricing." *Bell Journal of Economics* (Autumn 1976): 497.

18. Spinetto, R. D. "Fairness in Cost Allocations and Cooperative Games." *Decision Sciences* (July 1975): 482.

19. Washburn, A. R. "Search — Evasion Game in a Fixed Region." *Operations Research* (November–October 1980): 1290.

20. Wolf, G., and M. Shubik. "Market Structure, Opponent Behavior, and Information in a Market Game." *Decision Sciences* (July 1978): 421.

21. Zeleny, M. *Multiple Criteria Decision Making*. New York: McGraw-Hill, 1982.

22. Zusman, P., and M. Etgar. "The Marketing Channel as an Equilibrium Set of Contracts." *Management Science* (March 1981): 284.

Thought Exercises

1. What is the most appropriate payoff measure in each of the following situations? Explain.

   a. A company is considering a transfer of its headquarters to a different geographical region. The move will be based on a combination of economic, political, and personal preference considerations.

    b. A large department store is considering the introduction of its own brand of men's shirts. The profitability of this new product will depend on the level of demand.

    c. A young couple used all their savings to purchase a new home. They are trying to decide how much (if any) fire insurance to take on the house.

2. Describe each of the following decision makers' attitudes toward risk. Explain.

    a. Ann Arturin is approached by an associate with an investment proposition. She is given the option of getting a guaranteed return of 10% or a lottery ticket. The lottery involves a 20% chance of getting a 5% return. Ann would be equally happy with either option.

    b. Robert Sane is a great baseball fan with a moderate amount of wealth. He is thinking of buying a baseball team. The selling price is $500,000. Robert will be happy if the expected profit equals the sales price. There is a 50% chance that the team will have a $3 million profit and a 50% chance of a $2 million loss.

    c. A struggling student has just enough money to get through the school term. A friend offers an 80% chance at winning $5000. The bet will cost $1000, which happens to be the total value of the student's assets. The student does not take the bet.

3. Amy Carter owns a house worth $60,000. Insurance statistics indicate that there is a probability of only .002 that the house will burn down this year. Hence, her expected loss from a fire that totally destroys the house is $60,000 × .002 = $120.

    A Global Insurance Company representative wants to sell Amy a fire insurance policy with a $300 premium this year. Amy buys the policy even though its expected cost ($300) is larger than the expected loss from a major fire ($120). Can you explain her action?

4. Ken Care is interested in his state's lottery. A ticket costs $2. If Ken wins, he will get $1 million. However, the probability of winning is only .000001. Thus, the expected monetary value (EMV) of the lottery ticket is

$$\text{EMV (ticket)} = \$1,000,000 \,(.000001) + (-\$2)\,(.999999)$$

or

$$\text{EMV (ticket)} = -\$0.999998$$

    Ken buys the lottery ticket even though he can expect to lose about $1. That is, the expected monetary value of the lottery is negative ($-\$0.999998$). Can you explain his action?

5. A municipal library is considering the expansion of its reference section. The objectives are to attract federal grant money, provide increased community service, and enhance the library's reputation.

A composite utility measure, ranging in value between 0 and 100, will be used to evaluate the program. Ultimately, the program's success depends on whether there will be favorable or unfavorable community acceptance. The situation is represented by the following utility table.

Decision Alternatives	**States of Nature**	
	s_1 = favorable community acceptance	s_2 = unfavorable community acceptance
a_1 = expand the reference section	90	10
a_2 = do not expand	30	70

Utility value

Dianne Bookworth, the director of the library, is 80% confident that community acceptance will be favorable. On this basis, she decides to expand the reference section. Explain how Dianne arrived at her decision.

6. For each of the following, explain whether game theory is appropriate:
   a. A local gasoline station that wants to maximize its yearly profit
   b. Efforts of the postal service to maximize the "efficiency" of its delivery system
   c. The Vietnam War
   d. College football

7. What types of collusive arrangements or coalitions may exist in the following situations?
   a. Three major automobile manufacturers competing for a share of the market
   b. A running competition involving four teams each with three athletes
   c. The major petroleum companies competing for offshore drilling rights
   d. An auction

8. Explain whether each of the following games involves a zero sum:
   a. Two consumer products firms competing for a share of the laundry detergent market
   b. Two movie houses showing their major attractions at the same time
   c. Two men playing poker
   d. Two boxers' agents competing for a share of the purse

9. Adam McPhadom is known as the antibusiness congressperson. In a recent senate committee meeting, McPhadom presented the following game situation. Two firms must decide whether or not to advertise. If neither company advertises, each makes $3000 per month. When both advertise, each loses $10,000 per month. If company A advertises and company B does not, A gets $5000 profit per month and B loses $15,000. When B advertises and A does not, A loses $20,000 and B makes $8000 per month.

   According to McPhadom, this game shows that advertising leads to economically undesirable consequences. How did he arrive at this conclusion? Do you see anything wrong with his reasoning?

10. Two executives were participating in a seminar in game theory at a professional management conference. One said, "Game theory does attempt to show the actual competitive reactions we find in practice. However, it is inapplicable in all but exceptional circumstances." Can you explain this paradox? Use the tobacco, oil, and airline industries as guidelines in developing your answer.

11. Each year, a given number of new professional engineers join either Omicron or Phloton. The presidents of these societies want to select the recruitment policy that will maximize their new memberships. The situation is summarized in the following table, where entries represent the percentage of new engineers that join Phloton.

Phloton's Strategies	**Omicron's Strategies**	
	s_1 = a "hard sell" policy	s_2 = a "soft sell" policy
a_1 = use a "hard sell" recruitment policy	50	60
a_2 = use a "soft sell" recruitment policy	60	50

   Phloton's president uses game theory to develop the society's optimal mixed strategy. Based on the analysis, the society decides to use a "hard sell" policy for the first six months of the recruiting year and then shift to a "soft sell" policy for the last six months. Phloton expected 55% of the new engineers to join their society. In actual practice, only 50% became members.

   Show how Phloton arrived at its optimal mixed strategy and the expected payoff. Can you explain why actual membership did not meet expectations?

12. Do you agree or disagree with each of the following statements? Explain.

   a. There is a unique utility curve for every decision situation.

   b. We can select any initial utility values and still come up with relatively the same utility scale.

c. A risk avoider's utility curve will have the same shape in a cost problem or a return problem.
d. For a risk taker, the expected monetary value of the lottery is always greater than the guaranteed payoff.
e. For a risk-neutral decision maker, the expected monetary value of the lottery is always equal to the guaranteed payoff.
f. Game theory can be viewed as the special case of decision theory that involves active states of nature.
g. A game exists when one competitor knows the probabilities of the other's strategies.
h. Games may involve any number of players and any number of strategies for each competitor.
i. A pure strategy solution is really a special case of dominance.
j. Each of the game theory solution methods results in a saddle point.

Technique Exercises

1. A decision maker expresses the following indifference probabilities for a lottery having a payoff of $1000 with probability p and a payoff of $0 with probability $(1 - p)$.

Outcome	Lottery Indifference Probability (p)
$800	.95
$600	.80
$400	.50
$200	.25

Assign a utility of 100 to the $1000 payoff and a utility of 0 to the $0 outcome. Then find the utility value for each of the other outcomes.

2. Three decision makers express the following indifference probabilities for a lottery having a profit of $200,000 with probability p and a profit of $0 with probability $(1 - p)$.

Profit	Lottery Indifference Probability (p)		
	Person A	Person B	Person C
$150,000	.80	.60	.75
$100,000	.60	.40	.50
$50,000	.30	.10	.25

a. Find the utility value of the payoffs for each decision maker. Use a utility of 100 for the best payoff and 0 for the worst payoff.
b. Plot each decision maker's utility curve on the same graph.
c. Describe each decision maker's attitude toward risk.

3. A manager has the following decision table.

Decision Alternatives	States of Nature			
	s_1	s_2	s_3	s_4
a_1	$2,000	−$1,000	−$2,000	−$4,000
a_2	$6,000	$2,000	$0	−$1,000
a_3	$10,000	$6,000	$2,000	−$5,000

The manager has the following lottery indifference probabilities for the profits in the decision table.

Profit	Lottery Indifference Probability (p)
$6000	.60
$2000	.20
$0	.10
−$1000	.05
−$2000	.02
−$4000	.01

a. Find the utility value for each profit in the decision table. Assign a utility of 100 to the best payoff and 0 to the worst payoff.
b. Develop the utility table.
c. Graph the decision maker's utility curve.
d. Describe the decision maker's attitude toward risk.

4. A manager has the following decision table.

Decision Alternatives	States of Nature		
	s_1	s_2	s_3
a_1	$200	$400	$500
a_2	$500	$100	$100 ← Cost
a_3	$400	$200	$100

The manager also has the following lottery indifference probabilities: $p = .6$ for $200 and $p = .2$ for $400.

a. Find the utility value for each profit in the decision table, assigning a utility of 100 to the best payoff and 0 to the worst payoff. Develop the utility table.

b. Find the utility value for each profit in the decision table, assigning a utility of 200 to the best payoff and -100 to the worst payoff. Develop the utility table.

c. Assume that $P(s_1) = .3$, $P(s_2) = .4$, and $P(s_3) = .3$. What is the recommended expected monetary value decision?

d. Using the probabilities in part (c), what is the expected utility recommendation when we use the values in part (a)?

e. What is the expected utility recommendation when we use the values in part (b)?

f. Compare the results in parts (d) and (e). What do you find?

5. You are given the following decision data.

Decision Alternative	State of Nature	Value of Attribute (units)	
		A	B
a_1	s_1	100	50
a_1	s_2	250	25
a_1	s_3	400	10
a_2	s_1	300	60
a_2	s_2	200	80
a_2	s_3	150	150

a. Develop the decision table.

b. If $P(s_1) = .4$ and $P(s_2) = .5$, which decision alternative maximizes the value of attribute A? Which alternative minimizes the value of attribute B? Explain.

c. Suppose attribute A has the highest priority, but the expected value of B must not exceed 75. If it is desirable to have high values of A but low values of B, which alternative do you recommend?

d. Assume that a composite measure can be formed by dividing the value of attribute B into the value of attribute A. Develop an appropriate decision table and then select the alternative that maximizes the expected value of this composite measure. Which alternative minimizes the expected value of this measure?

e. Suppose the appropriate composite measure is found by dividing the value of attribute A into the value of attribute B. Show how this new composite measure changes the analysis in part (d).

f. What is the main decision-making implication of all these results?

6. A tire manufacturer is considering various locations in a particular geographical area for a franchise retail store. After careful

consideration, the company represents the problem with the following decision table. Note that there is a $P(s_1) = .6$ probability of economic growth.

Decision Alternatives	States of Nature	
	s_1 = economic growth	s_2 = economic stagnation
a_1 = locate in Beachtown	annual sales = $400,000 market share = 10% annual profit = $30,000	annual sales = $250,000 market share = 25% annual profit = $20,000
a_2 = locate in Sun City	annual sales = $200,000 market share = 20% annual profit = $31,000	annual sales = $150,000 market share = 8% annual profit = $18,500
a_3 = locate in Oldville	annual sales = $100,000 market share = 15% annual profit = $22,000	annual sales = $175,000 market share = 17.5% annual profit = $32,000

a. Suppose that the company's objectives, in rank order, are to maximize expected profit, attain the largest expected market share, and achieve the highest expected sales. Which decision alternative do you recommend? Explain.
b. Assume that management has the following lottery indifference probabilities.

Annual Profit		Market Share		Annual Sales	
Outcome ($)	Lottery Indifference Probability (p)	Outcome (%)	Lottery Indifference Probability (p)	Outcome ($)	Lottery Indifference Probability (p)
32,000	Does not apply	25	Does not apply	400,000	Does not apply
31,000	.95	20	.70	250,000	.50
30,000	.90	17.5	.50	200,000	1/3
22,000	.40	15	.35	175,000	.25
20,000	.25	10	.10	150,000	1/6
18,500	Does not apply	8	Does not apply	100,000	Does not apply

For each attribute, assign a utility value of 100 to the best outcome and a value of 0 to the worst payoff. Next, find the utility values for the other outcomes. Then describe the decision maker's attitude toward risk.
c. Suppose the company could sum the individual values for each attribute to form a multiattribute utility assessment. Develop the resulting multiattribute utility table. Which decision alternative leads to the maximum expected utility?

7. The production manager in an assembly plant has a problem that can be described by the following decision table. Note that there is a $P(s_1) = .7$ chance that operations will be normal.

Decision Alternatives	States of Nature	
	s_1 = normal operations	s_2 = extended operations
a_1 = use process X	production cost = $50,000 output = 450	production cost = $80,000 output = 550
a_2 = use process Y	production cost = $90,000 output = 500	production cost = $70,000 output = 700
a_3 = use process Z	production cost = $40,000 output = 400	production cost = $100,000 output = 200

a. Calculate the expected production cost and the expected output for each decision alternative. Which alternative minimizes the expected production cost? Which alternative maximizes the expected output?
b. Assume that output has the highest priority. However, management does not want the expected cost to exceed $60,000. Which alternative should management select? Explain.
c. Suppose management wanted to express the problem in terms of cost per unit of output. Develop the decision table that corresponds to this single composite measure. Which alternative minimizes the cost per unit of output? Explain.
d. The production manager has expressed the following lottery indifference probabilities.

Production Cost		Output	
Outcome ($)	Lottery Indifference Probability (p)	Outcome (units)	Lottery Indifference Probability (p)
40,000	Does not apply	700	Does not apply
50,000	.90	550	.65
70,000	.75	500	.50
80,000	.55	450	.35
90,000	.20	400	.10
100,000	Does not apply	200	Does not apply

For each attribute, assign a utility value of 100 to the best outcome and a value of 0 to the worst payoff. Next, find the utility values for the other outcomes. Then describe the manager's attitude toward risk. What do you find?
e. Suppose the manager assigns equal weight to each attribute.

Develop a multiattribute utility assessment for each decision outcome. Express each multiattribute utility assessment in terms of a value between 0 and 100. Use these results to transform the decision table into a multiattribute utility table. Which alternative leads to the maximum expected utility?

f. If the manager thought that output was three times as important as production cost, would you change the recommendation in part (e)? Explain.

8. In each of the following games, the entries represent payoffs to player A, and the constant sum is either 0 or 10. Determine whether any of the games involves a pure strategy solution. Identify the pure strategy solution if it exists.

A's Alternatives	B's Alternatives	
	s_1	s_2
a_1	2	-3
a_2	-4	1

Game 1

A's Alternatives	B's Alternatives	
	s_1	s_2
a_1	4	7
a_2	3	8

Game 2

A's Alternatives	B's Alternatives	
	s_1	s_2
a_1	3	-5
a_2	4	-10

Game 3

9. You are given the following zero sum game.

A's Alternatives	B's Alternatives	
	s_1	s_2
a_1	-18	25
a_2	30	-15

a. Find the $P(s_1)$ and $P(s_2)$ that equate the expected value of a_1 to the expected payoff of a_2. Show your results graphically.

b. Find the $P(a_1)$ and $P(a_2)$ that make the expected outcomes from s_1 and s_2 the same value. Show your results graphically.

c. Use the resulting probabilities to determine the value of the game. Show your results graphically.

10. You are given the following constant sum game. The constant sum is 25.

| | B's Alternatives | | |
A's Alternatives	s_1	s_2	s_3
a_1	10	15	20
a_2	15	10	5
a_3	8	6	5

a. Use the dominance concept to find the relevant game.
b. Determine each participant's optimal mixed strategies and the value of the game. Show the results graphically.

11. You are given the following zero sum game.

| | B's Alternatives | | | |
A's Alternatives	s_1	s_2	s_3	s_4
a_1	5	-3	2	4
a_2	0	-4	1	4
a_3	6	2	2	1

a. Use the dominance concept to find the relevant game.
b. Determine each participant's optimal mixed strategies and the value of the game. Show your results graphically.

12. Consider the following situation faced by two neighborhood gas stations, each of which wants weekly sales to be as large as possible.

| Union Stop's Alternatives | Mobiline's Alternatives | |
	s_1 = keep prices the same	s_2 = reduce prices
a_1 = keep prices the same	Union's weekly sales = 1300 gallons Mobiline's weekly sales = 1200 gallons	Union's weekly sales = 900 gallons Mobiline's weekly sales = 1400 gallons
a_2 = reduce prices	Union's weekly sales = 1500 gallons Mobiline's weekly sales = 800 gallons	Union's weekly sales = 1100 gallons Mobiline's weekly sales = 1050 gallons

a. Develop a separate game table for each participant.
b. Use game theory to determine the optimal strategies and the value of the game for each participant.
c. Is there a better solution? Explain.

1. Two management trainees for a department store chain are being evaluated for promotion. An important part of the evaluation process deals with the trainee's attitude toward risk. Each person is presented with the following situation. The chain has recently purchased land for a shopping center development in a suburban town. Various sizes of development are possible, but uncertain economic conditions make it difficult to ascertain the demand for the store's facilities. An oversized facility could be very costly to the chain. Yet an undersized store will unnecessarily limit the chain's profits. The possible profits are $2 million, $1 million, $500,000, $0, −$500,000, and −$1 million.

   The trainees are asked to state a preference between a guaranteed profit and the following lottery:

   Lottery: The trainee gets a $2 million profit with probability p and −$1 million with probability $(1 − p)$.

   Trainee A1 is indifferent between a guaranteed profit of $1 million and this lottery when $p = .8$. His other indifference probabilities are $p = .6$ when the guaranteed profit is $500,000, $p = .4$ when it is $0, and $p = .2$ when it is −$500,000. On the other hand, trainee Alice is indifferent between a guaranteed profit of $1 million and the lottery when $p = .6$. Her other indifference probabilities are $p = .45$ when the guaranteed profit is $500,000, $p = .3$ when it is $0, and $p = .1$ when it is −$500,000.

   If the company prefers risk-avoiding managers, which trainee has the best chance for promotion?

2. The public-service television network has been receiving low ratings for its 5–7 P.M. time slot. Currently, management is considering three alternatives for this slot: a sports show, travel films, or a political discussion program. The percent of viewing audience estimates depends on the demographic characteristics of the viewers. Audiences are demographically classified as "family oriented" or "sensation oriented." Market research indicates that the network can expect 10% of a "family-oriented" audience to view the sports show telecast; 5% of a "family-oriented" audience can be expected to view travel films; and 40% of this audience will watch the political discussion program. Among the "sensation-oriented" viewers, the network can expect 20% to watch the sports show, 25% to view travel films, and 5% to watch the political program.

   The network public relations executive is completely optimistic and wants to select the program that leads to the best percentage of the viewing audience. Which program should this executive select?

   The program manager points out the risk involved and believes that the network should incorporate this factor into the analysis. This manager suggests using utility as the appropriate payoff measure. He assigns a utility of 100 to the best payoff and a utility of 0 to the worst payoff. Then the manager assigns the following lottery indifference probabilities to the other payoffs:

Percent of Audience	Lottery Indifference Probability (p)
25	.7
20	.5
10	.2

The program manager wants the network to select the format that leads to the maximum expected utility. He believes that there is a 70% likelihood that audiences will be "sensation oriented." Which program should this executive select?

3. Storage Inc. is considering purchasing a theft insurance policy for its warehouse in New York. The policy has an annual cost of $20,000. If there is a minor theft, the company anticipates a cost of $200,000. A major theft would cost $1 million. Insurance records indicate that there is a 95% chance of no theft and a 4% chance of a minor theft.

After considering the risk and other related factors, company executives believe that utility is the appropriate payoff measure. The company president assigns a utility value of 100 to the best payoff and a utility value of 0 to the worst payoff. His indifference probabilities are $p = .01$ for the $20,000 cost and $p = .1$ for the $200,000 cost. The company president wants to maximize expected utility.

Should the company buy the policy? What is the price that the company president is apparently willing to pay to avoid the risk of theft?

4. An investor can buy stock in company A, company B, or both A and B. The return on investment depends on general economic conditions. Historically, there has been prosperity 10% of the time, stagnation 55% of the time, and recession 35% of the time. If she buys stock in A, the return will be $10,000 no matter what economic conditions occur. Stock in B has an expected return of $20,000 in prosperity, $2000 with stagnation, and a loss of $10,000 in recession.

However, the investor is also concerned with risk and other intangible factors. Consequently, the investments will be evaluated in terms of their utility to the decision maker. The investor's utility values are given as follows:

Return ($ thousand)	Utility
30	100
20	90
12	80
10	70
2	55
0	50
−10	0

a. Which investment leads to maximum expected utility?
b. Which investment leads to the maximum expected dollar return?
c. What is the difference in expected monetary value between the two recommendations? Can you rationalize this difference?

5. Sally Tally, a recent college graduate, is considering three job offers. The possibilities are a position in personnel management with the telephone company, a job as a financial analyst with a bank, and a job as a salesperson in real estate. Several factors are important to Sally. She is concerned with salary, fringe benefits, and advancement possibilities. Fringe benefits are expressed as a percentage of salary, while advancement opportunities are measured by the anticipated salary increments.

The attribute values for each position depend on economic conditions. After considering all relevant data, Sally has compiled the following information about the attributes:

Position	Growing Economy			Declining Economy		
	Annual Base Salary ($)	Annual Fringe Benefits ($)	Annual Salary Increments ($)	Annual Base Salary ($)	Annual Fringe Benefits ($)	Annual Salary Increments ($)
Telephone company personnel manager	20,000	6000	1000	18,000	5500	500
Bank financial analyst	24,000	4500	1500	16,000	3500	500
Real estate sales	25,000	4000	2000	15,000	3000	0

In this table, base salaries, fringe benefits, and salary increments are expressed as annual averages adjusted for inflation and discounted to present values over Sally's three-year planning horizon. Furthermore, government statistics indicate that there is a 50% likelihood of a growing economy.

If Sally wants to maximize the expected total dollar worth of the job attributes, which offer should she accept? Suppose that expected base salary has the highest priority and that the second most important attribute is the possibility of advancement. Also, Sally wants the position to provide at least $4000 in annual fringe benefits. Under these circumstances, which job offer should she accept?

6. A tornado has recently swept through a southwestern state, leaving vast areas utterly destroyed. Among such areas is one rural county with a long history of low income and high unemployment. The state planning commission is asked to recommend a general land-use program for the region. Public hearings are held to identify the priorities of such a program. The consensus is that the plan should

provide for recreation, encourage employment opportunities, and conserve the natural beauty of the area. After careful deliberation, the commission proposes the following alternatives:

♦ Fully exploit the recreational potential of the area with parks, beaches, campsites, and the like.

♦ Set aside the tillable land for agriculture only and use the rest for a community of vacation homes.

♦ Use the land only as a state forest preserve with hiking trails but very limited service facilities.

Each alternative is expected to provide some land for recreation, jobs, and wilderness areas. The specific amounts of these attributes will depend on future regional socioeconomic conditions. In this respect, it is possible to have either a growth in population density and per capita income or a stable population with declining per capita income. The commission feels that there is a 65% chance of population and income growth.

A preliminary study provides the following data:

	Population/Income Growth			**Stable Population/Declining Income**		
Land Use Alternatives	Recreational Land (Thousand Acres)	Jobs (Thousands)	Wilderness Area (Thousand Acres)	Recreational Land (Thousand Acres)	Jobs (Thousands)	Wilderness Area (Thousand Acres)
Parks/beaches	20	150	10	15	125	12
Agriculture	12	275	14	11	200	17
State forest	16	100	20	13	75	22

Alternatives will be evaluated by a utility measure that consolidates aspects of the consensus priorities. To facilitate such an analysis, the commission develops the following lottery indifference probabilities regarding the attribute outcomes. Each attribute is equally important to the commission.

Recreational Land		**Jobs**		**Wilderness Area**	
Outcome (Thousand Acres)	Lottery Indifference Probability (p)	Outcome (Thousand Jobs)	Lottery Indifference Probability (p)	Outcome (Thousand Acres)	Lottery Indifference Probability (p)
20	Does not apply	275	Does not apply	22	Does not apply
16	.50	200	.625	20	.95
15	.40	150	.375	17	.70
13	.20	125	.250	14	.50
12	.10	100	.125	12	.25
11	Does not apply	75	Does not apply	10	Does not apply

If the commissioners want to select the program that maximizes expected utility, which alternative should they recommend?

7. Southwest and Heartland railroads will each purchase a computerized dispatching system. Dynamo, Inc., and Electron Corp. are trying to get the railroads to adopt their systems. Research indicates that the probability of a sale is directly related to the relative number of sales calls. For example, if Dynamo sends two salespeople and Electron one, then Dynamo has a $\frac{2}{3}$, or about a 67%, chance of making a sale. When both send no salespeople, each has a 50% chance of obtaining the business. Currently, Dynamo has three salespeople available, while Electron has only two. Geography and time considerations make it necessary for the manufacturers to have different salespeople call on each railroad. For instance, one of Dynamo's alternatives would be to have all three people call on Southwest. Or the company could send two people to Southwest and one to Heartland. And so on. Similarly, Electron could send both its people to Southwest, one to each railroad, or both to Heartland.

Each manufacturer wants to get the largest expected number of sales. How many salespeople should each firm send to each railroad? What is the expected number of sales for each manufacturer?

8. Quesar is a developing oil sheikdom in the Middle East. Zambisee Motors and Stophagle, Inc., are the only two manufacturers granted permits to sell automobiles to the government staff. Zambisee calls its car the Executive, while Stophagle calls its car the Luxurus. Each company's profits depend on the marketing mix actions of the two firms. Past experience has enabled each to know the mixes that the other intends to adopt and the resulting market shares. However, each is still uncertain about the proportions of the mixes.

Zambisee's possible marketing policies are as follows:

♦ A price of $10,000 with annual marketing expenditures of $500,000

♦ A price of $15,000 with annual marketing expenditures of $600,000

Stophagle could adopt the following policies:

♦ A price of $12,000 with annual marketing expenditures of $1,200,000

♦ A price of $15,000 with annual marketing expenditures of $1,300,000

In similar markets in the past, when Zambisee has adopted the first policy, the company has obtained a 70% share if Stophagle has used its first policy. Zambisee has received a 60% share when Stophagle has employed its second action. When Zambisee has used its second policy, the company has obtained a 20% share if

Stophagle has gone with its first policy. Zambisee's market share has been 70% when Stophagle has played its second action.

What strategy should each employ? What market share can each firm expect?

9. Two lawyers are trying a civil suit involving substantial financial damages. The attorneys have faced each other under similar circumstances in the past. Sally Fine typically adopts one of three alternatives: aggression, a reconciling attitude, or a legally technical approach. On the other hand, Mort Tort usually uses either trickery or deceit.

The lawyers are representing the insurers of the litigants. The loser will have to pay financial damages to the winner of the trial. If Sally uses aggression, her client will win $50,000 when Mort tries trickery and $100,000 when Mort tries deceit. Furthermore, when Mort is deceitful, his client will win $30,000 if Sally takes a reconciling attitude and $50,000 if she takes a legally technical approach. Also, if Mort uses trickery, Sally's client will win $10,000 when she adopts a reconciling attitude and $60,000 when she uses the legally technical alternative.

What strategy should each lawyer adopt? What is each insurer's expected financial gain or loss?

10. The United States and the Soviet Union are negotiating a space territorial treaty. Samuel Spade, the American delegate, and Igor Ivanov, the Russian representative, have bargained many times in past similar circumstances. Igor knows that Samuel will be defiant or compromising, and Samuel knows that Igor has the same two alternatives.

In this particular session, the parties are negotiating the number of military craft each will allow in a given sector of outer space. Through previous similar bargaining, Samuel and Igor each have some idea of the possible outcomes for the various alternatives.

When Samuel is defiant, the United States will be allowed 10 craft if Igor is defiant and 26 if the Russian is compromising. But if Samuel is compromising, his country will obtain only 8 vehicles when Igor is defiant but 20 vehicles if the Russian compromises. On the other hand, when Igor is defiant, the Soviet Union will be allowed 10 craft if Samuel is defiant and 28 when the American compromises. However, if Igor is compromising, his country will obtain only 7 vehicles when Samuel is defiant but 20 if the American compromises.

Communication and cooperation are encouraged by the leaders of the two governments, but each country wants to obtain the best possible treaty. Which strategy should each negotiator adopt? What is the outcome that each country can expect from the resulting treaty?

CASE: Rural Vehicles, Inc.

Rural Vehicles, Inc., is a small rural distributor of agricultural vehicles in central Iowa. There are no competitors in the vicinity. Combines are the most popular vehicle, and the company places one order for this equipment each March. Although past experience indicates that Rural will sell no more than four combines during the season, the exact demand is unknown. However, historical records provide the following data:

Combines Sold	Probability
0	.0625
1	.2500
2	.3750
3	.2500
4	.0625

Rural will have the following expenses this year:

Mortgage	$20,000
Office supplies expense	500
Electricity, gas, and telephone	1,500
Salaries	30,000
Promotion	8,000
Total	$60,000

This year, a combine wholesales for $40,000. Rural will sell it for $50,000. There is also a rebate deal with the manufacturer. At the end of the season, all unsold combines are returned to the supplier. Rural then receives cost plus 5%. However, it costs Rural approximately 10% of its total expenses to hold a combine for the entire season.

In addition, if a combine is not available at Rural, a customer will buy elsewhere. A lost sale, including loss of potential service revenue, will cost Rural an estimated $12,000 per combine.

Rural's owner, U. R. Wright, wants to order the number of combines that will maximize the expected return on the economic investment. Wright defines this return as the ratio of profit to total costs, where costs are equal to expenses plus the combine holding cost plus lost service revenue. Wright's wife, Unifer, thinks that such a measure does not fully account for the risk and other intangibles involved in the problem. In her opinion, they first should separately establish the total worth of the profit and total cost attributes to the company. This total worth would reflect the monetary value of these attributes and U. R. and Unifer's personal assessment of the inherent risk and other intangibles. In this respect, Unifer wants to avoid risk. The individual total worths next could be consolidated into an overall assessment of total worth. Then the company would order the number of combines that maximizes the expected overall total worth.

Suppose that you are brought in as a consultant.

1. Develop the decision table in terms of U. R.'s return measure.

2. Set up the lotteries that would be involved in a utility analysis of this problem.

3. There are many sets of lottery indifference probabilities that a risk avoider might have for the monetary values in this problem. Assume that you and Unifer have exactly the same risk-avoiding viewpoint. Identify your (and Unifer's) lottery indifference probabilities for each attribute in this problem.

4. How many combines would the company order if it used U. R.'s return on economic investment measure? What is the probability that Rural will not satisfy demand with this policy?

5. How many combines would the company order if it used Unifer's overall total worth measure with U. R.'s view toward risk? Explain.

6. How many combines would you (and Unifer) order? What is the probability that Rural will not meet demand with this policy?

7. Demand for combines will depend on the age of existing machines, the amount farmers plant, and many other factors. Assume that the crop size is the only variable factor in this particular season. In this respect, there are many farmers from other areas competing with Rural's customers for shares of the same relatively fixed crop market. Consequently, the demand for the crops of Rural's customers, and thus its combine sales, could be determined by a game process between the two competing farmer groups. How would this possibility affect the analysis? Explain.

Prepare a report outlining this information in a form that would be understandable to U. R. and Unifer Wright.

Part III
Mathematical Programming

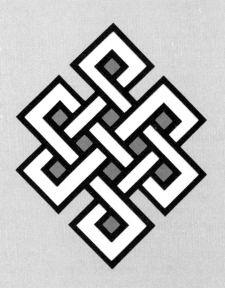

The previous chapters have dealt with the general topic of quantitative decision making. We showed how to identify and classify decision situations, develop a framework for analyzing each of these general situations, and generate a recommended solution. In the remainder of the text, our focus will shift from these general situations to specific types of decision problems.

Many of these problems are centered around the best way to achieve the objectives of the enterprise in the face of environmental constraints. These constraints can take the form of limited resources (such as time, labor, energy, material, and money) or restrictive guidelines (such as nutritional recipes and engineering specifications). Management scientists have developed a body of knowledge, known as mathematical programming, designed to solve such problems.

The most widely used mathematical programming approach, linear programming, is introduced in chapter 6. Typical linear programming models are formulated, characteristics are discussed, and the graphic solution method is developed. Chapter 7 discusses the simplex method, an efficient procedure for solving the large-scale problems encountered in practice. Other relevant solution topics and special situations are also considered.

Important products of a linear programming analysis are the economic values of the scarce resources. Chapter 8 shows how to determine and interpret these values. In addition, this chapter shows how to analyze the decision impact of potential changes in the values of the uncontrollable inputs. It also presents an appropriate computer analysis.

Linear programming is based on a set of rather restrictive assumptions. The final chapter of this part, chapter 9, discusses these assumptions and presents the limitations of a linear programming analysis. Other relevant methodologies, including integer, goal, and nonlinear programming, are then identified and developed.

After reading this part of the text, you should be able to:

♦ Identify situations that can be effectively analyzed with mathematical programming approaches
♦ Identify the relevant mathematical programming methodology
♦ Formulate various types of mathematical programming problems
♦ Solve these problems graphically, algebraically, and with the aid of available computer packages
♦ Interpret the results
♦ Develop other appropriate decision information from the results

This background will facilitate your understanding of later parts of the text.

Chapter 6
Linear Programming

Everyone, at one time or another, has the problem of allocating scarce resources among competing activities. As a student, for example, you must determine how to allocate your time among studying, sleeping, eating, and recreation. In addition, most of you are on a limited financial budget and must make difficult decisions regarding the utilization of funds.

Managers in all types of organizations have similar decision problems. Limited resources (including machinery, labor, materials, physical space, time, and money) are available to produce various products (such as furniture, food, and automobiles) or services (such as advertising strategies, investment plans, and shipping schedules). Typically, there are many competing ways to produce these products and services. Furthermore, the environment may impose guidelines (such as contract terms and engineering specifications) that restrict the ways in which the resources can be transformed into products or services. Management must decide which activities most effectively use the firm's resources and meet the restrictive guidelines.

Management scientists have developed a methodology, called **linear programming**, that offers one way of making such decisions in the best interests of the appropriate organizational unit. This unit may be the overall enterprise or some department within the firm. In fact, the methodology has been used successfully at many organizational levels in all types of industries, including manufacturing, transportation, energy, education, and government.

This chapter introduces linear programming. It describes the general nature of the model, outlines its characteristics, and develops a graphic solution procedure. Finally, special situations and other relevant concepts are presented and related to decision making. The material in this chapter is the foundation for the large-scale solution procedures and decision-making extensions of the basic model that are discussed in later chapters.

NATURE OF LINEAR PROGRAMMING

We can begin by considering Example 6.1.

EXAMPLE 6.1 Machine Shop Management

Saferly, Inc., manufactures two types of kitchen utensils: knives and forks. Both must be pressed and polished. The shop manager estimates that there will be a maximum of 70 hours available next week in the pressing machine center and 100 hours in the polishing center. Each case of knives requires an estimated 12 minutes (.2 hour) of pressing and 30 minutes (.5 hour) of polishing, while each case of forks requires 24 minutes (.4 hour) of pressing and 15 minutes (.25 hour) of polishing. The company can sell as many knives as it produces at the prevailing market price of $12 per case. Forks can be sold for $9 per case. It costs $4 to produce a case of knives and $3 to produce a case of forks. Saferly wants to determine how many cases of knives and forks the company should produce to maximize total dollar profit.

FORMULATING THE PROBLEM

As previous chapters have demonstrated, the first step in the decision-making process is to develop a clear and concise formulation of the problem. In Example 6.1, Saferly's problem is to determine the quantity of knives and forks that will maximize total dollar profit. However, the selected quantities cannot use more than the available pressing and polishing times.

Objective Saferly's total dollar profit will equal the contribution from knives plus the contribution from forks. Since it costs $4 to produce each case of knives, and since each case can be sold for $12, there is a contribution to profit of $12 − $4 = $8 per case of knives. The $8-per-case contribution multiplied by the number of cases will then give the total dollar profit from knives. Similarly, each case of forks can be produced for $3 and sold for $9. Hence, forks have a profit contribution of $9 − $3 = $6 per case. This $6-per-case contribution multiplied by the number of cases gives the total profit from forks.

By letting

X_1 = the number of cases of knives Saferly produces next week

X_2 = the number of cases of forks Saferly produces next week

Z = Saferly's total dollar profit

we can represent Saferly's total dollar profit by

(6.1) $Z = \$8X_1 + \$6X_2$

Company management has the discretion of setting the output levels (number of knives and forks produced). Thus, X_1 and X_2 represent the controllable inputs in this problem. In linear programming, these inputs are referred to as **decision variables**.

The company wants to choose the levels of the decision variables (X_1 and X_2) that maximize total dollar profit (Z). This objective can be expressed as

(6.2)   maximize $Z = \$8X_1 + \$6X_2$

In linear programming, such an expression is known as the **objective function**.

Restrictions   Available pressing and polishing capacity will limit the number of knives and forks that Saferly can produce. Since each case of knives uses .2 hour of pressing time, $.2 \times X_1$ is the total time required to press X_1 knives. In addition, each case of forks uses .4 hour of pressing time. Hence, $.4 \times X_2$ is the total time required to press X_2 forks. Consequently,

$.2X_1 + .4X_2$

gives the total time required to press X_1 knives and X_2 forks.

Saferly can select any product combination that does not require more total pressing time than the 70 hours available. In other words, management must satisfy the following condition:

(6.3) $\underbrace{.2X_1 + .4X_2}_{\substack{\text{Total pressing} \\ \text{time required}}} \quad \leq \quad \underbrace{70 \text{ hours}}_{\substack{\text{Total pressing} \\ \text{time available}}}$

where the symbol $\leq$ means "less than or equal to." In linear programming, such an expression is referred to as a **system constraint**.

Another system constraint deals with polishing operations. In particular, management knows that each case of knives uses .5 hour and each case of forks uses .25 hour of polishing time. Since there are only 100 hours of polishing time available,

(6.4) $\underbrace{.5X_1 + .25X_2}_{\substack{\text{Total polishing} \\ \text{time required}}} \quad \leq \quad \underbrace{100 \text{ hours}}_{\substack{\text{Total polishing} \\ \text{time available}}}$

That is, the demand for polishing time cannot exceed the available supply.

Also, it is physically impossible for Saferly to produce a negative number of knives and forks. Therefore, management must ensure that decision variables X_1 and X_2 have values greater than or equal to zero. Symbolically,

$$X_1 \geq 0 \quad \text{and} \quad X_2 \geq 0$$

or, in abbreviated form,

(6.5) $X_1, X_2 \geq 0$

where the symbol $\geq$ means "greater than or equal to." In linear programming, such expressions are called **nonnegativity conditions**.

Complete Formulation   By collecting objective function (6.2), system constraints (6.3) and (6.4), and nonnegativity conditions (6.5), Saferly's management can represent the machine shop problem with the following mathematical model:

maximize $Z = \$8X_1 + \$6X_2$ Objective function

subject to

$.2X_1 + .4X_2 \leq 70$ hours   (Pressing) $\Big\}$
$.5X_1 + .25X_2 \leq 100$ hours   (Polishing)   System constraints

$X_1, X_2 \geq 0$ Nonnegativity conditions

This type of model is called a **linear program**.

Saferly's linear program states that the company wants to produce the quantity of knives (X_1) and forks (X_2) that will maximize total dollar profit (Z). The output levels, however, are subject to some restrictions. For one thing, the demand for pressing and polishing time cannot exceed the available supply of these resources. Also, the output levels must be positive or zero.

The Process   Figure 6.1 outlines and summarizes the formulation process. Notice that an important step in the process is to gather relevant data. In Example 6.1, these data (product profit contributions per case, available resource supplies, and the utilization rates of these resources by each product) were already furnished. Typically, however, management must generate the required information. Although the nature of the problem will determine the specific data that are relevant, the following are usually included:

1. The available or required amount of each resource
2. How much of each resource is used by each decision variable
3. How much each decision variable contributes to the objective

Figure 6.1 Formulating a Linear Program

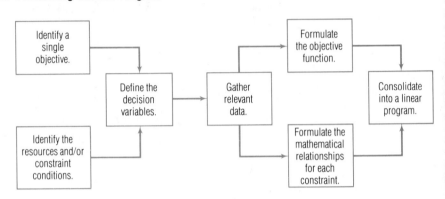

Appropriate sources of relevant data include sales invoices, production records, accounting and financial statements, and MIS reports. Relevant published documents include government records, trade studies, and commercially available market research reports. In addition, executive polls and surveys of employees and customers are also useful sources of information.

The case at the end of this chapter provides information in some of these forms, asks you to generate the relevant data from this information, and then requires an appropriate linear programming analysis.

CHARACTERISTICS   Scrutiny of Example 6.1 and the subsequent development will show that Saferly's problem has some specific characteristics. First, the company has a single, measurable criterion of maximizing total dollar profit, and several decision variables (X_1 and X_2) can be used to achieve this objective. Furthermore, each of the decision variables has an independent effect on the objective and contributes a constant, proportional amount to the objective.

For instance, Saferly's total profit equation (6.1),

$$Z = \$8X_1 + \$6X_2$$

shows that the contribution from the number of cases of knives (X_1) will be $8 per case regardless of the number of cases of forks (X_2). Also, the company will earn this same $8 per case no matter how many cases of knives (X_1) they produce and sell. Similarly, the $6-per-case profit contribution from the number of cases of forks (X_2) remains the same at all output/sales levels and is unaffected by knife production/demand.

Also, notice in Saferly's profit equation that each decision variable (X_1 and X_2) appears in a separate term and is raised to the first power (has an exponent of 1). In such cases, the decision variables are said to have a **linear relationship** to the total dollar profit criterion. Put another way, Saferly has a linear objective function.

Another basic property is the presence of restrictions that limit the value of the objective. Saferly, for example, has two scarce resources, available pressing time and available polishing time, that limit the output of knives and forks and hence restrict total dollar profit. There also is a linear relationship between decision variables X_1 and X_2 and each of these available times.

Consider, for instance, the pressing constraint of expression (6.3):

$$.2X_1 + .4X_2 \le 70 \text{ hours}$$

In this expression, each decision variable X_1 and X_2 appears in a separate term and has an exponent of one. Thus, each case of knives will utilize the same .2 hour of pressing time regardless of the quantity of forks (X_2). Furthermore, this pressing time utilization rate will remain at .2 hour per case no matter how many cases of knives (X_1) Saferly produces. In addition, the .4 hour per case utilization rate by forks remains the same at all output levels and is unaffected by knife production.

There is a similar linear relationship in the polishing constraint expression (6.4):

$$.5X_1 + .25X_2 \le 100 \text{ hours}$$

Namely, each decision variable X_1 and X_2 appears in a separate term and is raised to the first power. In fact, the linear relationships in the objective function and system constraint expressions are the special features of Saferly's model that make it a linear program.

There are additional important characteristics about Saferly's restrictions. For one thing, it is not necessary to satisfy each resource constraint exactly. For example, the company can use less than the available pressing or polishing time to produce knives and forks. That is why the constraint expressions are written as inequalities rather than as equations. Also, the linear program includes a formal statement of the nonnegativity conditions:

$$X_1, X_2 \ge 0$$

Although Saferly's problem involves the maximization of a criterion (profit), other linear programming situations could deal with a minimization process. A government planner, for instance, might want to select the

Table 6.1 Common Characteristics of Linear Programs

Objective Function	Restrictions
1. The decision maker has a single, measurable objective (such as maximizing profit or minimizing cost).	1. There is a finite number of restrictions on the objective.

2. Several activities (products, services, or processes) can be used to achieve the objective. These activities are called decision variables.	2. A restriction may involve:
	   a. A limited resource supply (such as a maximum budget)
	   b. A required resource demand (such as a minimum production standard)
	   c. A balance condition (such as a requirement that total sales demand equal total production supply)
	   d. Some other relationship (such as a requirement that the sales of one product be at least 40% of the sales of another product)

3. Each activity contributes to the objective. The mathematical relationship between the value of the criterion (such as total profit or cost) and the values of the decision variables is called the objective function.	3. Decision variable combinations must:
	   a. Use no more than an available resource supply
	   b. Have at least as much output as a required resource demand
	   c. Satisfy any other constraint conditions.
	 These relationships are called system constraint expressions when presented in mathematical form.

4. The objective function is linear. That is, each decision variable appears in a separate term and is raised to the first power.	4. There are linear relationships in each constraint.
5. The decision maker must determine the combination of decision variables that results in the most preferable value of the objective (such as maximum profit or minimum cost) and satisfies all constraints.	5. The decision variables must be positive or zero. These restrictions are called nonnegativity conditions.

program that minimizes budget costs. Also, Saferly's restrictions all involve "less than or equal to" ($\leq$) expressions. In practice, however, the constraint conditions can take several forms, including any or all of the following types:

1. An available input, such as machinery capacity, a money budget, or a labor supply

2. A required output, such as a minimum production level, a nutritional requirement, or a minimum building materials standard

3. A balancing condition, such as a requirement that total sales demand must exactly equal total production supply

4. Some other condition, such as a contract requirement specifying that the quantity of one product must be at least twice the amount of another

Indeed, the general format for a linear program is the following model:

$$\text{optimize} \quad Z = \sum_{j=1}^{n} c_j X_j$$

subject to $\displaystyle\sum_{j=1}^{n} a_{ij}X_j(\leq, \geq, =)b_i(i = 1, 2, \ldots, m)$

$X_j \geq 0 \; (j = 1, 2, \ldots, n)$

where X_j = the jth decision variable

c_j = per unit contribution of the jth decision variable to the objective

a_{ij} = the amount of the ith resource used to get one unit of the jth decision variable

b_i = the quantity of the ith resource

n = the number of decision variables

m = the number of resources

and the notation $\displaystyle\sum_{j=1}^{n}$ means that we must sum the effects of decision variables 1 through n. This format emphasizes that all linear programs optimize the value of the objective function. Optimization can mean either the maximization of a return or performance concept or the minimization of a cost or effort concept, depending on the nature of the problem. Also, there is a mixture of constraint forms. Some constraints can be less-than-or-equal-to ($\leq$) types, some can be equalities ($=$), and others can be greater-than-or-equal-to ($\geq$) types. All three types may appear in the same problem. Table 6.1 summarizes the common characteristics of all linear programs.

CLASSES OF PROBLEMS Linear programming has been applied most frequently to five general classes of decision problems: assignment, blending, planning and scheduling, resource allocation, and transportation.

Assignment In assignment problems, there are various facilities (people, machines, and so on) available to complete several required tasks (jobs, processes, and so on). Each facility can be assigned to only one task. The objective is to assign facilities to tasks in order to maximize performance or minimize costs. This type of problem is discussed in detail in chapter 10.

Blending In blending problems, several raw ingredients are mixed into a finished product that meets various specifications. Each ingredient contributes various properties to the finished product at a given cost. The objective is to determine the blend of ingredients that minimizes cost or maximizes contribution and meets technical specifications and supply requirements.

Planning and Scheduling   Many problems involve planning or scheduling. That is, the decision maker must plan or schedule present and future actions to achieve a future goal. In these cases, the problem is to identify the combination of decision activities that satisfies various time period constraints and maximizes return or minimizes costs.

Resource Allocation   Often, there are situations in which decision activities compete for various scarce resources. Each activity contributes a given amount to some objective and utilizes some of the resources. In these circumstances, a manager wants to allocate available resources among activities in a way that optimizes his or her decision objective.

Transportation   In distribution problems, it is necessary to transport goods or services from supply sources to various demand destinations. Each source has an available supply, and each destination requires a given demand. In addition, there are various costs or returns to transport a unit from each source to each destination. The problem is to determine the transportation pattern that minimizes total cost or maximizes total return and meets all demand and supply conditions. Chapter 10 presents a discussion of this problem in detail.

Table 6.2 gives examples of specific applications in these five areas.

GRAPHIC SOLUTION PROCEDURE

After properly formulating a linear program, the next step for the decision maker is to develop a recommended solution for the problem. There is a graphic approach that offers an easy way to solve simple linear programming problems with only two decision variables. Although the procedure is awkward in analyzing three-variable problems and cannot be used for larger problems, it provides an intuitive basis for more practical solution methods. In addition, the graphic approach will aid our understanding of advanced linear programming concepts.

The graphic solution process can be illustrated with the linear program for Saferly's machine shop problem:

maximize $Z = \$8X_1 + \$6X_2$

subject to $.2X_1 + .4X_2 \leq 70$ hours   (Pressing)

$.5X_1 + .25X_2 \leq 100$ hours   (Polishing)

$X_1, X_2 \geq 0$

where Z = Saferly's total dollar profit, X_1 = next week's output of knives (number of cases), and X_2 = next week's output of forks (number of cases).

Table 6.2 Linear Programming Applications*

Problem	Linear Programming Solution
Assignment	
Audit staffing [24]	Determines the assignment of senior accountants to audit supervisions that minimizes total people-hours of effort.
Police patrolling [14, 19]	Determines the assignment of police patrol cars to various areas of a city that minimizes the total time required to reach trouble spots.
Sales force deployment [4, 12, 25]	Determines the assignment of sales representatives to various districts that maximizes total sales.
Blending	
Diet selection [7]	Determines the least-cost menu or food mix that meets nutritional requirements.
Fertilizer composition [13]	Selects the least-cost mix of fertilizer ingredients that meets various quality and labeling requirements.
Waste management [2, 17]	Determines the combination of primary products, secondary goods produced from waste materials, and specially treated waste materials that maximizes total profit and meets various material constraints.
Planning and Scheduling	
Investment planning [3, 23]	Determines the combination of investment alternatives that maximizes total expected yield, subject to various financial considerations.
Production scheduling [10, 15]	Establishes the production schedule that minimizes overall production and inventory costs and satisfies labor, demand, and inventory requirements.
Purchasing [11, 19]	Minimizes the cost of obtaining products or services from several suppliers, subject to various demand and supply requirements.
Resource Allocation	
Media selection [26]	Allocates an available advertising budget among various communications media in a way that maximizes total audience exposure.
Capital budgeting [1, 22]	Maximizes the overall return from investments in various projects, subject to budgetary restrictions.
Product mix selection [6, 18]	Determines the kinds and quantities of products to manufacture that maximize total profit within capacity limitations.
Transportation	
Cargo loading [8, 21]	Determines the kinds and quantities of cargos to load in holds that maximize total revenue without violating weight and volume constraints.
School busing [16, 20]	Selects the routes that minimize the total transportation time to bus students from various neighborhoods to available schools.
Warehouse shipping patterns [5, 9]	Determines the quantities of products shipped from warehouses to sales outlets that minimize total transportation cost and meet demand and supply requirements.

* In this table, the numbers in brackets identify a reference that presents a direct or related application to the corresponding problem.

Figure 6.2 Saferly's Potential Solutions

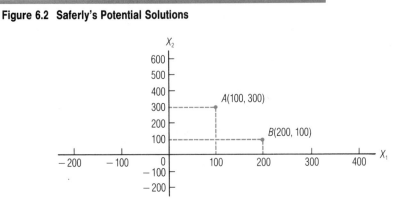

FEASIBLE SOLUTIONS We begin by developing a graph that will display the possible solutions to Saferly's linear program. Figure 6.2 presents this display. In this diagram, the values of X_1 are shown along the horizontal axis and the values of X_2 along the vertical axis. A point on the graph indicates the values of X_1 and X_2 by its position relative to the respective axes. Point A, for instance, signifies a combination of $X_1 = 100$ cases of knives and $X_2 = 300$ cases of forks. Similarly, point B corresponds to a combination of 200 cases of knives and 100 cases of forks. Each of these points identifies a potential solution to the problem and is therefore referred to as a **solution point**. The solution point where the values of the decision variables are zero is known as the origin.

Of course, it is possible to plot an infinite number of solution points. However, the decision maker is interested in only those solutions that satisfy all the restrictions in the linear program. Such solutions are called **feasible solutions**. In this respect, the nonnegativity conditions

$$X_1, X_2 \geq 0$$

require the values of the decision variables to be greater than or equal to zero. As Figure 6.3 demonstrates, these values are the solution points on or to the right of the vertical axis and on or above the horizontal axis. Put another way, the horizontal and vertical axes with zero or positive values bound the area of feasible solutions.

Additional boundaries are established from the other constraints. The inequality

$$.2X_1 + .4X_2 \leq 70 \text{ hours}$$

represents the pressing center restriction. Product combinations that use all the available hours will satisfy the equality

$$.2X_1 + .4X_2 = 70 \text{ hours}$$

Figure 6.3 Nonnegativity Conditions

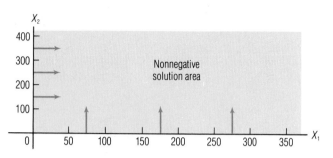

We can readily identify two such combinations. When no cases of knives are produced, $X_1 = 0$ and a maximum of

$$.2(0) + .4X_2 = 70$$

or

$$X_2 = \frac{70}{.4} = 175$$

cases of forks can be produced. The solution point ($X_1 = 0$, $X_2 = 175$) thus satisfies the pressing center equation. Alternatively, when no cases of forks are produced, $X_2 = 0$ and a maximum of

$$.2X_1 + .4(0) = 70$$

or

$$X_1 = \frac{70}{.2} = 350$$

cases of knives can be produced. Hence, a second point satisfying the equation is ($X_1 = 350$, $X_2 = 0$).

The pressing center restriction involves a linear relationship. As a result, Saferly can identify each output combination that uses exactly all the available pressing hours by plotting the two extreme points, ($X_1 = 0$, $X_2 = 175$) and ($X_1 = 350$, $X_2 = 0$), on a graph and connecting these two points with a straight line. If management does this, it will get the results shown in Figure 6.4.

Any point below the line in Figure 6.4 will use fewer than the available pressing hours. That is, such points will satisfy the relationship

$$.2X_1 + .4X_2 < 70 \text{ hours}$$

Figure 6.4 Pressing Center Restriction

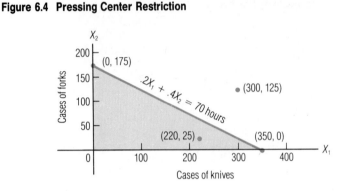

For example, the point $(X_1 = 220, X_2 = 25)$ uses

$$.2X_1 + .4X_2 = .2(220) + .4(25) = 54$$

pressing hours, which is less than the available 70 hours. Points above the line use more than the available hours and are thus unacceptable production alternatives. An example is the combination $X_1 = 300$ and $X_2 = 125$. This point uses

$$.2X_1 + .4X_2 = .2(300) + .4(125) = 110$$

hours, which is more than the available 70 pressing hours.

It should be evident that only solution points *on* or *below* the constraint line satisfy a less-than-or-equal-to constraint. In Figure 6.4, we indicate all such points by shading the area of the graph below the line. Any solution point outside the shaded area is infeasible.

The graph of the polishing center constraint

$$.5X_1 + .25X_2 \le 100 \text{ hours}$$

is constructed in a similar way. We start by graphing the line

$$.5X_1 + .25X_2 = 100 \text{ hours}$$

which shows the combinations of knives and forks using *all* available polishing hours. As before, we find two points that satisfy the equation. Then we connect the points with a straight line. One such point is when $X_1 = 0$ cases of knives and

$$.5(0) + .25X_2 = 100$$

or

$$X_2 = \frac{100}{.25} = 400$$

Figure 6.5 Polishing Center Restriction

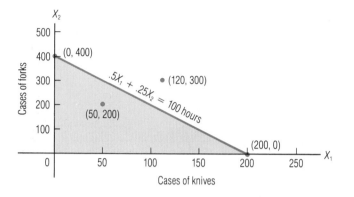

cases of forks. Another point is when $X_2 = 0$ cases of forks and

$$.5X_1 + .25(0) = 100$$

or

$$X_1 = \frac{100}{.5} = 200$$

cases of knives. Figure 6.5 shows the line connecting these points.

It is evident that only points on or below the line satisfy the polishing constraint. Thus, the point $(X_1 = 50, \; X_2 = 200)$ uses less than the available 100 polishing hours and is thus feasible. However, the point $(X_1 = 120, X_2 = 300)$ uses more than the available time and is therefore infeasible. The shaded area in Figure 6.5 identifies all feasible solution points for the polishing center restriction.

Linear programs consist of a system of constraints. Consequently, management must identify the solution points that simultaneously satisfy the entire group of restrictions. In Saferly's case, the decision maker must find the solution points that meet the nonnegativity conditions and are possible within the available pressing and polishing capacity. That is, the company wants to identify the solution points that are common to the shaded regions of Figures 6.3, 6.4, and 6.5.

By superimposing Figures 6.4 and 6.5 on Figure 6.3, Saferly's management will obtain a graph that simultaneously plots all restrictions. Figure 6.6 presents the results. The shaded region of Figure 6.6 identifies the solution points that simultaneously satisfy all of Saferly's restrictions. Such a region is referred to as the **feasible solution area**.

Any point on the boundary or within the feasible solution area is a feasible solution point. An example is the point involving the combination $X_1 = 100$ and $X_2 = 50$ in Figure 6.6. This combination is feasible because

Figure 6.6 Saferly's Feasible Solution Area

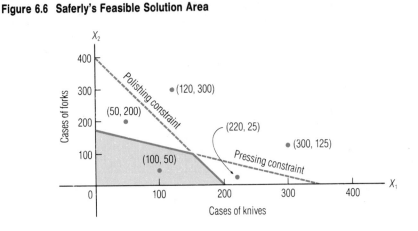

it uses less than the available polishing and pressing hours. Points outside the feasible solution area violate one or more constraints and are thus infeasible or unacceptable. Figure 6.6 shows several examples. Points $(X_1 = 120, X_2 = 300)$ and $(X_1 = 300, X_2 = 125)$ violate both constraints. Point $(X_1 = 50, X_2 = 200)$ satisfies the polishing restriction but uses more than the available pressing hours. On the other hand, a combination of $X_1 = 220$ cases of knives and $X_2 = 25$ cases of forks satisfies the pressing restriction but violates the polishing constraint.

In Saferly's problem, there are only two system constraints (pressing and polishing). Furthermore, each of these restrictions has the same less-than-or-equal-to format and involves both decision variables (X_1 and X_2). Consequently, the company's feasible solution area (the shaded region in Figure 6.6) takes a form that is common to many simple maximization problems.

Yet even simple linear programs can have any number of restrictions. In addition, some of the restrictions may involve only a single decision variable. And it is also possible to have less-than-or-equal-to, equality, and greater-than-or-equal-to restrictions all in the same problem. As a result, the feasible solution area can take a variety of forms. Figure 6.7 displays some of the possibilities. The shaded region in each graph indicates the appropriate feasible solution area.

Figure 6.7a depicts a situation in which each system constraint has a less-than-or-equal-to format but involves only a single decision variable. One of the constraints shows that X_1 must be less than or equal to some constant amount T, while the other restriction indicates that X_2 must not exceed the constant value K. Part (b) also displays a problem with two

Figure 6.7 Possible Feasible Solution Areas

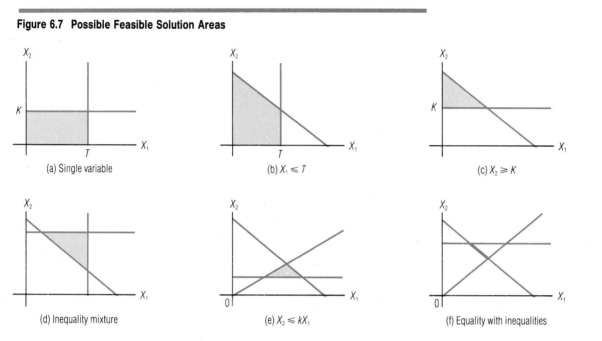

(a) Single variable   (b) $X_1 \leq T$ (c) $X_2 \geq K$

(d) Inequality mixture   (e) $X_2 \leq kX_1$ (f) Equality with inequalities

less-than-or-equal-to system constraints. Although one of the restrictions demonstrates that X_1 again must not exceed a constant amount T, the other involves both decision variables (X_1 and X_2). (Technique exercise 5 at the end of the chapter offers an example that resembles this situation.)

Parts (c) through (f) portray problems that involve a mixture of constraint formats. Furthermore, each of these graphs exhibits a unique feature. In part (c), for instance, one restriction indicates that decision variable X_2 must have a value greater than or equal to some constant amount K. (Thought exercise 2 at the end of the chapter illustrates a comparable situation.) Part (d) is a mixture of the elements from parts (a), (b), and (c). In part (e), the line emerging from the origin 0 identifies a restriction that shows that X_2 must not exceed some constant proportion k of X_1. (Technique exercise 2 offers an example that resembles this situation.) Finally, part (f) depicts a problem involving an equality restriction. In this graph, the solution points must be:

1. On or to the left of the line emerging from the origin 0
2. On or below the horizontal line
3. On the line that intersects both the X_1 and X_2 axes

As a result, the feasible solution area is merely the heavy colored line segment between the horizontal line and the line emerging from the origin. (Technique exercise 7 provides a similar illustration.)

Figure 6.7c–f also demonstrates that the origin 0 need not be in the feasible solution area. In addition, this brief description clearly demonstrates that the specific form of the feasible solution area will depend on the nature of the linear programming problem.

FINDING THE   Once the feasible solution area has been identified, the decision maker is
BEST SOLUTION   ready to find the best solution to the linear program. Such a solution will be the feasible solution that gives the most preferred value of the objective. Saferly's best solution, for instance, would be the output of knives (X_1) and forks (X_2) that maximizes total dollar profit within the available pressing and polishing time.

Trial and Error Method One method for finding the best solution is to use a simple trial and error approach. In this method, the decision maker first compiles an arbitrary list of feasible solution points and then computes the corresponding values of the objective function. Then management selects the feasible point that leads to the most preferred value of the criterion.

Unfortunately, this method can be very cumbersome and time-consuming to implement. Also, there may be an infinite number of feasible solutions. Since it is physically impossible to evaluate all of them, this trial and error approach cannot guarantee that the recommended solution will be optimal.

Isovalue Method These drawbacks have led management scientists to develop more systematic approaches. In one of these approaches, the decision maker first selects an arbitrary value for the objective function and identifies all feasible solution points that yield this value.

Suppose, for example, that Saferly wants to find the feasible solution points that would provide a $480 profit. That is, management seeks the values of X_1 and X_2 in the feasible solution area that will result in the objective function

$$Z = \$8X_1 + \$6X_2 = \$480$$

At one extreme, the company can produce $X_1 = 0$ cases of knives. To obtain a $Z = \$480$ profit, Saferly must then produce

$$\$480 = \$8X_1 + \$6X_2$$
$$= \$8(0) + \$6X_2$$

Figure 6.8 Saferly's $480 Profit Line

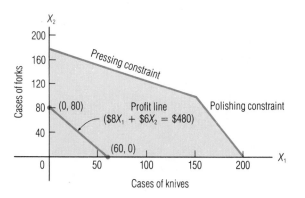

or

$$X_2 = \frac{\$480}{\$6} = 80$$

cases of forks. Hence, the solution point ($X_1 = 0$, $X_2 = 80$) yields a profit of $480. At the other extreme, the company can earn $480 profit by producing $X_2 = 0$ cases of forks and

$$\$480 = \$8X_1 + \$6(0)$$

or

$$X_1 = \frac{\$480}{\$8} = 60$$

cases of knives. Consequently, the solution point ($X_1 = 60$, $X_2 = 0$) also yields the $480 profit.

The profit equation

$$Z = \$480 = \$8X_1 + \$6X_2$$

is a linear relationship. As a result, management can identify each output combination that earns a $Z = \$480$ total dollar profit by plotting the two extreme points, ($X_1 = 0$, $X_2 = 80$) and ($X_1 = 60$, $X_2 = 0$), on a graph and connecting these two points with a straight line. Figure 6.8 presents such a graph of this $480 profit line superimposed on Saferly's feasible solution area. This type of line, depicting all combinations of the decision variables that yield the same specific criterion amount, is referred to as an **isovalue**

Figure 6.9 Saferly's Selected Isoprofit Lines

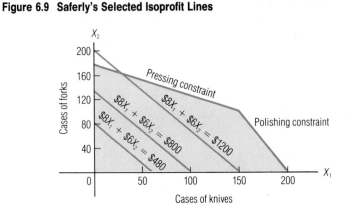

line. In Saferly's case, the criterion is profit. Hence, the $480 line in this graph may be called an **isoprofit line**.

As Figure 6.8 demonstrates, all points on the $480 isoprofit line are well within Saferly's feasible solution area. In fact, there are an infinite number of points on this line. Thus, the company has an unlimited number of feasible product combinations (values of X_1 and X_2) that will provide a $480 total dollar profit.

The next step in the evaluation process is to determine whether there are feasible solution points that yield more preferable values for this criterion. For example, Saferly might want to know if the company can feasibly earn an $800 profit or even a $1200 profit. To find out, management must construct the isoprofit lines for $Z = \$800$ and $Z = \$1200$ and superimpose the results on the feasible solution area. These $800 and $1200 isoprofit lines would be constructed in a manner similar to the development of the $480 isoprofit line. The results are shown in Figure 6.9.

Figure 6.9 demonstrates several important features. For one thing, all points on the $800, as well as $480, isoprofit line are well within the feasible solution area. Hence, there is an infinite number of feasible product combinations that will provide Saferly with an $800, as well as $480, total dollar profit. On the other hand, some points on the $1200 isoprofit line are beyond the pressing constraint line and thus are not feasible. As a result, the feasible product combinations that will provide a $1200 profit are the points on the $1200 isoprofit line between the pressing constraint line and the X_1 axis.

Figure 6.9 also shows that the isoprofit lines are parallel to one another, because each product's per-case contribution to profit remains the same, at $8 for knives and $6 for forks, regardless of the output levels X_1 and X_2. Put another way, each isoprofit line in the linear program will have an identical slope. In addition, notice that total dollar profit increases as the

Figure 6.10 Saferly's Best Solution

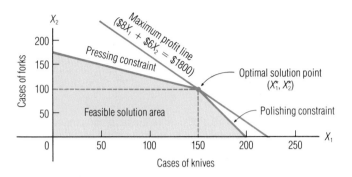

isoprofit lines are moved farther from the origin. This characteristic reflects the fact that lines farther from the origin involve more output of each product. Since larger output leads to higher total profit, the value of this criterion will increase as the isoprofit lines are shifted away from the origin.

In light of these features, Saferly should move the isoprofit line as far from the origin as feasible. That is, management now wants to find the highest-valued isoprofit line having at least one point in common with the feasible solution area. By continuing to shift the isoprofit line away from the origin, the company eventually will obtain the results shown in Figure 6.10.

As Figure 6.10 demonstrates, there is one point on the $1800 isoprofit line, labeled (X_1^*, X_2^*), that touches the boundary of the feasible solution area and thus can be achieved. If the isoprofit line was moved farther from the origin, however, it would be outside the feasible solution area and hence unattainable. Consequently, the (X_1^*, X_2^*) point represents the best solution to Saferly's machine shop problem.

Figure 6.10 shows that point (X_1^*, X_2^*) is at the intersection of the pressing constraint line

$$.2X_1 + .4X_2 = 70 \text{ hours}$$

and the polishing constraint line

$$.5X_1 + .25X_2 = 100 \text{ hours}$$

Therefore, the optimal solution point (X_1^*, X_2^*) must simultaneously satisfy both of these equations.

The polishing equation can be written as follows:

$$X_1 = 200 - .5X_2$$

By substituting this revised equation into the pressing expression and solving for X_2, management will find that

$$.2(200 - .5X_2) + .4X_2 = 70$$

$$.3X_2 = 30$$

$$X_2 = \frac{30}{.3} = 100$$

A substitution of this value into the revised polishing equation then reveals that

$$X_1 = 200 - .5X_2 = 200 - .5(100) = 150$$

Therefore, the optimal solution point is $X_1 = 150$ and $X_2 = 100$. Of course, if the graph is drawn accurately with graph paper and a ruler, as in Figure 6.10, these coordinates can simply be read from the X_1 and X_2 axes.

Since the total profit equation is

$$Z = \$8X_1 + \$6X_2$$

the optimal solution point, $X_1 = 150$ and $X_2 = 100$, yields a total dollar profit of

$$Z = \$8(150) + \$6(100) = \$1800$$

This result is also illustrated in Figure 6.10

According to the graphic analysis, then, Saferly can maximize total dollar profit at $Z = \$1800$ by producing $X_1 = 150$ cases of knives and $X_2 = 100$ cases of forks next week. As Figure 6.10 demonstrates, this solution point is at the intersection of the polishing and pressing constraint lines. Since a point on a line satisfies the restriction exactly, Saferly's optimal product combination uses all of the available 70 pressing hours and 100 polishing hours. Table 6.3 summarizes the isovalue approach to the graphic solution of linear programs.

Extreme Point Method   By examining Figure 6.10, you can see that Saferly's optimal solution point (X_1^*, X_2^*) occurs at the intersection of two (pressing and polishing) constraint lines. In other situations, however, such a point may be on one of the axes rather than at the intersection of system constraint lines. It all depends on the slope of the isovalue line.

Figure 6.11 shows some of the possibilities. In each graph, the shaded region identifies the relevant feasible solution area, the parallel lines are isovalue lines, and the dot represents the optimal solution point.

Note that when the optimal solution point is on one of the axes, the decision variable on this axis has a positive value. On the other hand, the other decision variable is equal to zero. In Figure 6.11a, for example, the

Table 6.3 Graphic Solution to Linear Programs with the Isovalue Approach

1. Prepare a graph of the feasible solution area for the linear program.
2. Draw lines that show all the values of the decision variables yielding the same specific amount of the criterion. These lines are the isovalue lines.
3. Move parallel isovalue lines toward more preferred amounts of the criterion until further movement would take such a line completely outside the feasible solution area. In a maximization problem, the decision maker should move the isovalue line as far from the origin as feasible. In a minimization situation, the isovalue line should be moved as close to the origin as possible.
4. The feasible solution point that touches the most preferred isovalue line represents the optimal solution to the linear program. In a maximization problem, the optimal solution point will touch the largest-valued feasible isovalue line. In a minimization situation, it will touch the smallest-valued feasible isovalue line.
5. Set decision variables equal to the values specified by the optimal solution point.

Figure 6.11 Possible Optimal Solution Points

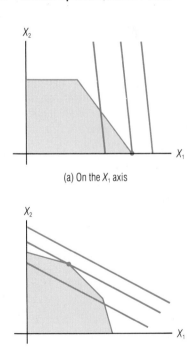

(a) On the X_1 axis

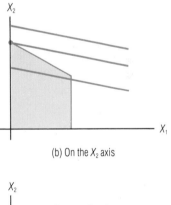

(b) On the X_2 axis

(c) At the intersection of the upper two restrictions

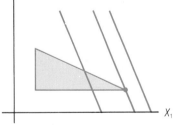

(d) At the intersection of the upper and lower restrictions

Figure 6.12 Saferly's Extreme Points

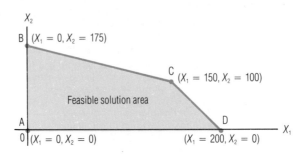

optimal solution point has $X_1 > 0$ and $X_2 = 0$, while in part (b), $X_1 = 0$ and $X_2 > 0$.

An examination of Figures 6.10 and 6.11 will show that in each case the optimal solution point occurs at a vertex, or corner, of the feasible solution area. The vertex, or intersection can occur:

1. Between two restriction lines (as at the optimal solution points in Figure 6.10 and Figure 6.11c and d)
2. Between a restriction line and one of the axes (as at the optimal solution points in Figure 6.11a and b)
3. At the origin of the graph (as at point 0 in Figure 6.10)

Such a vertex is also referred to as an **extreme point**.

The result is not a coincidence. Indeed, *an optimal solution to every linear program occurs at an extreme point of the feasible solution area.* As a result, when seeking the best linear programming solution, the decision maker need not always resort to the isovalue method (Table 6.3). Instead, if there are relatively few vertices, or because of user preference, it may be easier to identify and evaluate only the extreme points.

Consider Saferly's situation. This company's feasible solution area, which was originally shown as Figure 6.6, is reproduced in modified form in Figure 6.12. Note that Saferly's feasible solution area involves the extreme points labeled A, B, C, and D. By substituting the values of the decision variables at these points into the total profit equation

$$Z = \$8X_1 + \$6X_2$$

management will obtain the results presented in Table 6.4. These results indicate that extreme point C, $X_1 = 150$ and $X_2 = 100$, yields the largest total dollar profit at $Z = \$1800$.

According to the extreme point method, then, Saferly can maximize total profit at $1800 by producing 150 cases of knives and 100 cases of

Table 6.4 Evaluation of Saferly's Extreme Points

Extreme Point	Values of the Decision Variables		Value of the Criterion
	Cases of Knives	Cases of Forks	Total Dollar Profit
	X_1	X_2	$Z = \$8X_1 + \$6X_2$
A	0	0	$Z = \$8(0) + \$6(0) = \$0$
B	0	175	$Z = \$8(0) + \$6(175) = \$1050$
C	150	100	$Z = \$8(150) + \$6(100) = \$1800$
D	200	0	$Z = \$8(200) + \$6(0) = \$1600$

Table 6.5 Graphic Solution of Linear Programs with the Extreme Point Method

1. Prepare a graph of the feasible solution area for the linear program.
2. Identify the extreme points of the feasible solution area.
3. Substitute each extreme point into the objective function.
4. The optimal solution is the extreme point that leads to the most-preferred value of the objective.

forks next week. This recommendation, of course, is the same as the solution obtained from the isovalue approach. Hence, either approach offers an effective method to determine the optimal solution graphically for a simple linear program with only two decision variables. Table 6.5 summarizes the extreme point method.

MINIMIZATION PROBLEMS The isovalue and extreme point methods can also be applied to linear programs that involve two decision variables in a minimization situation. Example 6.2 illustrates.

EXAMPLE 6.2 A Diet Problem

Al Cook has learned from a nutrition book that his family needs at least 330 grams of protein and 45 milligrams of iron per day for sound health. These nutrients can be obtained from meat and vegetable products. Each pound of meat costs an average of $1.60 and contains an average of 150 grams of protein and 15 milligrams of iron, while each pound of vegetables costs 50 cents ($.50) and has 10 grams of protein and 5 milligrams of iron. Al wants to determine the quantities of food that meet the nutritional requirements at least cost.

Objective   It will cost Al $1.60 to purchase a pound of meat and $.50 per pound for vegetables. By letting

X_1 = the number of pounds of meat purchased per day

X_2 = the number of pounds of vegetables purchased per day

Z = Al Cook's total daily food expenditures

we can represent the total daily food cost by

(6.6) $Z = \$1.60X_1 + \$.50X_2$

Al has the discretion to determine how many pounds of meat and vegetables to purchase daily. Hence, X_1 and X_2 represent his decision variables. Also, since Al wants to purchase the least-cost diet (least-cost combination of X_1 and X_2), the objective can be expressed as follows:

(6.7)   minimize $Z = \$1.60X_1 + \$.50X_2$

Restrictions   Each pound of meat contains 150 grams of protein, while a pound of vegetables has 10 grams of protein. Consequently, there will be

$150X_1 + 10X_2$

total grams of protein supplied by the entire diet. Since Al must purchase a diet that contains at least the 330 grams of protein required by his family

(6.8) $150X_1 + 10X_2 \geq 330$ grams

In other words, the total protein content of the diet ($150X_1 + 10X_2$) must equal or exceed his family's daily requirements (330 grams).

   In addition, the diet must contain at least 45 milligrams of iron per day. Meat provides 15 milligrams per pound, while each pound of vegetables has 5 milligrams of iron. Thus,

(6.9) $15X_1 + 5X_2 \geq 45$ milligrams

That is, the total supply of iron ($15X_1 + 5X_2$) must equal or exceed the demand (45 milligrams) for this nutrient.

   Finally, Al cannot purchase a negative amount of meat or vegetables. Therefore, the expression

(6.10) $X_1, X_2 \geq 0$

represents the nonnegativity conditions.

Linear Program   By collecting objective function (6.7), system constraints (6.8) and (6.9), and nonnegativity conditions (6.10), Al Cook can represent his family's diet problem with the following linear program:

minimize $Z = \$1.60X_1 + \$.50X_2$ Objective function

Figure 6.13 Al Cook's Feasible Solution Area and Extreme Points

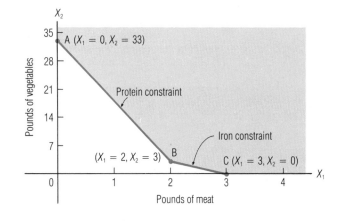

subject to

$$150X_1 + 10X_2 \geq 330 \text{ grams (Protein)}$$
$$15X_1 + 5X_2 \geq 45 \text{ milligrams (Iron)}$$

}System constraints

$$X_1, X_2 \geq 0$$

Nonnegativity
conditions

This linear program states that Al wants to purchase the diet of meats and
vegetables that will minimize total food expenditures. In doing so,
however, Al must ensure that the diet satisfies his family's minimum daily
protein and iron requirements.

Feasible Solution Area By plotting the protein and iron restrictions on
the same graph with the nonnegativity conditions, Al Cook will obtain the
graph in Figure 6.13. The shaded region in this graph identifies Al Cook's
feasible solution area. Also, notice that the feasible solution points must be
on or to the right of (above) both the protein and iron constraint lines,
because each of these constraints involves a greater-than-or-equal-to
relationship. In such cases, there will be no upper bound on the values of
the decision variables (X_1 and X_2).

Optimal Solution Suppose that Al uses the extreme point method to find
the least-cost diet. Figure 6.13 demonstrates that his feasible solution area
involves the extreme points labeled A, B, and C. By substituting the values
of the decision variables at these points into his total cost equation (6.6), Al
will obtain the results presented in Table 6.6. These results indicate that
extreme point B, $X_1 = 2$ and $X_2 = 3$, yields the smallest total expenditure
at $Z = \$4.70$.

Table 6.6 Evaluation of Al Cook's Extreme Points

| Extreme Point | Value of the Decision Variables | | Value of the Criterion |
	Pounds of Meat X_1	Pounds of Vegetables X_2	Total Daily Food Cost $Z = \$1.60X_1 + \$.50X_2$
A	0	33	$Z = \$1.60(0) + \$.50(33) = \$16.50$
B	2	3	$Z = \$1.60(2) + \$.50(3) = \$4.70$
C	3	0	$Z = \$1.60(3) + \$.50(0) = \$4.80$

According to the graphic analysis, then, Al Cook can minimize total food cost at $4.70 per day by purchasing 2 pounds of meat and 3 pounds of vegetables daily. Furthermore, in Figure 6.13, you can see that the minimum-cost food combination ($X_1 = 2$, $X_2 = 3$) is at the intersection of the protein and iron constraint lines. Thus, the optimal diet meets the minimum protein and iron requirements exactly. In other words, such a diet provides no excess amounts of either nutrient.

DECISION CONSIDERATIONS

In attempting to solve a linear programming problem, the decision maker may encounter some special situations, such as linear programs that involve one or more unnecessary restrictions, linear programs that have no practical solutions, or linear programs that have more than one optimal solution. Since these situations can affect the development of an optimal solution, they warrant the decision maker's attention.

REDUNDANT RESTRICTIONS

Consider Example 6.3.

EXAMPLE 6.3 Media Selection

The advertising agency promoting the new sports car the Zoommobile wants to get the best possible exposure for the product within the available $200,000 budget. To do so, the agency must decide how much to spend on its two most effective media: evening television spots and large magazine ads. Each television spot costs $20,000 and a magazine ad involves a $5000 expenditure. Based on industry ratings, each television spot is expected to reach 400,000 people, and a magazine ad 150,000 people.

Dawn Shawn, the agency director, knows from experience that it is important to use both media. In this way, the advertising will reach the broadest spectrum of potential Zoommobile customers. As a result, she decides to contract for at least four but no more than twelve television spots and a minimum of six magazine ads.

Consultations with the agency's research director, with the client, and with other experts have led Dawn to formulate the problem as the following linear program:

maximize

$$Z = 400,000X_1 + 150,000X_2$$

subject to

$$\$20,000X_1 + \$5000X_2 \leq \$200,000 \text{ (Budget)}$$

$$X_1 \leq 12 \text{ (Maximum TV)}$$

$$X_1 \geq 4 \text{ (Minimum TV)}$$

$$X_2 \geq 6 \text{ (Magazine)}$$

$$X_1, X_2 \geq 0$$

where Z = total audience exposure, X_1 = the number of evening television spots, and X_2 = the number of large magazine ads.

Dawn wants to select the media combination (values of X_1 and X_2) that will maximize total audience exposure (Z).

Figure 6.14 presents a graphic representation of the restrictions for the linear program in Example 6.3. The shaded region in this graph identifies the feasible solution area. You can see that the agency's feasible solution area is defined completely by the minimum TV, magazine, and budget constraint lines. The maximum TV restriction line, on the other hand, has no effect on this area. Dawn could satisfy this maximum TV constraint automatically by spending no more than the available budget on television and magazine advertising. In effect, then, the maximum TV restriction is unnecessary, or irrelevant, to the solution of the problem. A constraint such as this, which does not affect the feasible solution area, is known as a **redundant restriction**. It can be removed from the problem without affecting the optimal solution.

Figure 6.14 Dawn Shawn's Feasible Solution Area

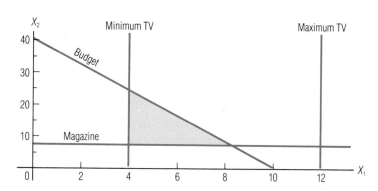

UNBOUNDED PROBLEMS In some linear programs, the restrictions do not put an effective limit on the values of the decision variables. Example 6.4 provides an illustration.

EXAMPLE 6.4 A Product Mix Problem

An office supply company manufactures two types of paper pads. The standard pad earns \$10 profit per box, and the legal pad yields \$25 profit per box. Customers require a combined total of at least 2000 boxes per month. The company's sales staff will have to work at least 20,000 hours per month to meet this demand. Past experience indicates that salespeople need 5 hours to sell a box of standard pads and 20 hours to sell a box of legal pads. Sales effort includes travel time, presentations, order taking, and follow-up. The company seeks the combination of pads that maximizes total monthly profit.

By letting

X_1 = the number of boxes of standard pads

X_2 = the number of boxes of legal pads

Z = the total monthly profit

we can express the company's problem by the following linear program:

maximize $Z = \$10X_1 + \$25X_2$

subject to $X_1 + X_2 \geq 2000$ boxes   (Demand)

$5X_1 + 20X_2 \geq 20{,}000$ hours   (Sales staff)

$X_1, X_2 \geq 0$

A graphic representation of this linear program is presented in Figure 6.15. As the figure demonstrates, the system constraints in the office supply company's linear program do not place an upper boundary on the feasible solution area. This region extends outward indefinitely from the demand and sales staff constraint lines. Hence, it is feasible for the company to produce an unlimited quantity of standard and legal pads. Also, look at the isoprofit lines in this graph. It is always possible to move toward a higher-valued isoprofit line and still have a feasible solution point. As a result, the company can obtain any monthly profit it wants, even one that is unlimited, or infinitely large. Such a linear program is known as an **unbounded problem**.

Few, if any, problems in practice are really unbounded. Experience tells us that it is impossible to increase profits indefinitely. Thus, when a linear program is unbounded, it typically means that the problem has been improperly formulated or the model is inappropriate.

Figure 6.15 The Office Supply Problem

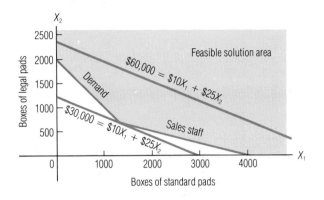

INFEASIBLE PROBLEMS In some linear programs, there is no combination of decision variables that simultaneously satisfies all the restrictions in the problem. Example 6.5 illustrates.

EXAMPLE 6.5 A Space Allocation Problem

I. M. Warm, an environmental design professor, has been given a federal grant to develop a prototype solar-powered home. Preliminary research indicates that the living area of such a home can be constructed for $40 per square foot. The house also requires a separate area for the installation and operation of solar energy equipment. This energy area can be constructed for $100 per square foot. The solar house must be competitive in the new housing market. To do so, it must have at least 1600 square feet of living area and cost no more than $60,000.

Under current solar technology, at least 300 square feet of energy area are needed to power such a home. The government wants Warm to determine the maximum feasible size of such a house.

By letting

X_1 = the number of square feet of living area

X_2 = the number of square feet of solar energy area

Z = the total number of square feet of the solar home

Figure 6.16 Warm's Space Allocation Restrictions

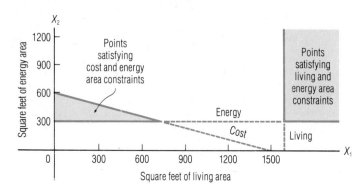

Warm can represent the problem with the following linear program:

maximize $Z = X_1 + X_2$

subject to $\$40X_1 + \$100X_2 \le \$60,000$ (Cost)

$X_1 \ge 1600$ square feet   (Living area)

$X_2 \ge 300$ square feet   (Energy area)

$X_1, X_2 \ge 0$

Figure 6.16 offers a graphic representation of the restrictions in Warm's linear program. You can see that there is no feasible solution area. That is, there are no solution points that simultaneously satisfy all the restrictions. The shaded area in the left-hand portion of the graph depicts the points satisfying the cost and energy area constraints, while the shaded region in the right-hand portion identifies the points that satisfy the living area and energy area restrictions. However, there are no points that satisfy all three constraints (cost, living area, and energy area). Therefore, there is no feasible solution to the linear program. Such a program is known as an **infeasible problem**.

As a result, Warm must advise the government that solar houses are not feasible under current cost, life-style, and technological conditions. In fact, the professor can utilize linear programming concepts to identify the causes of infeasibility. The government could then use such information to develop appropriate actions and policies.

For example, Figure 6.16 shows that the cost constraint line is to the left of (below) the living area restriction line. Feasible solution points for the

Figure 6.17 Feasible Living Area for Warm's House

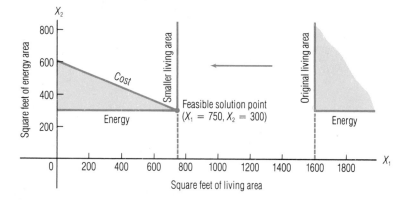

living area restriction, however, are to the right of (above) or on the living area constraint line. Thus, it is not possible to construct a solar house with the minimum desirable living area (1600 square feet) at the maximum acceptable cost ($60,000).

However, a solar house could be feasible if consumers would be satisfied with a smaller living area. The decision maker can find the feasible size by shifting the living area constraint line to the left. This shift should continue until a point of tangency is reached between the living area constraint line and the boundary of the shaded region in the left-hand portion of Figure 6.16. The appropriate movement is illustrated in Figure 6.17. As you can see, tangency would occur at the intersection of the cost and energy constraint lines. At this point,

$$\$40X_1 + \$100X_2 = \$60,000 \qquad \text{(Cost)}$$

$$X_2 = 300 \qquad \text{(Energy area)}$$

Thus, the feasible size would be

$$X_2 = 300 \text{ square feet of energy area}$$

and

$$\$40X_1 + \$100(300) = 60,000$$

$$X_1 = 750 \text{ square feet of living area}$$

for a total of

$$Z = X_1 + X_2 = 300 + 750 = 1050 \text{ square feet}$$

Figure 6.18 Feasible Cost for Warm's House

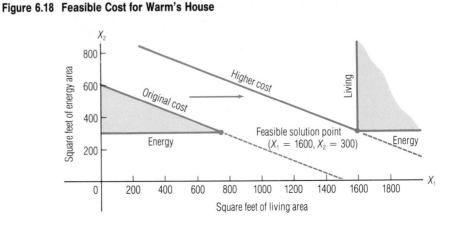

Alternatively, a solar home could be feasible if consumers would be willing to pay more for the house. Warm can find the higher cost by shifting the cost constraint line to the right. This shift should continue until a point of tangency is reached between the cost constraint line and the boundary of the shaded region in the right-hand portion of Figure 6.16. The appropriate movement is illustrated in Figure 6.18. You can see that the tangency would occur at the intersection of the living area and energy area constraint lines. At this point,

$X_1 = 1600$ square feet of living area

and

$X_2 = 300$ square feet of energy area

for a total of

$Z = X_1 + X_2 = 1600 + 300 = 1900$ square feet

The feasible cost would then be

$\$40X_1 + \$100X_2 = \$40(1600) + \$100(300) = \$94,000$

TIES FOR THE BEST SOLUTION A linear program can have two or more optimal solutions. In such cases, the program is said to have **multiple** or **alternative optima**. Example 6.6 illustrates.

EXAMPLE 6.6 A Blending Problem

A homeowner wants to paint the interior of his dwelling with flat and enamel finishes. Flat paint costs $6 per gallon, while each gallon of enamel costs $12. An average of 2 hours is needed to apply a gallon of flat, and 4 hours are needed for each gallon of enamel paint. The job will take at least 80 hours to complete. There are at least 2200 square feet of living area to paint. Each gallon of flat paint covers an average of 100 square feet, while a gallon of enamel covers 20 square feet. The homeowner wants to use the combination of paints that minimizes the cost of the job.

The homeowner's paint-blending problem can be represented by the following linear program:

$$\text{minimize} \quad Z = \$6X_1 + \$12X_2$$

$$\text{subject to} \quad 100X_1 + 20X_2 \geq 2200 \text{ square feet} \quad \text{(Size)}$$
$$2X_1 + 4X_2 \geq 80 \text{ hours} \quad\quad\quad \text{(Time)}$$
$$X_1, X_2 \geq 0$$

where Z = the total cost of the job, X_1 = the number of gallons of flat paint, and X_2 = the number of gallons of enamel paint.

Figure 6.19 provides a graphic solution to the homeowner's linear program using the isovalue approach. You can see that the minimum **isocost line**

$$Z = \$240 = \$6X_1 + \$12X_2$$

is parallel to, and hence coincides with, the time constraint line

$$2X_1 + 4X_2 = 80 \text{ hours}$$

As a result, $(X_1 = 20, X_2 = 10)$ and $(X_1 = 40, X_2 = 0)$ are both optimal solution points. In fact, any point on the line segment connecting these two points is optimal. Since there is an infinite number of such points, the homeowner has an unlimited number of paint blends (combinations of X_1 and X_2 values) that will minimize total cost at $240.

In a linear program with alternative optima, then, an infinite number of combinations for the decision variables will lead to the same best solution of the problem. Such a program offers an ideal situation because it enables management to consider additional criteria and then implement the most expedient solution.

For example, consider the optimal solution points $(X_1 = 20, X_2 = 10)$ and $(X_1 = 40, X_2 = 0)$. Both combinations result in the same minimum cost of $240. The first blend (20 gallons of flat paint and 10 gallons of

Figure 6.19 Optimal Solutions to the Homeowner's Blending Problem

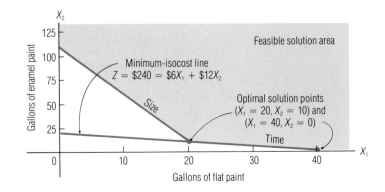

enamel) is at the intersection of the time and size constraint lines in Figure 6.19. Consequently, this blend requires the minimum hours and square feet to complete the job. On the other hand, the second blend (40 gallons of flat and 0 gallons of enamel paint) is on the time constraint line but to the right of (above) the size constraint line in Figure 6.19. Hence, this combination requires the minimum time but more than the minimum square footage to complete the job. In other words, the second blend involves painting excess space (probably reflecting a need to apply more than one coat) but avoiding the use of enamel. If the homeowner does not like to work with enamel, he could select this second blend. However, if the homeowner prefers to paint the minimum space, he could pick the first blend.

SUMMARY This chapter introduced a methodology, called linear programming, that can help decision makers solve a wide variety of management and economic problems. The initial section presented a discussion dealing with the nature of the methodology. We saw how to formulate the objective, system constraints, and nonnegativity conditions of a linear program, a process summarized in Figure 6.1. Next, we examined the common characteristics of all linear programs. These characteristics were summarized in Table 6.1. Then, this first section presented the major classes of linear programming problems: assignment, blending, planning and scheduling, resource allocation, and transportation. Table 6.2 gave some examples of specific applications in these five areas.

In the second section, several linear programs were formulated and solved by alternative graphic procedures. Among the methods we considered were the isovalue approach, summarized in Table 6.3, and the alternative, frequently preferable method of extreme points, summarized in Table 6.5. Each approach provides the optimal combination of decision variables in a linear program. Sometimes, the optimum is obtained by a maximization process, while in other situations it results from a minimization procedure.

The final section of the chapter presented some special situations that affect the development of an optimal solution. In one of these situations, the problem involves one or more unnecessary or redundant restrictions. Another special condition deals with linear programs that do not have effective bounds or limits on the values of the decision variables. A third situation involves infeasible linear programs. And the last condition deals with problems that have two or more optimal solutions. In each case, we showed how to identify and deal with the special condition.

The concepts presented in this chapter will be used extensively throughout the remainder of the text.

Glossary

decision variables The controllable inputs in a linear programming problem.

extreme point A vertex, or intersection point, on the graph of the feasible solution area for a linear program. The intersection can occur between two restriction lines, between a restriction line and one of the axes, or at the origin.

feasible solution A combination of values for the decision variables that simultaneously satisfies all the restrictions in a linear program.

feasible solution area The region of a graph that contains the feasible solution points for a linear programming problem.

infeasible problem A linear program in which there is no combination of decision variables that simultaneously satisfies all restrictions.

isocost line An isovalue line when the criterion is cost.

isoprofit line An isovalue line when the criterion is profit.

isovalue line The line on a graph that depicts all combinations of the decision variables yielding the same specific amount of the criterion variable.

linear program The complete formulation of a linear programming problem that includes the objective function, system constraints, and nonnegativity conditions.

linear programming A methodology for selecting the combination of activities that most effectively uses an organizational unit's resources and meets specified restrictive guidelines.

linear relationship A relationship in which each variable appears in a separate term and is raised to the first power (has an exponent of one). In a linear program, such a relationship indicates that each decision variable has an independent effect on the objective and the constraints and contributes a constant, proportional amount to the objective and each system constraint.

multiple (alternative) optima   The existence of more than one optimal solution to a linear program.

nonnegativity conditions   Constraints requiring the decision variables to have values greater than or equal to zero.

objective function   A mathematical expression that describes the objective of a problem.

redundant restriction   A system constraint that does not affect the feasible solution area and thus is irrelevant to the solution of a linear programming problem.

solution point   A point on a graph that identifies a particular value of each decision variable in a linear programming solution.

system constraint   A constraint on the linear programming solution that arises from limited resources, policy requirements, and the like.

unbounded problem   A linear program in which the constraints do not put an effective limit on the values of the decision variables.

References

1. Anderson, D. "Models for Determining Least-Cost Investments in Electricity Supply." *Bell Journal of Economics* (Spring 1972): 267.

2. Avani, S. "A Linear Programming Approach to Air-Cleaner Design." *Operations Research* (March–April 1974): 295.

3. Balbirer, S. D., and D. Shaw. "An Application of Linear Programming to Bank Financial Planning." *Interfaces* (October 1981): 77.

4. Bandyopadhyay, J. K., et al. "A Resource Allocation Model for an Employability Planning System." *Interfaces* (October 1980): 90.

5. Brosch, L. C., et al. "Boxcars, Linear Programming, and the Sleeping Kitten." *Interfaces* (December 1980): 53.

6. Byrd, J., and L. T. Moore. "The Application of a Product Mix Linear Programming Model in Corporate Policy Making." *Management Science* (September 1978): 1342.

7. Chappell, A. E. "Linear Programming Cuts Costs in Production of Animal Feeds." *Operational Research Quarterly* (March 1974): 19.

8. Darnell, D. W., and C. Loflin. "National Airlines Fuel Management and Allocation Model." *Interfaces* (February 1977): 1.

9. Drayer, W., and S. Seabury. "Facilities Expansion Model." Part 2. *Interfaces* (February 1975): 104.

10. Dyckhoff, H. "A New Linear Programming Approach to the Cutting Stock Problem." *Operations Research*

(November–December 1981): 1092.

11. Feldstein, M., and H. Luft. "Distribution Constraints in Public Expenditure Planning." *Management Science* (August 1973): 1414.

12. Freed, N., and F. Glover. "A Linear Programming Approach to the Discriminant Problem." *Decision Sciences* (January 1981): 68.

13. Glassey, C. R., and V. K. Gupta. "A Linear Programming Analysis of Paper Recycling." *Management Science* (December 1974): 392.

14. Heroux, R. L., and W. A. Wallace. "Linear Programming and Financial Analysis of the New Community Development Process." *Management Science* (April 1973): 857.

15. Hilal, S. S., and W. Erikson. "Matching Supplies to Save Lives: Linear Programming the Production of Heart Valves." *Interfaces* (December 1981): 48.

16. Koch, J. V. "A Linear Programming Model of Resource Allocation in a University." *Decision Sciences* (October 1973): 494.

17. Kohn, R. E. "Application of Linear Programming to a Controversy on Air Pollution Control." *Management Science* (June 1971): 609.

18. Kotak, D. B. "Applications of Linear Programming to Plywood Manufacture." Part

2. *Interfaces* (November 1976): 56.

19. Laidlaw, C. D. *Linear Programming for Urban Development and Plan Evaluation.* New York: Praeger, 1972.

20. McKeown, P., and B. Workman. "A Study in Using Linear Programming to Assign Students to Schools." *Interfaces* (August 1976): 96.

21. Nash, B. "A Simplified Alternative to Current Airline Fuel Allocation Models." *Interfaces* (February 1981): 1.

22. Rosenblatt, M. J., and J. V. Jucker. "Capital Expenditures Decision Making: Some Tools and Trends." *Interfaces* (February 1979): 63.

23. Schleef, H. J. "Using Linear Programming for Planning Life Insurance Purchases." *Decision Sciences* (July 1980): 522.

24. Summers, E. L. "The Audit Staff Assignment Problem: A Linear Programming Analysis." *The Accounting Review* (July 1972): 443.

25. Thie, H. J., and R. C. Lorbeer. "Better Personnel Management Through Applied Management Science." *Interfaces* (May 1976): 68.

26. Thomas, J. "Linear Programming Models for Production-Advertising Decisions." *Management Science* (April 1971): 474.

1. Determine if linear programming is appropriate in each of the following situations. Speculate on the nature of the objective function and constraints and how these factors influence your answer.

   a. A national steel manufacturer wants to know the number of units that should be produced each day in a sequential schedule so as to maximize total steel production while meeting certain contractual, budget, and order constraints.

   b. A student wants to know the combinations of foods to purchase in the university cafeteria so as to minimize the cost of his diet while meeting certain minimum nutritional constraints.

   c. A homeowner wants to place a second mortgage on her dwelling to obtain cash for investment in the stock market. She wants to know what combination of stocks in related industries to buy for her portfolio while meeting certain minimum investment requirements and her budget constraint.

   d. A regional electric utility wants to maximize its revenue from two customer groups while meeting certain service, budget, and capacity requirements.

2. Advertising Associates, Inc., handles radio and television promotional jobs and placements for a wide range of clients. The agency's objective is to maximize the total audience exposure for its clients' products. Research indicates that each radio spot results in 1000 exposures, while each television spot contributes an independent 3000 exposures. A radio spot costs $4000 and a television spot costs $20,000. Clients provide Associates with a maximum monthly budget of $1 million. Contracts with radio networks require a minimum of 100 spots per month. The agency employs account executives to place the spots. Past experience indicates that each radio spot takes 20 hours of executive effort and each television spot uses 50 hours. The agency's account executives are available for 4000 hours per month.

   a. Define the appropriate criterion and decision variables for this problem.

   b. Develop the relevant linear program.

3. A financial counselor wants to develop an investment portfolio that will maximize a customer's total dollar return. Two types of independent investments are available: stocks, whose average return is 10%, and bonds, which return an average 6% over cost. The customer has $1000 available and prefers to invest exactly twice as much in bonds as in stocks. As a result of other commitments, the counselor can devote no more than 90 hours to research and placement of the customer's portfolio. Past experience indicates that stocks require 6 minutes (.1 hour) of effort per dollar invested and bonds require 12 minutes (.2 hour).

    a. Define the appropriate criterion and decision variables for this
       problem.
    b. Develop the relevant linear program.

4. Intuitively explain why the optimal solution to a linear
programming problem must occur at an extreme point. Illustrate
your explanation graphically.

5. A government agency wants to maximize the total number of cases
it handles. Ordinarily, the agency deals with projects that are
labeled type A and type B. This agency has been provided with a
$10,000 budget, 100 staff hours, and 200 administrative hours. It
usually takes 5 staff hours to complete each type A case and 50 staff
hours for a type B case. Also, each type A and type B case costs the
same $100 to complete. A type A case uses 50 administrative hours,
while a type B case takes 40 administrative hours.

    a. Define the appropriate criterion and decision variables for this
       agency.
    b. Formulate the relevant linear program.
    c. After reviewing this linear program, a budget analyst in the
       government's accounting office advises the chair of the
       Congressional Appropriations Committee that this agency's
       budget can be reduced considerably. How did the analyst arrive
       at this conclusion? How much can the budget be reduced?

6. An airline executive seeks the combination of domestic and foreign
flights that will maximize total quarterly profit. Each domestic flight
contributes $2500 to profit, and a foreign flight contributes $5000 to
profit. Airline regulations require the company to schedule a total of
exactly 1000 flights per quarter. A second regulation requires the
number of foreign flights to be no more than 1/4 of the number of
domestic flights. This airline can staff as many as 10,000 hours per
quarter. Past experience indicates that a domestic flight takes 20
staff hours and each foreign flight takes 40 staff hours per quarter.

    a. Define the appropriate criterion and decision variables for the
       airline.
    b. Develop the relevant linear program.
    c. Determine the solution to this problem. How would this solution
       influence the company's case in future regulatory hearings?

7. The product mix problem given in Example 6.4 is represented by
the following linear program:

maximize $Z = \$10X_1 + \$25X_2$

subject to $X_1 + X_2 \geq 2000$ boxes   (Demand)

           $5X_1 + 20X_2 \geq 20{,}000$ hours   (Sales staff)

           $X_1, X_2 \geq 0$

where X_1 = the number of boxes of standard pads, X_2 = the number of boxes of legal pads, and Z = the total monthly profit. The office supply company finds that this problem is unbounded. After a careful reevaluation, the company concludes that the following constraint should have been included in the linear program:

$$20X_1 + 40X_2 \leq 80{,}000 \text{ units} \qquad \text{(Production capacity)}$$

How does this new constraint affect the problem? Explain and illustrate graphically.

8. If a linear program has multiple best solutions, does the optimal solution point still occur at an extreme point? Explain and illustrate graphically.

9. How can the existence of alternative optima aid the following decision makers?

    a. A plumbing contractor seeks the minimum cost combination of two types of fixtures while meeting legal requirements, budget constraints, and customer preferences.

    b. A plant manager seeks the maximum profit combination of two types of products while meeting capacity limitations and union contractual requirements.

    c. An amusement park director seeks the combination of hours of operation for two types of attractions that will maximize profit, subject to budget and capacity limitations and a union contractual requirement on minimum staff size.

10. Refer back to Example 6.3.

    a. Determine the optimal solution to this problem.

    b. In this problem, each television spot provides an audience exposure of 400,000 persons, while a magazine ad yields an exposure of only 150,000 persons. Yet you will find that the agency's optimal media plan involves six times as many magazine ads as television spots. Why?

    c. Does the optimal media plan exactly meet each constraint in the problem? Explain. How might the decision maker use this information?

11. We saw that the optimal solutions to Examples 6.1 and 6.2 each involved a combination of decision variables that exactly met all system constraints in the problem. Determine whether the solution to each of the following problems also meets all system constraints exactly. How might the decision maker in each of these examples utilize the additional information about constraint usage?

    a. Example 6.4

    b. Example 6.5

    c. Example 6.6.

12. Do you agree or disagree with each of the following statements? Explain.

a. Linear programming is a useless technique since its assumptions are so restrictive.
b. Minimization and maximization problems in linear programming do not differ in any way in terms of the graphic solution procedure.
c. A linear programming problem cannot be solved by the graphic solution method if there are three or more constraints.
d. The prime purpose of the linear programming analysis is to overload the decision maker with unnecessary information.
e. Points between corners on the boundary of the feasible solution area are never as desirable as points at the corners.
f. In a minimization problem, the graphic objective is to find the feasible activity combination as close to the origin as possible.
g. To find the optimal solution to a linear program, the decision maker must evaluate each extreme point.
h. A minimization problem cannot be unbounded.

Technique Exercises

1. Consider the following product mix problem:

maximize $Z = \$7X_1 + \$5X_2$

subject to $.2X_1 + .5X_2 \leq 60$ hours   (Labor)
$.4X_1 + .2X_2 \leq 40$ hours   (Capital)
$X_1, X_2 \geq 0$

where $Z =$ the total dollar profit per period, $X_1 =$ the number of units of product A, and $X_2 =$ the number of units of product B.

a. Determine the feasible solution area.
b. Show that any point lying within that area leads to lower profit contribution than any point on the boundary. Use a maximum of three such point comparisons in your demonstration.
c. Solve the problem.

2. Determine the optimal solution to the following problem for an investment counselor:

maximize $Z = .15X_1 + .1X_2$

subject to $X_1 + X_2 \leq \$1000$ (Investment)
$.1X_1 + .2X_2 \leq 90$ hours   (Counselor's time)
$X_1 = .5X_2$ (Customer preference)
$X_1, X_2 \geq 0$

where $Z =$ the total dollar return, $X_1 =$ the dollar amount invested in stocks, and $X_2 =$ the dollar amount invested in bonds. Explain the solution to the counselor's customer.

3. Determine the optimal solution to the following linear programming problem facing a small machine shop:

$$\text{maximize} \quad Z = \$10X_1 + \$30X_2$$

subject to
$$6X_1 + 12X_2 \leq 120 \text{ hours} \quad \text{(Center 1)}$$
$$12X_1 + 3X_2 \leq 120 \text{ hours} \quad \text{(Center 2)}$$
$$X_1, X_2 \geq 0$$

where Z = the total profit per period, X_1 = the number of units of product A, and X_2 = the number of units of product B.

4. Solve the following linear programming problem:

$$\text{minimize} \quad Z = \$100X_1 + \$50X_2$$

subject to
$$10X_1 + 40X_2 \geq 10{,}000 \text{ units} \quad \text{(Ingredient 1)}$$
$$80X_1 + 20X_2 \geq 20{,}000 \text{ units} \quad \text{(Ingredient 2)}$$
$$X_1, X_2 \geq 0$$

where Z = the total cost of a diet per period, X_1 = the number of units of food A, and X_2 = the number of units of food B.

5. Determine the optimal solution to the following linear programming problem:

$$\text{maximize} \quad Z = \$1000X_1 + \$250X_2$$

subject to
$$\$1X_1 + \$2X_2 \geq \$100 \quad \text{(Contract)}$$
$$\$3X_1 + \$2X_2 \leq \$600 \quad \text{(Budget)}$$
$$1\$1X_2 \leq \$200 \quad \text{(Legal)}$$
$$1\$1X_1 + \$10X_2 \geq \$300 \quad \text{(Request)}$$
$$1X_1, X_2 \geq 0$$

where Z = the total dollar return per period, X_1 = the number of units of product A, and X_2 = the number of units of product B.

6. Solve the following production technique problem:

$$\text{minimize} \quad Z = \$1X_1 + \$20X_2$$

subject to
$$100X_1 + 200X_2 \geq 1000 \text{ hours} \quad \text{(Contract)}$$
$$X_1 + X_2 = 20 \text{ units} \quad \text{(Order)}$$
$$X_1 \geq 5 \text{ units} \quad \text{(Policy)}$$
$$X_1, X_2 \geq 0$$

where Z = the total production cost per period, X_1 = the number of units produced by technique 1, and X_2 = the number of units produced by technique 2.

7. Solve the following linear programming problem facing the fire chief of a small rural community:

$$\text{minimize} \quad Z = X_1 + X_2$$

subject to $X_1 \geq \$10,000$ (Contract)
$X_1 + X_2 = \$30,000$ (Budget)
$X_2 \leq \$20,000$ (Chief's preference)
$X_1, X_2 \geq 0$

where Z = the total dollar cost of fire equipment, X_1 = additional dollars spent on labor, and X_2 = additional dollars spent on fire equipment. Explain the solution.

8. Refer back to Examples 6.2 through 6.6.
   a. In Example 6.2, show how Figure 6.13 was derived. Then solve the same problem with the isovalue approach.
   b. In Example 6.3, show how Figure 6.14 was derived. Then solve the same problem with the isovalue approach.
   c. In Example 6.4, show how Figure 6.15 was derived.
   d. Show how Figure 6.16 was derived for Example 6.5.
   e. In Example 6.6, show how Figure 6.19 was derived. Then solve this same problem with the extreme point method.

   Be sure to show all your work.

9. Refer back to thought exercises 2 and 3.
   a. Determine the optimal values of the decision variables and criteria for each of these problems.
   b. Determine whether the optimal solutions for each of these problems meet the system constraints exactly.

10. Determine the optimal solution to the following problem faced by a school district's finance director:

maximize $Z = .5X_1 + 2X_2$

subject to $X_1 + X_2 \leq \$400,000$ (Available funds)
$X_1 \geq 2X_2$ (Customer preference)
$X_1, X_2 \geq 0$

where Z = the total dollar return, X_1 = dollars invested in "conservative" ventures, and X_2 = dollars invested in "speculative" ventures. Also, determine whether the optimal solution involves a combination of decision variables that meets each system constraint exactly. Explain your results to the school board.

Applications Exercises

1. A computer systems manufacturer has just introduced two time-sharing programs for the generation of a wide range of statistical output useful to decision makers. Preliminary market research indicates that each hour of usage of STAT will result in $4 of profit, and each hour of REG will result in $10 of profit for the company. The company is capable of producing a combined total of 1000 hours per month for both programs. In addition, production requires

processing in two divisions, programming and storage. There is a maximum monthly budget of $40,000 for programming and $60,000 for storage. Each hour of STAT uses $20 of the programming budget and $50 of the storage budget, while each hour of REG uses $80 of the programming budget and $100 of the storage budget.

  a. What combination of STAT and REG should the manufacturer produce to maximize profit?
  b. What is the resulting profit level?
  c. Are there any idle resources at the optimum? If so, how would you interpret them?

2. A rancher raises milking cows and goats, which he feeds with two types of mixes, Boreto and Calfa. Each bag of Boreto costs $10 and contains 100 units of calcium and 400 units of protein; each bag of Calfa costs $15 and contains 200 units of calcium and 200 units of protein. The livestock need a minimum of 6000 units of calcium and 12,000 units of protein per day. Also, a contract with the feed producer requires the rancher to purchase at least 2 bags of Boreto for every bag of Calfa.

  a. What combination of mixes should the rancher buy to minimize daily feed cost?
  b. What is the daily feed cost?
  c. Are there any excess requirements? If so, how would you interpret them?

3. A politician running for a state senate seat in an upcoming election can spend his campaign contributions in two ways: on media promotions and on public appearances. Each media promotion costs an average of $10,000 per spot and is expected to "return" 1000 voters, while each public appearance costs $5000 and is expected to "return" 500 voters. The candidate has a maximum campaign budget of $1 million. In addition, the promotional messages require staff time for preparation. Each media spot requires 100 hours of preparation, and each personal appearance requires 20 hours of preparation. The size of the candidate's staff limits the number of total hours available to a maximum of 5000 hours.

  a. How many media spots and public appearances should the candidate make in order to maximize the total "return" of voters?
  b. If the candidate has a personal dislike for public appearances, how will this secondary goal influence his decision?

4. Union membership in the United Brotherhood of Brothers and Sisters entitles the cardholder to the fringe benefit of prepaid dental insurance. There are two separate plans: a fee plan and a deductible fully paid plan. Each member covered by the fee plan costs the union $200, while the other plan costs $100 per member. Total membership in the union is a minimum of 1000 people per month. Contracts

between the union and the insurance carrier also require a minimum of 500 covered members per month under the fee plan and a maximum of 800 members per month under the deductible plan. An additional constraint faced by the union is staff time required to administer the plans. The union estimates a minimum requirement of 2000 staff hours per month, with each member under the fee plan requiring 10 hours per month and each deductible member requiring 5 hours per month.

a. How many members under each plan should the union encourage in order to minimize its monthly dental insurance cost?

b. What is that monthly cost?

c. What does the optimal solution imply about the staff constraint? Explain.

5. County Purchasing Agency is responsible for procuring additional special-document copying machines to meet an anticipated increase in demand. There is not enough demand to justify an outright purchase, so the equipment is rented. Two brands are available: ABM and Texox. It is possible to rent each machine for any part of a month. An ABM rents for $120 per month and occupies 24 square feet of floor space. The Texox rents for $150 per month and requires 18 square feet. The total budget available for the expansion program is $1200 per month, and there is a maximum of 192 square feet of floor space available for the new machines. An ABM usually produces 150 copies of the special documents per day, while the Texox usually produces 185 copies per day.

a. How many machines of each type should the agency rent per month? Assume a 20-day work month.

b. Does it seem reasonable to use a fraction of a machine per month? Explain.

6. Channel Island Construction Company is developing a tract of new homes called Harbor Shores. Two models will be available: the luxury and the standard. Each luxury home is expected to contribute $5000 to the company's profits. It will be constructed on a 2/3-acre lot. The standard model will be constructed on a 1/4-acre lot and is expected to contribute $2000 to the builder's profit. Local ordinances restrict Harbor Shores to a 6-acre plot. There must also be twice as many luxury homes as standard types. Labor contracts require the company to use exactly 100 workers on the project. Each worker is expected to be available for 20 days next month. A luxury home requires 200 people-days to complete, while a standard home requires only 100 people-days.

a. How many homes can the company complete in the next month?

b. How would you interpret a solution with a fractional number of homes?

CASE: Aviation Unlimited

Aviation Unlimited is an airfreight carrier servicing the western region of the United States. It has 100 airplanes, 200 pilots, 20 ground crews of 10 workers per crew, and 150 administrators and other office personnel. T. T. Greedy, Aviation's chief accountant, has prepared a summary report of estimated expenses for the next quarter of operations, as shown in Table 6.7.

Aviation classifies its flights in either of two routes: long haul or short haul. Al Transport, Aviation's transportation engineer, has provided data on estimated tonnage and revenues for each of the route types. These data appear in Table 6.8.

You are asked to provide a management report to Hy Flyer, Aviation's president, containing the following information:

1. The number of each type of flight per quarter that will enable Aviation to maximize its total contribution to profit (revenue less variable cost)
2. The resulting profit contribution
3. The influence of fixed costs on the recommendation

In your report, it is important that you outline the procedure used in formulating your recommendation in a way that is understandable to Flyer. President Flyer is not interested in linear programming jargon, only in an intuitively appealing explanation of your recommendation.

Table 6.7 Estimated Expenses for Aviation

Item	Amount
Total fixed costs	$18,000,000
Administrative	1,500,000
Airplane maintenance	15,000,000
Pilots' salaries	1,500,000
Total variable costs per average flight	$6,000
Fuel	4,000
Ground personnel	2,000

Table 6.8 Estimated Tonnage and Revenues for Aviation

Route	Revenue Per Average Flight	Tonnage	Gallons of Fuel	Ground Crew Hours
Long haul	$9500	10	5,000	6
Short haul	$8500	30	3,000	4
Maximum available per quarter		450,000	75,000,000	96,000

Chapter 7
Simplex Method

CONCEPTS

♦ The nature of a popular method designed to solve large-scale linear programming problems

♦ Formulating problems in a format suitable for analysis by this method

♦ The step-by-step procedure involved in applying the method

♦ Interpreting and utilizing the results

♦ Dealing with special situations that can arise when implementing these approaches

By now, you should understand the nature of linear programming. Specifically, you should be able to recognize situations in which the methodology is applicable, formulate linear programs, and develop an optimal solution using a graphic approach. Of course, the graphic approaches are designed primarily for simple linear programs with only two decision variables. Practical problems, however, typically involve more than two decision variables. Indeed, there may be several thousand variables and hundreds of restrictions. In such cases, a graphic approach will not be useful. Fortunately, management scientists have developed systematic alternative methods designed to solve these large-scale linear programming problems. One of the most popular approaches is called the **simplex method**.

In this chapter we will examine the simplex method. The first section illustrates the fundamental methodology. It shows how to formulate a linear program in simplex format, identify an initial feasible solution, and then develop an optimal solution. The second section presents a tabular format that conveniently organizes, keeps track of, and helps perform the calculations involved in the simplex method. This section also demonstrates how the format can be used to develop an optimal solution of a linear program. The final section discusses some important decision considerations and extensions to the fundamental methodology.

Although the simplex methodology is designed for large-scale programs, the concepts will be illustrated with simple, small-scale problems. Such an approach is less cumbersome, and it enables us to see clearly the relationship between the graphic and simplex methods.

FUNDAMENTAL METHODOLOGY

The simplex method is an algebraic approach based on equality relationships. Yet linear programs typically involve inequalities. To use the simplex method, then, the decision maker first must convert each inequality restriction into an equality. There is a standard format for doing this, as Example 7.1 illustrates.

EXAMPLE 7.1 A Product Mix Problem

Daspling, Inc., manufactures two sizes of baseballs: little league and major league. The company earns a profit of $2 per box for little league baseballs and $3 per box for major league baseballs. Each product is assembled and packaged. There is a maximum of 1800 hours available in both the assembly and packaging departments during a given time period. It takes 9 minutes to assemble a box of little league baseballs and 15 minutes to assemble a box of major league baseballs. A box of little league balls requires 11 minutes of packaging (boxing, labeling, attaching promotional material, and so on). It takes 5 minutes to package a box of major league balls. Daspling seeks the combination of little league baseballs and major league baseballs that will maximize total profit within the available assembly and packaging time.

In Daspling's situation, each box of little league baseballs contributes $2 and each box of major league baseballs contributes $3 to profit. By letting

X_1 = the number of boxes of little league baseballs

X_2 = the number of boxes of major league baseballs

Z = the total dollar profit

we can express Daspling's total profit as

(7.1) $Z = \$2X_1 + \$3X_2$

Management can determine how many little league and major league baseballs to manufacture. Hence, X_1 and X_2 represent the decision variables.

Daspling wants to manufacture the most profitable product mix (combination of X_1 and X_2 values). This objective can be written as follows:

(7.2)   maximize $Z = \$2X_1 + \$3X_2$

However, there are some restrictions on the objective. Each box of little league baseballs takes 9 minutes to assemble, and a box of major league balls takes 15 minutes to assemble. As a result, it will take

$9X_1 + 15X_2$ minutes

to assemble the entire product mix. Since the total assembly time cannot exceed the available 1800 hours (108,000 minutes),

(7.3) $9X_1 + 15X_2 \leq 108{,}000$ minutes

In other words, the demand $(9X_1 + 15X_2)$ must be less than or equal to the available supply of assembly time (108,000 minutes).

Also, the product mix must use no more than the available 1800 hours (108,000 minutes) of packaging time. It takes 11 minutes to package a box of little league baseballs and 5 minutes to package a box of major league baseballs. Therefore,

(7.4) $11X_1 + 5X_2 \leq 108,000$ minutes

That is, the total demand $(11X_1 + 5X_2)$ must be less than or equal to the available supply of packaging time (108,000 minutes).

Finally, Daspling cannot manufacture a negative amount of little league or major league baseballs. Hence,

(7.5) $X_1, X_2 \geq 0$

represents the company's nonnegativity conditions.

By collecting expressions (7.2) through (7.5), management can represent Daspling's product mix problem with the following linear program:

maximize $Z = \$2X_1 + \$3X_2$

subject to $9X_1 + 15X_2 \leq 108,000$ minutes   (Assembly)

$11X_1 + 5X_2 \leq 108,000$ minutes   (Packaging)

$X_1, X_2 \geq 0$

This linear program states that Daspling wants to manufacture the number of little league (X_1) and major league (X_2) baseballs that will maximize total dollar profit (Z). In doing so, however, management must ensure that the output levels $(X_1$ and $X_2)$ do not utilize more than the available assembly and packaging time.

STANDARD FORM According to Daspling's assembly restriction (7.3), the company can produce a product mix (combination of X_1 and X_2 values) that utilizes less than the available 108,000 minutes. Put another way, there can be some unused, or idle, assembly time. In fact, this idle time can be any amount up to 108,000 minutes. The actual amount, of course, will depend on the output of little league (X_1) and major league (X_2) baseballs. In other words, the unused assembly time is a variable.

To account for any potential difference between the assembly time actually used $(9X_1 + 15X_2)$ and the amount available (108,000 minutes), management must define a new variable:

S_1 = unused assembly minutes

Such an activity, which accounts for any unused, or idle, amounts of a resource, is known as a **slack variable**. By adding this variable to the left-hand side of the original restriction (7.3), Daspling can write the assembly constraint as follows:

(7.6) $9X_1 + 15X_2 + S_1 = 108{,}000$ minutes

That is, the action transforms the original less-than-or-equal-to restriction into an equality relationship. Indeed, the addition of a slack variable to the left-hand side of a less-than-or-equal-to constraint always converts the original restriction into an equality.

The company's packaging restriction (7.4) can be transformed into an equality relationship by a similar process. First, management defines another slack variable,

S_2 = unused packaging minutes

to account for any potential difference between the packaging time actually utilized $(11X_1 + 5X_2)$ and the amount available (108,000 minutes). By adding S_2 to the left-hand side of the original restriction (7.4), Daspling can express the packaging constraint as follows:

(7.7) $11X_1 + 5X_2 + S_2 = 108{,}000$ minutes

Again, we have an equality relationship.

At this stage, management has introduced two new variables, S_1 and S_2, that have not been accounted for in the original objective function (7.2) or in the nonnegativity conditions (7.5). In addition, Daspling must define any potential impact of unused assembly minutes (S_1) on the original packaging restriction (7.4) and unused packaging minutes (S_2) on the original assembly constraint (7.3). Hence, the transformation process is not yet complete.

Unused assembly time (S_1) and unused packaging time (S_2) do not generate any output. Hence, neither of these slack variables will make any contribution to profit. That is, S_1 and S_2 each would have \$0 coefficients in the total profit equation (7.1). As a result, management can write Daspling's objective function as follows:

(7.8)   maximize $Z = \$2X_1 + \$3X_2 + \$0S_1 + \$0S_2$

Furthermore, unused packaging minutes (S_2) do not require any assembly time. In other words, S_2 would have a coefficient of 0 in either assembly constraint (7.3) or (7.6). Therefore, this constraint can be expressed as follows:

(7.9) $9X_1 + 15X_2 + S_1 + 0S_2 = 108{,}000$ minutes

Similarly, since unused assembly minutes (S_1) do not require any packaging time, the packaging restriction can be expressed in the following format:

(7.10) $11X_1 + 5X_2 + 0S_1 + S_2 = 108{,}000$ minutes

Table 7.1 Characteristics of the Standard Form

1. All variables are restricted to nonnegative values.
2. Each system constraint is expressed as an equality relationship.
3. There are variables on the left-hand side and a constant value on the right-hand side of each system constraint.
4. The value on the right-hand side of each system constraint is nonnegative.
5. One nondecision variable with a coefficient of $+1$ appears in each system constraint, and the nondecision variable with the $+1$ coefficient in a restriction has a coefficient of 0 in any other system constraint.
6. Each variable is accounted for in the objective function, in each system constraint, and in the nonnegativity conditions.

Finally, slack (like decision) variables must have values greater than or equal to zero. Consequently,

$$(7.11) \quad X_1, X_2, S_1, S_2 \geq 0$$

gives the expanded nonnegativity conditions.

By collecting expressions (7.8) through (7.11), management will find that Daspling's linear program now has the following format:

maximize $\quad Z = \$2X_1 + \$3X_2 + \$0S_1 + \$0S_2$

subject to $\quad 9X_1 + 15X_2 + S_1 + 0S_2 = 108{,}000$ minutes (Assembly)

$\qquad\qquad 11X_1 + 5X_2 + 0S_1 + S_2 = 108{,}000$ minutes (Packaging)

$\qquad\qquad X_1, X_2, S_1, S_2 \geq 0$

This format clearly shows that the decision maker must determine the values of the slack variables (S_1 and S_2) as well as the decision variables (X_1 and X_2) to obtain the optimal solution to the linear program.

Note that the revised format of the linear program has the properties summarized in Table 7.1. When a linear program has these characteristics, the model is said to be in its **canonical** or **standard form**.

The fifth property in Table 7.1 may require some clarification. When there is no number appearing before a variable, the corresponding value of the coefficient is $+1$. Hence, the term S_1 in the assembly restriction (7.9) actually has a coefficient of $+1$. Put another way, an unused assembly minute diverts 1 minute of the available time from baseball production. As a result, S_1 is the nondecision (slack) variable with a coefficient of $+1$ in the assembly equation (7.9). Furthermore, this S_1 variable has a coefficient of 0 in the packaging equation (7.10). Similarly, S_2 is the nondecision (slack) variable with a coefficient of $+1$ in the packaging restriction (7.10), but S_2 has a coefficient of 0 in the other (assembly) system constraint (7.9).

BASIC Once the decision maker has developed the standard form, the corre-
FEASIBLE SOLUTIONS sponding linear program can be solved with algebra. To see what is
involved, we will again consider the standard form of Daspling's product
mix problem:

$$\text{maximize} \quad Z = \$2X_1 + \$3X_2 + \$0S_1 + \$0S_2$$

$$\text{subject to} \quad 9X_1 + 15X_2 + S_1 + 0S_2 = 108{,}000 \text{ minutes} \quad \text{(Assembly)}$$
$$11X_1 + 5X_2 + 0S_1 + S_2 = 108{,}000 \text{ minutes} \quad \text{(Packaging)}$$
$$X_1, X_2, S_1, S_2 \geq 0$$

In the standard form, the assembly and packaging restrictions form a
system of two linear equations with four unknowns (X_1, X_2, S_1, and S_2).
To meet the system constraints, management must find a solution
(combination of X_1, X_2, S_1, and S_2 values) that satisfies both of these
equations. Such a solution can be obtained in two steps. First, the decision
maker can assign zero values arbitrarily to any two of the original four
variables. Then the assembly and packaging equations can be used to
solve for the remaining two variables.

Suppose, for example, that Daspling's management arbitrarily decides
to produce no little league baseballs and have no unused packaging
minutes. In this case, $X_1 = 0$ and $S_2 = 0$. By substituting these values into
the standard form assembly and packaging equations (7.9) and (7.10),
management will obtain the following system of two equations in two
unknowns:

$$15X_2 + S_1 = 108{,}000$$

$$5X_2 = 108{,}000$$

According to these equations,

$$X_2 = \frac{108{,}000}{5} = 21{,}600$$

and

$$15(21{,}600) + S_1 = 108{,}000$$

or

$$S_1 = 108{,}000 - 15(21{,}600) = -216{,}000$$

Consequently, $X_1 = 0$, $X_2 = 21{,}600$, $S_1 = -216{,}000$, and $S_2 = 0$ represent one solution to Daspling's standard form assembly and packaging
restrictions. In simplex method terminology, this combination of variables
is referred to as a **basic solution** to the linear program.

In general, a decision maker can find a basic solution to a standard form linear program with n variables and m system constraint equations by:

1. Arbitrarily setting $(n - m)$ variables equal to zero
2. Using the system constraint equations to solve for the remaining m variables

Furthermore, each of the $(n - m)$ zero-valued activities (X_1 and S_2 in the Daspling example) is known as a **nonbasic variable**. In addition, each of the remaining m activities (X_2 and S_1 for the product mix solution) is referred to as a **basic variable**. The combination of basic variables (X_2 and S_1 in our illustration) is called the **basis**.

Unfortunately, whenever a set of simultaneous linear expressions has more variables than equations, as in Daspling's standard form system constraints, there can be a large number of basic solutions. However, some of the solutions may not satisfy the nonnegativity conditions and thus may be infeasible. In fact, Daspling's basic solution of

$$X_1 = 0 \qquad\qquad S_1 = -216{,}000$$
$$X_2 = 21{,}600 \qquad S_2 = 0$$

involves a negative number of unused assembly minutes ($S_1 < 0$). Since S_1 does not satisfy the nonnegativity condition of $S_1 \geq 0$, this basic solution is not feasible. Decision makers, of course, should eliminate any such infeasible basic solution from further consideration.

Even then, there may be many remaining basic solutions that satisfy the system and nonnegativity restrictions in the standard form of a linear program. Indeed, in large-scale problems with thousands of variables and constraints, there may be hundreds of such **basic feasible solutions**. Furthermore, it would be cumbersome and time-consuming to identify and evaluate each of these solutions.

The simplex method avoids this difficulty by developing the optimal solution in stages. It begins with a basic feasible solution that is known to be nonoptimal. Then the method attempts to progressively improve each successive solution. Eventually, the process identifies the basic feasible solution, if it exists, that best meets the decision criterion.

INITIAL BASIC FEASIBLE SOLUTION

Daspling seeks the feasible combination of decision variables (X_1 and X_2) and nondecision variables (S_1 and S_2) that will maximize total dollar profit (Z). Management knows that the company cannot earn any profit without producing some baseballs. That is, a combination of

$X_1 = 0$ boxes of little league baseballs

and

$X_2 = 0$ boxes of major league baseballs

will not provide the optimal solution to the company's product mix problem.

On the other hand, when Daspling sets $X_1 = 0$ and $X_2 = 0$, the standard form assembly and packaging equations (7.9) and (7.10) indicate that the company will have

$$S_1 = 108,000 \text{ unused assembly minutes}$$

and

$$S_2 = 108,000 \text{ unused packaging minutes}$$

Consequently,

$$X_1 = 0 \qquad S_1 = 108,000$$

$$X_2 = 0 \qquad S_2 = 108,000$$

represents a basic solution to Daspling's standard form linear program that is known to be nonoptimal. Since this combination of variables satisfies the expanded nonnegativity conditions (7.11), it also is a basic feasible solution. As such, this solution provides a useful starting point for the simplex evaluation process.

In effect, then, when the standard form of a linear program contains only slack and decision variables, the decision maker should:

1. Set each decision variable equal to zero
2. Read the value of each slack variable from the right-hand side of the corresponding system constraint equation

The resulting combination of variables provides the nonoptimal basic feasible solution needed to begin the simplex evaluation process.

EVALUATING A SOLUTION To evaluate the initial solution, Daspling must determine the impact of the initial basis (S_1 and S_2) on the system (assembly and packaging) constraints and the profit criterion. In this regard, the value of $S_1 = 108,000$ is obtained from assembly constraint equation (7.9),

$$9X_1 + 15X_2 + S_1 + 0S_2 = 108,000$$

By solving (7.9) for S_1, management can obtain an equation

$$(7.12) \quad S_1 = 108,000 - 9X_1 - 15X_2 + 0S_2$$

that expresses the assembly restriction in terms of the corresponding basic variable S_1. Equation (7.12) can also be used to measure the idle assembly time (S_1) associated with any combination of the decision variables (X_1 and X_2).

Similarly, in the initial basic feasible solution, the value of $S_2 = 108,000$ is obtained from packaging constraint equation (7.10),

$$11X_1 + 5X_2 + 0S_1 + S_2 = 108,000$$

When the company solves (7.10) for S_2, it obtains an equation

(7.13) $S_2 = 108,000 - 11X_1 - 5X_2 + 0S_1$

that expresses the packaging restriction in terms of the corresponding basic variable S_2. Equation (7.13) can also be used to measure the idle packaging time (S_2) associated with any combination of the decision variables (X_1 and X_2).

If management substitutes equations (7.12) and (7.13) into the standard form objective function (7.8),

maximize $Z = \$2X_1 + \$3X_2 + \$0S_1 + \$0S_2$

it obtains a profit expression

(7.14)   maximize $Z = \$2X_1 + \$3X_2 + \$0$

that accounts for the initial basis (S_1 and S_2). Furthermore, by substituting the values of $X_1 = 0$ and $X_2 = 0$ into equation (7.14), Daspling will find that its initial basic feasible solution earns

$Z = \$2(0) + \$3(0) + \$0 = \$0$

total profit. In other words, the company will not earn anything when it produces no baseballs.

Equation (7.14), however, indicates that Daspling could increase this initial $Z = \$0$ total profit a net \$2 by producing a box of little league baseballs (X_1), or \$3 by producing a box of major league baseballs (X_2). In other words, the company can improve the initial criterion value by bringing either X_1 or X_2 into the basis. As a result, the initial basic feasible solution of

$X_1 = 0$ $S_1 = 108,000$

$X_2 = 0$ $S_2 = 108,000$

is not an optimum.

This result illustrates the following important property. *A basic feasible solution will be nonoptimal as long as it is possible to improve the criterion value by bringing a nonbasic variable into the basis.*

IMPROVING A SOLUTION Although the initial $Z = \$0$ total profit can be increased by producing either little league or major league baseballs, major league baseballs have a larger per-box contribution. Consequently, Daspling should first bring X_2, rather than X_1, into the basis. In the second solution, then, X_1 should remain nonbasic with a value of $X_1 = 0$, while X_2 becomes a basic variable. In simplex terminology, the activity that will be brought into the basis is referred to as the **entering variable**.

Daspling also knows that each box of major league baseballs contributes \$3 to profit. Since management wants to maximize total profit, it should produce as many boxes as feasible. In this regard, the initial basic feasible solution involves $S_1 = 108,000$ unused assembly minutes. According to the modified assembly constraint equation (7.12),

$$S_1 = 108,000 - 9X_1 - 15X_2 + 0S_2$$

the company must decrease idle assembly time (S_1) by 15 minutes to produce a box of major league baseballs (X_2). Thus, if management utilizes all available assembly time, it can manufacture as many as

$$\frac{108,000 \text{ unused assembly minutes}}{15 \text{ minutes per box}} = 7200$$

boxes of major league balls.

Similarly, the modified packaging constraint equation (7.13),

$$S_2 = 108,000 - 11X_1 - 5X_2 + 0S_1$$

shows that Daspling must decrease unused packaging time (S_2) by 5 minutes to produce a box of major league balls (X_2). Hence, if the company utilizes all available packaging time, it can manufacture as many as

$$\frac{108,000 \text{ unused packaging minutes}}{5 \text{ minutes per box}} = 21,600$$

boxes of these balls. Such values, which identify the maximum amounts of the entering variable that can be obtained for the entire quantities of the basic variables, are known as **trade ratios**.

Since 7200 and 21,600 are both positive values, either output would satisfy the nonnegativity condition of $X_2 \geq 0$. Also, since Daspling knows that larger output leads to higher profit, management would prefer to produce 21,600 rather than 7200 boxes of major league balls. Unfortunately, there is enough idle assembly time (S_1) to manufacture only 7200 boxes. That is, $X_2 = 7200$ is the maximum output that will satisfy all restrictions (be feasible) in Daspling's linear program. Therefore, the company should produce $X_2 = 7200$ boxes of major league baseballs.

According to equation (7.13), an output of $X_1 = 0$ boxes of little league baseballs and $X_2 = 7200$ boxes of major league baseballs would leave

$$S_2 = 108,000 - 11X_1 - 5X_2 + 0S_1$$

$$= 108,000 - 11(0) - 5(7200) + 0 = 72,000$$

unused packaging minutes. Yet equation (7.12) shows that this same output combination will leave

$$S_1 = 108{,}000 - 9X_1 - 15X_2 + 0S_2$$
$$= 108{,}000 - 9(0) - 15(7200) + 0 = 0$$

unused assembly minutes.

Daspling's second solution, then, consists of

$$X_1 = 0 \qquad S_1 = 0$$
$$X_2 = 7200 \qquad S_2 = 72{,}000$$

In this solution, two of the four standard form variables again are equal to zero. Also, the values of the remaining two variables are obtained from the two standard form system (assembly and packaging) constraint equations. In addition, the values of all four standard form variables are nonnegative. Therefore, this second combination of variables represents another basic feasible solution for Daspling's linear program.

ITERATION PROCESS A comparison of Daspling's first and second basic feasible solutions will show that a previous nonbasic variable X_2 becomes a basic variable with $X_2 = 7200$. In the process, a previous basic variable S_1 becomes a nonbasic variable with $S_1 = 0$. Put another way, X_2 replaces S_1 in the second basis. In simplex terminology, the activity that is removed from the basis is referred to as the **exiting** or **departing variable**.

Notice that the exiting variable (S_1) is the activity that generates the maximum feasible output (7200) of the entering variable (X_2). Furthermore, this output represents the smallest nonnegative trade ratio. In other words, the departing variable always corresponds to the activity with the smallest nonnegative trade ratio for the entering variable.

This interchange of roles between two variables is an essential simplex feature. Indeed, the simplex method always moves from one basic feasible solution to another by selecting a nonbasic variable to replace a basic variable. Such a process of moving from one basis to another is known as **iteration** or **pivoting**.

Figure 7.1 illustrates the iteration process involved in moving from Daspling's first basic feasible solution to its second basic feasible solution. The coordinates labeled A, B, C, and D identify the extreme points of Daspling's feasible solution area.

At extreme point A, which corresponds to the origin of the graph, $X_1 = 0$ and $X_2 = 0$. According to modified assembly constraint equation (7.12), this combination of decision variables generates

$$S_1 = 108{,}000 - 9X_1 - 15X_2 + 0S_2$$
$$= 108{,}000 - 9(0) - 15(0) + 0 = 108{,}000$$

unused assembly minutes. Also, equation (7.13) indicates that an $X_1 = 0$ and $X_2 = 0$ creates

Figure 7.1 Daspling's First Iteration

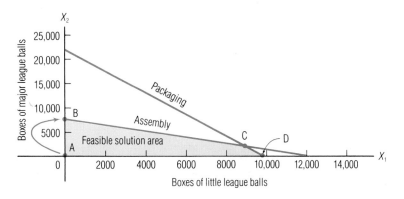

$$S_2 = 108,000 - 11X_1 - 5X_2 + 0S_1$$
$$= 108,000 - 11(0) - 5(0) + 0 = 108,000$$

unused packaging minutes. Extreme point A, then, involves

$$X_1 = 0 \qquad S_1 = 108,000$$
$$X_2 = 0 \qquad S_2 = 108,000$$

and thus corresponds to Daspling's initial basic feasible solution.

After evaluating this solution, management brings into the basis the variable X_2 with the largest net increase in total profit. In Figure 7.1, such a process corresponds to the movement indicated by the arrow along the X_2 axis. The movement continues until the assembly constraint line is reached at extreme point B. At this point, the company is using all available 108,000 idle assembly minutes to produce $X_2 = 7200$ boxes of major league baseballs. In the process, however, the company leaves $S_1 = 0$ unused assembly minutes and manufactures $X_1 = 0$ boxes of little league balls.

You can also see that extreme point B is below the packaging constraint line. Such a point, then, involves some unused packaging time (S_2). Indeed, Daspling can determine the quantity of S_2 by substituting the coordinates ($X_1 = 0$, $X_2 = 7200$) at this point into the modified packaging constraint equation (7.13):

$$S_2 = 108,000 - 11X_1 - 5X_2 + 0S_1$$
$$= 108,000 - 11(0) - 5(7200) + 0 = 72,000$$

unused packaging minutes. At extreme point B, then,

Table 7.2 Fundamental Simplex Methodology

1. Set up the standard form of the linear program.
2. Establish the initial basic feasible solution.
3. Evaluate the current basic feasible solution. To do so:
   a. Express each system constraint equation in terms of the corresponding basic variable.
   b. Substitute the modified version of the system constraint equations into the objective function.

   The coefficients of the resulting objective function will indicate whether it is possible to improve the criterion value.
4. Bring into the basis the variable that leads to the largest improvement in the value of the criterion. This activity is referred to as the entering variable.
5. Use the modified versions of the system constraint equations to calculate the trade ratios.
6. Remove from the basis the variable with the smallest nonnegative trade ratio. This activity is known as the existing, or departing, variable.
7. Establish the new basic feasible solution as follows:
   a. Set the entering variable equal to the smallest nonnegative trade ratio.
   b. Use the system constraint equations to find the values of the other basic variables.
8. Return to step 3 and repeat the procedure until it is impossible to improve the criterion value.

$$X_1 = 0 \qquad S_1 = 0$$
$$X_2 = 7200 \qquad S_2 = 72{,}000$$

Hence, this point corresponds to Daspling's second basic feasible solution.

Note that extreme points A and B in Figure 7.1 identify basic feasible solutions for the standard form of Daspling's linear program. In fact, so do extreme points C and D. This characteristic illustrates the following important property: *In a linear program involving only less-than-or-equal-to (≤) relationships, each basic feasible solution always occurs at an extreme point of the feasible solution area.* Put another way, in such programs, a basic feasible solution is the same thing as an extreme point solution.

The simplex method, then, is essentially a search procedure. It starts with a basic feasible solution, or extreme point, that will be nonoptimal. In linear programs with only two decision variables, like Daspling's, this initial basic feasible solution generally corresponds to the origin of the graph (extreme point A in Figure 7.1). Each preceding criterion value is improved by moving from one extreme point (basic feasible solution) to another. In Daspling's case, for instance, the initial criterion value is improved by moving from extreme point A to point B along the boundary of the feasible solution area in Figure 7.1. Such a search of the extreme points continues as long as it is possible to improve the criterion value. Table 7.2 outlines this fundamental simplex methodology.

FINDING THE Daspling can again use this fundamental methodology to evaluate the
OPTIMAL SOLUTION second basic feasible solution. In this solution, X_2 replaces S_1 in the basis.
As a result, the modified assembly constraint equation (7.12)

$$S_1 = 108,000 - 9X_1 - 15X_2 + 0S_2$$

which corresponds to the departing variable S_1, should be expressed in
terms of the entering variable X_2. If management does so, the assembly
contraint equation becomes

$$(7.15) \quad X_2 = 7200 - \tfrac{3}{5}X_1 - \tfrac{1}{15}S_1 + 0S_2$$

The modified packaging constraint equation (7.13)

$$S_2 = 108,000 - 11X_1 - 5X_2 + 0S_1$$

then can be written as follows:

$$S_2 = 108,000 - 11X_1 - 5(7200 - \tfrac{3}{5}X_1 - \tfrac{1}{15}S_1 + 0S_2) + 0S_1$$

or

$$(7.16) \quad S_2 = 72,000 - 8X_1 + \tfrac{1}{3}S_1 + 0X_2$$

In other words, equations (7.15) and (7.16) express Daspling's system
(assembly and packaging) constraints in terms of the company's second
basis (X_2 and S_2).

By substituting equations (7.15) and (7.16) into the modified objective
function (7.14)

$$\text{maximize } Z = \$2X_1 + \$3X_2 + \$0$$

Daspling obtains an expression

$$\text{maximize } Z = \$2X_1 + \$3(7200 - \tfrac{3}{5}X_1 - \tfrac{1}{15}S_1 + 0S_2) + \$0$$

or

$$(7.17) \quad \text{maximize } Z = \$21,600 + \$\tfrac{1}{5}X_1 - \$\tfrac{1}{5}S_1$$

that accounts for the second basis (X_2 and S_2). If management then
substitutes the values of the nonbasic variables, $X_1 = 0$ and $S_1 = 0$, into
expression (7.17), it will find that the second basic feasible solution earns

$$Z = \$21,600 + \$\tfrac{1}{5}(0) - \$\tfrac{1}{5}(0) = \$21,600$$

total profit.

Yet expression (7.17) also shows that Daspling can increase this
$Z = \$21,600$ profit a net $\$1/5 = \$.20$ by producing a box of little league
baseballs (X_1). That is, the company still can improve the criterion value
by bringing X_1 into the basis. Hence, the second basic feasible solution is
not an optimum.

Equation (7.15),

$$X_2 = 7200 - \tfrac{3}{5}X_1 - \tfrac{1}{15}S_1 + 0S_2$$

indicates that the company must decrease major league output (X_2) by 3/5 box to obtain a unit of the entering variable X_1. Thus, if Daspling reduces major league output as much as possible, it can produce as many as

$$\frac{7200 \text{ major league boxes}}{3/5 \text{ major per little league box}} = 12{,}000$$

boxes of little league balls.

Similarly, equation (7.16)

$$S_2 = 72{,}000 - 8X_1 + \tfrac{1}{3}S_1 + 0X_2$$

shows that Daspling must decrease unused packaging time (S_2) by 8 minutes to manufacture a box of little league baseballs (X_1). Therefore, if the company utilizes all available packaging time, it can produce as many as

$$\frac{72{,}000 \text{ unused packaging minutes}}{8 \text{ minutes per box}} = 9000$$

boxes of these balls.

Clearly, 9000 is a smaller nonnegative trade ratio than 12,000. Consequently, in the third solution, Daspling should produce $X_1 = 9000$ boxes of little league baseballs. Also, the nonbasic variable S_1 still should have a value of $S_1 = 0$. Then, as equation (7.15) indicates, an $X_1 = 9000$ and $S_1 = 0$ involves an output of

$$X_2 = 7200 - \tfrac{3}{5}X_1 - \tfrac{1}{15}S_1 + 0S_2$$
$$= 7200 - \tfrac{3}{5}(9000) - \tfrac{1}{15}(0) + 0 = 1800$$

boxes of major league balls. In addition, according to equation (7.16), this same combination of variables will leave

$$S_2 = 72{,}000 - 8X_1 + \tfrac{1}{3}S_1 + 0X_2$$
$$= 72{,}000 - 8(9000) + \tfrac{1}{3}(0) + 0 = 0$$

unused packaging minutes.

Daspling's third basic feasible solution, then, consists of

$$X_1 = 9000 \qquad S_1 = 0$$
$$X_2 = 1800 \qquad S_2 = 0$$

In the iteration from the second basic feasible solution to this third basic feasible solution, the entering variable X_1 becomes basic with an $X_1 = 9000$, while the departing variable S_2 becomes nonbasic with an $S_2 = 0$.

Figure 7.2 Daspling's Second Iteration

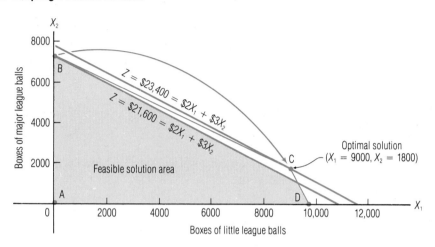

Also, if Daspling evaluates this solution (performs step 3 in Table 7.2), it will find that the expression

(7.18)   maximize $Z = \$23,400 - \$\frac{1}{60}S_2$

accounts for the third basis (X_1 and X_2). By substituting the value of the nonbasic variable $S_2 = 0$ into expression (7.18), management will then find that the third basic feasible solution earns

$Z = \$23,400 - \$\frac{1}{60}(0) = \$23,400$

total profit. Furthermore, expression (7.18) shows that Daspling cannot increase this profit by bringing S_2 back into the basis. As a result, the third basic feasible solution identifies the company's optimal product mix.

Figure 7.2 presents a graph of this second, and final, iteration. Extreme point B involves

$X_1 = 0$ $S_1 = 0$

$X_2 = 7200$ $S_2 = 72,000$

Hence, the point corresponds to Daspling's second basic feasible solution. After evaluating this solution, management brings into the basis the variable X_1 with the largest net increase in total profit. In Figure 7.2, such a process corresponds to the movement indicated by the arrow along the assembly constraint line. The movement continues until the packaging constraint line is reached at extreme point C. At this point, all available assembly and packaging time is being used to produce $X_1 = 9000$ boxes of little league balls and $X_2 = 1800$ boxes of major league balls. In the process, management leaves $S_1 = 0$ unused assembly minutes and $S_2 = 0$ unused packaging minutes. That is, at extreme point C,

$$X_1 = 9000 \qquad S_1 = 0$$
$$X_2 = 1800 \qquad S_2 = 0$$

Consequently, this point corresponds to Daspling's third basic feasible solution.

Figure 7.2 also shows that extreme point B is tangent to the $21,600 isoprofit line. That is, the second basic feasible solution provides Daspling with a $21,600 profit. Yet by moving from extreme point B to extreme point C, the company can reach the $23,400 isoprofit line. Since no higher-valued isoprofit line touches a point on the boundary of the feasible solution area, extreme point C represents the optimal solution.

Daspling, then, can maximize total profit at $Z = \$23,400$ by producing $X_1 = 9000$ boxes of little league baseballs and $X_2 = 1800$ boxes of major league baseballs. Furthermore, this optimal product mix will leave $S_1 = 0$ unused assembly minutes and $S_2 = 0$ idle packaging minutes.

SIMPLEX TABLES

Simplex calculations can be very complicated and confusing, especially in large-scale linear programs. Fortunately, management scientists have developed a tabular format that conveniently organizes, keeps track of, and helps perform the calculations necessary to get successive basic feasible solutions. Figure 7.3 presents the model for this type of format, which is known as a **simplex table**.

INITIAL SIMPLEX TABLE

The first simplex table always presents the decision information involved in the initial basic feasible solution of the standard form linear program. Table 7.3, for example, gives the simplex information corresponding to Daspling's initial basic feasible solution (extreme point A in Figures 7.1 and 7.2).

Part of this first simplex table merely restates the information contained in the standard form of the linear program. In Daspling's case, for instance, there are four variables: boxes of little league baseballs (X_1), boxes of major league baseballs (X_2), unused assembly minutes (S_1), and unused

Figure 7.3 Simplex Table

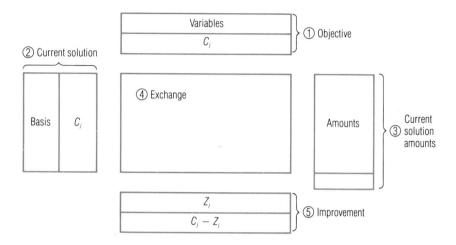

① *Objective*

 Variables: a list of all the variables (basic and nonbasic) in the linear program
 C_j: the per-unit contribution of each variable (basic and nonbasic) to the objective

② *Current solution*

 Basis: a list of the basic variables in the current solution
 C_j: the per-unit contribution of each basic variable to the objective

③ *Current solution amounts*

 Amounts: a list of the amounts of each basic variable and the total contribution of the current solution

④ *Exchange:* the amounts of each basic variable in the current solution that must be given up to get one unit of each variable (basic and nonbasic) in the linear program

⑤ *Improvement*

 Z_j: in the Variables columns, entries that give the contribution lost by bringing one unit of each variable (basic and nonbasic) into the basis; in the Amounts column, the Z_j entry that gives the total value of the objective for the current basic feasible solution
 $C_j - Z_j$: the net effect on the objective of bringing one unit of each variable (basic and nonbasic) into the basis

packaging minutes (S_2). Thus, Table 7.3 has four columns in the Variables row, and each of the company's activities is listed in a separate column of this row. The corresponding per-box contributions to profit are listed in the C_j row of the appropriate column. That is, the $2 contribution from little league balls is placed in the X_1 column of the C_j row, the $3 major league unit contribution is placed in the X_2 column of the C_j row, and so

Table 7.3   Daspling's First Simplex Table

Variables Basis	C_j	X_1 $2	X_2 $3	S_1 $0	S_2 $0	Amounts	Trade Ratios
S_1	$0	9	(15)	1	0	108,000	$\frac{108,000}{15} = 7200 \leftarrow$ Take out (pivot row)
S_2	$0	11	5	0	1	108,000	$\frac{108,000}{5} = 21,600$
Z_j		$0	$0	$0	$0	$0	
$C_j - Z_j$		$2	$3	$0	$0		

$\uparrow$
Bring in
(pivot column)

on. In effect, then, the Variables and C_j rows outline the information contained in the total profit equation

$$Z = \$2X_1 + \$3X_2 + \$0S_1 + \$0S_2$$

of Daspling's standard form linear program.

Each row of the Basis column lists a basic variable, S_1 and S_2, involved in Daspling's initial basic feasible solution. The C_j column gives the corresponding per-unit contributions to profit: \$0 for unused assembly minutes (S_1) and \$0 for unused packaging minutes (S_2). Each row of the Amounts column reports the quantity of the corresponding basic variables. Consequently, 108,000 is placed in the S_1 row and 108,000 in the S_2 row of the Amounts column of Table 7.3.

Any standard form variable that does not appear in the Basis column is nonbasic. Table 7.3, for example, shows that X_1 and X_2 are the nonbasic variables in Daspling's initial basic feasible solution. Since nonbasic variables have values of zero, $X_1 = 0$ and $X_2 = 0$ in this first solution.

Entries in the main body of Table 7.3 identify the amount of a basic variable that must be given up to get *one* unit of any variable in the program. The entry in the S_1 row and X_1 column, for instance, indicates that 9 minutes of unused assembly time (S_1) must be given up to produce one box of little league baseballs (X_1). Similarly, the entry in the S_2 row and X_2 column tells us that 5 minutes of unused packaging time (S_2) must be given up to produce one box of major league balls (X_2). A zero entry simply means that no exchange occurs. Hence, the entry in the S_1 row and S_2 column indicates that no unused assembly time (S_1) is needed to obtain one minute of unused packaging time (S_2). An entry of $+1$ means that there is an even (one-for-one) exchange between the variables. The entry in the S_1 row and S_1 column thus indicates that one unused assembly minute (S_1) will be given up to obtain one minute of the same slack (S_1). Put another way, Daspling can create an idle assembly minute only by diverting from baseball production one minute of available assembly time.

In the first simplex table, these exchange entries are simply the coefficients of the corresponding variables in the appropriate standard form system constraint equations. The S_1 row in Table 7.3, for instance, deals with unused assembly minutes. Hence, this row relates to the standard form of Daspling's assembly equation (7.9),

$$9X_1 + 15X_2 + 1S_1 + 0S_2 = 108{,}000$$

Since X_1 has a coefficient of 9 in this equation, there is a 9 in the X_1 column of the S_1 row of Table 7.3. Also, 15 appears in the X_2 column, 1 in the S_1 column, and 0 in the S_2 column of this row because these values are the coefficients of the corresponding variables in equation (7.9).

Similarly, the S_2 row in Table 7.3 deals with unused packaging minutes. Therefore, this row relates to the standard form of Daspling's packaging equation (7.10),

$$11X_1 + 5X_2 + 0S_1 + 1S_2 = 108{,}000$$

Consequently, 11 appears in the X_1 column, 5 in the X_2 column, 0 in the S_1 column, and 1 in the S_2 column of the S_2 row of Table 7.3.

The Z_j and $C_j - Z_j$ rows of the simplex table provide the information needed to evaluate the current solution. In Daspling's case, the Z_j row entries represent the decrease in total profit that will occur if one unit of each variable is brought into the basis. Consider, for example, the effects of producing little league baseballs. According to the X_1 column of Table 7.3, 9 unused assembly minutes (S_1) and 11 idle packaging minutes (S_2) must be given up to produce one box of little league balls. As the entries in the C_j column indicate, however, each unused assembly or packaging minute contributes \$0 to profit. Thus, the company will lose

$$\quad 9 \text{ unused assembly minutes @ \$0 profit/minute} = \$0$$

plus   11 unused packaging minutes @ \$0 profit/minute = \$0

for a total of   \$0

profit by utilizing this idle time (S_1 and S_2) to produce a box of little league baseballs (X_1). In other words, nothing is lost by putting idle time to productive use. As a result, there is a \$0 entry in the Z_j row of the X_1 column of Table 7.3.

Note that this Z_j row entry is obtained by multiplying the values in the C_j column by the corresponding elements in the appropriate variable column and then summing the results. In fact, the other entries in the Z_j row can be obtained by the same process, as Figure 7.4 illustrates. You can

Figure 7.4 Finding the Z_j Entries in Daspling's First Simplex Table

Basis C_j X_1

S_1	$0	9
S_2	$0	11
	Z_j	$0

9 of S_1 at $0 profit/minute $= $0

11 of S_2 at $0 profit/minute $= \underline{$0}$

Total $0

(a) Z_j entry for the X_1 column

Basis C_j X_1 X_2

S_1	$0		15
S_2	$0		5
	Z_j		$0

15 of S_1 at $0 profit/minute $= $0

5 of S_2 at $0 profit/minute $= \underline{$0}$

Total $0

(b) Z_j entry for the X_2 column

Basis C_j X_1 X_2 S_1

S_1	$0			1
S_2	$0			0
	Z_j			$0

1 of S_1 at $0 profit/minute $= $0

0 of S_2 at $0 profit/minute $= \underline{$0}$

Total $0

(c) Z_j entry for the S_1 column

Basis C_j X_1 X_2 S_1 S_2

S_1	$0				0
S_2	$0				1
	Z_j				$0

0 of S_1 at $0 profit/minute $= $0

1 of S_2 at $0 profit/minute $= \underline{$0}$

Total $0

(d) Z_j entry for the S_2 column

Basis C_j X_1 X_2 S_1 S_2 Amounts

S_1	$0					108,000
S_2	$0					108,000
	Z_j					$0

108,000 of S_1 at $0 profit/minute $= $0

108,000 of S_2 at $0 profit/minute $= \underline{$0}$

Total profit $0

(e) Z_j entry for the Amounts column

see that the entry in the Amounts column of the Z_j row is obtained by multiplying the C_j column values by the corresponding elements in the Amounts column and then summing the results. This entry identifies the criterion value associated with the simplex solution. Since Daspling's initial solution involves

$$X_1 = 0 \text{ boxes of little league baseballs @ \$2 profit/box} \quad = \$0$$
$$X_2 = 0 \text{ boxes of major league baseballs @ \$3 profit/box} \quad = \$0$$
$$S_1 = 108,000 \text{ unused assembly minutes @ \$0 profit/minute} = \$0$$
$$S_2 = 108,000 \text{ unused packaging minutes @ \$0 profit/minute} = \underline{\$0}$$
$$\text{for a total of} \qquad\qquad\qquad\qquad\qquad\qquad\qquad\qquad\qquad \$0$$

Table 7.3 has a \$0 entry in the Z_j row of the Amounts column. In other words, the company will not earn any profit when it produces no baseballs.

Now let us move to the $C_j - Z_j$ row of the simplex table. In Daspling's case, the C_j row entries represent the *increase* in total profit that will occur if one unit of each variable is brought into the solution. On the other hand, the corresponding Z_j row entries indicate how much the total profit will *decrease* in the process. Thus, the difference $C_j - Z_j$ gives the net effect on total dollar profit of any change in the basis.

Consider, for instance, the net effect of producing little league baseballs. This variable involves the X_1 column in Table 7.3. According to the C_j row of this table, each box of these balls will increase total profit by \$2. The corresponding Z_j row entry indicates that total profit will decrease by \$0 if one unit of the X_1 variable is brought into the basis. Hence, Daspling can increase total profit a net

$$C_j - Z_j = \$2 - \$0 = \$2$$

by producing a box of little league baseballs. As a result, there is a \$2 entry in the $C_j - Z_j$ row of the X_1 column of Table 7.3.

By subtracting each Z_j entry from the corresponding C_j row entry, Daspling can also determine the net effect of bringing one unit of the other variables into the basis. In this way, management will obtain the remainder of the entries in the $C_j - Z_j$ row of Table 7.3: \$3 in the X_2 column and \$0 in the S_1 and S_2 columns. These initial $C_j - Z_j$ row elements, in essence, identify the impact of the initial basis (S_1 and S_2) on the total profit criterion.

Table 7.4 summarizes the procedure for developing the initial simplex table.

In Table 7.3, you can see that the basic variables (S_1 and S_2) both have \$0 entries in the $C_j - Z_j$ row. These entries demonstrate that the criterion value (total profit) cannot be changed by replacing a variable with itself in the basis. The other $C_j - Z_j$ row entries, however, indicate that Daspling

Table 7.4　Developing the Initial Simplex Table

1. Set up the standard form of the linear program.
2. Establish the initial basic feasible solution.
3. Identify the data contained in the Objective segment of the initial simplex table. In this segment:
   a. The Variables row lists all variables in the standard form of the linear program.
   b. The C_j row gives each variable's per-unit contribution to the criterion.
4. Identify the information contained in the Current Solution segment of the initial simplex table. In this segment:
   a. The Basis column lists the basic variables involved in the initial basic feasible solution.
   b. The C_j column gives each basic variable's per-unit contribution to the criterion.
5. List the quantity of each basic variable in the Amounts column of the initial simplex table. In this table, each of these quantities will correspond to the constant value on the right-hand side of the appropriate standard form system constraint equation.
6. Identify the entries in the Exchange segment of the initial simplex table. The entries in each row of this table will be given by the coefficients of the corresponding variables on the left-hand side of the appropriate system constraint equation.
7. Compute the entries in the Improvement segment of the initial simplex table. In this segment, the Z_j row entries are found by:
   a. Multiplying each C_j column entry by the corresponding element in the appropriate Variables and/or Amounts column
   b. Summing the results
   The $C_j - Z_j$ row entries are then found by subtracting the Z_j row entries from the corresponding C_j row elements.

can increase profit a net \$2 by producing a box of little league baseballs (X_1), and a net \$3 by producing a box of major league baseballs (X_2). In other words, these other entries show that the initial $Z = \$0$ total profit will be increased by bringing either X_1 or X_2 into the basis. This result illustrates the following important property: *In a maximization problem, a basic feasible solution can be improved as long as there are positive entries in the $C_j - Z_j$ row of the simplex table.*

Although Daspling's initial criterion value can be increased by producing either little league or major league baseballs, major league balls have a larger per-box contribution. Consequently, the company should first bring X_2, rather than X_1, into the basis. *In a maximization problem, then, the decision maker always should bring into the basis the variable with the largest positive entry in the $C_j - Z_j$ row of the simplex table.* If there is a tie, management can arbitrarily designate any of the tied activities as the entering variable. The column in the simplex table that corresponds to this entering variable is referred to as the **pivot column**. Daspling's initial pivot column is labeled with the vertical arrow (↑) and "Bring in" notation in the X_2 column in Table 7.3.

Remember that entries in the Amounts column of Table 7.3 give the quantities of the basic variables (S_1 and S_2) involved in the initial simplex solution. Furthermore, the pivot column entries of this table identify the amounts of the corresponding basic variables that must be given up to obtain a unit of the entering variable (X_2). To find the relevant trade ratios, then, management must divide the entries in the Amounts column by the corresponding elements in the pivot column. Daspling's initial trade ratios, for example, are computed adjacent to the appropriate basic variable rows of Table 7.3. These ratios show that the company has enough idle assembly time (S_1) to produce $108,000/15 = 7200$ boxes of major league baseballs and sufficient unused packaging time (S_2) for $108,000/5 = 21,600$ boxes of major league baseballs.

The smallest nonnegative trade ratio of 7200 gives the maximum output of the entering variable (X_2) that will satisfy all restrictions in Daspling's linear program. By producing $X_2 = 7200$ boxes of major league balls, however, the company will utilize all the available assembly slack (S_1) in the initial basis. In other words, the ratio of 7200 also identifies the variable S_1 that should be removed from the basis. The row in the simplex table that corresponds to this departing variable is known as the **pivot row**. Daspling's initial pivot row is labeled with the horizontal arrow $(\leftarrow)$ and "Take out" notation alongside the S_1 row of Table 7.3.

The circled entry at the intersection of the pivot row and pivot column in Table 7.3 is also important. This value, which gives the amount of the departing variable that must be given up to obtain one unit of the entering variable, is called the **pivot element**. It will be used to find some of the entries in the second simplex table.

SECOND SIMPLEX TABLE At this stage, Daspling knows that the initial basic feasible solution, which is represented by Table 7.3, can be improved by replacing the departing variable S_1 with the entering variable X_2 in the basis. Table 7.5 presents the simplex information that would result from such an iteration.

Notice that the entries in the Variables and C_j rows of Table 7.5 are the same as the corresponding elements in the initial simplex table (Table 7.3). That is because these two rows outline the information contained in Daspling's *original* total profit equation

$$Z = \$2X_1 + \$3X_2 + \$0S_1 + \$0S_2$$

and this expression does not change from one basis to another. As a result, the Variables and C_j row entries always remain constant from one simplex table to another.

The remainder of the entries are another matter. In Daspling's second basic feasible solution, X_2 replaces S_1 as a basic variable, but packaging slack (S_2) is still in the basis. Hence, in Table 7.5, the Basis column lists X_2 (in place of S_1) and S_2. Also, since a box of major league baseballs (X_2) contributes \$3 to profit, there is a \$3 entry alongside X_2 in the C_j column. However, the C_j column entry for S_2 is still \$0 in Table 7.5.

Table 7.5   Daspling's Second Simplex Table

Variables		X_1	X_2	S_1	S_2	Amounts	Trade Ratios
Basis	C_j	$2	$3	$0	$0		
X_2	$3	$\frac{3}{5}$	1	$\frac{1}{15}$	0	7,200	$\dfrac{7200}{\frac{3}{5}} = 12{,}000$
S_2	$0	⑧	0	$-\frac{1}{3}$	1	72,000	$\dfrac{72{,}000}{8} = 9000 \leftarrow$ Take out (pivot row)
	Z_j	$\$\frac{9}{5}$	$3	$\$\frac{1}{5}$	$0	$21,600	
	$C_j - Z_j$	$\$\frac{1}{5}$	$0	$-\$\frac{1}{5}$	$0		

         ↑
Bring in
(pivot column)

Now let us consider the X_2 row of Table 7.5. By referring to the S_1 row in the first simplex table (Table 7.3), we can see that the circled 15 is Daspling's initial pivot element. This value indicates that 15 unused assembly minutes (S_1) must be given up to produce one box of major league baseballs (X_2). Since there are initially 108,000 idle assembly minutes available, the company can produce

$$\frac{108{,}000 \text{ of } S_1 \text{ available}}{15 \text{ of } S_1 \text{ for } 1X_2} = 7200$$

boxes of major league balls. As a result, there is a 7200 entry in the Amounts column of the X_2 row in Table 7.5.

There is a similar computation for the entry in the X_1 column of the X_2 row in Table 7.5. Again, refer back to the S_1 row in Table 7.3. These entries indicate that it takes 9 minutes to assemble a box of little league balls (X_1) and 15 minutes per unit of major league balls (X_2). Therefore, Daspling can assemble

$$\frac{9 \text{ of } S_1 \text{ for } 1X_1}{15 \text{ of } S_1 \text{ for } 1X_2} = \frac{9}{15} = \frac{3}{5} = .6$$

boxes of major league balls in the time needed to assemble one box of little league balls.

Now, the X_1 and X_2 activities both compete within the firm for the same limited available assembly time. When this time is being fully utilized, as in Daspling's second simplex solution (Table 7.5), one activity's

Figure 7.5 Finding the Entries in the X_2 Row of Daspling's Second Simplex Table

Basis	X_1	X_2	S_1	S_2	Amounts
S_1	9	(15)	1	0	108,000

← Pivot row

↑ Pivot column

(a) Entries in the S_1 row of the first simplex table (Table 7.3)

Basis	X_1	X_2	S_1	S_2	Amounts
X_2	$9 \div 15 = \frac{9}{15} = \frac{3}{5}$	$15 \div 15 = 1$	$1 \div 15 = \frac{1}{15}$	$0 \div 15 = 0$	$108{,}000 \div 15 = 7200$

(b) Entries in the X_2 row of the second simplex table (Table 7.5)

output can be increased only by reducing the production of the other activity. Consequently, there is an alternative interpretation of the 3/5, or .6, exchange rate. The .6 exchange rate indicates that management must cut major league output (X_2) by .6 box to free enough assembly time for the production of one box of little league baseballs (X_1). That is why there is an entry of 3/5 in the X_1 column of the X_2 row in Table 7.5.

Note that the $9/15 = 3/5$ value is simply the entry (9) in the X_1 column and S_1 row of Table 7.3 divided by the circled pivot element (15). Similarly, 7200 is the entry (108,000) in the Amounts column and S_1 row of Table 7.3 divided by the same pivot element (15). In fact, management can find each element in the X_2 row of Table 7.5 by the same process. That is, they can divide each entry in the S_1 row of the first simplex table (Table 7.3) by the circled pivot element. The calculations are shown in Figure 7.5.

A different process is required to find the entries in the S_2 row of the second simplex table. Consider, for example, the Amounts column. In Table 7.5, the entry in the X_2 row of this column shows that Daspling produces 7200 boxes of major league baseballs. Also, look back at the pivot (X_2) column entry in the S_2 row of Table 7.3. This entry indicates that it takes 5 minutes to package each box of major league balls. Hence, Daspling will need

$$\left(\begin{array}{c}\text{boxes of major} \\ \text{league balls}\end{array}\right) \times \left(\begin{array}{c}\text{minutes needed to package a} \\ \text{box of major league balls}\end{array}\right)$$

$$7200 \qquad \times \qquad 5$$

or a total of 36,000 minutes to package all 7200 boxes.

According to the Amounts column entry in the S_2 row of Table 7.3, there are initially 108,000 unused packaging minutes. After producing 7200 boxes of major league baseballs, however, there will be

$$\begin{pmatrix} \text{initial amount of} \\ \text{unused packaging} \\ \text{minutes} \end{pmatrix} - \left[\begin{pmatrix} \text{boxes of} \\ \text{major league} \\ \text{balls} \end{pmatrix} \times \begin{pmatrix} \text{minutes needed to} \\ \text{package a box of} \\ \text{major league balls} \end{pmatrix} \right]$$

$$108{,}000 \quad - \quad (7200 \quad \times \quad 5)$$

or a net difference of 72,000 unused packaging minutes (S_2) still remaining. As a result, management should enter 72,000 in the Amounts column of the S_2 row in Table 7.5.

The other entries in the S_2 row of Table 7.5 are determined in a similar manner. Consider, for instance, the X_1 variable. As the entry in the X_1 column of the S_2 row in Table 7.3 demonstrates, it initially takes 11 minutes to package a box of little league baseballs. However, this value does not take into account the impact of major league output (X_2) on the exchange process.

In this respect, management knows that it takes 5 minutes to package each box of major league balls. Furthermore, as the X_2 row of Table 7.5 demonstrates, Daspling must give up $3/5 = .6$ box of major league balls to produce one box of little league balls (X_1). By making such an exchange, the company will also free 3/5 of the time needed to package a box of major league baseballs. Under these circumstances, the company can have

$$\begin{pmatrix} \text{boxes of major league} \\ \text{balls given up for one box} \\ \text{of little league balls} \end{pmatrix} \times \begin{pmatrix} \text{minutes needed to} \\ \text{package a box of} \\ \text{major league balls} \end{pmatrix}$$

$$\frac{3}{5} \quad\quad \times \quad\quad 5$$

or 3 more minutes of packaging time available for little league output.

Consequently, after giving up 3/5 of a box of major league baseballs, Daspling will need

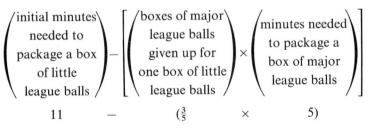

$$11 \quad - \quad (\tfrac{3}{5} \quad \times \quad 5)$$

or a net difference of 8 minutes to package a box of little league baseballs.

That is why management should enter 8 in the X_1 column of the S_2 row in Table 7.5.

This type of adjustment is analogous to an accounting inventory revaluation. In such cases, the value of inventory is established by the market prices of the items. When market prices change, an appropriate accounting adjustment is made to revalue the inventory. Similarly, a simplex exchange rate, like the 11 unused assembly minutes that must be given up for one box of little league balls, can be regarded as a kind of price. In this situation, it measures the amount of one variable that the firm barters internally to obtain a unit of another variable. Hence, when the basis changes, an appropriate simplex adjustment must be made to revalue these internal prices.

Notice that the 7200 in the Amounts column and the 8 in the X_1 column of the S_2 row in Table 7.5 are found by the same process. That is, management takes the

$$\begin{pmatrix} \text{entries in} \\ \text{the } S_2 \text{ row} \\ \text{of Table 7.3} \end{pmatrix} - \left[\begin{pmatrix} \text{corresponding entries} \\ \text{in the } X_2 \text{ row} \\ \text{of Table 7.5} \end{pmatrix} \times \begin{pmatrix} \text{pivot column} \\ \text{entry in the } S_2 \\ \text{row of Table 7.3} \end{pmatrix} \right]$$

This formula can also be used to find the other entries in the S_2 row of Table 7.5. The calculations are shown in Figure 7.6.

To calculate the Z_j row entries, the decision maker again uses the procedure outlined by step 7 in Table 7.4. That is, each C_j column entry is multiplied by the corresponding element in the appropriate Variables or Amounts column, and then the results are summed.

In Table 7.5, for example, entries in the Amounts column show that the second simplex solution involves 7200 boxes of major league baseballs (X_2) and 72,000 unused packaging minutes (S_2). As the C_j column entries indicate, each box of major league balls contributes $3, and each unused packaging minute $0, to profit. Therefore, Daspling will earn

$$\begin{array}{lr} \quad 7200 \text{ of } X_2 \text{ @ \$3 per unit} = \$21{,}600 \\ \text{plus} \quad 72{,}000 \text{ of } S_2 \text{ @ \$0 per unit} = \underline{\quad \$0} \\ \text{for a total of} \hspace{3.5cm} \$21{,}600 \end{array}$$

profit from this combination of variables. As a result, there is an entry of $21,600 in the Z_j row of the Amounts column in Table 7.5.

Similarly, there are entries of 3/5 alongside X_2 and 8 beside S_2 in the X_1 column of Table 7.5. Since X_2 has an entry of $3 and S_2 a $0 element in the C_j column, Daspling will lose

$$\begin{array}{lr} \quad 3/5 \text{ of } X_2 \text{ @ \$3 per unit} = \$9/5 \\ \text{plus} \quad 8 \text{ of } S_2 \text{ @ \$0 per unit} = \underline{\quad \$0} \\ \text{for a total of} \hspace{3.5cm} \$9/5 \end{array}$$

Figure 7.6 Finding the Entries in the S_2 Row of Daspling's Second Simplex Table (Table 7.5)

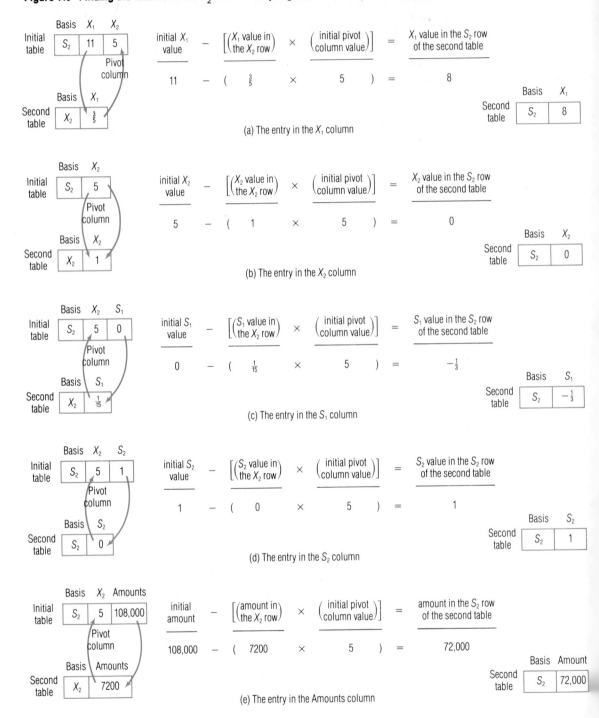

(a) The entry in the X_1 column

(b) The entry in the X_2 column

(c) The entry in the S_1 column

(d) The entry in the S_2 column

(e) The entry in the Amounts column

profit by bringing one box of little league baseballs (X_1) into the basis. Hence, there is an entry of $9/5 in the Z_j row of the X_1 column in Table 7.5.

The $C_j - Z_j$ row entries are then obtained by subtracting the Z_j row elements from the corresponding C_j row elements. For example, $2 appears in the C_j row and $9/5 in the Z_j row of the X_1 column in Table 7.5. Hence, Daspling can increase total profit a net

$$C_j - Z_j = \$2 - \$9/5 = \$1/5$$

by bringing one unit of X_1 into the basis. That is why there is a $1/5 entry in the $C_j - Z_j$ row of the X_1 column in Table 7.5.

Table 7.6 summarizes the procedure for developing the second and subsequent simplex tables.

The entries in the Basis and Amounts columns of Table 7.5 provide the solution information for the second simplex table. According to these entries, the second solution involves

$$X_2 = 7200 \text{ boxes of major league baseballs}$$

and

$$S_2 = 72,000 \text{ unused packaging minutes}$$

In addition, since X_1 and S_1 do not appear in the Basis column of the table, there will be

$$X_1 = 0 \text{ boxes of little league baseballs}$$

and

$$S_1 = 0 \text{ unused assembly minutes}$$

Also, the Z_j row entry in the Amounts column indicates that such a solution earns the company a total profit of $21,600.

In effect, then, Table 7.5 gives the simplex information corresponding to Daspling's second basic feasible solution (extreme point B in Figures 7.1 and 7.2). Furthermore, the iteration from the first simplex table (Table 7.3) to the second (Table 7.5) matches the movement indicated by the arrow from extreme point A to extreme point B in Figure 7.1.

In Table 7.5, you can also see that there are $0 entries in the X_2 and S_2 columns and a $-\$1/5$ element in the S_1 column of the $C_j - Z_j$ row. Such entries demonstrate that Daspling cannot increase the $Z = \$21,600$ total profit by bringing any of these variables into the basis. On the other hand, consider the $C_j - Z_j$ row entry in the X_1 column of the table. This element indicates that the company can increase profit a net $1/5 = $.20 for each box of little league baseballs (X_1) it produces. In other words, the second solution can be improved by bringing X_1 into the basis. As a result, X_1 is the pivot column for the second simplex table (Table 7.5).

By dividing the pivot (X_1) column entries into the corresponding

Table 7.6 Developing the Second and Subsequent Simplex Tables

1. Use the entries in the $C_j - Z_j$ row of the immediately preceding simplex table to determine if the current criterion value can be improved.

2. Identify the variable in the immediately preceding simplex table that leads to the largest net improvement in the criterion value. That is, identify the variable that has the most favorable $C_j - Z_j$ row entry in this table. The column that corresponds to this variable should be labeled as the pivot column.

3. Divide the entries in the Amounts column of the immediately preceding simplex table by the corresponding elements in the pivot column. The results identify the trade ratios of the basic variables for the entering (pivot column) variable.

4. Identify the basic variable in the immediately preceding simplex table that has the smallest nonnegative trade ratio. The row that corresponds to this variable should be labeled as the pivot row.

5. Circle the entry at the intersection of the pivot column and pivot row in the immediately preceding simplex table. This circled entry represents the pivot element.

6. Identify the data contained in the Objective segment of the new simplex table. In this segment, entries in the Variables and C_j rows are the same as the corresponding elements in the immediately preceding table.

7. Identify the information contained in the Current Solution segment of the new simplex table. In this segment:
   a. The entering (pivot column) variable replaces the departing (pivot row) variable in the Basis column.
   b. The per-unit contribution of the entering (pivot column) variable replaces the per-unit contribution of the departing (pivot row) variable in the C_j column.

   Other entries in this segment are the same as the corresponding elements in the immediately preceding simplex table.

8. Determine the entries in the Exchange and Amounts segment of the new simplex table for the row corresponding to the entering variable. To do so, divide the corresponding entries from the immediately preceding table by the pivot element.

9. Determine the entries in the Exchange and Amounts segments of the new simplex table for the rows corresponding to the other basic variables. To do so:
   a. List each entry from the corresponding row of the immediately preceding simplex table.
   b. Multiply each entry found in step 8 by the pivot column entry in the appropriate row of the immediately preceding simplex table.
   c. Subtract each of the values found in step b from the corresponding entry in step a.

10. Compute the entries in the Improvement segment of the new simplex table. In this segment, the Z_j row entries are found by:
    a. Multiplying each C_j column entry by the corresponding element in the appropriate Variables or Amounts column.
    b. Summing the results.

    The $C_j - Z_j$ row entries are then found by subtracting the Z_j row elements from the corresponding C_j row elements in the new simplex table.

11. Return to step 1 and repeat the procedure until it is impossible to improve the criterion value.

Amounts column elements, management will then find that the basic variable X_2 has a trade ratio of

$$\frac{7200}{\frac{3}{5}} = 12,000$$

and that the variable S_2 has a trade ratio of

$$\frac{72,000}{8} = 9000$$

These ratios are listed adjacent to the appropriate basic variable rows of Table 7.5.

Since the smallest nonnegative trade ratio of 9000 is associated with idle packaging time (S_2), this activity becomes the departing, or pivot row, variable in Table 7.5. Further, the circled entry of 8 at the intersection of the pivot row and pivot column becomes the pivot element for the second simplex table.

OPTIMAL SIMPLEX TABLE In the next (third) solution, the departing variable S_2 will be replaced by the entering variable X_1 in the basis. By using the procedure outlined in Table 7.6, Daspling can obtain the simplex information that would result from such an exchange. Table 7.7 presents this information.

The entries in the Basis and Amounts columns of Table 7.7 provide the solution information for the third simplex table. According to these entries, the third solution involves.

$X_2 = 1800$ boxes of major league baseballs

and

$X_1 = 9000$ boxes of little league baseballs

In addition, since S_1 and S_2 do not appear in the Basis column of the table, there will be

$S_1 = 0$ unused assembly minutes

and

$S_2 = 0$ unused packaging minutes

Also, the entry in the Z_j row of the Amounts column indicates that such a solution earns the company a total profit of $23,400.

In effect, then, Table 7.7 gives the simplex information corresponding to Daspling's third basic feasible solution (extreme point C in Figures 7.1 and 7.2). Further, the iteration from the second simplex table (Table 7.5) to the

Table 7.7 Daspling's Third (Optimal) Simplex Table

Basis	Variables C_j	X_1 $2	X_2 $3	S_1 $0	S_2 $0	Amounts
X_2	$3	0	1	$\frac{11}{120}$	$-\frac{3}{40}$	1,800
X_1	$2	1	0	$-\frac{1}{24}$	$\frac{1}{8}$	9,000
Z_j		$2	$3	$\frac{23}{120}$	$\frac{1}{40}$	$23,400
$C_j - Z_j$		$0	$0	$-\frac{23}{120}$	$-\frac{1}{40}$	

third (Table 7.7) matches the movement indicated by the arrow from extreme point B to extreme point C in Figure 7.2.

Finally, notice that all entries in the $C_j - Z_j$ row of Table 7.7 are either zero or negative. These entries demonstrate that Daspling cannot increase the $23,400 profit by bringing any variable into the basis. Consequently, the third basic feasible solution represents the optimal solution to the company's linear program. Put another way, Table 7.7 gives the optimal simplex table.

This result also illustrates the following important property: *The decision maker has found the maximum criterion value in a linear program when there are no positive entries in the $C_j - Z_j$ row of the simplex table.*

DECISION CONSIDERATIONS So far, the discussion has focused on a maximization problem that involves only less-than-or-equal-to restrictions. Practical linear programs, however, may have a variety of constraint formats and may involve a minimization objective. This next section shows how the simplex method deals with these additional formulations and other special situations that may be encountered in practice.

CONSTRAINT FORMATS A linear program may involve restrictions with negative right-hand-side values, greater-than-or-equal-to relationships, or equality expressions. In each of these cases, a special process is required to transform the original restriction into its standard form. Example 7.2 illustrates.

EXAMPLE 7.2 Work Force Planning

Shock, Inc., an electrical contractor, employs electricians for wiring commercial and residential structures. Including fringe benefits, master electricians earn $20 per hour and journeymen $10 per hour. Currently, business is expanding, so the manager plans to hire additional electricians. There is a $300,000 budget available for hiring purposes, and management plans to spend the entire amount. Union contracts require the number of journeyman hours to be at least twice the master hours. This same contract requires the employer to set aside 5000 master hours for company orientation and journeyman training. Also, Shock's management wants to employ additional journeymen for at least 10,000 hours during the proposed hiring period.

Past experience indicates that a master contributes $6 and a journeyman $2.50 per hour to profit. Shock wants to hire the combination of additional master and journeyman hours that will maximize total profit.

By letting

X_1 = additional master hours employed

X_2 = additional journeyman hours employed

Z = the total dollar profit

management can express Shock's problem as the following linear program:

maximize $Z = \$6X_1 + \$2.50X_2$

subject to $\$20X_1 + \$10X_2 = \$300,000$ (Budget)

$X_2 \geq 10,000$ hours   (Journeymen)

$X_2 \geq 2X_1 - 5000$ hours   (Union)

$X_1, X_2 \geq 0$

Negative Right-Hand Side   Recall from Table 7.1 that the proper standard form sets all variables on the left-hand side of each system constraint relationship. Yet in Shock's union restriction

$X_2 \geq 2X_1 - 5000$ hours

the decision variable X_1 appears on the right-hand side of the constraint. Management can remedy this situation by subtracting $2X_1$ from both sides of the inequality to obtain the revised union restriction

(7.19) $X_2 - 2X_1 \geq -5000$ hours

But expression (7.19) is still unacceptable. According to this expression, if $X_1 = 0$, then

$$X_2 \geq -5000$$

That is, X_2 could have a negative value and hence violate the nonnegativity condition that $X_2 \geq 0$.

Such a difficulty can be avoided by removing the negative (-5000) constant value from the right-hand side of expression (7.19). To do so, management should multiply both sides of the expression by -1. In the process, the original greater-than-or-equal-to constraint becomes

$$(X_2 - 2X_1) \times (-1) \geq (-5000) \times (-1)$$

or

$$(7.20) \quad 2X_1 - X_2 \leq 5000$$

which is a less-than-or-equal-to restriction. In fact, multiplying a greater-than-or-equal-to relationship by -1 will always convert the restriction into a less-than-or-equal-to expression, and vice versa.

To account for any potential difference between the hours $(2X_1 - X_2)$ actually employed and the 5000-hour training reserve, Shock must next define a slack variable:

$S_1 = $ unused training reserve hours

By adding S_1 to the left-hand side of inequality (7.20), management can then write the union constraint as follows:

$$(7.21) \quad 2X_1 - X_2 + S_1 = 5000$$

Furthermore, equation (7.21) has all variables on the left-hand side and a positive constant value on the right-hand side of the expression.

Excess Activity   According to Shock's journeymen constraint

$X_2 \geq 10,000$ hours

the company can use more than the minimum 10,000 hours desired by management. Put another way, there can be some excess, or extra, journeyman hours. Indeed, this excess can be any amount beyond the minimum requirement of 10,000 hours. The actual amount, of course, will depend on the selected value of decision variable X_2. In other words, the excess number of journeyman hours is a variable.

To account for any potential difference between the actual number of journeyman hours (X_2) and the minimum 10,000-hour specification, Shock can define another new variable:

$S_2 = $ excess journeyman hours

Such an activity, which accounts for any extra amount beyond a specified minimum requirement, is referred to as a **surplus variable**. By subtracting this variable from the left-hand side of the original journeyman hour constraint, management can rewrite the restriction as follows:

(7.22) $X_2 - S_2 = 10,000$ hours

That is, the action transforms the original greater-than-or-equal-to restriction into an equality relationship. In fact, the subtraction of a surplus variable from the left-hand side of a greater-than-or-equal-to restriction will always convert the original constraint into an equality.

Shock, of course, must account for the new variables (S_1 and S_2) in the objective function, system constraints, and nonnegativity conditions of the linear program. In this regard, neither unused training reserve hours (S_1) nor excess journeyman hours (S_2) make any contribution to profit. Also, neither of these variables requires any budgetary expenditures. Furthermore, the unused training reserve hours (S_1) do not directly provide any journeyman hours, and the excess journeyman hours (S_2) have no direct impact on the union contractual requirement. In addition, slack and surplus variables, as well as decision variables, must have values greater than or equal to zero. As a result, the company's linear program can be expressed in the following format:

maximize $Z = \$6X_1 + \$2.50X_2 + \$0S_1 + \$0S_2$

subject to $\$20X_1 + \$10X_2 + \$0S_1 + \$0S_2 = \$300,000$ (Budget)

$\quad\quad\quad\quad 0X_1 + X_2 + 0S_1 - S_2 = 10,000$ hours   (Journeymen)

$\quad\quad\quad\quad 2X_1 - X_2 + S_1 + 0S_2 = 5000$ hours   (Union)

$\quad\quad\quad\quad X_1, X_2, S_1, S_2 \geq 0$

Fictitious Activity   Although all system constraints are expressed as equalities and all variables are accounted for throughout the problem, Shock's linear program is not yet in a suitable standard form. To see why, let us reconsider the preliminary stages of the fundamental simplex methodology.

In the simplex method, the decision maker obtains an initial basic feasible solution by first setting the decision variables equal to zero. The values of the remaining variables are then read from the right-hand side of the corresponding system constraint equations. In Shock's case, for instance, management sets $X_1 = 0$ and $X_2 = 0$. Under these circumstances, the standard form union constraint shows that there will be

$2X_1 - X_2 + S_1 + 0S_2 = 5000$

or

$S_1 = 5000 - 2X_1 + X_2 + 0S_2$

$\quad = 5000 - 2(0) + 0 + 0 = 5000$

unused training reserve hours. Also, the standard form journeymen restriction demonstrates that when $X_2 = 0$, there will be

$$0X_1 + X_2 + 0S_1 - S_2 = 10,000$$

or

$$S_2 = X_2 - 10,000 + 0X_1 + 0S_1$$
$$= 0 - 10,000 + 0 + 0 = -10,000$$

excess journeyman hours.

However, there are $n = 4$ variables ($X_1, X_2, S_1,$ and S_2) and $m = 3$ system (budget, journeymen, and union) constraint equations in the second version of Shock's linear program. To obtain a basic solution, then, management must set $n - m = 4 - 3 = 1$ variable equal to zero. Yet, initially, we have

$$X_1 = 0 \qquad S_1 = 5000$$
$$X_2 = 0 \qquad S_2 = -10,000$$

or two variables (X_1 and X_2) with zero values. Hence, such a combination of variables does not represent a basic solution. Also, in this solution, the $-10,000$ excess journeyman hours violate the nonnegativity condition that $S_2 \geq 0$. In addition, when $X_1 = 0$, $X_2 = 0$, $S_1 = 5000$, and $S_2 = -10,000$, the total employment expenditure becomes

$$\$20X_1 + \$10X_2 + \$0S_1 + \$0S_2 = \$20(0) + \$10(0) + \$0 + \$0 = \$0$$

which does not equal the planned $300,000 budget. As a result, the solution is not even feasible.

Figure 7.7 presents a representation of the difficulty. The colored line segment on the budget constraint line identifies Shock's feasible solution area. The extreme points of this area are labeled B and C, while the origin of the graph is depicted as point A. At point A, $X_1 = 0$ and $X_2 = 0$. This point lies below the journeymen constraint line and, as the standard form of this constraint demonstrated, involves an $S_2 = -10,000$. In addition, point A is to the left of the union constraint line and, as indicated by the standard form of the restriction, generates an $S_1 = 5000$. But as Figure 7.7 shows, the origin (point A) does not lie in Shock's feasible solution area. Thus, the combination $X_1 = 0$, $X_2 = 0$, $S_1 = 5000$, and $S_2 = -10,000$ does not provide a feasible solution to the problem.

The difficulty results from the presence of greater-than-or-equal-to constraints and equality constraints. Whenever such constraints appear in a linear program, management will be unable to obtain an appropriate standard form with only slack and surplus variables. Instead, another kind of variable is needed.

Let us again consider the budget constraint equation

$$\$20X_1 + \$10X_2 + \$0S_1 + \$0S_2 = \$300,000$$

Figure 7.7 Shock's Feasible Solution Area and Extreme Points

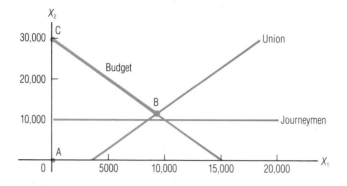

As noted previously, when $X_1 = 0$ and $X_2 = 0$, such as at point A in Figure 7.7, total employment expenditures

$$\$20(0) + \$10(0) + \$0 + \$0 = \$0$$

will not equal the planned $300,000 budget. On the other hand, suppose management adds a fictitious new variable A_1 to the left-hand side of the budget restriction. The constraint can then be written as

(7.23) $\$20X_1 + \$10X_2 + \$0S_1 + \$0S_2 + A_1 = \$300,000$

Then, if $X_1 = 0$ and $X_2 = 0$,

$$\$20(0) + \$10(0) + \$0 + \$0 + A_1 = \$300,000$$

or

$$A_1 = \$300,000$$

In other words, the A_1 variable accounts for the difference between the possible $0 and the planned $300,000 budgetary expenditures.

Similarly, when $X_1 = 0$ and $X_2 = 0$, the journeymen constraint equation

$$0X_1 + X_2 + 0S_1 - S_2 = 10,000 \text{ hours}$$

demonstrates that there will be $S_2 = -10,000$, or a negative number of excess hours. However, if management adds another fictitious variable A_2 to the left-hand side of the restriction, the constraint becomes

(7.24) $0X_1 + X_2 + 0S_1 - S_2 + A_2 = 10,000 \text{ hours}$

Then, when $X_1 = 0$ and $X_2 = 0$,

$$0 + 0 + 0 - S_2 + A_2 = 10,000 \text{ hours}$$

or, since there are no excess journeyman hours ($S_2 = 0$) with this combination of variables,

$A_2 = 10,000$ hours

That is, A_2 accounts for the difference between the possible 0 hours and the minimum 10,000-hour specification.

Fictitious activities, such as A_1 and A_2, are referred to as **artificial variables**. Although these variables are irrelevant for the original problem, they enable the decision maker to develop an appropriate standard form and an initial basic feasible solution.

The artificial variables (A_1 and A_2) do not directly affect the union contractual requirement. Also, A_1 has no direct relevance to the journeymen constraint, while A_2 does not deal with the budget relationship. In addition, artificial variables (as well as slack, surplus, and decision variables) must have values greater than or equal to zero. Consequently, Shock's set of restrictions can be written as follows:

$$20X_1 + \$10X_2 + \$0S_1 + \$0S_2 + A_1 + \$0A_2 = \$300,000 \qquad \text{(Budget)}$$

$$0X_1 + X_2 + 0S_1 - S_2 + 0A_1 + A_2 = 10,000 \text{ hours} \qquad \text{(Journeymen)}$$

$$2X_1 - X_2 + S_1 + 0S_2 + 0A_1 + 0A_2 = 5000 \text{ hours} \qquad \text{(Union)}$$

$$X_1, X_2, S_1, S_2, A_1, A_2 \geq 0$$

A check of Table 7.1 will show that this group of restrictions possesses all the characteristics of a proper standard form.

Shock's restrictions now consist of $n = 6$ variables ($X_1, X_2, S_1, S_2, A_1,$ and A_2) and $m = 3$ system (budget, journeymen, and union) constraint equations. Hence, management can obtain a basic solution by giving $n - m = 6 - 3 = 3$ variables zero values and using the $m = 3$ system constraint equations to find the remaining variable amounts. In particular, if management sets

$$X_1 = 0 \qquad X_2 = 0 \qquad S_2 = 0$$

the system constraint equations will show that

$$A_1 = \$300,000 \qquad A_2 = 10,000 \text{ hours} \qquad S_1 = 5000 \text{ hours}$$

Also, this combination of variables satisfies all standard form restrictions, including the nonnegativity conditions, and thereby represents a basic feasible solution. Furthermore, since such a solution is known to be nonoptimal, it provides a useful starting point for the simplex method.

To find an initial basic feasible solution for a standard form linear program, then, the decision maker should:

1. Set all decision and surplus variables equal to zero

2. Set the slack and artificial variables equal to the constant values on the right-hand side of the corresponding system constraint equations

There is another important consideration. Whenever the decision maker uses artificial variables, the resulting standard form will be a fictitious representation, not an equivalent, of the original linear program. As a result, a basic feasible solution for the standard form may not be a feasible solution to the original linear program. Indeed, Shock's initial basic feasible solution of

$$X_1 = 0 \quad S_1 = 5000 \quad A_1 = 300{,}000$$

$$X_2 = 0 \quad S_2 = 0 \quad A_2 = 10{,}000$$

corresponds to point A in Figure 7.7. Yet, as the graph illustrates, such a point does not satisfy the company's original budget or journeymen constraints.

Fortunately, the optimal combination of standard form variables is the only solution that must be feasible in terms of the original linear program. Therefore, if management can guarantee that the artificial variables do not appear in the optimal basis, the discrepancy between the standard and original forms will not be critical. One way of doing this is to make each artificial variable an unattractive decision alternative. In a minimization problem, for instance, the decision maker can assign a very large positive per-unit criterion contribution to each artificial variable. Although any huge number would be appropriate, the symbol M (for mammoth) is customarily used to represent the very large unit contribution. An artificial variable would then lead to a substantial increase in the criterion value. Yet, in a minimization problem, the objective is to reduce (not increase) the criterion value as much as possible. Consequently, the M unit contributions will force management to eliminate the artificial variables from the basis early in the iteration process. Such an approach is known as the **big M method**.

The big M method is also applicable to maximization problems. Shock, for example, can assign a $-\$M$ (very large negative) per-unit profit contribution to each artificial variable (A_1 and A_2) in its linear program. The company's total profit objective can then be expressed as follows:

$$(7.25) \quad \text{maximize } Z = \$6X_1 + \$2.50X_2 + \$0S_1 + \$0S_2 - \$MA_1 - \$MA_2$$

Since each artificial variable now leads to a substantial reduction in total profit, management should eliminate these fictitious activities from the basis early in the iteration process.

Further, note that all six variables (X_1, X_2, S_1, S_2, A_1, and A_2) are accounted for in expression (7.25). Hence, this expression represents the standard form of Shock's objective function. As a result, the following model gives the complete standard form of the company's linear program:

maximize $\quad Z = \$6X_1 + \$2.50X_2 + \$0S_1 + \$0S_2 - \$MA_1 - \$MA_2$

subject to

$\$20X_1 + \$10X_2 + \$0S_1 + \$0S_2 + A_1 + \$0A_2 = \$300,000 \quad$ (Budget)

$0X_1 + X_2 + 0S_1 - S_2 + 0A_1 + A_2 = 10,000 \text{ hours} \quad$ (Journeymen)

$2X_1 - X_2 + S_1 + 0S_2 + 0A_1 + 0A_2 = 5000 \text{ hours} \quad$ (Union)

$X_1, X_2, S_1, S_2, A_1, A_2 \geq 0$

Table 7.8 summarizes the procedures for establishing the standard form of a linear program. These procedures use the big M method to deal with artificial variables. S. P. Bradley and others [2], N. P. Loomba [9], and R. Rottenberg [11] discuss alternative methods for eliminating the artificial variables.

As noted previously, the initial basic feasible solution to Shock's standard form linear program involves

$X_1 = 0 \qquad S_1 = 5000 \qquad A_1 = 300,000$

$X_2 = 0 \qquad S_2 = 0 \qquad A_2 = 10,000$

By using the procedures outlined in Table 7.4, management will find that this solution generates the simplex information presented in Table 7.9. As you can see, there are artificial variables in the Basis column with positive values in the Amounts column. Furthermore, Shock knows that the initial basic feasible solution, and thereby Table 7.9, corresponds to point A in Figure 7.7. Yet Figure 7.7 demonstrates that such a point does not satisfy the budget and journeymen restrictions in the original linear program. This result illustrates the following important property: *If an artificial variable appears in the Basis column of a simplex table with a positive Amounts entry, the corresponding solution will be infeasible for the original linear program.*

Table 7.9 does not provide the optimal simplex solution. As you can see, there are positive entries in the X_1 and X_2 columns of the $C_j - Z_j$ row. These entries indicate that Shock can increase the initial total profit a net $\$6 + \$20M$ by employing an additional master hour (X_1) and $\$2.50 + \$11M$ by employing an additional journeyman hour (X_2).

Since $\$6 + \$20M$ is a larger positive number then $\$2.50 + \$11M$, the company can obtain the largest net increase in total profit by first bringing X_1 into the basis. That is why X_1 is labeled as the entering, or pivot column, variable in Table 7.9. Also, the smallest negative trade ratio is the 2500 value associated with unused training reserve hours (S_1). Hence, S_1 becomes the departing, or pivot row, variable in this first simplex table.

Table 7.8 Establishing the Standard Form of a Linear Program

Original Constraint	Adjustment of Constraint	Adjustment of Non-negativity Conditions	Adjustment of Objective Function
The value of the right-hand side is negative.	Multiply the left-hand and right-hand sides of the constraint by -1. This procedure converts a less-than-or-equal-to relationship into a greater-than-or-equal-to relationship, or a greater-than-or-equal-to relationship into a less-than-or-equal-to form. An equality remains an equality relationship.	None	None
A less-than-or-equal-to relationship	Add a slack variable S to the left-hand side of the restriction. The slack variable accounts for unused amounts of the constraint.	The value of the slack variable must be greater than or equal to zero.	Add a slack variable with a coefficient of 0 to the objective function.
An equality relationship	Add an artificial variable A to the left-hand side of the restriction. When the decision variables have values of zero, the artificial variable accounts for the difference between zero and the amount of the constraint.	The value of the artificial variable must be greater than or equal to zero.	Add the artificial variable to the objective function. The artificial variable has a very large negative $(-M)$ coefficient in a maximization problem and a very large positive (M) coefficient in a minimization problem. This procedure makes the artificial variable undesirable as a decision alternative for the optimal solution.
A greater-than-or-equal-to-relationship	Subtract a surplus variable S and add an artificial variable A on the left-hand side of the restriction. The surplus variable accounts for any amount above the minimum constraint requirement. The artificial variable again accounts for the difference between zero and the amount of the constraint.	The values of the artificial and surplus variables must be greater than or equal to zero.	Add the artificial variable to the objective function. The artificial variable again has a very large negative $(-M)$ coefficient in a maximization problem and a very large positive (M) coefficient in a minimization problem. Add a surplus variable with a coefficient of 0 to the objective function.

Table 7.9 Shock's First Simplex Table

Variables		X_1	X_2	S_1	S_2	A_1	A_2		
Basis	C_j	$6	$2.5	$0	$0	-$M	-$M	Amounts	Trade Ratios
A_1	-$M	20	10	0	0	1	0	300,000	$\frac{300,000}{20} = 15,000$
A_2	-$M	0	1	0	-1	0	1	10,000	$\frac{10,000}{0}$ = undefined
S_1	$0	②	-1	1	0	0	0	5,000	$\frac{5000}{2} = 2500 \leftarrow$ Take out (pivot row)
	Z_j	-$20M	-$11M	$0	$M	-$M	-$M	-$310,000M	
	$C_j - Z_j$	$6 + $20M	$2.5 + $11M	$0	-$M	$0	$0		

$\uparrow$
Bring in
(pivot column)

Table 7.10 Shock's Optimal Simplex Table

Variables		X_1	X_2	S_1	S_2	A_1	A_2	
Basis	C_j	$6	$2.5	$0	$0	-$M	-$M	Amounts
S_2	$0	0	0	$-\frac{1}{2}$	1	$\frac{1}{20}$	-1	2,500
X_2	$2.5	0	1	$-\frac{1}{2}$	0	$\frac{1}{20}$	0	12,500
X_1	$6	1	0	$\frac{1}{4}$	0	$\frac{1}{40}$	0	8,750
	Z_j	$6	$2.5	$.25	$0	$.275	$0	$83,750
	$C_j - Z_j$	$0	$0	-$.25	-$0	-$M - $.275	-$M	

Finally, the circled entry of 2 at the intersection of the pivot row and pivot column becomes the pivot element for Table 7.9.

By using the procedures outlined in Table 7.6, Shock will eventually obtain the simplex information presented in Table 7.10. Notice that all entries in the $C_j - Z_j$ row are either negative or zero. These entries demonstrate that Shock cannot increase total profit by bringing any variable into the basis. As a result, Table 7.10 provides the optimal basic feasible solution to the company's linear program.

The entries in the Basis and Amounts columns of Table 7.10 identify the optimal solution. According to these entries, management should employ

$$X_1 = 8750 \text{ additional master hours}$$

and

$$X_2 = 12,500 \text{ additional journeyman hours}$$

which creates

$$S_2 = 2500 \text{ excess journeyman hours}$$

above the minimum proposed by management. In addition, since A_1, A_2, and S_1 do not appear in the Basis column of the table, there will be no fictitious activity and

$$S_1 = 0 \text{ unused training reserve hours}$$

in this solution. Also, the entry in the Z_j row of the Amounts column indicates that such a solution earns the company a total profit of $83,750.

A check of Figure 7.7 will show that the optimal combination of standard form variables corresponds to extreme point B of the feasible solution area. Thus, the optimal simplex table (Table 7.10) provides a solution that is feasible for Shock's original linear program. In fact, such a solution represents the optimal solution to the original linear program.

Minimization Problems The simplex method is also applicable to linear programs that involve a minimization objective. However, the decision maker must be careful in interpreting two steps in the procedure. Example 7.3 illustrates.

EXAMPLE 7.3 A Mine Planning Problem

The Northeastern Company operates two separate coal mines. It costs $5000 a day to operate the Alpha shaft and $3000 a day to operate the Beta mine. After crushing, coal ore is processed into premium and standard grades. Dealer contracts call for at least 300 tons of premium and 600 tons of standard in a given time period. The Alpha shaft averages 30 tons of premium grade and 90 tons of standard grade per day. The Beta mine averages 50 tons of premium and 25 tons of standard per day. Management wants to determine the least costly mine-operating plan.

After careful deliberation, management has been able to formulate the problem as the following linear program:

minimize

$$Z = \$5000X_1 + \$3000X_2$$

subject to

$$30X_1 + 50X_2 \geq 300 \text{ tons}$$
$$\text{(Premium)}$$
$$90X_1 + 25X_2 \geq 600 \text{ tons}$$
$$\text{(Standard)}$$
$$X_1, X_2 \geq 0$$

where $Z =$ Northeastern's total operating cost, $X_1 =$ the number of days of operation for the Alpha shaft, and $X_2 =$ the number of days of operation for the Beta mine.

By using the procedures outlined in Table 7.8, management will establish the standard form of Northeastern's linear program. In this form, the company's problem is to:

minimize $Z = \$5000X_1 + \$3000X_2 + \$0S_1 + \$0S_2$
$\qquad\qquad + \$MA_1 + \$MA_2$

subject to

$$30X_1 + 50X_2 - S_1 + 0S_2 + A_1 + 0A_2 = 300 \text{ tons} \qquad \text{(Premium)}$$
$$90X_1 + 25X_2 + 0S_1 - S_2 + 0A_1 + A_2 = 600 \text{ tons} \qquad \text{(Standard)}$$
$$X_1, X_2, S_1, S_2, A_1, A_2 \geq 0$$

where $S_1 =$ excess tons of premium coal, $S_2 =$ excess tons of standard coal, $A_1 =$ artificial tons of premium coal, and $A_2 =$ artificial tons of standard coal. Note that to make the fictitious activities unattractive, management gives A_1 and A_2 very large ($\$M$) per-unit costs in the objective function.

Northeastern's standard form consists of $n = 6$ variables ($X_1, X_2,$ $S_1, S_2, A_1,$ and A_2) and $m = 2$ system (premium and standard) constraint equations. Thus, management can obtain an initial basic solution first by assigning zero values to $n - m = 6 - 2 = 4$ variables. Then the $m = 2$ system constraint equations can be used to find the values of the remaining variables.

If Northeastern initially gives zero values to the decision variables (X_1 and X_2) and surplus variables (S_1 and S_2), the fictitious activity amounts (A_1 and A_2) can be read from the right-hand side of the corresponding system restrictions. Further, the resulting initial basic feasible solution of

$$X_1 = 0 \qquad S_1 = 0 \qquad A_1 = 300$$
$$X_2 = 0 \qquad S_2 = 0 \qquad A_2 = 600$$

will be nonoptimal. Hence, it provides a convenient starting point for the simplex method.

By using the procedure outlined in Table 7.4, management will find that the initial basic feasible solution generates the simplex information contained in Table 7.11. As you can see, there are negative entries in the X_1 and X_2 columns of the $C_j - Z_j$ row. These entries indicate that Northeastern can reduce the initial total cost a net $5000 - \$120M$ by mining a day in Alpha (X_1) and a net $3000 - \$75M$ by mining a day in Beta (X_2). In other words, management can improve the initial basic feasible solution by bringing either X_1 or X_2 into the basis. This result illustrates the following important property: *In a minimization problem, a basic feasible solution can be improved as long as there are negative entries in the $C_j - Z_j$ row of the corresponding simplex table.*

Although Northeastern's initial cost can be decreased by mining either the Alpha or Beta shaft, the $5000 - \$120M$ from Alpha represents a larger daily expense reduction than the $3000 - \$75M$ from Beta. Consequently, the company should first bring X_1 into the basis. *In a minimization problem, then, the decision maker should always bring into the basis the variable with the largest negative entry in the $C_j - Z_j$ row of the simplex table.* That is why X_1 is labeled as the entering, or pivot column, variable in Table 7.11.

The rule for taking a variable out of the basis is the same in a minimization or maximization problem. The smallest nonnegative trade ratio is the 20/3 value associated with the artificial tons of standard coal (A_2). Thus, A_2 becomes the departing, or pivot row, variable in Table 7.11. In addition, the circled entry of 90 at the intersection of the pivot row and pivot column becomes the pivot element for this simplex table.

By using the procedure outlined in Table 7.6, Northeastern will eventually obtain the simplex information presented in Table 7.12. You can see that all entries in the $C_j - Z_j$ row are either zero or positive. These entries demonstrate that Northeastern cannot decrease total cost by bringing any variable into the basis. As a result, Table 7.12 provides the optimal basic feasible solution to the company's linear program. This result also illustrates the following important property: *The decision maker has found the minimum criterion value when there are no negative entries in the $C_j - Z_j$ row of the simplex table.*

The entries in the Basis and Amounts columns of Table 7.12 identify the optimal solution. According to these entries, Northeastern should schedule

$X_1 = 6$ days of operation in the Alpha shaft

and

$X_2 = \frac{12}{5} = 2.4$ days of operation in the Beta mine

Since A_1, A_2, S_1, and S_2 do not appear in the Basis column of this table, there also will be no fictitious activities and

Table 7.11 Northeastern's First Simplex Table

Variables		X_1	X_2	S_1	S_2	A_1	A_2		
Basis	C_j	$5000	$3000	$0	$0	$M	$M	**Amounts**	**Trade Ratios**
A_1	$M	30	50	−1	0	1	0	300	$\frac{300}{30}=10$
A_2	$M	⑨⓪	25	0	−1	0	1	600	$\frac{600}{90}=\frac{20}{3}$ ← Take out (pivot row)
	Z_j	$120M	$75M	−$M	−$M	$M	$M	$900M	
	$C_j - Z_j$	$5000 − $120M	$3000 − $75M	−$M	$M	$0	$0		

Bring in
(pivot column)

Table 7.12 Northeastern's Optimal Simplex Table

Variables		X_1	X_2	S_1	S_2	A_1	A_2	
Basis	C_j	$5000	$3000	$0	$0	$M	$M	**Amounts**
X_2	$3000	0	1	$-\frac{3}{125}$	$\frac{1}{125}$	$\frac{3}{125}$	$-\frac{1}{125}$	$\frac{12}{5}$
X_1	$5000	1	0	$\frac{1}{150}$	$-\frac{6}{450}$	$-\frac{1}{150}$	$\frac{6}{450}$	6
	Z_j	$5000	$3000	$-$\frac{116}{3}$	$$\frac{128}{3}$	$$\frac{116}{3}$	$$\frac{128}{3}$	$37,200
	$C_j - Z_j$	$0	$0	$$\frac{116}{3}$	$-$\frac{128}{3}$	$M − $\frac{116}{3}$	$M − $\frac{128}{3}$	

$S_1 = 0$ excess tons of premium coal

and

$S_2 = 0$ excess tons of standard coal

in the optimal solution. In addition, the Z_j row entry in the Amounts column indicates that such a solution involves a total cost of $37,200.

Special Situations As chapter 6 demonstrated, when attempting to solve a problem, the decision maker may encounter linear programs that have redundant restrictions, are unbounded, are infeasible, or have alternative optima. We will briefly examine how these special situations affect the simplex method.

Redundant Restrictions Ordinarily, an unnecessary, or redundant, restriction will not create any serious difficulty in the simplex method. Under some circumstances, however, the condition can force a tie for the departing, or pivot column, variable during the iteration process. Example 7.4 illustrates.

EXAMPLE 7.4 Production Planning

A small firm has the problem represented by the following linear program:

maximize

$Z = \$30X_1 + \$20X_2$

subject to

$X_1 \le 2000$ units   (Process 1)

$X_2 \le 2000$ units   (Process 2)

$X_1 + X_2 \le 4000$ units (Process 3)

$X_1, X_2 \ge 0$

where $Z =$ the total dollar profit, $X_1 =$ the number of units of product A, and $X_2 =$ the number of units of product B.

Management wants to evaluate the problem with the simplex method.

In Example 7.4, the process 3 system constraint ($X_1 + X_2 \le 4000$ units) is already accounted for by the other (process 1 and 2) restrictions. Hence, the process 3 restriction is redundant, or irrelevant, to the solution of the problem. Furthermore, by using the procedures outlined in Tables 7.4 and 7.6, management will eventually obtain the simplex information contained in Table 7.13. The entries in the $C_j - Z_j$ row indicate that management should bring X_2 into the basis. However, there is a tie between the S_2 and S_3 rows for the smallest nonnegative trade ratio. As a result, it is unclear which of these two slack variables should be taken out of the basis.

Table 7.13   Second Simplex Table for the Production-Planning Problem

Variables		X_1	X_2	S_1	S_2	S_3		
Basis	C_j	$30	$20	$0	$0	$0	**Amounts**	**Trade Ratios**
X_1	$30	1	0	1	0	0	2,000	$\frac{2000}{0}$ = undefined
S_2	$0	0	1	0	1	0	2,000	$\frac{2000}{1}$ = 2000
S_3	$0	0	1	−1	0	1	2,000	$\frac{2000}{1}$ = 2000
	Z_j	$30	$0	$30	$0	$0	$60,000	
	$C_j - Z_j$	$0	$20	−$30	$0	$0		

↑
Bring in
(pivot column)

Table 7.14   Third Simplex Table for the Production-Planning Problem

Variables		X_1	X_2	S_1	S_2	S_3	
Basis	C_j	$30	$20	$0	$0	$0	**Amounts**
X_1	$30	1	0	1	0	0	2,000
S_2	$0	0	0	1	1	−1	0
X_2	$20	0	1	−1	0	1	2,000
	Z_j	$30	$20	$10	$0	$20	$100,000
	$C_j - Z_j$	$0	$0	−$10	$0	−$20	

A typical way of dealing with this situation is to arbitrarily designate
any of the activities with the tied trade ratio as the departing, or pivot row,
variable. In Table 7.13, for example, management can label S_3 as the
exiting variable. After completing the next iteration, the company can then
obtain the simplex information contained in Table 7.14. As Table 7.14
demonstrates, when X_2 replaces S_3 in the third basis, the basic variable S_2
ends up with a zero value. In other words, the number of standard form
variables with nonzero values (X_1 and X_2) is now less than the number of

Table 7.15 Fourth Simplex Table for the Office Supply Problem

Variables		X_1	X_2	S_1	S_2	A_1	A_2		
Basis	C_j	$10	$25	$0	$0	$-\$M$	$-\$M$	**Amount**	**Trade Ratios**
X_1	$10	1	4	0	$-\frac{1}{5}$	0	$\frac{1}{5}$	4,000	$4000/-\frac{1}{5} = -20,000$
S_1	$0	0	3	1	$-\frac{1}{5}$	-1	$\frac{1}{5}$	2,000	$2000/-\frac{1}{5} = -10,000$
	Z_j	$10	$40	$0	$-\$2$	$0	$2	$40,000	
$C_j - Z_j$		$0	$-\$15$	$0	$2	$-\$M$	$-\$M - \$2$		

↑
Bring in
(pivot column)

system (process 1, 2, and 3) constraint restrictions. Such a condition is referred to as **degeneracy**.

Theoretically, degeneracy can lead to a situation in which the iteration process alternates between the same nonoptimal solutions. Under these circumstances, it may be impossible to obtain the optimal solution using standard simplex procedures. Fortunately, such a phenomenon rarely occurs. Nevertheless, L. Cooper and D. Steinberg [3], R. I. Levin and R. P. Lamone [8], and G. E. Thompson [12] discuss the phenomenon, as well as other causes of degeneracy, and present some methods for resolving the difficulty.

Unbounded Problems As demonstrated in chapter 6, some linear programs involve an unbounded problem. In such programs, the restrictions do not put an effective limit on the values of the decision variables. Under the simplex method, this condition will ultimately make it impossible to determine the departing, or pivot row, variable in one of the iterations. The office supply problem in Example 6.4 of chapter 6 provides an illustration.

By using the procedures outlined in Tables 7.4 and 7.6, the office manager will eventually obtain the simplex information contained in Table 7.15. Remember, the objective in this problem is to maximize total dollar profit. Since the $2 in the S_2 column is the largest (and only) positive $C_j - Z_j$ row entry, management should bring S_2 into the basis. Also, the entries in the S_2 column show that the company must give up $-1/5$ unit of X_1 and $-1/5$ unit of S_1 to get one unit of the entering variable (S_2). Yet giving up a negative amount is the same as obtaining a positive quantity.

Hence, the company actually obtains extra amounts of X_1 and S_1 when S_2 is brought into the basis. That is, there will be an increase in the values of X_1 and S_1 whenever S_2 grows in value.

In this situation, then, X_1 or S_1 will never be driven out of the basis (forced to zero values), no matter how large S_2 becomes. Put another way, none of the basic variables will have a nonnegative trade ratio for the entering variable. Indeed, that is why X_1 and S_1 have negative trade ratios alongside Table 7.15. Under these circumstances, management can bring an infinite amount of S_2 into the basis and still have a feasible solution. Since each unit of S_2 increases total profit by \$2, this condition means that the company can get an infinitely large profit. In other words, the problem is unbounded.

As noted in chapter 6, an unbounded linear program usually indicates that the problem has been improperly formulated or the model is inappropriate. H. G. Daellenbach and E. G. Bell [4] and B. Kolman and R. E. Beck [6] discuss this issue in detail.

Infeasibility Chapter 6 also showed that some linear programs are infeasible. In this case, there is no combination of the decision variables that simultaneously satisfies all restrictions in the problem. The simplex method uses the artificial variables to identify any infeasible conditions. To see how, let us reconsider the space allocation problem in Example 6.5 of chapter 6.

If I. M. Warm uses the procedures outlined in Tables 7.4 and 7.6, the professor will eventually obtain the simplex information presented in Table 7.16. As you can see, there are artificial variables (A_1 and A_2) in the Basis column. Further, each of these fictitious activities has a positive entry in the Amounts column of the table. Recall that under these conditions, the corresponding solution will be infeasible for the original linear program.

Warm's objective is to increase the criterion value as much as possible. Yet all entries in the $C_j - Z_j$ row of Table 7.16 are either negative or zero. These entries indicate that Warm cannot improve the criterion value by changing the basis given in this table. Since such a basis includes artificial variables, the professor must conclude that there is no feasible solution to the space allocation problem.

Table 7.16 also identifies the infeasible conditions. In the standard form of Warm's linear program,

A_1 = artificial square feet of living area

and

A_2 = artificial square feet of energy area

Table 7.16 Warm's Second Simplex Table

Variables Basis	C_j	X_1 1	X_2 1	S_1 0	S_2 0	S_3 0	A_1 $-M$	A_2 $-M$	Amounts
X_1	1	1	$\frac{5}{2}$	$\frac{1}{40}$	0	0	0	0	1500
A_1	$-M$	0	$-\frac{5}{2}$	$-\frac{1}{40}$	-1	0	1	0	100
A_2	$-M$	0	1	0	0	-1	0	1	300
Z_j		1	$\frac{5}{2} + \frac{5}{2}M$	$\frac{1}{40} + \frac{1}{40}M$	M	M	$-M$	$-M$	$1500 - 400M$
$C_j - Z_j$		0	$-\frac{3}{2} - \frac{5}{2}M$	$-\frac{1}{40} - \frac{1}{40}M$	$-M$	$-M$	0	0	

In addition, the Basis and Amounts columns of Table 7.16 show that $A_1 = 100$ and $A_2 = 300$ in this solution. These entries demonstrate that the solar home has 100 fewer square feet of living area and 300 fewer square feet of energy area than the government's minimum specifications.

Infeasibility ordinarily indicates that the problem has been formulated improperly or the model is inappropriate. S. I. Gass [5] and R. E. Machol [10] discuss this issue in detail.

Alternative Optima   As chapter 6 illustrated, a linear program may have two or more optimal solutions. In the simplex procedure, we can identify this situation by examining the entries in the $C_j - Z_j$ row of the final simplex table. The homeowner's blending problem in Example 6.6 of chapter 6 provides an illustration.

By using the procedures outlined in Tables 7.4 and 7.6, the homeowner will ultimately obtain the simplex information contained in Table 7.17. The homeowner's objective is to decrease the criterion value (total cost) as much as possible. Yet all entries in the $C_j - Z_j$ row of Table 7.17 are either positive or zero. These entries indicate that the homeowner cannot decrease total cost by bringing any variable into the basis. As a result, Table 7.17 provides an optimal solution to the paint-blending problem.

On the other hand, notice that there is a \$0 entry in the S_1 column of the $C_j - Z_j$ row. According to this entry, if the homeowner brings a unit of the nonbasic variable S_1 into the basis, there will be a \$0 net change in total cost. In other words, there is an alternative combination of variables that will lead to the same \$240 minimum cost given in the Z_j row of the Amounts column.

To find one such alternative, the homeowner should treat S_1 as the entering, or pivot column, variable for Table 7.17. The resulting trade

Table 7.17 Homeowner's Final Simplex Table

Variables		X_1	X_2	S_1	S_2	A_1	A_2		
Basis	C_j	$6	$12	$0	$0	$M	$M	**Amounts**	**Trade Ratios**
X_1	$6	1	0	$-\frac{1}{90}$	$\frac{1}{18}$	$\frac{1}{90}$	$-\frac{1}{18}$	20	$20/-\frac{1}{90} = -1800$
X_2	$12	0	1	$\left(\frac{1}{180}\right)$	$-\frac{5}{18}$	$-\frac{1}{180}$	$\frac{5}{18}$	10	$10/\frac{1}{180} = 1800 \leftarrow$ Take out (pivot row)
	Z_j	$6	$12	$0	$-$3	$0	$3	$240	
	$C_j - Z_j$	$0	$0	$0	$3	$M	$M - $3		

$\uparrow$

Bring in
(pivot column)

Table 7.18 Homeowner's Alternative Optimal Simplex Table

Variables		X_1	X_2	S_1	S_2	A_1	A_2	
Basis	C_j	$6	$12	$0	$0	$M	$M	**Amounts**
X_1	$6	1	2	0	$-\frac{1}{2}$	0	$\frac{1}{2}$	40
S_1	$0	0	180	1	-50	-1	50	1800
	Z_j	$6	$12	$0	$-$3	$0	$3	$240
	$C_j - Z_j$	$0	$0	$0	$3	$M	$M - $3	

ratios alongside this table demonstrate that X_2 will be the departing, or pivot row, variable. After completing the next iteration, the homeowner will obtain Table 7.18.

Since all entries in the $C_j - Z_j$ row of Table 7.18 are positive or zero, this table provides an alternative optimal solution to the homeowner's blending problem. In fact, any weighted average of the basic variables from Tables 7.17 and 7.18 will also be optimal. D. R. Anderson and others [1] and S. M. Lee [7] illustrate such weighted averages and discuss the decision-making implications of alternative optima in detail.

SUMMARY This chapter has presented the simplex method for solving large-scale linear programs. The method was shown to be an algebraic approach based on equality relationships. Yet linear programs typically involve inequality relationships. To use the simplex method, then, the decision maker first must convert each inequality relationship into an equality. The result, which has the characteristics summarized in Table 7.1, is called the standard form of the linear program. Table 7.8 outlined the procedures for transforming a linear program into its standard form.

Once in standard form, the linear program consists of n variables and m system constraint equations. The decision maker then develops a basic feasible solution by assigning zero values to $n - m$ variables. Then the system constraint equations are used to find the values of the remaining m variables.

The simplex method essentially is a search procedure. It starts with a known nonoptimal basic feasible solution. Then each preceding criterion value is improved by successively moving from one basic feasible solution to another. Such a search continues as long as it is possible to improve the criterion value. Table 7.2 summarized the steps involved in this fundamental simplex methodology.

As the chapter demonstrated, simplex calculations can be very complicated and confusing, especially in large-scale linear programs. Hence, management scientists have developed a simplex table, described in Figure 7.3, that conveniently organizes, keeps track of, and helps perform the calculations necessary to get successive basic feasible solutions. Table 7.4 outlined the procedures for establishing the initial simplex table, while Table 7.6 summarized the methods for developing second and subsequent simplex tables.

The procedures indicated that the criterion value can be improved for a maximization problem as long as there are positive $C_j - Z_j$ row entries in the simplex table. In a minimization problem, improvement is possible as long as this $C_j - Z_j$ row contains negative elements. The solution is improved by bringing into the basis the variable that leads to the largest net improvement in the criterion value. In a maximization problem, such a variable has the largest positive $C_j - Z_j$ row entry. In a minimization problem, the decision maker brings into the basis the variable with the largest negative $C_j - Z_j$ row element. Furthermore, management knows that it has found the maximum criterion value when there are no positive $C_j - Z_j$ row entries. Alternatively, the minimum criterion value involves an absence of negative entries in the $C_j - Z_j$ row.

In the final portion of the chapter, we saw how redundant restrictions, unbounded problems, infeasibility, and alternative optima affect the simplex method. We saw that redundant restrictions can lead to degeneracy or a condition in which a basic variable has a value of zero in a simplex solution. In an unbounded problem, none of the basic variables has a nonnegative trade ratio for the entering variable. As a result, it is impossible to determine the departing, or pivot row, variable in one of the simplex iterations. On the other hand, a problem is infeasible if there are artificial variables in the Basis column with positive values in the Amounts column of the last simplex table. Further, the values of these artificial variables identify the infeasible conditions. Finally, when there is a zero $C_j - Z_j$ entry in a nonbasic variable column of the last simplex table, the linear program involves alternative optima. One of these alternatives can be found by treating the zero-valued nonbasic activity as the entering, or pivot column, variable in the next simplex iteration.

Glossary

artificial variables   Fictitious variables that enable the decision maker to develop an appropriate standard form and an initial feasible solution in the simplex method.

basic feasible solution   A combination of decision and nondecision (slack, surplus, and artificial) variables that simultaneously satisfies all system constraints and the nonnegativity conditions in the standard form of a linear program.

basic solution   A combination of decision and nondecision (slack, surplus, or artificial) variables that simultaneously satisfies all system constraints in the standard form of a linear program.

basic variable   A variable that has a nonzero value in the basic solution of a linear program.

basis   The combination of basic variables in a solution for a linear program.

big M method   Assigning the artificial variables very large per-unit contributions to the criterion value.

canonical (standard) form   The form in which each nondecision variable (slack, surplus, or artificial variable) and decision variable is accounted for in the objective function, system constraints, and nonnegativity conditions of a linear program.

degeneracy   A condition in which the number of standard form variables with nonzero values is less than the number of system constraint equations.

entering variable The variable that is brought into the basis in the simplex method.

exiting (departing) variable The variable that is taken out of the basis in the simplex method.

iteration (pivoting) The process of moving from one basis to another in the simplex method.

nonbasic variable A variable that is set equal to zero in the basic solution of a linear program.

pivot column The column in the simplex table that corresponds to the entering variable.

pivot element The entry in a simplex table that is at the intersection of the pivot row and pivot column. It identifies the quantity of the exiting variable that must be given up to obtain one unit of the entering variable.

pivot row The row in the simplex table that corresponds to the exiting, or departing, variable.

simplex method A methodology designed to systematically solve large-scale linear programming problems.

simplex table A tabular format that conveniently organizes, keeps track of, and helps perform the calculations involved in the simplex method.

slack variable A variable that accounts for any unused, or idle, amounts of a resource.

surplus variable A variable that accounts for any excess, or extra, amount beyond some specified minimum requirement.

trade ratio A ratio that identifies the maximum amount of the entering variable that can be obtained for the entire amount of a basic variable.

References

1. Anderson, D. R., et al. *Linear Programming for Decision Making*. St. Paul: West, 1974.
2. Bradley, S. P., et al. *Applied Mathematical Programming*. Reading, Mass.: Addison-Wesley, 1977.
3. Cooper, L., and D. Steinberg. *Linear Programming*. Philadelphia: Saunders, 1974.
4. Daellenbach, H. G., and E. G. Bell. *User's Guide to Linear Programming*. Englewood Cliffs, N.J.: Prentice-Hall, 1970.
5. Gass, S. I. *An Illustrated Guide to Linear Programming*. New York: McGraw-Hill, 1970.
6. Kolman, B., and R. E. Beck. *Elementary Linear Programming with Applications*. New York: Academic Press, 1980.
7. Lee, S. M. *Linear Optimization for Management*. New York: Petrocelli/Charter, 1976.
8. Levin, R. I., and R. P. Lamone. *Linear Programming for Management Decisions*. Homewood, Ill.: Irwin, 1969.
9. Loomba, N. P. *Linear Programming: A Managerial Perspective*. 2d ed. New York: Macmillan, 1976.
10. Machol, R. E. *Elementary Systems Mathematics: Linear Programming for Business and*

Social Sciences. New York: McGraw-Hill, 1976.

11. Rottenberg, R. *Linear Programming.* New York: Elsevier North-Holland, 1980.

12. Thompson, G. E. *Linear Programming.* New York: Macmillan, 1971.

Thought Exercises

1. A marketing executive seeks the brand combination that maximizes total profit contribution. The combination must also satisfy a production cost constraint imposed by top management, a minimum contractual requirement, and a maximum staff availability. A marketing analyst is able to formulate the problem as the following linear program:

maximize $\quad Z = \$100X_1 + \$200X_2 + \$300X_3$

subject to

$\$50X_1 + \$100X_2 + \$40X_3 = \$40,000 \quad$ (Production cost)

$X_1 + X_2 + X_3 \geq 500 \text{ units} \qquad\quad$ (Contract)

$X_1 + 4X_2 + 2X_3 \leq 1000 \text{ hours} \qquad$ (Staff availability)

$X_1, X_2, X_3 \geq 0$

where $Z = $ the total profit contribution per time period, $X_1 = $ the number of units of brand A, $X_2 = $ the number of units of brand B, and $X_3 = $ the number of units of brand C. Explain the nature of the objective and constraints in this linear program in a way that is understandable to a non-quantitatively oriented decision maker.

2. Explain whether slack, surplus, and/or artificial activities are appropriate in the following situations, and give their decision-making interpretations. Assume that the problems have feasible solutions. (To answer this question properly, trace out a rough sketch of your conception of the objective function and constraints.)

   a. A fire department seeks the combination of trucks, fire fighters, and equipment that minimizes the cost of fire protection in a community, subject to constraints on the minimum number of calls per month, a maximum budget, and a maximum number of personhours available per month.

   b. An advertising agency seeks the combination of different types of industry accounts that maximizes its sales revenue, subject to constraints on a maximum annual operating budget, maximum staff capacity, and minimum account coverage requests from each industry classification.

   c. A major national soap manufacturer seeks the combination of soap types that will maximize profit, subject to constraints of maximum production capacity, distribution contracts requiring minimum production levels for each type of soap, and a maximum operating budget.

d. A retail sporting goods store seeks the combination of wearing apparel and equipment that maximizes profit per period while still meeting budget, hours of operation, and size of staff constraints.

e. A nursery school seeks the combination of elementary and intermediate classes that minimizes operating cost per period while meeting minimum schedule and staff requirements.

3. Towilly, Inc., is a manufacturer of pollution control equipment. The company offers three products: a converter, a synthesizer, and an evaporator. Each product is produced and marketed by separate divisions. Monthly production, marketing, and administrative information is summarized in the following report:

Management Report

	Budget Required to Produce One Unit			Available Budget
Budget	Converter	Synthesizer	Evaporator	
Production	$10	$5	$20	$30,000
Marketing	$5	$10	$40	$40,000
Administration	$20	$10	$5	$10,000
Per-unit profit contribution	$100	$40	$50	

Management wants the combined quantity of converters and synthesizers to be at least as large as the quantity of evaporators. The company also is going to save ten crates of evaporators for promotional purposes. In light of the restrictions, the company seeks the combination of equipment that will maximize total profit.

a. Formulate the company's problem as a linear program.

b. Develop the appropriate standard form.

4. Use Examples 7.1 and 7.2 to explain, in language understandable to management, why slack, surplus, and artificial variables must have nonnegative values.

5. Refer back to Example 7.1. In Daspling's second basic feasible solution, there is an entry of $-1/3$ in the S_1 column of the S_2 row of the corresponding simplex table (Table 7.5). Give an intuitive explanation of the derivation and meaning of this entry.

6. State Senator J. M. McConnell has been investigating highway construction from three independent projects, coded A, B, and C. Project A costs $200 per hour to complete, project B costs $100 per hour to complete, and project C costs $500 per hour to complete. There must be a total of at least 2500 hours spent on the projects in order to satisfy contractual requirements of the construction bidders. In addition, the total expenditures on the projects cannot exceed the maximum politically determined budget of $200,000 for the given time period. Each hour devoted to project A adds .2 mile to highway development, each hour devoted to project B adds .1 mile, and each hour devoted to project C adds .6 mile. The governor's stated objective is to maximize the number of additional miles of highway development for the given time period.

Senator McConnell's staff includes an operations research analyst. After a linear programming analysis of the problem, the analyst advises the senator that the governor's objective is not attainable. How did he arrive at this conclusion? Do you see any way of overcoming this difficulty?

7. Custom Costumes manufactures and distributes tuxedos, theatrical costumes, and seasonal costumes at a profit of $100, $50, and $30 per carton, respectively. The company has a minimum total demand of 5000 cartons of tuxedos per month and a minimum total demand of 8000 cartons of each type of costume per month. Also, the company must operate its facilities at a minimum of 20,000 hours to meet these demands. Each carton of tuxedos requires 2 hours of facility operation, each carton of theatrical costumes requires 5 hours, and each carton of seasonal costumes requires 2 hours.

I. M. Bewilder, the company's general manager, has been unable to determine the combination of products that leads to maximum monthly profit. It appears to him that the company should produce an unlimited number of cartons of each type of product, but this conclusion is contrary to his experience in these circumstances. Can you see how he arrived at his conclusion? Can you think of any other factors that may account for his experience to the contrary? Use linear programming analysis to answer these questions.

8. There is a close analogy between the simplex procedure and the movement between the extreme points of the graphic feasible solution area. The simplex method, in effect, starts at the origin of the graph and proceeds toward the optimal solution by searching extreme points of the feasible solution area. Use Examples 7.2 and 7.3 to illustrate this analogy.

9. Brightstar, Inc., is a manufacturer of three types of television picture tubes: black and white, solid-state color, and tube color. Each type is produced and marketed independently. Each tube also goes

through the same three processes: it is produced in the manufacturing center, packaged in a distribution center, and sold through a wholesale center.

The company wants to produce and market the combination of tubes that maximizes total profit and satisfies the available capacity constraints in each center. Brightstar's general manager, with assistance from the corporate operation's research analyst, has formulated the problem as a linear program. An optimal solution is reported in the following simplex table:

Variables		X_1	X_2	X_3	S_1	S_2	S_3	
Basis	C_j	$50	$100	$75	$0	$0	$0	**Amounts**
X_1	$50	1	0	0	$-\frac{3}{10}$	$\frac{1}{10}$	$\frac{1}{5}$	700
X_2	$100	0	1	0	$\frac{1}{5}$	$\frac{2}{5}$	$-\frac{2}{5}$	1,500
X_3	$75	0	0	1	$\frac{1}{5}$	$-\frac{1}{3}$	$\frac{2}{5}$	1,000
	Z_j	$50	$100	$75	$20	$20	$0	$260,000
	$C_j - Z_j$	$0	$0	$0	$-20	$-20	$0	

In this problem, Z = the total dollar profit, X_1 = the number of crates of black and white picture tubes, X_2 = the number of crates of solid-state color tubes, X_3 = the number of crates of tube color types, S_1 = unused manufacturing hours, S_2 = unused distribution hours, and S_3 = unused wholesaling hours.

a. Explain why the solution presented in this table is optimal.
b. How many black and white, solid-state color, and tube color picture tubes should the company produce and sell?
c. What is the maximum total profit the company can expect? Are there any alternative ways to achieve this maximum profit? Explain.
d. How can such knowledge be of benefit to the marketing executive?

10. A company wants to determine the optimal production and inventory schedule for the coming year. The general manager has formulated the problem as the following linear program:

minimize $\quad Z = \$10X_1 + \$15X_2 + \$5X_3$

subject to $\quad X_1 + X_2 + X_3 \geq 2000$ units $\qquad$ (Demand)

$\qquad\qquad\quad 3X_1 + 2X_2 + 6X_3 \leq 3000$ hours $\quad$ (Production capacity)

$\qquad\qquad\quad X_1, X_2, X_3 \geq 0$

The final solution is given in the following simplex table:

Variables Basis	C_j	X_1 $10	X_2 $15	X_3 $5	S_1 $0	S_2 $0	A_1 $M	Amounts
A_1	$M	$-\frac{1}{2}$	0	-2	-1	$-\frac{1}{2}$	1	500
X_2	$15	$\frac{3}{2}$	1	3	0	$\frac{1}{2}$	0	1500
Z_j		$-\$\frac{1}{2}M + \$\frac{45}{2}$	$15	$-\$2M + \$45$	$-\$M$	$-\$\frac{1}{2}M + \$\frac{15}{2}$	$M	$\$500M + 22{,}500$
$C_j - Z_j$		$\$\frac{1}{2}M - \$\frac{45}{2}$	$0	$\$2M - \$40$	$M	$\$\frac{1}{2}M - \$\frac{15}{2}$	$0	

In this problem, Z = the total manufacturing cost, X_1 = the number of units produced in the first half of the year, X_2 = the number of units produced in the second half of the year, X_3 = the number of units held in inventory at the end of the year, S_1 = the number of units produced in excess of yearly demand, S_2 = unused hours of production capacity, and A_1 represents the artificial variable for the demand constraint.

What does this table tell the general manager? Explain.

11. Century Products, Inc., produces citizens band (CB) radios. There are three models: deluxe, standard, and economy. The products are sold to commercial enterprises (governments and companies), as well as to private citizens. Commercial demand is at least 2000 units in a given time period. Private citizen demand is at least 1000 units in that same time period.

The company wants to produce and market the combination of CB radios that maximizes total profit and satisfies consumer demand. Century's manager has formulated the problem as a linear program. The last solution is reported in the following table:

Variables Basis	C_j	X_1 $20	X_2 $30	X_3 $10	S_1 $0	S_2 $0	A_1 $-\$M$	A_2 $-\$M$	Amounts
S_2	$0	0	0	0	-1	1	1	-1	2,000
X_2	$30	1	1	1	-1	0	1	0	3,000
Z_j		$30	$30	$30	$-\$30$	$0	$30	$0	$90,000
$C_j - Z_j$		$-\$10$	$0	$-\$20$	$30	$0	$-\$M - \$30$	$-\$M$	

In this problem, Z = the total profit, X_1 = the number of deluxe units, X_2 = the number of standard units, X_3 = the number of economy units, S_1 = unmet commercial demand, S_2 = unmet citizen demand, and A_1 and A_2 represent the artificial variables for the commercial and citizen demand constraints, respectively.

What can Century conclude from this last table? Explain.

12. Explain why you agree or disagree with each of the following statements:

a. There can be an infinite number of basic and/or basic feasible solutions.

b. The Basis and C_j columns in a simplex table are segments of the Variables and C_j rows.

c. In a simplex table, there must always be an even (one-for-one) exchange between a basic variable and itself.

d. In the first simplex table, the exchange segment corresponds to the left-hand side and the Amounts column to the right-hand side of the appropriate standard form system constraint equations.

e. All Z_j elements in a simplex table will be zero when there are only slack variables in the basis.

f. Basic variables always have zero entries in the $C_j - Z_j$ row of a simplex table.

g. In a simplex table, each basic variable column will have an entry of 1 in one row and zeros elsewhere.

h. When a surplus variable and an artificial variable appear in the same constraint, these variables will have exchange segment entries in the simplex tables that are the same value but opposite in sign.

i. Redundant restrictions always lead to degeneracy.

j. In the simplex method, there can only be a finite number of alternative optima.

Technique Exercises

1. Consider this brand mix problem given in thought exercise 1:

maximize $Z = \$100X_1 + \$200X_2 + \$300X_3$

subject to

$\$50X_1 + \$100X_2 + \$40X_3 = \$40,000$ (Production cost)

$X_1 + X_2 + X_3 \geq 500$ units   (Contract)

$X_1 + 4X_2 + 2X_3 \leq 1000$ hours   (Staff availability)

$X_1, X_2, X_3 \geq 0$

Convert this problem into its standard form. Then solve by the simplex method.

2. Show how the fundamental simplex methodology of Table 7.2 was used to derive the final total profit expression (7.18) in Daspling's

problem. Also, demonstrate the relationship between this fundamental methodology and the simplex tables. In so doing, relate the system constraint equations and objective function for each basic feasible solution for the Daspling problem to the corresponding rows of the appropriate simplex tables.

3. Consider the following maximization problem:

maximize $\quad Z = 2X_1 + .1X_2$

subject to $\quad X_1 + X_2 \leq 100$

$\qquad\qquad X_1 \leq 1.5X_2$

$\qquad\qquad X_1, X_2 \geq 0$

Solve the linear program by the graphic solution procedure. Then convert the program into its standard form and solve by the simplex procedure. Compare the two solutions. What observations can you make?

4. Consider the following minimization problem:

minimize $\quad Z = 2X_1 + 1.5X_2$

subject to $\quad 400X_1 + 200X_2 \geq 2000$

$\qquad\qquad 300X_1 + 600X_2 \geq 2400$

$\qquad\qquad X_1, X_2 \geq 0$

Solve the linear program by the graphic and simplex solution procedures. Compare the results. Are they the same? Explain. Do you see any advantage for the simplex procedure?

5. Solve the following linear programming problem by the simplex method:

maximize $\quad Z = 12X_1 + 8X_2 + 9X_3$

subject to $\quad 2X_1 + 4X_2 + 4X_3 \leq 260$

$\qquad\qquad 3X_1 + 2X_2 + X_3 \geq 300$

$\qquad\qquad X_1 + X_2 \leq 200$

$\qquad\qquad X_1, X_2, X_3 \geq 0$

6. Solve the following linear programming problem by the simplex method:

minimize $\quad Z = X_1 + 2X_2 + 3X_3$

subject to $\quad 20X_1 + 10X_2 + 5X_3 \geq 3500$

$\qquad\qquad X_1 + X_3 \geq 600$

$\qquad\qquad 100X_1 + 200X_2 \geq 50,000$

$\qquad\qquad X_1, X_2, X_3 \geq 0$

7. Ivy College must purchase footballs, baseballs, and basketballs for its athletic department for the coming academic year. The athletic director wants the combination of balls that minimizes total purchase cost and meets the department's educational and team competition requirements. Ivy's problem is formulated as the following linear program:

minimize $Z = \$20X_1 + \$15X_2 + \$30X_3$

subject to
$$10X_1 + 30X_2 + 20X_3 \geq 200 \text{ trips} \quad \text{(Competition)}$$
$$20X_1 + 10X_2 + 40X_3 \geq 200 \text{ classes} \quad \text{(Education)}$$
$$X_1, X_2, X_3 \geq 0$$

where Z = the total purchase cost, X_1 = the number of packages of footballs, X_2 = the number of packages of baseballs, and X_3 = the number of packages of basketballs.

Solve this problem by the simplex method. Explain your findings in language that the athletic director will understand.

8. You are given the following linear program:

maximize $Z = X_1 + X_2$

subject to $50X_1 + 100X_2 \leq 55,000$
$$X_1 + X_2 \geq 1200$$
$$X_2 \leq 300$$
$$X_1, X_2 \geq 0$$

a. Graph this problem. Do you notice anything unusual? Explain.
b. Set up the standard form of the linear program and attempt to solve the problem by the simplex method.
c. Compare the graph and the resulting simplex tables. What observations can you make?

9. Demonstrate how the linear program or standard form of the following problems was derived:
a. Example 7.2
b. Example 7.3
c. Example 7.4
d. Show how Tables 7.9 and 7.10 for Example 7.2 were derived; Tables 7.11 and 7.12 for Example 7.3; and Tables 7.13 and 7.14 for Example 7.4.
e. What is the optimal solution for Example 7.4?

10. You are given the following linear program:

maximize $Z = \$300X_1 + \$200X_2 + \$1000X_3$

subject to $X_1 + 2X_2 + 8X_3 \leq 8000 \text{ hours} \quad \text{(Plant 1)}$

$$5X_1 + 6X_2 + 45X_3 \leq 45{,}000 \text{ hours} \qquad \text{(Plant 2)}$$
$$16X_1 + 8X_2 + X_3 \leq 80{,}000 \text{ hours} \qquad \text{(Plant 3)}$$
$$X_1, X_2, X_3 > 0$$

where Z = the total profit, X_1 = the number of units of product A, X_2 = the number of units of product B, and X_3 = the number of units of product C.

a. Develop the appropriate standard form of the linear program.
b. Determine the first and second simplex tables. Do you notice anything unusual in the second simplex table? Explain.
c. Determine the optimal solution.

11. Consider the office supply problem given in Example 6.4 of chapter 6:

maximize	$Z = \$10X_1 + \$25X_2$	
subject to	$X_1 + X_2 \geq 2000 \text{ boxes}$	(Demand)
	$5X_1 + 20X_2 \geq 20{,}000 \text{ hours}$	(Sales staff)
	$X_1, X_2 \geq 0$	

where X_1 = the number of boxes of standard pads; X_2 = the number of boxes of legal pads, and Z = the total monthly profit. Note that this problem is unbounded.

a. Develop the standard form for this problem.
b. You are given the fourth simplex solution for this problem in Table 7.15. Determine the first, second, and third simplex tables.

12. Consider the space allocation problem given in Example 6.5 of chapter 6:

maximize	$Z = X_1 + X_2$	
subject to	$\$40X_1 + \$100X_2 \leq \$60{,}000$	(Cost)
	$X_1 \geq 1600 \text{ square feet}$	(Living area)
	$X_2 \geq 300 \text{ square feet}$	(Energy area)
	$X_1, X_2 \geq 0$	

Note that this problem is infeasible.

a. Develop the standard form for this problem.
b. You are given the second simplex solution in Table 7.16. Determine the first simplex table.

13. The blending problem given in Example 6.6 of chapter 6 is represented in the following linear program:

minimize	$Z = \$6X_1 + \$12X_2$	
subject to	$100X_1 + 20X_2 \geq 2200 \text{ square feet}$	(Size)
	$2X_1 + 4X_2 \geq 80 \text{ hours}$	(Time)
	$X_1, X_2 \geq 0$	

You are given two optimal solutions to this problem in Tables 7.17 and 7.18 in the text. Set up the standard form for the problem and then show how these tables were derived. Are there any other optimal solutions to this problem? Explain.

14. Refer back to thought exercise 3. Solve this problem with the simplex method. Show all your work.

15. The first basic feasible solution to a linear program is given in the following simplex table:

Variables		X_1	X_2	X_3	X_4	S_1	S_2	S_3	A_1	A_2	A_3	
Basis	C_j	1.5	.15	.5	.1	0	0	0	M	M	M	**Amounts**
A_1	M	.1	.25	.1	.05	-1	0	0	1	0	0	1000
A_2	M	.25	.2	.02	.3	0	-1	0	0	1	0	2000
A_3	M	.05	.05	.15	1.5	0	0	-1	0	0	1	3000
Z_j		.4M	.5M	.27M	1.85M	$-M$	$-M$	$-M$	M	M	M	6000M
$C_j - Z_j$		1.5 − .4M	.15 − .5M	.5 − .27M	.1 − 1.85M	M	M	M	0	0	0	

You want to minimize the value of the objective. Determine the optimal solution. Show all the simplex tables.

Applications Exercises

1. Tough Crack Concrete Packagers must decide how many packages of each type of concrete mix to distribute. There are three types of packages—large, medium, and small—and there are two types of mixes—regular and premium. Each large package holds 100 pounds of regular mix or 90 pounds of premium; a medium package holds 50 pounds of regular or 40 pounds of premium; and a small package holds 30 pounds of regular or 20 pounds of premium. Production and inventory capacity in the given time period limits the available regular mix to 600,000 pounds and the premium mix to 500,000 pounds. Also, the company must mix a minimum of 3000 small packages to meet consumer demand. In addition, the number of large packages must equal the total quantity of medium and small packages.

The company can obtain $6 of profit for each large package, $4 for each medium package, and $2 for each small package.

a. What quantity of each size package should Tough Crack distribute to maximize its profit?

b. What is that profit level?

    c. Does that combination involve any idle regular or premium mix capacity? Does it involve any surplus packages above the minimum demand?

2. A hospital uses three major types of fuel in its normal activities: electricity, natural gas, and uranium (for X-ray and other related medical equipment). Each kilowatt of electricity costs 3 cents, each cubic foot of natural gas 2 cents, and each gram of uranium $100. The fuels are used for three basic functions: medical, administrative, and patient environmental (room heating, air conditioning, and the like). The hospital administrator forecasts a minimum requirement of 2000 hours for the medical function, 1000 hours for the administrative function, and 3000 hours for environmental functions in a given time period. Each kilowatt of electricity provides $\frac{1}{4}$ hour of medical function, $\frac{1}{3}$ hour of administrative function, and $\frac{4}{5}$ hour of environmental function. A cubic foot of natural gas gives $\frac{1}{2}$ hour of medical, $\frac{2}{5}$ hour of administrative, and $\frac{1}{2}$ hour of environmental function. Each gram of uranium supports 5 hours of medical, $\frac{1}{10}$ hour of administrative, and $\frac{1}{5}$ hour of environmental function. Research and patient care typically generate a demand for at least 10 grams of uranium during the given time period.

    What combination of fuels should the administrator use to minimize the total cost of meeting the three hospital needs? Is there any surplus of medical, administrative, or environmental hours associated with the minimum cost? Explain, giving your interpretation of the results and a recommendation for future activities.

3. TRT Association is a private research organization specializing in the development of new chemical and physical processes. In the coming quarter, the association can work on three independent projects dealing with the development of commercial uses of solar energy. Project Alpha involves the development of a home-heating device and is expected to generate $10 of profit to the association for every hour of research effort. Project Beta deals with the conversion of office-lighting equipment and is expected to yield $30 of profit per hour of research effort. Project Centurion, which involves the development of a military weapon, is expected to give the association a profit of $5 per research hour.

    The association does have research capacity, budget, and administrative report-writing restrictions, however. They are specified in the following table, along with the utilization rates of these resources by each research activity:

Project	**Quantity of Resource Used Per Hour of Research**		
	Capacity	Budget	Administration
Alpha	1	$50	2
Beta	1	$30	4
Centurion	1	$100	40
Maximum available	8000 hours	$300,000	20,000 hours

Internal corporate commitments also require the Alpha project to be at least as large as the Beta research effort, while Beta's should not exceed Centurion's endeavors.

a. How many hours of research should be used on each project to maximize quarterly profit?

b. What is that total profit level?

c. Does the maximum profit project combination involve any idle research capacity, unspent budget dollars, or unused administrative hours? Explain.

4. A university cafeteria hires student employees to assist in three shifts of operation: breakfast, lunch, and dinner. Scheduling of classes and other considerations necessitate hiring different students for each shift. Employee costs are also different for each shift, because the work quantity and quality differ. It costs the cafeteria $2 per hour for student assistance at the breakfast shift, $3 per hour at lunch, and $4 per hour at dinner.

Past experience and recent cafeteria forecasts indicate that a minimum of 500 meals will be served per day. The breakfast shift is capable of serving 10 meals per student hour employed, the lunch shift 20 meals per hour, and the dinner shift 5 meals per hour. Policy of the university limits the total hours employed to a maximum of 75 per day.

To ensure that all meals are properly covered, the cafeteria has a policy that the number of student hours employed during the dinner shift must equal the combined effort at the other two meals. Also, management wants to use at least 6 student hours during the breakfast shift.

How many hours of student assistance should the cafeteria employ during each shift to minimize its total daily cost of assistance? Are there any surplus meals prepared or idle student hours employed under this policy?

5. Garbat Baby Foods, Inc., is in the midst of an advertising campaign and must decide its television promotional schedule. Management must decide on the number of advertising spots to place in the Saturday morning lineup, weekday afternoon period, weekday prime-time period, and weekend prime-time period. Spots are defined as one-minute messages, but it is also possible to use fractional spots at proportionately lower rates and with proportionately less audience exposure.

Audience exposure is measured by a proportional index of audience points. Each Saturday morning spot has an estimated 1500 audience points, each weekday afternoon spot 2000 points, a weekday prime-time spot 1200 points, and a weekend prime-time spot 2100 points. Garbat is restricted in its placements by an advertising budget of $6 million and by a network contract requiring a minimum of 250 total spots. There is also a network limitation that requires the number of prime-time spots in a given time period to be at least as large as the sum of all other spots less 180. Also, the network requires a commitment for a minimum of 10 spots in each time slot. Each Saturday morning spot costs $20,000, each weekday afternoon spot $12,000, each weekday prime-time spot $30,000, and each weekend prime-time spot $40,000.

a. How many spots of each type should the company place to maximize total audience points?

b. Does this combination use the entire advertising budget?

c. Are there any surplus spots?

6. Delicious Pastries is a local bakery shop that makes its products on the premises and sells them to the public. The shop uses four basic ingredients: milk, sugar, eggs, and flour. Milk costs $1.50 per gallon, sugar 25 cents a pound, eggs 75 cents a dozen, and flour 15 cents a pound. The bakery sells three basic types of product: cakes, pies, and breads. Each week the shop has a minimum demand for 150 packages of cakes, 150 packages of pies, and 300 packages of bread. It takes 6.4 fluid ounces (.05 gallon) of milk, 8 ounces (.5 pound) of sugar, 3 ($\frac{1}{4}$ dozen) eggs, and 9.6 ounces (.6 pound) of flour to make a package of cakes. Each package of pies requires 19.2 fluid ounces (.15 gallon) of milk, 6.4 ounces (.4 pound) of sugar, 2 (1/6 dozen) eggs, and 8 ounces (.5 pound) of flour. It takes 7.68 fluid ounces (.06 gallon) of milk, 1.6 ounces (.1 pound) of sugar, 1 (1/12 dozen) egg, and 1.5 pounds of flour to make a package of bread.

Also, according to the bakery's recipe policy, the total ingredients of any product must contain no more than 10% sugar, at least 5% milk, no more than 60% flour, and a minimum 15% eggs.

a. How many gallons of milk, pounds of sugar, dozens of eggs, and pounds of flour should Delicious buy to minimize its total purchase cost?

b. What is that total purchase cost?

c. Are there any surplus packages of cakes, pies, or breads at this minimum cost ?

CASE: Lowe Chemical, Inc.

Lowe Chemical, Inc., is a large international manufacturer of chemical products. A subsidiary division produces military bombs and explosives for the armed services, foreign governments, and other parties. Products are classified into three independent categories: plastic explosives, aircraft-delivered bombs, and ground-vehicle-delivered bombs.

An executive planning committee has assembled data on estimated revenues, costs, and technical production rates for the three units, which may include several complete bombs or spare bomb parts (fractions of a purchase unit). Costs and selling prices are presented in the Data Report (Table 7.19). Units are manufactured with the company's limited production facilities and labor

and then marketed within the constraints of the available promotional budget. The per-unit usage rate of each of these resources by each product and the levels of the available resources are also given in the Data Report.

The company wants to produce and market the combination of products that will maximize its profit for the planning period. As a secondary goal, it would like a product mix that involves some idle productive, labor, or marketing capacity to use as a reserve for unforeseen contingencies.

You are employed as a management consultant by the company's executive committee, and you are asked to prepare a decision report that includes the following information:

1. A formulation of the company's problem as a linear programming model

2. An explanation of the applicability of that model to the problem

3. An explanation of the role of the company's fixed costs in the problem

4. A recommendation concerning the optimal product mix

5. A recommendation concerning any potential alternative product mix that would incorporate management's secondary goal

6. The role that fixed costs play in this choice between alternatives

Remember that your report is directed to an executive committee, so be careful to define all terms. Also, make sure that you present your report in language understandable to that committee.

Table 7.19   Data Report

Accounting Classification	Plastic	Product Aircraft	Ground
Fixed costs	$100,000	$600,000	$200,000
R & D	$ 60,000	$500,000	$170,000
Administrative	$ 40,000	$100,000	$ 30,000
Per-unit variable costs	$ 6,000	$ 50,000	$ 35,000
Labor	$ 3,000	$ 10,000	$ 5,000
Materials	$ 2,000	$ 30,000	$ 20,000
Testing	$ 500	$ 6,000	$ 9,000
Other	$ 500	$ 4,000	$ 1,000
Per-unit selling price	$ 36,000	$120,000	$ 85,000

Monthly Per-Unit Usage Rate of Resource			
Product	Production Capacity	Labor Availability	Marketing Budget
Plastic	20 hours	500 hours	$100
Aircraft	100 hours	200 hours	$200
Ground	40 hours	100 hours	$280
Maximum resource available	10,000 hours	50,000 hours	$60,000

Chapter 8
Postoptimality Analysis

CHAPTER OUTLINE

- The Dual
  Shadow Prices
  Dual Linear Program
  Minimization Problems
- Sensitivity Analysis
  Objective Function
  System Constraint Amount
  Exchange Coefficients
  Other Postoptimality Analysis
- Computer Analysis
  User Input
  Computer Output
  Management Benefits
- **Case:** The Tennis Shop

CONCEPTS

- Measuring the economic value of scarce resources and restrictive guidelines
- Interpreting and utilizing these economic values in decision making
- Measuring the sensitivity of the optimal solution to changes in the parameters of the original linear program
- Interpreting and utilizing such sensitivity information for decision making
- Using a computer program to generate the linear programming information

APPLICATIONS

- Antiques refurbishing
- Oil refining
- Tobacco farming
- Hamburger sales
- Bike manufacturing
- Staff scheduling
- Mutual fund investments
- Dog racing
- Thrift shop operations
- Making or buying batteries
- Meal planning
- Production scheduling

Frequently, management is concerned primarily with the optimal solution to a linear program. Yet such a solution provides input for additional analyses that can generate information useful for management planning and control.

Some of the further knowledge is obtained by examining the original linear program from an alternative perspective. In a typical product mix problem, for example, the decision maker seeks the product or service combination that maximizes profit from available resources. Under these circumstances, management usually concentrates on the products or services that generate the maximum profit. Nevertheless, the firm cannot produce any products or services unless it acquires the necessary resources at a reasonable cost. Furthermore, the appropriate cost will depend on the economic value of these resources to the firm. Consequently, the resource values are important additional aspects of the product mix problem. To obtain these values, however, management must focus on the resources rather than on the products or services. In the first section of this chapter, we discuss the two ways of looking at a linear program and show how such an analysis can benefit the decision maker.

Decisions are made in a dynamic environment. Prices and costs change over time, new machines and processes are developed, people change jobs, and so on. These variations can change the variables' unit contributions, restriction amounts, and constraint utilization rates in the original linear program. Hence, management must determine how such changes might affect the optimal solution and identify any revisions that are needed to accommodate the variations. The chapter's second section demonstrates how to obtain this important additional information without reworking the entire problem.

The alternative viewpoint and variation knowledge are gained from an examination of the optimal solution to the original linear program. As a result, these further evaluations can be referred to as **postoptimality analysis**.

A complete linear programming analysis, including the postoptimality evaluation, can be very time-consuming and cumbersome. Fortunately, there are several computer packages available to perform the necessary calculations. The third section of this chapter presents one such package and demonstrates how it is used to help solve linear programming problems and perform the postoptimality analysis.

THE DUAL We begin by considering Example 8.1.

EXAMPLE 8.1 A Product Mix Problem

Ancient Enterprises specializes in the refurbishing and sale of antique clocks and stoves. Each refurbished clock can be sold for an estimated average profit of $20, and each stove for $40. A clock requires 3 labor hours and 1 capital hour for restoration, while a stove needs 5 labor hours and 5 capital hours for restoration. In addition, 25 pounds of a particular cast iron are needed to refurbish a typical antique stove. There are an estimated 1000 capital hours and 1800 labor hours available per month with current facilities. Also, management will provide funds sufficient to purchase a maximum 3750 pounds of cast iron per month. It is possible to start the restoration in one month and complete the project in a subsequent time period. The company wants to refurbish the number of clocks and stoves that will maximize total monthly profit.

By letting

Z = the total monthly profit

X_1 = the number of clocks refurbished

X_2 = the number of stoves refurbished

Ancient's problem can be expressed as the following linear program:

maximize $\quad Z = \$20X_1 + \$40X_2$

subject to $\quad 3X_1 + 5X_2 \leq 1800$ hours $\quad$ (Labor)

$\qquad\qquad 1X_1 + 5X_2 \leq 1000$ hours $\quad$ (Capital)

$\qquad\qquad 25X_2 \leq 3750$ pounds $\qquad$ (Cast iron)

$\qquad\qquad X_1, X_2 \geq 0$

That is, the company seeks the antique mix (combination of X_1 and X_2 values) that will maximize total monthly profit (Z). However, management must ensure that the optimal mix does not utilize more than the available labor, capital, and cast-iron capacities.

Figure 8.1 Ancient's Optimal Solution

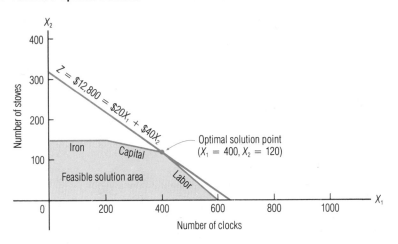

The graph in Figure 8.1 depicts the company's linear programming problem. As you can see, Ancient can maximize total monthly profit at $Z = \$12{,}800$ by refurbishing

$$X_1 = 400 \text{ clocks}$$

and

$$X_2 = 120 \text{ stoves}$$

Furthermore, the optimal solution point ($X_1 = 400$, $X_2 = 120$) is at the intersection of (lies on both) the labor and capital constraint lines. As a result, such a combination of decision variables utilizes all available labor and capital hours. In other words, Ancient's optimal product mix involves no idle labor or capital resources.

Figure 8.1 also shows that the optimal solution point lies below the iron constraint line. Consequently, this combination of decision variables involves some idle or unused pounds of cast iron. That is, Ancient has more than enough cast iron to generate the optimal product mix.

SHADOW PRICES Current resource capacity limits Ancient's profit to a total of $12,800 per month. On the other hand, if management procures additional resources, the company can refurbish more clocks and/or stoves and possibly increase profits. In other words, it may be worthwhile for the firm to expand capacity. To evaluate this issue properly, however, the decision maker must determine the economic value of an additional unit of each resource.

Figure 8.2 Ancient's Optimal Solution with One Additional Labor Hour

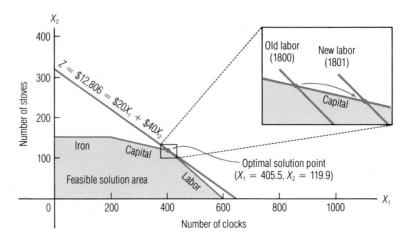

Consider Ancient's labor resource. If management acquires one additional labor hour, the labor constraint expression becomes

$$3X_1 + 5X_2 \leq 1801 \text{ hours}$$

When other conditions (available capital hours, unit profits, and so on) remain the same, such a change produces the effects shown in Figure 8.2. The square in the upper right-hand portion of the figure shows that the additional capacity shifts the labor constraint line to the right. This shift makes the feasible solution area wider than before. Nevertheless, as the graph demonstrates, the optimal solution point of

$$X_1 = 405.5$$

and

$$X_2 = 119.9$$

is still at the intersection of the labor and capital constraint lines.

Figure 8.2 also indicates that the shift in the labor constraint line enables Ancient to reach the $Z = \$12,806$ isoprofit line. Before the shift, the company was able to earn only a $Z = \$12,800$ total profit. Ancient will therefore obtain a

$$\$12,806 - \$12,800 = \$6$$

increase in monthly profit if it can procure one additional labor hour.

This $6 increase in profit, in effect, represents the marginal, or incremental, economic value of the labor resource. As a result, it also identifies the maximum price that management should pay to acquire one additional

Table 8.1 Ancient's Optimal Simplex Table

Basis	Variables C_j	X_1 $20	X_2 $40	S_1 $0	S_2 $0	S_3 $0	Amounts
S_3	$0	0	0	$\frac{5}{2}$	$-\frac{15}{2}$	1	750
X_1	$20	1	0	$\frac{1}{2}$	$-\frac{1}{2}$	0	400
X_2	$40	0	1	$-\frac{1}{10}$	$\frac{3}{10}$	0	120
Z_j		$20	$40	$6	$2	$0	$12,800
$C_j - Z_j$		$0	$0	$-$6	$-$2	$0	

labor hour. Such a price, which measures the criterion value change that results from a one-unit change in a restriction amount, is known as a **shadow price**. In fact, each system constraint in a linear program will have its own shadow price.

Using the Optimal Simplex Table The decision maker can also obtain the relevant shadow prices from the information contained in the optimal simplex table. Table 8.1, for instance, presents the simplex data corresponding to Ancient's optimal basic feasible solution (the $X_1 = 400$ and $X_2 = 120$ point in Figure 8.1). In this table, S_1 denotes unused labor hours and S_2 idle capital hours, while S_3 represents the slack pounds of cast iron. As the Basis and Amounts columns demonstrate, Ancient can maximize total profit at $Z = \$12,800$ by restoring

$X_1 = 400$ clocks

and

$X_2 = 120$ stoves

while leaving

$S_3 = 750$ unused pounds of cast iron

However, since S_1 and S_2 do not appear in the Basis column of the table, the optimal solution will involve

$S_1 = 0$ unused labor hours

and

$S_2 = 0$ unused capital hours

That is, Ancient's optimal product mix utilizes all currently available labor and capital capacity.

Now, suppose the company wants to use 1799 rather than the available 1800 labor hours. In that case, $S_1 = 1$ unused labor hour must be brought into the optimal basis. According to the $C_j - Z_j$ row entry in the S_1 column of Table 8.1, this smaller labor capacity would decrease the company's total profit by \$6. On the other hand, assume that the decision maker can increase labor capacity from 1800 to 1801 hours. Under these circumstances, the \$6 represents the increase in Ancient's total profit that can be obtained from an additional labor hour. In other words, the $C_j - Z_j$ row entry in the S_1 column of Table 8.1 indicates that labor has a shadow price of \$6 per hour.

Such a result illustrates the following important property: *Each system constraint's shadow price is given by the absolute value of the $C_j - Z_j$ row entry in the corresponding nondecision (slack or surplus) variable column in the optimal simplex table.* In this regard, there is a $-\$2$ entry in the unused capital (S_2) column in the $C_j - Z_j$ row of Table 8.1. Hence, Ancient's capital has a shadow price equal to the absolute value of the $-\$2$ entry, or

$$|-\$2| = \$2$$

per hour. Similarly, the $C_j - Z_j$ row entry in the S_3 column indicates that unused cast iron has a shadow price of \$0 per pound.

Managerial Applications   Shadow price information is useful for management planning and control. The decision maker can establish from these prices the relative importance to the organization of various scarce resources or restrictive guidelines. In Ancient's case, cast iron has a shadow price of \$0 per pound. This price indicates that an extra pound would increase the resource's idle capacity but generate no further product output or profit. In other words, the company currently has more than enough cast iron to refurbish the optimal mix of clocks and stoves. As a result, additional cast-iron capacity will have no immediate economic value to the firm.

On the other hand, labor has a \$6 shadow price and capital a \$2 shadow price. Hence, both of these resources are more valuable to Ancient than cast iron. Furthermore, these prices indicate that an additional hour of labor will increase monthly profit by $\$6 - \$2 = \$4$ more than an equivalent amount of capital. Consequently, management knows that additional labor capacity is $\$6/\$2 = 3$ times more valuable to the company than extra capital.

In addition, the decision maker can use the shadow prices to help evaluate proposed changes in resource capacity or restrictive guidelines. Suppose Ancient is considering the use of overtime as a means of increasing labor capacity. Each overtime hour will cost an additional \$5 in wages and benefits. Another option is to increase capital capacity by renting extra machinery for \$3 per hour.

Let us first consider the overtime option. When management utilizes overtime, Ancient's labor cost will increase by $5 per hour. Yet the shadow price of labor indicates that an additional hour of this resource will increase profit by $6 per hour. Overtime, then, will result in a net $6 − $5 = $1 per hour increase in monthly profit. Thus, such an option represents a worthwhile endeavor for the company.

The machinery option is a different matter. If the company rents extra machinery, capital cost will increase by $3 per hour. However, the shadow price of capital indicates that an additional hour of this resource will increase profit by only $2 per hour. The extra machinery, then, will generate

$$\$2 - \$3 = -\$1$$

or a $1 per hour decrease in Ancient's monthly profit. Therefore, such an option is not advisable for the firm.

Shadow prices are also useful in evaluating new decision variables. For example, suppose Ancient is thinking about adding table refurbishing to its antiques business. Each table is expected to contribute a $30 profit. Yet experience indicates that it will take an average of 4 labor hours and 2 capital hours, but no cast iron, to restore a typical table. All other conditions in the problem remain the same.

Ancient's available labor and capital hours currently are being used to refurbish the optimal mix of $X_1 = 400$ clocks and $X_2 = 120$ stoves. To obtain the capacity necessary for table restoration, management must divert its resources from the other projects. In the process, however, the company will reduce clock and/or stove output and thus lose some profit.

Now, remember that Ancient's shadow prices measure the changes in monthly profit that result from unit changes in the resource amounts. In particular, the shadow price of labor indicates that the company will lose $6 in profit for each one-hour reduction in labor availability. Since each table diverts 4 labor hours for restoration, the new product will result in a

$$4 \text{ labor hours @ } \$6 \text{ per hour} = \$24$$

loss in profit from the other projects. Similarly, the shadow price of capital suggests that the firm will lose $2 in profit for each hour reduction in capital availability. In addition, management knows that each table diverts 2 capital hours from clock and/or stove refurbishing. Therefore, when the company restores one table, it will lose

$$2 \text{ capital hours @ } \$2 \text{ per hour} = \$4$$

in profit from the other projects.

In refurbishing each table, then, Ancient must divert enough resources to reduce the monthly profit from the other projects by a total of $28.

Table 8.2 Shadow Price Applications Procedures

Establishing Constraint Priorities	Evaluating Changes in the Constraint Amounts	Evaluating a New Decision Variable
1. Identify the shadow price for each constraint. 2. Establish from these shadow prices the relative importance of each constraint to the decision criterion.	1. Identify the cost or benefit obtained from changing the constraint amount by one unit. 2. Identify the shadow price corresponding to the constraint. 3. Compute the difference between the shadow price and the per-unit cost or benefit. 4. Adopt the proposal only if this difference represents a desirable change in the criterion value.	1. Identify the constraints affected by the new decision variable. 2. Identify the shadow prices corresponding to the affected constraints. 3. Identify the quantity of each constraint needed for (or contributed by) one unit of the new decision variable. These quantities represent exchange coefficients. 4. Multiply each shadow price by the corresponding exchange coefficient and sum the results. This sum represents the decrease in the criterion value that results from the addition of one unit of the new decision variable. 5. Identify the new decision variable's per-unit contribution to the criterion value. 6. Take the difference between the value identified in step 5 and the sum found in step 4. This difference represents the net effect on the criterion value of adding one unit of the new decision variable. 7. Add the new decision variable only if this net effect is desirable.

Nevertheless, the company can earn $30 gross profit each month for each table it refurbishes, leaving a net profit of

$$30 - $28 = $2$$

per table. Thus, the proposed product expansion is a worthwhile endeavor for Ancient Enterprises.

Table 8.2 summarizes the various managerial applications procedures. A. R. Abdel-Khalik [1], D. B. Crane and others [5], and J. F. Sharp [10] present additional business and economic applications of shadow prices.

DUAL
LINEAR PROGRAM Further insights can be gained by examining the product mix problem (Example 8.1) from a resource perspective. In the original problem, management focuses on the products (clocks and stoves) that generate the maximum profit from the available resources (labor, capital, and cast iron). Yet Ancient would be unable to refurbish any products if it could not acquire the necessary resources at a reasonable cost. A related problem, then, is to determine how much the company should pay for its resources.

Wages, interest, and cast-iron purchase costs are already accounted for in the product (clock and stove) per-unit profit contributions. Furthermore, such expenses primarily measure external market prices rather than the internal profit gains accruing from increments in the firm's resources. As a result, these market prices may not reflect the true economic worth of the resources to the company.

On the other hand, Ancient's shadow prices give the profit gains obtained from unit changes in the firm's resources. In effect, then, these prices measure the marginal, or incremental, economic values of the resources to the company. Hence, such values represent the appropriate prices to use in the resource valuation phase of the product mix problem.

Ancient currently has 1800 labor hours available. Now, let U_1 denote labor's shadow price, or the maximum price that management should pay for an additional labor hour. The company should therefore pay a total of

$$1800 \times U_1$$

for the entire labor capacity. Similarly, if U_2 represents capital's shadow price and U_3 cast iron's shadow price, then Ancient should pay a total of

$$1000 \times U_2$$

for all 1000 capital hours and

$$3750 \times U_3$$

for the entire 3750 pounds of cast iron.

The payments for all three resources, then, will total

(8.1) $C = 1800U_1 + 1000U_2 + 3750U_3$

where C = Ancient's total resource payments. Since the company would want to minimize such payments, the following expression represents Ancient's resource objective:

(8.2) minimize $C = 1800U_1 + 1000U_2 + 3750U_3$

There are restrictions on the resource objective (8.2). One constraint deals with clock restoration. In particular, it takes 3 labor hours to refurbish a clock, and labor has a shadow price of U_1 per hour. Hence, Ancient should pay $3U_1$ for the labor hours used in the restoration process. Also, it takes 1 capital hour, but no cast iron, to refurbish a clock.

Since U_2 gives capital's shadow price and U_3 represents cast iron's shadow price, the company should pay $1U_2$ for the capital and $0U_3$ for the cast iron used in clock restoration. Management should therefore pay a total of

$$3U_1 + 1U_2 + 0U_3$$

to refurbish one clock.

Furthermore, resource payments for clock restoration cannot be less than the product's $20 per unit profit. That is,

(8.3) $\underbrace{3U_1 + 1U_2 + 0U_3}_{\text{Resource payments per clock}} \geq \underbrace{\$20}_{\substack{\text{Profit} \\ \text{per} \\ \text{clock}}}$

Otherwise, Ancient would want to refurbish an unlimited number of clocks. Put another way, if management does not satisfy expression (8.3), the company will be encouraged to perform more clock restoration than the current limited resource capacity allows.

There is a similar constraint for stove restoration. Specifically, it takes 5 labor hours and 5 capital hours plus 25 pounds of cast iron to refurbish one stove. Consequently, management should pay a total of

$$5U_1 + 5U_2 + 25U_3$$

to refurbish one stove. Since these payments must be greater than or equal to the $40 profit per stove, the following expression gives the stove restriction on resource payments:

(8.4) $5U_1 + 5U_2 + 25U_3 \geq \$40$

Finally, shadow prices, like most monetary measures, must have values greater than or equal to zero. That is,

(8.5) $U_1, U_2, U_3 \geq 0$

gives the nonnegativity conditions for the resource payments.

By consolidating the objective function (8.2), system constraints (8.3) and (8.4), and nonnegativity conditions (8.5), Ancient can express its resource problem as the following linear program:

minimize $C = 1800U_1 + 1000U_2 + 3750U_3$

subject to $3U_1 + 1U_2 + 0U_3 \geq \$20$ (Clocks)

$5U_1 + 5U_2 + 25U_3 \geq \$40$ (Stoves)

$U_1, U_2, U_3 \geq 0$

According to this linear program, the company seeks the shadow prices $(U_1, U_2,$ and $U_3)$ that minimize the total cost (C) of providing resources for antiques refurbishing. However, management must ensure that each

Table 8.3 Ancient's Primal and Dual Linear Programs

Primal	Dual
maximize $\quad Z = \$20X_1 + \$40X_2$	minimize $\quad C = 1800U_1 + 1000U_2 + 3750U_3$
subject to $\quad 3X_1 + 5X_2 \le 1800$ hours $\quad$ (Labor)	subject to $\quad 3U_1 + 1U_2 + 0U_3 \ge \$20 \quad$ (Clocks)
$\quad\quad\quad\quad 1X_1 + 5X_2 \le 1000$ hours $\quad$ (Capital)	$\quad\quad\quad\quad 5U_1 + 5U_2 + 25U_3 \ge \$40 \quad$ (Stoves)
$\quad\quad\quad\quad 0X_1 + 25X_2 \le 3750$ pounds $\quad$ (Cast iron)	$\quad\quad\quad\quad U_1, U_2, U_3 \ge 0$
$\quad\quad\quad\quad X_1, X_2 \ge 0$	where $\quad C$ = the total resource payments
where $\quad Z$ = the total monthly profit	$\quad\quad\quad\quad U_1$ = shadow price per labor hour
$\quad\quad X_1$ = the number of refurbished clocks	$\quad\quad\quad\quad U_2$ = shadow price per capital hour
$\quad\quad X_2$ = the number of refurbished stoves	$\quad\quad\quad\quad U_3$ = shadow price per pound of cast iron

product's (clock's and stove's) unit profits do not exceed the corresponding resource payments. Such a program is referred to as the **dual** of the original product mix problem, while the original program is known as the **primal**.

Primal and Dual Relationships Table 8.3 presents Ancient's primal and dual linear programs side by side. As the table shows, there are some important relationships between the primal and dual linear programs. In the primal, Ancient maximizes total monthly profit (Z) by using the available resources (labor, capital, and cast iron) to refurbish clock and stove products. The dual objective is to minimize the total payments (C) for these resources. In so doing, the company must ensure that each product's unit profit does not exceed the corresponding resource payments. Hence, the product quantities $(X_1$ and $X_2)$ are the decision variables in the primal, whereas the resource shadow prices $(U_1, U_2,$ and $U_3)$ are the dual's decision activities.

Also, in the primal, the system (labor, capital, and cast-iron) constraints involve less-than-or-equal-to relationships. But in the dual, the system (clock and stove) constraints are greater-than-or-equal-to expressions. Furthermore, the resource amounts (1800, 1000, and 3750) in the primal's system constraints become the coefficients of the corresponding shadow prices $(U_1, U_2,$ and $U_3)$ in the dual objective function. Similarly, the profit coefficients (\$20 and \$40) in the primal's objective function become the amounts of the corresponding system (clock and stove) constraints in the dual.

Table 8.3 illustrates another important relationship between primal and dual. Notice that the product coefficients (3 for X_1 and 5 for X_2) in the primal's labor restriction become labor's shadow price (U_1) coefficients in the dual's system (clock and stove) constraints. In addition, the product

Table 8.4 Transforming the Primal into the Dual Linear Program

1. Identify the dual's decision criterion.
2. Define the dual's decision variables.
3. If the objective is to maximize the primal's criterion value, then the decision maker should minimize the dual's criterion value. Conversely, when the objective is to minimize the primal's criterion value, management should maximize the dual's criterion value.
4. If the system constraints in the primal involve less-than-or-equal-to relationships, the corresponding system constraints in the dual must be greater-than-or-equal-to restrictions. Conversely, when the primal's system constraints involve greater-than-or-equal-to relationships, the corresponding system constraints in the dual must be less-than-or-equal-to restrictions.
5. The amounts on the right-hand side of the primal system constraints become the coefficients of the decision variables in the dual's objective function.
6. The coefficients of the decision variables in the primal's objective function become the amounts on the right-hand side of the dual system constraints.
7. The coefficients of the decision variables in the rows of the primal system constraints become the coefficients in the corresponding columns of the dual system constraints.
8. The decision variables in the dual must be restricted to nonnegative values.

coefficients (1 for X_1 and 5 for X_2) in the primal's capital restriction become capital's shadow price (U_2) coefficients in the dual's system constraints. Also, the primal's cast-iron restriction coefficients (0 for X_1 and 25 for X_2) become the cast-iron shadow price (U_3) coefficients in the dual's system constraints. In other words, the coefficients in the rows of the primal system constraints become the coefficients in the columns of the dual system constraints. The decision maker can use these relationships to readily transform any primal into its dual linear program. Table 8.4 summarizes the procedure.

Some linear programs have a mixture of constraint formats. That is, there may be greater-than-or-equal-to, equality, and less-than-or-equal-to restrictions in the same problem. In such cases, the decision maker must put the system constraints in the same format before setting up the dual. Otherwise, it may be difficult to establish and solve the dual linear program. C. Kim [7] and T. H. Naylor and others [8] discuss this and other situations in detail and present some methods for resolving the difficulties.

Decision Relevance   There are several important reasons for studying primal and dual relationships. For one thing, the dual provides useful insights into the economic nature and decision implications of the primal linear program. In addition, the optimal dual solution generates information that is valuable for management planning and control of the primal problem. Table 8.5 presents the simplex information corresponding to Ancient's optimal dual solution. The entries in the Basis and Amounts

Table 8.5 Simplex Table for Ancient's Optimal Dual Solution

Variables		U_1	U_2	U_3	S_4	S_5	A_1	A_2	
Basis	C_j	1800	1000	3750	0	0	M	M	**Amounts**
U_1	1800	1	0	$-\frac{5}{2}$	$-\frac{1}{2}$	$\frac{1}{10}$	$\frac{1}{2}$	$-\frac{1}{10}$	$6
U_2	1000	0	1	$\frac{15}{2}$	$\frac{1}{2}$	$-\frac{3}{10}$	$-\frac{1}{2}$	$\frac{3}{10}$	$2
	Z_j	1800	1000	3000	-400	-120	400	120	$12,800
$C_j - Z_j$		0	0	750	400	120	$M - 400$	$M - 120$	

columns identify the optimal dual solution. According to these entries, Ancient can minimize the total resource payments at $C = \$12,800$ by paying

$U_1 = \$6$ per labor hour

and

$U_2 = \$2$ per capital hour

Since U_3 does not appear in the Basis column of the table, management should also pay

$U_3 = \$0$ per pound of cast iron

Furthermore, such values represent the appropriate shadow prices for the resources in the company's primal linear program.

This result illustrates the following important property: *The optimal values of the dual decision variables always give the appropriate shadow prices for the corresponding primal system constraints.* In some planning situations, the decision maker may be more interested in shadow prices than in primal information. In such cases, management can find the appropriate shadow prices directly by formulating and solving the dual linear program.

The optimal dual solution also provides other relevant decision information that is not directly available from the primal linear program. In Table 8.5, for example, the products' excess resource payments are represented by S_4 for a clock and S_5 for a stove. Since neither of these surplus variables appears in the Basis column of the table, Ancient's optimal shadow price combination involves

$S_4 = \$0$ excess resource payments per clock

and

$S_5 = \$0$ excess resource payments per stove

The S_4 value indicates that the resources used in restoring a clock should be paid a sum exactly equal to the $20 profit contribution from the product. Similarly, the S_5 value suggests that the resources used in refurbishing a stove should be paid a total exactly equal to the product's $40 profit contribution.

Finally, the primal and dual relationships yield some practical procedural benefits. Kim [7], for example, describes how the dual can be used to test the optimal primal solution. Also, Naylor and others [8] discuss ways by which the dual can help reduce the computational burden involved in solving the primal linear program. In fact, these authors show that it is sometimes easier to solve the dual rather than the primal linear program. In such circumstances, the decision maker may prefer to solve the dual and then derive the optimal primal solution from the results.

Solving the Primal from the Dual Ancient's optimal dual solution recommends that management pay a $U_3 = \$0$ shadow price, or nothing, to acquire an additional pound of cast iron. Yet such a recommendation would be valid only if the company currently has more than enough resource capacity to refurbish the optimal antiques mix. Consequently, the $0 shadow price implies that this mix involves some unused cast iron ($S_3 > 0$). That is, *when an optimal shadow price is equal to zero, the corresponding nondecision (slack or surplus) variable will have a positive value in the optimal primal solution.*

In addition, the optimal S_3 value can be found from the information contained in Table 8.5. To see how, suppose management proposes a $U_3 = \$1$ rather than $U_3 = \$0$ shadow price for cast iron. According to the $C_j - Z_j$ row entry in the U_3 column of the table, this $1 shadow price increase would utilize 750 pounds of cast iron. On the other hand, if the shadow price remains at $U_3 = \$0$, the 750 will represent the unused, or idle, resource capacity. In other words, the $C_j - Z_j$ row entry in the U_3 column of Table 8.5 indicates that Ancient's optimal antiques mix involves $S_3 = 750$ unused pounds of cast iron.

Such a result illustrates the following important property: *Each primal nondecision (slack or surplus) variable's optimal value is given by the $C_j - Z_j$ row entry in the corresponding shadow price column in the dual's optimal simplex table.* In this regard, there is a zero entry in the labor shadow price (U_1) column of the $C_j - Z_j$ row of Table 8.5. Thus, Ancient's optimal primal solution involves $S_1 = 0$ unused labor hours. Similarly, the $C_j - Z_j$ row entry in the capital shadow price (U_2) column indicates that the optimal antiques mix generates $S_2 = 0$ unused capital hours.

Ancient's optimal dual solution also involves $S_4 = \$0$ excess resource payments per clock. This value indicates that each clock earns enough money to compensate labor, capital, and cast iron the exact sum these resources contribute in additional profit. As a result, the company could not gain by shifting these resources away from clock restoration to competing antiques projects. The $0 excess resource payment, then, implies that the optimal antiques mix will include some clock refurbishing ($X_1 > 0$). That is, *if a nondecision (slack or surplus) variable is equal to zero in the optimal dual solution, the corresponding decision variable must have a positive value in the optimal primal solution.*

Furthermore, the optimal X_1 value can be found from the information presented in Table 8.5. Assume that management proposes an $S_4 = \$1$ rather than an $S_4 = \$0$ excess resource payment per clock. According to the $C_j - Z_j$ row entry in the S_4 column, this $1 payment will divert to more profitable projects enough resources for the restoration of 400 clocks. On the other hand, if there is no excess resource payment, or $S_4 = \$0$, the company will have sufficient resources to refurbish $X_1 = 400$ clocks.

This result illustrates the following property: *Each primal decision variable's optimal value is given by the $C_j - Z_j$ row entry in the corresponding nondecision (slack or surplus) variable column in the dual's optimal simplex table.* In this respect, there is an entry of 120 in the excess resource payments per stove (S_5) column of the $C_j - Z_j$ row of Table 8.5. Hence, Ancient's optimal antiques mix involves $X_2 = 120$ refurbished stoves.

Finally, Ancient's optimal product mix must earn enough money to compensate labor, capital, and cast iron the exact sum these resources contribute in total additional profit. Otherwise, the company could gain by shifting the resources away from clock and stove restoration to more profitable activities. Consequently, the optimal dual criterion value generally will equal the optimal criterion value for the primal. In other words, Ancient's minimum total payments ($C = \$12,800$) for the resources utilized in refurbishing antiques should equal the maximum total monthly profit ($Z = \$12,800$) obtained from the products.

Table 8.6 summarizes the principles used in solving the primal from the dual. Converse principles can be used to solve the dual from the primal. In fact, such converse principles have already been used to find Ancient's shadow prices from the optimal simplex table (Table 8.1) for its primal problem. Another illustration will be provided shortly. Collectively, the relationships between the optimal values of the primal and dual variables are known as **complementary slackness**.

MINIMIZATION PROBLEMS   In the case of Ancient Enterprises, shadow price and dual concepts are used to examine the impact of scarce resources on a maximization objective. The same concepts can also be applied to minimization problems involving restrictive guidelines. Example 8.2 illustrates.

Table 8.6 Solving the Primal from the Dual

1. If an optimal shadow price is positive, set the corresponding nondecision (slack or surplus) variable equal to zero in the optimal primal solution.

2. When an optimal shadow price is equal to zero, the corresponding nondecision (slack or surplus) variable must have a positive value in the optimal primal solution. Furthermore, the optimal value of the primal nondecision variable is given by the $C_j - Z_j$ row entry in the corresponding shadow price column in the dual's optimal simplex table.

3. If a nondecision (slack or surplus) variable has a positive value in the optimal dual solution, set the corresponding decision variable equal to zero in the optimal primal solution.

4. When a nondecision (slack or surplus) variable is equal to zero in the optimal dual solution, the corresponding decision variable must have a positive value in the optimal primal solution. Moreover, the optimal value of the primal decision variable is given by the $C_j - Z_j$ row entry in the corresponding nondecision (slack or surplus) variable column in the dual's optimal simplex table.

5. Set the primal's optimal criterion value equal to the optimal criterion value in the dual. This value is given by the entry in the Amounts column of the $C_j - Z_j$ row of the dual's optimal simplex table.

EXAMPLE 8.2 A Blending Problem

Millips Oil Company plans to develop a new engine additive called Wear Prevention. The additive will be a blend of what the company calls types A and B crude oil. Both types of oil contain the same two secret compounds, coded JT and WY, that are required to produce the additive. However, the percentage of the compounds in each type of crude oil differs. Each gallon of type A crude has 30% of compound JT and 10% of WY. A gallon of type B contains 20% of JT and 40% of WY. Millips will need at least 2000 gallons of JT and at least 3000 gallons of WY daily to produce the new additive. Each gallon of type A costs 15 cents, while a gallon of type B costs 20 cents. The company wants to purchase the quantity of each type of crude that will satisfy production requirements at least cost.

After careful consideration, management has been able to express the problem as the following linear program:

minimize

$$Z = \$.15X_1 + \$.20X_2$$

subject to

$$.3X_1 + .2X_2 \geq 2000 \text{ gallons (JT)}$$
$$.1X_1 + .4X_2 \geq 3000 \text{ gallons (WY)}$$
$$X_1, X_2 \geq 0$$

where Z = the total daily purchase cost, X_1 = the number of gallons of type A crude oil, and X_2 = the number of gallons of type B crude oil.

Optimal Primal Solution   The model given in Example 8.2 represents the Millips primal linear program. Table 8.7 presents the simplex data corresponding to the optimal basic feasible solution to such a program. In

Table 8.7 Optimal Simplex Table for the Millips Primal Linear Program

Variables		X_1	X_2	S_1	S_2	A_1	A_2	
Basis	C_j	$.15	$.20	$0	$0	$M	$M	Amounts
X_1	$.15	1	0	−4	2	4	−2	2000
X_2	$.20	0	1	1	−3	−1	3	7000
Z_j		$.15	$.20	−$.40	−$.30	$.40	$.30	$1700
$C_j - Z_j$		$0	$0	$.40	$.30	$M − $.40	$M − $.30	

this table, S_1 denotes the excess gallons of compound JT and S_2 the surplus for WY. Artificial variables A_1 and A_2 are the fictitious activities used only to establish an initial basic feasible solution to the standard form of the primal linear program.

The entries in the Basis and Amounts columns of Table 8.7 identify Millips's optimal primal solution. According to these entries, the company can minimize total daily purchase cost at $Z = \$1700$ by blending

$X_1 = 2000$ gallons of type A crude oil

and

$X_2 = 7000$ gallons of type B crude oil

Also, since S_1 and S_2 do not appear in the Basis column of the table, the optimal solution involves

$S_1 = 0$ surplus gallons of JT

and

$S_2 = 0$ surplus gallons of WY

That is, Millips's optimal oil blend utilizes the minimum required gallons of each compound.

Dual Linear Program Current production requirements make it impossible for Millips to reduce purchase costs below $1700 a day. On the other hand, if management uses less of either compound in the blending process, the company can buy less oil and hence save some purchase cost. To find out how much can be saved, however, the decision maker must determine the marginal economic value, or shadow price, of each compound.

In this regard, let

U_1 = cost savings obtained by using one less gallon of JT

and

U_2 = cost savings obtained by using one less gallon of WY

That is, these variables give the decreases in purchase costs that result from unit changes in Millips's production requirements. In effect, then, they measure the marginal economic values, or shadow prices, of the compounds.

Millips's problem now is to determine the shadow price values (U_1 and U_2) that maximize the total cost savings obtained by using the compounds for oil blending. In so doing, however, management must ensure that each oil's per-gallon cost savings do not exceed the product's corresponding unit purchase cost. Otherwise, the company will be encouraged to use less of each compound than the current minimum production specifications for the Wear Prevention engine additive.

By using the principles outlined in Table 8.4, the decision maker will find that this shadow price, or dual, problem can be expressed as the following linear program:

maximize $C = 2000U_1 + 3000U_2$

subject to $.3U_1 + .1U_2 \leq \$.15$ (Type A oil)

$.2U_1 + .4U_2 \leq \$.20$ (Type B oil)

$U_1, U_2 \geq 0$

where C denotes the total cost savings obtained by using the compounds for oil blending.

Optimal Dual Solution   Management can find the optimal solution to the dual linear program from the information contained in the primal's optimal simplex table. Consider, for example, the surplus JT compound (S_1) column in Table 8.7. According to the $C_j - Z_j$ row entry, Millips will increase total daily purchase cost a net 40 cents by bringing an extra gallon of JT into the optimal oil blend. On the other hand, suppose that the decision maker can use one gallon less of the compound in the blending process. Under these circumstances, the \$.40 represents the decrease in purchase expense, or cost savings, per gallon of the JT compound. In other words, the $C_j - Z_j$ row entry in the S_1 column of Table 8.7 indicates that JT has an optimal shadow price of $U_1 = \$.40$ per gallon. Similarly, the $C_j - Z_j$ row entry in the S_2 column of this table indicates that the WY compound has an optimal shadow price of $U_2 = \$.30$ per gallon.

Also, the JT and WY compounds must generate enough total cost savings to purchase the optimal oil blend. Otherwise, Millips could gain by shifting types A and B oil away from Wear Prevention blending to more cost-effective activities. As a result, the company's maximum total cost savings from the production compounds should equal the minimum total cost of purchasing the blending oils. In other words, the optimal dual criterion value (C) will be equal to the optimal criterion value (Z) in the primal.

Finally, Millips's optimal primal criterion value is given by the Z_j row entry in the Amounts column in Table 8.7. Therefore, according to this entry, the company's optimal shadow price combination involves a maximum total cost savings of $C = Z = \$1700$ per day.

SENSITIVITY ANALYSIS

To properly formulate a linear program, the decision maker must know the values of the following key parameters:

1. Each variable's unit contribution to the criterion value
2. The system restriction amounts
3. Each variable's constraint utilization rate

In Example 8.2, for example, Millips needs each crude oil's per-gallon purchase cost, each compound's production requirement, and the amount of the compounds in each oil. Yet these values rarely are known with complete certainty. Instead, they often represent estimates made at a selected point in time. Oil purchase costs, for example, may be the average quotation of several suppliers on a specific date. Similarly, production requirements and oil content data might come from experiments with current technology.

Unfortunately, conditions change, and the changes can make the original estimates inaccurate. If some oil suppliers go out of business and others alter their price quotations, Millips's purchase cost approximations may be seriously in error. And changes in technology might substantially alter the company's production requirement and oil content estimates.

In spite of the uncertainties, the decision maker will need the original estimates to develop an initial solution to the linear programming problem. After identifying the solution, however, management should also determine how changes in the parameters could affect the optimal primal and dual results. Otherwise, the company may be unprepared for changes in the problem conditions. Furthermore, it should be possible to carry out such an analysis without completely reworking the problem. The methodology used for this process is referred to as a **linear programming sensitivity analysis**.

Consider Example 8.3.

EXAMPLE 8.3 A Resource Allocation Problem

Country Farms, in North Carolina, grows tobacco and cotton on its 200 acres of land. An acre of tobacco brings a $100 profit, and an acre of cotton earns a $50 profit. Government regulations limit tobacco farming to a maximum of 40 acres. During the planting season, there are 500 people-hours of time available. Each acre of tobacco requires 6 people-hours, while each acre of cotton requires 2 people-hours

for cultivation. Country wants to plant the number of tobacco and cotton acres that will maximize total profits.

After careful consideration, management has been able to express Country's problem as the following linear program:

maximize

$$Z = \$100X_1 + \$50X_2$$

subject to

$$X_1 + X_2 \leq 200 \text{ acres (Land)}$$

$X_1 \leq 40$ acres
(Tobacco regulation)

$6X_1 + 2X_2 \leq 500$ people-hours
(Planting)

$X_1, X_2 \geq 0$

where Z = the total profit, X_1 = the number of acres of tobacco, and X_2 = the number of acres of cotton.

The model presented in Example 8.3 represents Country's primal linear program. Table 8.8 gives the simplex data corresponding to the optimal basic feasible solution to such a program. In this table, S_1 denotes the unused acres of farmland, S_2 the idle acres of tobacco, and S_3 the slack people-hours. According to the entries in the Basis and Amounts columns, Country can maximize total profit at $Z = \$11,250$ by planting

$$X_1 = 25 \text{ acres of tobacco}$$

and

$$X_2 = 175 \text{ acres of cotton}$$

while leaving

$$S_2 = 15 \text{ unused acres of tobacco}$$

Also, since S_1 and S_3 do not appear in the Basis column of the table, the optimal crop mix will provide

$$S_1 = 0 \text{ unused acres of farmland}$$

and

$$S_3 = 0 \text{ unused people-hours}$$

OBJECTIVE FUNCTION   In one form of sensitivity analysis, management examines the potential impact of changes in each decision variable's unit contribution to the objective. Consider, for example, Country's per-acre tobacco profit. The C_j row entry in the X_1 column of Table 8.8 indicates that this crop originally yields $100 profit per acre. Now, if the decision maker lets

Table 8.8 Optimal Simplex Table for Country Farms' Primal Linear Program

Variables		X_1	X_2	S_1	S_2	S_3	
Basis	C_j	$100	$50	$0	$0	$0	**Amounts**
S_2	$0	0	0	$\frac{1}{2}$	1	$-\frac{1}{4}$	15
X_1	$100	1	0	$-\frac{1}{2}$	0	$\frac{1}{4}$	25
X_2	$50	0	1	$\frac{3}{2}$	0	$-\frac{1}{4}$	175
	Z_j	$100	$50	$25	$0	$\frac{25}{2}$	$11,250
	$C_j - Z_j$	$0	$0	$-$25	$0	$-$\frac{25}{2}$	

Table 8.9 The Effects of Changes in Tobacco Profit on Country's Optimal Simplex Table

Variables		X_1	X_2	S_1	S_2	S_3	
Basis	C_j	$100 + \Delta c_1$	$50	$0	$0	$0	**Amounts**
S_2	$0	0	0	$\frac{1}{2}$	1	$-\frac{1}{4}$	15
X_1	$100 + \Delta c_1$	1	0	$-\frac{1}{2}$	0	$\frac{1}{4}$	25
X_2	$50	0	1	$\frac{3}{2}$	0	$-\frac{1}{4}$	175
	Z_j	$100 + \Delta c_1$	$50	$25 - \$\frac{1}{2}\,\Delta c_1$	$0	$\frac{25}{2} + \$\frac{1}{4}\,\Delta c_1$	$11,250 + \$25\,\Delta c_1$
	$C_j - Z_j$	$0	$0	$-$25 + \$\frac{1}{2}\,\Delta c_1$	$0	$-$\frac{25}{2} - \$\frac{1}{4}\,\Delta c_1$	

$\Delta c_1 =$ the change in tobacco's per-acre profit

then the unit contribution becomes

$100 + \Delta c_1$

or the original $100 objective function coefficient plus the Δc_1 change. Furthermore, such a revision will alter some of the entries in the optimal simplex table.

Specifically, the new coefficient ($100 + \Delta c_1$) replaces the old coefficient ($100) in the C_j row of the X_1 column and alongside X_1 in the C_j column of Table 8.8. These substitutions will in turn change some Z_j and $C_j - Z_j$ row entries. In fact, by making the pertinent substitutions and resulting computations, management will obtain the revised optimal simplex data presented in Table 8.9.

Country's linear program involves a maximization objective. As a result, the farm's current basis will remain optimal as long as there are no positive entries in the $C_j - Z_j$ row of Table 8.9. To determine the range over which tobacco's per-acre profit could fluctuate without altering the optimal basis, management must find the Δc_1 values that keep all

$$C_j - Z_j \leq 0$$

Each basic variable in the table (S_2, X_1, and X_2) already has a $C_j - Z_j$ row entry of zero. Hence, none of these variables will have any impact on the Δc_1 calculations.

On the other hand, Table 8.9 shows that the nonbasic variable S_1 has a $C_j - Z_j$ row entry of

$$-\$25 + \$\tfrac{1}{2}\, \Delta c_1$$

Consequently, this entry will be negative or zero, and S_1 will not be brought into the basis as long as

$$-\$25 + \$\tfrac{1}{2}\, \Delta c_1 \leq 0$$

or

$$\Delta c_1 \leq \$50$$

In other words, tobacco's per-acre profit could increase by as much as $50 without altering the optimal basis for Country's original linear program.

Similarly, the nonbasic variable S_3 has a $C_j - Z_j$ row entry of

$$-\$\tfrac{25}{2} - \$\tfrac{1}{4}\, \Delta c_1$$

Therefore, this entry will be negative or zero, and hence S_3 will not be brought into the basis as long as

$$-\$\tfrac{25}{2} - \$\tfrac{1}{4}\, \Delta c_1 \leq 0$$

or

$$\Delta c_1 \geq -\$50$$

In other words, tobacco's per-acre profit could decrease by as much as $50 without altering the optimal basis for Country's original linear program. Coincidentally, this allowable decrease happens to be the same $50 as the permitted increase.

In effect, then, the basis in Table 8.9 will remain optimal as long as

$$-\$50 \leq \Delta c_1 \leq \$50$$

or if there is no more than a $\Delta c_1 = \pm \$50$ change in tobacco's per-acre profit. As a result, this product's actual profit could equal the original $100 estimate plus or minus $50 without affecting Country's optimal crop mix.

Figure 8.3 illustrates the sensitivity analysis for tobacco's per-acre profit. You can see that the $\Delta c_1 = \$50$ change in tobacco's per-acre profit makes

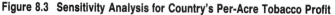

Figure 8.3 Sensitivity Analysis for Country's Per-Acre Tobacco Profit

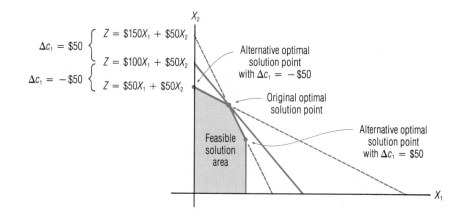

Country's isoprofit line steeper. Consequently, when the crop's profit rises to \$150 per acre, the farm has an alternative for the original optimal solution point. Further increases, then, would exclude this point as a recommended solution to the original linear program. That is, \$150 represents the upper limit to which tobacco's per-acre profit can rise without changing the optimal crop mix for Country's original farming problem.

Figure 8.3 also demonstrates that the $\Delta c_1 = -\$50$ change in the crop's unit contribution makes the isoprofit line flatter. As a result, when tobacco's profit falls to \$50 per acre, Country has another alternative for the original optimal solution point. Further decreases in the unit contribution, then, would exclude this point as a recommended solution to the original linear program. Therefore, \$50 represents the lower limit to which tobacco's per-acre profit can fall without altering the optimal crop mix in Country's original farming problem.

These limits, measuring the scope over which an objective function coefficient can fluctuate without altering the optimal basis in a linear program, form a so-called **range of optimality**. It is important to realize that such a range is obtained by changing only the parameter of interest—in Country's case, tobacco's per-acre profit. All other program parameters (such as cotton's per-acre profit or available land) must remain at their original values during the sensitivity analysis.

Nonbasic Decision Variables   Country's primal linear program contains two decision variables (X_1 and X_2), and both are included in the farm's optimal crop mix. In other cases, however, one or more decision variables may not be in the optimal basis. Fortunately, it is relatively easy to find the range of optimality for the objective function coefficient of such a nonbasic decision variable.

Consider, for example, a maximization problem. In this situation, a decision activity will be nonbasic because it makes an insufficient contribution to the objective. Hence, there is no possible decrease in the contribution that would encourage the decision maker to bring the activity into the basis. Put another way, the variable's unit contribution could be reduced to an infinitely small negative value without affecting the optimal basis. The lower limit on the range of optimality for such a parameter, then, will equal negative infinity $(-\infty)$.

The range's upper limit can be found from the information presented in the optimal simplex table. In particular, the nonbasic activity's $C_j - Z_j$ row entry in the table gives the decrease in the criterion value obtained when a unit of the variable is brought into the basis. The entry's absolute value, then, effectively measures the smallest amount by which the activity's unit contribution must increase before the variable becomes attractive enough to be included in the optimal basis. As a result, the upper limit on the range of optimality for such a parameter will equal the original objective function coefficient plus this smallest required increase.

There would be a similar analysis for a minimization problem. In this case, a decision activity will be nonbasic because it makes an excessive contribution to the objective. Thus, there is no possible increase in the contribution that would encourage the decision maker to bring the activity into the basis. That is, the variable's unit contribution could be increased to an infinitely large value without affecting the optimal basis. The upper limit on the range of optimality for such a parameter, then, will equal positive infinity (∞).

The corresponding lower limit again can be found from the data contained in the optimal simplex table. Specifically, the pertinent $C_j - Z_j$ row entry identifies the smallest amount by which the nonbasic activity's unit contribution must decrease before the variable becomes attractive enough to include in the optimal basis. Therefore, the lower limit on the range of optimality for such a parameter will equal the difference between the original objective function coefficient and this smallest required decrease.

General Procedure   Table 8.10 summarizes the general procedure to find the range of optimality for the objective function coefficient of a decision variable. The general procedure is applicable for basic and nonbasic variables in maximization or minimization problems. Indeed, management can use this procedure to determine the range of optimality for the objective function coefficient of the second decision variable (X_2) in Country's optimal basis. By so doing, management will find that cotton's actual profit could fluctuate between \$33.33 and \$100 per acre without

Table 8.10 Finding an Objective Function Coefficient's Range of Optimality

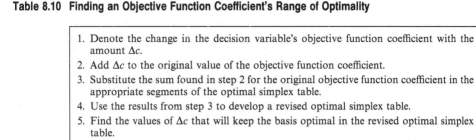

1. Denote the change in the decision variable's objective function coefficient with the amount Δc.
2. Add Δc to the original value of the objective function coefficient.
3. Substitute the sum found in step 2 for the original objective function coefficient in the appropriate segments of the optimal simplex table.
4. Use the results from step 3 to develop a revised optimal simplex table.
5. Find the values of Δc that will keep the basis optimal in the revised optimal simplex table.
6. Set the range of optimality's upper limit equal to the sum of the original objective function coefficient plus the smallest positive Δc value. If there is no positive Δc value, set this upper limit equal to an infinitely large positive number (∞).
7. Set the range of optimality's lower limit equal to the sum of the original objective function coefficient minus the smallest absolute value of the negative Δc amounts. If there is no negative Δc value, set this lower limit equal to an infinitely large negative number ($-\infty$).

affecting the optimal crop mix. In addition, the farm's optimal basis includes $S_2 = 15$ unused acres of tobacco. Such slack (S_2) activity, however, does not contribute anything to profit. Consequently, it is meaningless to develop a range of optimality for the unit profit of the S_2 variable. In fact, there usually will be no good reason to perform a sensitivity analysis on the objective function coefficient of any nondecision (slack or surplus) variable.

Evaluating Parameter Changes   The optimal basis and corresponding basic variable amounts will not change as long as the pertinent activity's objective function coefficient remains within its range of optimality. Moreover, if the activity is a nonbasic variable, such fluctuations do not alter the optimal criterion value. When the activity is a basic variable, however, parameter movements within the range will change this value.

Consider, for example, Country's tobacco activity (X_1). Since X_1 appears in the Basis column of Table 8.9, this activity is a basic variable in the farm's optimal crop mix. Also, the Z_j row entry in the Amounts column of the table shows that such a mix leads to a maximum total profit of

$11,250 + $25 \Delta c_1$

In other words, the entry indicates that the optimal criterion value will depend on the change in tobacco's per-acre profit (Δc_1).

Now, recall that Country's recommended crop mix remains optimal as long as tobacco's per-acre profit remains within its \$50-to-\$150 range of optimality. At the range's \$50 lower limit, there is a

$\Delta c_1 = \$50 - \$100 = -\$50$

change from the parameter's original $100 estimate. Hence, the farm would earn a maximum total profit of

$$\$11,\!250 + \$25\,\Delta c_1 = \$11,\!250 + \$25(-50) = \$10,\!000$$

when tobacco yields a $50 per-acre profit. Yet, at the range's $150 upper limit,

$$\Delta c_1 = \$150 - \$100 = \$50$$

and the maximum total profit is

$$\$11,\!250 + \$25\,\Delta c_1 = \$11,\!250 + \$25(50) = \$12,\!500$$

As a result, actual total profit will fluctuate between $10,000 and $12,500 within the range of optimality for tobacco's objective function coefficient.

If an activity's objective function coefficient is outside its range of optimality, there will be changes in the optimal basis, in the basic variable amounts, and in the optimal criterion value. As an illustration, suppose that favorable market conditions increase Country's tobacco profit from $100 to $180 per acre. This new $180 contribution is beyond the relevant range of optimality's $150 upper limit and represents a

$$\Delta c_1 = \$180 - \$100 = \$80$$

increase from the original $100 estimate. According to the $C_j - Z_j$ row entry in the S_3 column of Table 8.9, such a change will alter Country's optimal total profit by

$$-\$\tfrac{25}{2} - \$\tfrac{1}{4}\,\Delta c_1 = -\$\tfrac{25}{2} - \$\tfrac{1}{4}(80) = -\$32.50$$

for each unused people-hour brought into the basis. That is, if tobacco earns $180 per acre, the farm will decrease profit a net $32.50 by keeping a people-hour idle. Consequently, management still should not bring S_3 into the basis.

On the other hand, observe the $C_j - Z_j$ row entry in the S_1 column of Table 8.9. This entry indicates that $\Delta c_1 = \$80$ will alter the optimal criterion value by

$$-\$25 + \$\tfrac{1}{2}\,\Delta c_1 = -\$25 + \$\tfrac{1}{2}(80) = \$15$$

for each unused acre of farmland brought into the basis. That is, when tobacco earns $180 per acre, Country can increase total profit a net $15 by keeping an acre of farmland idle. Therefore, the decision maker should now bring S_1 into the basis.

To find the revised optimal solution, Country must treat S_1 as the entering variable and then complete the simplex iteration process. If management does this, it will obtain the results presented in Table 8.11. The entries in the Basis and Amounts columns identify the revised optimal solution. These entries indicate that if tobacco earns $180 per acre, Country can maximize total profit at $Z = \$13,700$ by planting

Table 8.11 Country's Optimal Solution When Profit Per Acre of Tobacco Is $180

Variables Basis	C_j	X_1 $180	X_2 $50	S_1 $0	S_2 $0	S_3 $0	Amounts
S_1	$0	0	0	1	2	$-\frac{1}{2}$	30
X_1	$180	1	0	0	1	0	40
X_2	$50	0	1	0	-3	$\frac{1}{2}$	130
Z_j		$180	$50	$0	$30	$25	$13,700
$C_j - Z_j$		$0	$0	$0	$-30	$-25	

Table 8.12 Evaluating a Change in an Objective Function Coefficient

1. Determine whether the objective function coefficient is within its range of optimality.
2. If the coefficient is within its range, do not change the optimal basis or basic variable amounts. To find the optimal criterion value:
   a. Substitute the new coefficient for the old coefficient in the appropriate segments of the optimal simplex table.
   b. Recompute the Amounts column entry in the Z_j row of this table.
   Such an entry identifies the revised optimal criterion value.
3. If the coefficient is outside its range:
   a. Replace the old unit contribution with the new unit contribution in the appropriate segments of the optimal simplex table.
   b. Recalculate the Z_j and $C_j - Z_j$ row entries in this table.
   c. Use the simplex iteration process to develop a revised optimal simplex table.
   The entries in the Basis and Amounts columns in the revised optimal simplex table identify the new optimal solution.

$X_1 = 40$ acres of tobacco

and

$X_2 = 130$ acres of cotton

while leaving

$S_1 = 30$ unused acres of farmland

Also, since S_2 and S_3 do not appear in the Basis column of the table, such a crop mix will involve no unused acres of tobacco or idle people-hours.

Table 8.12 summarizes the general procedure for evaluating a change in an objective function coefficient. This general procedure is applicable to basis and nonbasic variables in maximization or minimization problems.

In another form of sensitivity analysis, the decision maker examines the impact of changes in each system constraint amount. Consider, for instance, Country's farmland restriction. Example 8.3 tells us that the farm originally has 200 acres of land available for planting. Now, if management lets

Δb_1 = the change in the available acres of farmland

the constraint amount becomes

$200 + \Delta b_1$

or the original 200 acres plus the Δb_1 change. Furthermore, such a revision will alter some of the entries in the optimal simplex table. For example, look at the entries in the S_1 and Amounts columns of Table 8.8. The Amounts column entry indicates that Country's original optimal basis involves $S_2 = 15$ unused acres of tobacco. According to the S_1 column entry, however, management must exchange $1/2 = .5$ unused tobacco acre (S_2) for each idle farmland acre (S_1) brought into the optimal basis. Moreover, in the optimal simplex table, Δb_1 can be viewed as the change in idle farmland or the quantity of S_1 that will be brought into the basis. Thus, after the Δb_1 change in farmland acreage, there will be

$S_2 = 15 + \frac{1}{2} \Delta b_1$ unused acres of tobacco

or the original quantity (15) plus the impact of the alteration [$(1/2) \Delta b_1$]. Consequently, the new entry [$15 + (1/2) \Delta b_1$] should replace the old entry (15) in the S_2 row in the Amounts column.

The change in farmland acreage (Δb_1) will revise the Amounts column entries in the X_1 and X_2 rows of Table 8.8 in a similar manner. That is, the new Amounts column entries will equal the original quantities plus a multiple of the Δb_1 change. Furthermore, the appropriate multiple is given by the corresponding exchange segment entry in the S_1 column. For instance, there is an entry of $-1/2$ in the S_1 column of the X_1 row of Table 8.8. As a result, the new entry of

$25 + (-\frac{1}{2}) \Delta b_1 = 25 - \frac{1}{2} \Delta b_1$

should replace the original 25 acres in the X_1 row of the Amounts column of the optimal simplex table. These revisions, in turn, will alter the Z_j row entry in the Amounts column of Table 8.8. In fact, by making the appropriate Amounts column changes, the decision maker will obtain the revised optimal simplex data presented in Table 8.13.

Note that each basic variable in Table 8.13 must have a nonnegative quantity to remain in the optimal basis. To determine the range over which available farmland can fluctuate without altering the optimal basis, management must find the Δb_1 values that satisfy such conditions. That is, Country seeks the Δb_1 values that keep

$S_2, X_1, X_2 \geq 0$

Table 8.13 The Effect of Changes in Acres of Land on Country's Optimal Simplex Table

Variables		X_1	X_2	S_1	S_2	S_3	
Basis	C_j	$100	$50	$0	$0	$0	**Amounts**
S_2	$0	0	0	$\frac{1}{2}$	1	$-\frac{1}{4}$	$15 + \frac{1}{2}\Delta b_1$
X_1	$100	1	0	$-\frac{1}{2}$	0	$\frac{1}{4}$	$25 - \frac{1}{2}\Delta b_1$
X_2	$50	0	1	$\frac{3}{2}$	0	$-\frac{1}{4}$	$175 + \frac{3}{2}\Delta b_1$
	Z_j	$100	$50	$25	$0	$\frac{25}{2}$	$11,250 + \$25\,\Delta b_1$
	$C_j - Z_j$	$0	$0	$-\$25	$0	$-\$\frac{25}{2}$	

in the Amounts column of Table 8.13. In this regard, the basic variable S_2 has an Amounts column entry of

$$15 + \tfrac{1}{2}\,\Delta b_1$$

Therefore, S_2 will be positive or zero as long as

$$15 + \tfrac{1}{2}\,\Delta b_1 \geq 0$$

or

$$\Delta b_1 \geq -30$$

That is, S_2 will remain in the optimal basis as long as available farmland does not decrease by more than 30 acres.

There is a similar finding for the X_2 basic variable. Its Amounts column entry in Table 8.13 is

$$175 + \tfrac{3}{2}\,\Delta b_1$$

Hence, X_2 will be positive or zero as long as

$$175 + \tfrac{3}{2}\,\Delta b_1 \geq 0$$

or

$$\Delta b_1 \geq -\tfrac{350}{3}$$

In other words, X_2 will remain in the optimal basis as long as available farmland does not decrease by more than 116.67 acres.

As available farmland decreases, then, both S_2 and X_2 will eventually be driven out of the optimal basis. However, it takes only a 30-acre reduction to exclude S_2, rather than the 116.67-acre decrease required for X_2. Consequently, 30 acres represents the largest amount by which available farmland can be reduced without altering the optimal basis for Country's original linear program.

Figure 8.4 Sensitivity Analysis for Country's Available Farmland

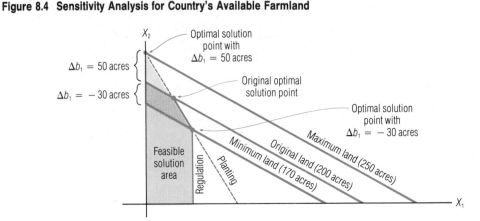

On the other hand, the basic variable X_1 has an Amounts column entry of

$$25 - \tfrac{1}{2} \Delta b_1$$

in Table 8.13. Thus, X_1 will be positive or zero as long as

$$25 - \tfrac{1}{2} \Delta b_1 \geq 0$$

or

$$\Delta b_1 \leq 50$$

Put another way, 50 acres represents the largest amount by which available farmland can be increased without altering the optimal basis for Country's original linear program.

In effect, then, the basis in Table 8.13 will remain optimal as long as

$$-30 \leq \Delta b_1 \leq 50$$

or if there is no more than a 30-acre reduction or a 50-acre increase in available farmland. As a result, this resource's actual quantity can equal the original 200 acres plus 50 acres or minus 30 acres without affecting Country's optimal basis.

Figure 8.4 illustrates the sensitivity analysis for available farmland. To make the graph easier to read, the farm's isoprofit lines are omitted. If these lines did appear, they would indicate that the optimal solution points are as shown in the graph.

In Figure 8.4, you can see that the $\Delta b_1 = 50$-acre change in available acreage shifts the land constraint line to the right and expands the feasible solution area. Yet, the optimal solution point remains at the intersection of the land and planting constraint lines until the farmland increases to 250 acres. At such a point, Country has no idle farmland or unused people-hours, and further increases in available acreage will exclude the land constraint line from the feasible solution area. Any optimal solution point, then, will involve some unused acres of farmland. In other words, 250 acres represents the upper limit to which available farmland can rise without changing the optimal basis for Country's original linear program.

Figure 8.4 also demonstrates that the $\Delta b_1 = -30$-acre change in available acreage shifts the land constraint line to the left and shrinks the feasible solution area. Yet the optimal solution point remains at the intersection of the land and planting constraint lines until the farmland decreases to 170 acres. At such a point, Country has no idle farmland or unused people-hours, and further decreases will exclude the planting constraint line from the feasible solution area. Any optimal solution point, then, will involve some idle people-hours. Put another way, 170 acres represents the lower limit to which available farmland can fall without altering the optimal basis for Country's original linear program.

These limits, measuring the scope over which a constraint amount can fluctuate without altering the optimal basis in a linear program, form a so-called **range of feasibility**. It is important to note that such a range is obtained by changing only the parameter of interest—in Country's case, the available acres of farmland. All other program parameters (such as the crops' per-acre profits or available people-hours) must remain at their original values during the sensitivity analysis.

Basic Slack Variables The change in Country's land constraint amount is reflected in its optimal simplex table as an alteration in unused acreage (S_1). Similarly, a change in the farm's tobacco regulation can be viewed as an alteration in the idle acres of tobacco (S_2). However, S_1 is a nonbasic variable, while S_2 is included in Country's optimal basis. Fortunately, it is relatively easy to find the range of feasibility for the constraint amount corresponding to such a basic slack variable.

Let us again consider the original linear program. Example 8.3 tells us that government regulations initially limit Country's tobacco farming to a maximum of 40 acres. Yet Table 8.8 indicates that the farm's optimal crop mix leaves $S_2 = 15$ unused acres of tobacco. Government could therefore reduce the allowance by as much as 15 acres to a lower limit of

$$40 - 15 = 25 \text{ acres}$$

without affecting the optimal basis. That is, the lower limit on the range of feasibility for such a parameter will equal the original constraint amount (40) minus the optimal quantity (15) of the corresponding basic slack variable (S_2).

Moreover, the value of S_2 indicates that Country does not plant 15 of the 40 acres allowed by current government regulations. Thus, the government can increase the tobacco regulation quantity to an infinitely large amount without altering the farm's optimal basis. In other words, positive infinity (∞) represents the upper limit on the range of feasibility for such a parameter.

General Procedures   A strict equality system constraint will involve an artificial rather than a slack variable. Nevertheless, if the fictitious activity is treated as a slack variable, the same concepts can be used to find the range of feasibility for a less-than-or-equal-to or equality restriction.

On the other hand, a greater-than-or-equal-to system constraint involves a surplus variable rather than a slack variable. Furthermore, a surplus activity identifies the amount by which the corresponding constraint requirement will be exceeded or overachieved. A slack variable, however, gives the quantity by which the corresponding constraint amount is underachieved. Consequently, changes in restriction amounts will cause opposite reactions in surplus and slack variables. Now, remember that such reactions are used to compute the limits on the corresponding ranges of feasibility. When calculating these limits, then, the decision maker must interpret reactions to changes in a greater-than-or-equal-to restriction amount in the reverse manner of the reactions for a less-than-or-equal-to constraint. In other words, an allowable increase for a less-than-or-equal-to restriction amount represents a permitted decrease for a greater-than-or-equal-to constraint quantity, and vice versa.

Table 8.14 summarizes the general procedures to find the range of feasibility for the amount on the right-hand side of a system constraint. The general procedures are applicable to system constraints that involve basic and nonbasic slack, surplus, and artificial variables. Indeed, management can use these procedures to determine the range of feasibility for the system constraint amount dealing with Country's other nonbasic slack variable (S_3). By so doing, management will find that available people-hours can fluctuate between 400 and 560 hours without changing the optimal basis for the farm's original linear program.

Evaluating Parameter Changes   The optimal basis will not change as long as the relevant constraint amount remains within its range of feasibility. In addition, if the constraint corresponds to a basic slack or surplus variable, such fluctuations do not alter the optimal criterion value. Parameter movements within the range of feasibility, however, will change the amounts of the basic variables. Moreover, when the restriction involves a nonbasic activity, these movements alter the optimal criterion value.

Consider, for example, the change in Country's available farmland (Δb_1), which, in the optimal simplex table, corresponds to an alteration of

Table 8.14 Finding the Range of Feasibility for a System Constraint Amount

1. Denote the change in the system constraint amount with the variable Δb.
2. Identify the nondecision (slack, surplus, or artificial) variable that corresponds to this system constraint.
3. Identify the exchange segment entries in the appropriate nondecision variable column in the optimal simplex table.
4. Multiply each exchange segment entry by Δb.
5. Add the products found in step 4 to the corresponding entries in the Amounts column of the optimal simplex table.
6. Find the values of Δb that keep each Amounts column entry greater than or equal to zero.
7. Set the limits on the range of feasibility according to the following formulas:

Type of System Constraint	Lower Limit	Upper Limit
Less than or equal to ($\leq$) or equality ($=$)	$\begin{bmatrix} \text{original} \\ \text{constraint} \\ \text{amount} \end{bmatrix} - \begin{bmatrix} \text{smallest absolute} \\ \text{value of the} \\ \text{negative } \Delta b \text{ amounts} \end{bmatrix}$ or $-\infty$ if there is no negative Δb	$\begin{bmatrix} \text{original} \\ \text{constraint} \\ \text{amount} \end{bmatrix} + \begin{bmatrix} \text{smallest} \\ \text{positive} \\ \Delta b \text{ value} \end{bmatrix}$ or ∞ if there is no positive Δb
Greater than or equal to ($\geq$)	$\begin{bmatrix} \text{original} \\ \text{constraint} \\ \text{amount} \end{bmatrix} - \begin{bmatrix} \text{smallest positive} \\ \Delta b \\ \text{value} \end{bmatrix}$ or $-\infty$ if there is no positive Δb	$\begin{bmatrix} \text{original} \\ \text{constraint} \\ \text{amount} \end{bmatrix} + \begin{bmatrix} \text{smallest absolute} \\ \text{value of the} \\ \text{negative } \Delta b \text{ amounts} \end{bmatrix}$ or ∞ if there is no negative Δb

the nonbasic slack variable S_1. As the entries in the Basis and Amounts columns of Table 8.13 demonstrate, such a change generates optimal basic variable amounts of

$$S_2 = 15 + \tfrac{1}{2} \Delta b_1$$
$$X_1 = 25 - \tfrac{1}{2} \Delta b_1$$

and

$$X_2 = 175 + \tfrac{3}{2} \Delta b_1$$

and an optimal criterion value of

$$\$11{,}250 + \$25 \, \Delta b_1$$

In other words, these entries indicate that the optimal basic variable amounts and optimal criterion value depend on the change (Δb_1) in the farm's available acreage.

Recall that Country's basis will remain optimal as long as available land remains within its 170-to-250-acre range of feasibility. At the 170-acre lower limit,

$$\Delta b_1 = 170 - 200 = -30 \text{ acres}$$

Hence, there is a -30-acre change from the parameter's original 200-acre estimate, and the optimal solution involves

$$S_2 = 15 + \tfrac{1}{2} \Delta b_1 = 15 + \tfrac{1}{2}(-30) = 0 \text{ unused acres of tobacco}$$

$$X_1 = 25 - \tfrac{1}{2} \Delta b_1 = 25 - \tfrac{1}{2}(-30) = 40 \text{ acres of tobacco}$$

and

$$X_2 = 175 + \tfrac{3}{2} \Delta b_1 = 175 + \tfrac{3}{2}(-30) = 130 \text{ acres of cotton}$$

with a maximum total profit of

$$\$11{,}250 + \$25 \, \Delta b_1 = \$11{,}250 + \$25(-30) = \$10{,}500$$

when the farm consists of 170 acres. Yet, at the 250-acre upper limit,

$$\Delta b_1 = 250 - 200 = 50 \text{ acres}$$

and the optimal solution involves

$$S_2 = 15 + \tfrac{1}{2} \Delta b_1 = 15 + \tfrac{1}{2}(50) = 40 \text{ unused acres of tobacco}$$

$$X_1 = 25 - \tfrac{1}{2} \Delta b_1 = 25 - \tfrac{1}{2}(50) = 0 \text{ acres of tobacco}$$

and

$$X_2 = 175 + \tfrac{3}{2} \Delta b_1 = 175 + \tfrac{3}{2}(50) = 250 \text{ acres of cotton}$$

with a maximum total profit of

$$\$11{,}250 + \$25 \, \Delta b_1 = \$11{,}250 + \$25(50) = \$12{,}500$$

That is, idle tobacco acreage (S_2) will fluctuate between 0 and 40 acres, tobacco (X_1) from 40 to 0 acres, and cotton (X_2) from 130 to 250 acres within the range of feasibility for Country's available land. As a result, total profit will fluctuate between \$10,500 and \$12,500 within this range.

There is also an important relationship between an optimal shadow price and the range of feasibility for the corresponding system constraint amount. Remember that a constraint's shadow price is given by the absolute value of the $C_j - Z_j$ row entry in the pertinent nondecision variable column in the optimal simplex table. In this regard, there is a $-\$25$ entry in the idle farmland (S_1) column of the $C_j - Z_j$ row of Table 8.13. Thus, Country's farmland has a shadow price equal to the absolute value of $-\$25$, or

$$|-\$25| = \$25 \text{ per acre}$$

According to this shadow price, Country's total profit increases a net \$25 for each acre that the decision maker adds to the original farm size. Such a profit increase, however, cannot continue indefinitely. As management acquires additional acreage, increasingly more farmland is made available for planting crops. Eventually, the available acreage will reach the 250-acre upper limit on the range of feasibility for Country's farmland.

Any further increase in available acreage will lead to a change in the optimal basis.

In addition, this shadow price indicates that Country's total profit decreases a net $25 for each acre that the decision maker subtracts from the original farm size. Yet such a profit decrease cannot continue indefinitely. As management disposes of additional acreage, less and less farmland is made available for planting crops. Eventually, the available acreage will reach the 170-acre lower limit on the range of feasibility for Country's farmland. Any further decrease in available acreage will lead to a change in the optimal basis.

Any change in the optimal basis will in turn alter the $-$25$ entry in the S_1 column of the $C_j - Z_j$ row of Table 8.13. In effect, then, Country's land has a shadow price of $25 per acre only if the farm does not shrink below 170 acres or expand above 250 acres. Put another way, *an optimal shadow price is valid only within the range of feasibility for the corresponding system constraint amount.*

When the system constraint amount is outside its range of feasibility, there will be changes in the optimal basis, basic variable amounts, optimal criterion value, and optimal shadow prices. Unfortunately, the appropriate analysis involves an elaboration that is well beyond the scope of this text. T. Gal [6] and Kim [7] provide an in-depth discussion of such an analysis for the interested reader.

EXCHANGE COEFFICIENTS In a third form of sensitivity analysis, the decision maker examines the potential impact of changes in each decision variable's system constraint utilization rate. Consider, for instance, Country's planting restriction. According to Example 8.3, it originally takes 6 people-hours to plant one acre of tobacco. Now, suppose a technological innovation reduces this time by 1 hour. In that case, the expression

$$5X_1 + 2X_2 \le 500 \text{ people-hours}$$

would represent the new planting restriction. That is, the X_1 decision variable will have an exchange coefficient of 5 rather than 6.

Figure 8.5 illustrates the effects of the increase in tobacco-planting efficiency. To make the graph easier to read, the farm's isoprofit lines are omitted. If these lines did appear, they would indicate that the optimal solution points are as shown in the graph.

In Figure 8.5, you can see that the reduction in the X_1 variable's exchange coefficient makes the planting constraint line steeper. Such a shift enables Country to plant more acres of tobacco than before with the same work force capacity. For example, the farm originally could plant a maximum of

$$\frac{500 \text{ available people-hours}}{6 \text{ people-hours per acre of tobacco}}$$

Figure 8.5 The Effect of a Decrease in the People-hours Needed to Plant One Acre of Country's Tobacco

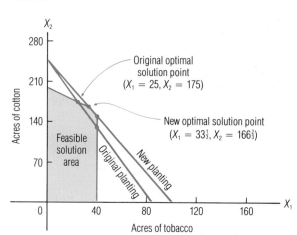

or 83.33 acres of tobacco with 500 people-hours. After the technological innovation, however, management can produce $500/5 = 100$ acres of this crop with the same work force. Figure 8.5 also demonstrates that the increased efficiency alters the shape of the feasible solution area. As a result, Country's optimal solution point changes from $(X_1 = 25, X_2 = 175)$ to $(X_1 = 33\frac{1}{3}, X_2 = 166\frac{2}{3})$.

Example 8.3 shows that total profit is given by the expression

$$Z = \$100X_1 + \$50X_2$$

Hence, the farm obtains a total profit of

$$Z = \$100(33\tfrac{1}{3}) + \$50(166\tfrac{2}{3}) = \$11,666.67$$

after the technological innovation, rather than the original

$$Z = \$100(25) + \$50(175) = \$11,250$$

In other words, the innovation increases profit by encouraging Country to plant more tobacco but less cotton than before the change.

A similar approach can be used to determine the effects of an increase in the time needed for planting an acre of tobacco. In fact, it is possible to find the range over which this exchange coefficient could fluctuate without altering Country's optimal basis. Unfortunately, such a sensitivity analysis again involves an elaboration that is beyond the scope of the text. Gal [6] and Kim [7] present the details for the interested reader.

OTHER POSTOPTIMALITY ANALYSIS Our sensitivity analyses have been confined to the consideration of a discrete change in a single parameter for the original linear program. All other parameters are assumed to remain at their original values during the sensitivity analysis. In some cases, however, the decision maker may want to examine the effects of:

1. Continuous, rather than discrete, variations in a program parameter
2. A change in the form of the linear program (such as the addition of a new constraint)
3. Simultaneous changes in several program parameters

Management scientists have developed methodologies that are helpful in executing these additional forms of postoptimality analysis. One of these methodologies, called **parametric programming**, examines how specified continuous variations in the parameters influence the optimal linear programming solution. Regretfully, such methodologies are again beyond the scope of this text. Gal [6] and Kim [7] discuss these approaches in detail, while S. C. Bhatnagar [3] and R. A. Cabraal [4] provide some practical business and economic applications.

COMPUTER ANALYSIS

Most practical linear programming problems are too complex for solution with the graphic or manual simplex procedures. As a result, management scientists have developed computer programs especially designed to solve large-scale linear programs. Moreover, these canned (prewritten) programs are widely available through computer manufacturers, distributors, and service companies to academic, business, and government organizations. Some of the most popular manufacturer-supplied programs include General Electric's LINPRO, IBM's MPSX, Control Data's OPTIMA, Honeywell's ALPS, Univac's 1107 LP, and Grumman's LINPROG and SIMPLEX. In addition, numerous universities provide students with variations of these and other linear programming computer packages. One such package is the Linear Interactive Discrete Optimizer, or LINDO, program [9].

Although each computerized linear programming package is slightly different, the basic features are essentially the same. In each package, the user must access the program, supply the pertinent data, and request the appropriate analysis. To provide this information, of course, the user must fully understand the nature and purpose of a linear program. The computer will then perform the necessary linear programming computations, typically with some version of the simplex method, and generate the requested output. Such output may include:

1. The simplex tables

2. The optimal level of each variable

3. The criterion value

4. The optimal shadow prices

5. A complete sensitivity analysis

Naturally, a fundamental knowledge about simplex and sensitivity analysis concepts would enhance the user's ability to accurately interpret and completely utilize the computer output.

This section demonstrates the process of running a typical computerized linear programming package. In particular, we will show how the LINDO program available on the California State University and College System (CSUC) computer system can be used to solve Country Farm's linear program. This package may not be identical to the one in use at your institution. However, the vast majority of available packages essentially have the same standard components. Hence, what you learn here should be transferable to your own system.

USER INPUT Figure 8.6 presents the solution to Country's linear program by the LINDO computer package on the CSUC system. In this figure, X_1 denotes the acres of tobacco and X_2 the acres of cotton. Figure 8.6 shows that the user accesses the computer package with the command FIND, LINDO. The program next prompts an input with a colon (:). At this point, the user inputs Country's objective function: MAX $100X_1 + 50X_2$. By striking the carriage return on the computer terminal's keyboard, the user will then receive the prompt indicated with the symbol >. This symbol is a request by the computer for the restriction segment of the linear program. The appropriate response is the ST command. In the subsequent > prompt, LINDO is requesting a system constraint expression. Hence, the user could input the land restriction: $X_1 + X_2 < 200$. Also, notice that a less-than-or-equal-to ($\leq$) relationship is identified by < in the input phase of LINDO.

After providing the last system constraint expression, the user inputs the word END following the > prompt. Such a command informs the computer that it has received the complete linear program. LINDO then prompts an action with the : symbol. At this point, the user may wish to check the linear program for any input errors. To do this, the user types the phrase LOOK ALL after the : symbol. The computer will then print the complete linear program supplied by the user. In the printout, the objective function becomes row 1, while the land restriction is labeled row 2. Similarly, the regulation constraint is denoted as row 3 and the planting restriction as row 4 in the LOOK ALL printout.

Figure 8.6 Solution of Country's Linear Program with LINDO

```
 /FIND,LINDO
 : MAX 100X1 + 50X2

 > ST

 > X1 + X2 < 200

 > X1 < 40

 > 6X1 + 2X2 < 500

 > END


 : LOOK ALL


  MAX      100 X1 + 50 X2
  SUBJECT TO
     2)      X1 +, X2 <=    200
     3)      X1 <=   40
     4)     6 X1 + 2 X2 <=    500
  END


 : GO

       LP OPTIMUM FOUND  AT STEP     3

            OBJECTIVE FUNCTION VALUE

   1)          11250.0000

  VARIABLE          VALUE         REDUCED COST
        X1        25.000000         0.000000
        X2       175.000000         0.000000


  ROW          SLACK OR SURPLUS    DUAL PRICES
     2)           0.000000         25.000000
     3)          15.000000          0.000000
     4)           0.000000         12.500000

  NO. ITERATIONS=       3

   DO RANGE(SENSITIVITY) ANALYSIS?
 > YES


     RANGES IN WHICH THE BASIS IS UNCHANGED

                       OBJ COEFFICIENT RANGES
  VARIABLE       CURRENT        ALLOWABLE       ALLOWABLE
                 COEF           INCREASE        DECREASE
        X1     100.000000      50.000000       50.00000
        X2      50.000000      50.000000       16.66666 ·

                     RIGHTHAND SIDE RANGES
     ROW        CURRENT        ALLOWABLE       ALLOWABLE
                RHS            INCREASE        DECREASE
      2       200.000000      50.000000       30.00000
      3        40.000000      INFINITY        15.00000
      4       500.000000      60.000000       100.00000
 : QUIT
```

COMPUTER OUTPUT After printing the complete linear program, LINDO prompts a command with another : symbol. If the LOOK ALL printout reveals no errors, the user executes the solution phase of LINDO by typing the word GO following the : symbol. The computer will then include the appropriate nonnegativity conditions, solve the linear program, and print the following information:

1. The optimal objective function value
2. The optimal value of each decision and nondecision (slack or surplus) variable
3. The optimal shadow prices for the dual linear program
4. The number of simplex iterations required to reach the optimal solution

The LP optimum in Figure 8.6, for example, demonstrates that Country can maximize total profit at $11,250 by planting $X_1 = 25$ acres of tobacco and $X_2 = 175$ acres of cotton. In addition, the optimal solution involves $S_1 = 0$ unused acres of farmland, $S_2 = 15$ unused acres of tobacco, and $S_3 = 0$ unused people-hours. Furthermore, such an optimum, which requires three simplex iterations, generates shadow prices of $25 per acre of farmland, $0 per acre of tobacco, and $12.50 per people-hour.

LINDO also prints the reduced costs associated with the optimal values of each decision variable. Such a cost represents the amount by which the variable's unit contribution must be improved before the activity will enter the optimal basis. In other words, these reduced costs give the optimal values of the nondecision (slack or surplus) variables in the dual linear program. A decision variable that already appears in the optimal primal basis, as in the case of X_1 and/or X_2, will have a zero reduced cost.

At this stage, LINDO asks if the user wants a sensitivity analysis. By typing the word YES after the > prompt, the user commands LINDO to find the ranges over which the optimal basis remains unchanged. The resulting printout includes the range of optimality data for each objective function coefficient and the range of feasibility data for each system constraint amount. The sensitivity analysis of Figure 8.6, for instance, shows that cotton's (X_2) current $50 profit contribution can increase by $50 or decrease by $16.67 without affecting Country's optimal basis. LINDO, however, does not ordinarily perform a sensitivity analysis of the exchange coefficients on the left-hand side of the system constraints.

When LINDO finishes the sensitivity analysis, it prompts other desired actions with another : symbol. Some of the possibilities include the printing of selected simplex tables, the deletion of a specified constraint, and the addition of a new restriction. If no further analyses are required, the user exits the computer program by typing the word QUIT after the : symbol.

MANAGEMENT BENEFITS In linear programming's early development, its business and economic applications were restricted by the cost of solving large-scale, practical linear programs and the expense of collecting the necessary input data. The relatively modest purchase or lease cost, low processing expenses, and wide availability of computer packages like LINDO have done much to alleviate the first difficulty. For example, LINDO can be obtained at a nominal expense from a variety of sources. Moreover, this package solves a very large-scale linear program in minutes for as little as $5 worth of computer time and related expenses.

The continuous development by many firms of integrated management information systems (MIS) and decision support systems (DSS) should help to overcome the second difficulty. D. Avramovich and others [2] demonstrate how a decision support system can be used in conjunction with linear programming to effectively manage fleet operations.

SUMMARY In this chapter we saw how postoptimality analysis generates information useful for management planning and control. Some of the knowledge is obtained by examining the original or primal linear program from its dual perspective. Table 8.4 summarized the procedure for transforming the primal into the dual linear program.

By studying the dual, the decision maker obtains valuable insights about the economic nature and management implications of the primal linear program. In addition, the dual solution generates the optimal shadow prices for the primal system constraints. These prices, which measure the variations in the optimal criterion value that result from unit changes in the constraint amounts, can be applied to decision making, as summarized in Table 8.2. Also, the primal and dual relationships offer practical procedural benefits. In fact, sometimes it is easier to solve the dual rather than the primal linear program. Under such circumstances, management should solve the dual and then derive the optimal primal solution from the results. Table 8.6 summarized the principles for doing so.

The optimal primal and dual solutions are based on the original estimates of the linear program parameters. Yet variations in decision conditions often change these original estimates. As a result, the decision maker must determine the effects of such changes on the optimal primal and dual results. The second section of the chapter demonstrated how sensitivity analysis can provide this information without the decision maker having to completely rework the problem.

In one form of sensitivity analysis, management examines the potential impact of changes in each decision variable's unit contribution to the objective. Such an analysis establishes the variable's range of optimality, or the scope over which its objective function coefficient could change without altering the optimal basis in the linear program. The general procedure for finding this range was summarized in Table 8.10, while Table 8.12 outlined the approach to evaluate changes in these coefficients.

In another form of sensitivity analysis, the decision maker examines the impact of changes in each system constraint amount. Such an analysis establishes the range of feasibility, or the scope over which a constraint amount can fluctuate without altering the optimal basis in the linear program. The general procedures for finding this range were summarized in Table 8.14. Also, we saw that the optimal basis and the restriction's shadow price do not change as long as the relevant system constraint amount remains within its range of feasibility. Parameter movements within the range, however, alter the optimal quantities of the basic variables.

It is also possible to investigate the potential impact of changes in each decision variable's system constraint utilization rate. By performing this and the other forms of sensitivity analysis, management is able to determine how sensitive the optimal solution is to variations in the linear program parameters. Consequently, management is in a better position to evaluate the efficiency of obtaining better parameter estimates.

Most practical linear programming problems are too complex for solution with the graphic or manual simplex procedures. As a result, management scientists have developed computer programs especially designed to solve large-scale linear programs. These canned (prewritten) programs are available through computer manufacturers, distributors, and service companies to academic, business, and government organizations. The final section of the chapter showed how a typical computerized package, called LINDO, is used to solve a linear program and perform the corresponding sensitivity analysis.

Glossary

complementary slackness The relationships between the optimal values of the primal and dual variables.

dual A linear programming problem that provides an alternative and complementary way of looking at the original (primal) program.

linear programming sensitivity analysis A methodology for investigating the impact of parameter changes on the optimal primal and dual solutions to a linear program.

parametric programming A form of postoptimality analysis in which the decision maker examines how specified continuous variations in the uncontrollable inputs influence the optimal linear programming solution.

postoptimality analysis The examination of the optimal solution to an original linear program to identify the economic values of scarce resources and restrictive guidelines and to determine the effect of parameter changes on the problem.

primal The original linear programming problem.

range of feasibility The range of values over which a constraint amount can fluctuate without altering the optimal basis in a linear program.

range of optimality The range of values over which an objective function coefficient can fluctuate without altering the optimal basis and basic variable amounts in a linear program.

shadow price The change in the criterion value that results from a one-unit change in the amount of a constraint.

References

1. Abdel-Khalik, A. R. "Using Sensitivity Analysis to Evaluate Materiality—An Exploratory Approach." *Decision Sciences* (July 1977): 616.

2. Avramovich, D., et al. "A Decision Support System for Fleet Management: A Linear Programming Approach." *Interfaces* (June 1982): 1.

3. Bhatnagar, S. C. "Implementing Linear Programming in a Textile Unit: Some Problems and a Solution." *Interfaces* (April 1981): 87.

4. Cabraal, R. A. "Production Planning in a Sri Lanka Coconut Mill Using Parametric Linear Programming." *Interfaces* (June 1981): 16.

5. Crane, D. B., et al. "An Application of Management Science to Bank Borrowing Strategies." Part 2. *Interfaces* (November 1977): 70.

6. Gal, T. *Postoptimal Analyses, Parametric Programming, and Related Topics.* New York: McGraw-Hill, 1978.

7. Kim, C. *Introduction to Linear Programming.* New York: Holt, Rinehart, & Winston, 1971.

8. Naylor, T. H., et al. *Introduction to Linear Programming.* 2d ed. Belmont, Calif.: Wadsworth, 1971.

9. Schrage, L. *Linear Programming Models with LINDO .* Palo Alto, Calif.: The Scientific Press, 1981.

10. Sharp, J. F. "The Effects of Income Taxes on Linear Programming Models." *Decision Sciences* (July 1975): 462.

1. An opportunity cost is defined as the difference between the outcomes of the best and next best alternatives. Why are the optimal values of the dual variables or shadow prices considered opportunity costs?

2. Interpret the dual for each of the following primal linear programs. (Give a verbal interpretation of the dual objective function and system constraints.)

   a. A winery wants to determine the product mix of wines that will maximize profit. Labor, grapes, and sugar are used to make the wines, and each of these resources is in limited supply.

   b. A dog kennel wants to determine the minimum cost mix of various dog food products. A dog food mix must contain minimum amounts of various nutrients to provide a balanced dog diet.

   c. An armed forces public relations agency wants to determine how many "spots" to place in various medium so as to maximize audience exposure. Total dollars spent cannot exceed the available budget. Also, the total number of spots placed in each medium cannot exceed the quantity offered for armed forces public-service messages.

3. Interpret the optimal value of the dual variable for the specified system constraint in each of the following decision situations:

   a. A company wants to determine how many machines of each type it should purchase so as to maximize the machines' daily output (in units). One constraint specifies that the total floor space used by the machines must be less than or equal to the available square footage.

   b. A market research company wants to determine a plan that will minimize interview costs. A contractual constraint specifies that the company must contact a minimum number of households with a given set of characteristics.

   c. A university credit union wants to determine how much of its funds to allocate to various investments so as to maximize dollar return. The company cannot invest more than the available funds.

   d. A government agency wants to determine how many professionals of various types to hire to fill the agency's positions at minimum recruiting cost. One constraint specifies that the total recruitment of two of the professional groups must meet a minimum agency quota.

4. The primal of a linear program has six decision variables but only two constraints. You are interested only in the optimal criterion value. Your instructor suggests that it may be easier to solve the dual rather than the primal of this problem. Why do you think your instructor made such a recommendation?

5. Smooth Cycles, Inc., manufactures three types of bicycles: the Lady Ride, the Neutral, and the Macho Man. The bikes must be manufactured and assembled. There is limited available capacity for each of these operations. The company's planning department formulates the problem as the following linear program:

$$\text{maximize} \quad Z = \$20X_1 + \$30X_2 + \$40X_3$$

$$\text{subject to} \quad .2X_1 + .2X_2 + .1X_3 \leq 120 \text{ hours} \quad \text{(Manufacturing)}$$
$$.4X_1 + .1X_2 + .3X_3 \leq 120 \text{ hours} \quad \text{(Assembly)}$$
$$X_1, X_2, X_3 \geq 0$$

where Z = the total profit, X_1 = the number of cartons of Lady Ride, X_2 = the number of cartons of Neutral, and X_3 = the number of cartons of Macho Man. Smooth's planning director provides the following optimal dual solution information:

C = total resource payments = $24,000

U_1 = shadow price of a manufacturing hour = $100

U_2 = shadow price of an assembly hour = $100

S_4 = excess cost of a Lady Ride = $40

The director also indicates that neither the Neutral nor the Macho Man model involves any excess cost.

You are called in as a consultant and asked the following questions:

a. How many bikes of each type should Smooth produce to maximize profit?
b. What is the maximum profit?
c. Is there any unused capacity?
d. Smooth is considering a new product: Kiddy Cycles. A Kiddy would earn $25 profit and take 6 minutes to manufacture and 3 minutes to assemble. Should Smooth manufacture the Kiddy Cycle?

Prepare a report that provides this information.

6. Pioneer Hamburger House specializes in three types of burgers: regular, whopper, and double whopper. Labor, meat, and seasoning ingredients are used to make each type of burger. Pioneer's management has not been satisfied with recent profits and has therefore employed a local management consulting firm. The consultant has formulated an appropriate linear program and has arrived at the optimal simplex table on the following page.

Variables		X_1	X_2	X_3	S_1	S_2	S_3	
Basis	C_j	$.10	$.12	$.20	$0	$0	$0	**Amounts**
X_2	$.12	2	1	0	−3	6	0	200
S_3	$0	−4	0	0	1	−3	1	1000
X_3	$.20	1	0	1	2	4	0	150
	Z_j	$.44	$.12	$.20	$.04	$1.52	$0	$54
	$C_j - Z_j$	−$.34	$0	$0	−$.04	−$1.52	$0	

In this table,

X_1 = regulars sold per quarter (in thousands)

X_2 = whoppers sold per quarter (in thousands)

X_3 = double whoppers sold per quarter (in thousands)

Z = profit (in thousands of dollars)

S_1 = idle labor hours

S_2 = unused pounds of meat

S_3 = idle packages of seasoning ingredients

On the basis of these results, the consultant advises Pioneer to discontinue selling regular hamburgers unless the profit per regular can be increased by at least 34 cents. The consultant also advises Pioneer to use more meat and labor. Meat is said to be a much more profitable source of expansion than labor.

How did the consultant arrive at these recommendations?

7. Hamilton Bender, Inc., manufactures three main health care products: packaged brewer's yeast, multiple vitamins, and protein powder. Plants in Springfield and McAllister manufacture sufficient quantities of these products to meet forecasted monthly demand at least cost. However, management has not been satisfied with recent cost experience. As a result, management has referred the problem to its planning staff for consideration and analysis. The staff has formulated an appropriate linear program and has arrived at the following optimal simplex table:

Variables		X_1	X_2	S_1	S_2	S_3	A_1	A_2	A_3	
Basis	C_j	$6000	$4500	$0	$0	$0	M	M	M	**Amounts**
X_2	$4500	0	1	0	$\frac{1}{5}$	$\frac{3}{5}$	0	$-\frac{1}{5}$	$-\frac{3}{5}$	25
S_1	$0	0	0	1	$\frac{2}{3}$	-4	1	$-\frac{2}{3}$	4	3,000
X_1	$6000	1	0	0	$-\frac{1}{6}$	$-\frac{1}{2}$	0	$\frac{1}{6}$	$\frac{1}{2}$	20
	Z_j	$6000	$4500	$0	$-$100	$-$300	$0	$100	$300	$232,500
	$C_j - Z_j$	$0	$0	$0	$100	$300	M	$M + $100	$M + $300	

In this table, A_1, A_2, and A_3 are artificial variables, while

X_1 = days worked per month at the Springfield plant

X_2 = days worked per month at the McAllister plant

Z = total monthly production cost

S_1 = excess cases of brewer's yeast

S_2 = excess cases of multiple vitamins

S_3 = excess cases of protein powder

On the basis of these results, the planning director advises management to reduce yeast output by 3000 cans per month. In addition, the director offers the following suggestions:

♦ A decrease in protein powder demand will be more cost effective than an equivalent reduction in multiple vitamin sales.

♦ The company should operate the Springfield plant 20 days per month and the McAllister facility 25 days per month as long as protein powder demand is between 160 and 241.67 cases per month. Sales were originally forecasted to be 200 cases per month.

♦ The same production schedule will be appropriate as long as the actual demand for brewer's yeast does not exceed the original 8000-case forecast by more than 3000 cases.

How did the planning director arrive at these recommendations?

8. Refer back to Ancient Enterprises's product mix problem (Example 8.1). By using the LINDO computer package to solve the linear program for this problem, the decision maker will get the following output:

```
        LP OPTIMUM FOUND  AT STEP      3

             OBJECTIVE FUNCTION VALUE

   1)          12800.0000

   VARIABLE          VALUE          REDUCED COST
         X1       400.000000          0.000000
         X2       120.000000          0.000000


   ROW          SLACK OR SURPLUS      DUAL PRICES
      2)             0.000000          6.000000
      3)             0.000000          2.000000
      4)           750.000000          0.000000

   NO. ITERATIONS=       3

    DO RANGE(SENSITIVITY) ANALYSIS?
   > YES



      RANGES IN WHICH THE BASIS IS UNCHANGED

                          OBJ COEFFICIENT RANGES
   VARIABLE         CURRENT        ALLOWABLE       ALLOWABLE
                     COEF          INCREASE        DECREASE
         X1       20.000000        4.000000       12.000000
         X2       40.000000       60.000000        6.666667

                          RIGHTHAND SIDE RANGES
   ROW             CURRENT        ALLOWABLE       ALLOWABLE
                     RHS           INCREASE        DECREASE
      2          1800.000000     1200.000000      300.000000
      3          1000.000000      100.000000      400.000000
      4          3750.000000       INFINITY       750.000000
```

Interpret the computer output in language that would be understandable to Ancient's management.

9. Refer back to Millips Oil Company's blending problem (Example 8.2). By using the LINDO computer package to solve the linear program for this problem, the decision maker will obtain the following output:

```
     LP OPTIMUM FOUND  AT STEP

          OBJECTIVE FUNCTION VALUE

   1)          1700.00000

 VARIABLE         VALUE         REDUCED COST
       X1      2000.000000        0.000000
       X2      7000.000000        0.000000


 ROW         SLACK OR SURPLUS    DUAL PRICES
    2)           0.000000          -.400000
    3)           0.000000          -.300000

 NO. ITERATIONS=        2

  DO RANGE(SENSITIVITY) ANALYSIS?
 > YES



     RANGES IN WHICH THE BASIS IS UNCHANGED

                         OBJ COEFFICIENT RANGES
 VARIABLE        CURRENT      ALLOWABLE        ALLOWABLE
                  COEF        INCREASE         DECREASE
       X1        .150000        .150000         .100000
       X2        .200000        .400000         .100000

                         RIGHTHAND SIDE RANGES
 ROW             CURRENT      ALLOWABLE        ALLOWABLE
                  RHS         INCREASE         DECREASE
    2         2000.000000    7000.000000      500.000000
    3         3000.000000    1000.000000     2333.333333
```

Interpret the computer output in language that would be understandable to Millips's management.

Suppose that the company can purchase a new crude oil (type C) to include in the blend of the Wear Prevention additive. A gallon of type C crude oil costs 18 cents and has 15% of compound JT and 30% of WY. All other conditions are the same as in the original problem. Should Millips purchase the new type of oil? Explain.

10. Do you agree or disagree with each of the following statements? Explain.

a. A shadow price is the same as an accounting, or nominal, cost, such as a wage or interest payment.

b. The dual of the dual is the primal.

c. If the primal is an unbounded problem, then the dual will have no feasible solution.

d. The dual plays no role in postoptimality analysis.

e. The dual is a form of sensitivity analysis.

f. The optimal values of the dual variables remain the same for changes that are within the various ranges of optimality.

g. The range of feasibility's upper and lower limits each result in degeneracy.

Technique Exercises

1. You are given the following product mix problem:

maximize $Z = \$13X_1 + \$8X_2$

subject to $4X_1 + X_2 \le 48$ units   (Resource A)

$3X_1 + 2X_2 \le 72$ units   (Resource B)

$X_1, X_2 \ge 0$

where Z = the total profit, X_1 = the number of units of product 1, and X_2 = the number of units of product 2.

Formulate the dual and solve it graphically. Interpret the optimal values of the dual variables.

2. You are given the following blending problem:

minimize $Z = \$60X_1 + \$20X_2 + \$75X_3$

subject to $20X_1 + 8X_2 + 10X_3 \ge 275$ units   (Compound A)

$5X_1 + 2X_2 + 10X_3 \ge 250$ units   (Compound B)

$X_1, X_2, X_3 \ge 0$

where Z = the total cost, X_1 = the number of units of ingredient 1, X_2 = the number of units of ingredient 2, and X_3 = the number of units of ingredient 3.

Formulate the dual and solve it graphically. Interpret the optimal values of the dual variables.

3. Consider the following resource allocation problem:

maximize $Z = \$10X_1 + \$20X_2 + \$30X_3$

subject to $X_1 + 4X_2 + 5X_3 \le 70$ hours   (Labor)

$2X_1 + 4X_2 + 10X_3 \le 100$ hours   (Capital)

$X_1, X_2, X_3 \ge 0$

where Z = the revenue from gizmos, X_1 = the number of units produced by the economy method, X_2 = the number of units produced by the regular method, and X_3 = the number of units produced by the quality method. You are given the following optimal simplex table for this problem:

Variables		X_1	X_2	X_3	S_1	S_2	
Basis	C_j	$10	$20	$30	$0	$0	**Amounts**
X_2	$20	0	1	0	$\frac{1}{2}$	$-\frac{1}{4}$	10
X_1	$10	1	0	5	-1	1	30
Z_j		$10	$20	$50	$0	$5	$500
$C_j - Z_j$		$0	$0	$-$10	$0	$-$5	

In this table, S_1 represents unused labor hours and S_2 gives unused capital hours.

Formulate the dual linear program, and determine the optimal dual solution from this optimal simplex table. Do you notice anything unusual? Explain. Interpret the optimal values of the dual variables.

4. Refer back to Ancient Enterprises' product mix problem (Example 8.1).
   a. Show how Figure 8.1 was developed.
   b. Develop graphs similar to Figure 8.2 for the company's iron and capital constraints.
   c. Show how Tables 8.1 and 8.5 were derived.

5. Refer back to Millips Oil Company's blending problem (Example 8.2).
   a. Show how Table 8.7 was derived.
   b. Develop a graphic interpretation of the shadow price concept for each system constraint in this problem. Use Figure 8.2 as a guide in the development.

6. Consider the sales problem of a local ice cream parlor:

$$\text{maximize} \quad Z = \$.20X_1 + \$.30X_2 + \$.40X_3$$

subject to

$4X_1 + 2X_2 + 2X_3 \leq 800$ units	(Ingredient A)
$8X_2 + 4X_3 \leq 400$ units	(Ingredient B)
$X_1, X_2, X_3 \geq 0$	

where Z = profit, X_1 = the number of containers of vanilla ice cream sold, X_2 = the number of containers of chocolate ice cream sold, and X_3 = the number of containers of butterscotch ice cream sold.

   a. Formulate the standard form of this primal program.
   b. Formulate the dual linear program and its standard form.

c. Solve the dual graphically.
d. Use the primal-dual relationships and the principles of complementary slackness to find the optimal primal solution.

7. You are given the following staff-scheduling problem:

$$\text{minimize} \quad Z = \$30X_1 + \$45X_2 + \$70X_3$$

$$\text{subject to} \quad X_1 + 2X_2 + 3X_3 \geq 3000 \text{ hours} \qquad \text{(Project A)}$$
$$2X_1 + X_2 + 6X_3 \geq 3000 \text{ hours} \qquad \text{(Project B)}$$
$$X_1, X_2, X_3 \geq 0$$

where Z = cost, X_1 = the number of units of output by group 1, X_2 = the number of units of output by group 2, and X_3 = the number of units of output by group 3.

a. Formulate the standard form of this primal linear program.
b. Formulate the dual linear program and its standard form.
c. Solve the dual graphically.
d. Use the primal-dual relationships and the principles of complementary slackness to find the optimal primal solution.

8. Refer back to Country Farms's resource allocation problem (Example 8.3).
a. Show how Table 8.8 was derived.
b. Show how Figure 8.3 was developed.
c. Show how Tables 8.11 and 8.13 were developed.
d. Show how Figures 8.4 and 8.5 were derived.
e. Set up the dual linear program for this problem.
f. Use the results from Table 8.8, the primal-dual relationships, and the principles of complementary slackness to find the optimal dual solution.

9. Again refer to Example 8.3.
a. Show how the range of optimality for cotton's unit profit contribution was determined.
b. Suppose unfavorable market conditions decrease cotton's unit profit contribution from $50 to $20. How will this change affect Country's plans? Explain.
c. Show how the range of feasibility for available people-hours was determined.
d. Suppose that Country is thinking about adding a soybean crop. It would take 2 people-hours to plant one acre of soybeans. Yet each acre of the crop would provide a $60 profit. All other conditions are the same as in the original problem. Should management plant soybeans? Explain.

10. Quality Products, Inc., has the product mix problem represented by the following linear program:

$$\text{maximize} \quad Z = \$20X_1 + \$40X_2$$
$$\text{subject to} \quad 3X_1 + 5X_2 \leq 1800 \text{ hours} \qquad \text{(Labor)}$$

$$X_1 + 5X_2 \le 1000 \text{ hours} \qquad \text{(Capital)}$$
$$X_1, X_2 \ge 0$$

where Z = the total monthly profit, X_1 = the quantity of product A, and X_2 = the quantity of product B. The optimal simplex table for this program is as follows, where S_1 represents unused labor hours and S_2 gives unused capital hours.

Variables		X_1	X_2	S_1	S_2	
Basis	C_j	$20	$40	$0	$0	**Amounts**
X_1	$20	1	0	$\frac{1}{2}$	$-\frac{1}{2}$	400
X_2	$40	0	1	$-\frac{1}{10}$	$\frac{3}{10}$	120
	Z_j	$20	$40	$6	$2	$12,800
$C_j - Z_j$		$0	$0	$-$6	$-$2	

a. Find the range of optimality for the profit per unit of product A.
b. Suppose that the profit per unit of product A decreases to $10. What will be the effect on the optimal solution? Suppose that the profit per unit of product A decreases to $6. What will be the effect on the optimal solution?
c. Find the range of optimality for the profit per unit of product B.
d. Suppose that the profit per unit of product B increases to $80. What will be the effect on the optimal solution? Suppose that the profit per unit of product B increases to $120. What will be the effect on the optimal solution?
e. Find the ranges of feasibility for labor and capital hours.
f. Suppose that it takes 5 (instead of 3) labor hours to produce a unit of product A. Graphically illustrate the effect of this change on the optimal solution.

11. Mertz Components, Inc., will soon begin making and selling a new stereo model at its Archadelphia plant. The product-marketing plan calls for distribution through department stores, a national chain of stereo shops, and discount retail stores. Mertz gets $25 profit from a sale in department stores, $30 from a sale in the chain, and $15 from a sale in the discount stores. The product is promoted with advertising and sales force effort. It takes an estimated $5 of advertising to get a department store sale, $10 of advertising for a sale in the chain shop, and $4 of advertising for the discount store sale. The sales force spends an estimated 2 hours of effort on this product in department stores, 1 hour in chain shops, and 4 hours in the discount stores. Advertising and sales force figures are based on past experience with similar products. Mertz expects to have an

advertising budget of $20,000 per month for the new stereo. The
sales manager will also allocate 10,000 hours of sales force time per
month for the new product. Mertz wants to know how many
stereos should be distributed through each outlet in order to
maximize monthly profits.

The optimal simplex table for this problem is presented as
follows, where S_1 denotes the unused advertising dollars and S_2 the
idle hours of sales effort.

Variables		X_1	X_2	X_3	S_1	S_2	
Basis	C_j	$25	$30	$15	$0	$0	**Amounts**
X_1	$25	1	2	$\frac{4}{5}$	$\frac{1}{5}$	0	4,000
S_2	$0	0	-3	$\frac{12}{5}$	$-\frac{2}{5}$	1	2,000
	Z_j	$25	$50	$20	$5	$0	$100,000
	$C_j - Z_j$	$0	$-20	$-$5	$-$5	$0	

a. Show how the optimal simplex table was derived.
b. Find the range of optimality for the profit per stereo sold
   through department stores.
c. Suppose that the profit per department store sale increases to
   $50. What will be the effect on the optimal solution? Suppose
   that the profit per department store sale decreases to $15. What
   will be the effect on the optimal solution?
d. Find the range of optimality for the profit per stereo sold
   through chain shops.
e. Suppose that the profit per chain shop sale increases to $45.
   What will be the effect on the optimal solution?
f. Find the range of optimality for the profit per stereo sold
   through discount stores.
g. Suppose that the profit per discount store sale increases to $30.
   What will be the effect on the optimal solution?
h. Find the ranges of feasibility for advertising dollars and hours of
   sales force effort.

12. Millips Oil Company's blending problem is given in Example 8.2 as

   minimize $Z = \$.15X_1 + \$.20X_2$
   subject to $.3X_1 + .2X_2 \geq 2000$ gallons   (JT)
                $.1X_1 + .4X_2 \geq 3000$ gallons   (WY)
                $X_1, X_2 \geq 0$

where $Z =$ the total daily purchase cost, $X_1 =$ the number of
gallons of type A crude oil, and $X_2 =$ the number of gallons of type
B crude oil. The optimal simplex table (Table 8.7) for the problem is

reproduced as follows, where S_1 measures the surplus gallons of JT, S_2 gives the surplus gallons of WY, and A_1 and A_2 are artificial variables.

Variables		X_1	X_2	S_1	S_2	A_1	A_2	
Basis	C_j	$.15	$.20	$0	$0	$M	$M	Amounts
X_1	$.15	1	0	-4	2	4	-2	2000
X_2	$.20	0	1	1	-3	-1	3	7000
	Z_j	$.15	$.20	$-\$.40$	$-\$.30$	$.40	$.30	$1700
$C_j - Z_j$		$0	$0	$.40	$.30	$M - \$.40$	$M - \$.30$	

a. Find the range of optimality for the cost per gallon of type A crude oil.
b. Suppose that the cost per gallon of type A crude oil increases to $.20. What will be the effect on the optimal solution? Suppose that the cost per gallon of type A crude oil increases to $.30. What will be the effect on the optimal solution?
c. Find the range of optimality for the cost per gallon of type B crude oil.
d. Suppose that the cost per gallon of type B crude oil decreases to $.05. What will be the effect on the optimal solution?
e. Find the ranges of feasibility for gallons of compounds JT and WY.
f. Suppose that each gallon of type B crude oil has 20% (instead of 40%) of compound WY. Graphically illustrate the effect of this change on the optimal solution.

Applications Exercises

1. Equity Security Corporation is a mutual fund. The corporation has just obtained $200,000 by converting industrial bonds to cash and is now looking for other investment opportunities for these funds. Equity's financial analysis department has identified three investment opportunities and has projected their annual rates of return. The information is summarized as follows:

Investment	Projected Annual Return (% of Investment)
Eastern Oil's preferred stock	9
Mammoth Steel's common stock	7
City of Los Angeles municipal bonds	6

Equity's management has imposed the following investment guidelines:

♦ Both types of stock should receive no more than 60% of the total new investment.

♦ Municipal bonds should receive no more than 20% of the stock investment plus $50,000.

♦ It is not necessary to invest the entire $200,000.

The company wants to know how much to invest in each type of opportunity so as to maximize total dollar return. Equity management is also interested in the planning aspects of this problem. Specifically, management would like to know:

a. The additional dollar return that can be expected from an additional dollar of available funds
b. The additional dollar return that can be expected from an additional dollar invested in stocks
c. The additional dollar return that can be expected from an additional dollar invested in bonds.

Prepare a proposal that provides all the desired information.

2. Caliente Kennels, Inc., raises greyhound dogs for the dog races in Miami, Florida. This company is experimenting with a special diet for its race dogs. The feed components available for the diet are a standard dog feed product, a vitamin-enriched biscuit, and a new vitamin and mineral additive. Nutritional values and cost of each component are summarized as follows:

	Units of Diet Ingredient per Pound of Feed Component		
Diet Requirement	Standard	Enriched Biscuit	Additive
Ingredient A	.3	.4	.6
Ingredient B	.2	.6	.3
Ingredient C	.2	.1	.1
Cost per pound	$.30	$.60	$1

The dog trainer sets the minimum daily diet requirement at 1.2 units of ingredient A, 1.2 units of ingredient B, and .4 unit of ingredient C.

Caliente Kennels' management wants to mix the feed components in a way that will produce the desired product at least cost. The company is also interested in the cost savings that can be realized from one-unit reductions in each of the three diet ingredients (A, B, and C).

Prepare a diet analysis that provides all the desired information.

3. Goodhope Army operates a specialty thrift shop that sells used, seconds (rejects from large mills), and damaged-freight carpeting. Each square yard of used carpeting yields a $2 profit, while seconds net $3 per square yard, and the damaged-freight merchandise earns $1 per square yard. This service organization has a policy of earning 50% markups on the wholesale costs of seconds and damaged-freight carpeting and 100% on used carpeting. The thrift shop can spend no more than its $36,000 projected purchase budget this year.

The thrift shop's operations are also limited by its available work force. It takes an estimated .4 people-hour of work force effort to prepare and sell one square yard of used carpeting. Preparation includes collection, processing, and packaging. Selling includes sales force effort and invoicing. It takes .3 people-hour for a square yard of seconds, and .6 hour per square yard of damaged-freight carpeting. The thrift shop will have a maximum of 6000 people-hours available this year.

Goodhope Army is currently evaluating the thrift shop's operations. As part of the evaluation, Goodhope Army wants the following information:

a. The number of square yards of each type of carpeting that the shop should buy and the resulting maximum profit
b. The effect of a proposed deal with an insurance company that would increase the profit from damaged-freight carpeting by $2 per square yard
c. The effect of a proposed deal with a mill that would increase the profit from seconds by $3 per square yard
d. The effect of unfavorable market conditions that would decrease the profit from used carpeting by $2.50 per square yard
e. The range of the purchase budget over which the optimal purchase plan remains valid
f. The range of the available work force over which the optimal purchase plan remains valid

The manager of the thrift shop is asked to provide the desired information. What responses should be in her report?

4. The Silent Alarm Company is experiencing a tremendous growth in demand for its household burglar alarm. Silent produces both an AC-operated model and a battery-operated model. It has an opportunity to be the exclusive supplier for a major department store chain, the M. W. Panny Company. Panny wants at least 800 cartons of the AC model and 400 cartons of the battery model each week.

Previously, Silent manufactured all of its own products. However, the unanticipated opportunity has left the company with insufficient capacity to satisfy the Panny contract. There is a local subcontractor who can make the same type of alarms for Silent. The subcontractor will charge Silent $150 per carton of the AC model and $90 per carton of the battery model. Also, the subcontractor can supply any combination of AC and battery models up to 600 cartons total per week.

When Silent does its own work, it costs $120 to manufacture a carton of the AC model and $80 per carton of the battery model. Other manufacturing data are summarized in the following table:

Department	Hours Required per Carton of Each Model		Hours Available per Week
	AC	Battery	
Production	4	2	1800
Packaging	2	4	2400

Silent's management wants to determine the make-or-buy decision that will meet the contract demands at a minimum total cost. How many cartons of each model should be made and how many purchased?

Management is also interested in the sensitivity of the optimal solution to potential changes in the data. Specifically, the company wants to consider the following possibilities:

a. Suppose that labor negotiations increase the cost of making a battery model to $86. What is the effect on the optimal solution?
b. Suppose that increased efficiency allows the subcontractor to supply the battery model at $84 a carton. What is the effect on the optimal solution?
c. What department is limiting manufacturing volume?
d. Suppose that a plant accident decreases available production time to 1650 hours. What is the effect on the optimal solution?
e. Suppose that increased efficiency allows the subcontractor to supply 700 cartons per week. What is the effect on the optimal solution?
f. How much would available packaging time have to decrease before there is an effect on the optimal solution?

Suppose that you are hired by Silent as a management consultant. How would you answer each of the company's questions?

5. Golden Age Senior Citizens Center advertises itself as a fun place to gather and have a healthy meal. In keeping with this policy, the director of the center wants the meals to have the highest nutritional value possible. Consequently, the director orders the cook to use as much as possible of the ingredients on hand. Currently, there are 80 pounds of ingredient A, 60 pounds of ingredient B, and 120 pounds of ingredient C available.

The cook knows how to cook just two different recipes: the Chef's Special and the Center's Standard. Each serving of the Special calls for 2 pounds of A, 1 pound of B, and 4 pounds of C. Each serving of the Standard requires 2 pounds of A, 4 pounds of B, and 2 pounds of C. One serving of the Special contains 30 nutritional units, while a serving of the Standard has 60 nutritional units.

Answer the following questions for the director:

a. How many servings of each recipe should the cook make to maximize the nutritional value of the meals made?

b. Suppose that the nutritional value of a Chef's Special is decreased to 10 units. What is the effect on the optimal solution?

c. Suppose that the nutritional value of a Center's Standard is increased by 20 units. What is the effect on the optimal solution?

d. How many pounds of ingredient A would have to be taken away before there would be a change in the optimal solution?

e. Suppose that each serving of the Standard meal calls for 4 (instead of 2) pounds of ingredient C. What is the effect on the optimal solution?

f. A new recipe is being planned. It will contain 40 nutritional units and require 7 pounds of ingredients B and C. Should the Center introduce the new recipe? Explain.

6. Swain Products, Inc., plans to develop a new hair shampoo called Form of Essence. The new product is a blend of the company's regular shampoo base and a new conditioning agent. Three raw materials are used in the blending process: sudsing, conditioning, and perfume ingredients. The final product must have at least 60 grams of the sudsing agent, exactly 40 grams of the conditioning ingredient, and no more than 15 grams of perfume. There are 100 grams of the sudsing agent, 5 grams of the conditioning ingredient, and 10 grams of the perfume in each gallon of the regular shampoo base. Each gallon of the conditioning agent has 200 grams of the conditioning ingredient but none of the sudsing or perfume ingredients. It costs $2 to blend a gallon of the regular shampoo base and $5 for a gallon of the conditioning agent. Swain wants to know how much of each raw material there should be in each gallon of the new shampoo to meet product requirements at minimum cost.

Management is also interested in the sensitivity of the optimal solution to potential changes in the data. In particular, the company wants to consider the following possibilities:

a. Suppose that materials inflation increases the cost of blending the regular shampoo by 30 cents per gallon. What is the effect on the optimal solution?

b. Suppose that a technological innovation reduces the cost of blending the conditioning agent by $1.50. What is the effect on the optimal solution?

c. Which ingredient offers the largest potential cost savings? Explain.

d. Suppose that a new formula reduces the amount of suds in Form of Essence by 40 grams. What is the effect on the optimal solution?

e. How much would the available perfume content of Form of Essence have to increase before there is an effect on the optimal solution?

f. How much would the conditioning agent content in Form of Essence have to change before there is an effect on the optimal solution?

Answer these questions for Swain's management.

CASE: The Tennis Shop

The Tennis Shop is a specialty sporting goods store that makes and sells tennis rackets. There are three models: the Junior, the Intermediate, and the Advanced. The shop operates on a made-to-order basis. Since there is a heavy backlog of orders for the Juniors and Intermediates, the store can sell all these models that are produced.

The Tennis Shop is planning the production schedule for next month. Each racket must be molded, painted, and finished. Next month, the manager expects to have 240 hours available for molding, 70 hours for painting, and 40 hours for finishing. Production of a batch of 120 Juniors requires 2 hours of molding, 4 hours of painting, and 1 hour of finishing. It takes 4 hours to mold 120 Intermediates, 2 hours for painting, and 2 hours for finishing. A batch of 120 Advanced models uses 8 hours of molding, 1 hour of painting, and 1 hour of finishing.

The shop expects to make $350 per batch (120) of the Juniors, $600 per batch of the Intermediates, and $1000 per batch of the Advanced model. Since there is a limited number of outstanding players, the shop expects to sell no more than 4800 (40 batches of 120 each) of the Advanced racket.

Tennis Shop's manager consults with you and asks you to answer the following questions:

1. How many rackets of each type should be produced next month to maximize profit?

2. Suppose that the unexpected popularity of Juniors increases its profit per batch to $400. What is the effect on the optimal solution?

3. Suppose that a decline in demand decreases Intermediate's profit per batch to $480. What is the effect on the optimal product mix?

4. Suppose that unexpected popularity increases the Advanced model's profit per batch to $1600. What is the effect on the optimal solution?

5. How much can the anticipated demand for Advanced rackets decrease before there is an effect on the optimal product mix?

6. Suppose that a machine failure reduces molding capacity to 100 hours. What is the effect on the optimal product mix?

7. Suppose that an increase in employee efficiency increases painting capacity to 75 hours. What is the effect on the optimal solution?

8. Suppose that a new process creates 20 additional finishing hours. What is the effect on the optimal product mix?

9. A new model is being considered. It will earn $800 per batch and require 6 hours of molding and 3 hours each for painting and finishing. Should the new model be introduced?

Prepare a management report that gives your recommendations on these issues.

Chapter 9
Mathematical Programming Topics

CHAPTER OUTLINE

◆ Linear Programming Limitations
  Indivisibility
  Multiple Objectives
  Uncertainty
  Nonlinear Relationships
  Sequential Problems
  Decision Situations

◆ Integer Programming
  Rounding Fractional Solutions
  Graphic Approach
  Enumeration
  Cutting Plane Method
  Branch and Bound Method
  Computer Analysis
  Extensions

◆ Goal Programming
  Formulating the Problem
  Graphic Solution
  Computer Analysis
  Extensions

◆ **Case:** Federated Motors, Inc.

CONCEPTS

◆ The assumptions and limitations of a
  linear programming analysis

◆ The nature and purpose of alternative
  methodologies

◆ Dealing with situations in which some
  or all decision variables must have
  whole-unit values

◆ Incorporating multiple criteria into a
  mathematical programming analysis

APPLICATIONS

◆ Production scheduling
◆ Distribution strategy
◆ Regional work force planning
◆ Affirmative action recruiting
◆ Store location
◆ Public health
◆ Cutting stock
◆ Cable television programming
◆ Carnival safety
◆ Production and labor planning

Linear programming is based on a set of rather restrictive assumptions. Although these assumptions will be valid for many practical problems, there are numerous other situations in which one or more of the suppositions may not be factual. The first section of this chapter presents the fundamental linear programming assumptions, identifies circumstances that could invalidate each supposition, and outlines appropriate alternative methodologies.

In one potential circumstance, some or all of the decision variables in the linear program must have whole-unit values only (no fractional values). For example, when an airline decides how many Boeing 767s or DC-10s to purchase, management cannot order 6.29 Boeings and 5.93 DC-10s. Instead, the airline must buy 5, 6, 7, 8, or some other whole-unit amount of each aircraft. The second section of this chapter shows how to formulate and solve such whole-unit problems.

Also, the decision maker may have several objectives, not just one. For example, management may want to minimize costs and maintain product quality as well as maximize profit. Furthermore, some of the criteria (such as product quality) may be difficult to quantify, and some of the objectives (such as maintaining product quality and minimizing costs) may conflict. The third section of this chapter demonstrates how multiple criteria can be incorporated into a mathematical programming analysis. Specifically, it shows how to formulate, solve, and interpret such multiple-objective programs.

LINEAR PROGRAMMING LIMITATIONS

As chapters 6 through 8 demonstrated, linear programming is a powerful and readily available methodology for solving a wide variety of decision problems. Moreover, it provides a great deal of information that is very useful for management planning and control. However, the methodology is based on a set of rather restrictive assumptions that limit its application. To avoid the misuse of linear programming, the decision maker must thoroughly understand these suppositions and resulting limitations of the analysis. Example 9.1 will illustrate the concepts.

EXAMPLE 9.1 Production Scheduling

Quantum Enterprises is thinking of manufacturing and selling video games on an experimental basis over the next three months. Management projects the schedule of manufacturing data and selling prices shown in Table 9.1.

There are no video games on hand at the beginning of December. Furthermore, the quantity manufactured during any month will be accumulated and shipped out in one large load at the end of the month. As a result, it takes one month to gear up and ship out the first batch. Thus, Quantum cannot sell any games during December. Also, the company does not want any video games on hand at the end of February. Consequently, management decides to manufacture no games during February.

Although Quantum can sell as many games as it produces,

operations are limited by the size of the company warehouse. Currently, this facility can hold no more than 1500 video games. Management wants to manufacture and sell the monthly quantities that will maximize total profit for the three-month test period.

After a careful study of the situation, the management staff has been able to formulate the problem as the following linear program:

maximize

$$Z = \$150X_2 + \$125X_3 \\ - \$50Y_1 - \$45Y_2$$

subject to

$10Y_1 \leq 20{,}000$ hours
(December capacity)

$8Y_2 \leq 24{,}000$ hours
(January capacity)

$Y_1 \leq 1500$
(December inventory)

$Y_1 + Y_2 - X_2 \leq 1500$
(January inventory)

$Y_1 + Y_2 - X_2 - X_3 = 0$
(February inventory)

$X_2, X_3, Y_1, Y_2 \geq 0$

where $Y_1 =$ the number of video games manufactured during December, $Y_2 =$ the number of video games manufactured during January, $X_2 =$ the number of video games sold during January, $X_3 =$ the number of video games sold during February, and $Z =$ the total dollar profit.

Table 9.1 Manufacturing Data and Selling Prices for Quantum Enterprises

Month	Manufacturing Cost ($)	Production Time per Game (Hours)	Capacity (Hours)	Selling Price ($)
December	50	10	20,000	—
January	45	8	24,000	150
February	—	—	—	125

INDIVISIBILITY The linear programming model assumes that each decision variable is divisible into a fractional value. Such an assumption generally will be valid when these variables represent a physical measure (weight, capacity, length, area, or volume), time, monetary values, or percentages.

Under some circumstances, quantity also is divisible into fractions. Consider the linear program in Example 9.1. By using this program to schedule production, management assumes that X_2, X_3, Y_1, and Y_2 each can have a fractional value such as 944.06 or 1298.98. Such an assumption may be valid if Quantum can (1) manufacture a portion of the video game during one month and complete the process later and (2) initiate a sale during one month and terminate the transaction in the future. For example, an $X_2 = 42.54$ might indicate that the company has sold 42 games and completed .54, or 54%, of the transaction work for another game during January. The remaining 46% of January's incomplete sales transaction, which may involve delivery and installation, can then be terminated during February. Similarly, a $Y_1 = 956.23$ would mean that 956 complete games and .23, or 23%, of another game are manufactured during December. The remaining 77% of the production work for December's unfinished game could be completed in January.

On the other hand, Quantum's video game experiment is scheduled to last for only three months. As a result, all sales transactions must be terminated by the end of the test in February. Salespeople, then, will be unable to initiate a transaction during February and complete the sale later. In addition, management does not want to manufacture any games during February. Therefore, manufacturing personnel should not have any unfinished games on hand at the end of January.

These test conditions may force the company to manufacture complete, rather than portions of, video games during January. The same circumstances could also compel management to fully, instead of partially, terminate sales transactions during February. In other words, at least two (X_3 and Y_2) of Quantum's four (X_2, X_3, Y_1, and Y_2) decision variables might have to be whole-unit rather than fractional values.

Moreover, Quantum's circumstances are not unusual. Indeed, practical problems often involve situations in which some or all of the decision variables must have whole-unit rather than fractional values. For example, it is impossible for an automobile dealer to stock 11.33 station wagons and 35.89 sedans, because only whole cars will be kept in inventory. Hence, management must stock 10, 11, 12, or some other whole-unit, or integer, number of automobiles. Similarly, when a company decides how many people should be assigned to various projects, the supervisor cannot place 1.8 or 2.55 people in each job. Rather, the supervisor must assign 1, 2, 3, or some other integer number of people to a task.

Linear programming, however, may not provide such whole-unit, or integer, solutions. Fortunately, management scientists have developed a methodology that is designed specifically for situations in which some or all of the decision variables must have integer values. This methodology, which is referred to as **integer programming**, will be presented in the second section of this chapter.

MULTIPLE OBJECTIVES The linear programming model also assumes that there is only a single objective in the problem. Furthermore, it presumes that the objective can be expressed in terms of a numerical criterion such as quantity, time, or revenue. In the linear program of Example 9.1, for instance, Quantum's single objective is to maximize the numerical criterion of total dollar profit (Z).

Frequently, however, practical problems involve several objectives. In addition, each objective may be expressed in terms of a different criterion. A textile company, for example, may want to select the manufacturing process that generates the most output in the shortest possible time frame. Moreover, some criteria can be difficult, if not impossible, to quantify. For instance, it is hard to measure social benefit, customer satisfaction, quality, and similar criteria in numerical terms. Also, there might be a conflict between the objectives, as in the case of a city that is faced with the problem of providing the maximum community safety with the smallest possible police budget.

As demonstrated in chapter 5, management scientists have developed methodologies for dealing with these multiple-criteria decision problems. One of the approaches, called **goal programming**, is designed to accommodate multiple criteria within the mathematical programming framework. This approach will be presented in the third section of this chapter.

UNCERTAINTY Linear programming further assumes that the value of each uncontrollable input is known with perfect certainty. That is, the decision maker must have the exact per-unit contribution of each variable to the objective, the exact amount of each system constraint, and the exact rate at which each system constraint amount is transformed into each variable. Put another way, the linear program should be a deterministic model.

Consider the linear program in Example 9.1. Quantum knows the exact per-game profit contribution of each decision variable: $150 for X_2, $125 for X_3, $-$50 for Y_1, and $-$45 for Y_2. Also, the company knows the precise capacity limitations (20,000 hours for December and 24,000 for January) and inventory limitations (1500 games each in December and January and 0 in February). In addition, management knows the exact rates (10 hours for December and 8 for January) at which each month's manufacturing capacity is transformed into a video game. Hence, Quantum's linear program is a deterministic model.

In practice, such uncontrollable input information typically comes from managerial estimates and formal forecasts. But estimates and forecasts are, by their very nature, imprecise. Quantum's selling prices, for example, will be influenced by uncertain future demand conditions in the video game market. Unforeseen changes in these conditions, such as a shift in consumer recreational habits, may result in prices that are considerably different from the estimates. Similarly, unanticipated supply circumstances, such as a strike at a raw-material supplier, may invalidate the forecasted manufacturing costs.

There are other sources of uncertainty that can affect the accuracy of Quantum's system constraint amount and utilization rate estimates. A plant accident, for example, might reduce the company's forecasted production capacity during December or January. Moreover, the industrial engineering department could erroneously estimate the times needed to manufacture a video game during December and January. And an unplanned business deal may provide more warehouse space for inventory than the forecasts for December and January indicate.

One way of dealing with parameter uncertainty is to perform post-optimality analyses on the original linear program. As demonstrated in chapter 8, sensitivity analysis can be used to evaluate the effects of discrete changes in the uncontrollable inputs on the optimal linear programming solution. In addition, parametric programming can be used to investigate how specified continuous variations in the parameters influence the optimal solution to the original linear program. S. P. Bradley and others [3], N. P. Loomba and E. Turban [20], and J. F. Shapiro [26] discuss these methods for dealing with parameter uncertainty in detail.

Postoptimality analysis, however, does not utilize any probability information that may be available concerning the uncontrollable inputs. As a result, this analysis can only partially account for the potential impact of parameter uncertainty on the linear programming problem. The difficulty is especially apparent when the uncontrollable inputs depend on the values of the decision variables. Such a situation might arise, for instance, in a model where future profit levels depend on earlier output decisions.

To fully overcome the difficulty, the decision maker must formulate a mathematical programming model that explicitly includes the parameter uncertainty and then use the resulting stochastic model to develop the optimal solution. As B. J. Hansotia [10] demonstrates, **stochastic programming** offers one methodology for doing this. In this approach, the objective function and system constraint segments of the original linear program are expanded to incorporate the impact of the parameter uncertainty on the problem. Such an approach converts the stochastic elements of the problem into an equivalent deterministic form. By solving the enlarged linear program, management obtains an optimal solution that fully considers and directly accounts for the parameter uncertainty.

Several classes of models have been developed to handle specific cases of the general stochastic programming problem. Unfortunately, each model requires an elaboration that is well beyond the scope of this text. I. M. Stancu-Minasian and M. J. Wets [28] provide a research bibliography on these methodologies for the interested reader. Yet, as these references will illustrate, there are some difficulties in applying the stochastic programming approach. For one thing, the decision maker must enlarge the original mathematical program to include each possible consequence of the parameter uncertainty. In practice, managers may not be willing or able to identify and precisely define these consequences. Also, the enlarged mathematical program may have an extremely large number of variables and constraints. In fact, the size of the stochastic program might make it difficult, if not practically impossible, to find the optimal solution to the problem.

As a result of these difficulties, an alternative methodology, known as **chance-constrained programming,** has been developed to deal with parameter uncertainty. In this approach, each original system constraint is reformulated in a way that ensures that the optimal solution provides a high probability of meeting the restriction. Typically, such a probability is specified by management judgment or some other relevant analysis.

The chance-constrained reformulation usually has the same size and structure as the original mathematical program. Hence, such a methodology avoids the computational burden associated with the alternative stochastic programming approach. Nevertheless, chance-constrained programming involves some serious practical and conceptual difficulties. First, it only indirectly evaluates the economic consequences of violating each system constraint. More important, there may be virtually no way to ensure that a chance-constrained formulation will give an optimal solution to the original mathematical programming problem.

Regretfully, the development of the chance-constrained methodology would take us well beyond the scope of the text. Instead, the interested reader is referred to A. J. Hogan and others [11]. This reference presents the chance-constrained methodology, compares it with stochastic programming, and discusses the resulting issues in detail.

NONLINEAR RELATIONSHIPS The linear programming model assumes that each decision variable makes a constant and independent contribution to the objective. In Example 9.1, for instance, each video game sold during January (X_2) contributes the same $150 to profit regardless of the sales level. Thus, if Quantum doubles January sales, it will double total profit. Indeed, any specified change in X_2 will result in a proportional change in the criterion value Z. That is, a 10% decrease in January sales reduces total profit by 10%, a tripling of these sales triples the criterion value, and so on. Furthermore, the $150 per-game profit contribution from January sales (X_2) is not influenced by February sales (X_3) or by manufacturing activity (Y_1 and Y_2). In other words, January sales' total contribution to profit ($150X_2$) is independent of the corresponding returns from the other decision variables.

Similarly, February sales (X_3) make a constant per-game contribution ($125) and an independent total contribution ($125X_3$) to profit. Also, December output (Y_1) contributes a constant per-game ($-$50$) and an independent total ($-$50Y_1$) contribution to the criterion value Z. In a similar manner, January output (Y_2) makes a constant per-game ($-$45$) and an independent total ($-$45Y_2$) contribution to profit. As a result, management can determine total profit

$$Z = \$150X_2 + \$125X_3 - \$50Y_1 - \$45Y_2$$

by adding the independent contributions of each decision variable.

Note that each decision variable (X_2, X_3, Y_1, and Y_3) has an exponent of 1 in the resulting profit function. Indeed, that is how the expression mathematically accounts for the proportional contribution of each month's sales or output to total profit. Moreover, each decision variable appears in a separate term of the expression. In fact, that is how the function mathematically accounts for the assumed independence between the monthly sales and output levels. When the decision variables have these additive and proportionality properties, the expression is said to involve a **linear relationship**.

Linear programming also assumes that there are linear relationships in each system constraint expression. Consider, for instance, the restrictions of the linear program in Example 9.1. In the February inventory constraint

$$Y_1 + Y_2 - X_2 - X_3 = 0$$

each decision variable appearing in the restriction has an exponent of 1 and appears in a separate term of the expression. The same is true for the January inventory constraint.

December output (Y_1) is the only decision variable that appears in both the December capacity and December inventory restrictions. Furthermore, Y_2 is the single decision variable that appears in the January capacity constraint. Nevertheless, in each of these three cases, the relevant decision variable has an exponent of 1 and appears in a separate term of the expression. For example, in the December capacity restriction

$$10Y_1 \leq 20,000 \text{ hours}$$

December output (Y_1) utilizes a constant per-game amount (10 hours) and an independent total amount ($10Y_1$) of the 20,000 available hours.

Each system constraint in Quantum's program, then, involves a linear relationship. In practice, however, each decision variable does not always utilize a constant and independent amount of capacity. Expansion frequently enables work groups to specialize in particular tasks. This specialization, in turn, creates productive efficiencies that can reduce resource utilization rates as the level of activity increases. Under these circumstances, a growth in resource usage will result in a greater-than-proportional increase in output. Tripling production, for example, might require only a doubling rather than a tripling of resource utilization.

In other situations, expansion creates coordination problems for management. Such problems, in turn, can lead to inefficiencies that increase resource usage as the level of activity expands. Under these circumstances, an increase in resource usage will result in a less-than-proportional increase in output. Doubling production, for instance, may require a tripling rather than a doubling of resource utilization.

Thus, as a result of factors such as expansion, a decision variable's constraint utilization rate may fluctuate, rather than remain constant, as the level of activity changes. Moreover, decision variables often have interrelated, instead of independent, effects on the system constraint relationships. An electric utility, for instance, typically uses the same personnel to service residential and commercial customers. That is, each customer group utilizes joint rather than separate resources and facilities. For this reason, an increase in commercial calls could divert available service personnel from residential customer requests. If such a diversion delays service, the completion time per residential request would depend on the number of commercial calls. Put another way, residential and commercial calls have an interrelated effect on the usage of service capacity.

In addition, each decision variable does not always make a constant and independent contribution to the objective. A company, for example, can usually sell a larger quantity by lowering its price. That is, revenue per unit will decrease as the sales quantity increases. Also, learning by doing and other related factors often enable work groups to produce larger quantities at a lower unit cost. In other words, manufacturing cost per unit may decline as the output level increases. Thus, a product's or service's per-unit contribution to a profit criterion will fluctuate rather than remain constant as the level of activity changes.

Furthermore, decision variables frequently have interrelated, rather than independent, effects on the criterion value. For example, suppose that a shaving equipment firm sells razors and blades. Since these products complement each other in the market, management may find that a growth in razor sales increases the demand for blades. Consequently, the profit from blades may depend on the number of razor sales. In other words, razor and blade sales make interrelated contributions to a profit criterion.

When any decision activity makes a variable unit contribution or interrelated contribution to the criterion value, the mathematical program's objective function will not involve a linear relationship. That is, a decision variable will have an exponent different than 1, and/or more than one activity will appear in a single term of the function. In such cases, the expression is said to exhibit a **nonlinear relationship**.

A variable utilization rate or interactions among the decision activities also create a nonlinear relationship in the corresponding system constraint expression. As a result, a company can have a mathematical program that

Table 9.2 Examples of Nonlinear Programs

Nonlinear Program	Characteristics	Category	Reference
minimize $Z = 5X_1 + 5X_2 - X_1X_2$ subject to $X_1 + 2X_2 = 10$	Nonlinear objective function (X_1 and X_2 both appear in the third term of the expression) Linear system constraint equality	Calculus	B. D. Sivazlian and L. E. Stanfel [27]
maximize $Z = 10X_1 - 10X_1^2$ $\quad + 20X_1 - 2X_2^2 + 10X_1X_2$ subject to $2X_1 + 2X_2 \le 12$ $4X_1 + X_2 \le 24$ $X_1, X_2 \ge 0$	Nonlinear objective function (X_1 has an exponent of 2 in the second term, X_2 has an exponent of 2 in the fourth term, and X_1 and X_2 both appear in the last term) Highest exponent of any decision variable is 2 Linear system constraint inequalities Nonnegativity conditions	Quadratic programming	M. Avriel [1]; F. J. Fabozzi and J. Valente [8]
maximize $Z = 3X_1 + 2X_2$ subject to $X_1^4 + 4X_2 \le 200$ $X_1 + 2X_2^3 \le 40$ $X_1, X_2 \ge 0$	Linear objective function Nonlinear system constraint inequalities (X_1 has an exponent of 4 in the first restriction, and X_2 has an exponent of 3 in the second constraint) Nonlinear terms can be approximated by linear expressions Nonnegativity conditions	Separable programming	Avriel [1]

consists of a nonlinear objective function and/or at least one nonlinear system constraint expression. Such a problem, which is referred to as a **nonlinear program**, can take several different forms. Table 9.2 presents some of the possibilities.

Sometimes, the interactions between the decision variables and nonproportional effects are minor. In such cases, it may be possible to reformulate these nonlinearities as linear relationships. Linear programming, then, could still provide a reasonable approximation of the optimal solution to the problem. Bradley and others [3], Loomba and Turban [20], and Shapiro [26] discuss this approach in detail.

On the other hand, when the nonproportionalities and interrelationships are significant, the decision maker must formulate and solve the

Table 9.2 continued

Nonlinear Program	Characteristics	Category	Reference
minimize $$Z = \frac{1200}{X_1 X_2} + 40 X_1^2 X_2^3$$ subject to $$6 X_1 X_2 + X_1 X_2 \leq 5400$$ $$X_1, X_2 \geq 0$$	Nonlinear objective function (X_1 has an exponent of -1 in the first term and 2 in the second term, X_2 has an exponent of -1 in the first term and 3 in the second term, and X_1 and X_2 both appear in each term of the expression) Nonlinear system constraint inequality (X_1 and X_2 both appear in each term of the expression) Nonlinear terms generally involve the product of some decision variable combination Nonnegativity conditions	Geometric programming	M. Corstjens and P. Doyle [6]
maximize $$Z = 5X_1 - X_2^2 - 2X_1 X_2$$ subject to $$X_1^2 + X_1 X_2 + X_2^2 \leq 50$$ $$X_1 + X_2 \leq 75$$ $$X_1, X_2 \geq 0$$	Nonlinear objective function (X_2 has an exponent of 2 in the second term, while X_1 and X_2 both appear in the third term of the expression) Nonlinear system constraint inequality (X_1 has an exponent of 2 in the first term, X_2 has an exponent of 2 in the third term, and X_1 and X_2 both appear in the second term of the expression) Linear system constraint inequality Nonnegativity conditions	Convex programming	M. S. Bazaraa and C. M. Shetty [2]; J. H. Grotte [9]

corresponding nonlinear program. Unlike the simplex method for linear programming problems, however, there is no efficient general-purpose algorithm that can be used to solve all nonlinear programs. In fact, some of these problems cannot be solved in a satisfactory manner by any method. Nevertheless, various computational techniques have been developed to solve some important categories of nonlinear programs. Such methodologies are known collectively as **nonlinear programming**.

Each nonlinear programming category has its own special name. Indeed, many of the important categories are identified in Table 9.2. Unfortunately, these methodologies all involve a mathematical elaboration that is well beyond the scope of this text. Nonetheless, the references listed in Table 9.2 present the relevant analyses for the interested reader.

SEQUENTIAL PROBLEMS The linear programming model assumes that the problem involves a single, one-time decision. In Example 9.1, for instance, Quantum wants to develop a video game production/sales schedule for only the three-month experiment. Moreover, the optimal experimental plan will be unaffected by previous management actions, nor should it have a direct impact on other concurrent or future company activities. Instead, the selected schedule will be the result of an independent decision made at the beginning of the three-month planning period.

Yet, as chapter 3 demonstrated, many problems involve a series of interrelated decisions. Consider, for example, a military training program. In such programs, all recruits are expected to complete various training phases, such as military indoctrination and physical development. Also, each phase usually contains a specified number of tasks. Physical development, for instance, might consist of 2000 push-ups, 4000 knee bends, and so on. Hence, each trainee can be assigned a wide variety of tasks at each stage of the program. Since all training phases are necessary, however, each assignment is influenced by the pattern of previously completed and future required tasks. Put another way, the recruit task assignments entail a series of interrelated, rather than independent, decisions. As a result, camp management must determine the sequence of assignments that minimizes recruits' total time in the training program.

As illustrated in chapter 3, management scientists have developed methodologies for dealing with these sequential decision problems. One of the approaches, called dynamic programming, decomposes the original problem into smaller multiple stages. Each smaller part is then solved in sequence through the use of information from each preceding stage.

Unlike the other models presented in this chapter, however, dynamic programming is not a special type of mathematical program. Instead, the methodology represents a general type of approach to problem solving. It would be useful, then, to present the methodology in conjunction with the problem situations for which the technique is best suited. Consequently, the discussion on dynamic programming is deferred until chapter 15.

DECISION SITUATIONS In effect, then, linear programming is best suited for problems in which:

1. Each decision variable is divisible into a fractional value
2. There is a single objective that can be expressed in terms of a numerical criterion
3. The value of each uncontrollable input is known with perfect certainty
4. There are linear relationships in the objective function and each system constraint
5. Management must make a single, one-time decision

Table 9.3 Alternative Solution Methodologies

Linear Programming Assumption	Actual Situation	Alternative Approach
Divisible decision variables	Indivisibility	Integer programming
Single objective	Multiple objectives	Goal programming
Deterministic information	Uncertainty	Postoptimality analyses, stochastic programming, chance-constrained programming
Proportional relationships, independent decision variables	Nonproportional relationships, interactions among decision variables	Nonlinear programming
Single, one-time decision	Sequential problems	Dynamic programming

When the actual decision situation does not have each of these characteristics, management should consider an alternative solution methodology. Table 9.3 summarizes the alternatives.

INTEGER PROGRAMMING

Often, a mathematical programming problem may deal with a one-time decision, have a single objective, involve linear relationships, and contain deterministic information. Yet some or all of the decision variables may be required to have integer values. Example 9.2 illustrates.

EXAMPLE 9.2 Distribution Strategy

Quality Foods Corporation operates a regional chain of supermarkets in the Midwest. Recently, its board of directors approved a $15.5 million budget to be used for the construction of additional stores and/or warehouses. Each store will cost $1 million to construct and contribute an estimated monthly profit of $30,000. On the other hand, every warehouse will contribute an expected $72,000 monthly profit but cost $3 million to construct. Nevertheless, the board wants to build at least one additional warehouse and no more than five new stores. Quality's objective is to construct the number of additional stores and warehouses that maximizes total profit.

Management realizes that Quality cannot build a fraction of a warehouse or store. After a thorough deliberation, however, the staff has been able to formulate the problem as the following mathematical program:

maximize

$$Z = \$30{,}000X_1 + \$72{,}000X_2$$

subject to

$$\$1{,}000{,}000X_1 + \$3{,}000{,}000X_2$$
$$\leq \$15{,}500{,}000 \quad \text{(Budget)}$$
$$X_1 \leq 5 \quad\quad \text{(New stores)}$$

$$X_2 \geq 1$$
$$\text{(Additional warehouses)}$$
$$X_1, X_2 \geq 0 \text{ and are integers}$$

where $Z =$ the total monthly profit, $X_1 =$ the number of new stores, and $X_2 =$ the number of additional warehouses.

In Example 9.2, Quality's problem deals with the isolated action of developing an optimal distribution strategy. Moreover, the single objective of this strategy is to maximize total profit. Also, there are linear relationships in the objective function and system constraints of the corresponding mathematical program. In addition, management knows the exact values of the uncontrollable inputs (unit profit, budget, new store, and additional warehouse guidelines).

The mathematical program in Example 9.2, then, has nearly all the characteristics of a linear programming problem. The only exception is that Quality must build an integer rather than fractional number of new stores and/or additional warehouses. That is, each decision variable is required to have a whole-unit value. As a result, the company's situation represents an integer, instead of linear, programming problem.

In fact, there is a special name for Quality's situation. Problems in which all the decision variables must have whole-unit solutions are referred to as **pure integer programming** problems. Moreover, several methods have been developed to solve such problems.

ROUNDING FRACTIONAL SOLUTIONS If management temporarily ignores the integer restrictions on the X_1 and X_2 values, Quality's problem can be expressed as follows:

maximize $Z = \$30{,}000X_1 + \$72{,}000X_2$

subject to
$$\$1{,}000{,}000X_1 + \$3{,}000{,}000X_2 \leq \$15{,}500{,}000 \quad\quad \text{(Budget)}$$
$$X_1 \leq 5 \quad\quad \text{(New stores)}$$
$$X_2 \geq 1 \quad\quad \text{(Additional warehouses)}$$
$$X_1, X_2 \geq 0$$

That is, the mathematical program becomes an ordinary linear programming problem. As such, it can be solved with the simplex method or graphic linear programming procedure. By using the graphic procedure,

Figure 9.1 Quality's Optimal Linear Programming Solution

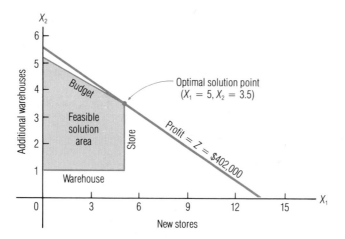

the company will obtain the results shown in Figure 9.1. The shaded region of the diagram identifies the feasible solution area for the linear programming formulation of Quality's mathematical program.

Sometimes, the optimal solution to the temporary linear programming formulation will provide whole-unit values for each decision variable. If so, this solution also represents the optimal answer for the original integer programming problem. Usually, however, the linear programming answer contains one or more fractional values, as in Quality's case. As Figure 9.1 demonstrates, the company's optimal linear programming solution involves

$$X_1 = 5 \text{ new stores}$$

and

$$X_2 = 3.5 \text{ additional warehouses}$$

for a total monthly profit of $Z = \$402,000$. But the firm must build a complete structure, not a partial structure. Hence, the recommendation of $X_2 = 3.5$ additional warehouses is an impractical answer for Quality's original integer programming problem.

Often, the fractional portion of a noninteger decision variable has little effect on the optimal recommendation. Consider the following situation encountered by a pencil manufacturer. Each pencil earns 2 cents profit, and the optimal output is 42,196.38 pencils. But it is impossible to sell an unfinished pencil. Under these circumstances, the company will not lose much money by manufacturing 42,196 rather than 42,196.38 pencils. In making its production decision, management will simply round the fractional value to the nearest feasible integer and hence recommend an output of 42,196 pencils.

Quality, on the other hand, is faced with a different situation. Each additional warehouse will cost $3 million and contribute $72,000 to monthly profit. Even a fraction of these amounts would have a substantial financial impact on the company. Still, management might be tempted to find an integer solution by rounding the fractional values in the optimal linear programming answer of $X_1 = 5$ new stores and $X_2 = 3.5$ additional warehouses.

In particular, the decision maker could round $X_2 = 3.5$ to either $X_2 = 3$ or $X_2 = 4$. The alternative recommendations, then, would be to build

$X_1 = 5$ new stores

$X_2 = 4$ additional warehouses

or

$X_1 = 5$ new stores

$X_2 = 3$ additional warehouses

In fact, there generally will be two possible integer combinations for each fractional decision variable in the solution. Unfortunately, this characteristic can lead to a large number of rounded combinations. For instance, a problem with just three fractional solution values would involve $2^3 = 2 \times 2 \times 2 = 8$ rounded combinations.

However, some of the rounded combinations may not satisfy all the system constraints in the mathematical program. For example, the alternative integer combinations of

$X_1 = 5, \quad X_2 = 4$

and

$X_1 = 5, \quad X_2 = 3$

each satisfy both the new store restriction

$X_1 \le 5$

and the additional warehouse restriction

$X_2 \ge 1$

The $X_1 = 5$ and $X_2 = 3$ combination also meets the

$\$1,000,000X_1 + \$3,000,000X_2 \le \$15,500,000$

budget restriction. On the other hand, a recommendation of $X_1 = 5$ and $X_2 = 4$ involves an expenditure of

$\$1,000,000(5) + \$3,000,000(4) = \$17,000,000$

Since the company has only a $15,500,000 budget, this $X_1 = 5$ and $X_2 = 4$ combination is infeasible.

Any infeasible rounded solutions, such as the $X_1 = 5$ and $X_2 = 4$ combination in Example 9.2, should be eliminated from further consideration. The decision maker can then choose from among the remaining feasible alternatives the rounded solution that best meets the objective. In Quality's case, the elimination of the $X_1 = 5$ and $X_2 = 4$ mixture leaves the $X_1 = 5$ and $X_2 = 3$ combination as the only feasible rounded solution. Thus, the company knows that a distribution strategy of $X_1 = 5$ new stores and $X_2 = 3$ additional warehouses is the feasible rounded solution that provides the largest total profit. In fact, the objective function relationship

$$Z = \$30{,}000X_1 + \$72{,}000X_2$$

from the mathematical program indicates that this $X_1 = 5$ and $X_2 = 3$ combination leads to a

$$Z = \$30{,}000(5) + \$72{,}000(3) = \$366{,}000$$

total monthly profit.

Unfortunately, the rounding approach has some serious shortcomings. When there are many fractional values, it is very time-consuming to develop the rounded combinations, check each for feasibility, and identify the best feasible rounded solution. Furthermore, this best rounded solution is only one among many feasible integer combinations. Consequently, the best rounded combination may not represent the optimal solution to the original integer programming problem. To see why, let us examine the graphic approach to pure integer programming.

GRAPHIC APPROACH Quality knows that the feasible solution area of Figure 9.1 contains all the decision variable combinations (X_1 and X_2) satisfying the system constraints in its mathematical program. Although there is an infinite number of points in this area, management is interested only in the integer combinations. Each of these feasible integer combinations is identified with a heavy dot (.) in Figure 9.2. The shaded region of the diagram again shows the feasible solution area for the linear programming formulation of Quality's mathematical program.

One of the feasible integer combinations (heavy dots) in Figure 9.2 represents the optimal solution to Quality's mathematical program. To find this solution, management uses a variation of the isovalue line method presented in chapter 6. The company's objective function relationship

$$Z = \$30{,}000X_1 + \$72{,}000X_2$$

Figure 9.2 Quality's Feasible Integer Combinations

can be used to construct a series of isoprofit lines. Recall that each of these lines gives the decision variable combinations (X_1 and X_2) that generate a specified profit level (Z). Moreover, every line in the series will move progressively away from the origin toward a higher profit level. The decision maker then identifies the largest-valued isoprofit line that passes through an integer combination in the feasible solution area. This combination is the optimal solution to the pure integer programming problem.

Figure 9.3 illustrates the graphic approach for Quality's mathematical program. As the figure shows, the company's best rounded solution of

$X_1 = 5$ new stores

and

$X_2 = 3$ additional warehouses

is on the isovalue line that corresponds to a $Z = \$366,000$ total monthly profit. Yet management can move to the $Z = \$378,000$ isoprofit line by constructing

$X_1 = 3$ new stores

and

$X_2 = 4$ additional warehouses

Furthermore, there is no other feasible integer combination that provides a profit larger than $378,000. Thus, this integer combination ($X_1 = 3$,

Figure 9.3 Quality's Optimal Integer Programming Solution

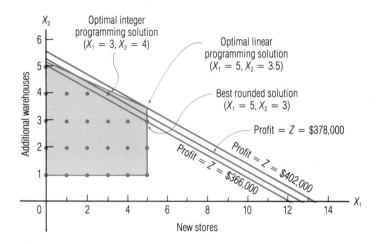

$X_2 = 4$), rather than the best rounded recommendation ($X_1 = 5$, $X_2 = 3$), provides the optimal solution to the integer programming problem. Indeed, by using the best rounded instead of the optimal integer solution, Quality will get

$$\$378,000 - \$366,000 = \$12,000$$

less per month in profits.

Nonetheless, Figure 9.3 shows that the optimal linear programming solution ($X_1 = 5$, $X_2 = 3.5$) generates a larger criterion value (lies on a higher-valued isoprofit line) than the optimal integer combination ($X_1 = 3$, $X_2 = 4$). This result is not a coincidence. In fact, *the optimal integer combination will never provide a criterion value that is superior to the best linear programming solution*, because the integer restrictions add additional constraints to the problem and thereby effectively reduce the decision maker's feasible alternatives. Such lost opportunities, in turn, usually lead to lower efficiency, higher costs, and diminished profits.

In Quality's case, the optimal linear programming solution ($X_1 = 5$, $X_2 = 3.5$) is on the isovalue line that corresponds to a $Z = \$402,000$ total monthly profit. The integer restrictions on the X_1 and X_2 values, however, prevent the company from reaching this $402,000 isoprofit line. Instead, the optimal integer combination ($X_1 = 3$, $X_2 = 4$) allows the company to achieve a $Z = \$378,000$ total monthly profit. Consequently, the integer restrictions create a monthly opportunity cost of

$$\$402,000 - \$378,000 = \$24,000$$

This graphic approach can be used to solve only those integer programming problems that have two decision variables. Most practical situations, however, involve many decision activities. Consequently, the decision maker will need an alternative solution procedure for these larger integer programming problems.

ENUMERATION Remember that each decision variable in a pure integer programming problem must have a whole-unit solution. As a result, there will be a finite number of feasible integer combinations. Thus, the decision maker can list, or enumerate, each combination, calculate the corresponding criterion value, and then identify the feasible integer combination that leads to the best criterion value.

Figure 9.2, for example, demonstrates that there are twenty-three feasible integer combinations (heavy dots) in Quality's mathematical program. Hence, the company can easily list each combination and calculate the corresponding total monthly profit. Indeed, if management does this, it will obtain the results presented in Table 9.4.

As the enumeration in Table 9.4 demonstrates, $X_1 = 3$ and $X_2 = 4$ is the feasible integer combination that leads to the best criterion value. Specifically, it shows that Quality can maximize total monthly profit at $Z = \$378,000$ by constructing

$X_1 = 3$ new stores

and

$X_2 = 4$ additional warehouses

This optimal integer solution, of course, is the same as the recommendation obtained from the graphic approach.

Although the enumeration method will provide the optimal solution to any pure integer programming problem, it is best suited for small-scale situations, since large problems may involve thousands, even millions, of feasible integer combinations. It would be impractical, even with a computer, to list and evaluate each of these combinations. Consequently, the decision maker needs some systematic way to solve large-scale integer programming problems.

CUTTING PLANE METHOD By examining Figure 9.3, you can see that Quality's optimal integer answer ($X_1 = 3, X_2 = 4$) lies within the linear programming formulation's feasible solution area. This characteristic suggests the following solution procedure. First, management again can temporarily ignore the integer restrictions on the decision variables and treat the problem as a linear program. If the best linear programming recommendation provides

Table 9.4 Quality's Feasible Integer Solutions

Feasible Integer Combinations		Total Monthly Profit ($ thousand) $Z = \$30{,}000X_1 + \$72{,}000X_2$
New Stores X_1	Additional Warehouses X_2	
0	1	72
0	2	144
0	3	216
0	4	288
0	5	360
1	1	102
1	2	174
1	3	246
1	4	318
2	1	132
2	2	204
2	3	276
2	4	348
3	1	162
3	2	234
3	3	306 Optimal
3	4	378 ← integer
4	1	192 solution
4	2	264
4	3	336
5	1	222
5	2	294
5	3	366

whole-unit values for each decision variable, then it represents the optimal solution to the original integer programming problem.

Quality's distribution problem is not such a case. As Figures 9.1 and 9.3 demonstrate, the linear programming formulation leads to an optimal solution ($X_1 = 5$, $X_2 = 3.5$) that contains a fractional decision variable. Under these circumstances, management then adds to the linear programming formulation a new constraint that eliminates some noninteger answers. Specifically, this new restriction, called a **Gomory cut**, should exclude the optimal fractional answer but include each integer combination in the linear program's feasible solution area.

Figure 9.4 illustrates the process. By inspecting this diagram, you can see that the dashed line excludes all decision variable combinations in the unshaded triangle of Quality's feasible solution area. Moreover, this eliminated (unshaded) region contains the optimal fractional answer ($X_1 = 5$, $X_2 = 3.5$) to the company's original linear programming formulation. Yet all attainable integer combinations (heavy dots) still remain within the feasible solution area (shaded region) of the graph. Consequently, the dashed line, which corresponds to a total structures restriction of

Figure 9.4 Quality's First Gomory Cut

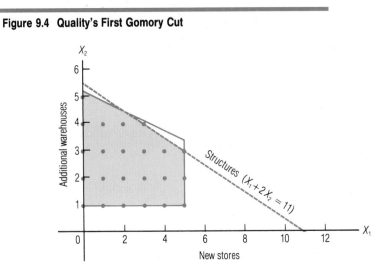

$X_1 + 2X_2 \leq 11$, provides an appropriate first Gomory cut for the original linear programming formulation.

After constructing a Gomory cut, the decision maker then must solve the revised linear program. If the resulting recommendation involves whole-unit values for each decision variable, the revised answer represents the optimal integer programming solution. Otherwise, management must add other Gomory cuts, one at a time, and solve each successive linear program. Eventually, one of these linear programs will yield an all-integer solution. Put another way, this process, which is known as the **cutting plane method**, ultimately generates the optimal integer programming answer.

In Quality's case, for example, the first Gomory cut ($X_1 + 2X_2 = 11$) creates the following linear program:

maximize $Z = \$30{,}000X_1 + \$72{,}000X_2$

subject to $\$1{,}000{,}000X_1 + \$3{,}000{,}000X_2 \leq \$15{,}500{,}000$ (Budget)

$X_1 \leq 5$ (New stores)

$X_2 \geq 1$ (Additional warehouses)

$X_1 + 2X_2 \leq 11$ (Structures)

$X_1, X_2 \geq 0$

By using the graphic procedure to solve this linear program, the company will obtain the results presented in Figure 9.5. The shaded region identifies the feasible solution area for the revised linear program.

Figure 9.5 Quality's Optimal Linear Programming Solution with the First Gomory Cut

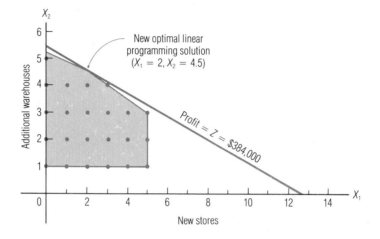

Figure 9.5 shows that the first Gomory cut (structures constraint) leads to a new optimal linear programming solution of

$X_1 = 2$ new stores

$X_2 = 4.5$ additional warehouses

Since this solution also contains a fractional decision variable, however, it does not provide the optimal integer programming solution. As a result, the decision maker must add another Gomory cut to the linear programming formulation.

Quality's management can again construct the appropriate Gomory cut from an inspection of Figure 9.5. By so doing, in fact, it will find that a second total structures restriction of

$$X_1 + 3X_2 \le 15$$

provides a suitable additional cut. Furthermore, this second Gomory cut will create a revised linear program that, in turn, leads to the solution identified in Figure 9.6.

As Figure 9.6 demonstrates, the optimal linear programming solution with the second Gomory cut involves whole-unit values for each decision variable ($X_1 = 3$, $X_2 = 4$). Thus, this answer represents the optimal solution to Quality's integer programming problem. The result is also the same as the recommendation obtained by the more cumbersome enumeration approach.

In Example 9.2, the decision maker can construct a Gomory cut by inspecting the graph of the corresponding linear program's feasible

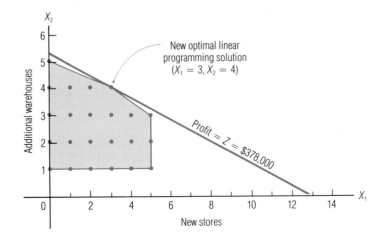

Figure 9.6 Quality's Optimal Linear Programming Solution with the Second Gomory Cut

solution area. Still, the process requires a great deal of judgment and skill. More important, it can be used only for integer programming problems that have only two decision variables. Practical situations, however, typically involve many activities that are restricted to whole-unit values. In these cases, management will be unable to graph the feasible solution region. As a result, the simplex method or some other efficient algorithm must be used to construct the Gomory cuts and develop the resulting linear programming solutions. There are methodologies available for doing this. H. Salkin [24] and H. A. Taha [29] present the details for the interested reader.

Unfortunately, there is a more serious difficulty. Each Gomory cut can turn out to be a small reduction of a very large feasible solution region. Consequently, the decision maker may need a large number of Gomory cuts (additional constraints) to develop the optimal integer solution from a linear programming formulation. Indeed, experience indicates that an integer programming problem of a relatively modest size can involve thousands of cuts. Under these circumstances, it might be impractical, even with a computer, to complete the search for the optimal whole-unit answer.

BRANCH AND BOUND METHOD The implementation difficulties encountered with the cutting plane method have led management scientists to develop alternative integer programming solution procedures. One of these alternatives, called the **branch and bound method**, has some similarities to the cutting plane procedure. Like the Gomory approach, the branch and bound method begins by temporarily treating the integer programming problem as a linear program. If the best linear programming recommendation provides whole-unit values for each decision variable, such an answer represents the optimal integer solution. Otherwise, the decision maker again conducts an intelligent search of the linear programming formulation's feasible solution region. Unlike Gomory's approach, however, the branch and bound method bases the search on a partitioning rather than cutting process.

Consider Quality's distribution problem. Figure 9.3 shows that the optimal linear programming solution recommends a fractional number of $X_2 = 3.5$ additional warehouses. Since the company needs integer rather than fractional recommendations, management must exclude this answer from further consideration. Nevertheless, the $X_2 = 3.5$ recommendation suggests that the optimal integer solution should have a value of either $X_2 \leq 3$ or $X_2 \geq 4$. In other words, the $X_2 \leq 3$ constraint places an upper bound and the $X_2 \geq 4$ restriction a lower bound on the number of additional warehouses.

As a result, the decision maker can move toward the optimal integer solution by partitioning the original linear programming formulation into two complementary subproblems. One of these subproblems is created by adding the upper-bound constraint ($X_2 \leq 3$) to the original linear program. The other is generated by adding the lower-bound restriction ($X_2 \geq 4$) to the original linear program. By performing this initial partitioning, or branching, action, Quality will form the subproblems presented in Figure 9.7.

If the company uses the graphic linear programming solution procedure to solve these two subproblems, it will obtain the results shown in Figure 9.8. The unshaded region in this diagram gives the portion of the original feasible solution area that is eliminated by the initial partitioning, or branching, action. On the other hand, the upper shaded region represents the feasible solution area for subproblem 2. Similarly, the lower shaded region identifies the feasible solution area for subproblem 1.

As Figure 9.8 demonstrates, the initial partitioning process excludes the original optimal linear programming answer ($X_1 = 5$, $X_2 = 3.5$) from the feasible solution area (shaded region) of each subproblem. Yet all attainable integer combinations (heavy dots) still remain within these areas. Consequently, the feasible solution areas (shaded regions) for the subproblems must contain the optimal integer solution.

The partitioning process, however, creates additional restrictions that effectively reduce the decision maker's feasible alternatives. Thus, each subproblem has a solution that involves a smaller criterion value than the original optimal linear programming answer. Figure 9.8, for instance, shows that the optimal subproblem 1 and 2 solutions both lead to smaller earnings (lie on lower-valued isoprofit lines) than the optimal linear programming solution. In effect, then, the $Z = \$402,000$ total monthly profit from the original optimal linear programming solution provides an initial upper bound on the criterion value for the best integer answer.

Figure 9.8 also shows that subproblem 1 has an optimal solution

Figure 9.7 Quality's Initial Partitioning Process

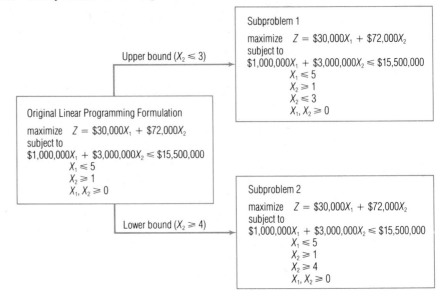

Figure 9.8 Quality's Initial Subproblem Solutions

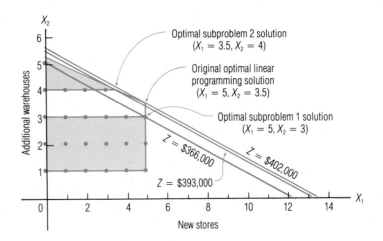

($X_1 = 5$, $X_2 = 3$) that involves integer values for each decision variable. The optimal subproblem 2 solution, on the other hand, involves a fractional answer ($X_1 = 3.5$, $X_2 = 4$). Yet the best profit ($Z = \$393,000$) from subproblem 2 is larger than the optimal criterion value ($Z = \$366,000$) for subproblem 1. Hence, the whole-unit recommendation of subproblem 1 does not necessarily represent the optimal solution to Quality's original integer programming problem. Instead, there may be an integer combination within subproblem 2's feasible solution area (the upper shaded region in Figure 9.8) that provides a profit greater than $366,000. To find out, the company must partition subproblem 2 into its two complementary subproblems. The $X_1 = 3.5$ recommendation suggests that subproblem 2's optimal integer solution should have a value of either $X_1 \leq 3$ or $X_1 \geq 4$. One branch, then, is created by adding the upper-bound constraint ($X_1 \leq 3$) to the linear program in subproblem 2. The other branch is generated by adding the lower-bound restriction ($X_1 \geq 4$) to this program. Such actions also mean that the best subproblem 2 profit ($Z = \$393,000$) replaces the previous largest return ($Z = \$402,000$) as the upper bound on the optimal criterion value.

If management forms these two additional subproblems and then finds the corresponding optimal solutions, it will obtain the results shown in Figure 9.9. As the figure illustrates, the second partitioning process creates subproblems 3 and 4 from subproblem 2. However, since subproblem 4 has an infeasible solution, it can be eliminated from further consideration. In the diagram, this exclusion is indicated by drawing a jagged line (pruning the branch) leading to subproblem 4.

On the other hand, subproblem 3 has an optimal solution ($X_1 = 3$, $X_2 = 4$) that contains integer values for each decision variable. Hence, this combination represents the best integer answer within subproblem 2's feasible solution area. Figure 9.9 also shows that such an answer provides a profit ($Z = \$378,000$) that is greater than the earnings ($Z = \$366,000$) from the best previous integer recommendation (subproblem 1). As a result, the decision maker can now eliminate subproblem 1 from consideration. In the diagram, the exclusion again is indicated by drawing a jagged line (pruning the branch) leading to subproblem 1.

These actions mean that the best subproblem 3 profit ($Z = \$378,000$) replaces the previous largest return (the $Z = \$393,000$ from subproblem 2) as the upper bound on the optimal criterion value. By following the unpruned branches in Figure 9.9, you can also see that there are no further subproblems that could provide an integer solution with a profit greater than $378,000. Therefore, the best subproblem 3 solution ($X_1 = 3$, $X_2 = 4$) must represent the optimal answer for Quality's integer programming problem. This branch and bound recommendation, of course, is the same result obtained by the usually more cumbersome enumeration and cutting plane approaches. Table 9.5 summarizes the branch and bound method for solving integer programming problems.

Figure 9.9 Branch and Bound Solution of Quality's Integer Program

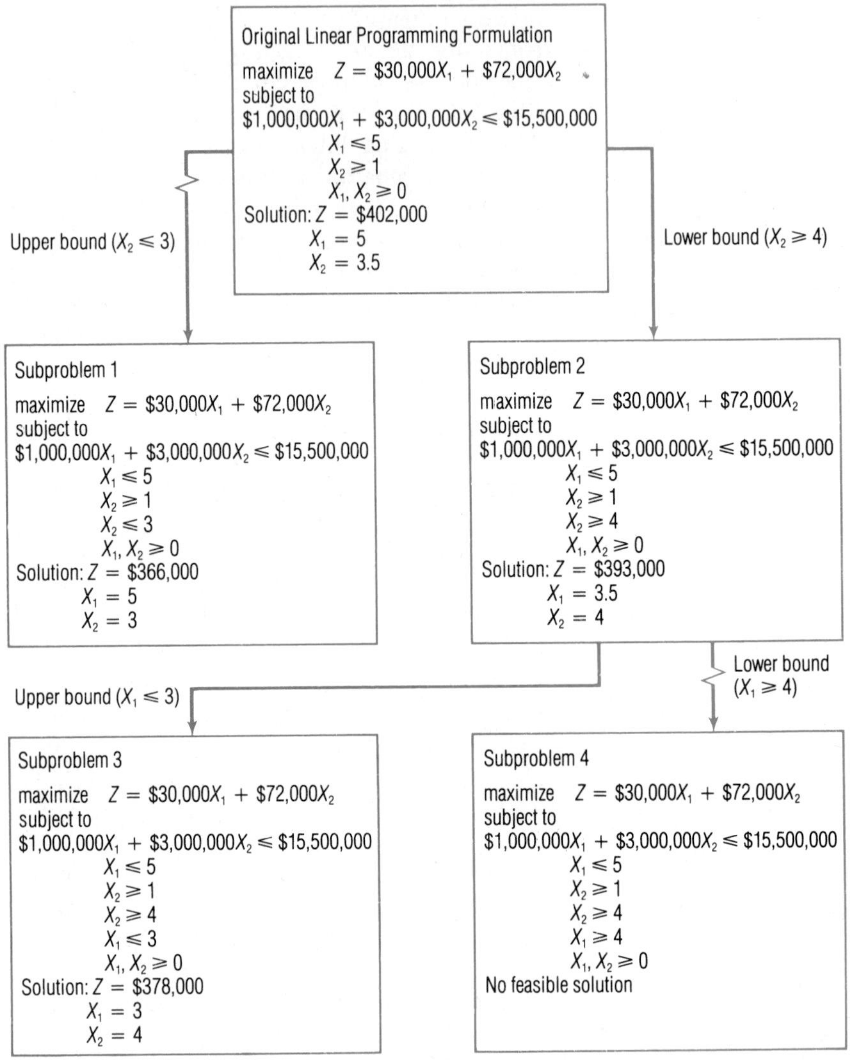

Original Linear Programming Formulation

maximize $Z = \$30,000X_1 + \$72,000X_2$
subject to
$\$1,000,000X_1 + \$3,000,000X_2 \leqslant \$15,500,000$
$X_1 \leqslant 5$
$X_2 \geqslant 1$
$X_1, X_2 \geqslant 0$
Solution: $Z = \$402,000$
$X_1 = 5$
$X_2 = 3.5$

Upper bound ($X_2 \leqslant 3$)

Lower bound ($X_2 \geqslant 4$)

Subproblem 1

maximize $Z = \$30,000X_1 + \$72,000X_2$
subject to
$\$1,000,000X_1 + \$3,000,000X_2 \leqslant \$15,500,000$
$X_1 \leqslant 5$
$X_2 \geqslant 1$
$X_2 \leqslant 3$
$X_1, X_2 \geqslant 0$
Solution: $Z = \$366,000$
$X_1 = 5$
$X_2 = 3$

Subproblem 2

maximize $Z = \$30,000X_1 + \$72,000X_2$
subject to
$\$1,000,000X_1 + \$3,000,000X_2 \leqslant \$15,500,000$
$X_1 \leqslant 5$
$X_2 \geqslant 1$
$X_2 \geqslant 4$
$X_1, X_2 \geqslant 0$
Solution: $Z = \$393,000$
$X_1 = 3.5$
$X_2 = 4$

Lower bound
($X_1 \geqslant 4$)

Upper bound ($X_1 \leqslant 3$)

Subproblem 3

maximize $Z = \$30,000X_1 + \$72,000X_2$
subject to
$\$1,000,000X_1 + \$3,000,000X_2 \leqslant \$15,500,000$
$X_1 \leqslant 5$
$X_2 \geqslant 1$
$X_2 \geqslant 4$
$X_1 \leqslant 3$
$X_1, X_2 \geqslant 0$
Solution: $Z = \$378,000$
$X_1 = 3$
$X_2 = 4$

Subproblem 4

maximize $Z = \$30,000X_1 + \$72,000X_2$
subject to
$\$1,000,000X_1 + \$3,000,000X_2 \leqslant \$15,500,000$
$X_1 \leqslant 5$
$X_2 \geqslant 1$
$X_2 \geqslant 4$
$X_1 \geqslant 4$
$X_1, X_2 \geqslant 0$
No feasible solution

Table 9.5 The Branch and Bound Method of Integer Programming

1. Treat the problem as a linear program by temporarily ignoring any integer restrictions on the decision variables.
2. Solve the linear program. If the answer provides whole-unit values for each integer-restricted variable, it represents the optimal solution to the integer programming problem. Otherwise, go to step 3.
3. Use the following procedure to partition the linear program into two complementary subproblems:
    a. Select an integer-restricted decision variable that has a fractional value in the optimal linear programming solution. If there is more than one such activity, select the variable that makes the most favorable contribution to the objective.
    b. Formulate an upper-bound constraint that requires the selected variable to have a value no greater than the integer portion of the fractional answer.
    c. Create one subproblem by adding the upper-bound constraint to the linear program.
    d. Formulate a lower-bound restriction that requires the selected variable to have a value at least as large as 1 plus the integer portion of the fractional answer.
    e. Generate the second subproblem by adding the lower-bound restriction to the linear program.
4. Solve each subproblem. Record any solution that contains whole-unit values for each integer-restricted variable.
5. Select a subproblem with a solution that contains fractional decision variables but generates a criterion value superior to any recorded integer answer. If there is a choice, select the subproblem with the best criterion value. Then return to step 3. If there is no such subproblem, go to step 6.
6. Compare all subproblem solutions that provide whole-unit values for each integer-restricted variable. The whole-unit answer with the best criterion value represents the optimal integer programming solution. If no subproblem contains a whole-unit answer, then there is no feasible solution to the integer programming problem.

Example 9.2 involves only two decision variables and three system constraints. Moreover, the fractional linear programming answer is relatively close to the best integer solution. As a result, the decision maker must complete only a few branch and bound calculations to find the optimal integer programming solution. On the other hand, typical large-scale situations may require hundreds of computations. Thus, the branch and bound method, in practice, is usually implemented with the aid of a computer.

COMPUTER ANALYSIS Management scientists have developed several prewritten computer packages that are designed to solve relatively large-scale integer programming problems. Most employ some form of the cutting plane and/or branch and bound methods. One such package, called **Multi Purpose Optimization System (MPOS)**, is available on the California State University and College System (CSUC) Computer System.

Figure 9.10 illustrates the MPOS solution to Quality's distribution

Figure 9.10 Solving Quality's Problem with MPOS

```
/FIND,MPOS
? TITLE
? QUALITY ENTERPRISES
        TITLE
        QUALITY ENTERPRISES
? INTEGER
        INTEGER
? X1
X2
        X1
?       X2
? MAXIMIZE
        MAXIMIZE
? 30000X1 + 72000X2
        30000X1 + 72000X2
? CONSTRAINTS
        CONSTRAINTS
? 1000000X1 + 3000000X2 < 15500000
    1.   1000000X1 + 3000000X2 < 15500000
? X1 < 5
    2.   X1 < 5
? X2 > 1
    3.   X2 > 1
? OPTIMIZE
        OPTIMIZE
--- CONTINUOUS SOLUTION ---



            SUMMARY OF RESULTS  AT ITERATION        2

            OBJECTIVE FUNCTION =     402000.000000

    VARIABLE        BASIS/   INTEG/      ACTIVITY              OPPORTUNITY
    TAG    NAME     BOUNDS   CONTIN      LEVEL                 COST
    9002   X2       B        C            3.5000000             --
    9001   X1       B        C            5.0000000             --
    -3    --SLACK   B        C            2.5000000             --
    -2    --SLACK   NB       C             ---           -6000.0000000
    -1    --SLACK   NB       C             ---              -.0240000


        TIME =      .032 SECONDS.

--- NEW INTEGER-FEASIBLE SOLUTION ---
```

problem. The decision maker executes the computer program with the
FIND,MPOS command. The package then prompts another command
with the ? symbol. An appropriate response is BBMIP. This statement tells
MPOS that the branch and bound method will be used to solve an integer
programming problem. The next two statements give the title QUALITY
ENTERPRISES to the problem.

At this stage, the user must input the integer programming data. The

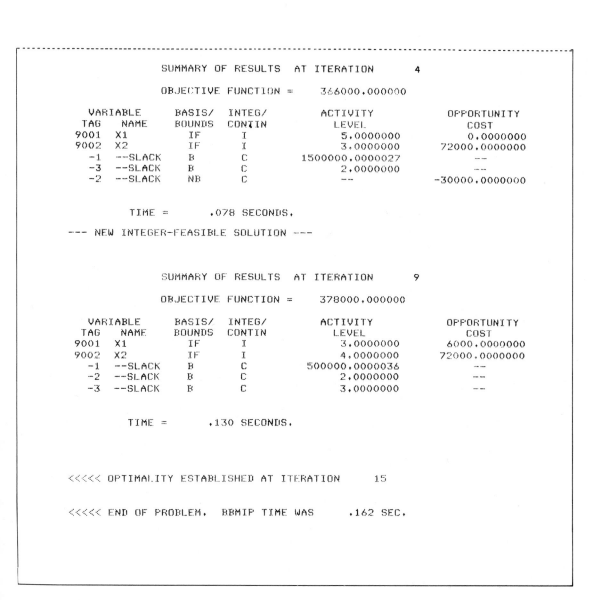

```
              SUMMARY OF RESULTS  AT ITERATION      4

              OBJECTIVE FUNCTION =    366000.000000

     VARIABLE      BASIS/   INTEG/        ACTIVITY          OPPORTUNITY
   TAG    NAME     BOUNDS   CONTIN         LEVEL               COST
   9001   X1         IF       I          5.0000000          0.0000000
   9002   X2         IF       I          3.0000000       72000.0000000
    -1   --SLACK     B        C       1500000.0000027          ---
    -3   --SLACK     B        C          2.0000000             ---
    -2   --SLACK     NB       C             ---           -30000.0000000

        TIME =      .078 SECONDS.

 --- NEW INTEGER-FEASIBLE SOLUTION ---


              SUMMARY OF RESULTS  AT ITERATION      9

              OBJECTIVE FUNCTION =    378000.000000

     VARIABLE      BASIS/   INTEG/        ACTIVITY          OPPORTUNITY
   TAG    NAME     BOUNDS   CONTIN         LEVEL               COST
   9001   X1         IF       I          3.0000000        6000.0000000
   9002   X2         IF       I          4.0000000       72000.0000000
    -1   --SLACK     B        C        500000.0000036          ---
    -2   --SLACK     B        C          2.0000000             ---
    -3   --SLACK     B        C          3.0000000             ---

        TIME =      .130 SECONDS.



 <<<<< OPTIMALITY ESTABLISHED AT ITERATION      15

 <<<<< END OF PROBLEM.  BBMIP TIME WAS     .162 SEC.
```

INTEGER command instructs MPOS that X_1 and X_2 are restricted to whole-unit values. These inputs are followed by the objective function and constraints. Then the OPTIMIZE command tells MPOS to solve the previously stated integer programming problem.

The BBMIP routine first will ignore the integer restrictions and develop the linear programming or CONTINUOUS solution. Figure 9.10 shows that such a solution involves

$X_1 = 5$ new stores

and

$X_2 = 3.5$ additional warehouses

and generates a total monthly profit, or objective function value, of $402,000. It also involves 2.5 slack units in the third constraint, or a surplus of 2.5 additional warehouses. After four iterations, BBMIP next identifies an integer solution. Another nine iterations then provide the optimal integer solution of

$X_1 = 3$ new stores

and

$X_2 = 4$ additional warehouses

Furthermore, such a solution generates a $378,000 objective function value (total monthly profit) and a first constraint slack (usused budget) of $500,000. In addition, it involves a second constraint slack of 2 new stores and a surplus (third restriction slack) of 3 additional warehouses.

EXTENSIONS Many practical integer programming problems involve decision variables that represent yes or no choices. Consider, for example, the problem of determining the location of police stations within a new community. Typically, management must select from among a set of potential locations the sites that provide the necessary service at least cost. Under these circumstances, each decision variable (police station location) might be depicted as a yes or no choice. In particular, the variable could be assigned a value of 1 if the site is selected and 0 when the city bypasses the location. Such a situation, in which each decision variable must have a solution value of 0 or 1, is known as a **zero/one** or **binary integer programming problem**.

In other integer programming cases, some decision variables may be fractional while others are required to have either binary or pure integer solution values. A company, for instance, might use a portion of a work period to manufacture a product. Yet management must either use or not use each alternative from among a set of potential manufacturing processes. Furthermore, only an integer number of people can be employed on any project team. In other words, the work period variable can be fractional, but each manufacturing process must have a binary integer value. Furthermore, the project team sizes are restricted to whole-unit solutions. Such a situation, in which some, but not all, of the decision variables must have integer values, is called a **mixed integer programming problem**.

Table 9.6 **Integer Programming Applications**

Area	Application	Reference
Financial management	Selecting the projects that minimize the net interest cost for a required investment	R. M. Nauss and B. R. Keeler [22]
Work flow planning	Determining the order in which a set of jobs is to be processed through a work center	F. J. Fabozzi and J. Valente [8]
Transportation	Dispatching service equipment in the way that meets customer needs	G. G. Brown and G. W. Graves [4]
Advertising	Determining the most efficient distribution of direct-mail advertising	F. R. Dwyer and J. R. Evans [7]
Vision care	Testing for vision loss in patients	P. Kolesar [16]
Health care	Planning hospital services	R. J. Ruth [23]

Mixed and binary problems can be solved with the same branch and bound concepts used for pure integer programming situations (Table 9.5). As in the pure integer case, these concepts are usually implemented with computer assistance.

Even the branch and bound method, however, may require an excessive amount of computer cost and time to find the optimal integer programming solution. In these cases, it is common to employ some rule of thumb for stopping the branch and bound search. Such stopping rules typically limit the computer time and cost that will be expended on the search. Management scientists also have been working on approaches for finding "good" approximate, though not necessarily optimal, solutions to integer programming problems. The general concept underlying these approaches will be presented in chapter 16. In addition, Salkin [24] and Taha [29] provide specific details for the interested reader.

In spite of the computational difficulties, pure, binary, and mixed integer programming have been applied to a variety of business and economic problems. Table 9.6 presents a small sample of these applications.

Progress is also being made in dealing with integer programming problems that involve nonlinear relationships. M. W. Cooper [5] gives a survey of these new developments.

GOAL PROGRAMMING
Traditional mathematical programming models assume that the decision maker has a single, measurable objective such as maximizing profit or minimizing cost. Instead of posing a single objective, however, managers frequently use multiple criteria in decision making. Moreover, they typically set concrete goals, targets, or aspiration levels as a tactic in the pursuit of objectives. Such goals establish a clear point of reference, provide a keen sense of direction, and measure the progress toward the company's objectives. Example 9.3 illustrates.

EXAMPLE 9.3 Regional Work Force Planning

The State Department of Transportation (SDOT) plans on launching a vast construction project to complete various urban freeway systems. Department engineers estimate that the project will require at least one million skilled labor hours. This work force is to be drawn from unemployed skilled industrial and/or residential construction personnel.

Unemployed industrial personnel can be put to work on local phases of the project immediately at an average wage of $6 per hour. On the other hand, residential construction workers must be retrained for the project at government expense. The retrained labor would then be available locally at an average hourly wage of $10. This amount includes the government training expense. State legislators have allocated a budget of no more than $12 million for project labor costs.

The primary goal of the SDOT project is to alleviate unemployment among construction workers in the state's urban areas. Union and political pressures will also force the department to pursue two additional but less important targets. Specifically,

the governor has directed the SDOT to:

1. Employ skilled residential workers for at least as many hours as construction workers

2. Supply no more than 400,000 labor hours for the project from the retraining program

Moreover, the employment ratio target is considered more important than the retraining aspiration level.

Department officials want to identify the employment levels that best satisfy the project goals.

In Example 9.3, the SDOT must consider three criteria: total employment, the industrial/residential construction worker mix, and the retraining program supply. Furthermore, each criterion is stated in terms of a concrete goal. The primary goal, for instance, is to alleviate unemployment in the state's urban areas by using at least one million idle skilled labor hours for the freeway project. That is, if department officials let

X_1 = skilled labor hours allocated to unemployed industrial construction workers

and

X_2 = skilled labor hours allocated to unemployed residential construction personnel

Figure 9.11 The SDOT Budget and Goal Constraints

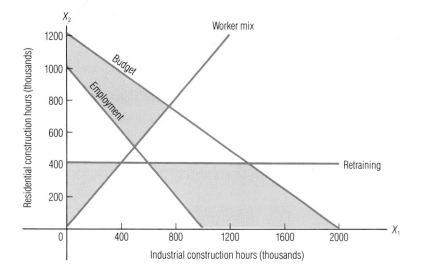

then the first priority is the employment goal of

$$X_1 + X_2 \geq 1{,}000{,}000 \text{ hours}$$

After satisfying the first goal, the next target is to employ skilled residential workers for at least as many hours as industrial construction personnel. This worker mix can be written as

$$X_2 \geq X_1$$

The lowest-priority goal is to supply no more than 400,000 labor hours from the retraining program, or

$$X_2 \leq 400{,}000 \text{ hours}$$

In addition to these three goal constraints (employment, worker mix, and retraining constraints), the SDOT must ensure that

$$\$6X_1 + \$10X_2 \leq \$12{,}000{,}000$$

That is, the department cannot spend more than the $12 million budget on project labor costs. Such an expression, which deals with a resource capacity or nongoal-oriented limitation, is known as a **technological** or **structural constraint**.

The goal and budget constraints are depicted graphically in Figure 9.11. You can see that the upper shaded region identifies the decision variable combinations (X_1 and X_2) that satisfy the budget restriction and the employment and worker mix aspirations. Similarly, the lower right shaded region gives the work force mix that meets the budget constraint and the employment and retraining targets. Finally, the lower left shaded region represents the employment levels that fulfill the budget restriction and the worker mix and retraining goals.

Note, however, that there is no decision variable combination in Figure 9.11 that meets the budget restriction and simultaneously satisfies all three goal constraints. Instead, the retraining target conflicts with either the worker mix or employment aspiration level. To find a feasible project plan, then, SDOT officials must concentrate on the deviations from the specified goals.

FORMULATING THE PROBLEM The SDOT employment goal is to use at least one million idle skilled labor hours for the freeway project, or have

$$X_1 + X_2 \geq 1,000,000 \text{ hours}$$

In practice, however, officials may need more skilled labor or be required to settle for less skilled labor than the one-million-hour target. To account for these possibilities, the department first should let

d_1^+ = employment above the one-million-hour aspiration level

and

d_1^- = employment below the one-million-hour aspiration level

Such activities, which measure the amounts by which the goal will be exceeded (d^+) or underachieved (d^-), are known as **deviational variables**.

By subtracting d_1^+ from, and adding d_1^- to, the left-hand side of the employment target expression, the SDOT will obtain the goal equation

$$X_1 + X_2 - d_1^+ + d_1^- = 1,000,000 \text{ hours}$$

This relationship accounts for all possible goal circumstances. For instance, if the department meets the one-million-hour target exactly, then

$$X_1 + X_2 = 1,000,000 \text{ hours}$$

and d_1^+ and d_1^- equal zero. On the other hand, when project employment exceeds the aspiration level, then

$$X_1 + X_2 > 1,000,000 \text{ hours}$$

with d_1^- equal to zero and d_1^+ equal to the excess of the actual ($X_1 + X_2$) work force over the one-million-hour goal. Alternatively, if employment falls below the target, then d_1^+ will equal zero, but d_1^- will equal the difference between the one-million-hour goal and the actual work force.

The SDOT must reformulate the other two (worker mix and retraining) goal constraints in a similar manner. Hence, officials should define

d_2^+ = residential construction personnel employment above the worker mix aspiration level

and

d_2^- = residential construction personnel employment below the worker mix aspiration level

By subtracting d_2^+ from, and adding d_2^- to, the left-hand side of the worker mix target expression ($X_2 \geq X_1$), the department will obtain an equation

$$X_2 - d_2^+ + d_2^- = X_1$$

or

$$-X_1 + X_2 - d_2^+ + d_2^- = 0 \text{ hours}$$

that accounts for all possible goal circumstances. Also, the SDOT can define

d_3^+ = retraining above the 400,000-hour aspiration level

and

d_3^- = retraining below the 400,000-hour aspiration level

Then, by subtracting d_3^+ from, and adding d_3^- to, the left-hand side of the retraining program target expression ($X_2 \leq 400{,}000$ hours), the department will get an equation

$$X_2 - d_3^+ + d_3^- = 400{,}000 \text{ hours}$$

that accounts for all potential retraining goal conditions.

Department officials must also spend no more than $12 million on freeway construction labor costs. Unlike the three other constraints (employment, worker mix, and retraining), this budget restriction does not involve a project goal. As a result, the SDOT will be unable to consider labor costs that exceed the budget. In other words, the only relevant deviational variable in this situation is

d_4^- = labor expenditures below the $12 million budget

Indeed, by adding d_4^- to the left-hand side of the budget expression ($\$6X_1 + \$10X_2 \leq \$12{,}000{,}000$), the department will obtain an equation

$$\$6X_1 + \$10X_2 + d_4^- = \$12{,}000{,}000$$

that accounts for all possible budget conditions.

The SDOT is now in a position to formulate an objective function for the freeway project. Remember that the department's main goal is to alleviate unemployment among construction workers in the state's urban areas, or have

$$X_1 + X_2 \geq 1{,}000{,}000 \text{ hours}$$

Employment below the one-million-hour target, or any positive d_1^- value, would represent a very undesirable goal deviation. Thus, the officials' first priority, denoted by P_1, is to make d_1^- as small as possible. This objective is written as follows:

minimize $P_1 d_1^-$

P_1, which is called a **preemptive weight**, generally does not have a numerical value in the expression. It merely indicates that the decision maker's highest priority is to minimize the value of the d_1^- deviational variable.

After satisfying the highest-priority goal, officials next consider the second most important target—to employ skilled residential workers for at least as many hours as industrial construction personnel, or have

$X_2 \geq X_1$

Since residential employment below the worker mix target would be undesirable, the department's second priority P_2 is to minimize the value of d_2^-. This objective is written as follows:

minimize $P_2 d_2^-$

The preemptive weight P_2 in the expression simply indicates that the decision maker's second-highest priority is to minimize the value of the d_2^- deviational variable.

After fulfilling, in order, the higher-priority goals, the SDOT can finally consider the least important target—to supply no more than 400,000 labor hours from the retraining program, or have

$X_2 \leq 400,000$ hours

Retraining above the 400,000-hour aspiration level (any positive d_3^+ value) would represent a very undesirable goal deviation. Therefore, the third priority P_3 is to make d_3^+ as small as possible, or

minimize $P_3 d_3^+$

The preemptive weight P_3 in this expression indicates that the decision maker's third-highest priority is to minimize the value of the d_3^+ deviational variable.

In pursuing each lower-ranked goal, however, the SDOT must not select employment levels that jeopardize the attainment of any higher-priority targets. Hence, officials should first find the minimum value of the most important (P_1) deviational variable d_1^-. While maintaining d_1^- at its minimum value, they should next minimize the quantity of the second most important (P_2) deviational variable d_2^-. Finally, while sustaining the P_1 and P_2 goal achievements, the department should seek the minimum value of the least important (P_3) deviational variable d_3^+. This hierarchy of objectives can be written as follows:

minimize $P_3 d_3^+$ | minimum $P_2 d_2^-$ | minimum $P_1 d_1^-$

The statement after each vertical bar identifies the condition regarding a higher-priority goal that must be satisfied while pursuing the lower-ranked target listed before the bar. Such an expression clearly shows that the decision maker must minimize each goal deviation (d_1^-, d_2^-, and d_3^+) individually in its order of priority (P_1, P_2, and P_3).

Traditionally, however, the hierarchy of objectives has been treated in a different manner. In the conventional approach, the decision maker is assumed to minimize the sum of the preemptively weighted goal deviations, or, in the SDOT case, to

minimize $Z = P_1 d_1^- + P_2 d_2^- + P_3 d_3^+$

Unfortunately, this objective function suggests that management has a single criterion (Z) rather than a series of individual goals ($P_1 d_1^-$, $P_2 d_2^-$, and $P_3 d_3^+$). Thus, it is misleading. Moreover, the deviational variables, in many applications, are expressed in different units of measurement. As a result, the sum Z is often meaningless. Nevertheless, such notation is prevalent in the literature and hence cannot be ignored.

By collecting the traditional objective function and constraint equations and adding the appropriate nonnegativity conditions, SDOT officials can express the work force problem as follows:

minimize $\quad Z = P_1 d_1^- + P_2 d_2^- + P_3 d_3^+$

subject to $\quad X_1 + X_2 - d_1^+ + d_1^- = 1{,}000{,}000$ hours $\qquad$ (Employment)

$\qquad\qquad -X_1 + X_2 - d_2^+ + d_2^- = 0$ hours $\qquad\qquad$ (Worker mix)

$\qquad\qquad X_2 - d_3^+ + d_3^- = 400{,}000$ hours $\qquad\qquad$ (Retraining)

$\qquad\qquad \$6 X_1 + \$10 X_2 + d_4^- = \$12{,}000{,}000 \qquad\qquad$ (Budget)

$\qquad\qquad X_1, X_2, d_1^+, d_1^-, d_2^+, d_2^-, d_3^+, d_3^-, d_4^- \geq 0$

Such a statement is referred to as a **goal programming problem**. Table 9.7 summarizes the procedures for formulating a goal programming problem.

GRAPHIC SOLUTION The SDOT can use the employment, worker mix, retraining, and budget equations to identify all feasible work force alternatives. Officials first should set

$d_1^+ = d_1^- = d_2^+ = d_2^- = d_3^+ = d_3^- = d_4^- = 0$

and then graph the resulting constraint equations. By so doing, they will get the results presented in Figure 9.12. In this graph, decision variable combinations (X_1 and X_2) on the constraint lines provide zero values for the corresponding deviational (d^+ or d^-) activities. Each point above a

Table 9.7 Formulating a Goal Programming Problem

1. Express each goal and technological constraint in mathematical programming format.
2. Use the following rules to convert each constraint into goal programming format.

Type of Constraint	Original Form	Rule
Goal	Any	Subtract a d^+ deviational variable from, and add a d^- deviational variable to, the left-hand side of the original expression.
Technological	$\leq$	Add a d^- variable to the left-hand side of the original expression.
	$=$	Leave the expression in its original form.
	$\geq$	Subtract a d^+ variable from the left-hand side of the original expression.

3. Form nonnegativity conditions for the decision and deviational variables.
4. Identify all undesirable goal deviations.
5. Assign a preemptive weight P to each goal deviation.
6. Minimize each goal deviation individually in the order of its priority or preemptive weight.

line represents a positive d^+ quantity, and any combination below a line corresponds to a positive d^- value.

According to the budget equation in the goal programming formulation, the SDOT cannot choose decision variable combinations that require an expenditure in excess of the $12 million budget. Consequently, officials must select points that are on or below the budget constraint line in Figure 9.12. Although there is an infinite number of such points, many will not satisfy the hierarchy of goals specified in the problem's objective function.

In particular, SDOT's highest priority (P_1) is to minimize employment below the one-million-hour target (d_1^-). To fully achieve this objective, the department must set $d_1^- = 0$ or select points that are on or above the employment constraint line in Figure 9.12. Yet some of these points will not meet the next-highest priority (P_2) of minimizing residential construction employment below the worker mix aspiration level (d_2^-). In fact, points on or above the worker mix line in Figure 9.12 represent the only decision variable combinations that can completely attain the second-ranked objective.

In effect, then, the shaded region of Figure 9.12 identifies the employment levels that satisfy the budget restriction and fully achieve the project's top two $(P_1$ and $P_2)$ goals. Management, however, still must consider the

Figure 9.12 The SDOT Goal Programming Solution

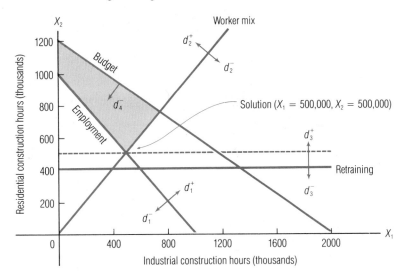

third priority (P_3) of minimizing retraining time above the 400,000-hour aspiration level (d_3^+). This time, of course, will be minimized if $d_3^+ = 0$ or when the department chooses points on or below the retraining constraint line in Figure 9.12.

Unfortunately, none of the points on or below the retraining line are in the shaded region of Figure 9.12. In other words, there is no work force plan that will satisfy the budget restriction, fully achieve SDOT's top two (P_1 and P_2) goals, and still completely attain the lowest priority (P_3) target. To operate within the budget and fully accomplish the two highest priorities, then, the department must have some excess retraining hours.

Nevertheless, the SDOT still should seek the work force plan that keeps the excess retraining hours (d_3^+) at a minimum. To find such a plan, officials can shift the retraining constraint line upward in parallel fashion until it touches the boundary of the shaded region in Figure 9.12. The parallel shift, which is indicated with the dashed line in the diagram, identifies the point that minimizes d_3^+ without violating the budget restriction and two highest priority goals. In short, this graphical analysis determines the solution to the department's goal programming problem.

By examining Figure 9.12, you can see that the solution point involves

$X_1 = 500,000$ skilled labor hours allocated to unemployed industrial construction workers

Table 9.8 Graphic Solution of a Goal Programming Problem

1. Set each deviational variable equal to zero.
2. Use the constraint equations to graph the goal and technological restrictions.
3. Identify the decision variable combinations (points on the graph) that satisfy all technological constraints. Shade this portion of the graph. If there is no such region, the problem does not have a feasible solution. Otherwise, go to step 4.
4. Eliminate from the shaded region all points that involve any undesirable deviation from the highest-priority goal.
5. Find the points within this shaded region that provide a zero undesirable deviation from the next-highest priority goal. If there are no such points, move the corresponding goal constraint line in a parallel fashion until it touches the boundary of the shaded region.
6. Repeat step 5 in order of priority for each goal in the problem.
7. Identify the point (or points) on the boundary of the shaded area that best meets the hierarchy of goals. This point (decision variable combination) represents the solution to the goal programming problem.
8. Substitute the solution point into each constraint and solve the resulting equations for the corresponding values of the deviational variables.

and

$X_2 = 500,000$ skilled labor hours allocated to unemployed residential construction personnel

Moreover, this point is on both the employment and worker mix constraint lines. Hence, the work force plan will have

$$d_1^+ = d_1^- = d_2^+ = d_2^- = 0$$

That is, the SDOT can fully achieve both the employment and worker mix targets with the freeway project.

Figure 9.12 also shows that the solution point ($X_1 = 500,000$, $X_2 = 500,000$) is above the retraining constraint line. As a result, $d_3^- = 0$, but there will be some excess retraining hours. Indeed, according to the retraining constraint equation, the goal programming plan will involve

$$X_2 - d_3^+ + d_3^- = 400,000 \text{ hours}$$

or

$$d_3^+ = X_2 + d_3^- - 400,000 = 500,000 + 0 - 400,000 = 100,000$$

retraining hours above the 400,000-hour target.

Finally, Figure 9.12 demonstrates that the goal programming solution point ($X_1 = 500,000$, $X_2 = 500,000$) is below the budget constraint line. Consequently, the SDOT project will come in under budget. In fact, according to the budget constraint equation, the freeway project will cost

$$\$6X_1 + \$10X_2 + d_4^- = \$12,000,000$$

or

$$d_4^- = \$12{,}000{,}000 - \$6(500{,}000) - \$10(500{,}000) = \$4{,}000{,}000$$

less than the $12 million budgeted for labor expenditures.

Table 9.8 summarizes the graphic approach for solving goal programming problems. Unfortunately, the graphic approach can only be used to solve goal programming problems that have only two decision variables. Yet most practical situations involve many decision activities. In such cases, management will be unable to graph the constraints and pictorially develop the goal programming solution. Fortunately, management scientists have developed a modified version of the simplex method to deal with these large-scale goal programming problems. J. P. Ignizio [13] and S. M. Lee [18] present the details for the interested reader.

COMPUTER ANALYSIS The modified version of the simplex method is usually implemented with the aid of a computer. In fact, there are several prewritten computer packages designed to solve relatively large-scale goal programming problems. One such package, called **GOAL**, is available on the California State University and College System (CSUC) computer system.

Figure 9.13 illustrates the GOAL solution to the SDOT work force problem. The decision maker executes the computer program with the FIND, GOAL command. Next, the package prompts another command with the ? symbol. The appropriate response is 'PROB,' 4,2,3. This statement tells GOAL that the problem consists of 4 constraints, 2 decision variables, and 3 goal priorities. The 'B,' 'B,' 'B,' 'L' command then describes the nature of each constraint. Specifically, the B symbols indicate that the first three constraints each contain both a positive (d^+) and a negative (d^-) deviational variable. The L tells GOAL that the fourth constraint involves only a negative deviational variable (d^-).

The 'OBJ' command tells the computer program that the user will next supply the data from the objective function. Each of the following three commands gives the specific information. For example, the 'NEG,' 1,1,1 statement informs GOAL that the negative deviational variable for the first constraint (d_1^-) is the highest-priority (P_1) target. It also assigns a weight of 1.0 to this variable. Similarly, the 'POS,' 3,3,1 command indicates that the positive deviational variable for the third constraint (d_3^+) is the third-highest priority (P_3) goal. Furthermore, this d_3^+ activity has the same 1.0 weight as each other deviational variable in the objective function.

The 'DATA,' $-0,-0,-0$ statement informs the computer program that the decision maker will next input the data on the left-hand side of the constraints. Each of the following seven commands provides the specific information. The 'DATA,' 1,1,1 statement, for instance, tells GOAL that the first decision variable (X_1) in the initial constraint has a coefficient of 1.

Figure 9.13 Solving the SDOT Problem with GOAL

```
/FIND,GOAL
? 'PROB',4,2,3
?'B','B','B'.'L'
? 'OBJ'
? 'NEG',1,1,1
? 'NEG'.2,2,1
? 'POS',3,3,1
? 'DATA',-0,-0,-0
? 'DATA',1,2,1
? 'DATA',2,2,-1
? 'DATA',2,2,1
? 'DATA',3,2,1
? 'DATA',4,1,6
? 'DATA',4,2,10
? 'RIGHT',-0,-0,-0
? 1000000,0,400000,12000000
```

                                          SLACK ANALYSIS

ROW	AVAILABLE	POS-SLK	
1	1000000.00000	0.00000	0.00000
2	.00001	0.00000	0.00000
3	400000.00000	100000.00000	0.00000
4	12000000.00000	0.00000	3999999.99998

                                          VARIABLE ANALYSIS

VARIABLE	AMOUNT
1	500000.00000
2	500000.00000

ANALYSIS OF THE OBJECTIVE

PRIORITY	UNDER-ACHIEVEMENT
3	100000.00000
2	0.00000
1	0.00000

Similarly, the 'DATA,' 4,2,10 command indicates that the second decision variable in the fourth constraint has a coefficient of 10.

Finally, the 'RGHT,' $-0, -0, -0$ statement tells the computer program that the user will input the data on the right-hand side of the four constraints. Such information is supplied in consecutive order. Hence, the last line in the problem definition section indicates that 1000000 or 1,000,000 is the right-hand-side amount in the first constraint. It also instructs the program that 0, 400,000, and 12,000,000 are the right-hand-side amounts, respectively, of the second, third, and fourth constraints.

At this point, the computer program processes the data and solves the corresponding goal programming problem. It next evaluates, under the SLACK ANALYSIS heading, the impact of the solution on the positive (d^+) and negative (d^-) deviational variables. Figure 9.13, for example, shows that the SDOT solution involves no positive or negative slack in the first and second constraints. Consequently, $d_1^+ = d_1^- = d_2^+ = d_2^- = 0$ in the recommended plan. Moreover, the solution leaves no negative slack $(d_3^- = 0)$ in the third constraint and zero positive slack $(d_4^+ = 0)$ in the fourth constraint.

On the other hand, the 100,000 positive slack in the third restriction indicates that the plan will involve $d_3^+ = 100,000$ retraining hours above the 400,000-hour target. Similarly, the 3999999.99998 negative slack value in the fourth row tells us that the recommended decision variable combination costs $d_4^- = \$4$ million less than the \$12 million budget. The recommended work force plan of $X_1 = 500,000$ and $X_2 = 500,000$ skilled labor hours is listed under the VARIABLE ANALYSIS segment of Figure 9.13.

The final portion of the printout, which is labeled ANALYSIS OF THE OBJECTIVE, gives the degree of achievement for the hierarchy of goals. As Figure 9.13 demonstrates, the recommended solution completely achieves the top two priority (P_1 and P_2) targets. It also indicates that the third-priority (P_3) goal will not be achieved by $d_3^+ = 100,000$ hours.

EXTENSIONS In Example 9.3, each undesirable deviational variable has a different priority to the SDOT. Frequently, however, two or more deviational variables are given the same priority in the problem. Furthermore, management might want to give some of the equally ranked deviational variables more importance or weight than others. Still, the decision maker can solve these more complex problems with the same principles used in the basic goal programming situation. Ignizio [13] and Lee [18] again present the details for the interested reader.

These goal programming concepts have been applied to a wide variety of business and economic problems. W. T. Lin [19], in fact, lists at least seventy illustrations reported from 1972 through 1980 in the management

Table 9.9 Goal Programming Applications

Area	Application	Reference
Human resource management	Allocating human resources to meet specified regulatory practices	L. Jones and N. K. Kwak [14]
Recruiting	Selecting college students who satisfy prescribed admission standards	K. E. Kendall and R. L. Leubbe [15]
Military defense	Developing a ballistic missile strategy that meets stated mission standards	J. M. Mellichamp et al. [21]
Site selection	Identifying the facility location that best satisfies prescribed selection goals	M. J. Schniederjans et al. [25]

science literature. A small sample of other typical applications is presented in Table 9.9.

In addition, there have been some interesting extensions to the fundamental goal programming methodology. J. S. H. Kornbluth and R. E. Steuer [17], for instance, introduce some fractional goal considerations, while V. M. Trivedi [30] extends the principles to integer-restricted decision variables. Research also continues on nonlinear goal programming approaches.

Most of this current methodology emphasizes the preemptive version of goal programming. Specifically, undesirable goal deviational variables are minimized one by one in the order of their priority. As originally conceived, however, the objective is to minimize a composite measure of divergence. Such a measure simultaneously considers the set of undesirable deviational variables but weights each according to its relative importance in the problem. Some management scientists believe that the decision maker should use the original rather than the preemptive version of goal programming.

There are also other alternative methodologies available to deal with multiple-criteria decision-making problems. In one approach, called **multiobjective programming**, management first establishes a separate objective for each relevant combination of decision variables. Next, management finds all feasible solutions that will not improve the value of one criterion without diminishing the quantity of at least one other criterion. The decision maker can then analyze these solutions to identify the most preferable variable combination. C. L. Hwang and A. Masud [12] provide an overview of this multiobjective approach and other more advanced multiple-criteria mathematical programming methodologies.

SUMMARY In this chapter, we examined certain mathematical programming topics that are important to practical decision making. We learned to identify the fundamental assumptions of linear programming and discussed circumstances that could invalidate each supposition, outlining appropriate alternative methodologies. The concepts were summarized in Table 9.3.

One of the most common situations involves a mathematical programming problem in which some or all of the decision variables are required to have integer values. One approach to such problems is to treat the situation as an ordinary linear problem and then round any fractional solution to whole-unit values. As the second section of the chapter demonstrated, however, this rounding procedure is sometimes very time-consuming and often does not provide the optimal solution to the original problem. Consequently, management scientists have developed alternative methodologies to solve these integer programming problems. We reviewed the most popular of these procedures, including the graphic approach, enumeration, the cutting plane method, and the branch and bound procedure. The branch and bound method was summarized in Table 9.5. In addition, we saw how a prewritten computer package such as MPOS can be used to solve integer programming problems. We concluded with some important practical extensions to the fundamental methodology. Typical integer programming applications were presented in Table 9.6.

In the third section of the chapter, we discussed mathematical programming problems in which management has multiple decision criteria expressed in terms of concrete targets, or goals. First we saw how to formulate these goal programming problems. The procedures were summarized in Table 9.7. Next, we examined a graphic solution methodology designed for small-scale situations. Table 9.8 summarized the approach. Then we saw how a prewritten computer package such as GOAL can be used to solve large-scale goal programming problems. Finally, the last section outlined some important practical extensions to the fundamental methodology and presented some typical applications of goal programming in Table 9.9.

Glossary *branch and bound method* An approach that develops an optimal solution by successively partitioning a problem into progressively smaller segments.

chance-constrained programming A methodology that accounts for parameter uncertainty by reformulating each original system constraint in a way that ensures that a mathematical programming solution provides a high probability of meeting the restriction.

cutting plane method A procedure that obtains an optimal integer solution by successively adding constraints that eliminate fractional answers from a linear programming formulation of the problem.

deviational variables Variables that measure the amounts by which the target in a goal constraint will be exceeded or underachieved.

GOAL A prewritten computer package that can be used to solve relatively large-scale goal programming problems.

goal programming A methodology designed to incorporate multiple criteria within the mathematical programming framework.

goal programming problem A mathematical programming problem that involves a hierarchy of specified, concrete targets or aspiration levels.

Gomory cut A new constraint that eliminates some fractional decision variable combinations from a linear programming solution.

integer programming A methodology designed to deal with mathematical programming problems in which some or all of the decision variables must have whole-unit values.

linear relationship A relationship in which each decision variable has an exponent of 1 and appears in a separate term of the relevant mathematical expression.

mixed integer programming problem An integer programming problem in which some, but not all, decision variables must have integer solution values.

multiobjective programming A methodology designed to solve mathematical programming problems that involve separate objective functions for each relevant combination of decision variables.

Multi Purpose Optimization System (MPOS) A prewritten computer package that can be used to solve relatively large-scale integer programming problems.

nonlinear program A mathematical program that consists of a nonlinear objective function and/or at least one nonlinear system constraint.

nonlinear programming Any methodology designed to solve a nonlinear program.

nonlinear relationship A relationship in which a decision variable has an exponent different than 1 and/or more than one activity appears in a single term of the relevant mathematical expression.

preemptive weight A symbol indicating the priority assigned by the decision maker to the corresponding deviational variable.

pure integer programming A situation in which all the decision variables in the mathematical program must have integer solutions.

stochastic programming A methodology that accounts for parameter uncertainty by incorporating stochastic elements into an expanded version of the original mathematical program.

technological (structural) constraint A restriction that deals with a resource capacity or other nongoal-oriented limitation.

zero/one (binary integer) programming problem An integer programming problem in which each decision variable must have a solution value of one or zero.

References

1. Avriel, M. *Nonlinear Programming: Analysis and Methods.* Englewood Cliffs, N. J.: Prentice-Hall, 1976.

2. Bazaraa, M. S., and C. M. Shetty. *Nonlinear Programming: Theory and Algorithms.* New York: Wiley, 1979.

3. Bradley, S. P., et al. *Applied Mathematical Programming.* Reading, Mass.: Addison-Wesley, 1977.

4. Brown, G. G., and G. W. Graves. "Real-Time Dispatch of Petroleum Tank Trucks." *Management Science* (January 1981): 19.

5. Cooper, M. W. "A Survey of Methods for Pure Nonlinear Integer Programming." *Management Science* (March 1981): 353.

6. Corstjens, M., and P. Doyle. "A Model for Optimizing Retail Space Allocations." *Management Science* (July 1981): 822.

7. Dwyer, F. R., and J. R. Evans. "A Branch and Bound Algorithm for the List Selection Problem in Direct Mail Advertising." *Management Science* (June 1981): 658.

8. Fabozzi, F. J., and J. Valente. "Mathematical Programming in American Companies: A Sample Survey." Part 1. *Interfaces* (November 1976): 93.

9. Grotte, J. H. "An Optimizing Nuclear Exchange Model for the Analysis of Nuclear War and Deterrence." *Operations Research* (May–June 1982): 428.

10. Hansotia, B. J. "Stochastic Linear Programming with Recourse: A Tutorial." *Decision Sciences* (January 1980): 151.

11. Hogan, A. J., et al. "Decision Problems Under Risk and Chance Constrained Programming: Dilemmas in the Transition." *Management Science* (June 1981): 698.

12. Hwang, C. L., and A. Masud. *Multiple Objective Decision Making—Methods and Applications.* New York: Springer-Verlag, 1979.

13. Ignizio, J. P. *Goal Programming and Extensions.* Lexington, Mass.: Heath, 1976.

14. Jones, L., and N. K. Kwak. "A Goal Programming Model for Allocating Human Resources for the Good Laboratory Practice Regulations." *Decision Sciences* (January 1982): 156.

15. Kendall, K. E., and R. L. Leubbe. "Management of College Student Recruiting Activities Using Goal Programming." *Decision Sciences* (April 1981): 193.

16. Kolesar, P. "Testing for Vision Loss in Glaucoma Suspects." *Management Science* (May 1980): 439.

17. Kornbluth, J. S. H., and R. E. Steuer. "Multiple Objective Linear Fractional Programming." *Management Science* (September 1981): 1024.

18. Lee, S. M. *Goal Programming for Decision Analysis.* Philadelphia: Auerbach, 1972.

19. Lin, W. T. "A Survey of Goal Programming Applications." *OMEGA* (January 1980): 115.

20. Loomba, N. P., and E. Turban. *Applied Programming for Management.* New York: Holt, Rinehart, & Winston, 1974.

21. Mellichamp, J. M., et al. "Ballistic Missile Defense Technology Management with Goal Programming." *Interfaces* (October 1980): 68.

22. Nauss, R. M., and B. R. Keeler. "Minimizing Net Interest Cost in Management Bond Bidding." *Management Science* (April 1981): 365.

23. Ruth, R. J. "A Mixed Integer Programming Model for Regional Planning of a Hospital Inpatient Service." *Management Science* (May 1981): 521.

24. Salkin, H. *Integer Programming.* Reading, Mass.: Addison-Wesley, 1975.

25. Schniederjans, M. J., et al. "An Application of Goal Programming to Resolve a Site Location Problem." *Interfaces* (June 1982): 65.

26. Shapiro, J. F. *Mathematical Programming: Structures and Algorithms.* New York: Wiley, 1979.

27. Sivazlian, B. D., and L. E. Stanfel. *Optimization Techniques in Operations Research.* Englewood Cliffs, N. J.: Prentice-Hall, 1975.

28. Stancu-Minasian, I. M., and M. J. Wets. "A Research Bibliography in Stochastic Programming, 1955–75." *Operations Research* (November–December 1976): 1078.

29. Taha, H. A. *Integer Programming: Theory, Applications, and Computations.* New York: Academic Press, 1975.

30. Trivedi, V. M. "A Mixed-Integer Goal Programming Model for Nursing Service Budgeting." *Operations Research* (September–October 1981): 1019.

Thought Exercises

1. Which mathematical programming methodology seems most appropriate in each of the following situations? Explain.

   a. The Air Force is considering five types of attack missiles to equip its fighter aircraft. Missile effectiveness is determined by the military value of the target destroyed during a specified operation. The effectiveness ratings, personnel requirements, and maintenance costs for each missile are constant and exactly known. Fighter capacity and support requirements are also readily available from design specifications. The problem is to find the quantity of each missile that will maximize the "attack value" of the fighter.

   b. Eastern Regional Savings and Loan Association is preparing to invest no more than 10% of its cash reserves. Several alternatives are available, each with its own probability distribution of returns. Association policy, however, places some clear restrictions on any investment portfolio. Management wants to determine the portfolio that maximizes the expected return on the investment while satisfying these policy restrictions.

   c. An overnight delivery service utilizes a fleet of vans in its operations. The company knows the exact purchase price, annual operating cost, and yearly resale value of each van. Management wants to determine the replacement policy (age for replacing a van) that will minimize total fleet cost.

   d. A large cooperative in the western part of the state operates a group of farms. Each farm utilizes available acreage, current personnel, and existing equipment to plant and harvest several distinct crops. The cooperative wants to find the crop mix on each farm that will maximize total profit.

   e. Government officials currently are considering alternative fiscal (spending and/or tax) and monetary policies to improve national economic conditions. The policies will be evaluated in terms of their effect on gross national product, inflation, unemployment, the international trade balance, and interest rates. All selected policies must also meet prescribed political, social, and economic constraints.

   f. A large department store chain plans to allocate some or all of its monthly advertising budget in your town. It can purchase local radio messages, television spots, or newspaper insertions. Although these placements should provide some audience exposure to the advertising message, it is unlikely that the effects will be uniform or independent. Specifically, the company believes that larger placements will lead to increased exposure. Moreover, it thinks that the exposure from radio spots will depend on the number of television and newspaper placements. Management wants to find the media mix that provides the largest audience exposure.

2. Examine each of the nonlinear programming problems listed in the following table:

Problem	Definitions
maximize $Z = 40X_1 + 60X_2 - 10X_1^3 - 20X_2^2$ subject to $5X_1 + 15X_1 \le 40$ hours (Plant 1) $30X_1 + 12X_2 \le 84$ hours (Plant 2) $X_1, X_2 \ge 0$	Z = total profit X_1 = quantity of product A X_2 = quantity of product B
minimize $Z = \$5\left(\dfrac{1000}{X_1 X_2 X_3}\right) + \$30\left(\dfrac{1000}{X_1}\right) + \$25\left(\dfrac{1000}{X_3}\right)$ subject to $X_1 X_3 + 2X_1 X_2 \le 26$ square feet	Z = total shipping cost X_1 = container length X_2 = container width X_3 = container height
maximize $Z = 12X_1 - 2X_1^2 + 15X_2 - X_1 X_2$ subject to $2X_1 + 4X_2 \ge 160$ hours (Labor) $X_1, X_2 \ge 0$	Z = total profit X_1 = yards of high-quality fabric X_2 = yards of low-quality fabric
minimize $Z = 20X_1^2 + 10X_2^2 + 20X_1 X_2 - 40X_1 - 30X_2$ subject to $5X_1 + 4X_2 = 500$ gloves (Output)	Z = total production cost X_1 = shift 1 labor hours X_2 = shift 2 labor hours

a. Identify the category of nonlinear programming that best describes each problem. (Table 9.2 may be useful in the identification process.)

b. Explain the nonlinear relationships in the objective function and/ or constraints of each problem in language that would be understandable to management.

3. Grandy Prancer, the administrator of the South Hills Sanatorium, is interested in enhancing the organization's cash flow situation by expanding its profitable health resort facilities. Unfortunately, her proposal was not completely endorsed by the board of directors. Instead, it authorized only $120,000 in funds to be used for not more than seven additional health resort rooms. Although Grandy was disappointed with the authorization, she decided to try and make the most of this additional budget.

    After examining sanatorium operations for a couple of days, Grandy concluded that the additional rooms could be best utilized in the "Blue" and/or "Green" wings of the resort. Since each additional "Green" room would generate $60 and every "Blue" chamber only $30 profit per day, she was tempted to expand only the "Green" wing. However, Grandy remembered that the board insisted on at least three additional "Blue" rooms. Also, expansion will cost

$19,000 per "Green" room and only $10,000 for each additional "Blue" chamber. Thus, she can build more "Blue" rooms than "Green" rooms for the same expenditure. The problem is to determine the room mixture that maximizes total additional daily profit.

Dolph Mojon, the administrative assistant at South Hills, had recently completed an executive education seminar in management science methodologies. Hence, Grandy thought that he could offer some useful advice on the problem. Consequently, she provided Dolph with the available information and instructed him to work on the problem while Grandy conducted her weekly staff meeting.

Dolph realized that he was dealing with an allocation problem that could be formulated as a linear program. Yet the optimal solution did not provide an integer number of additional "Green" rooms. As a result, Dolph decided to reexamine the problem from an integer programming perspective. Before he could do so, however, Grandy returned from the meeting and became very upset with Dolph. In particular, she felt that Dolph's management science "background" should have enabled him to develop a recommendation during the hour Grandy spent in the staff meeting.

Grandy then began to examine the problem in her own way. She rationalized that the only alternatives were the following room mixes:

Room Mix		Room Mix	
Blue	Green	Blue	Green
0	9	5	4
1	8	6	3
2	7	7	2
3	6	8	1
4	5	9	0

According to Grandy's analysis of these alternatives, the most profitable plan would consist of six additional "Blue" rooms and three more "Green" rooms. Furthermore, she claimed that "common sense" is the only approach needed to find this plan.

Although disheartened by Grandy's criticism, Dolph continued with his integer programming analysis. Such further analysis revealed that an alternative room mix provided the same maximum profit as Grandy's "common sense" solution. More important, Dolph's recommendation required a $1000 lower capital outlay than Grandy's plan. When confronted with these new data, Grandy admitted that the management science seminar "perhaps was worth the investment."

a. What was the linear programming solution?
b. How did Grandy obtain her "common sense" solution?
c. Explain how Dolph was able to save $1000 in capital outlay.
d. What is your recommendation? Explain and show all your work.

4. Karen Scatlis, manager of the local college women's softball team, will soon take the varsity on an interconference road trip. There are twenty players on the team, but the school can afford to send only fifteen women on the trip.

The coaching staff feels that the team will need at least two catchers, three pitchers, five outfielders, and five infielders to be "competitive" on the trip. Karen also believes that her team must hit well to beat the opposition on the schedule. As a result, she would prefer to select the players that have the highest composite batting average. In this regard, the coaching staff has compiled the following statistics on the team roster:

Player	Position	Batting Average	At Bats	Player	Position	Batting Average	At Bats
Jones	Pitcher	.210	50	White	Catcher	.150	30
Thomas	Infielder	.280	100	Green	Outfielder	.360	110
Adams	Catcher	.320	100	Smith	Outfielder	.310	100
Simmons	Outfielder	.400	120	Kajowski	Catcher	.200	50
Rupp	Outfielder	.350	70	Olivera	Pitcher	.500	10
Tolliver	Infielder	.220	50	Tonti	Infielder	.270	90
Abraham	Infielder	.250	80	Queen	Infielder	.300	80
Flint	Pitcher	.100	20	King	Pitcher	.180	60
Black	Infielder	.450	100	Howley	Outfielder	.290	120
Brown	Infielder	.260	150	Scott	Outfielder	.340	80

The composite measure is defined as the sum of each player's weighted batting average. In addition, the appropriate weight equals the player's at bats divided by total team at bats.

Formulate the coach's team selection problem.

5. Refer back to Example 9.1. As noted in the text discussion, test conditions will likely force at least two (X_3 and Y_2) of Quantum's four (X_2, X_3, Y_1, and Y_2) decision variables to have integer rather than fractional values. Under these circumstances, then, management should add the restriction

X_3, $Y_2 \geq 0$ and are integers

to the original linear program.

Suppose that management did this, then solved the resulting program with MPOS and obtained the results displayed in the following figure. According to this MPOS printout, what is the recommended solution for Quantum's integer programming problem? Express your answer in language that would be understandable to management.

```
*******************
* PROBLEM NUMBER  1 *
*******************

USING BBMIP
QUANTUM ENTERPRISES



- - - CONTINUOUS SOLUTION - - -



                    SUMMARY OF RESULTS AT ITERATION   5

                 OBJECTIVE FUNCTION =   465000.000000

        VARIABLE        BASIS/    INTEG/    ACTIVITY          OPPORTUNITY
      TAG    NAME        BOUNDS    CONTIN     LEVEL               COST
      9003  X2             B         C     4500.0000000           - -
         4  Y1             B         C     1500.0000000           - -
        -1  --SLACK        B         C     5000.0000000           - -
        -4  --SLACK        B         C     1500.0000000           - -
         2  Y2             B         C     3000.0000000           - -
        -3  --SLACK        NB        C        - -             -100.0000000
        -2  --SLACK        NB        C        - -              -13.1250000
         1  X3             NB        C        - -              -25.0000000


           TIME =          .039 SECONDS.



    <<<<< CONTINUOUS SOLUTION IS INTEGER SOLUTION. >>>>>
```

6. A southwestern university's business school must fill at least twenty faculty positions for the next academic year. The highest priority is to remain within the $1 million budget provided for faculty additions. In this regard, it will cost an average of $30,000 to recruit and pay the first-year salary and benefits of each new faculty member.

Also, the business school faculty currently does not meet Equal Employment Opportunity Commission (EEOC) affirmative action requirements. Thus, the second most important goal is that at least

30% of the new employees be minorities. Latins, blacks, women, and native Americans qualify as minorities under EEOC guidelines. Experience indicates that specialized recruiting procedures and salary inducements for such faculty typically add $16\frac{2}{3}$% to the school's recruitment and first-year employment costs.

The administration's lowest priority is to limit total faculty positions as much as possible. Fractional (part-time) faculty appointments are acceptable. Formulate this affirmative action problem. Define each variable and label all expressions.

7. Refer back to Example 9.3. Suppose that the problem is reformulated as the following linear program:

$$\text{minimize} \quad Z = d_3^+$$

$$\begin{array}{lll} \text{subject to} & X_1 + X_2 \geq 1{,}000{,}000 \text{ hours} & \text{(Employment)} \\ & X_2 \geq X_1 & \text{(Worker mix)} \\ & \$6X_1 + \$10X_2 \leq \$12{,}000{,}000 & \text{(Budget)} \\ & X_1, X_2 \geq 0 \end{array}$$

where $d_3^+ = X_2 - 400{,}000$ and Z represents retraining above the 400,000-hour aspiration level.

What is the optimal solution to the reformulated problem? How does this recommendation compare to the goal programming solution? Explain. What is the implication of your finding?

8. Alright Corporation of Zonton is considering four new household products to replace recently discontinued brands. The problem is to determine the product mix that will best achieve a range of corporate goals. After consulting with the firm's management staff, the firm's System Analysis Group has expressed the new product problem as follows:

$$\text{minimize} \quad Z = P_1 d_1^- + P_2(d_2^+ + d_2^-) + P_3 d_3^+ + P_4 d_4^-$$

subject to

$$\$.2X_1 + \$.5X_2 + \$.4X_3 + \$1X_4 + d_1^- - d_1^+ = \$8 \text{ million}$$
$$\text{(Profit goal)}$$

$$.4X_1 + 1X_2 + .2X_3 + .7X_4 + d_2^- - d_2^+ = 10{,}000$$
$$\text{(Employment goal)}$$

$$\begin{array}{ll} X_1 + X_2 - X_3 - X_4 + d_3^- - d_3^+ = 0 & \text{(Brand mix goal)} \\ \$.3X_1 + \$.2X_2 + \$.6X_3 + \$.4X_4 + d_4^- - d_4^+ = \$20 \text{ million} \end{array}$$
$$\text{(Investment goal)}$$

$$2X_1 + 10X_2 + 5X_3 + 4X_4 + d_5^- = 70{,}000 \text{ hours} \quad \text{(Machinery)}$$

$$X_1, X_2, X_3, X_4, d_1^-, d_1^+, d_2^-, d_2^+, d_3^-, d_3^+, d_4^-, d_4^+, d_5^- \geq 0$$

where X_1 = the number of bars of soap (in millions), X_2 = the number of cans of deodorant spray (in millions), X_3 = the number of tubes of toothpaste (in millions), and X_4 = the number of bottles of mouthwash (in millions). In addition, the d_1^- through d_4^+ deviational variables represent the degree of achievement for the corresponding corporate goals. On the other hand, the d_5^- deviational variable gives the firm's unused machinery hours.

The Systems Analysis Group has also provided the following GOAL solution for the company's new product problem:

SLACK ANALYSIS

ROW	AVAILABLE	POS-SLK	NEG-SLK
1	8.00000	2.68292	0.00000
2	10.00000	0.00000	0.00000
3	.00001	0.00000	0.00000
4	20.00000	0.00000	11.48780
5	70.00000	0.00000	0.00000

1

VARIABLE ANALYSIS

VARIABLE	AMOUNT
4	6.82926
1	10.97562
3	4.14634

1

ANALYSIS OF THE OBJECTIVE

PRIORITY	UNDER-ACHIEVEMENT
4	11.48780
3	0.00000
2	0.00000
1	0.00000

0
0
0
0

Interpret the group's mathematical programming formulation and this resulting GOAL computer printout for the management staff. Use language that would be understandable to these executives.

9. Explain why you agree or disagree with each of the following statements:

a. In a linear program, the same change in all decision variables will result in a proportional change in the criterion value and each system constraint amount.

b. Integer programming problems generally have fewer feasible solutions than similar linear programs.

c. An integer programming problem is easier to solve than a similar linear program.

d. The optimal integer programming solution will not be as good as the best linear programming solution for the same problem.

e. The deviational variables in goal programming serve the same purpose as the slack and surplus activities in linear programming.

f. Whenever a goal programming solution has zero values for all deviational variables, all postulated goals have been met.

g. Goal programming attempts to optimize the multiple objectives of management.

h. At least one of the deviational variables in a goal constraint must equal zero.

Technique Exercises

1. Consider the following integer programming problem faced by an aircraft manufacturer:

$$\text{maximize} \quad Z = \$30X_1 + \$60X_2$$

$$\begin{array}{lll} \text{subject to} & \$12X_1 + \$20X_2 \leq \$120 \text{ million} & \text{(Budget)} \\ & X_1 + X_2 \leq 7 & \text{(Total output)} \\ & X_1 \leq X_2 & \text{(Product mix)} \\ & X_1 \geq 1 & \text{(Product requirement)} \\ & X_1, X_2 \geq 0 \text{ and are integers} \end{array}$$

where Z = the profit in millions of dollars, X_1 = the number of T-757s, and X_2 = the number of T-767s.

a. Use the graphic method to find the optimal linear programming solution. Does this recommendation provide an integer solution? If not, round the linear programming solution.

b. Next, determine the optimal integer programming solution first by enumeration and then with the graphic approach. Show all your work.

c. How does the optimal integer programming solution compare to the rounded linear programming recommendation?

2. Refer back to Example 9.2.

a. Show how the optimal linear programming solution in Figure 9.1 was developed.

b. Show how the cutting plane solutions in Figures 9.5 and 9.6 were derived.

c. Show how the branch and bound subproblem 3 and 4 solutions in Figure 9.9 were developed.

Show all your work.

3. You are given the following integer programming problem:

maximize $\quad Z = 20X_1 + 50X_2$

subject to $\quad 1X_1 + 3X_2 \le 12$

$\quad\quad\quad\quad X_1 + X_2 \le 7$

$\quad\quad\quad\quad X_1, X_2 \ge 0$ and are integers

a. Use the graphic method to find the optimal linear programming solution.
b. Determine the optimal integer programming solution first by enumeration and next with the cutting plane method. Show all your work.
c. How does the optimal integer programming solution compare to the best linear programming recommendation?

4. Consider the following integer programming problem:

maximize $\quad Z = 75X_1 + 50X_2$

subject to $\quad 10X_1 + 20X_2 \le 100$

$\quad\quad\quad\quad 12X_1 + 6X_2 \le 80$

$\quad\quad\quad\quad X_1, X_2 \ge 0$ and are integers

Use the cutting plane and branch and bound methods to find the optimal integer programming solution. Show all your work.

5. Use the branch and bound method to solve the following integer programming problem. Show all your work.

minimize $\quad Z = 110X_1 + 4X_2 + 2X_3$

subject to $\quad 6X_1 - 4X_2 + 8X_3 \ge 16$

$\quad\quad\quad\quad 6X_1 + 8X_2 - 4X_3 \ge 12$

$\quad\quad\quad\quad X_1, X_2, X_3 \ge 0$ and are integers

6. A small town must determine the location of three additional ambulance dispatch stations within the community. The administration wants to select from among a set of potential locations the sites that provide the necessary service at least cost. In this regard, the staff has formulated the problem as follows:

minimize $\quad Z = \$300{,}000X_1 + \$260{,}000X_2 + \$340{,}000X_3$

subject to $\quad X_1 + X_2 \ge 1 \quad\quad\quad$ (Neighborhood A)

$\quad\quad\quad\quad X_2 + X_3 \ge 1 \quad\quad\quad$ (Neighborhood B)

$\quad\quad\quad\quad X_1 + X_2 + X_3 \ge 1 \quad$ (Neighborhood C)

$\quad\quad\quad\quad X_1 + X_3 \ge 1 \quad\quad\quad$ (Neighborhood D)

$\quad\quad\quad\quad X_1, X_2, X_3 = 0$ or 1

where Z = the total costs for the ambulance sites, $X_1 = 1$ if the Omega site is selected and 0 otherwise, $X_2 = 1$ if the Delta site is selected and 0 otherwise, and $X_3 = 1$ if the Epsilon site is selected and 0 otherwise.

Find the optimal set of ambulance sites.

7. Wallington Company, Inc., manufactures two industrial chemicals. Management wants to determine the product mix that will maximize total revenue. Its staff has formulated the problem as follows:

maximize $Z = \$170X_1 + \$3X_2$

subject to $60X_1 + 1X_2 \le 4000$ pounds   (Ingredient 1)
                 $36X_1 + .8X_2 \le 1600$ pounds   (Ingredient 2)
                 $4X_1 + .2X_2 \le 400$ pounds   (Ingredient 3)
                 $X_1, X_2 \ge 0$
                 X_1 must be an integer

where Z = the total revenue, X_1 = the number of 100-pound bags of leadoline, and X_2 = the number of dry mixed pounds of philon.
Find the optimal product mix.

8. Consider the following goal programming problem:

minimize $Z = P_1 d_3^- + P_2 d_1^+$

subject to $X_1 + X_2 + d_1^- - d_1^+ = 1800$
                 $X_1 + d_2^- = 1000$
                 $2000X_1 + 1500X_2 + d_3^- - d_3^+ = 3,000,000$
                 $X_1, X_2, d_1^-, d_1^+, d_2^-, d_3^-, d_3^+ \ge 0$

Find the optimal goal programming solution.

9. Refer back to thought exercise 6. Determine the faculty mixture that best satisfies the business school's multiple goals. Suppose that the administration changes its priorities to the following order:

   ◆ Have at least 30% of the new employees be minorities.
   ◆ Limit total faculty positions as much as possible.
   ◆ Remain within the $1 million budget.

   How will this change affect your recommendation? Explain.

10. A discount department store is considering several locations for a new outlet. Since management wants to draw as many customers as possible, it will select the most centrally located site. The staff has formulated the problem as follows:

minimize $Z = d_1^- + d_1^+ + d_2^- + d_2^+ + d_3^- + d_3^+ + d_4^- + d_4^+$
                $+ d_5^- + d_5^+ + d_6^- + d_6^+$

subject to

$$X_1 + d_1^- - d_1^+ = 5 \text{ miles} \qquad \text{(Population center A)}$$
$$X_2 + d_2^- - d_2^+ = 3 \text{ miles} \qquad \text{(Population center A)}$$
$$X_1 + d_3^- - d_3^+ = 7 \text{ miles} \qquad \text{(Population center B)}$$
$$X_2 + d_4^- - d_4^+ = 8 \text{ miles} \qquad \text{(Population center B)}$$
$$X_1 + d_5^- - d_5^+ = 2 \text{ miles} \qquad \text{(Population center C)}$$
$$X_2 + d_6^- - d_6^+ = 10 \text{ miles} \qquad \text{(Population center C)}$$
$$X_1, X_2, d_1^-, d_1^+, d_2^-, d_2^+, d_3^-, d_3^+,$$
$$d_4^-, d_4^+, d_5^-, d_5^+, d_6^-, d_6^+ \geq 0$$

where Z = the total miles from all population centers, X_1 = the north/south coordinate of the outlet (miles from the map reference point), and X_2 = the east/west coordinate of the outlet (miles from the map reference point). Also, the d^- and d^+ deviational variables represent the distances in miles of the outlet from the corresponding population centers.

Find the linear programming solution to this store location problem. Next, use the goal programming approach to develop a recommended outlet site. How does the goal programming solution compare to the best linear programming recommendation? Explain.

Suppose that management feels that the size of the population center should determine the priority of site selection. In this respect, population center B has more people than A, which in turn contains a larger potential market than C. Under these circumstances. the highest priority is to minimize the total distance from population center B. Similarly, the second most important objective is to minimize the total distance from population center A. How would such considerations affect the analysis and your recommendation? Explain. Interpret all solutions in language that would be understandable to management.

11. You are given the following goal programming problem.

minimize $\qquad Z = 2P_1 d_4^- + P_1 d_5^- + P_2(d_3^- + d_3^+)$

subject to $\qquad 5X_1 + 3X_2 + d_1^- = 30$
$$4X_1 + 5X_2 + d_2^- = 40$$
$$10X_1 + 10X_2 + d_3^- - d_3^+ = 120$$
$$X_1 + d_4^- - d_4^+ = 1$$
$$X_2 + d_5^- - d_5^+ = 3$$
$$X_1, X_2, d_1^-, d_2^-, d_3^-, d_3^+, d_4^-, d_4^+, d_5^-, d_5^+ \geq 0$$

In the formulation, notice that the d_4^- and d_5^- deviational variables are on the same P_1 priority level. However, d_4^- is given twice as much weight (considered twice as important) within the priority level as the d_5^- variable.

Find the solution to this goal programming problem.

12. Jentron, Inc., manufactures two brands of a particular medical product. Management wants to determine the brand mix that will best satisfy the hierarchy of goals expressed in the following problem:

minimize $\quad Z = P_1 d_1^- + 10P_2 d_2^- + 4P_2 d_3^- + P_3 d_4^+$

subject to $\quad 4X_1 + 3X_2 + d_1^- - d_1^+ = 480$ hours

$\hspace{7cm}$ (Production capacity)

$\quad\quad\quad\quad X_1 + d_2^- - d_2^+ = 80{,}000 \quad\quad$ (Brand A demand)

$\quad\quad\quad\quad X_2 + d_3^- - d_3^+ = 100{,}000 \quad\quad$ (Brand B demand)

$\quad\quad\quad\quad d_1^+ + d_4^- - d_4^+ = 40$ hours $\quad\quad\quad$ (Overtime)

$\quad\quad\quad\quad X_1, X_2, d_1^-, d_1^+, d_2^-, d_2^+, d_3^-, d_3^+, d_4^-, d_4^+ \geq 0$

where

$\quad X_1 =$ output of brand A (in thousands)

$\quad X_2 =$ output of brand B (in thousands)

$\quad d_1^- =$ unused capacity hours

$\quad d_1^+ =$ overtime hours

$\quad d_2^- =$ output below brand A's 80,000 demand target

$\quad d_2^+ =$ output above brand A's 80,000 demand target

$\quad d_3^- =$ output below brand B's 100,000 demand target

$\quad d_3^+ =$ output above brand B's 100,000 demand target

Also, the d_4^- and d_4^+ deviational variables represent the degree of achievement for the company's 40-hour overtime goal.

Find the solution to this goal programming problem.

Applications Exercises

1. Downtown Memorial Clinic has recently added the latest medical care equipment to its public health service facility. The facility is currently available for only two types of patients: indigents and welfare referrals. To enhance health care opportunities for the community, the clinic will process as many patients as possible through the new facility. In this regard, the staff can handle up to 72 indigents and at least 20 welfare referrals per day.

The clinic is the only health care facility readily available to the indigent, while welfare referrals have alternative sources of medical treatment. Hence, the staff believes that indigent care is far more important to the community than the treatment of welfare referrals. In fact, it considers each indigent as the equivalent of three welfare referrals. For similar reasons, the staff wants the clinic to treat at least 42 indigents but no more than 120 welfare referrals per day.

Another important consideration is the available supply of medication. In particular, the clinic receives no more than 1800 fluid ounces per day of the most popular medication. Moreover, experience indicates that each indigent requires 24 ounces of this medication, and each welfare referral requires 33 ounces.

What is the patient mixture that will provide the maximum benefit to the community? Benefit is defined as the total number of people in the community to be treated in the clinic per day, as per staff guidelines.

2. The Bethel Company manufactures rolls of paper for use in computer printers. These rolls, which are 80 feet long, can be produced only in a 50-inch width. Yet customers demand widths of varying sizes. In fact, the company has committed orders for the following roll sizes in the coming month:

Roll Width (Inches)	Rolls Ordered
10	760
15	590
20	880

Since additional orders may be received during the month, these commitments represent minimum demand levels. Nevertheless, any additional demand will be for one of the three roll sizes listed. In other words, there is no demand for any other width.

Bethel, then, must cut the rolls to the desired final product sizes. What is the minimum number of 50-inch rolls that will be required to satisfy customer demand? Suppose that management decides to minimize the waste (unused paper). How would this objective affect the recommendation? Explain.

3. Cable Television Network (CTN) is preparing its schedule of programs for the new season. These programs can be classified as news, sports, movies, and variety. Potential earnings from each category differ because of production cost and commercial rate differentials. Typical revenue and cost data are given in the following table:

Program Category	Commercial Revenue ($ million)	Production Costs ($ million)			
		Operations	Equipment	Talent	Technical Support
News	18	3	4	4	3
Sports	25	2	5	6	3
Movies	9	1	0.5	0.5	1.5
Variety	12	2.5	1.5	1	2

Administrative activities, such as accounting, financial analysis, and marketing, make up the operations function. Equipment expenses include camera, videotape, microphone, and other sound/video instrument costs. Talent costs consist of the salaries and benefits for performers, broadcasters, and commentators. Technical support involves activities such as engineering, film processing, and electrical work.

The network has budgeted $5 million for operations, $7 million for equipment, $8 million for talent, and $6 million for technical support activities. Which program categories should management select to maximize total commercial revenue for the new season?

4. The Spilding Company, a major sporting goods manufacturer, is bringing out a new line of aluminum baseball bats. This product will be launched with a national advertising campaign consisting of inserts in the *Baseball News* magazine and ads during the television game of the week. Each magazine insert costs $15,000 and is expected to reach an estimated 500,000 potential customers. On the other hand, each television ad costs $25,000 but reaches an expected one million possible consumers. These fees are for full-message placements. Nevertheless, it also is possible to buy a fraction (partial) magazine insert and/or television ad.

Spilding has budgeted $600,000 for the advertising campaign. Management has also agreed that this campaign should achieve several goals in the following order of priority:

♦ Stay within the budget.
♦ Run at least nine television ads.
♦ Place at least five magazine insertions.
♦ Reach at least twelve million potential customers.

How many ads must Spilding place in each medium to attain these goals? What advertising strategy do you recommend? Explain.

5. Bungling Brothers Carnival provides a portable amusement park for church fairs, shopping center promotions, and social clubs. Recently, the carnival's facilities were inspected by government agents enforcing the Occupational Safety and Health Act (OSHA). The inspectors found violations in two major categories: equipment maintenance and fire protection. Moreover, these agents have proposed safety guidelines designed to reduce the carnival's frequency of accidents and mishap cost per person.

Of course, it will cost Bungling money to achieve the relevant compliance levels. Indeed, the following table presents the cost of achieving a percentage increase in compliance as well as the resulting accident frequency and per-person mishap cost reductions:

Violation Category	Accident Frequency Reduction (Accidents per 10,000 Hours of Exposure)	Reduction in Mishap Cost (per Person)	Compliance Cost (per Percentage Point Increase in Compliance Level)
Equipment Maintenance	.25	$100	$300
Fire Protection	.40	$500	$450

To fully achieve the OSHA guidelines in both categories, the carnival must increase the equipment maintenance compliance level by 25 percentage points and reduce violations in the fire protection category by 50 percentage points. Yet Bungling can afford to spend only $15,000 on safety. The government agents recognize this dilemma. Hence, they are willing to delay punitive action as long as Bungling makes progress toward full compliance. In particular, the agents have established the following goals in the order of their priority:

♦ Decrease total accident frequency by at least ten mishaps per 10,000 hours of exposure.

♦ Reduce the total mishap cost per worker by at least $6000.

♦ Achieve at least 95% compliance in each violation category.

How many percentage points of compliance in each violation category are needed to achieve these OSHA goals? Suppose the government considers equipment maintenance to be twice as desirable for the carnival as fire protection. How would this preference change the recommendation? Explain.

6. Outlands East, one store of a chain in a major metropolitan area, specializes in the sale of hobby supplies. It operates with a staff of nine people: a manager who is compensated by a fixed salary plus bonuses and eight full-time salespeople who are paid an hourly wage. Each salesperson typically works 180 hours per month, while the manager has a regular working schedule of 192 hours per month.

Store operations are based on sales quotas set by top management. Outlands East, for instance, has a sales quota of $35,000 in the current month. The store manager receives a 5% bonus on all sales above the monthly quota. To motivate the individuals, the manager sets a sales quota for the entire full-time staff and also pays a 6% commission on all sales above the group quota. Moreover, commissions are split equally among the sales staff. In this regard, the manager has established a $28,800 sales quota in the current month for the full-time staff. Past experience indicates that each salesperson can sell, on average, $30 worth of merchandise per hour. On the other hand, the manager has been able to average $40 in sales per hour.

Here are the manager's priorities, in their order of importance:

◆ Achieve the store sales quota.

◆ Have the staff attain the group sales quota.

◆ Provide a commission of $50 for each salesperson and a $150 bonus for the manager.

For motivation reasons, the commissions are considered to be three times as important as the bonus. How many hours should the manager and sales staff work to achieve the hierarchy of goals?

The salespeople, on the other hand, believe that the commissions and bonuses would provide the motivation necessary to attain the store and staff quotas. Consequently, they propose the following reordering of priorities:

◆ Provide a commission of $50 for each salesperson.

◆ Give the manager a $150 bonus.

◆ Achieve the store sales quota.

◆ Have the staff attain the group sales quota.

How would such a priority reordering affect the work plan? Which goal structure do you recommend? Explain.

CASE: Federated Motors, Inc.

Federated Motors, Inc., is a major automobile manufacturer. One of its major subsidiaries has a labor-planning problem. A decision must be made involving departmental staffing requirements for the next month's production. Since some employees have been cross-trained on two or more jobs, the subsidiary has some labor flexibility. At least some labor can be assigned to more than one department or work center.

The subsidiary is planning to produce truck and automobile batteries during the next month. Batteries are processed in two departments. It takes .2 labor hour to process a truck battery and .1 labor hour for an automobile battery in department 1. It takes .1 labor hour to process a truck battery and .2 labor hour for an automobile battery in department 2.

Excess equipment capacity is available and will not be a restriction. However, the subsidiary's labor is limited. After careful consideration of the training and experience qualifications of the workers, the subsidiary's management devises the possible labor assignments presented in Table 9.10. Hence, 2500 of the 15,000 people-hours available for the month's production can be allocated with some management discretion. That is, the labor assignments to departments are variables. The company makes a profit of $10 per truck battery and $8 per automobile battery. Labor assignment variables do not directly affect profit.

The subsidiary submits the problem to the company's planning department. The subsidiary asks this department to provide recommendations on the following questions:

a. How many batteries of each type should be produced next month to maximize profit?

b. How many people-hours should be allocated to each department as part of the optimal product mix?

What would you recommend?

Suppose management establishes the following hierarchy of goals:

◆ Earn at least $300,000 profit.

◆ Produce an equal number of truck and automobile batteries.

◆ Utilize at least 5000 people-hours in department 2.

How would these considerations affect your recommendation? Explain.

Table 9.10 Possible Labor Assignments for Federated Motors

Labor Assignment	People-hours Available
Department 1 only	5,000
Department 2 only	7,500
Department 1 or 2	2,500
Total	15,000

Part IV
Networks

Many decision problems can be depicted as a set of junction points interconnected by a series of lines. The junction points may represent geographic locations (such as cities), physical facilities (like warehouses), or activities. Connecting lines may portray routes, layout designs, or job relationships. Usually, management wants to find the series of connections that best achieves some specified objective.

Such problems have been solved successfully with network analysis. This part of the text presents some of the most widely used network techniques. Chapter 10 introduces approaches designed to optimally distribute products and services from sources of supply to demand destinations. The chapter shows how to formulate typical distribution problems and develop the recommended solutions. It also outlines the assumptions and limitations of the analysis.

Chapter 11 presents network approaches directed at the flow of items, objects, or people through a system. In this chapter, we see how to design an optimal layout, identify the preferred route, and establish the best flow through the system. The final chapter, chapter 12, develops the network approaches to project management. In particular, it examines the methods to plan and schedule large-scale projects, control the time and cost aspects of the plan, and analyze the effects of uncertainty.

After reading this part of the text, you should be able to:

◆ Identify problems suitable for network analysis
◆ Formulate the appropriate decision model
◆ Develop a recommended solution mathematically and with the aid of a computer
◆ Recognize the assumptions and limitations of the network analysis.

This background will also facilitate your understanding of subsequent chapters of the text.

Chapter 10
Distribution

M any decision problems involve the allocation of supplies from their origins to centers of demand. Because supplies are scarce resources and transportation is expensive, it is important for any organization to move its supplies from source to destination at minimum cost. Constraints on demand and supply further complicate the allocation problem. Decision scientists have developed quantitative models that help managers analyze these situations. This chapter presents these models.

We begin with the more general situation—the transportation problem—discussing its nature, the most efficient solution procedures, and extensions to the basic model. Then the assignment problem is contrasted with the transportation model, and its appropriate solution procedures and extensions are developed. As the chapter demonstrates, these approaches apply to a wide range of problems in the modern enterprise.

TRANSPORTATION

In modern economies, firms are often physically separated from their customers. Production facilities typically are located at the source of raw materials, within inexpensive labor markets, in low tax areas, and near transportation facilities. On the other hand, purchase centers may be situated within large population centers that are convenient to customers and close to competition. Seldom are the manufacturing facilities close to the purchase centers. As a result, firms develop distribution systems to overcome these physical separations.

In such systems, items are transported from the supply sources (plants, storage areas, and so on) to the demand destinations (wholesalers, retail outlets, and so forth). Furthermore, each source has an available supply of items, while every destination has a particular demand. Management must therefore select the plan that most effectively distributes available supplies to the requesting destinations. Example 10.1 presents a typical illustration of this resource allocation problem.

EXAMPLE 10.1 Product Shipment

Tyler Incorporated makes men's suits for a midwestern chain of department stores. The company has production facilities at the sources of its raw materials and labor suppliers in the cities of Milwaukee, Gary, and Flint. It has warehouses in the Chicago, Minneapolis, and Detroit metropolitan areas, where there are concentrations of the department store chain's retail outlets. Milwaukee's plant can supply 1000 suits per month, Gary's 800, and Flint's 1200. The Chicago warehouse has a demand for 1500 suits per month, Minneapolis 500, and Detroit 1000. Transportation costs per suit, including freight, handling, and insurance, are presented in Table 10.1. Tyler's management seeks the distribution plan that will satisfy all plant capabilities and warehouse demands at least cost.

Table 10.1 Cost of Transporting One Suit to Each Tyler Warehouse

	Warehouse Location		
Plant Location	Chicago	Minneapolis	Detroit
Milwaukee	$2	$4	$5
Gary	$1	$6	$2
Flint	$4	$7	$1

NATURE OF THE PROBLEM As Example 10.1 demonstrates, Tyler has a specified demand for suits at each of its three metropolitan area warehouses. The company can satisfy these demands by transporting the available supplies from its three manufacturing plants to the warehouses. Several alternative routes, each with a specific per-suit transportation cost, can be used to make these shipments. These alternatives are depicted in Figure 10.1 as a set of labeled circles (plant and warehouse locations) interconnected by a series of lines (shipping routes). Also, the lines reflect the flow (movement of Tyler suits) that will occur through the distribution system. Such a map, or diagram, is known as a **network**. In network terminology, the circles are called **nodes**, while the lines are referred to as **arcs, branches, links,** or **edges**. Moreover, when the flows can occur in only one direction, as in Tyler's case, the diagram is known as a **directed network**.

In Figure 10.1, each number next to a node represents a supply available at a plant or a demand emanating from a warehouse. Every value on an arc identifies the cost of transporting one suit along the corresponding shipping route. Management, then, must determine the least costly way of shipping the required quantities of suits over these arcs.

According to Figure 10.1, Tyler can transport a suit over each specified route for a known and constant cost. For example, it costs $2 to ship a suit from Gary to Detroit, regardless of the shipment size. Consequently, the

Figure 10.1 Tyler's Shipping Alternatives

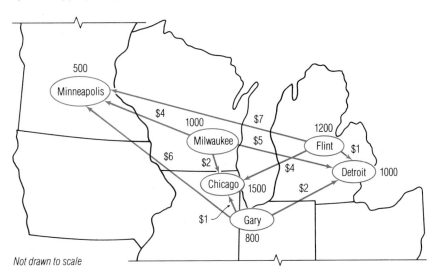

Not drawn to scale

total transportation cost between each plant and warehouse will be directly proportional to the quantity in the shipment. By letting

  i = the plant index (1 = Milwaukee, 2 = Gary, and 3 = Flint)

  j = the warehouse index (1 = Chicago, 2 = Minneapolis, and 3 = Detroit)

  X_{ij} = the number of suits transported from plant i to warehouse j each month

  Z = total transportation cost

management can use the expression

$$\text{minimize } Z = \$2X_{11} + \$4X_{12} + \$5X_{13} + \$1X_{21} + \$6X_{22} \\ + \$2X_{23} + \$4X_{31} + \$7X_{32} + \$1X_{33}$$

to denote the company's cost minimization objective.

There will be constraints on the objective, some involving the supplies available at each plant. Specifically, the total quantity of suits transported to all warehouses cannot exceed the available supply at each plant. That is,

  $X_{11} + X_{12} + X_{13} \leq 1000$ suits per month (Milwaukee)

  $X_{21} + X_{22} + X_{23} \leq 800$ suits per month (Gary)

  $X_{31} + X_{32} + X_{33} \leq 1200$ suits per month (Flint)

Another set of restrictions deals with the demand requirements at each warehouse. In particular, the total number of suits shipped from all plants must be greater than or equal to the demand at each warehouse. Put another way,

$$X_{11} + X_{21} + X_{31} \geq 1500 \text{ suits per month (Chicago)}$$

$$X_{12} + X_{22} + X_{32} \geq 500 \text{ suits per month (Minneapolis)}$$

$$X_{13} + X_{23} + X_{33} \geq 1000 \text{ suits per month (Detroit)}$$

The nonnegativity conditions

$$X_{11}, X_{12}, X_{13}, X_{21}, X_{22}, X_{23}, X_{31}; X_{32}, X_{33} \geq 0$$

are the final restrictions on the problem.

If management collects the objective function, supply and demand constraints, and nonnegativity conditions, it will formulate the following model:

minimize $\quad Z = \$2X_{11} + \$4X_{12} + \$5X_{13} + \$1X_{21} + \$6X_{22}$
$\qquad\qquad\quad + \$2X_{23} + \$4X_{31} + \$7X_{32} + \$1X_{33}$

subject to $\quad X_{11} + X_{12} + X_{13} \leq 1000 \text{ suits per month (Milwaukee)}$
$\qquad\qquad X_{21} + X_{22} + X_{23} \leq 800 \text{ suits per month (Gary)}$
$\qquad\qquad X_{31} + X_{32} + X_{33} \leq 1200 \text{ suits per month (Flint)}$
$\qquad\qquad X_{11} + X_{21} + X_{31} \geq 1500 \text{ suits per month (Chicago)}$
$\qquad\qquad X_{12} + X_{22} + X_{32} \geq 500 \text{ suits per month (Minneapolis)}$
$\qquad\qquad X_{13} + X_{23} + X_{33} \geq 1000 \text{ suits per month (Detroit)}$
$\qquad\qquad X_{11}, X_{12}, X_{13}, X_{21}, X_{22}, X_{23}, X_{31}, X_{32}, X_{33} \geq 0$

This model completely describes Tyler's resource allocation problem. Such a model is known as a **transportation problem**.

As you can see, the transportation problem has the same general structure as any ordinary linear program. There is an objective function that relates a single numerical criterion (total transportation cost) to a group of decision variables (amounts shipped over each arc in the transportation network). This objective is subject to a finite number of constraints, with one restriction for each supply source and demand destination (node) in the transportation network. Moreover, these constraints and the objective function each involve linear relationships. Finally, the decision variables are restricted to nonnegative values.

The decision maker, then, can use the simplex method to solve the transportation problem. However, transportation problems tend to have a large number of decision variables and constraints. Thus, even relatively simple transportation problems, such as Tyler's, may involve considerable computational effort.

Table 10.2 Tyler's Transportation Table

From Plant Location	To Warehouse Location			Plant Supply (Suits per Month)
	Chicago	Minneapolis	Detroit	
Milwaukee	$2 X_{11}	$4 X_{12}	$5 X_{13}	1000
Gary	$1 X_{21}	$6 X_{22}	$2 X_{23}	800
Flint	$4 X_{31}	$7 X_{32}	$1 X_{33}	1200
Warehouse Demand (Suits per Month)	1500	500	1000	3000

Cell corresponding to shipments from Flint to Chicago

Total supply and total demand

Fortunately, there is a key feature that distinguishes the transportation problem from other linear programs. Consider, for instance, the Milwaukee plant constraint

$$X_{11} + X_{12} + X_{13} \leq 1000 \text{ suits per month}$$

In this restriction, each of the X_{11}, X_{12}, and X_{13} decision variables has a coefficient of 1. Since the other decision variables (X_{21}, X_{22}, X_{23}, X_{31}, X_{32}, and X_{33}) do not appear, they all have coefficients of 0 in the Milwaukee constraint. Tyler's other plant and warehouse restrictions have a similar coefficient pattern. In fact, the coefficients of the decision variables in the supply and demand constraints of a transportation problem generally will be either 0 or 1. As a result, it is possible to use streamlined procedures that provide substantial computational shortcuts over the ordinary simplex method.

Although the computations differ in each approach, all streamlined procedures utilize a standard table to conveniently record the data and keep track of the calculations. This standard format, called the **transportation table**, is illustrated with Tyler's product shipment information in Table 10.2. Each row corresponds to a supply source (node) and every column to a demand destination (node) in Tyler's transportation network. For example, the first row portrays the Milwaukee plant, and the third column depicts the Detroit warehouse. Also, each cell corresponds to one of the decision variables (X_{ij}) in the problem. The cell at the intersection of the third row and first column, for instance, gives the number of suits (X_{31})

transported from the Flint plant to the Chicago warehouse. Since the company has three plants and three warehouses, there are $3 \times 3 = 9$ cells (decision variables) in the table.

The entry in the upper right-hand corner of each cell represents the cost of transporting one suit over the corresponding arc of the network. Observe, for example, the cell at the intersection of the second row and second column in Table 10.2. The entry in the upper right-hand corner indicates that Tyler must pay $6 to ship one suit from the Gary plant to the Minneapolis warehouse.

In addition, the quantities in the right-hand border give the supply available at each source, while the numbers in the bottom margin identify the demand at every destination. For instance, the entry in the right margin of the first row of Table 10.2 shows that the Milwaukee plant can supply 1000 suits per month. Similarly, the border value under the first column indicates that the Chicago warehouse demands 1500 suits per month. Furthermore, the table is set up in a way that ensures that total supply exactly equals total demand. In Tyler's case, the three plants can supply a total of 3000 suits per month, while the three warehouses demand the same monthly total. Hence, the required balance between total demand and total supply is a characteristic of the company's problem. Cases that contain imbalances between these totals will be dealt with in a later section of the chapter.

FIRST FEASIBLE SOLUTION   As in the ordinary simplex method, management begins the search for the optimal distribution pattern by identifying a solution that satisfies all constraints in the problem. Moreover, the customary methodology can be used to identify this first feasible solution. However, there are streamlined procedures available that will provide the solution more quickly and effectively than the ordinary simplex method.

Northwest Corner Method   One of the simplest ways to find an initial feasible solution is with the **northwest corner method**. In this approach, the decision maker starts with the cell in the upper left-hand (northwest) corner of the transportation table. Allocations are then made by moving down and to the right (or to the right and down). The process continues until the allocations satisfy all demand and supply requirements.

Table 10.3 illustrates this method with Tyler's product shipment data. The cell in the northwest corner corresponds to the route between the Milwaukee plant and the Chicago warehouse. Management begins by shipping as many suits as possible over such a route. There are 1500 suits required each month by the Chicago warehouse. Yet the Milwaukee plant is capable of supplying only 1000 suits per month. Consequently, the company can ship only 1000 suits per month from the Milwaukee plant to the Chicago warehouse.

Table 10.3 Tyler's Northwest Corner Solution

From Plant Location	To Warehouse Location			Plant Supply (Suits per Month)
	Chicago	Minneapolis	Detroit	
Milwaukee	$2 1000	$4	$5	1000 − 1000 = 0
Gary	$1 500 ────→	$6 300	$2	800 − 500 = 300 − 300 = 0
Flint	$4	$7 200 ────→	$1 1000	1200 − 200 = 1000 − 1000 = 0
Warehouse Demand (Suits per Month)	1500 − 1000 = 500 − 500 = 0	500 − 300 = 200 − 200 = 0	1000 −1000 = 0	

Such an initial allocation is denoted by writing 1000 in the Milwaukee/Chicago (northwest corner) cell of Table 10.3. As you can see, the shipment also reduces the supply at the Milwaukee plant from 1000 to 0 suits per month. Nevertheless, it still leaves an unsatisfied demand for 1500 − 1000 = 500 suits per month at the Chicago warehouse. Management must therefore find an additional source of supply for this warehouse.

Management can arrive at the next source of supply by moving down the Chicago column to the next row in the transportation table. As Table 10.3 demonstrates, such a movement will bring management to the Gary plant. It also shows that the remaining Chicago demand of 500 suits per month is less than the 800-suit supply available at this plant. To satisfy the demand, then, management must ship only 500 suits per month over the Gary-to-Chicago route.

This second allocation is denoted by writing 500 in the Gary/Chicago cell of Table 10.3. Such a shipment also reduces the demand at the Chicago warehouse from 500 to 0 suits per month. Yet it still leaves a supply of 800 − 500 = 300 suits per month available at the Gary plant.

The decision maker can identify another destination for this plant's supply by moving along the Gary row to the next column in the transportation table. Table 10.3 shows that such a movement will bring the decision maker to the Minneapolis warehouse. It also indicates that the remaining Gary supply of 300 suits per month is insufficient to completely satisfy the 500-suit demand at the Minneapolis warehouse. Nevertheless, the company ships its 300 suits over the Gary-to-Minneapolis route.

Table 10.4 Summary of Tyler's Northwest Corner Solution

Route		Suits Shipped per Nonth (X_{ij})	Transportation Cost per Suit ($)	Suits Shipped × Transportation Cost per Suit ($)
From	To			
Milwaukee	Chicago	$X_{11} = 1000$	2	$1000 \times 2 = 2000$
Milwaukee	Minneapolis	$X_{12} = 0$	4	$0 \times 4 = 0$
Milwaukee	Detroit	$X_{13} = 0$	5	$0 \times 5 = 0$
Gary	Chicago	$X_{21} = 500$	1	$500 \times 1 = 500$
Gary	Minneapolis	$X_{22} = 300$	6	$300 \times 6 = 1800$
Gary	Detroit	$X_{23} = 0$	2	$0 \times 2 = 0$
Flint	Chicago	$X_{31} = 0$	4	$0 \times 4 = 0$
Flint	Minneapolis	$X_{32} = 200$	7	$200 \times 7 = 1400$
Flint	Detroit	$X_{33} = 1000$	1	$1000 \times 1 = 1000$

Total transportation cost = $6700

This third allocation is denoted by writing 300 in the Gary/Minneapolis cell of Table 10.3. Moreover, the shipment reduces the supply at the Gary plant from 300 to 0 suits per month. However, it still leaves an unsatisfied demand for $500 - 300 = 200$ suits per month at the Minneapolis warehouse.

Management discovers another source of supply by moving down the Minneapolis column to the Flint row in Table 10.3. Tyler can meet the unsatisfied Minneapolis demand by transporting 200 suits per month from the Flint plant. Furthermore, such a shipment will leave $1200 - 200 = 1000$ suits available at the Flint plant. The residual Flint stock can then be used to satisfy the entire 1000-suit demand at the Detroit warehouse.

At this stage of the process, the allocations satisfy all of Tyler's supply and demand requirements. Therefore, the distribution pattern depicted in Table 10.3 represents a feasible solution to the company's product shipment problem. Its details are summarized in Table 10.4.

Although the northwest corner method is relatively quick and easy to use, its allocation process totally ignores Tyler's transportation costs. The first feasible solution, then, is not likely to be the minimum-cost distribution pattern. In fact, a great deal of effort may be required to improve the northwest corner solution. However, management can overcome this shortcoming by incorporating cost considerations into the allocation decisions.

Vogel Approximation Method   As M. H. Beilby [3] and H. H. Shore [19] demonstrate, there are several ways to account for transportation costs in the initial allocation process. One of the most popular approaches is based on the opportunity loss concept originally introduced in chapter 3. Table

Table 10.5 Tyler's Initial VAM Allocation

From Plant Location	To Warehouse Location			Plant Supply (Suits per Month)	Plant Penalty per Suit
	Chicago	Minneapolis	Detroit		
Milwaukee	$2	$4	$5	1000	$4 − $2 = $2
Gary	$1	$6	$2	800	$2 − $1 = $1
Flint	$4	$7	$1 1000	1200 −1000 = 200	$4 − $1 = $3*
Warehouse Demand (Suits per Month)	1500	500	1000 −1000 = 0		
Warehouse Penalty per Suit	$2 − $1 = $1	$6 − $4 = $2	$2 − $1 = $1		

10.5 illustrates this approach, which is known as the **Vogel approximation method (VAM)**, with Tyler's product shipment data.

As Table 10.5 demonstrates, the least expensive shipping route from the Milwaukee plant is to the Chicago warehouse, with a transportation cost of $2 per suit. The next best alternative is the Milwaukee-to-Minneapolis route. However, it costs Tyler $4 to ship a suit over this route. Thus, if management does not utilize the least expensive route from the Milwaukee plant, the company will incur an opportunity loss of at least $4 − $2 = $2 per suit. This penalty is recorded in the far-right margin of the Milwaukee plant row in Table 10.5.

Management can determine the opportunity losses for the other (Gary and Flint) plants in a similar manner. That is, management can identify the two least expensive shipping routes and then compute the difference in the corresponding per-suit transportation costs. Indeed, by so doing, the decision maker will obtain the plant penalties shown in the far-right margin of Table 10.5.

There will also be opportunity losses associated with each demand destination. Consider, for instance, the Chicago warehouse. The least expensive way to satisfy this warehouse's demand is with shipments from the Gary plant, which involves a transportation cost of $1 per suit. The next best alternative is the Milwaukee-to-Chicago route, with a transportation cost of $2 per suit. Therefore, if management does not utilize the least expensive route to the Chicago warehouse, the company will incur an opportunity loss of at least $2 − $1 = $1 per suit. This penalty is recorded at the bottom of the Chicago warehouse column in the table. By performing similar calculations for the other demand destinations (Minneapolis and Detroit), the decision maker will obtain the warehouse penalties shown in the bottom margin of the table.

A comparison of these plant and warehouse penalties demonstrates that the largest opportunity loss is the $3 associated with the Flint plant (denoted with the asterisk in Table 10.5). To avoid such a penalty, Tyler must ship as many suits as possible over the lowest-cost route from the Flint plant.

You can see from Table 10.5 that the least expensive shipping route from the Flint plant is to the Detroit warehouse. Furthermore, the Detroit demand of 1000 suits per month is less than the 1200-suit supply available at the Flint plant. To satisfy this demand, then, management must ship only 1000 suits per month over the Flint-to-Detroit route.

Such an initial allocation is denoted by writing 1000 in the Flint/Detroit cell in Table 10.5. As you can see, the shipment still leaves a supply of 1200 − 1000 = 200 suits per month available at the Flint plant. Nevertheless, it completely satisfies the Detroit demand. In other words, this warehouse cannot be a destination for any other shipment.

These results also lead to the allocation seen in Table 10.6. This table shows that the elimination of the Detroit destination leaves the remaining (Chicago and Minneapolis) warehouse penalties unchanged. Yet it forces Tyler to recompute the supply source opportunity losses. Indeed, the new plant penalties given in the far-right margin of the table show that the largest opportunity loss is now the $5 associated with the Gary plant. (Once more, it is denoted with an asterisk.) To avoid such a penalty, the company must ship as many suits as possible over the lowest-cost route from the Gary plant. The least expensive shipping route from the Gary plant is to the Chicago warehouse, where there are 1500 suits demanded each month. However, the Gary plant is capable of supplying only 800 suits per month. Consequently, Tyler can ship only 800 suits per month over the Gary-to-Chicago route.

This second allocation is depicted by writing 800 in the Gary/Chicago cell in Table 10.6. As you can see, such a shipment reduces the demand at the Chicago warehouse from 1500 to 700 suits per month. In addition, it completely exhausts the supply available at the Gary plant. Hence, the Gary plant can no longer be a source of any shipment.

These results lead to the allocation illustrated in Table 10.7. As the table demonstrates, the elimination of the Gary source leaves the remaining (Milwaukee and Flint) plant penalties unchanged. However, it forces Tyler to recompute the demand destination opportunity losses. The new warehouse penalties are calculated in the bottom margin of the table.

Table 10.6 Tyler's Second VAM Allocation

From Plant Location	To Warehouse Location		Plant Supply (Suits per Month)	Plant Penalty per Suit
	Chicago	Minneapolis		
Milwaukee	$2	$4	1000	$4 − $2 = $2
Gary	$1 800	$6	800 − 800 = 0	$6 − $1 = $5*
Flint	$4	$7	200	$7 − $4 = $3
Warehouse Demand (Suits per Month)	1500 − 800 = 700	500		
Warehouse Penalty per Suit	$2 − $1 = $1	$6 − $4 = $2		

Table 10.7 Tyler's Third VAM Allocation

From Plant Location	To Warehouse Location		Plant Supply (Suits per Month)	Plant Penalty per Suit
	Chicago	Minneapolis		
Milwaukee	$2	$4 500	1000 − 500 = 500	$4 − $2 = $2
Flint	$4	$7	200	$7 − $4 = $3*
Warehouse Demand (Suits per Month)	700	500 − 500 = 0		
Warehouse Penalty per Suit	$4 − $2 = $2	$7 − $4 = $3*		

Table 10.8 Tyler's VAM Solution

From Plant Location	To Warehouse Location			Plant Supply (Suits per Month)
	Chicago	Minneapolis	Detroit	
Milwaukee	$2 500	$4 500	$5	1000 − 500 = 500 500 − 500 = 0
Gary	$1 800	$6	$2	800 − 800 = 0
Flint	$4 200	$7	$1 1000	1200 − 1000 = 200 200 − 200 = 0
Warehouse Demand (Suits per Month)	1500 − 800 = 700 − 500 = 200 − 200 = 0	500 − 500 = 0	1000 −1000 = 0	

As you can see, the largest opportunity loss in Table 10.7 is the $3 associated with either the Flint plant or the Minneapolis warehouse. Tyler can therefore choose either of two ways to avoid such a penalty. On the one hand, the company can ship as many suits as possible over the lowest-cost route from the Flint plant. Alternatively, the company can utilize the most inexpensive route to the Minneapolis warehouse.

Although each alternative allocation will eventually lead to the same result, there may be some computational advantage in selecting the route with the largest potential shipment. In this respect, the Minneapolis warehouse needs 500 suits, while the Flint plant can ship only 200 suits per month. The larger potential shipment, then, will be to the Minneapolis warehouse rather than from the Flint plant. Consequently, the company should transport as many suits as possible over the lowest-cost route to the Minneapolis warehouse.

According to Table 10.7, the least expensive shipping route to Minneapolis is from the Milwaukee plant, which is capable of supplying the entire 500 suits required each month at the Minneapolis warehouse. Therefore, Tyler should ship 500 suits per month from the Milwaukee plant to the Minneapolis warehouse.

This third VAM allocation is denoted by writing 500 in the Milwaukee/ Minneapolis cell in Table 10.7. Such a shipment completely satisfies the

Table 10.9 Summary of Tyler's Vogel Approximation Solution

Route		Suits Shipped per Month (X_{ij})	Transportation Cost per Suit ($)	Suits Shipped × Transportation Cost per Suit ($)
From	To			
Milwaukee	Chicago	$X_{11} = 500$	2	$500 \times 2 = 1000$
Milwaukee	Minneapolis	$X_{12} = 500$	4	$500 \times 4 = 2000$
Milwaukee	Detroit	$X_{13} = 0$	5	$0 \times 5 = 0$
Gary	Chicago	$X_{21} = 800$	1	$800 \times 1 = 800$
Gary	Minneapolis	$X_{22} = 0$	6	$0 \times 6 = 0$
Gary	Detroit	$X_{23} = 0$	2	$0 \times 2 = 0$
Flint	Chicago	$X_{31} = 200$	4	$200 \times 4 = 800$
Flint	Minneapolis	$X_{32} = 0$	7	$0 \times 7 = 0$
Flint	Detroit	$X_{33} = 1000$	1	$1000 \times 1 = 1000$
			Total transportation cost = $5600	

demand at the Minneapolis warehouse. Yet it still leaves a monthly supply of $1000 - 500 = 500$ suits available at the Milwaukee plant.

Milwaukee's residual stock next can be used to satisfy 500 of the 700-suit demand at the Chicago warehouse. The remaining Chicago demand can then be provided by the 200-suit supply still available from the Flint plant. At this stage of the process, Tyler will have the complete Vogel approximation solution presented in Table 10.8. The five VAM allocations satisfy all of Tyler's supply and demand requirements. Thus, the distribution pattern depicted in Table 10.8 represents a feasible solution to the company's product shipment problem. Its details are summarized in Table 10.9.

By comparing Tables 10.4 and 10.9, you will find that the VAM solution generates a lower total transportation cost for Tyler's problem than the northwest corner recommendation. Such a result is not a coincidence. In fact, the Vogel approximation method usually provides a more economical first feasible solution than the northwest corner approach. As a result, VAM minimizes the calculations necessary to reach an optimal solution. Nevertheless, the Vogel method requires more computations than the northwest corner approach to identify a first feasible solution. When considering these alternative methodologies, then, management must weigh the northwest corner's ease of use against VAM's potential efficiency for reaching an optimal transportation solution. Table 10.10 summarizes the northwest corner and Vogel approximation methods of finding a first feasible solution to the transportation problem.

Table 10.10 Finding a First Feasible Solution to the Transportation Problem

Northwest Corner Method (NWC)	Vogel Approximation Method (VAM)
1. Allocate as many units as possible to the cell in the left-hand (northwest) corner of the transportation table. The maximum amount that can be allocated is the smaller of the source supply or destination demand.	1. Compute a penalty cost for each source (row) and destination (column) in the transportation table. The penalty is the difference between the unit cost on the second-best and the best route in the row or column.
2. Reduce the source supply and destination demand by the amount allocated to the cell.	2. Identify the source or destination with the largest overall penalty.
3. If the source supply is now zero, move down the destination column to the next cell. If the destination demand is now zero, move to the right on the source row to the next cell. If both the source supply and destination demand are zero, move down and right one cell to the next cell.	3. Identify the most desirable cell in the identified row or column.
4. Assign as many units as possible to the next cell identified by step 3.	4. Allocate as many units as possible to the identified cell. The maximum amount that can be allocated is the smaller of the source supply or destination demand.
5. Repeat steps 2 to 4 until a first feasible solution is obtained.	5. Reduce the source supply and destination demand by the amount allocated to the cell.
	6. If the source supply is now zero, eliminate the source. If the destination demand is now zero, eliminate the destination. If both the source supply and demand are zero, eliminate both the source and destination.
	7. Compute the new penalties for each source and destination in the revised transportation table formed by step 6.
	8. Repeat steps 2 to 7 until a first feasible solution is obtained.

EVALUATING THE SOLUTION Neither the northwest corner nor the Vogel approximation method guarantees an optimal solution. Instead, further calculations are usually necessary to determine if improvements can be made in the initial distribution pattern. To see what is involved, we will again consider the northwest corner solution given in Table 10.3.

You can see that Tyler's northwest corner solution fills five cells of the transportation table. These filled cells, which are equivalent to the basic variables in a simplex solution, represent the shipping routes utilized in the initial distribution pattern. This pattern leaves four empty cells in Table 10.3. These empty cells, which correspond to the nonbasic variables in a simplex solution, portray the currently unused transportation routes. Yet such unused routes (empty cells) may be more economical than the currently selected channels (filled cells). To find out, management must evaluate the economic effects of reallocating shipments from the filled cells to the empty cells in the transportation table.

Stepping Stone Method There are several ways to perform the evaluation process. One of the easiest approaches to understand is known as the

Table 10.11 Flint-to-Chicago Reallocation of the Northwest Corner Solution

From Plant Location	To Warehouse Location			Plant Supply (Suits per Month)
	Chicago	Minneapolis	Detroit	
Milwaukee	$2 1000	$4	$5	1000
Gary	$1 500 − 1 = 499	$6 300 + 1 = 301	$2	800
Flint	$4 + 1	$7 200 − 1 = 199	$1 1000	1200
Warehouse Demand (Suits per Month)	1500	500	1000	3000

stepping stone method. In this approach, the decision maker begins by tracing the pattern of changes required with each reallocation. Next, the patterns are used to determine the economic consequences of the corresponding reallocations. Management then utilizes the economic data to evaluate the current feasible solution.

Suppose that Tyler ships one suit over the currently unused route from the Flint plant to the Chicago warehouse. Such a reallocation creates the changes shown in Table 10.11. Note that the Flint plant has 1200 suits available each month. Moreover, the Detroit warehouse receives 1000 of this 1200-suit supply. As a result, the one-suit shipment to the Chicago warehouse means that the company must transport $200 - 1 = 199$ rather than 200 suits over the Flint-to-Minneapolis route. Since Minneapolis still demands 500 suits, such a shipment, in turn, will require Tyler to ship $300 + 1 = 301$ instead of 300 suits over the Gary-to-Minneapolis route. To avoid exceeding Gary's 800-suit supply, management should then transport $500 - 1 = 499$ rather than 500 suits over the Gary-to-Chicago route.

In effect, this method treats the transportation table as a kind of pond with the filled cells representing stones across the water. Also, the series of adjustments (directed lines in Table 10.11) traces a path over the filled cells that guides management safely across the pond. The path, which preserves all demand and supply requirements, begins at an empty cell. It then moves in horizontal and vertical fashion over filled cells in directions that lead back to the starting point. Such a series of horizontal and vertical lines is referred to as a **closed path** or **loop**.

By its nature, there will be only one loop associated with each unused route (empty cell) in the transportation network. Furthermore, the closed path provides the information needed to evaluate the economic consequences of the corresponding reallocation. By examining the closed path in Figure 10.11, for instance, we can see that each suit shipped over the currently unused Flint-to-Chicago route will affect transportation cost as indicated in Table 10.12. That is, Tyler will increase transportation cost a net $2 for each suit shipped over the currently unused route from the Flint plant to the Chicago warehouse. Such a net effect, which can be called an **improvement index**, is equivalent to a $C_j - Z_j$ value in the ordinary simplex method.

Tyler can use the same general approach to evaluate the other unused routes in its northwest corner solution. That is, the decision maker can trace the closed path and then compute the corresponding improvement index for each empty cell in Table 10.3. In fact, if management does this, it will obtain the results shown in Table 10.13. The circled numbers in the table represent the improvement indexes associated with the corresponding empty cells.

As Table 10.13 demonstrates, the empty cells corresponding to the Flint-to-Chicago, Milwaukee-to-Detroit, and Gary-to-Detroit routes each have positive improvement indexes. Such positive values indicate that Tyler would increase costs by transporting suits over these routes. Consequently, the currently unused Flint-to-Chicago, Milwaukee-to-Detroit, and Gary-to-Detroit routes are all unattractive alternatives to the distribution pattern (filled cells) in the company's northwest corner solution.

On the other hand, Table 10.13 shows that the empty cell corresponding to the Milwaukee-to-Minneapolis route has an improvement index of −$3. This value means that the northwest corner solution is not Tyler's minimum-cost distribution pattern. Rather, management can reduce the northwest corner solution's $6700 total cost a net $3 for each suit transported over the currently unused Milwaukee-to-Minneapolis route.

These results illustrate the following important principle: *In a minimization problem, the decision maker can better the current solution as long as at least one unused transportation route has a negative improvement index.* Later in the chapter we will see how to make the improvements.

Modified Distribution Method Although the stepping stone method is relatively easy to understand, it can be very tedious and time-consuming. After all, the decision maker must trace a closed path for every empty cell to find the corresponding improvement indexes. Moreover, such loops are often quite complicated. Fortunately, there is an alternative way to

Table 10.12 Effect of Flint-to-Chicago Reallocation on Cost

Route	Change	Effect on Cost
Flint to Chicago	Add 1 suit	+$4
Flint to Minneapolis	Subtract 1 suit	−$7
Gary to Minneapolis	Add 1 suit	+$6
Gary to Chicago	Subtract 1 suit	−$1
	Net effect on transportation cost $2	

Table 10.13 Tyler's Northwest Corner Solution Improvement Indexes

From Plant Location	To Warehouse Location			Plant Supply (Suits per Month)
	Chicago	Minneapolis	Detroit	
Milwaukee	$2 1000	$4 (−$3)	$5 ($4)	1000
Gary	$1 500	$6 300	$2 ($2)	800
Flint	$4 ($2)	$7 200	$1 1000	1200
Warehouse Demand (Suits per Month)	1500	500	1000	3000

determine these indexes. Again let us consider Tyler's northwest corner solution given in Table 10.3.

Each utilized route (filled cell) in Table 10.3 involves two important cost considerations. First, there is the cost of transporting one suit directly from a plant to a warehouse. This expense is given in the upper right-hand corner of the filled cell. For example, it costs $2 to ship a suit over the Milwaukee-to-Chicago route.

In addition, when Tyler ships one suit over a particular route, the company has one less suit to transport over alternative channels. Therefore, the company saves the expenses involved in moving the suit over these alternative channels. As a result, there will be cost savings associated with each utilized route (filled cell) in the transportation network. For example, you can see that Tyler's northwest corner solution utilizes the route from the Milwaukee plant to the Chicago warehouse. By shipping a suit from Milwaukee, the company saves the expenses involved in transporting the merchandise from the Gary and/or Flint plants. Let U_1 denote this cost savings. Moreover, the acceptance at Chicago saves the expenses involved in shipping the suit to the Minneapolis and/or Detroit warehouses. Let V_1 represent such cost savings. Consequently, the shipment of one suit over the Milwaukee-to-Chicago route will generate a total cost savings of $U_1 + V_1$ dollars.

If these total savings $(U_1 + V_1)$ exceeded the $2 cost of transporting a suit directly from Milwaukee to Chicago, Tyler would ship an unlimited quantity over the route. Put another way, the problem would be unbounded. Yet there is a bound on Milwaukee's plant capacity and a limited demand at the Chicago warehouse. Consequently, the cost savings must be no greater than the corresponding direct transportation expense, or

$$U_1 + V_1 \leq \$2$$

for the Milwaukee-to-Chicago route. This expression, which represents a constraint in the dual linear programming formulation of the problem, places an upper boundary on the total savings.

Furthermore, Tyler would have no incentive to ship a suit over the Milwaukee-to-Chicago route if the $2 direct transportation expense surpassed the $U_1 + V_1$ total cost savings. That is, management must set $X_{11} = 0$ when

$$U_1 + V_1 < \$2$$

These conditions imply that the company should utilize the Milwaukee-to-Chicago route only when

$$U_1 + V_1 = \$2$$

or when the total cost savings $(U_1 + V_1)$ exactly equal the direct transportation expense ($2) of the shipment.

There is a similar relationship between the cost savings and the direct expense for each utilized route in a transportation network. Thus, every filled cell in a transportation table will entail the following general equation:

$$U_i + V_j = C_{ij}$$

where U_i = the cost savings associated with supply source i, V_j = the cost savings associated with demand destination j, and C_{ij} = the direct expense of transporting one unit from source i to destination j. Indeed, when management applies this formula to the utilized routes (filled cells) in Tyler's northwest corner solution (Table 10.3), it gets the equations given in Table 10.14. Notice that there is one equation for each utilized route (filled cell) in the company's northwest corner solution.

These equations form a simultaneous system of five equations in six unknowns (U_1, U_2, U_3, V_1, V_2, and V_3). Since there are more unknowns than equations, management will be unable to find unique values for the

Table 10.14 Tyler's Cost Savings Equations

Utilized Route	Equation	Definition
Milwaukee to Chicago	$U_1 + V_1 = \$2$	U_1 = cost savings associated with a one-suit shipment from the Milwaukee plant
		V_1 = cost savings associated with a one-suit shipment to the Chicago warehouse
Gary to Chicago	$U_2 + V_1 = \$1$	U_2 = cost savings associated with a one-suit shipment from the Gary plant
Gary to Minneapolis	$U_2 + V_2 = \$6$	V_2 = cost savings associated with a one-suit shipment to the Minneapolis warehouse
Flint to Minneapolis	$U_3 + V_2 = \$7$	U_3 = cost savings associated with a one-suit shipment from the Flint plant
Flint to Detroit	$U_3 + V_3 = \$1$	V_3 = cost savings associated with a one-suit shipment to the Detroit warehouse

cost savings from these equations. This condition occurs because one of the supply or demand constraints in the transportation model is redundant or implied by the other restrictions in the problem. However, the decision maker can determine relative (rather than unique) values of cost savings first by arbitrarily setting one of the unknowns equal to zero. Then the decision maker uses the simultaneous system of equations to solve for the other unknowns.

Although ultimately it will not matter which unknown is set equal to zero, the computations can be reduced by selecting the variable that appears in the most equations. An examination of Tyler's five simultaneous cost savings equations shows that U_2, U_3, V_1, and V_2 are the variables that occur most often in the system. Hence, any one of these variables can be set equal to zero.

Suppose that management arbitrarily fixes the Chicago warehouse's cost savings at $V_1 = \$0$. According to the Milwaukee/Chicago equation, the cost savings associated with the Milwaukee plant will be

$$U_1 + V_1 = \$2$$
$$U_1 = \$2 - V_1 = \$2 - \$0 = \$2$$

Similarly, the Gary/Chicago equation gives us

$$U_2 + V_1 = \$1$$
$$U_2 = \$1 - V_1 = \$1 - \$0 = \$1$$

By using this value in the Gary/Minneapolis equation, the decision maker finds that

$$U_2 + V_2 = \$6$$
$$V_2 = \$6 - U_2 = \$6 - \$1 = \$5$$

Moreover, this value, when substituted in the Flint/Minneapolis equation, yields

$$U_3 + V_2 = \$7$$
$$U_3 = \$7 - V_2 = \$7 - \$5 = \$2$$

The Flint/Detroit equation then shows that

$$U_3 + V_3 = \$1$$
$$V_3 = \$1 - U_3 = \$1 - \$2 = -\$1$$

which is the cost savings associated with a one-suit shipment to the Detroit warehouse.

These cost savings, along with the resulting evaluation of Tyler's northwest corner solution, are presented in Table 10.15. Note that the cost savings can be positive (like U_1, U_2, U_3, and V_2), zero (like V_1), or negative (like V_3).

At this stage, management has the information it needs to evaluate the economic consequences of altering the existing distribution pattern. Consider, for instance, the currently unused route from the Milwaukee plant to the Minneapolis warehouse. As Table 10.15 demonstrates, it costs Tyler $4 to ship one suit directly over such a route. Nevertheless, the shipment generates a cost savings of $U_1 = \$2$ for the Milwaukee plant and $V_2 = \$5$ for the Minneapolis warehouse. Thus, the company will change transportation cost by

$$\$4 - U_1 - V_2 = \$4 - \$2 - \$5 = -\$3$$

or reduce it a net $3 for each suit shipped over the Milwaukee-to-Minneapolis route.

Such a net effect represents the improvement index associated with the route. In other words, an empty cell's improvement index will equal

or

$$C_{ij} - U_i - V_j$$

Table 10.15 Cost Savings Evaluation of Tyler's Northwest Corner Solution

From Plant Location	To Warehouse Location			Plant Supply (Suits per Month)	Plant Cost Savings
	Chicago	Minneapolis	Detroit		
Milwaukee	$2 1000	$4 (−$3)	$5 ($4)	1000	$U_1 = \$2$
Gary	$1 500	$6 300	$2 ($2)	800	$U_2 = \$1$
Flint	$4 ($2)	$7 200	$1 1000	1200	$U_3 = \$2$
Warehouse Demand (Suits per Month)	1500	500	1000	3000	
Warehouse Cost Savings	$V_1 = \$0$	$V_2 = \$5$	$V_3 = -\$1$		

This procedure for calculating the improvement indexes is called the **modified distribution (MODI) method.**

By applying such a method to the unused routes in Tyler's northwest corner solution, management will get the improvement indexes circled in the corresponding empty cells of Table 10.15. The positive indexes in the Flint/Chicago, Milwaukee/Detroit, and Gary/Detroit cells indicate that the direct expense of transporting a suit over each of these routes exceeds the cost savings from the shipment. Consequently, Tyler would only increase costs by shipping suits over such routes.

On the other hand, Table 10.15 shows that the Milwaukee/Minneapolis cell has an improvement index of − $3. This negative value means that the cost savings from transporting a suit over such a route are $3 more than the direct expense of the shipment. In other words, Tyler could reduce the northwest corner solution's $6700 total cost a net $3 for each suit shipped over the currently unused Milwaukee-to-Minneapolis route.

Moreover, notice that Table 10.15 provides the same circled numbers as Table 10.13. Such a result is not a coincidence. Indeed, it demonstrates that the modified distribution and stepping stone methods give identical improvement indexes. After all, both approaches perform the same evaluation process—only in different ways. In large-scale applications, however, the MODI method usually requires fewer and less complex calculations than the stepping stone approach. Table 10.16 summarizes the stepping stone and modified distribution methods of evaluating a transportation solution.

Table 10.16 Evaluating a Transportation Solution

Stepping Stone Method	Modified Distribution (MODI) Method
1. Identify the closed path for each unused route in the transportation network. This path begins with the corresponding empty cell in the transportation table and moves in horizontal and vertical directions from one filled cell to another until it returns to the starting point.	1. Set up the equation $U_i + V_j = C_{ij}$ for each *filled* cell in the transportation table. In this equation, U_i = the cost savings associated with source i, V_j = the cost savings for the destination j, and C_{ij} = the cost of allocating one unit to the filled cell. The result is a simultaneous system of equations.
2. For each closed path, put a plus sign $(+)$ in the empty cell and a minus sign $(-)$ in the first filled cell on a corner of the path.	2. Identify the U_i or V_j that appears in the most equations of the system formed in step 1.
3. Alternate plus and minus signs in sequence for the remainder of the filled cells on the corners of the path in step 2.	3. Set the most frequent U_i or V_j variable equal to zero.
4. Sum the unit transportation costs for the plus $(+)$ cells of the path in step 2.	4. Use the system of equations formed in step 1 to solve for the other U_i and V_j variables.
5. Sum the unit transportation costs for the minus $(-)$ cells of the path in step 2.	5. Calculate the improvement index $C_{ij} - U_i - V_j$ for each *empty* cell in the transportation table.
6. Calculate the improvement index for each closed path by subtracting the sum in step 5 from the sum in step 4.	6. In a minimization problem, the current solution can be improved as long as at least one unused transportation route has a negative improvement index.
7. In a minimization problem, the current solution can be improved as long as at least one unused transportation route has a negative improvement index.	

IMPROVING THE SOLUTION Tables 10.13 and 10.15 both show that the Milwaukee/Minneapolis cell has the improvement index with the largest negative value. In fact, it is the only empty cell in these tables with a negative index. Such a condition means that a shipment over the currently unused Milwaukee-to-Minneapolis route will lead to the greatest possible reduction in the northwest corner solution's total transportation cost. It also illustrates the following important principle: *In a minimization problem, management can better the current solution the most by utilizing the unused transportation route with the largest negative improvement index.* When two or more empty cells meet this test, the decision maker can break the tie arbitrarily.

Tables 10.13 and 10.15 therefore indicate that Tyler can best improve the northwest corner solution by utilizing the Milwaukee-to-Minneapolis route. Furthermore, these tables show that each suit shipped over this route will reduce total transportation cost a net $3. Since the company still wants to minimize such cost, management should transport as many suits as possible over this route.

Each suit reallocated to the Milwaukee-to-Minneapolis route will create the pattern of changes given by the closed path in Table 10.17. Note that a closed path will be required regardless of whether the modified distribution or stepping stone method is used in the evaluation process. If

Table 10.17 Milwaukee-to-Minneapolis Closed Path

From Plant Location	To Warehouse Location			Plant Supply (Suits per Month)
	Chicago	Minneapolis	Detroit	
Milwaukee	$2 1000 − 1 = 999	$4 +1	$5	1000
Gary	$1 500 + 1 = 501	$6 300 − 1 = 299	$2	800
Flint	$4	$7 200	$1 1000	1200
Warehouse Demand (Suits per Month)	1500	500	1000	3000

management uses the MODI approach, however, it needs the loop only for the empty cell with the most desirable improvement index. On the other hand, in the stepping stone method, the decision maker must trace a closed path for every unused route in the transportation network.

According to the closed path in Table 10.17, each suit shipped along the Milwaukee-to-Minneapolis route takes away a suit from the Milwaukee-to-Chicago and Gary-to-Minneapolis channels. Moreover, Tyler is currently transporting 1000 suits from Milwaukee to Chicago but only 300 over the Gary-to-Minneapolis route. As a result, management should reallocate no more than 300 suits from these currently utilized channels to the Milwaukee-to-Minneapolis route. Otherwise, the company will have to take away more suits than are available along the Gary-to-Minneapolis route.

In making the reallocation, management must also trace the pattern of changes prescribed by the closed path in Table 10.17. That is, the company must add 300 suits on the Milwaukee-to-Minneapolis route, subtract 300 suits from the Milwaukee-to-Chicago shipment, add 300 suits to the Gary-to-Chicago allocation, and subtract 300 suits along the Gary-to-Minneapolis channel. Otherwise, the company will violate one or more of the plant supply and warehouse demand requirements.

By making the prescribed changes, Tyler will obtain the revised solution

Table 10.18 Tyler's Revised Transportation Solution

Route		Suits Shipped per Month	Transportation Cost per Suit	Suits Shipped × Transportation Cost per Suit
From	To	(X_{ij})	($)	($)
Milwaukee	Chicago	$X_{11} = 700$	2	$700 \times 2 = 1400$
Milwaukee	Minneapolis	$X_{12} = 300$	4	$300 \times 4 = 1200$
Milwaukee	Detroit	$X_{13} = 0$	5	$0 \times 5 = 0$
Gary	Chicago	$X_{21} = 800$	1	$800 \times 1 = 800$
Gary	Minneapolis	$X_{22} = 0$	6	$0 \times 6 = 0$
Gary	Detroit	$X_{23} = 0$	2	$0 \times 2 = 0$
Flint	Chicago	$X_{31} = 0$	4	$0 \times 4 = 0$
Flint	Minneapolis	$X_{32} = 200$	7	$200 \times 7 = 1400$
Flint	Detroit	$X_{33} = 1000$	1	$1000 \times 1 = 1000$

Total transportation cost = $5800

Table 10.19 Improving a Transportation Solution

1. Identify the unused transportation route that leads to the largest improvement in the value of the objective.
2. Identify the closed path corresponding to this route.
3. Identify the *smallest* amount for the filled cells in a minus position along the closed path.
4. Allocate that amount according to the directions of the closed path. That is, add the amount to cells in a plus position and subtract the amount from cells in a minus position along the path. The result is a revised transportation solution.

listed in Table 10.18. As the table shows, the company now ships 300 suits over the previously unused Milwaukee-to-Minneapolis route. Since such a route has an improvement index of $-$3, the total cost of this revised solution should then be

$$300 \times (-\$3) = -\$900$$

of $900 less than before. Indeed, a comparison of Tables 10.18 and 10.4 demonstrates that the revised solution, $Z = \$5800$, is $900 below the corresponding expense of $6700 from the northwest corner distribution pattern.

Table 10.19 summarizes the procedure for improving a transportation solution. The procedure is equivalent to the pivoting process in the

Table 10.20 Tyler's Optimal Transportation Solution

From Plant Location	To Warehouse Location			Plant Supply (Suits per Month)
	Chicago	Minneapolis	Detroit	
Milwaukee	$2 500	$4 500	$5 ($6)	1000
Gary	$1 800	$6 ($3)	$2 ($4)	800
Flint	$4 200	$7 ($1)	$1 1000	1200
Warehouse Demand (Suits per Month)	1500	500	1000	3000

simplex method of linear programming. In particular, the original distribution pattern corresponds to a basic feasible solution in the simplex procedure. Thus, utilizing the unused transportation route with the best improvement index represents the process of bringing into the basis the nonbasic variable with the most desirable $C_j - Z_j$ value. Furthermore, reallocating the smallest quantity in a minus position along the closed path is analogous to the process of removing from the basis the basic variable with the smallest nonnegative trade ratio. Finally, the resulting revised distribution pattern corresponds to another basic feasible solution in the simplex procedure.

FINDING THE OPTIMAL SOLUTION At this point, Tyler must use either the stepping stone or MODI method to evaluate the revised transportation solution (Table 10.18). If management does this, it will find that this solution can be improved by utilizing the currently unused Flint-to-Chicago route. Moreover, by applying the principles outlined in Table 10.19, the company will obtain the second revised transportation solution presented in Table 10.20.

As you can see, each empty cell in Table 10.20 has a positive improvement index (circled number). These indexes indicate that Tyler would only increase costs by shipping suits over any of the currently unused (Milwaukee-to-Detroit, Gary-to-Minneapolis, Gary-to-Detroit, or Flint-to-Minneapolis) transportation routes. Thus, the distribution pattern given in Table 10.20 must represent the company's minimum-cost solution.

This result demonstrates the following important principle: *In a minimization problem, a solution is optimal when the improvement index for each*

Table 10.21 Finding an Optimal Transportation Solution

> 1. Use the procedures outlined in Table 10.10 to develop an initial solution.
> 2. Utilize the principles outlined in Table 10.16 to evaluate the current transportation solution. If improvement is possible, go to step 3.
> 3. Use the procedure listed in Table 10.19 to improve the current transportation solution.
> 4. Repeat steps 2 ad 3 until you find the optimal solution. In a minimization problem, a solution is optimal when the improvement index for each unused transportation route is greater than or equal to zero.

unused transportation route is greater than or equal to zero. Table 10.21 summarizes the procedure for finding such an optimum.

Compare Tables 10.8 and 10.20. Note that the second revision of the northwest corner solution (Table 10.20) gives the same distribution pattern as the Vogel approximation recommendation (Table 10.8). Recall that Table 10.20 depicts the company's best product shipment plan. In this case, then, the VAM answer detailed in Table 10.9 gives the optimal solution to Tyler's transportation problem.

DECISION CONSIDERATIONS

There are several special conditions that can occur in transportation situations, including problems with unbalanced supply and demand, prohibited routes, a maximization objective, degenerate solutions, and multiple optima. In this section we will see how to identify and deal with such conditions. We will also see how transportation problems can be solved with the aid of a computer, examine the assumptions of the solution methodology, and consider some important managerial applications.

UNBALANCED SUPPLY AND DEMAND

In Example 10.1, Tyler's total plant supply of 3000 suits per month is exactly equal to the total warehouse demand. But such balance is unlikely in practice. Companies often maintain an excess supply to prepare for potential raw-material shortages, strikes, or unforeseen demand. On the other hand, favorable economic conditions, changes in customer preferences, and decreased competition can lead to an excess in total demand over total supply.

The transportation solution methodology, however, requires the total source supply to exactly equal the total destination demand. To use this methodology, then, the decision maker first must eliminate any imbalance between total supply and total demand. Fortunately, there is an easy way to do this without changing the basic structure of the problem.

Excess Supply   Consider Example 10.2.

EXAMPLE 10.2 Automobile Distribution

Gem Enterprises has created a new automobile: the Jetstream. The car is produced in three plants and sold through three major franchise dealerships throughout the United States.

Annual plant supplies and franchise demands are given in Table 10.22, while the costs of transporting a car from each plant to each dealership are given in Table 10.23. Gem

wants to minimize the total cost of transporting the Jetstream. How many cars should be shipped from each plant to each franchise dealership?

Table 10.22 Annual Plant Supplies and Franchise Demands for Gem Enterprises

Cars Supplied		Cars Demanded	
Plant	Cars per Year	Franchise	Cars per Year
P_1	3000	F_1	10,000
P_2	7000	F_2	1,000
P_3	5000	F_3	2,000
Total supply 15,000		Total demand 13,000	

Table 10.23 Gem's Transportation Costs

From Plant	To Franchise		
	F_1	F_2	F_3
P_1	$250	$300	$200
P_2	$100	$200	$350
P_3	$300	$100	$50

In Example 10.2, Gem's total plant supply is $15,000 - 13,000 = 2000$ cars more than the total franchise demand. To account for this super-fluity, the decision maker can create a fictitious franchise destination that demands the exact excess supply of 2000 automobiles. Such a destination is known as a **dummy demand point**.

Since the dummy is imaginary, there actually will be no shipments to this point. Thus, it really costs nothing to transport a car to the fictitious franchise. Consequently, the decision maker should assign a transporta-tion cost of $0 per car to each dummy route.

Table 10.24 Gem's Transportation Table

From Plant	To Franchise Dealership				Plant Supply (Cars per Year)
	F_1	F_2	F_3	Dummy	
P_1	$250	$300	$200	$0	3,000
P_2	$100	$200	$350	$0	7,000
P_3	$300	$100	$50	$0	5,000
Franchise Demand (Cars per Year)	10,000	1000	2000	2000	15,000

By incorporating these considerations into the problem formulation process, Gem will obtain Table 10.24. You can see that the dummy demand point is depicted as a franchise column in Gem's transportation table. Each cell in this column will give the number of cars that will be transported from the corresponding plant to the dummy franchise. In other words, each of these cells represents an unused plant supply. Hence, the cells are equivalent to the slack variables in ordinary linear programming. As with a slack variable, each dummy route is assigned a shipment cost of $0 per car in the upper right-hand corner of the matching cell in Table 10.24.

After balancing total demand and total supply in this manner, management can use the conventional methodologies outlined in Tables 10.10, 10.16, 10.19, and 10.21 to determine the best transportation solution. In the process, the dummy franchise will be treated like any other demand destination. Moreover, the quantity shipped to a dummy destination is interpreted as the corresponding source's supply that cannot be economically utilized under current conditions.

Excess Demand   Now consider Example 10.3.

EXAMPLE 10.3 A Purchase Decision

Omnibus Hardware sells two main groups of products: interior and exterior items. The items are supplied by three manufacturers, and each sells both types of products. Omnibus has a monthly demand of 4000 units for interior equipment and 3000 units for exterior items. Recent union practices and economic conditions have limited the manufacturers' supplies to the amounts given in Table 10.25. The average per-unit purchase costs are given in Table 10.26.

Omnibus wants to determine how many of each product it should purchase from each manufacturer. The objective is to minimize the total purchase cost.

Table 10.25 Manufacturers' Supplies

Manufacturer	Units Supplied This Month
Olex	2200
Tilet	2500
Zanc	1300
Total supply	6000

Table 10.26 Purchase Costs for Interior and Exterior Items

Product	Manufacturer		
	Olex	Tilet	Zanc
Interior	$2	$3	$1
Exterior	$4	$3	$6

In this problem, there again is a physical movement of merchandise (hardware items) from various supply sources (manufacturers). However, the demand destinations are now product (exterior and interior) categories rather than geographic locations. Moreover, the focus is on purchase costs instead of transportation costs. Still, the situation can be treated as a transportation problem.

There is only one complication. In Example 10.3, the 4000 + 3000 = 7000 unit total demand is 1000 units greater than the manufacturers' total 6000-unit supply. To account for this superfluity, management can create a fictitious manufacturing source that will supply the exact excess demand for 1000 hardware items. Such a source is referred to as a **dummy supply point**.

Since the dummy is imaginary, there actually will be no shipments from this point. Therefore, it really will cost nothing to purchase a hardware item from the fictitious manufacturer. As a result, the decision maker should assign a purchase cost of $0 per unit to each dummy route.

By incorporating these considerations into the problem formulation process, Omnibus will obtain Table 10.27. You can see that the dummy

Table 10.27 Omnibus's Transportation Table

| From Manufacturer | To Product | | Manufacturer's Supply (Units per Month) |
	Interior	Exterior	
Olex	$2	$4	2200
Tilet	$3	$3	2500
Zanc	$1	$6	1300
Dummy	$0	$0	1000
Product Demand (Units per Month)	4000	3000	7000

supply point is portrayed as a manufacturer row in Omnibus's transportation table. Each cell in this row will give the number of corresponding hardware items that will be purchased from the dummy manufacturer. That is, each of these cells represents an unsatisfied demand. Thus, the cells are equivalent to the slack variables in ordinary linear programming. As with a slack variable, each dummy route is assigned a purchase cost of $0 per unit.

After balancing total demand and total supply in this manner, management can use the conventional transportation methodologies to find the minimum-cost solution. In the process, the dummy manufacturer will be treated like any other supply source. Furthermore, the amount purchased from the dummy source is interpreted as the corresponding product's demand that cannot be economically satisfied with the currently available resources.

PROHIBITED ROUTES In practice, it may not be possible or desirable to transport merchandise over one or more routes. This situation may result from consumer or management preferences, carrier strikes, poor weather conditions, road restrictions, or government regulations. Such prohibitions can also arise in transportation-type problems that do not involve the physical shipment of merchandise from one geographic location to another. Example 10.4 illustrates.

EXAMPLE 10.4 A Job Order Problem

The Pamphlet Printing Company has three orders for single-page advertising leaflets. Order A calls for 30,000 copies, order B for 20,000, and order C for 30,000. The company has two presses available. Each press can produce 40,000 copies per day. The variable costs (per thousand) in running the orders on the various presses are given in Table 10.28. Management's preventive maintenance policy prohibits the use of press 1 on the jobs required by order B or the use of press 2 on the jobs required by order C. Pamphlet wants to know how many leaflets of each type it should print on each press. The objective is to minimize cost.

Table 10.28 Pamphlet's Costs per Thousand Leaflets

	Order		
Press	A	B	C
1	$4	—	$8
2	$6	$3	—

Example 10.4 involves an allocation of job requests to printing presses rather than a physical movement of merchandise over shipping routes. As a result, the supply sources and demand destinations are no longer geographic locations. Instead, the job requests are completed by the presses to satisfy the demands from the advertising orders. Also, the focus is on printing costs rather than transportation costs. Nevertheless, the situation can be treated as a transportation problem.

There is only one complication. As Example 10.4 indicates, the preventive maintenance policy prohibits the use of press 1 on any B order or the use of press 2 for a C request. Hence, Pamphlet must devise a method that will exclude such unacceptable allocations from the recommended job order solution. Management can do this by allocating a very large per-unit cost to each prohibited allocation in the problem. Although any mammoth number would work, it is customary to use the symbol M for this purpose.

By incorporating these considerations into the problem formulation process, Pamphlet will obtain Table 10.29, where the prohibited allocations (press 1/order B and press 2/order C) are portrayed as cells. Such an approach is equivalent to the use of artificial variables in linear programming. Moreover, as with an artificial variable, each prohibited allocation is assigned M per thousand-copy printing cost.

At this point, Pamphlet can use the conventional transportation methodologies to find the minimum-cost printing plan. In the process, the

Table 10.29 Pamphlet's Transportation Table

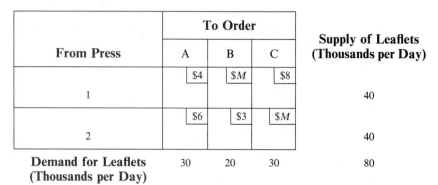

From Press	To Order			Supply of Leaflets (Thousands per Day)
	A	B	C	
1	$4	$M	$8	40
2	$6	$3	$M	40
Demand for Leaflets (Thousands per Day)	30	20	30	80

symbol M must be interpreted as a number so large that M less any cost still is approximately equal to M. Thus, an empty cell with an M per-unit printing cost will always generate the largest VAM penalties and result in undesirable stepping stone or MODI improvement indexes. As a result, such a cell (prohibited allocation) can never be part of the optimal solution to the problem.

MAXIMIZATION The objective in Examples 10.1 through 10.4 was to minimize cost. Nevertheless, there are many situations in which the decision maker wants to maximize profit, output, or some other measure of return. Example 10.5 illustrates.

EXAMPLE 10.5 Consumer Protection

Nardi's Sardis is a nonprofit organization that specializes in consumer protection issues. Recently, concerned citizens have brought four cases (labeled 1, 2, 3, and 4) to the attention of the agency. Nardi estimates that case 1 will require 2000 hours per month, case 2 will require 4000 hours per month, case 3 will require 1000 hours per month, and case 4, 3000 hours per month.

Currently, Sardis has three research groups (coded A, B, and C) available to work on these cases. Group A can expend 4000 hours per month, group B can expend 5000 hours per month, and group C can expend 1000 hours per month. Moreover, there are many similarities between the cases. Hence, it will be possible for each group to work on several cases simultaneously.

Assignments are based on an index of job performance. The index is a composite of the following criteria: thoroughness and accuracy of research, selection of appropriate remedial recommendations, and success of implementation. After reviewing personnel records, Nardi and his executive committee assign a rating to each group for each potential case. The rating scale goes from a low of zero to a high of 100 points per hour of effort. Nardi believes that the groups will achieve the ratings depicted in Table 10.30. Nardi wants to determine the staff allocation pattern that will maximize the total job performance index.

Table 10.30 Ratings for Nardi's Sardis by Group and Case

Research Group	Case 1	2	3	4
A	90	70	60	80
B	70	60	80	40
C	20	80	70	60

In Example 10.5, there is an allocation of work effort rather than a physical distribution of merchandise. Also, the supply sources and demand destinations are no longer geographic locations. Instead, the work effort is supplied by the three research groups in response to the demand from the four consumer cases. Moreover, the focus is on a return measure (employee job performance) rather than a cost measure. Still, the situation can be treated as a transportation problem. Indeed, by using the conventional formulation process, Nardi will obtain Table 10.31, where the number in the upper right-hand corner of each cell represents a job performance score.

On the other hand, most of the conventional solution methodologies are designed for transportation problems involving a minimization objective, whereas Nardi wants to maximize the job performance index. Management must therefore adapt the conventional solution methodology to accommodate this maximization objective.

Several methods are available. In general, these approaches either transform the problem from a maximization objective to a minimization objective or modify the procedure for evaluating and improving a transportation solution. Although either approach will work, it is usually easier to convert the objective. Furthermore, the opportunity loss concept offers a convenient vehicle for making this transformation. To see why, we will continue with Nardi's transportation table.

According to the data in the upper right-hand corners of Table 10.31, 90 points is the highest overall rating attainable by any of the research groups. Consequently, such a score gives a standard that Nardi can use to judge job performance. In particular, if management computes the difference between each actual index and the highest overall rating, it will measure the degree to which the corresponding allotments deviate from this standard. These differences, which represent the opportunity costs associated with the matching staff allocations, are calculated in Table 10.32.

Table 10.31 Nardi's Transportation Table

From Research Group	To Case				Supply of Research (Hours per Month)
	1	2	3	4	
A	90	70	60	80	4,000
B	70	60	80	40	5,000
C	20	80	70	60	1,000
Demand for Research (Hours per Month)	2000	4000	1000	3000	10,000

Table 10.32 Opportunity Costs for Nardi's Sardis

Research Group	Case			
	1	2	3	4
A	$90 - 90 = 0$	$90 - 70 = 20$	$90 - 60 = 30$	$90 - 80 = 10$
B	$90 - 70 = 20$	$90 - 60 = 30$	$90 - 80 = 10$	$90 - 40 = 50$
C	$90 - 20 = 70$	$90 - 80 = 10$	$90 - 70 = 20$	$90 - 60 = 30$

Management should then substitute these differences for the corresponding numbers in the upper right-hand corners of the cells in Table 10.31. That is, 0 should replace 90 in the A/1 cell, 10 should replace 80 in the B/3 cell, and so on. In this way, the problem will be expressed in terms of opportunity costs rather than job performance indexes. Since the decision maker must seek the smallest opportunity costs, such a process also transforms the situation from a maximization objective to a minimization objective. Nardi can then use the conventional transportation methodologies to find the optimal staff allocation.

In Nardi's situation, the total demand exactly equals the total supply of research effort. However, the opportunity cost approach is also applicable to maximization problems that involve an imbalance between total supply and demand. In such problems, however, the dummy source or destination must be added *before* the decision maker computes the opportunity costs. Otherwise, the dummy erroneously will appear to have the smallest opportunity costs, and the conventional methodologies may not generate the optimal transportation solution.

Also, Nardi's situation does not involve any prohibited allocations. Nevertheless, such allocations can arise in transportation problems with maximization objectives. In these cases, the decision maker must denote a prohibited allocation by allotting a very large negative $(-M)$ per-unit return to the corresponding cell in the transportation table. Furthermore, the $-M$ allotments must be made *before* the decision maker computes the opportunity costs. Otherwise, the prohibited route erroneously will appear to have a negative opportunity loss, and the conventional methodologies may not generate the optimal transportation solution.

DEGENERACY Example 10.1 dealt with a transportation problem involving three supply (plant) sources and three demand (warehouse) destinations. Reexamining Tables 10.3 and 10.8, you will find that each solution to the problem utilized exactly five transportation routes. That is, the number of filled cells in these transportation tables equals one less than the sum of supply sources and demand destinations. In fact, *a problem with m supply sources and n demand destinations will usually have a solution that fills $m + n - 1$ cells in the transportation table.* This condition is equivalent to having a basic feasible solution in the simplex method of linear programming.

In many cases, however, the conventional methodologies will generate a solution that fills fewer than $m + n - 1$ cells in the transportation table. Furthermore, this condition, which is equivalent to degeneracy in linear programming, can arise either in the initial transportation solution or during the reallocation process. Example 10.6 illustrates.

EXAMPLE 10.6 Tennis Instruction

Leaftown's recreation department hires local amateur and professional players on a part-time basis to conduct its tennis education program. Ace Serve is available for 20 hours per week, Julie Baseline for 40 hours, and Chris King for 40 hours. Three classes are offered at municipal courts: beginning, intermediate, and advanced. Leaftown plans to offer 50 hours of beginning classes per week, 20 hours of intermediate classes, and 30 hours of advanced instruction. The cost of offering each class depends on the instructor's relative teaching skill, class size, and other related factors. These costs are summarized in Table 10.33. Leaftown wants to allocate instructors to classes in the way that minimizes the total cost of offering the tennis education program.

Table 10.33 Costs of Tennis Classes in Leaftown

Instructor	Hourly Cost of Offering Each Class		
	Beginning	Intermediate	Advanced
Ace Serve	$5	$4	$2
Julie Baseline	$3	$6	$1
Chris King	$2	$3	$10

Example 10.6 involves an allocation of instruction rather than a physical distribution of merchandise. Also, the supply sources and demand destinations are not geographic locations. Instead, the education is supplied by the three instructors in response to the demand from the three classes. In addition, the focus is on instruction costs rather than transportation costs. Nevertheless, the situation can be treated as a transportation problem. Indeed, by using the customary formulation process and the methodologies outlined in Tables 10.10, 10.16, and 10.19, Leaftown will eventually obtain the transportation solution presented in Table 10.34.

Leaftown's problem involves $m = 3$ supply sources (instructors) and $n = 3$ demand destinations (classes). Thus, each solution should fill $m + n - 1 = 3 + 3 - 1 = 5$ cells in the corresponding transportation table. As Table 10.34 demonstrates, however, the city's second transportation solution has only four filled cells. Consequently, this second solution is degenerate.

Even though a degenerate solution will usually be feasible (satisfy all demand and supply requirements), it causes special difficulties for the conventional transportation methodologies. In particular, such a solution does not provide the number of filled cells necessary to identify all relevant stepping stone paths or MODI cost savings (U_i and V_j values). As a result, it will be impossible to calculate the pertinent improvement indexes.

In Table 10.34, for instance, the allocation of 20 hours to the Ace/intermediate cell simultaneously satisfies Ace Serve's supply and the intermediate class demand. In fact, that is why Leaftown's second transportation solution is degenerate. Consequently, the city will not have enough data to calculate the improvement indexes for the Ace/beginning, Ace/advanced, Julie/intermediate, and Chris/intermediate empty cells. Therefore, management will not be able to evaluate this second (degenerate) solution.

Fortunately, there is a relatively simple way to handle the difficulty. The decision maker can artificially create enough additional filled cells to resolve the degeneracy in the transportation solution. This task is accom-

Table 10.34 Leaftown's Second Transportation Solution

From Instructor	To Class			Supply of Instruction (Hours per Week)
	Beginning	Intermediate	Advanced	
Ace Serve	$5	$4 20	$2	20
Julie Baseline	$3 10	$6	$1 30	40
Chris King	$2 40	$3	$10	40
Demand for Instruction (Hours per Week)	50	20	30	100

Table 10.35 Leaftown's Nondegenerate Second Transportation Solution

From Instructor	To Class			Supply of Instruction (Hours per Week)
	Beginning	Intermediate	Advanced	
Ace Serve	$5	$4 20	$2 ε	20
Julie Baseline	$3 10	$6	$1 30	40
Chris King	$2 40	$3	$10	40
Demand for Instruction (Hours per Week)	50	20	30	100

plished by allotting some small quantity, denoted by ε (epsilon), to the empty cells that provide the relevant improvement index data.

Leaftown, for example, can avoid degeneracy in the second transportation solution by allotting ε hours to the Ace/beginning, Ace/advanced, Julie/intermediate, or Chris/intermediate cell in Table 10.34. Although any one of these empty cells will suffice, the Ace/advanced cell has the smallest per-unit cost ($2) among the four. Hence, the decision maker may prefer to utilize this cell and obtain the transportation solution presented in Table 10.35. As you can see, this table has five filled cells. Thus, Leaftown's second transportation solution is no longer degenerate.

After resolving the degeneracy in this manner, management can use the conventional transportation methodologies to find the minimum-cost tennis education program. In the process, ε is interpreted as a quantity large enough to be considered an allocation but sufficiently minuscule to be treated as a zero in any computation. When improving a transportation solution, then, the decision maker must regard ε as the smallest of the amounts in a minus position along the pertinent closed path. On the other hand, an ε allocation is equivalent to adding or subtracting zero units from the corresponding transportation table. Furthermore, there will be a $0 cost of allocating ε units.

MULTIPLE OPTIMA   As with any ordinary linear programming situation, a transportation problem may involve more than one optimal solution. Example 10.7 illustrates.

EXAMPLE 10.7 Bus Scheduling

A small-town municipally operated bus line services three main areas designated as zones A, B, and C. There are two main service facilities: the downtown and uptown terminals. Each route involves a particular operating cost, and there is a different number of buses available from each terminal and demanded at each zone. The bus line's prime goal is to minimize the cost of providing the necessary service. However, there are also political and social considerations. Hence, if several alternatives have the same minimum total cost, the bus line would prefer a scheduling pattern that provides the maximum number of uptown buses for zone B.

After much deliberation, the management staff realizes that the situation can be treated as a transportation problem.

Moreover, by using the conventional transportation methodologies, management develops the solution shown in Table 10.36. Each number in the upper right-hand corner of every cell represents the cost of operating a bus along the corresponding route. Also, the circled numbers give the improvement indexes associated with each empty cell in the solution.

Table 10.36 Optimal Bus-Scheduling Solution

From Terminal	To Zone			Supply of Service (Buses)
	A	B	C	
Downtown	$200 10	$300 30	$200 20	60
Uptown	$200 40	$300 ⓈО	$300 Ⓢ100	40
Demand for Service (Buses)	50	30	20	100

Table 10.37 Alternative Optimal Bus-Scheduling Solution

From Terminal	To Zone			Supply of Service (Buses)
	A	B	C	
Downtown	$200 40	$300 ($0)	$200 20	60
Uptown	$200 10	$300 30	$300 ($100)	40
Demand for Service (Buses)	50	30	20	100

In Table 10.36, every empty cell has a nonnegative improvement index (circled number). These indexes indicate that the town cannot decrease operating costs by sending buses over any of the currently unused routes. Therefore, the distribution pattern given in this figure portrays a minimum-cost bus schedule.

Nevertheless, the currently unused bus route between the uptown terminal and zone B has a $0 improvement index. The situation is equivalent to having a $C_j - Z_j = 0$ for a nonbasic variable in the simplex method. It means that the town will not change total costs by allocating buses to such a route. Furthermore, the distribution pattern given in Table 10.36 is an optimal solution. As a result, the $0 improvement index implies that there must be alternative ways to minimize the total operating cost of the bus service.

To find one of the alternative optimal solutions, management should treat the empty uptown/zone B cell as the unused transportation route with the best improvement index. Management can then use the procedure outlined in Table 10.19 to "improve" the current optimal (Table 10.36) distribution pattern. By doing this, the decision maker will obtain the solution shown in Table 10.37. The circled numbers in the table again give the improvement indexes associated with the empty cells in the solution.

Notice that every empty cell in Table 10.37 has a nonnegative improvement index (circled number). Hence, this table, as well as Table 10.36, portrays an optimal distribution pattern. Put another way, Tables 10.36 and 10.37 identify alternative minimum-cost bus schedules.

There may be many considerations that management is unable or unwilling to express explicitly as costs or constraints. Yet these considerations may be important in choosing among solutions that have the same minimum costs. The existence of alternative optima provides management with greater flexibility in selecting and using resources.

The municipal bus line, for example, has political and social considerations that are not directly incorporated into operating costs, terminal supply requirements, or zone demand requirements. However, if several alternatives have identical optimal total costs, management will prefer the scheduling pattern that provides the maximum number of uptown buses for zone B. The distribution pattern given in Table 10.37 provides better service (more buses) over the uptown-to-zone B route than the solution portrayed in Table 10.36. Thus, management will prefer the bus schedule in Table 10.37 to the schedule in Table 10.36.

COMPUTER ANALYSIS Practical transportation problems often involve hundreds of supply sources and demand destinations. In such situations, it would be cumbersome and time-consuming to perform the transportation calculations by hand. Fortunately, management scientists have developed canned, or prewritten, computer packages designed to solve these large-scale transportation problems. One of the packages, **TRANLP**, is available on the California State University and College System (CSUC) computer system. Figure 10.2 illustrates how this program can be used to solve the bus-scheduling problem in Example 10.7.

The decision maker executes the program with the LIB command. This command instructs the computer that the program is contained in a library file. Next, the program asks for the name of the library program. The appropriate response is TRANLP.

At this point, the computer notes that TRANLP is a system for transportation problems and asks if the decision maker wants instructions. Then it begins requesting input data. First, the decision maker types the supplies available at each source (row) in the transportation table. These supplies, 60 for row 1 (the downtown terminal) and 40 for row 2 (the uptown terminal), are inputted after the question (?) prompt. Then the computer requests the demands required at every destination (column) in the transportation table. These demands, 50 for column 1 (zone A), 30 for column 2 (zone B), and 20 for column 3 (zone C), again are inputted after the question (?) prompt.

Next, TRANLP asks for the type of output desired, the nature of the objective function, and the cost data. The answers once more are typed after the appropriate question (?) prompts. Figure 10.2, for instance, gives only the final solution (type 1 output). It also indicates that the bus line wants to minimize the objective function (total operating cost). Moreover, the relevant cost data for each row in the transportation table are entered from the keyboard (KB). Operating costs per bus from the downtown (row 1) terminal, for example, are $200 to zone A, $300 to zone B, and $200 to zone C. Hence, these values are inputted after the row 1 question (?) prompt.

Next, the computer requests an initial solution code. As Figure 10.2 demonstrates, the decision maker responds by entering the number 1, 2, or

Figure 10.2 TRANLP Solution of the Bus Scheduling Problem

```
LIB

Name of Library Program?  TRANLP

T R A N L P

A  SYSTEM FOR TRANSPORTATION PROBLEMS

DO YOU WANT INSTRUCTIONS?  NO


TYPE IN DATA FOR THE FOLLOWING ITEMS--
SEPARATE EACH ITEM BY A COMMA OR A LINE FEED.

NUMBER OF ROWS AND COLUMNS?  2, 3
INPUT SUPPLY DATA FOR EACH ROW:
? 60,40
INPUT DEMAND DATA FOR EACH COLUMN:
? 50,30,20

PRINT CODE:  TYPE 1 FOR FINAL SOLUTION ONLY.
             TYPE 2 FOR INPUT DATA AND FINAL SOLUTION.
             TYPE 3 FOR FULL PRINTOUT AND SOLUTION TRACE.
1, 2, OR 3?  1
IS THE OBJECTIVE FUNCTION TO BE MINIMIZED?  YES

THE COST DATA MATRIX MUST BE ENTERED BY ROW!
WILL YOU ENTER COST DATA MATRIX FROM FILE OR KB:?  KB:
ENTER COST DATA MATRIX BY ROW:
  ROW  1?  200,300,200
  ROW  2?  200,300,300

INITIAL SOLUTION:
       TYPE 1 FOR NORTHWEST CORNER METHOD.
       TYPE 2 FOR COLUMN OPTIMIZATION.
       TYPE 3 IF YOU WILL INPUT INITIAL SOLUTION.
1, 2, OR 3?  1

FINAL SOLUTION MATRIX
ROW/COL              1          2          3

  1                40.0        0.0       20.0

  2                10.0       30.0        0.0

OBJECTIVE FUNCTION =     23000

DO YOU HAVE ANOTHER PROBLEM?  NO
```

3 after the question (?) prompt. In this case, for instance, the user asks TRANLP to find the initial solution by the northwest corner method. The computer than prints the final solution.

According to Figure 10.2, the bus line should send 40 buses over the route from the downtown (row 1) terminal to zone A (column 1). In addition, the bus line should allocate 0 buses from downtown to zone B, 20 buses from downtown to zone C, 10 buses from uptown to zone A, 30 buses from uptown to zone B, and 0 buses from uptown to zone C. Furthermore, this solution, which is identical to the distribution pattern shown in Table 10.37, minimizes total operating costs at $23,000.

LIMITATIONS   The transportation problems in Examples 10.1 through 10.7 all have the same fundamental characteristics. These characteristics, which are summarized in Table 10.38, limit the applicability of the transportation model. The decision maker must know the exact source supplies, destination demands, and per-unit transportation costs to properly implement this model. Yet these cost, demand, and supply parameters typically are based on estimates or forecasts. Moreover, changes in consumer tastes, shipping difficulties, and other unforeseen circumstances can create substantial inaccuracies in these estimates. As a result, the conventional transportation methodology may not provide an optimal or even "good" solution for such uncertain or risky distribution situations.

Other limitations arise from the linear nature of the transportation model. Specifically, the model assumes that the per-unit transportation cost remains constant, regardless of the quantity shipped over a route. Such an assumption, however, rules out the possibility of a quantity discount or other similar inducement. In addition, the methodology presumes that each route's per-unit transportation cost will be unaffected by the shipments made over alternative channels. Yet some carriers offer discounts or require premiums for utilizing various channel or route combinations. In these cases, the per-unit transportation costs will be influenced by the distribution pattern. Thus, the conventional methodology may not provide an optimal or even "good" solution to these nonlinear transportation problems.

In spite of these limitations, management scientists have reported many successful applications of the transportation methodology. For example, Beilby [3] and T. K. Zierer and others [20] show how the methodology can be used to solve the typical problem of transporting merchandise between sources and destinations. Moreover, the transportation model has been flexible enough to accommodate a wide variety of other situations. Indeed, the approach may be applicable whenever the supply of an item is being used to meet a specified demand.

Table 10.38 Characteristics of the Transportation Problem

1. There is a finite number of supply sources and demand destinations.
2. Each source has a known supply and each destination has a known demand.
3. A decision variable represents the quantity transported from a source to a destination.
4. Each decision variable makes a constant and independent contribution to the objective.
5. The total quantity transported from each source to a particular destination will be at least as large as the demand required at the destination.
6. The total quantity transported to each destination from a particular source will not exceed the supply available at the source.

Examples 10.3 through 10.7 have provided some insight into these nontypical applications. In addition, O. Aarvik and P. Randolph [1] use the methodology to determine transmission fees in an electrical power network. Also, F. Glover and others [9] and P. Gray [10] utilize the approach to allocate raw materials among various production tasks, while P. Hansen and L. Kaufman [11] and R. F. Love and L. Yerex [15] show how the model is useful in selecting facility locations. Other interesting implementations are reported by A. Dutta and others [6], S. W. Hess [13], and M. Segal and D. B. Weinberger [18].

ASSIGNMENT In many distribution situations, the resources available from each supply source and the tasks required at each demand destination are indivisible. That is, each resource can be assigned to one and only one task, while each job must be completed by one and only one resource. Example 10.8 illustrates.

EXAMPLE 10.8 Maintenance Dispatching

The maintenance department of a small manufacturing firm has three available repairpersons: Tom, Alice, and Sam. There are three jobs that must be done in a given time period. Owing to the nature and location of the jobs, only one person can be assigned to one job at any given time. Since each repairperson has different skills and each job requires different tasks, there is a different per-hour cost of assigning each person to each job. The relevant costs are presented in Table 10.39. The maintenance manager wants to establish the maintenance plan that will minimize total repair cost.

Table 10.39 Job Costs in Maintenance-Dispatching Problem

| | Job Cost per Hour | | |
Repairperson	A	B	C
Tom	$3	$6	$10
Alice	$5	$12	$7
Sam	$8	$4	$2

NATURE OF THE PROBLEM According to Example 10.8, the manufacturing firm has a demand for one and only one repairperson at each of the three unique jobs. Management can satisfy these demands by assigning one and only one repairperson to each job. Several alternative personnel assignments, each with a specific per-hour cost, can be used to perform the necessary maintenance. These alternatives are depicted in Figure 10.3, where each node (circle) represents a supply source (repairperson) or demand destination (job). The arcs (lines) reflect the flow (movement of repairpersons to jobs) that will occur through the maintenance system. The number above each node depicts the supply available at that source or the demand emanating from that destination. As you can see, there is exactly one repairperson available at each source and precisely one job required at each destination. Every value on an arc identifies the cost of assigning the repairperson to the corresponding job. Because management must determine the least costly way of making the assignments, such a situation is known as an **assignment problem**.

Compare the assignment diagram in Figure 10.3 with the transportation network in Figure 10.1. Notice that the assignment situation is merely a special case of the transportation problem in which only one unit is supplied from each source and only one unit is demanded at each destination. Therefore, the decision maker can use the conventional transportation methodologies to solve the assignment problem. However, these methodologies typically generate a large number of degenerate solutions when applied to assignment problems. In such cases, the solution process will require numerous iterations that do nothing more than reallocate an ε quantity between empty cells.

Fortunately, the unique nature of the assignment problem makes it possible to use streamlined procedures that provide substantial computational shortcuts over the conventional transportation methodologies. Although the computations differ in each approach, all streamlined procedures utilize a standard table to conveniently record the data and keep track of the calculations. This standard format, which can be called

Figure 10.3 Maintenance Assignment Alternatives

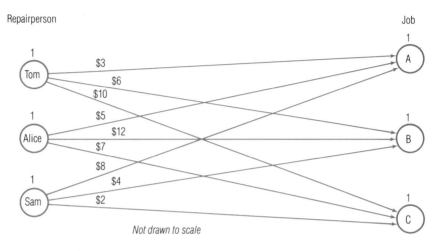

Not drawn to scale

Table 10.40 Maintenance-Dispatching Assignment Table

From Repairperson	To Job		
	A	B	C
Tom	$3	$6	$10
Alice	$5	$12	$7
Sam	$8	$4	$2

Job cost per hour

the **assignment table**, is illustrated with the maintenance-dispatching information in Table 10.40.

Each row in the table represents a supply source (node) and every column a demand destination (node) in the manufacturing firm's assignment network. For example, the second row portrays repairperson Alice, and the third column depicts job C. The cells correspond to the potential assignments (arcs) in the maintenance network. The cell at the intersection of the second row and first column, for instance, corresponds to the possible assignment of Alice to job A. Since the firm has three repairpersons and three jobs, there are $3 \times 3 = 9$ cells (possible assignments) in the table.

Entries in the cells of Table 10.40 give the costs of the corresponding assignments. The entry at the intersection of the second row and first column, for instance, indicates that it costs $5 to assign Alice to job A. Similarly, the entry at the intersection of the third row and second column shows that it costs $4 for Sam to do job B.

In addition, Table 10.40 shows that the number of rows (repairpersons) is exactly equal to the number of columns (jobs). This required balance is a characteristic of the manufacturing firm's maintenance-dispatching problem. Nevertheless, there are cases that involve imbalances between the number of resources (rows) and tasks (columns) in the assignment table. Such cases will be dealt with later in the chapter.

SOLVING THE PROBLEM As Beilby [3] and R. Chandrasekaran and S. S. Rao [5] demonstrate, there are several ways to develop a distribution pattern from the information contained in the assignment table. One method is to list all possible assignment combinations, compare the outcomes, and then select the most preferable combination. Indeed, this enumeration procedure will work very well for problems that involve a small number of potential assignment combinations.

Typical situations, however, have a very large number of possible alternatives. For example, a problem with only ten resources and tasks will require the decision maker to evaluate $10 \times 9 \times 8 \times 7 \times 6 \times 5 \times 4 \times 3 \times 2 \times 1 = 3{,}628{,}800$ possible assignment combinations! Since it is highly impractical to compare so many alternatives, management will need a more systematic solution procedure. One of the most popular approaches is based on the opportunity loss concept originally introduced in chapter 3. To see how this procedure works, let us examine the position of each repairperson and job in the maintenance-dispatching problem.

Resource Penalties Table 10.40 shows that the least expensive assignment for Tom is to job A at $3 per hour. Alternatively, he can be assigned to job B or C. However, it costs $6 for Tom to perform an hour of job B and $10 per hour for C. Therefore, the manufacturing firm will incur an hourly regret, or opportunity loss, of $6 - $3 = $3 if Tom is assigned to job B and $10 - $3 = $7 if he is assigned to job C.

In a minimization problem, then, the resource (row) penalties can be found by subtracting the smallest entry in each row from all costs in that row of the assignment table. Table 10.41 presents these opportunity loss calculations for the three repairpersons in the maintenance-dispatching problem.

By comparing Tables 10.40 and 10.41, you will find that these row opportunity loss computations leave the entries in the same relative positions in each table. In both tables, for example, A is the smallest-cost, B the next smallest-cost, and C the highest-cost job for Tom. Also, each

Table 10.41 Repairperson (Row) Opportunity Loss Table

From Repairperson	To Job		
	A	B	C
Tom	$3 − $3 = $0	$6 − $3 = $3	$10 − $3 = $7
Alice	$5 − $5 = $0	$12 − $5 = $7	$7 − $5 = $2
Sam	$8 − $2 = $6	$4 − $2 = $2	$2 − $2 = $0

Table 10.42 Task (Column) Opportunity Loss Table

From Repairperson	To Job		
	A	B	C
Tom	$0 − $0 = $0	$3 − $2 = $1	$7 − $0 = $7
Alice	$0 − $0 = $0	$7 − $2 = $5	$2 − $0 = $2
Sam	$6 − $0 = $6	$2 − $2 = $0	$0 − $0 = $0

repairperson's least expensive assignment (Tom to A, Alice to A, and Sam to C) involves no regret (a $0 opportunity loss).

Task Penalties   Although Table 10.41 shows the regrets associated with repairperson assignments, it does not account for the job opportunity losses. Nevertheless, the table does provide the data necessary to find such losses.

Consider job B. Table 10.41 shows that the least expensive way to perform job B is with Sam at $2 per hour. Alternatively, the job can be assigned to Alice or Tom. But there is a $7 opportunity loss for Alice to complete an hour of job B and a $3 opportunity loss per hour for Tom. Thus, the manufacturing firm will incur an hourly regret, or opportunity loss, of $7 − $2 = $5 if Alice is assigned to job B and $3 − $2 = $1 if Tom is assigned to job B. In other words, the task (column) penalties can be found by subtracting the smallest entry in each column from all costs in that column of the row opportunity cost table. Table 10.42 presents these penalty computations for the maintenance problem.

Table 10.43 Maintenance Assignments with $0 Penalties

	Job		
Repairperson	A	B	C
Tom	$0	$1	$7
Alice	$0	$5	$2
~~Sam~~	~~$6~~	~~$0~~	~~$0~~

By comparing Tables 10.41 and 10.42, you will find that these column penalty calculations leave the entries in the same relative positions in each table. In both tables, for example, Sam is the least expensive, Tom the next lowest, and Alice the most expensive repairperson to assign to job B. Also, there is a $0 penalty associated with the least costly way to perform each job (A by Tom or Alice, B by Sam, and C by Sam).

Optimality Test   Naturally, management would like to avoid any of these opportunity losses. To do so, however, the manufacturing firm must assign each repairperson to a job that he or she can perform with a $0 penalty. Table 10.42 indicates that job A is the only job Tom can perform with a $0 opportunity loss. Hence, the decision maker may be inclined to assign Tom to job A.

Of course, such a decision will exclude job A as a candidate for any other repairperson. We can depict this fact by drawing a line through A's column in the task opportunity loss table, as shown in Table 10.43.

In addition, Table 10.42 shows that Sam is the only repairperson who can perform job C with a $0 opportunity loss. Therefore, management may be inclined to assign Sam to job C. By so doing, management eliminates Sam as a candidate for any other job assignment. We depict this fact by drawing a line through Sam's row in Table 10.43.

The nature and location of the maintenance jobs require each repairperson to be assigned a separate job. Therefore, the assignment of Tom to job A and Sam to job C will leave Alice as the only repairperson available for the remaining job B. As Table 10.43 demonstrates, however, Tom's and Sam's assignments create two lines that cross out all the $0 penalties in the task opportunity loss table. Consequently, Alice would not be able to perform job B with a $0 penalty.

Management still might be inclined to assign Alice to job B. After all, such a policy would enable the manufacturing firm to assign Tom and Sam to jobs that these repairpersons can perform with $0 penalties.

Nevertheless, Table 10.43 shows that Alice's assignment to job B generates an hourly opportunity loss of $5 for the company.

On the other hand, there are assignments with hourly penalties smaller than $5 available for Alice and job B. Table 10.43 shows that Alice can perform job C with only a $2 hourly regret, while job B can be done by Tom for a $1 per hour opportunity loss. These values indicate that the manufacturing firm will incur less regret if it assigns a repairperson other than Alice to job B. As a result, the maintenance plan suggested by the line pattern in Table 10.43 (Tom to job A, Alice to job B, and Sam to job C) is not the optimal assignment.

These results illustrate the following important principle: *Management will not have an optimal assignment unless the minimum number of lines required to cover all zeros equals the number of rows in the current opportunity loss table.* In Table 10.43, for instance, only two lines are needed to cover all the $0 entries. Yet there are three rows in this table. Consequently, the decision maker has $3 - 2 = 1$ line less than the number required to identify the optimal assignment.

Revision Process Although Table 10.43 will not identify the optimal maintenance plan, it does provide the data necessary to improve the assignment pattern. In particular, the cell entries covered by lines depict the assignments that can be made with $0 opportunity losses (Tom or Alice to job A, and job B or C to Sam). Entries not covered by lines represent the penalties associated with the remaining assignments (Tom or Alice to job B, and job C to Tom or Alice). Since all these remaining elements are positive, the manufacturing firm will incur some opportunity loss in making the remaining assignments. Still, management should try to minimize such penalties.

Table 10.43 shows that the smallest unlined hourly penalty is the $1 associated with the assignment of Tom to job B. Hence, such an allocation is the best candidate for one of the remaining assignments. To encourage the selection of the assignment, management should create a $0 penalty in the Tom/B cell of the current opportunity loss table. Once more, this task can be accomplished by subtracting the $1 penalty from all the opportunity losses in the job B column of Table 10.42. These computations and the resulting impact on other penalties are presented in Table 10.44.

In Table 10.44, the subtraction of $1 from the penalties in the job B column initially leaves a $-$1 opportunity loss in Sam's row. Yet it is impossible for Sam to perform job B with a negative penalty. To avoid this possibility, the decision maker adds a $1 opportunity loss to each penalty in Sam's row.

As Table 10.44 demonstrates, such arithmetic still enables Sam to perform job B for the same $0 penalty that existed before the computations. Moreover, it creates the desired $0 opportunity loss entry in the

Table 10.44 Revised Opportunity Loss Table

From Repairperson	To Job		
	A	B	C
Tom	$0	$1 − $1 = $0	$7 − $1 = $6
Alice	$0	$5 − $1 = $4	$2 − $1 = $1
Sam	$6 + $1 = $7	$0 − $1 = − $1 + $1 = $0	$0 + $1 = − $1 + $1 = $0

Tom/B cell of the table. These calculations, however, eliminate the only $0 penalty in job C's column. To restore this no-regret assignment, management must then subtract the smallest penalty of $1 from the other opportunity losses in job C's column.

A comparison of Table 10.43 with Table 10.44 will reveal another perspective. Notice that the entries in Table 10.44 are found by:

1. Subtracting the smallest penalty ($1) not covered by a line from all unlined opportunity losses in Table 10.43

2. Adding this smallest unlined penalty to every entry at the intersection of any two lines in Table 10.43

3. Leaving the remaining covered entries in Table 10.43 unchanged

Such rules offer a shortcut way of accomplishing the series of opportunity loss adjustments involved in the revision process.

Optimal Assignment   After completing the revision process, the manufacturing firm again should check for an optimal assignment. Table 10.44 indicates that job A is the only job that Alice can perform with a $0 opportunity loss. Therefore, management will be inclined to assign Alice to job A.

Naturally, such a policy excludes job A from any other assignments. We can depict this fact by enclosing the $0 penalty with a square and drawing a line through A's column in the revised opportunity loss table, as shown in Table 10.45. Furthermore, Table 10.44 shows that Sam is the only repairperson who can perform job C with a $0 penalty. Therefore, the manufacturing firm will be inclined to assign Sam to job C. By so doing, the firm excludes Sam from any other assignment. As illustrated in Table 10.46, we can portray this fact by enclosing the $0 penalty with a square and drawing a line through Sam's row.

Table 10.45 Alice to Job A

Repairperson	Job		
	A	B	C
Tom	$0	$0	$6
Alice	[$0]	$4	$1
Sam	$7	$0	$0

Table 10.46 Sam to Job C

Repairperson	Job		
	A	B	C
Tom	$0	$0	$6
Alice	[$0]	$4	$1
Sam	$7	$0	[$0]

According to Table 10.44, these two assignments (Alice to A and Sam to C) leave Tom as the only repairperson who can perform the remaining job B with a $0 penalty. Hence, management will have to assign Tom to job B. In the process, job B is eliminated from any other assignment. We depict this fact in Table 10.47 by enclosing the $0 penalty with a square and then drawing a line though job B's column.

As Table 10.47 demonstrates, the assignments create three lines that cross out all the $0 penalties in Table 10.44. In other words, each of the three repairpersons is assigned to a separate job that he or she can perform with a $0 opportunity loss. Consequently, the maintenance plan suggested by the line pattern in Table 10.47 represents the optimal assignment. By utilizing the line pattern in Table 10.47 and the data from the original assignment table (Table 10.40), management will find that the minimum-cost maintenance plan is as presented in Table 10.48.

Table 10.49 summarizes the procedure to find an optimal assignment. This procedure is based on a theorem developed by the Hungarian mathematician D. Konig. In honor of the nationality of the originator, the approach has come to be known as the **Hungarian method**. It is also called **Flood's technique** and **matrix reduction**.

Table 10.47 Tom to Job B

	Job		
Repairperson	A	B	C
Tom	$0	$0	$6
Alice	$0	$4	$1
Sam	$7	$0	$0

Table 10.48 Minimum-Cost Maintenance Plan

Assignment		Hourly Cost
Repairperson	Job	
Tom	B	$6
Alice	A	$5
Sam	C	$2
Total hourly repair cost = $13		

Table 10.49 Finding an Optimal Assignment

1. Formulate the assignment table.
2. Develop the row penalty cost table. To do so, take the difference between the most preferable entry in each row and every element in that row of the assignment table.
3. Develop the column penalty cost table. To do so, subtract the smallest entry in each column from every element in that column of the row penalty cost table.
4. Find the minimum number of horizontal and vertical lines necessary to cover all the zeros in the column penalty cost table.
5. If the minimum number of lines is the same as the number of rows, the optimal solution can be found by using the zero-value cells in the final table. Otherwise, go to step 6.
6. Identify the smallest entry not covered by a line.
7. Subtract the smallest uncovered entry from all unlined entries and add it to every entry that is at the intersection of two lines.
8. Repeat steps 3 through 7 until an optimal solution is found.

SPECIAL SITUATIONS There are several special conditions that may arise in assignment situations, including problems with an unequal number of resources and tasks, prohibited assignments, a maximization objective, and multiple optimal solutions. Let us begin our review of these conditions by considering Example 10.9.

EXAMPLE 10.9 Sales Force Allocation

A small clothing store has four salespeople and three departments. Since each person has a different level of experience and ability, each will generate different sales in each department. The store's manager has estimated the sales volume that can be expected from each person in each department. The data are given in Table 10.50.

Joe does not have the interest, knowledge, or ability to sell accessories. Jim has always had trouble selling shoes. Therefore, the store manager does not want to assign Joe to accessories or Jim to shoes. The manager wants to know which salesperson to assign to which department to maximize sales.

Table 10.50 Sales Force Data

| Salesperson | Monthly Sales Volume | | |
	Suits	Shoes	Accessories
Nancy	$300	$300	$200
Joe	$600	$600	—
Barbara	$400	$400	$100
Jim	$200	—	$500

Resource-Task Imbalances In Example 10.8, the manufacturing firm had three repairpersons available to perform three maintenance jobs. That is, the number of resources (repairpersons) was exactly equal to the number of tasks (maintenance jobs). Yet such balance does not always occur in practice. Instead, there may be more resources than tasks, or vice versa. The sales force allocation problem in Example 10.9 offers just such a situation. The store manager has four salespeople but only three departments. That is, there are more resources (salespeople) than tasks (departments).

The assignment methodology, however, requires the resources and tasks to be in balance. To utilize this methodology, then, the decision maker first must eliminate any imbalances between the number of resources and tasks. As with the transportation problem, the use of fictitious sources or destinations provides an easy way to correct the imbalance without changing the basic structure of the problem.

The store manager, for instance, has $4 - 3 = 1$ more salesperson (resource) than department (task). To account for this excess resource, the manager can create a fictitious department that would demand the extra salesperson. Such a department, which is similar to a fictitious demand point in the transportation problem, can be called a **dummy task**.

Since the dummy is imaginary, there actually will be no assignment to this task. Thus, the store really gets nothing by assigning a salesperson to the fictitious department. Consequently, the manager should list a $0 sales volume for each dummy task assignment.

On the other hand, suppose that the manager of a different store has five salespeople and eight departments. In this case, there are $8 - 5 = 3$ more tasks (departments) than resources (salespeople). Hence, the store executive must create a separate fictitious salesperson to handle each extra department. That is, there would be a need for three imaginary resources. In assignment terminology, each of these fictitious salespeople is referred to as a **dummy resource**. Since each dummy is imaginary, there actually will be no assignment of this resource. Therefore, the store really gets nothing by assigning a fictitious salesperson to a department. As a result, the manager would list a $0 sales volume for each dummy resource assignment.

Prohibited Assignments   It may not always be possible or desirable to assign a particular resource to a selected task. This situation can happen because of resource capabilities, task requirements, or management preferences. Example 10.9 is a case in point.

Joe does not have the interest, knowledge, or ability to sell accessories, while Jim has trouble selling shoes. Therefore, the store manager prefers to avoid an assignment of Joe to the accessory department and Jim to the shoe department. As in the transportation situation, such unacceptable allocations can be denoted by allotting a very large negative ($-\$M$) sales volume to each prohibited assignment in the problem.

By incorporating the prohibited assignment and dummy task considerations into the problem formulation process, the clothing store manager will obtain Table 10.51. Note that the dummy task (department) is portrayed as a column in the sales force assignment table. Each entry in this column gives the cost ($0) of assigning a salesperson to such a task. Also, the prohibited assignments (Joe to accessories and Jim to shoes) are depicted as cells with $-\$M$ sales volumes.

Maximization   In Example 10.9, the clothing store manager wants to select the salesperson assignments that will maximize sales volume. The conventional solution procedure, however, is designed for assignment problems involving minimization. Management must therefore adapt the

Table 10.51 Sales Force Assignment Table

From Salesperson	To Department			
	Suits	Shoes	Accessories	Dummy
Nancy	$300	$300	$200	$0
Joe	$600	$600	$-M$	$0
Barbara	$400	$400	$100	$0
Jim	$200	$-M$	$500	$0

Table 10.52 Revised Sales Force Assignment Table

From Salesperson	To Department			
	Suits	Shoes	Accessories	Dummy
Nancy	$600 - 300 = $300	$600 - 300 = $300	$600 - 200 = $400	$600 - 0 = $600
Joe	$600 - 600 = $0	$600 - 600 = $0	$600 - (-$M)$ = $600 + M	$600 - 0 = $600
Barbara	$600 - 400 = $200	$600 - 400 = $200	$600 - 100 = $500	$600 - 0 = $600
Jim	$600 - 200 = $400	$600 - (-$M)$ = $600 + M	$600 - 500 = $100	$600 - 0 = $600

customary methodology to accommodate the sales volume objective. As in the transportation situation, management can either transform the objective or modify the analysis. Once more, it is usually easier to transform the objective. Furthermore, the opportunity loss concept still offers a convenient vehicle for making the transformation.

Table 10.51 indicates that $600 is the largest overall volume attainable by any of the salespeople. Such a score, then, establishes a standard that the store manager can use to measure job performance. In particular, if management computes each difference between the actual and highest volume, it will measure the degree to which the corresponding allotment deviates from the standard. These differences, which represent the opportunity losses associated with the matching staff allocations, are calculated in Table 10.52.

As Table 10.52 shows, these differences become substitutes for the corresponding sales volume entries in Table 10.51. That is, $600 + $M replaces the $-$M entry in the Jim/shoes cell, $500 supplants the $100 entry in the Barbara/accessories cell, and so on. In this way, the problem will be expressed in terms of opportunity losses rather than sales volumes. Since the decision maker must seek the smallest opportunity losses, such a process also transforms the situation from a maximization objective to a minimization objective.

Management can then use the conventional solution procedure to find the optimal sales force assignment. In the process, the dummy department will be treated like any other task. Moreover, the salesperson sent to the dummy department is interpreted as the resource that cannot be economically assigned under current conditions.

In addition, the symbol M should be construed as a number so large that M less any opportunity loss is still approximately equal to $M. Thus, a cell with an entry of $M will always generate the largest remaining opportunity loss in the assignment table. As a result, such a cell (prohibited assignment) can never be part of the optimal solution to the problem.

Although the sales force situation deals with a maximization objective, prohibited assignments can also arise in minimization problems. In these problems, we denote a prohibited assignment by allotting a very large positive (M) entry to the corresponding cell in the assignment table. Furthermore, the M allotment again must be made *before* the decision maker computes the opportunity losses.

Multiple Optima As in the transportation situation, an assignment problem may have more than one optimal solution. Example 10.9 is such a problem. To see why, we will need the opportunity losses associated with the revised sales force assignment table (Table 10.52).

By using the data from Table 10.52 and the conventional assignment procedure, the store manager will eventually obtain the opportunity losses given in Table 10.53. Note that Jim is the only salesperson who can sell accessories with a $0 penalty. Therefore, the store manager should assign Jim to the accessory department. Of course, such a policy will exclude Jim from any other assignment. We depict this fact by enclosing the $0 opportunity loss in a square and drawing a line through Jim's row in the table. Also, Nancy is the only salesperson who can perform the dummy task with a $0 penalty. Hence, the store manager should assign her to the dummy department. In effect, this policy means that Nancy will remain idle. Yet it excludes her from any other assignment. We indicate this fact by enclosing the $0 opportunity loss in a square and drawing a line through Nancy's row in the table.

These two assignments (Jim to accessories and Nancy to the dummy

Table 10.53 Optimal Sales Force Assignment

From Salesperson	To Department			
	Suits	Shoes	Accessories	Dummy
Nancy	$0	$0	$100	[$0]
Joe	$0	[$0]	$600 + M	$300
Barbara	[$0]	$0	$300	$100
Jim	$300	$500 + M	[$0]	$200

department) leave Barbara and Joe for the remaining shoe and suit departments. Moreover, Table 10.53 indicates that Barbara can sell suits and Joe can sell shoes with $0 penalties. Thus, the store manager can assign Joe to shoes and Barbara to suits. We denote such assignments by enclosing the $0 opportunity losses in squares and drawing lines through the suit and shoe columns.

As Table 10.53 demonstrates, the assignments create four lines that cover all the $0 penalties. That is, each of the salespeople is assigned to a separate sales task that he or she can perform with no opportunity loss. Consequently, the following sales force assignment plan suggested by the line pattern in Table 10.53 represents an optimal assignment:

- Nancy to the dummy department
- Joe to shoes
- Barbara to suits
- Jim to accessories

On the other hand, there are also $0 entries in the Barbara/shoes and Joe/suits cells of Table 10.53. These entries indicate that Barbara can sell shoes and Joe can sell suits with no opportunity loss. As a result, the following assignment is an alternative that will provide the clothing store with the same optimal sales volume as the plan suggested by the enclosed $0 penalties in Table 10.53:

- Nancy to the dummy department
- Joe to suits
- Barbara to shoes
- Jim to accessories

Such alternative optima are important because they provide the decision maker with greater flexibility in selecting and utilizing resources. For

Figure 10.4 ALP Solution of the Sales Force Assignment Problem

```
/FIND,ALP

A L P
ASSIGNMENT FORM LINEAR PROGRAMMING


 DO YOU WANT A DESCRIPTION OF THE PROGRAM
 ? NO

 NUMBER OF ROWS
 ? 4
 IS THIS A MINIMIZATION PROBLEM
 ? NO
 WILL YOU ENTER THE PROFIT DATA MATRIX FROM FILE OR TERMINAL
 ? TERMINAL
 ENTER THE PROFIT DATA BY ROW,  4 ITEMS PER ROW.

 ROW 1:
 ? 300,300,200,0
 ROW 2:
 ? 600,600,-1000,0
 ROW 3:
 ? 400,400,100,0
 ROW 4:
 ? 200,-1000,500,0
 WOULD YOU LIKE THE DATA LISTED
 ? YES

 PROFIT MATRIX
 ROW/COLUMN              1     2     3     4
 1                      300   300   200    0
 2                      600   600 - 1000   0
 3                      400   400   100    0
 4                      200-1000   500     0
```

example, suppose that clothing store experience indicates that suit customers are more likely to harass male salespeople than female salespeople. To promote employee morale, the manager may prefer the optimal assignment that has Barbara rather than Joe at the suit department.

COMPUTER ANALYSIS Practical assignment problems may involve hundreds, even thousands, of resources and tasks. In such situations, it will be cumbersome and time-consuming to perform the assignment calculations by hand. Fortunately,

```
DO YOU WANT A SOLUTION TRACE
? NO

OPPORTUNITY LOSS MATRIX:  ITERATION   2
ROW/COLUMN                1    2    3    4
        ALLOC.   LINE
    1      4        0     100  100  100    0
    2      1        0       0    0 1500  200
    3      2        0       0    0  200    0
    4      3        0     400 1600    0  200

                  LINE      0    0    0    0

OPTIMUM ASSIGNMENT
      ROW TO COLUMN C(I,J)
        I          J
        1          4          0
        2          1        600
        3          2        400
        4          3        500

    TOTAL                   1500

DO YOU HAVE ANOTHER PROBLEM
? NO
```

management scientists have developed prewritten computer packages designed to solve these large-scale assignment problems.

One of the packages, **ALP**, is available on the California State University and College System (CSUC) computer system. Figure 10.4 illustrates how this program can be used to solve the sales force assignment problem of Example 10.9. The decision maker executes the program with the FIND,ALP command. After locating the program and printing the descriptive title of ALP, the computer asks if the user wants instructions. Then it begins requesting input data.

First the decision maker must type the number of rows in the assignment table. This number, 4 in the case of the sales force problem, is inputted after the question (?) prompt. Next, the computer asks for the nature of the objective function and the source of the data. The answers once more are typed after the appropriate question (?) prompts. Figure 10.4, for instance, indicates that the clothing store wants to maximize (not minimize) sales volume. Moreover, the user informs ALP that the relevant data will be entered from the computer terminal.

At this point, the package begins requesting the cell entries in each row of the assignment table. The answers again are typed after the appropriate question (?) prompts. Table 10.51, for example, indicates that Nancy (row 1) generates a \$300 sales volume on suits, \$300 on shoes, \$200 on accessories, and \$0 in the dummy department. Consequently, these values are inputted after the row 1 question (?) prompt. Similarly, Jim produces a \$200 sales volume on suits, $-\$M$ on shoes, \$500 on accessories, and \$0 in the dummy department. Hence, values of 200, -1000, 500, and 0 are typed after the row 4 question (?) prompt. (The number -1000—or any other large negative value—must be substituted for $-M$, because ALP is not programmed to interpret such a symbol.)

The program then asks if the user wants to see ALP's version of the original assignment and resulting opportunity loss tables. As Figure 10.4 demonstrates, the decision maker responds by entering a YES or a NO. In this case, the user asks the program for the original listing but not the subsequent opportunity loss tables.

The computer then prints the final opportunity loss table and the optimal assignment. Figure 10.4 shows that ALP recommends the following assignment:

◆ Nancy (row 1) to the dummy (column 4)
◆ Joe (row 2) to suits (column 1)
◆ Barbara (row 3) to shoes (column 2)
◆ Jim (row 4) to accessories (column 3)

Furthermore, it indicates that this solution, which is identical to one of the alternative optimal assignments identified in Table 10.53, maximizes total sales at \$1500.

APPLICATIONS As in the transportation situation, the decision maker must know the exact costs or returns to properly implement the assignment model. Yet these values typically are based on estimates or forecasts. Moreover, unforeseen circumstances can create substantial inaccuracies in these estimates and thereby invalidate the recommended solution.

The assignment model, like the transportation model, also assumes that the costs or returns are linear in nature. Companies, however, can often

Table 10.54 Assignment Applications

Area	Application	References
Computer operations	Assigning personnel to programming jobs	V. Balachandran [2]
University planning	Assigning faculty to courses	S. D. Bloomfield and M. M. McSharry [4]; G. B. Harwood and R. W. Lawless[12]
Vehicle routing	Assigning delivery vehicles to routes	M. L. Fisher et al. [7]; Z. F. Lansdowne and D. W. Robinson [14]
Hospital operations	Assigning nurses to duty shifts	H. E. Miller et al. [16]
Manufacturing	Assigning personnel to machines	J. G. Miller and W. L. Berry [17]

utilize resources more efficiently in a joint rather than separate manner. Similarly, tasks frequently have a complementary instead of independent effect on costs or returns. In these cases, costs or returns are likely to be influenced by the assignment pattern. As A. M. Geoffrion and G. W. Graves [8] demonstrate, management must alter the methodology to accommodate such nonlinear relationships.

In spite of its limitations, the assignment model has been successfully applied to a wide variety of business and economic problems. Table 10.54 lists a small sample of the reported applications.

SUMMARY This chapter presented the transportation and assignment problems. It began with a discussion of the nature and relevance of the transportation situation and proceeded to show how to solve these problems. The conventional methodology involves a multiple-stage procedure. First, the decision maker obtains an initial feasible solution, typically with either the northwest corner method or the Vogel approximation method (VAM), summarized in Table 10.10. Then the initial solution is evaluated, usually with either the stepping stone method or the modified distribution (MODI) method, summarized in Table 10.10. If no improvements are possible, then the current distribution pattern represents the optimal transportation solution. Otherwise, management must utilize the procedure outlined in Table 10.19 to improve the distribution pattern. This entire procedure for finding an optimal transportation solution was summarized in Table 10.21.

In the second section of the chapter, we saw how to deal with some special conditions that can arise in transportation situations. These include problems with unbalanced supply and demand (which are handled with dummy demand and supply points), prohibited routes (handled with the M allotments), maximization objectives (which are handled by transforming the objective), degenerate solutions (which are handled with the epsilon (ε) allocations, and multiple optima. This section also illustrated how transportation problems can be solved with the aid of a computer, examined the assumptions of the solution methodology, and presented some important managerial applications.

In the final section, we discussed the assignment situation. We began with a discussion of the nature and relevance of the problem and then proceeded to the method used to solve these problems. Table 10.49 summarized the conventional procedure. This section also demonstrated how to recognize and handle the special conditions that can arise in assignment situations. These include problems with resource/task imbalances, prohibited assignments, maximization objectives, and multiple optimal solutions. Finally, we saw how assignment problems can be solved with the aid of a computer and considered some reported management applications of the model.

Glossary

ALP   A prewritten computer package designed to solve large-scale assignment problems.

arcs (branches, links, edges)   The lines connecting the nodes in a network.

assignment problem   A problem whose objective is to find the most effective way of assigning a group of indivisible resources to a set of indivisible tasks.

assignment table   A standard tabular format used to conveniently record the data and keep track of the calculations in an assignment problem analysis.

closed path (loop)   The series of horizontal and vertical lines that traces the pattern of changes required by a reallocation in the transportation problem.

directed network   A network in which flows can occur in only one direction.

dummy demand point   A fictitious destination created to account for any excess supply in a transportation problem.

dummy resource   A fictitious resource created to account for an excess task in an assignment problem.

dummy supply point   A fictitious source created to account for any excess demand in a transportation problem.

dummy task   A fictitious task created to account for an excess resource in an assignment problem.

Hungarian method (Flood's technique, matrix reduction)   The standard procedure used to find an optimal solution to an assignment problem.

improvement index   A value that measures the net effect on the objective of shipping one unit over a currently unused route in the transportation network.

modified distribution (MODI) method A procedure that evaluates a transportation solution by comparing direct expenses to the cost savings associated with each unused route in the network.

network A diagram consisting of junction points interconnected by a series of lines that carry a flow through the system.

nodes The junction points (circles) of a network.

northwest corner method A procedure that finds an initial feasible solution to a transportation problem through making allocations by moving down and to the right through the transportation table.

stepping stone method A procedure that evaluates a

transportation solution by tracing the pattern of changes required with each reallocation.

TRANLP A prewritten computer package designed to solve large-scale transportation problems.

transportation problem A problem whose objective is to find the most effective way of distributing a commodity from a group of supply sources to a set of demand destinations.

transportation table A standard tabular format used to conveniently record the data and keep track of the calculations in a transportation problem analysis.

Vogel approximation method (VAM) A procedure that utilizes the opportunity loss concept to find an initial feasible solution to a transportation problem.

References

1. Aarvik, O., and P. Randolph. "The Application of Linear Programming to the Determination of Transmission Fees in an Electrical Power Network." Part 1. *Interfaces* (November 1975): 47.

2. Balachandran, V. "An Integer Generalized Transportation Model for Optimal Job Assignment in Computer Networks." *Operations Research* (July–August 1976): 742.

3. Beilby, M. H. *Economics and Operations Research*. New York: Academic Press, 1976. Chaps. 6–8.

4. Bloomfield, S. D., and M. M. McSharry. "Preferential Course Scheduling." *Interfaces* (August 1979): 24.

5. Chandrasekaran, R., and S. S. Rao. "A Special Case of the Transportation Problem." *Operations Research* (May–June 1977): 525.

6. Dutta, A., et al. "On Optimal Allocation in a Distributed Processing Environment." *Management Science* (August 1982): 839.

7. Fisher, M. L., et al. "A Computerized Vehicle Routing Application." *Interfaces* (August 1982): 42.

8. Geoffrion, A. M., and G. W. Graves. "Scheduling Parallel Production Lines with Changeover Costs: Practical Application of a Quadratic Assignment/LP Approach." *Operations Research* (July–August 1976): 595.

9. Glover, F., et al. "An Integrated Production, Distribution, and Inventory Planning System." *Interfaces* (November 1979): 21.

10. Gray, P. "The Shirt Allocation Problem." *Operations Research* (July–August 1976): 788.

11. Hansen, P., and L. Kaufman. "Public Facilities Location Under an Investment Constraint." *Operational Research*. Amsterdam: North-Holland Publishing Company, 1975.

12. Harwood, G. B., and R. W. Lawless. "Optimizing Organizational Goals in Assigning Faculty Teaching Schedules." *Decision Sciences* (July 1975): 513.

13. Hess, S. W. "Design and Implementation of a New Check Clearing System for the Philadelphia Federal Reserve District." Part 2. *Interfaces* (February 1975): 22.

14. Lansdowne, Z. F., and D. W. Robinson. "Geographic Decomposition of the Shortest Path Problem, with an Application to the Traffic Assignment Problem." *Management Science* (December 1982): 1380.

15. Love, R. F., and L. Yerex. "An Application of a Facilities Location Model in the Prestressed Concrete Industry." *Interfaces* (August 1976): 45.

16. Miller, H. E., et al. "Nurse Scheduling Using Mathematical Programming." *Operations Research* (September–October 1976): 857.

17. Miller, J. G., and W. L. Berry. "The Assignment of Men to Machines: An Application of Branch and Bound." *Decision Sciences* (January 1977): 56.

18. Segal, M., and D. B. Weinberger. "Turfing." *Operations Research* (May–June 1977): 367.

19. Shore, H. H. "The Transportation Problem and Vogel Approximation Method." *Decision Sciences* (July–October 1970): 441.

20. Zierer, T. K., et al. "Practical Applications of Linear Programming to Shell's Distribution Problems." *Interfaces* (August 1976): 13.

Thought Exercises

1. Explain the specific similarities and differences between the transportation and assignment problems. Why do these decisions arise in modern enterprises?

2. Specify whether each of the following circumstances is a transportation situation or an assignment situation. Explain.

   a. A nonprofit research organization's geographic allocation of project engineers to independent projects

b. A municipal sanitation department's weekly geographic allocation of trucks to streets

c. A toy manufacturer's allocation of its supply of a given toy from a group of its warehouses to a group of wholesalers

d. A cigar importer's allocation of its supply of various types of cigars from a given country to a group of distribution outlets

3. Let

m = the number of sources
i = the source index ($i = 1, 2, \ldots, m$)
n = the number of destinations
j = the destination index ($j = 1, 2, \ldots, n$)
X_{ij} = the number of units transported from source i to destination j
c_{ij} = the contribution to the objective of transporting one unit from source i to destination j
Z = the transportation pattern's total contribution to the objective
S_i = the supply in units at source i
D_j = the demand in units at destination j

Use these symbols to develop a general linear programming formulation for the transportation problem. If you utilized the simplex method to solve this problem, what would be the initial basic feasible solution? Explain.

4. Consider the following transportation situation, where entries in the upper right-hand corner of the cells are per-unit allocation costs. What are the penalty costs for the source? Explain.

	Farm	Supermarket	Milk Stand	Health Store
Milk Truck	$3	$10	$4	$3

5. Pamphlet Printing's (Example 10.4) optimal job order plan is given by the following transportation table. Interpret this solution for the company's management. That is, how many leaflets for each job should be printed on each press? What is the resulting minimum total cost?

	To Order			Supply of Leaflets (Thousands per Day)
From Press	A	B	C	
1	$4 10	$M	$8 30	40
2	$6 20	$3 20	$M	40
Demand for Leaflets (Thousands per Day)	30	20	30	80

6. Let

m = the number of resources
i = the resource index $(i = 1, 2, \ldots, m)$
n = the number of tasks
j = the task index $(j = 1, 2, \ldots, n)$
$$X_{ij} = \begin{cases} 1 \text{ if resource } i \text{ is assigned to task } j \\ 0 \text{ otherwise} \end{cases}$$
c_{ij} = the contribution to the objective from assigning resource i to task j
Z = the assignment pattern's total contribution to the objective

Use these symbols to develop a general linear programming formulation for the assignment problem. If you utilized the simplex method to solve this problem, what would be the initial basic feasible solution? Explain.

7. What is the interpretation of the dummy source (resource) or dummy destination (task) in the following circumstances?

   a. An excess number of test pilots for new test aircraft
   b. Excess demand for a group of consumer products in given geographic areas
   c. Excess supply of sugar in international trading markets from particular supplying countries
   d. An inadequate number of football positions for potential high school football players

8. How would the existence of alternative optima help the following decision makers? Speculate on the nature of appropriate secondary goals and their influence on the selection of alternative optima.

   a. A police captain whose prime goal is to assign various officers over particular patrol zones in a way that maximizes some index of performance
   b. A travel agent whose prime goal is to allocate a group of tourists over a group of travel areas in a way that minimizes their travel costs
   c. A manufacturer who seeks the minimum transportation cost for various raw materials from particular suppliers

9. General Commando, chief operations officer for the Third Airlift Command, must deliver three types of new aircraft to three air bases. Only one plane can be delivered to one base at a time. Delivery costs differ because of distance, fuel efficiency, crew size, and so on. Captain Britton, the general's aid, has formulated the problem as an assignment situation and developed the following final opportunity loss table:

From Plane	To Air Base		
	Alton AFB	Bart NAS	Clove AFB
Fighter	$0	$0	$5000
Bomber	$0	$2000	$1000
Transport	$2000	$0	$0

According to this table, which plane should be assigned on each air base? Explain.

Suppose the total delivery costs of each distribution are given as follows:

From Plane	To Air Base		
	Alton AFB	Bart NAS	Clove AFB
Fighter	$3000	$4000	$9000
Bomber	$2000	$5000	$4000
Transport	$2000	$1000	$1000

What is the total delivery cost for the optimal assignment?

10. Do you agree or disagree with each of the following statements? Explain.

   a. An assignment problem may need both dummy resources (rows) and dummy tasks (columns).

   b. VAM instead of the northwest corner method should always be used to find the first feasible solution for a transportation problem.

   c. We cannot find the optimal solution to a transportation problem with VAM or the northwest corner method.

   d. Degeneracy cannot exist in an assignment problem.

   e. Row and column reductions leave the amounts in the same relative positions of the opportunity loss table.

   f. In a transportation problem with a minimization objective, penalties are found by taking the difference between the lowest and next lowest costs for each source and destination.

   g. In the Hungarian method, you will never need more lines to cover all zero entries than the number of rows in the assignment table.

   h. The number of decision variables in a transportation problem will equal the number of supply sources multiplied by the number of demand destinations.

Technique
Exercises

1. You are given the following transportation table, where entries in the upper right-hand corner of the cells are per-unit costs.

From Origin	To Destination		Supply
	D_1	D_2	
O_1	5	9	100
O_2	7	4	200
Demand	200	100	300

   a. Use the northwest corner method to find a first feasible solution.
   b. Use the stepping stone method to find the optimal solution.

2. Consider the following transportation problem, where entries in the upper right-hand corner of the cells are per-unit costs.

From Origin	To Destination		Supply
	D_1	D_2	
O_1	4	2	30
O_2	1	3	10
O_3	5	6	30
Demand	30	40	70

   a. Use the Vogel approximation method to find a first feasible solution.
   b. Use the modified distribution method to find the optimal solution.

3. Refer back to Example 10.1.
   a. Solve the corresponding linear problem with the simplex method.
   b. Interpret the resulting linear programming solution.
   c. Show how Tables 10.13 and 10.15 were developed.
   d. Show how Tables 10.18 and 10.20 were derived.

4. You are given the following transportation problem, where entries in the upper right-hand corner of the cells are per-unit revenues.

From Plant	To Retail Outlet			Production Capacity (Units)
	Springfield	Lincoln	Montclair	
La Cross	$20	$80	$100	5000
Columbia	$60	$110	$60	4000
Colton	$120	$70	$90	3000
Forecasted Demand (Units)	4500	1500	3000	12,000 / 9000

    a. Use the northwest corner method to find a first feasible solution.
    b. Identify any degenerate solutions.
    c. Use the modified distribution method to find the optimal solution.

5. Refer back to Examples 10.2 and 10.3.

    a. Determine the optimal solution to each problem.
    b. Interpret the solution in language that would be understandable to management.

6. Refer back to Examples 10.4 and 10.5.

    a. Use the conventional transportation methodologies to determine the optimal solution to each problem.
    b. Interpret the solution for Example 10.5 in language that would be understandable to management.

7. Refer back to Examples 10.6 and 10.7.

    a. Determine the optimal solution for Example 10.6.
    b. Show how Tables 10.36 and 10.37 were derived.

8. Refer back to Example 10.9.

    a. List each alternative assignment.
    b. Select the alternative that maximizes sales.
    c. Show how Table 10.53 was developed.
    d. How does the recommendation from Table 10.53 compare with the answer from part (b)? Explain.

9. Consider the assignment problem given in the following table, where entries in the cells give the times needed by each resource to complete each task.

From Resource	To Task			
	T_1	T_2	T_3	T_4
R_1	6	5	5	2
R_2	3	4	5	7
R_3	4	3	6	1
R_4	5	4	2	6

Find the optimal assignment by the Hungarian method. What is the total time for this optimal assignment?

10. You are given the following assignment table, where entries in the cells give the rankings (from 1 to 3) associated with each assignment. A lower-valued rank is preferred to a higher-valued rank.

From Resource	To Task		
	T_1	T_2	T_3
R_1	3	M	2
R_2	2	3	1
R_3	1	1	M

Use the Hungarian method to find the resource/task assignments that minimize the sum of the rankings. Are there any alternative optima? Explain.

Applications Exercises

1. Smooth Ride Tire Company stores its radial tires in three centrally located warehouses for distribution to its prime markets. Supply availabilities and demand requirements are as follows:

Warehouse	Supply Available (Thousands of Tires per Week)
Wilmington, Delaware	20
Gary, Indiana	50
Norwalk, California	30

Market	Demand (Thousands of Tires per Week)
New York	30
Chicago	30
Los Angeles	40

Physical handling and freight rates make up most of the following distribution costs between each warehouse and market (costs are in dollars per tire):

From	To		
	New York	Chicago	Los Angeles
Wilmington	3	4	6
Gary	4	2	4
Norwalk	8	5	1

Assuming that Smooth Ride wants to minimize its total distribution costs, how many tires should be allocated from each warehouse to each market? Can you give some possible reasons why Smooth Ride might have located its markets and warehouses in the given locations? List some reasons why the cost, supply, and demand structures for warehouses and markets might be as shown.

2. Fresh Milk Dairy is a small, rural dairy with only three delivery trucks and three geographically separated routes. It is impossible for one truck to handle more than one route per day, but each truck is capable of completing each route in a given day. The dairy pays its drivers on a straight-time basis, with "working time" including driving time from the driver's house (where he or she keeps the truck overnight) to the route and back again. Each driver is paid $5 per hour, but it is estimated that other operating costs for each truck differ (because of the truck's age, make, and so on). Specifically, truck A costs $2 an hour to operate, truck B costs $3 an hour, and truck C costs $4 an hour (a prorated cost per hour based on the total miles driven over the useful life of the truck).

   Each truck is mechanically more efficient in different topographical conditions and can therefore complete each route in a different amount of time per day. Company records indicate that the hours per day that each truck requires to complete each route are as follows:

Truck	Route		
	1	2	3
A	8	6	8
B	4	10	3
C	5	6	8

   Which truck should be assigned to each route to minimize total delivery cost? What is that cost?

3. Crimetown's police chief wants to allocate three tactical patrol units to three precincts that have recently been experiencing large increases in crime. The three teams have different numbers of officers, years of experience, and modes of operation. Crime analysts have determined an index of crime deterrence for each team. This index represents the portion of crimes that is expected to be deterred as a result of the tactical unit's effort. The index is from a low of zero to a high of 100. The following table gives the index of crime deterrence for the patrol units and precincts:

	To Precinct		
From Tactical Unit	1	2	3
A	90	80	40
B	20	60	80
C	50	70	20

Team A will be available for 50 hours next month, team B for 40 hours, and team C for 60 hours. Based on the projected number of serious crimes, the chief expects to need 30 hours of effort in precinct 1, 70 hours in precinct 2, and 50 hours in precinct 3. The chief wants to allocate the three teams in such a way as to maximize the index of crime deterrence. How many hours should each team be assigned to each precinct in order to accomplish this goal?

4. A major European city has four incinerator sites for processing solid waste. There are four garbage collection areas within the city. The city wants to determine the least-cost method of disposing of its trash. Each incinerator is characterized by an operating cost for processing each ton of waste. There is also a cost of transporting each ton of waste from each collection area to each incinerator. The total (operating plus transportation) cost per ton is summarized in the following table:

	To Incineration Site			
From Collection Area	1	2	3	4
A	$75	$80	$60	$40
B	$70	$70	$100	$60
C	$90	$40	$50	$100
D	$60	$50	$40	$30

Incinerator site 1 has a monthly capacity of 6000 tons, site 2 has a capacity of 5000 tons, and site 3 has a capacity of 8000 tons. There are 2000 tons of waste generated at area A, 8000 tons at area B, and

9000 tons at area C per month. A total of 20,000 tons of waste per month are generated from all four areas. How many tons of waste from each collection area should be processed at each site in order to minimize the total cost?

5. Adam Hoop is a professional basketball coach who knows that he must play a different combination of his players for each opposing team if he is to maximize his probability of winning any given game. Only one combination can be employed against any given team at any given time in the game. After careful consideration of his scouting reports and evaluation of his personnel, Adam formulates the following matrix of probabilities of winning:

Player Combination	Opposing Team		
	Dunkers	Burners	Musclemen
Tall	.90	.30	.60
Quick	.40	.50	.80
Strong	.70	.20	.90

Which combination should Hoop employ against each team?

6. A local radio station is considering its new daily programming schedule. The station plans to have three separate formats: 5 hours of news, 10 hours of sports, and 9 hours of music in each 24-hour period. Research indicates that there are four reasonably distinct audiences: 12 midnight to 6 A.M., 6 A.M. to 2 P.M., 2 P.M. to 8 P.M., and 8 P.M. to midnight. Per-hour audience point ratings for each format in each time segment are estimated to be as follows:

Format	Hour			
	12–6	6–2	2–8	8–12
News	100	400	600	200
Sports	600	200	400	300
Music	800	600	300	700

How many hours of each format should the station schedule in each time segment so as to maximize total audience points?

7. Jackson Roykirk, a project director in a NASA program, has three engineers available for assignment to two projects. Only one engineer can be assigned to a project at any given time. Each engineer has special skills and thus does not have the same degree of efficiency on each project. Roykirk has used past experience to set the following project costs:

	Costs of Project	
Engineer	Spacecraft	Computer
Atomon	$10,000	$10,000
Electrot	$20,000	$10,000
Wafe	$5,000	$30,000

The director wants to assign each engineer to a project in a way that minimizes the total cost of the projects. What assignments do you suggest?

Atomon has a recent medical problem. Hence, if possible, Roykirk would prefer not to use this engineer. How does this situation influence your recommendation?

8. A political candidate can make three different speeches: conservative, moderate, or liberal. There are three audiences: a professional society of business people, a university group, and a construction union conference. Her aides know that each speech will have a different impact on each audience. The potential percent of favorable responses from each audience for each speech is estimated as follows:

	Audience		
Speech	Business	College	Union
Conservative	70%	20%	40%
Moderate	60%	40%	50%
Liberal	30%	80%	60%

What speech should be given to each audience to maximize the percent of favorable responses?

CASE: Oriental Carpets, Inc.

Oriental Carpets is a large multinational manufacturer and distributor of custom carpets. It locates its production facilities at the source of the raw materials and labor supply in five cities: Tokyo, Seoul, Hong Kong, Taipei, and Bangkok. Distribution is carried out by four large import-export merchants located in four major market centers: New York, London, Buenos Aires, and Cairo.

Transportation costs, including freight rates and handling, are constant on a monthly basis between each facility and merchant center. Currently, they are as follows:

Production Facility	Per-Carpet Transportation Cost			
	New York	London	Buenos Aires	Cairo
Tokyo	$50	$30	$60	$20
Seoul	$60	$40	$40	$10
Hong Kong	$30	$40	$70	$40
Taipei	$20	$30	$40	$20
Bangkok	$40	$30	$60	$10

The Tokyo plant is capable of supplying 30,000 rugs per month, Seoul 10,000, Hong Kong 30,000, Taipei 20,000, and Bangkok 10,000. The New York merchant center requires 40,000 rugs per month, London 30,000, Buenos Aires 10,000, and Cairo 20,000.

There are three loading cranes available in each supplying city to accommodate production in three locations. Each of the three locations requires only one loading crane at a time. Cranes are dispatched from a central staging area, and the per-crane allocation cost to each production site varies by its geographic location, the demand for the crane at the site, and maintenance required after use at a site. Oriental management has found that allocation costs do not differ by city and are given on a weekly basis as follows:

Crane	Per-Crane Allocation Cost to Site		
	1	2	3
A	$5000	$2000	$6000
B	$3000	$5000	$2000
C	$4000	$4000	$1000

1. How many carpets per month should be shipped from each production facility to each merchant center to minimize the total transportation cost under current conditions?

2. What are some of the uncertainties involved in this allocation pattern? How might they affect the decision?

3. Which crane should be assigned to each site in each supplying city to minimize the total loading cost per week?

4. Does the assumption about constant crane allocation cost for each city seem realistic? What other factors seem to be ignored, and how might they affect the decision?

Prepare answers to these questions in a report suitable for a management audience.

Chapter 11
Network Topics

CONCEPTS

♦ Minimizing the total length of connections in a network

♦ Finding the shortest route through a network

♦ Finding the shortest round trip from a specified origin to a given destination

♦ Finding the largest possible flow through a system

♦ Working with a distribution strategy that best meets the demand and supply requirements at various points in a network

APPLICATIONS

♦ Designing equestrian trails
♦ Tram routing
♦ Computer system design
♦ Plant layout
♦ Theater wiring
♦ Transmitting gas
♦ Scheduling replacements
♦ Planning communications

In many situations, there are several geographic junction points (such as work stations, warehouses, or plants) that can be connected in a variety of ways. Typically, the decision maker wants to find the series of connections that most efficiently utilizes scarce resources. The problem may involve the design of an effective layout for physical facilities or the selection of a desirable route for people and materials. Network analysis has been successfully applied to such layout design and routing problems.

This chapter presents some of the most widely used network techniques. In the first section, we discuss the nature of a network and its application to layout design. In particular, we show how to select the layout that minimizes the total length of connections in a network.

The second section focuses on routing problems. First, a technique is developed for finding the shortest route from a given origin to a specified location. In another situation, we find the minimum cost, time, or distance involved in making a round trip through the network.

In the final situation, we are presented with a resource flow from a specified origin through various junction points to a given destination. Further, the flow has restricted capacities in both directions. This final section develops a procedure for finding the largest possible flow through the system and illustrates its application. It also shows how to determine the distribution strategy that best meets the demand and supply requirements at various points in a network.

LAYOUTS Often, a decision maker must design the layout that most effectively joins the locations or activities in a network. Example 11.1 illustrates.

EXAMPLE 11.1 Designing an Equestrian Layout

Prestige Builders, Inc., has set aside a portion of its exclusive housing development, Sunrise, for an equestrian/jogging park. The park will consist of a system of trails between the controlled entrance and various sites. Figure 11.1 shows the proposed trail system. In this

Figure 11.1 Sunrise's Equestrian Trail System

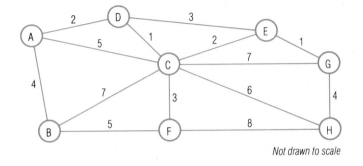

Not drawn to scale

diagram, location A is the entrance into the park. Sites B through H are various rest stations located at scenic points in the park. There is also a scenic overlook at the park entrance and a popular swimming and skating pond at site H. The numbers give the distances of the winding trails in miles.

Water and sewer pipes must be installed under the trails so as to connect all locations (including the park entrance). Since installation is both expensive and disturbing to the natural environment, Prestige wants to connect all sites with the minimum number of miles of pipe.

NATURE OF THE PROBLEM Figure 11.1 depicts a network in which a set of park sites (nodes) is interconnected by a series of trails (branches). The flow in these branches (over the trails) represents the movement of people between the sites. Moreover, each branch value (number on the line) measures the distance in miles between the corresponding park sites.

Prestige needs to join all sites (nodes) in the park system, a process known as **spanning** the network, with water and sewer pipes. Although each pipe must lead from one site to another, this spanning can be accomplished without installing a line under every trail (branch) in the park. Furthermore, refuse and water can flow in any direction through the lines between sites. Consequently, there is no need for a **loop** or **cycle**, a sequence of lines that leads from a site back to itself through other stations.

Instead, management wants to utilize the series of trails (branches) that will connect all sites (nodes) in the park system with the minimum total number of miles of pipe. Such a series of connections is referred to as the **minimal spanning tree**. In effect, then, Prestige's problem is to find the minimal spanning tree for the equestrian park network.

Table 11.1 summarizes the general characteristics of the minimal spanning tree problem.

Table 11.1 Characteristics of the Minimal Spanning Tree Problem

1. The problem can be portrayed as a network in which a set of nodes is interconnected by a series of branches.
2. Each branch depicts a potential link between nodes.
3. There is a movement of items or people over the branches.
4. The movement can flow in any direction over the links.
5. Branch values measure the distance, time, cost, or capacity associated with the flow over the corresponding links.
6. Each node represents a junction point or location.
7. All nodes must be connected by branches or links.
8. It is not necessary to utilize every potential link nor have any loop between nodes.
9. The objective is to find a series of links that will minimize the total length of the branches used in connecting all the nodes.

FINDING THE OPTIMAL DESIGN As M. S. Bazaraa and J. J. Jarvis [3] and K. Murtz [16] demonstrate, most network flow problems can be formulated as linear programs and then solved with the simplex method. Yet even small-scale network situations, like Prestige's equestrian park, may generate relatively large linear programming problems. As a result, it may be very time-consuming and costly, even with the aid of a computer, to determine an optimal network solution with linear programming methodologies.

Fortunately, management scientists have developed specialized procedures to solve network flow problems. One of these approaches makes it possible to determine the minimal spanning tree in a relatively straightforward manner. To see what is involved, let us again examine Prestige's equestrian network.

The analysis can begin at any site (node) in the network. For ease of reference, however, we will start at the park entrance (site A in Figure 11.1). Prestige can install a line under the trail from site A to station B, C, or D. Moreover, B is 4 miles, C is 5 miles, and D is 2 miles from node A.

Now, recall that management wants to minimize the total miles of pipe utilized on the project. Since D is nearest to A, the first connection should join these two sites. Figure 11.2 illustrates this first connection.

The next phase of construction may begin from either of the connected sites (A or D). Although A has already been connected to D, Figure 11.1 shows that Prestige can still install pipes from A to B, from A to C, from D to C, or from D to E. Also, site C is 1 mile from D and site E is 3 miles from D. Sites B and C are 4 and 5 miles, respectively, from A. Among these unconnected sites (B, C, and E), C is the closest in miles to a connected node (D). Thus, as indicated in Figure 11.3, management next should connect site C to site D.

At this stage, Prestige has connected A to D and D to C. Since A to D is

Figure 11.2 Prestige's First Connection (A to D)

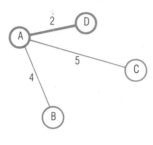

Figure 11.3 Prestige's Second Connection (D to C)

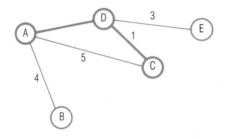

Table 11.2 Potential Connections Following Prestige's Second Connection

From Site	To Station	Distance (Miles)
A	B	4
D	E	3
C	E	2
C	G	7
C	H	6
C	F	3
C	B	7

2 miles and D to C is another 1 mile, the system currently has $2 + 1 = 3$ miles of pipe. In the third phase, Prestige can start a pipeline from any of the three connected sites (A, C, or D).

According to Figure 11.1, the company can now join the three already-connected sites to various unconnected sites. These potential connections

Figure 11.4 Prestige's Third Connection (C to E)

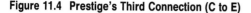

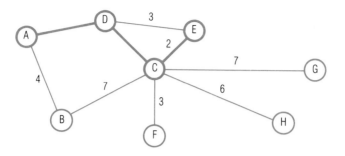

Table 11.3 Finding the Minimal Spanning Tree

1. Arbitrarily select any node in the network.
2. Connect the branch between the starting node and the nearest distinct node. Ties may be broken arbitrarily.
3. Identify the branch values from the connected to the unconnected nodes. Do not consider branches to nodes that have already been connected by other lines.
4. Identify the unconnected node that is closest to a connected node. Ties may be broken arbitrarily.
5. Connect the branch between the two nodes.
6. Repeat steps 3 through 5 until all nodes in the network have been connected.
7. The resulting series of branches is the minimal spanning tree.

are listed in Table 11.2. Notice that A to C is not being considered, because nodes A and C already have been connected by other branches (lines). Among the possibilities, E is the closest site to a connected site (C). Hence, as shown in Figure 11.4, the third connection is between sites C and E.

Such a process, which is summarized in Table 11.3, must be repeated until all the nodes in the network are connected with branches. Indeed, by completing this so-called **greedy algorithm**, Prestige will obtain the minimal spanning tree presented in Figure 11.5. The figure shows that Prestige can minimize the total miles of pipe required in the park system by installing lines under the following trails:

♦ 2 miles from A to D
♦ 1 mile from D to C
♦ 2 miles from C to E
♦ 1 mile from E to G
♦ 3 miles from C to F

Figure 11.5 Prestige's Minimal Spanning Tree

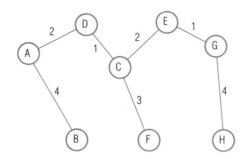

♦ 4 miles from A to B
♦ 4 miles from G to H

By adding these mileages, you can see that such a network will involve a total of 17 miles of pipe.

COMPUTER ANALYSIS In large-scale problems, it can be tedious and time-consuming to find the minimal spanning tree by hand. Moreover, the process may be prone to error. Consequently, management scientists have developed prewritten computer packages designed to perform the necessary computations. One such package, called **SPNT1**, is available on a diskette for personal computers with the purchase of the W. J. Erikson and O. P. Hall [6] book. Figure 11.6 illustrates the SPNT1 solution to Prestige's equestrian layout problem.

The user executes the program by typing the code number for SPNT1 on the computer keyboard. Although not shown in Figure 11.6, this number will be identified on the screen display of the available programs in the Erikson and Hall computer diskette. The program then requests the information about the network.

As Figure 11.6 demonstrates, the user first must enter the number of nodes and links (branches) in the network. In this regard, there are eight sites (nodes) and fourteen trails (links) in Prestige's equestrian/jogging park (network). Hence, the decision maker should type the value 8 after the prompt for the number of nodes and 14 following the prompt for the number of links.

At this point, SPNT1 asks the user to identify the starting node, ending node, and branch value (link length) for each link in the network. In the process, all nodes and links must be identified by integers rather than letters. Moreover, the integers should start with the number 1 and contain no gaps.

Figure 11.6 Prestige's SPNT1 Solution

```
        ** INFORMATION ENTERED **

        NUMBER OF NODES: 8
        NUMBER OF LINKS: 14

   LINK      START      END        LINK
  NUMBER     NODE       NODE       LENGTH
    1          1          2          4
    2          1          3          5
    3          1          4          2
    4          2          3          7
    5          2          6          5
    6          3          4          1

    7          3          5          2
    8          3          6          3
    9          3          7          7
   10          3          8          6
   11          4          5          3
   12          5          7          1
   13          6          8          8
   14          7          8          4


        ** RESULTS **

  MINIMUM SPANNING TREE

   START     END        LINK
   NODE      NODE       LENGTH
    1          4          2
    4          3          1
    3          5          2
    5          7          1
    3          6          3
    1          2          4
    7          8          4

  TOTAL LENGTH = 17


        ** END OF ANALYSIS **
```

Consider, for instance, the trail (link) between the park entrance (node A) and station B in Sunrise's equestrian network (Figure 11.1). Management can label this trail as link 1, the park entrance as node 1, and station B as node 2. Hence, this particular trail (link 1) starts at node 1, ends at node 2, and is 4 miles long. Therefore, the user should enter these numbers after the corresponding link 1 prompts in Figure 11.6.

Similarly, the trail between stations C and E in the equestrian network (Figure 11.1) can be denoted as link 7. In such a scheme, C is depicted as node 3 and E as node 5. The trail joining these sites (link 7) then starts at node 3, ends at node 5, and is 2 miles long. These numbers are entered after the corresponding link 7 prompts in Figure 11.6.

After receiving all the network information, SPNT1 processes the data and generates the minimal spanning tree. In particular, the program identifies the starting node, ending node, and length of each link (branch) in this tree. It also lists the total length (sum) of the branch values for the minimal spanning tree.

Figure 11.6, for example, shows that Prestige's minimal spanning tree involves a total of 17 miles of pipe. Furthermore, this tree is obtained by utilizing the links between the following sites:

- ◆ 1 (A) and 4 (D)
- ◆ 4 (D) and 3 (C)
- ◆ 3 (C) and 5 (E)
- ◆ 5 (E) and 7 (G)
- ◆ 3 (C) and 6 (F)
- ◆ 1 (A) and 2 (B)
- ◆ 7 (G) and 8 (H)

By comparing Figures 11.5 and 11.6, you will find that SPNT1 has generated the same minimal spanning tree recommendation as the more cumbersome hand calculation.

APPLICATIONS The minimal spanning tree methodology is usually applied to design or construction problems. It is most useful when the decision maker must identify or establish the best series of links between all the nodes in a network. In practice, such problems arise frequently and in a wide variety of business and economic situations. Table 11.4 presents a few typical illustrations.

In addition, the basic minimal spanning tree concepts can be extended and then applied to related problems. Some of these extensions are discussed by D. Klingman [13] and E. Lawler [14]. Moreover, D. A. Schilling [19] and P. J. Slater [22] show how modified versions of this network analysis can be used for facility planning.

ROUTES In Prestige's problem, the equestrian layout did not have to start or end at a designated location. However, many problems involve both a specified origin and a specified destination. In one case, the objective may be to find the shortest route from a source to a destination. In another case, a resource may start from a particular location, visit each facility only once,

Table 11.4 Minimal Spanning Tree Applications

Network	Nodes	Branches	Problem
Cable television	Transmitting and receiving stations	Wire cables	Use the minimum amount of wire to link all stations.
Computer	Terminals	Wires	Use the minimum amount of wire to link all terminals.
Circuit board	Circuits	Copper strips	Use the minimum quantity of strips to connect all circuits on the board.
Rapid transit	Communities	Subway lines	Utilize the least costly subway layout that will join all communities.
Electric power	Neighborhoods	Power lines	Utilize the least costly distribution layout that will join all neighborhoods.
Air conditioning	Rooms	Air ducts	Use the air duct layout that will connect all rooms at least cost.

and then return to the origin. In this second situation, the decision maker may want to find the minimum cost, time, or distance involved in following such a loop. In this section, we will see how to formulate and deal with these routing problems.

SHORTEST ROUTE PROBLEM Consider Example 11.2.

EXAMPLE 11.2 Tram Routing

This example deals with the equestrian trail system portrayed in Figure 11.1. Suppose that the scenery is so beautiful that some Sunrise residents would like to use the park without horseback riding or jogging. Consequently,

Prestige has agreed to provide tram service from the park entrance to each site.

In operation, the line will send a different tram from the park entrance to each station. Expenses will be paid from revenues generated by a

distance-related fare charged to the users. Therefore, the residents want each tram to follow a route that is the least total number of miles from the park entrance.

Prestige's tram-routing situation is very similar to its equestrian layout problem (Example 11.1). In fact, the situation can again be portrayed as a network in which a set of park sites (nodes) is linked by a series of trails (branches). Each branch depicts a potential link (tram route) between nodes. There will be a flow (movement of trams) along the branches, and this movement will flow in any direction over the links.

Also, the branch values once more measure the distances in miles between the corresponding nodes in the network. Each node represents a park site, and every site is joined by at least one trail (potential tram route). Furthermore, it is not necessary to utilize every potential link or have a loop in any tram line route.

Nevertheless, there are some key differences between Examples 11.1 and 11.2. One distinction deals with the nature of the decision. In Example 11.1, Prestige must build the pipelines (links) that connect the sites (nodes) in the park system (network). On the other hand, the links (trails) between the nodes (stations) already exist in the tram-routing situation. Hence, the residents simply must choose among these available links. Put another way, Example 11.2 involves an operations problem, while Example 11.1 is concerned with a design or construction situation.

Another difference deals with the nature of the flow over the branches. In Example 11.1, the water and sewer pipes could originate from and terminate at any site in the park system. Each tram in the routing situation, however, must begin from the park entrance and finish at a particular station. This specified origin (the park entrance) is known as the **source node**, and the particular destination (station) is the **sink node**. In other words, Example 11.2 has both a source of and sink for every flow over the links in the park system.

There is also a distinction between the requirements in the two examples. In Example 11.1, Prestige's pipelines must connect all sites in the park system. On the other hand, a different tram will be sent from the Sunrise entrance to each station in the park. Consequently, each tram in Example 11.2 will not be required to join every node of the network. Moreover, the residents want every tram route to follow the series of trails (branches) that gives the fewest total miles between the park entrance and the specified station. Such a series of links is called the **shortest route**. In effect, then, the problem is to find the shortest route for each different tram.

Table 11.5 summarizes the key differences between the shortest route and minimal spanning tree problems.

FINDING THE SHORTEST ROUTE   As R. Hesse [10] demonstrates, it is possible to solve the shortest route problem with the assignment methodologies of chapter 10. Yet the assignment approach is designed primarily to find the shortest distance between the origin and only one (rather than all) destination. Further-

Table 11.5 Comparison of the Shortest Route and Minimal Spanning Tree Problems

Factor	Minimal Spanning Tree	Shortest Route
Nature of the decision	Decision maker must design the layout of the links in the network.	Decision maker must choose among the already-existing links in the network.
Nature of the flow	There is no source node or sink node.	There is both a source node and a sink node.
Requirements	Decision maker must join all nodes in the network with links.	Decision maker must join only the source node with each sink node.

Figure 11.7 First Tram Line Route (A to D)

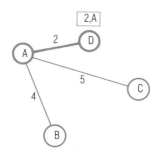

more, even small-scale shortest route situations, like Prestige's tram problem, may generate relatively large assignment problems. As a result, it may be very time-consuming and costly, even with the aid of a computer, to determine the shortest route with the assignment procedures.

Fortunately, management scientists have developed specialized methodologies to solve the shortest route problem. Moreover, one of these methodologies enables the decision maker to determine the solution in a relatively straightforward manner. To examine the procedure, we will again consider the equestrian trail system in Figure 11.1.

Prestige's tram service originates at the park entrance. Thus, node A is the source node for every tram line in the residents' shortest route problem. As Figure 11.1 indicates, the tram can travel from A over the trails to station B, C, or D. Among these sites, D is the nearest to A. In other words, the shortest route to station D is directly from the park entrance at site A.

Figure 11.7 illustrates the first tram line route. The shortest distance to

Table 11.6 Possibilities for Second Tram Route

Route	Distance (Miles)
A to B	4
A to C	5
A through D to C	$2 + 1 = 3$
A through D to E	$2 + 3 = 5$

Figure 11.8 Second Tram Line Route (A through D to C)

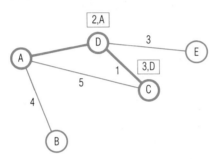

the origin is enclosed in a box above the connected node. The box also identifies the immediately preceding station on the shortest route from the origin.

There are several possibilities for the next route. A tram still can go from the park entrance at A to site B or C. As Figure 11.1 indicates, B is 4 miles from A and C is 5 miles from A. In addition, site D has already been connected to A, and so the tram can travel from the park entrance through D to site C or E. Since A to D is 2 miles and D to C another 1 mile, the route from A through D to C is a total of $2 + 1 = 3$ miles. Similarly, A through D to E is a total of $2 + 3 = 5$ miles. In other words, the possibilities given in Table 11.6 are all candidates for the second tram route. Among these four candidates, the route to site C through station D is the fewest total miles from the park entrance (node A). That is, the shortest route from A to C would be through site D. Figure 11.8 illustrates this second tram line route. The shortest distances to the origin are again enclosed in boxes above the corresponding connected nodes. And once more, each box identifies the immediately preceding station on the shortest route from the origin.

Since the shortest route to site C is through D, the decision maker can eliminate the trail from A to C from further consideration. However, there

Table 11.7 Possibilities for Third Tram Route

Route	Distance (Miles)
A to B	4
A through D to E	2 + 3 = 5
A through D through C to E	2 + 1 + 2 = 5
A through D through C to B	2 + 1 + 7 = 10
A through D through C to G	2 + 1 + 7 = 10
A through D through C to H	2 + 1 + 6 = 9
A through D through C to F	2 + 1 + 3 = 6

Figure 11.9 Third Tram Line Route (A to B)

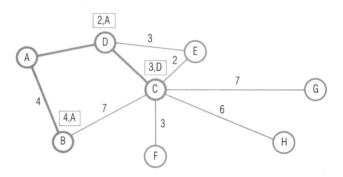

are still many candidates for the third tram line route. Again, the tram can travel the 4 miles from site A to B and the 5 miles from A through D to E. Also, C connects the origin A to many other stations. In fact, Figure 11.1 shows that the residents can utilize any of the routes given in Table 11.7 for this third tram line connection. Among these seven possibilities, the direct route to B is the shortest from origin A. That is, the shortest route to park station B is straight from the Sunrise entrance. Figure 11.9 illustrates this third tram line route.

Such a process, which is summarized in Table 11.8, can be repeated until the decision maker finds the shortest route from the origin to each node in the network. Indeed, by completing this modified version of the **labeling technique**, the decision maker will obtain the shortest tram line routes shown in Figure 11.10.

Figure 11.10 indicates that 9 miles is the shortest distance from the origin A to site H. By utilizing the boxed node labels to backtrack through the network, the decision maker can also determine the route associated

Table 11.8 Finding the Shortest Routes

1. Identify the specified origin and destination nodes in the network.
2. Connect the branch between the origin node and the nearest distinct node. Ties may be broken arbitrarily.
3. Write the branch length to the origin node in a box above the connected node. The box should also identify the immediately preceding node on the shortest route from the origin.
4. Identify the total branch lengths from the origin, either directly or through connected nodes, to unconnected nodes. Do not consider links to nodes that have already been connected by other branches.
5. Identify the unconnected node that is the shortest total branch length from the origin. Ties may be broken arbitrarily.
6. Join the unconnected node from step 5 with the immediately preceding node on the shortest route from the origin.
7. Write the total branch length to the origin in a box next to the connected node. The box should also identify the immediately preceding node on the shortest route from the origin.
8. Repeat steps 4 through 7 until all nodes in the network have been connected.
9. The resulting set of branches gives the shortest routes from the origin to every other node in the network.

Figure 11.10 Shortest Tram Routes

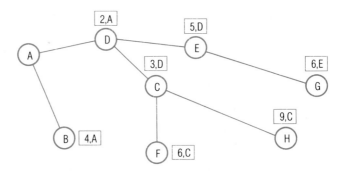

with this shortest distance. In particular, the boxed label above site H shows that C is the immediately preceding node on the shortest route from the origin. Furthermore, the boxed label above C lists site D as the preceding node, and station A precedes D. Therefore, the shortest tram line route to the swimming and skating pond at site H is the 9 miles from the park entrance at A, through station D, then through site C. A similar examination of Figure 11.10 will reveal that the shortest tram line routes from the park entrance to the other park sites are as given in Table 11.9.

Table 11.9 Shortest Tram Routes

Route	Distance (Miles)
A to B	4
A to D	2
A through D to C	3
A through D to E	5
A through D through C to F	6
A through D through E to G	6

COMPUTER ANALYSIS In large-scale problems, it can be tedious and time-consuming to find the shortest route by hand. Moreover, the process may be prone to error. As in the minimal spanning tree situation, however, management scientists have developed prewritten computer packages designed to solve the shortest route problem. One such package, called **SHOR1**, is available on a diskette for personal computers with the purchase of the Erikson and Hall [6] book. Figure 11.11 illustrates the SHOR1 solution for the swimming and skating pond (site H) destination in Prestige's tram-routing problem.

The user executes the program by typing the code number for SHOR1 on the computer keyboard. Although not shown in Figure 11.11, this number will appear on the screen display of the available programs in the Erikson and Hall computer diskette. The program then requests the information about the network that describes the decision problem.

As Figure 11.11 shows, the user first must enter the number of nodes and links in the network. In this regard, there are eight sites (nodes) and fourteen trails (links) in the Sunrise park system. Therefore, the decision maker should type the value 8 after the prompt for the number of nodes and 14 following the prompt for the number of links.

Next, the user specifies the type of network that describes the problem. There are two alternatives. In an **asymmetric network**, the branch between at least one pair of nodes is restricted to one-way traffic and/or has a different length in each flow direction. On the other hand, a network is **symmetric** when the link between any pair of nodes has an identical length in either flow direction.

In Sunrise's park network (Figure 11.1), a tram line running between stations C and D will travel 1 mile regardless of the route direction. Similarly, a movement between C and H will require a 6-mile trip regardless of the route direction. In fact, the trail (branch) between any pair of park stations is an identical length in either route direction. Hence, the decision maker enters the word SYMMETRIC after the computer prompt for network type.

Figure 11.11 Tram Line SHOR1 Solution

```
        ** INFORMATION ENTERED **

        NUMBER OF NODES 8
        NUMBER OF LINKS 14
        TYPE:  SYMMETRIC

   LINK START END    DISTANCE      REVERSE
        NODE  NODE                 DISTANCE

     1    1    2      4              4
     2    1    3      5              5
     3    1    4      2              2
     4    2    3      7              7
     5    2    6      5              5
     6    3    4      1              1
     7    3    5      2              2
     8    3    6      3              3
     9    3    7      7              7
    10    3    8      6              6
    11    4    5      3              3
    12    5    7      1              1
    13    6    8      8              8
    14    7    8      4              4


        ** RESULTS **

    START          END          DISTANCE
    NODE           NODE

     1              4              2
     4              3              1
     3              8              6

        TOTAL DISTANCE 9


        ** END OF ANALYSIS **
```

At this point, SHOR1 asks the user to identify the starting node, ending node, and distance (branch value) for each link in the network. In the process, all nodes and links must be identified by integers rather than letters. Moreover, the decision maker should designate the origin (source) as node 1, label the intermediate nodes with consecutive integers, and assign the highest identification number to the destination (sink) node. Link identification numbers also must start with the number 1 and contain no gaps.

Consider, for example, the trail (link) between the park entrance (node A) and station D in Sunrise's park system (Figure 11.1). Management can label this trail as link 3, the park entrance as node 1, and station D as node 4. Such a trail (link 3) then starts at node 1, ends at node 4, and is 2 miles long. Thus, the user enters these numbers after the corresponding link 3 prompts in Figure 11.11.

Similarly, the trail between stations C and D in the park network can be denoted as link 6. In such a scheme, site C is depicted as node 3 and station D as node 4. The trail joining these sites (link 6) then starts at node 3, ends at node 4, and is 1 mile in length. Consequently, these numbers are entered after the corresponding link 6 prompts in Figure 11.11.

The swimming and skating pond at H is the destination site in the SHOR1 computer run of Figure 11.11, so the user assigns the highest node identification number to site H. Since there are eight nodes in Sunrise's park network, station H must be labeled as node 8 in Figure 11.11.

After receiving all the network information, SHOR1 processes the data and generates the shortest route from the origin (source) to the specified destination (sink). The program prints the starting node, ending node, and length of each link in this route. Moreover, it lists the total length (sum of the branch values) for the shortest route.

The RESULTS segment of Figure 11.11, for example, shows that 9 miles is the shortest distance from the park entrance at node 1 (A) to the swimming and skating pond at node 8 (H). Furthermore, this distance is obtained by utilizing the trails (links) between the following nodes:

♦ node 1 (site A) and node 4 (site D)
♦ node 4 (site D) and node 3 (site C)
♦ node 3 (site C) and node 8 (site H)

In other words, the shortest tram line route to the swimming and skating pond at site H is the 9 miles from the park entrance at A, through station D, then through site C. By comparing Figures 11.11 and 11.10, you will find that SHOR1 has generated the same shortest route recommendation for site H as the more cumbersome hand calculation.

APPLICATIONS The shortest route methodology is usually applied to operations problems. It is most useful when management seeks the shortest route over the existing links between two specified nodes in a network. In practice, such problems arise frequently and in a wide variety of business and economic situations. Table 11.10 presents a few typical illustrations.

In addition, the basic shortest route concepts can be extended and then applied to related problems. Some of these extensions, including asymmetric network situations, are discussed by Lawler [14] and Murtz [16]. Moreover, M. L. Fisher and R. Jaikumar [7] show how a modified version of this network analysis can be used for space shuttle scheduling.

Table 11.10 Shortest Route Applications

Network	Nodes	Branches	Problem
Highway	Cities and towns	Roads	Find the shortest route between specified cities.
Parts	Work stations	Pneumatic tube system	Specify the shortest route between a central parts depository and various work stations.
Natural gas	Distribution stations	Pipelines	Determine the shortest route from the main distributor to specified regional stations.
Air travel	Airports	Air lanes	Find the shortest routes between specified airports.
Equipment replacement	Time periods	Replacement options	Determine the times during which the equipment can be replaced at least cost.

TRAVELING SALESPERSON PROBLEM   Example 11.3 illustrates another type of routing situation.

EXAMPLE 11.3 Traveling Salesperson

Jenny Float is a salesperson for Dynamite Exercise Equipment Company. As part of her customer service responsibilities, she must travel each month from the regional sales office in Townson to consumer seminars in Roystertown, Annadel, Colutia, Ophan, and Hunter Valley.

Table 11.11 lists the driving times in minutes required to

Table 11.11 Jenny Float's Travel Times (in Minutes)

From	To					
	Townson	Roystertown	Annadel	Colutia	Ophan	Hunter Valley
Townson	—	11	23	19	13	25
Roystertown	11	—	49	7	46	39
Annadel	20	49	—	12	55	70
Colutia	19	7	12	—	55	57
Ophan	13	46	59	55	—	12
Hunter Valley	28	39	82	57	13	—

travel over the existing routes between the towns. As the table indicates, the intercity travel times are not all symmetrical. For example, it takes 23 minutes to travel from Townson to Annadel, but only 20 minutes from Annadel to Townson. Such a situation arises because of traffic patterns, construction detours, and other diversions.

Sales management considers travel time to be costly and unproductive effort. Therefore, it wants Jenny to minimize her travel time. In particular, the sales manager requests that she start at Townson, visit each seminar site only once, and then return to the regional office in the smallest possible total number of minutes.

Dynamite's situation is similar to Prestige's tram-routing problem (Example 11.2). That is, the salesperson situation can be portrayed as a network in which a set of nodes (cities) is linked by a series of branches (roads). Each branch depicts a potential link (salesperson route) between nodes. There will be a flow (Jenny's movement) along the branches, and this movement will flow in any direction over the links. Also, the branch values measure the travel time in minutes between the corresponding nodes in the network.

In addition, the flow vehicle (Jenny) once more starts at a source (Townson) and travels over the existing links (roads) to a sink (the regional office). Furthermore, the decision maker (regional sales manager) still wants to select the series of links between the source and sink that minimizes a criterion value. In Example 11.3, this criterion is travel time in minutes.

Nevertheless, there are some key differences between Examples 11.2 and 11.3. One distinction deals with the nature of the route from source to sink. In Example 11.2, each tram is sent from the park entrance to a specified station. In the process, it is not necessary to utilize every potential trail (link) or have a loop in any tram route. On the other hand, Jenny starts at Townson, visits each seminar site only once, and then returns to the regional sales office. Such a sequence of visits, known as a **tour**, will form a loop from Townson back to itself in the corresponding network of towns. Put another way, Jenny must follow a loop or cycle.

Another difference deals with the number of routes from source to sink. In Example 11.2, Prestige sends a different tram from the park entrance to each station. Hence, each destination can receive a tram through a distinct route. In other words, there is a need for several tram routes. But Jenny's tour can be completed with a single route from Townson through the sequence of assigned seminar sites. Indeed, the sales manager wants to find the tour that will minimize her total travel time. Such a situation is referred to as the **traveling salesperson problem**.

Figure 11.12 Towns on Jenny's Tour

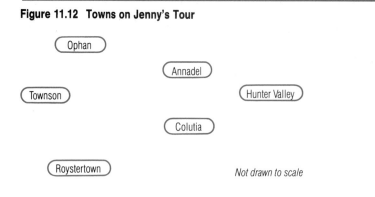

Not drawn to scale

Table 11.12 Jenny's Assignment Table

From	To					
	Townson	Roystertown	Annadel	Colutia	Ophan	Hunter Valley
Townson	M	11	23	19	13	25
Roystertown	11	M	49	7	46	39
Annadel	20	49	M	12	55	70
Colutia	19	7	12	M	55	57
Ophan	13	46	59	55	M	12
Hunter Valley	28	39	82	57	13	M

Driving time in minutes

FINDING THE BEST TOUR   As E. Minieka [15] demonstrates, there is a variety of methods available to solve the traveling salesperson problem. One of the most popular approaches utilizes the assignment procedure from chapter 10 in conjunction with a modified version of chapter 9's branch and bound methodology.

To see how this approach works, let us take a look at Figure 11.12, which shows the towns that Jenny must visit to complete her customer service responsibilities. If this group of towns is viewed as a distribution system, then Jenny's situation can be treated as the assignment problem depicted by Table 11.12. In this table, each town represents both an origin for and a destination of Jenny's travels. Table entries identify the driving times in minutes between towns. The problem is to determine the town assignments that will minimize Jenny's total driving time.

Since it is pointless to make any intratown assignments (such as from Townson to Townson or Annadel to Annadel), management should assign

Table 11.13 Jenny's Optimal Assignment Table

	To					
From	Townson	Roystertown	Annadel	Colutia	Ophan	Hunter Valley
Townson	M	$\boxed{0}$	4	8	2	11
Roystertown	$\boxed{0}$	M	34	0	39	29
Annadel	4	37	M	$\boxed{0}$	43	55
Colutia	11	3	$\boxed{0}$	M	51	50
Ophan	0	37	42	46	M	$\boxed{0}$
Hunter Valley	11	26	61	44	$\boxed{0}$	M

Opportunity losses in minutes

a very large driving time to each intratown route. In this way, such routes will become extremely unattractive alternatives, and the decision maker will be inclined to avoid these pointless routes. Although any very large value will work, it is customary to use an arbitrary number denoted by the symbol M. Once more, M represents a number so large that M minus any value still equals M. Each intratown route will have an entry of M in Table 11.12.

By applying the methodology from chapter 10, Dynamite's management will obtain the optimal assignment pattern shown in Table 11.13. In this table, the zero values enclosed in boxes identify the optimal assignments. Table 11.13 indicates that Dynamite will minimize Jenny's total travel time by assigning her as follows:

♦ From Townson to Roystertown
♦ From Roystertown to Townson
♦ From Annadel to Colutia
♦ From Colutia to Annadel
♦ From Ophan to Hunter Valley
♦ From Hunter Valley to Ophan

Moreover, according to Table 11.12, these optimal assignments will involve $11 + 11 + 12 + 12 + 12 + 13 = 71$ minutes of driving time.

Figure 11.13 presents a representation of Jenny's optimal assignment pattern. Notice how the optimal assignment pattern creates three separate sequences of links, or **subtours**, between the towns. In each case, Jenny starts at a particular city, visits some (but not all) towns, and returns to the starting point. The Townson/Roystertown subtour, for instance, starts at

Figure 11.13 Jenny's Optimal Assignments

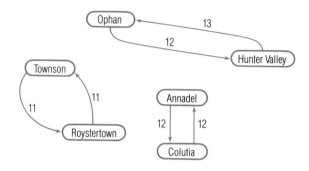

the regional office in Townson, visits only Roystertown, and then returns to the office. Similarly, the Ophan/Hunter Valley subtour begins at Ophan, visits only Hunter Valley, and then returns to Ophan.

The sales manager, however, wants Jenny to make a complete tour. She must start at Townson, visit each seminar site only once, and then return to the regional office. Since the optimal assignment pattern fails to form such a tour, it does not constitute a feasible solution to Dynamite's traveling salesperson problem. Nevertheless, this solution provides the data needed to form a complete tour from the three subtours depicted in Figure 11.13.

Although the tour formation process can begin anywhere, it is usually most convenient to start with the subtour that involves the fewest nodes. In this regard, Figure 11.13 shows that each of the three subtours has the same number of towns. Thus, any one of these subtours can be used to initiate the formation process.

Suppose that Dynamite's sales manager selects the Townson/Roystertown subtour. By replacing the 0 with an M entry in the Townson/Roystertown cell in Table 11.13, the sales manager effectively prohibits any assignment along the Townson-to-Roystertown link of this subtour. In the process, management creates a new assignment problem. Similarly, the decision maker can prevent any allocation along the Roystertown-to-Townson branch of the subtour by replacing the 0 with an M entry in the Roystertown/Townson cell. Moreover, such a procedure creates a second new assignment problem.

If Dynamite performs this partitioning, or branching, action and solves the resulting new assignment problems, it will obtain the results shown in Figure 11.14. Note that the initial branching action creates two new solutions to the problem. Furthermore, both of these solutions exclude the Roystertown/Townson subtour and, in the process, generate more complete sequences of towns for Jenny to visit. New problem 1's optimal assignment, for instance, includes visits to Townson and Roystertown

Figure 11.14 Dynamite's Initial Partitioning Process

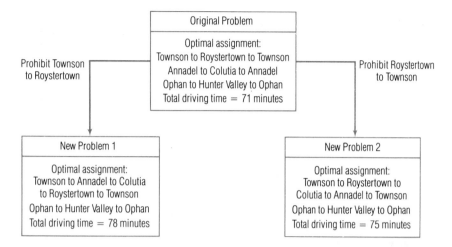

within a larger Townson/Annadel/Colutia/Roystertown/Townson subtour. That is, the new problems come closer than the original assignment structure to forming a complete tour (feasible solution) for Dynamite's traveling salesperson situation.

The partitioning process, however, adds prohibitions that effectively reduce the decision maker's available assignments. As a result, both new problems have solutions that involve longer total driving times than the answer to the original assignment formulation. Figure 11.14, for example, shows that new problem 1's subtours require Jenny to drive for $78 - 71 = 7$ minutes longer than the total time associated with the original problem subtours. In effect, then, the 71-minute value from the original assignment problem solution represents an initial lower bound on Jenny's optimal total travel time.

Figure 11.14 also indicates that the optimal travel time (75 minutes) from new problem 2 is shorter than the corresponding answer (78 minutes) for new problem 1. Yet neither of these two new problems provides a solution that forms a complete tour of the towns on Jenny's itinerary. This result suggests that there are no complete tours with a total travel time of less than 75 minutes. Consequently, 75 replaces 71 minutes as the lower bound on Jenny's optimal total travel time.

At this stage, however, Dynamite does not know if a complete tour can be formed from the two subtours associated with the lower bound structure (new problem 2). To find out, management must partition new problem 2 into its complementary assignment formulations and then solve the resulting new problems. By so doing, it will obtain the results depicted in Figure 11.15. (In Figure 11.15, the first letter is used to identify the town.

Figure 11.15 Dynamite's Second Partitioning Process

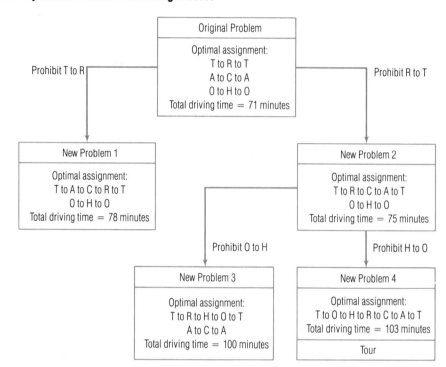

Townson, for example, is represented by the letter T, Roystertown by the letter R, and so on.)

As Figure 11.15 indicates, the second partitioning process starts with the Ophan/Hunter Valley/Ophan subtour. Once more, this subtour is selected primarily for convenience, since this sequence has fewer towns than the other (Townson/Roystertown/Colutia/Annadel/Townson) subtour associated with new problem 2's solution. By prohibiting the visit from Ophan to Hunter Valley, Dynamite creates new problem 3. This problem involves an optimal assignment that incorporates visits to Ophan and Hunter Valley within a larger Townson/Roystertown/Hunter Valley/Ophan/Townson subtour. Still, new problem 3's solution forms two subtours rather than a complete tour of towns. Moreover, these subtours require Jenny to drive $100 - 75 = 25$ minutes longer than the total time needed for new problem 2's solution.

On the other hand, consider the other branch emanating from new problem 2 in Figure 11.15. As you can see, when Dynamite prohibits the visit from Hunter Valley to Ophan, it creates new problem 4. Furthermore, this problem involves an optimal assignment that forms the Townson/Ophan/Hunter Valley/Roystertown/Colutia/Annadel/Townson complete tour of towns on Jenny's itinerary.

The Townson/Ophan/Hunter Valley/Roystertown/Colutia/Annadel/ Townson sequence is the only complete tour formed by any of the assignment problems shown in Figure 11.15. In other words, Dynamite has not yet identified a feasible solution that is better than new problem 4's recommendation. Consequently, the 103-minute value from new problem 4's solution represents an initial upper bound on Jenny's optimal total travel time.

Still, there are two remaining new problem solutions that have shorter total travel times than the 103-minute initial upper bound. Figure 11.15, for example, shows that new problem 1's optimal assignment requires Jenny to drive $103 - 78 = 25$ minutes less than the total time associated with the initial upper bound (new problem 4) recommendation. Similarly, the optimal travel time from new problem 3 is $103 - 100 = 3$ minutes less than the initial upper bound. Yet neither new problem 1 nor new problem 3 provides a solution that forms a complete tour of the towns on Jenny's itinerary. This suggests that there are no complete tours with a total travel time of less than 78 minutes. Therefore, new problem 1's recommendation (78 minutes) replaces new problem 2's answer (75 minutes) as the lower bound on Jenny's optimal travel time.

At this stage, then, Dynamite knows that the optimal tour will require Jenny to drive at least 78 minutes (the lower bound) but no more than 103 minutes (the upper bound). Furthermore, it may be possible to form such a tour from the two subtours associated with the lower bound (new problem 1) solution. To find out, management must continue with the branching process to eventually obtain the results depicted in Figure 11.16.

Figure 11.16 shows that the partitioning of new problem 1 creates new problems 5 and 6. Moreover, the optimal assignment for new problem 5 forms a complete tour (Townson/Annadel/Colutia/Roystertown/Hunter Valley/Ophan/Townson) of the towns on Jenny's itinerary. However, this tour requires her to drive $107 - 103 = 4$ minutes longer than the total time associated with the upper bound (new problem 4) recommendation. In the diagram, we denote such an exclusion by drawing a jagged line (pruning the branch) leading to new problem 5. On the other hand, new problem 6's solution requires Jenny to drive $103 - 99 = 4$ minutes less than the upper bound tour time. Moreover, new problem 6's optimal travel time is $100 - 99 = 1$ minute less than the corresponding answer to new problem 3. Neither of these new solutions, however, forms a complete tour of towns. These results imply that there are no such tours with a driving time shorter than 99 minutes. Hence, the 99-minute recommendation from new problem 6 becomes the lower bound on Jenny's optimal travel time.

By partitioning new problem 6 into its complementary assignment formulations, Dynamite then creates new problems 7 and 8. As Figure 11.16 indicates, the optimal assignment from new problem 8 requires Jenny to drive $121 - 103 = 18$ minutes longer than the upper bound tour

Figure 11.16 Dynamite's Branch and Bound Solution

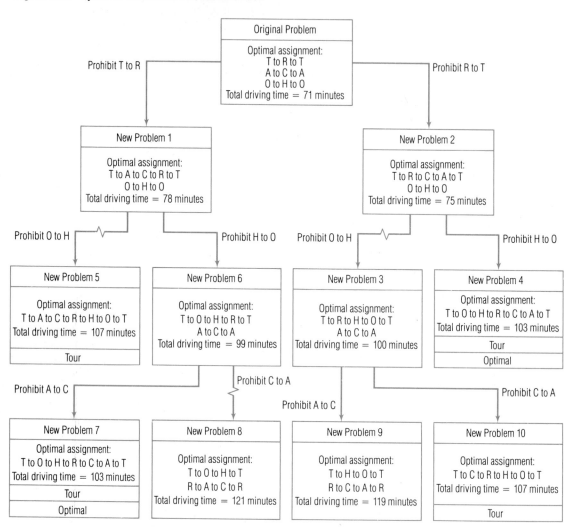

time. Consequently, this problem can be eliminated from further consideration. Once more, we denote such an exclusion in the diagram by drawing a jagged line (pruning the branch) leading to new problem 8.

The optimal assignment for new problem 7 forms a complete tour (Townson/Ophan/Hunter Valley/Roystertown/Colutia/Annadel/Townson) of the towns on Jenny's itinerary. Yet Figure 11.16 shows that this solution is the same recommendation provided by the upper bound (new problem 4) structure. Such a result confirms that 103 minutes represents the upper bound on Jenny's optimal travel time.

Nevertheless, Figure 11.16 indicates that new problem 3's optimal

Figure 11.17 Dynamite's Optimal Traveling Salesperson Solution

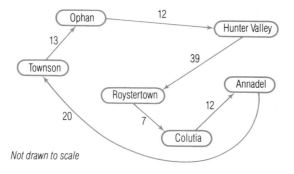

Not drawn to scale

assignment requires Jenny to drive $103 - 100 = 3$ minutes less than the upper bound tour time. Although this assignment consists of two subtours, such a result suggests that Dynamite still may be able to form a tour with a travel time between 100 and 103 minutes. To find out, management must continue with the branching action. In the process, the 100-minute recommendation from new problem 3 becomes the lower bound on the optimal total travel time.

When Dynamite partitions new problem 3 into its complementary assignment formulations, it creates new problems 9 and 10. As Figure 11.16 shows, however, the optimal assignments from new problems 9 and 10 both require Jenny to drive longer than the upper bound tour time. The optimal assignment for new problem 10, for instance, demands $107 - 103 = 4$ more minutes than the upper bound. As a result, both of these problems can be eliminated (pruned) from further consideration.

At this stage, there are no other new problems that can form a tour with a driving time shorter than 103 minutes. Hence, 103 minutes becomes the lower bound on the optimal total travel time. Since the lower and upper bounds now have the same value, 103 minutes also must represent Jenny's optimal travel time.

By following the unpruned branches in Figure 11.16, you can see that the 103-minute recommendation is obtained from the solution to new problems 4 and 7. According to these solutions, Jenny should be assigned as follows:

- From Townson to Ophan
- From Opnan to Hunter Valley
- From Hunter Valley to Roystertown
- From Roystertown to Colutia
- From Colutia to Annadel
- From Annadel to Townson

This optimal tour is depicted in Figure 11.17.

Table 11.14 Finding the Optimal Tour

1. Treat the situation as an assignment problem. Each site should be denoted as both an origin and a destination. Cell entries in the assignment table identify the costs, times, or distances between sites. Unacceptable or prohibited routes are assigned very large positive (M) entries in the table.

2. Solve the assignment problem. If the answer forms a complete tour, it represents the optimal solution to the traveling salesperson situation. Otherwise, go to step 3.

3. Determine the lower bound on the optimal criterion value. To do so:
   a. Identify all assignment problem solutions that involve subtours.
   b. Select the solution with the best criterion value.
   c. Set the lower bound equal to this value.

4. Find the upper bound on the optimal criterion value as follows:
   a. Identify all assignment problem solutions that involve complete tours.
   b. Select the solution with the best criterion value.
   c. Set the upper bound equal to this value. If there are no solutions with complete tours, set the upper bound equal to infinity (∞).

5. Use the following procedure to partition the lower bound problem into its complementary assignment formulations:
   a. Select the subtour with the least number of sites. Any ties can be broken arbitrarily.
   b. List each intercity trip in the subtour.
   c. Create a new assignment problem from the lower bound structure by prohibiting one of the listed intercity trips.
   d. Formulate one such new problem from the lower bound formulation for each of the intercity trips.

6. Solve each new assignment problem. Then return to step 3.

7. Repeat steps 3 through 6 until the lower bound is equal to the upper bound on the optimal criterion value. When the two bounds are equal, the optimal tour will be given by the assignment problem solution that corresponds to that criterion value.

Table 11.15 Traveling Salesperson Extensions and Applications

Area	Application	Reference
Trucking	Planning truck fleet size	M. O. Ball et al. [2]
Municipal sanitation operations	Routing and scheduling street sweepers	L. D. Brodin and S. J. Kursh [4]
Airline operations	Developing passenger mix flight plans	F. Glover et al. [9]
Maintenance	Scheduling of vehicle maintenance	H. K. Schultz [20]
Training	Scheduling crew personnel for recurrent training	M. Shapiro [21]

Table 11.14 summarizes this branch and bound procedure for solving the traveling salesperson problem. Such a solution procedure is referred to as the **Eastman/Shapiro algorithm**.

EXTENSIONS The traveling salesperson methodology originally was developed to find the optimal tour of sites on a company itinerary. In addition, the basic methodology has recently been extended and applied to a variety of related business and economic problems. Table 11.15 presents a small sample of the extensions and applications. Also, H. Crowder and M. W. Padberg [5] and F. Glover and others [8] have developed efficient methodologies for solving many of these traveling salesperson problem extensions.

FLOWS In the previous layout and route problems, there were no limits placed on the number of items that could flow over the network branches. However, many network situations involve links that do have limited flow capacities.

MAXIMAL FLOW PROBLEM When there are flow restrictions, the decision maker frequently must determine the maximum number of items that can move from a specified origin to a particular destination in the network. Example 11.4 illustrates.

EXAMPLE 11.4 Transmitting Natural Gas

The Atlantic Pacific Company owns a pipeline network that is used to transmit natural gas between its main exploration site and several storage facilities. A portion of the network is depicted in Figure 11.18. In this diagram, the numbers on the branches give the flow capacities in each direction. These numbers are expressed in thousands of cubic feet per hour. Consider, for example, the two numbers on the branch from the exploration site to facility 1. The 10 indicates that the company can transmit 10,000 cubic feet of

Figure 11.18 Atlantic Pacific's Pipeline Network

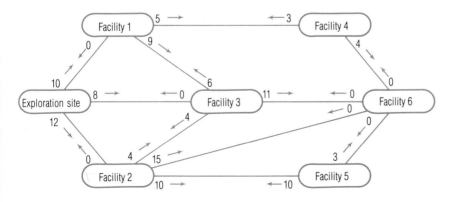

natural gas from the source to facility 1, while the 0 means that it can send nothing in the reverse direction. Similarly, the two numbers on the branch between facilities 2 and 3 show that 4000 cubic feet of natural gas can be transmitted in each direction between these sites.

Flow capacities differ because of varying pipe sizes. By selectively opening and closing sections of the pipeline network, Atlantic can supply any of the storage locations. Currently, management seeks the maximum quantity of natural gas that can be transmitted from the exploration site to storage facility 6.

Atlantic's gas transmission situation has some characteristics in common with routing problems. Figure 11.18 demonstrates that the gas transmission situation can be portrayed as a network in which a set of nodes (the exploration and storage sites) is linked by a series of branches (pipelines). Each branch depicts a potential link between nodes, and there is a flow (movement of natural gas) along the links. Also, the flow once more starts at a source (the exploration site) and moves over the existing links to a sink (storage facility 6). In transmitting the flow, Atlantic may not have to utilize every potential link (pipeline) in the network.

Nevertheless, there are some key differences between routing problems and Example 11.4. One distinction deals with the branch values. In the previous routing (shortest route and traveling salesperson) problems, the branch values measured the distance or time required to travel between the network nodes. But the numbers on Atlantic's links give the quantity of natural gas that can be transmitted between the exploration site and the storage facilities.

Another difference deals with the flow capabilities. In the prior routing problems, there were no restrictions on the quantities that could be moved over the network links. Atlantic's pipeline sizes, however, limit the volume of natural gas that can be transmitted between the exploration and storage sites. That is, Example 11.4 involves restricted branch flow capacities.

In addition, there is a distinction between the decision objectives for these problems. In the previous routing situations, management wanted the minimum distance or time required to link the network source and sink. Atlantic also wants to link the source (the exploration site) and sink (storage facility 6) in its pipeline network. But management's objective is to transmit as much natural gas as possible between the source and sink. This largest possible quantity is known as the **maximal flow**. In effect, then, Atlantic's problem is to determine the maximal flow of natural gas through the pipeline network.

FINDING THE MAXIMAL FLOW As Bazaraa and Jarvis [3] and Murtz [16] demonstrate, the maximal flow problem can be formulated as a linear program and then solved with the simplex method. Yet even small-scale maximal flow situations, like

Figure 11.19 Maximal Flow over Atlantic's Exploration Site/Facility 3/Facility 6 Path

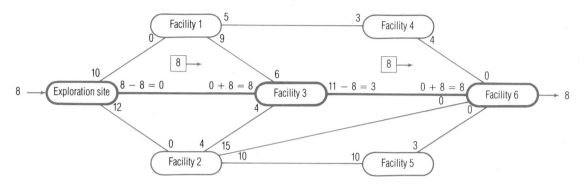

Atlantic's pipeline network, may generate relatively large linear programming problems. Thus, it can be very time-consuming and expensive, even with the aid of a computer, to determine the maximal flow with linear programming methodologies.

For this reason, management scientists have developed specialized procedures to solve the maximal flow problem. One of these procedures enables the decision maker to determine the solution in a relatively straightforward manner. To see what is involved, let us again examine Atlantic's pipeline network (Figure 11.18).

There are many ways for the company to transmit natural gas between the source (exploration site) and sink (storage facility 6). One possibility is to send the gas from the exploration site through storage facility 3 and on to storage facility 6. Such a series of links is known as a **path** from the source to the sink of the network.

According to Figure 11.18, Atlantic can transmit 11,000 cubic feet of natural gas per hour along the facility 3/facility 6 branch of the exploration site/facility 3/facility 6 path. The exploration site/facility 3 pipeline, however, is big enough to handle only 8000 cubic feet per hour. To meet this branch flow constraint, then, management must send no more than 8000 cubic feet over each link in the exploration site/facility 3/facility 6 path. In other words, the maximal flow along a path will equal the smallest of all current branch capacities associated with the path.

If the company transmits the maximal flow over the exploration site/facility 3/facility 6 path, it will obtain the results shown in Figure 11.19. The colored links identify the exploration site/facility 3/facility 6 path. The maximal flows over these links are enclosed in boxes above the corresponding path branches. Also, the number entering the source (exploration site) and exiting the sink (facility 6) represents the total quantity of natural gas currently flowing through Atlantic's pipeline network. Once more, the flows are measured in thousands of cubic feet per hour.

Figure 11.20 Maximal Flow over Atlantic's Exploration Site/Facility 1/Facility 4/Facility 6 Path

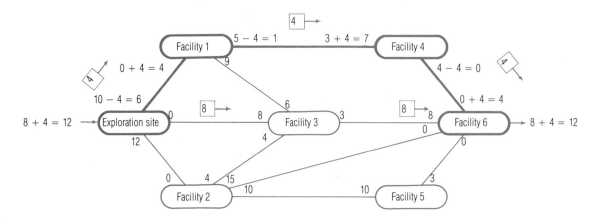

As Figure 11.19 demonstrates, the maximal flow over the exploration site/facility 3/facility 6 path is 8000 cubic feet of natural gas per hour. If Atlantic sends this quantity over the denoted path, it will reduce the exploration site/facility 3 pipeline capacity from 8000 cubic feet to $8000 - 8000 = 0$ cubic feet per hour. Moreover, the facility 3/facility 6 branch capacity will drop from 11,000 cubic feet to $11,000 - 8000 = 3000$ cubic feet per hour.

On the other hand, such an action might adversely affect the flow along the potential paths in the system. Furthermore, these alternative paths could enable Atlantic to increase the total flow of natural gas between the source and sink of its pipeline network. As a result, management eventually may want to divert some or all of the exploration site/facility 3/facility 6 flow to the alternative paths.

The divergence can be accounted for by sending the flow back over the links joining the sink and source of the path. In this regard, the exploration site/facility 3/facility 6 path has a maximal flow of 8000 cubic feet of natural gas per hour. Hence, Atlantic could send as much as 8000 cubic feet back over the facility 6/facility 3 and facility 3/exploration site links of the path. Figure 11.19 shows that such an accounting will increase the facility 6/facility 3 pipeline capacity from 0 (the original limit) to $0 + 8000 = 8000$ cubic feet (the original limit plus maximal diverted flow). Similarly, the facility 3/exploration site branch capacity would rise from 0 to $0 + 8000 = 8000$ cubic feet per hour.

Figure 11.19 also indicates that the natural gas can follow additional paths from the source to the sink of the company's pipeline network. The flow can move from the exploration site through facility 1, then 4, and on to facility 6. In addition, Figure 11.19 shows that 4000 cubic feet per hour

Table 11.16 Branch Flow Capacities

Branch	Original Capacity (Cubic Feet per Hour)	Flow Change (Cubic Feet per Hour)	Revised Capacity (Cubic Feet per Hour)
Exploration site to facility 1	10,000	−4000	6000
Facility 1 to facility 4	5,000	−4000	1000
Facility 4 to facility 6	4,000	−4000	0
Facility 6 to facility 4	0	4000	4000
Facility 4 to facility 1	3,000	4000	7000
Facility 1 to exploration site	0	4000	4000

is the smallest branch flow capacity associated with this path. Therefore, the maximal flow over the exploration site/facility 1/facility 4/facility 6 path is 4000 cubic feet of natural gas per hour.

When management transmits the maximal flow over this path, it obtains the results shown in Figure 11.20. Again, the colored links identify the exploration site/facility 1/facility 4/facility 6 path, and the maximal flows over these links once more are enclosed in boxes above the corresponding path branches. Also, the number entering the source (exploration site) and exiting the sink (facility 6) again represents the total quantity of natural gas (in thousands of cubic feet per hour) currently flowing through Atlantic's pipeline network.

As Figure 11.20 demonstrates, the maximal flow over the exploration site/facility 1/facility 4/facility 6 path is 4000 cubic feet per hour. If Atlantic sends this quantity over the denoted path, branch flow capacities will change as indicated in Table 11.16. In the process, the total flow through the pipeline network will increase from 8000 cubic feet per hour (the exploration site/facility 3/facility 6 maximal flow) to 8000 + 4000 = 12,000 cubic feet per hour.

This process, which is summarized in Table 11.17, must be repeated until management finds the maximal total flow through the network. Indeed, by completing this process, management will obtain the maximal flow pattern shown in Figure 11.21. According to this diagram, management should utilize the flow pattern presented in Table 11.18. The quantity entering the source (exploration site) and exiting the sink (facility 6) gives the maximal total flow resulting from the optimal pattern. In particular, it shows that the company can transmit no more than 30,000 cubic feet of natural gas per hour through the existing pipeline network.

Table 11.17 Finding the Network's Maximal Total Flow

1. Identify the source and the sink of the network.
2. Select any path that has flow capacities greater than zero on all branches from the source to the sink.
3. Identify the smallest of all current branch capacities associated with the path. This smallest branch capacity represents the maximal flow along the path.
4. Write the path's maximal flow in a box above each branch on the path. Use an arrow to indicate the quantity's direction of flow.
5. Subtract the path's maximal flow from the capacity of each path branch leading from the source to the sink.
6. Add the path's maximal flow to the capacity of each path branch leading from the sink to the source.
7. Repeat steps 2 through 6 until there are no more paths with positive flow capacities on all branches from the source to the sink.
8. The resulting diagram identifies the maximal flow along each branch and the maximal total flow through the network.

Figure 11.21 Atlantic's Maximal Flow Pattern

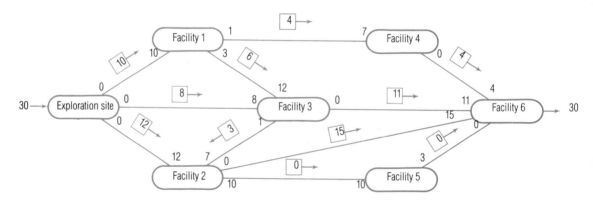

COMPUTER ANALYSIS In large-scale problems, it can be tedious and time-consuming to find the maximal flow by hand. Moreover, the process is prone to error. Consequently, management scientists have developed prewritten computer packages designed to perform the necessary computations. One such package, called **MAXF1**, is available on a diskette for personal computers with the purchase of the Erikson and Hall [6] book. Figure 11.22 illustrates the MAXF1 solution to Atlantic's natural gas transmission problem.

The user executes the program by typing the code number for MAXF1 on the computer keyboard. Although not shown in Figure 11.22, this

Table 11.18 Atlantic's Maximal Flow Pattern

Pipeline	Natural Gas Transmitted (Cubic Feet per Hour)
Exploration site to facility 1	10,000
Exploration site to facility 2	12,000
Exploration site to facility 3	8,000
Facility 1 to facility 3	6,000
Facility 1 to facility 4	4,000
Facility 2 to facility 5	0
Facility 2 to facility 6	15,000
Facility 3 to facility 2	3,000
Facility 3 to facility 6	11,000
Facility 4 to facility 6	4,000
Facility 5 to facility 6	0

number will be identified on the screen display of the available programs in the Erikson and Hall computer diskette. The program then requests the information about the network that describes the decision problem.

As Figure 11.22 demonstrates, the user first must enter the number of nodes and links in the network. In this regard, there are seven sites (nodes) and eleven pipelines (links) in Atlantic's network. However, four of the links can accommodate a two-way flow of natural gas. The MAXF1 program treats each such link as two one-way pipelines. For MAXF1 purposes, then, there are fifteen links in the pipeline system. Hence, the decision maker should type the value 7 after the prompt for the number of nodes and 15 following the prompt for the number of links.

At this point, MAXF1 asks the user to identify the starting node, ending node, and maximum possible flow for each link in the network. In the process, all nodes and links must be identified by integers rather than letters. Moreover, the decision maker should designate the source as node 1, label the intermediate nodes with consecutive integers, and assign the highest identification number to the sink node. Link identification numbers also must start with the number 1 and contain no gaps.

Consider, for instance, the link between the exploration site (source) and facility 3 in Atlantic's pipeline network (Figure 11.18). Management can label this pipeline as link 2, the exploration site as node 1, and facility 3 as node 3. Such a pipeline (link 2) starts at node 1, ends at node 3, and has a maximum possible flow of 8000 cubic feet per hour. Thus, the user should enter these numbers after the corresponding link 2 prompts in Figure 11.22.

Similarly, the pipeline between facilities 4 and 1 in Atlantic's network can be denoted as link 9. In such a scheme, facility 4 is depicted as node 5

Figure 11.22
Atlantic's MAXF1 Solution

** INFORMATION ENTERED **

NUMBER OF NODES: 7
NUMBER OF LINKS: 15

LINK	START NODE	END NODE	FLOW
1	1	2	10
2	1	3	8
3	1	4	12
4	4	3	4
5	3	4	4
6	2	3	9
7	3	2	6
8	2	5	5
9	5	2	3
10	4	6	10
11	6	4	10
12	4	7	15
13	3	7	11
14	5	7	4
15	6	7	3

** RESULTS **

OPTIMAL FLOW OVER ALL PATHS FROM

NODE 1 TO NODE 7 :

FLOW	NODES THAT DEFINE EACH PATH			
8	1	3	7	
3	1	2	3	7
12	1	4	7	
3	1	2	3	4	7
4	1	2	5	7

OPTIMAL FLOW OVER EACH LINK:

START NODE	END NODE	FLOW
1	2	10
1	3	8
1	4	12
2	3	6
2	5	4
3	4	3
3	7	11
4	7	15
5	7	4

MAXIMUM TOTAL NETWORK FLOW: 30

** END OF ANALYSIS **

and facility 1 as node 2. The pipeline joining these facilities (link 9) then starts at node 5, ends at node 2, and has a maximum possible flow of 3000 cubic feet per hour. Consequently, these numbers are entered after the corresponding link 9 prompts in Figure 11.22.

Also, facility 6 is the sink of Atlantic's pipeline network. Hence, the user should assign the highest node identification number to facility 6. Since there are seven nodes in the company's network, facility 6 must be labeled as node 7 in Figure 11.22.

After receiving all the network information, MAXF1 processes the data and generates the maximal flow pattern. In particular, the program first lists a table of all flow paths from the source to the sink of the network. This table contains the total flow over each path and the node identification numbers of all nodes on the corresponding paths. Next, MAXF1 identifies the starting node, ending node, and optimal flow over each link utilized in the network. Then it gives the resulting maximal total network flow.

The RESULTS segment of Figure 11.22 shows that Atlantic can transmit no more than 30,000 cubic feet of natural gas per hour through the pipeline network. Furthermore, this maximal flow is achieved by sending the following quantities:

♦ 10,000 from node 1 (exploration site) to node 2 (facility 1)
♦ 8000 from node 1 (exploration site) to node 3 (facility 3)
♦ 12,000 from node 1 (exploration site) to node 4 (facility 2)
♦ 6000 from node 2 (facility 1) to node 3 (facility 3)
♦ 4000 from node 2 (facility 1) to node 5 (facility 4)
♦ 3000 from node 3 (facility 3) to node 4 (facility 2)
♦ 11,000 from node 3 (facility 3) to node 7 (facility 6)
♦ 15,000 from node 4 (facility 2) to node 7 (facility 6)
♦ 4000 from node 5 (facility 4) to node 7 (facility 6)

Since links 4, 7, 9, 10, 11, and 15 are not included in the optimal flow pattern, Atlantic should transmit 0 cubic feet of natural gas from node 4 (facility 2) to node 3 (facility 3), from node 3 (facility 3) to node 2 (facility 1), from node 5 (facility 4) to node 2 (facility 1), from node 4 (facility 2) to node 6 (facility 5), and from node 6 (facility 5) to node 4 (facility 2). By comparing Figures 11.21 and 11.22, we see that MAXF1 has generated the same maximal flow recommendation as the more cumbersome hand calculation.

APPLICATIONS The maximal flow methodology is usually applied to operations problems. It is most useful when management seeks the maximal flow over the existing links in a network. In practice, such problems arise frequently and

Table 11.19 Maximal Flow Applications

Network	Nodes	Branches	Problem
Sewage	Pumping stations	Pipes	Find the maximal flow of sewage through the system.
Waterway	Locks	Canals	Determine the maximal flow of barges through the waterway.
Automobile traffic	Lights and intersections	Roads	Specify the maximal flow of automobiles through the system.
Production	Manufacturing processes	Work flow links	Determine the total number of units that can flow through the system.
Communication	Message receivers and senders	Communication lines	Find the maximal flow of messages through the system.
Computer	Terminals	Cable/lines	Determine the total quantity of jobs that can flow through the network.

in a wide variety of business and economic situations. Table 11.19 presents a few typical illustrations.

In addition, the basic maximal flow concepts can be extended and applied to related problems. For example, suppose that Atlantic partitions its pipeline network into the complementary parts divided by the wavy line in Figure 11.23. If management separates the part on the left from the part on the right, it will completely disconnect the network source (exploration site) and sink (facility 6). In the process, the company will eliminate any flow through the network. Consequently, this partitioning process is known as a **cut** of the network.

By making the cut indicated by the wavy line in Figure 11.23, Atlantic prevents the flow of 30,000 cubic feet of natural gas away from the exploration site. Nevertheless, any other cut would stop more than this quantity from flowing to the sink of the pipeline network. Therefore, 30,000 cubic feet represents the minimum total capacity that can be cut from the company's pipeline system, and the break in the network that generates such a capacity is referred to as the **minimal cut**. Thus, the wavy line in Figure 11.23 denotes Atlantic's minimal cut.

Furthermore, notice that the 30,000 cubic feet capacity of the minimal cut is exactly equal to the company's maximal total flow through the pipeline system. This result is not a coincidence. Rather, it illustrates the

Figure 11.23 Atlantic's Minimal Cut

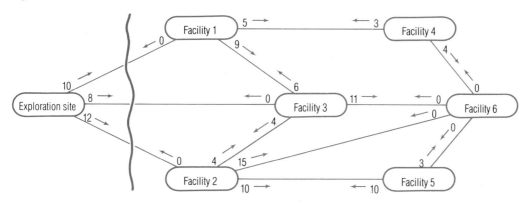

following important principle: *For any network with a single source and sink, the maximal total flow will equal the total capacity of the minimal cut.* In linear programming terms, the minimal cut problem is the dual of the maximal flow formulation. As a result, minimal cut problems can be formulated as maximal flow situations and then solved with maximal flow methodologies. Bazaraa and Jarvis [3] and Murtz [16] demonstrate the concepts and discuss the advantages of the approach. Also, some illustrations and applications are presented in the Lawler [14] and Minieka [15] books.

Additional extensions to the basic maximal flow concepts are discussed by Y. P. Aneja and K. P. K. Nair [1], J. J. Jarvis and H. D. Ratliff [11], and J. L. Kennington [12]. Moreover, R. J. Paul [17] shows how a modified version of this network analysis can be used for production scheduling. In addition, R. E. Rosenthal [18] applies an extended form of the analysis to electric utility distribution management.

TRANSFER SHIPPING In the maximal flow problem, management focuses on the quantity that can be sent over the links from a specified origin to a particular destination in the network. Often, the concern is also with the route of the flow and the corresponding allocation costs or returns. Consider Example 11.5.

EXAMPLE 11.5 Truck Routing

The JBT Company processes and distributes a variety of canned vegetables throughout the Pacific Coast states. One of its main products, corn, is prepared at two canneries (near Seattle and near San Francisco) and then shipped by truck to two distributing warehouses (in

Portland and Los Angeles). Common carriers are used to truck the canned corn. Cannery supplies and warehouse demands for the upcoming season are estimated as in Table 11.20.

Unfortunately, there is no single trucking company that serves the entire area containing all the canneries and warehouses. Therefore, many of the shipments will have to be transferred to another carrier at least once along the way. Moreover, the carriers are willing to make transfer only at the Portland warehouse, San Francisco cannery, and/or trucking depots in Redding and Fresno.

The costs of transporting a truckload of canned corn between the various shipping points are given in Table 11.21. As the cost data indicate, some shipments are either inappropriate (IA), not available from the carriers (NA), or involve a $0 actual expenditure. Management wants to determine the distribution pattern that will minimize total transportation cost.

Table 11.20 Estimated Cannery Supply and Warehouse Demand

Output		Demand	
Cannery	Truckloads	Warehouse	Truckloads
Seattle	2500	Portland	1200
San Francisco	1500	Los Angeles	2800

Table 11.21 Transportation Costs per Truckload

	To					
From	Seattle Cannery	San Francisco Cannery	Redding Depot	Fresno Depot	Portland Warehouse	Los Angeles Warehouse
Seattle Cannery	$0	NA	$500	NA	$350	NA
San Francisco Cannery	IA	$0	$250	$300	$700	$550
Redding Depot	IA	$260	$0	$480	$450	NA
Fresno Depot	IA	$310	$480	$0	NA	$280
Portland Warehouse	IA	$700	$430	NA	$0	NA
Los Angeles Warehouse	IA	IA	IA	IA	IA	$0

The company's truck-routing situation has several characteristics in common with chapter 10's transportation problem. In particular, the situation can be portrayed as a network in which a set of nodes (canneries, trucking depots, and warehouses) is linked by a series of branches (shipping routes). There will be a flow (movement of corn) along these branches, and the flow will move in only one direction. Since each node supplies and/or demands a limited quantity, there are restrictions on the network flows. Furthermore, JBT incurs a cost for transporting a truck-load of corn along each shipping route. Management, then, must deter-mine the least costly way of shipping the required quantities of corn over these branches.

Nevertheless, there is one key difference between the transportation problem and Example 11.5. The transportation problem deals with a situation in which each shipping point (node) is either a supply source or a demand destination. In Example 11.5, however, the Redding and Fresno depots, Portland warehouse, and San Francisco cannery each act as a transfer point in JBT's distribution network. That is, these locations can receive canned corn from some source and then reship it to another destination. Such locations are called **transshipment points**.

In effect, then, the vegetable company wants to find the transportation pattern that incorporates these transshipment considerations. Hence, the situation can be viewed as a transportation problem that allows transfer shipping. This extension is referred to as a **transshipment problem**.

OPTIMAL DISTRIBUTION PATTERN

As Bazaraa and Jarvis [3] show, it is possible to solve the transshipment problem with the transportation methodologies of chapter 10. To do so, however, the decision maker must convert the transshipment problem into a transportation format. One popular approach modifies the standard format to account for the transshipment capability.

In this approach, each transshipment point is treated as both a supply source and a demand destination. JBT management, for instance, would view the San Francisco cannery as a demand destination as well as supply source for the corn. Similarly, the Portland warehouse and the Redding and Fresno depots each should be treated as both a supply source and a demand destination.

The decision maker must then identify the supplies available and demands required at each of these transshipment points. Consider, for example, the San Francisco cannery. Although this cannery is not a warehouse, it can serve as a transfer point for shipments from the Portland warehouse and the Redding and Fresno depots. Unfortunately, manage-ment does not know in advance how much demand there will be for such a service. Nevertheless, the data in Table 11.20 indicate that the total corn demand for the upcoming season is 4000 truckloads. Since it would be inefficient to send merchandise through the same transshipment point more than once, a quantity of 4000 truckloads is a safe upper bound on San Francisco's demand.

The San Francisco cannery supply is another matter. According to Table 11.20, this cannery can produce 1500 truckloads of corn for the upcoming season. Yet it also can transship the truckloads received from

Table 11.22 JBT's Transportation Table

From	To					Supply (Truckloads)
	Portland	Los Angeles	Redding	Fresno	San Francisco	
Seattle	$350	$M	$500	$M	$M	2500
San Francisco	$700	$550	$250	$300	$0	5500
Redding	$450	$M	$0	$480	$260	4000
Fresno	$M	$280	$480	$0	$310	4000
Portland	$0	$M	$430	$M	$700	4000
Demand (Truckloads)	5200	2800	4000	4000	4000	20,000

Table 11.23 JBT's Optimal Transportation Table

From	To					Supply (Truckloads)
	Portland	Los Angeles	Redding	Fresno	San Francisco	
Seattle	$350 1200	$M ($M)	$500 1300	$M ($M)	$M ($M)	2500
San Francisco	$700 ($1060)	$550 1500	$250 ($460)	$300 ($30)	$0 4000	5500
Redding	$450 ($600)	$M ($M)	$0 2700	$480 1300	$260 ($50)	4000
Fresno	$M ($M)	$280 1300	$480 ($960)	$0 2700	$310 ($580)	4000
Portland	$0 4000	$M ($M)	$430 ($280)	$M ($M)	$700 ($340)	4000
Demand (Truckloads)	5200	2800	4000	4000	4000	20,000

the Portland warehouse and the Redding and Fresno depots. Therefore, the San Francisco cannery may have a supply equal to its own output plus the potential transshipments, or $1500 + 4000 = 5500$ truckloads.

In effect, then, the supply at each transshipment, point can be set equal to the original output plus the total demand at all final destinations. Now, the Portland warehouse and the Redding and Fresno depots are not canneries and therefore have no original outputs. Hence, JBT should plan for a $0 + 4000 = 4000$ truckload supply at each of these transfer locations.

Similarly, the demand at each transshipment point can be set equal to the original requirement plus the total demand at all final destinations. In this regard, the Redding and Fresno depots are not warehouses and therefore have no original requirements. Thus, the company should plan for a $0 + 4000 = 4000$ truckload demand at each of these transfer locations.

On the other hand, Table 11.20 indicates that the Portland warehouse has an original demand for 1200 truckloads of corn during the upcoming season. However, this warehouse can also transship as many as 4000 truckloads received from other locations. Therefore, the total demand may be equal to the original requirement plus the transshipments, or $1200 + 4000 = 5200$ truckloads.

The demand and supply at the locations that are not transshipment points will remain at their original levels. In particular, Table 11.20 shows that the Seattle cannery can supply 2500 truckloads of corn for the upcoming season and the Los Angeles warehouse has a demand for 2800 truckloads. The costs of transporting a truckload of canned corn between the various shipping and receiving points are given in Table 11.21.

If management utilizes this information to formulate the problem, it will obtain Table 11.22. Inappropriate (IA) and nonavailable (NA) shipments should be treated as prohibited routes in such a formulation. As a result, these shipments are assigned very large positive (M) per-unit costs in Table 11.22.

By applying the transportation solution methodology from chapter 10, JBT will obtain the optimal distribution pattern shown in Table 11.23. In this table, the circled numbers identify the improvement indexes associated with the corresponding empty cells (unused routes). Table 11.23 indicates that JBT will minimize its total transportation cost by shipping 1200 truckloads at \$350 per load directly from the Seattle cannery to the Portland warehouse and 1500 truckloads at \$550 per load directly from the San Francisco cannery to the Los Angeles warehouse. The optimal plan also recommends that the company transship 1300 truckloads at \$500 per load from the Seattle cannery to the Redding depot, 1300 truckloads at \$480 per load from the Redding depot to the Fresno depot, and 1300 truckloads at \$280 per load from the Fresno depot to the Los Angeles warehouse. In other words, management should transship 1300 truckloads of corn from the Seattle cannery, through the Redding and Fresno depots, and on to the Los Angeles warehouse. Moreover, this optimal distribution pattern will involve a

$$(1200 \times \$350) + (1500 \times \$550) + 1300 (\$500 + \$480 + \$280)$$
$$= \$2,883,000$$

total transportation cost.

In addition, Table 11.23 shows that some locations receive shipments from themselves. In particular, the optimal plan recommends that JBT transport 4000 truckloads at $0 per load from the San Francisco cannery to itself, 2700 truckloads at $0 per load from the Redding depot to itself, 2700 truckloads at $0 per load from the Fresno depot to itself, and 4000 truckloads at $0 per load from the Portland warehouse to itself. These allocations, however, are not actual shipments. After all, the corn never leaves the premises and therefore is assigned a $0 per load transportation cost. Rather, these intrasite allocations should be interpreted as unused transshipment capacity.

SUMMARY   In this chapter we have considered some of the most widely used network techniques. We began with a discussion of the nature of the minimal spanning tree problem. The general characteristics of this problem were summarized in Table 11.1. Then we saw how to select the layout that minimized the total length of connections in a network. Table 11.3 summarized the process. The first section of the chapter also illustrated how minimal spanning tree problems can be solved with the aid of a computer. In addition, we reviewed the typical situations in which the methodology has been applied as well as a small sample of the applications. These applications were summarized in Table 11.4.

In the second section, the discussion focused on network problems in which the flow begins at a particular origin and proceeds to a specified destination. Two such routing situations were examined. In one case, the objective was to find the shortest route from a source to a sink of the network. Table 11.5 summarized the key differences between this problem and the minimal spanning tree situation, while Table 11.8 outlined the procedure for finding the shortest routes. We also considered typical managerial uses of the methodology and saw how shortest routes can be found with the aid of a computer. Table 11.10 presented a small sample of the reported applications. The other routing problem dealt with the situation in which a resource could start from a particular location, visit each facility only once, and then return to the origin. In this case, the objective was to find the route that minimized the cost, time, or distance involved in completing such a tour. Table 11.14 summarized the procedure for finding the optimal tour, while Table 11.15 presented a small sample of the methodology's extensions and applications.

The final section of the chapter showed how to formulate and solve some important restricted flow network problems. In one case, the decision maker had to determine the maximum quantity that could flow from a specified origin to a particular destination in the network. Table 11.17 summarized the procedure for finding this maximal total flow. We then considered some typical applications of the methodology, presented in Table 11.19, and reviewed the procedure for finding maximal flow with the aid of a computer.

A second problem dealt with the route of the flow and the corresponding allocation costs or returns. As the third section demonstrated, the problem resembled a transportation situation that allows transfer shipping. Consequently, it was possible to solve this transshipment problem with a modified version of chapter 10's transportation methodology.

Glossary

asymmetric network A network in which the link between at least one pair of nodes is restricted to one-way traffic and/or has a different length in each flow direction.

cut A break that separates the source from the sink and thereby eliminates any flow through a network.

Eastman/Shapiro algorithm A branch and bound methodology designed to solve traveling salesperson problems.

greedy algorithm A procedure that can be used to find the minimal spanning tree.

labeling technique A procedure that can be used to find the shortest route through a network.

loop (*cycle*) A sequence of branches that leads from a node back to itself through other nodes.

MAXF1 A prewritten computer package designed to find the maximal flow through a network.

maximal flow The largest quantity that can be sent through a network with branch flow capacities.

minimal cut The network cut with the smallest total capacity.

minimal spanning tree A series of links that will minimize the total length of the branches required to connect all the nodes in a network.

path The series of links that leads from the source to the sink of a network.

SHOR1 A prewritten computer package designed to find the shortest routes through a network.

shortest route A series of links that will minimize the total length of the branches required to connect a specified origin with a particular destination in a network.

sink node The specified destination node for the flow over the branches in a network.

source node The specified origin node of the flow over the branches in a network.

spanning The process of connecting all nodes in a network.

SPNT1 A prewritten computer package designed to find the minimal spanning tree in a network.

subtour A sequence of links that starts at the source, visits some (but not all) nodes in the network only once, and then returns to the origin.

symmetric network A network in which the link between any pair of nodes has an identical length in either flow direction.

tour A sequence of links that starts at the source, visits each node in the network only once, and then returns to the origin.

transshipment point A location in a distribution network that can receive merchandise from one shipping point and then reship it to another destination.

transshipment problem A problem in which the objective is to find the most effective way of distributing merchandise from a group of supply sources, through transshipment points, and on to a set of demand destinations.

traveling salesperson problem A problem whose objective is to find the minimum-length tour through a network.

References

1. Aneja, Y. P., and K. P. K. Nair. "Multicommodity Network Flows with Probabilistic Losses." *Management Science* (September 1982): 1080.

2. Ball, M. O., et al. "Planning for Truck Fleet Size in the Presence of a Common-Carrier Option." *Decision Sciences* (January 1983): 103.

3. Bazaraa, M. S., and J. J. Jarvis. *Linear Programming and Network Flows*, chaps. 9–11. New York: Wiley, 1977.

4. Brodin, L. D., and S. J. Kursh. "A Computer-Assisted System for the Routing and Scheduling of Street Sweepers." *Operations Research* (July–August 1978): 525.

5. Crowder, H., and M. W. Padberg. "Solving Large-Scale Symmetric Traveling Salesman Problems to Optimality." *Management Science* (May 1980): 495.

6. Erikson, W. J., and O. P. Hall. *Computer Models for Management Science*. Reading: Addison-Wesley, 1983.

7. Fisher, M. L., and R. Jaikumar. "An Algorithm for the Space-Shuttle Scheduling Problem." *Operations Research* (January–February 1978): 166.

8. Glover, F., et al. "Improved Computer-Based Planning Techniques." *Interfaces* (August 1979): 12.

9. Glover, F., et al. "The Passenger-Mix Problem in the Scheduled Airlines." *Interfaces* (June 1982): 73.

10. Hesse, R. "Solution of the Shortest Route Problem Using the Assignment Technique." *Decision Sciences* (January 1972): 1.

11. Jarvis, J. J., and H. D. Ratliff. "Some Equivalent Objectives for Dynamic Network Flow Problems." *Management Science* (January 1982): 106.

12. Kennington, J. L. "A Survey of Linear Cost Multi-commodity Network Flows." *Operations Research* (March–April 1978): 209.

13. Klingman, D. "Finding Equivalent Network Formulations for Constrained Network Problems." *Management Science* (March 1977): 737.

14. Lawler, E. *Combinatorial Optimization.* New York: Holt, Rinehart, & Winston, 1976.

15. Minieka, E. *Optimization Algorithms for Networks and Graphs.* New York: Marcel Dekker Publications, 1978.

16. Murtz, K. *Linear and Combinatorial Programming.* New York: Wiley, 1976.

17. Paul, R. J. "A Production Scheduling Problem in the Glass-Container Industry." *Operations Research* (March–April 1979): 290.

18. Rosenthal, R. E. "A Nonlinear Network Flow Algorithm for Maximization of Benefits in a Hydroelectric Power System." *Operations Research* (July–August 1981): 763.

19. Schilling, D. A. "Strategic Facility Planning: The Analysis of Options." *Decision Sciences* (January 1982): 1.

20. Schultz, H. K. "A Practical Method for Vehicle Scheduling." *Interfaces* (May 1979): 13.

21. Shapiro, M. "Scheduling Crewmen for Recurrent Training." *Interfaces* (June 1981): 1.

22. Slater, P. J. "On Locating a Facility to Service Areas Within a Network." *Operations Research* (May–June 1981): 523.

Thought Exercises

1. Identify the nodes, branches, and flows in each of the following networks:

   a. A highway system   b. A telephone network
   c. A forest   d. A pipeline
   e. A factory

2. Identify the nature of the arc values in each of the following situations:

   a. A logging company must use a limited budget to construct a series of roads between various logging centers.
   b. A research and development center must develop a new vaccine within a certain schedule.
   c. A defense contractor with a certain budget must plan and schedule work activity on a new air force bomber.

    d. An international household goods manufacturer must develop a distribution plan for its new bath soap.

3. Indicate whether each of the following situations is a minimal spanning tree or shortest route problem. Explain.

    a. A parcel delivery service wants to find the minimum cost of delivering packages to various cities in the state.

    b. A municipal golf course wants to find the minimum number of water lines to the sprinkler heads.

    c. A troop master wants to find the shortest distance between the boy scout center and the summer camp.

    d. A trucking company wants to use the minimum number of roads between its dispatching center and various delivery points.

4. The minimal spanning tree is often referred to as the "greedy algorithm" because you can try to find the shortest connection each time and still get the optimal solution. How does this fact help you to break ties in using the procedure outlined in Table 11.3? Demonstrate with Example 11.1.

5. A local high school principal has asked a planning committee to design the layout of the institution's fire sprinkler system. Potential links between the main water supply and sprinkler fixtures are shown in the following network:

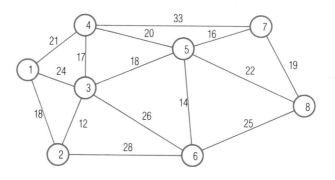

In this diagram, the nodes denote the potential pipelines between the fixtures. The numbers above the branches give the distances in feet between the nodes. Site 5 is the location of the institution's main water supply.

    In view of the school's limited budget, the principal wants the design to include the least possible total feet of pipeline. Hence, she has asked the institution's chief financial officer to serve on the committee with the head of the science and mathematics department. After a careful review and evaluation of the problem, they have developed the following SPNT1 solution:

```
        ** INFORMATION ENTERED **

        NUMBER OF NODES: 8
        NUMBER OF LINKS: 15

    LINK      START      END        LINK
    NUMBER    NODE       NODE       LENGTH
      1         1          2          18
      2         1          3          24
      3         1          4          21
      4         2          3          12
      5         2          6          28
      6         3          4          17

      7         3          5          18
      8         3          6          26
      9         4          5          20
     10         4          7          33
     11         5          6          14
     12         5          7          16
     13         5          8          22
     14         6          8          25
     15         7          8          19


        ** RESULTS **

    MINIMUM SPANNING TREE

    START     END        LINK
    NODE      NODE       LENGTH
      1         2          18
      2         3          12
      3         4          17
      3         5          18
      5         6          14
      5         7          16
      7         8          19

    TOTAL LENGTH = 114


        ** END OF ANALYSIS **
```

Interpret this solution for the planning committee. What design should the committee recommend to the principal? How many total feet of pipeline will be used in their recommended design?

6. Although ties may be broken arbitrarily in the shortest route procedure (Table 11.8), they may indicate the presence of alternative optimal solutions. The tram-routing situation for Sunrise residents (Example 11.2) is a case in point. Can you identify the alternative

optimal solution? Show your work. Can you think of any reasons why the residents might prefer one solution over another? Explain.

7. Refer again to Example 11.2. Suppose that Prestige lets X_{ij} represent the flow (movement of a tram) over the trail (branch) connecting site i with site j. For example, X_{12} would denote the movement of a tram from the park entrance at A (node 1) to site B (node 2). Similarly, X_{68} would give the flow between site F (node 6) and the swimming and skating pond at H (node 8). Also, assume

$$X_{ij} = \begin{cases} 1 \text{ if the link is used} \\ 0 \text{ otherwise} \end{cases}$$

and that the flow can go only from a lower- to a higher-numbered node. Use the symbols and assumptions to develop a linear program for Sunrise's shortest route problem.

8. A company is interested in employing a recent college graduate for an operations management opening at its headquarters. As part of the evaluation process, the firm will fly the graduate to the headquarters for a series of interviews. The available flight routes are shown in the following network:

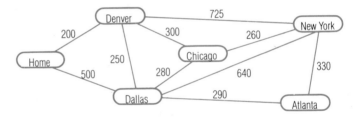

In the diagram, the branches denote the potential links, and the nodes identify the connecting cities in the flight network. The numbers above the branches give the first-class air fare in dollars between the nodes. Company headquarters are located in New York.

As the flight network indicates, there is no direct flight from the graduate's home to the company headquarters. Nevertheless, management wants its travel staff to determine the least costly round-trip first-class flight route for the candidate. After a careful review and evaluation of the problem, the staff has developed the following SHOR1 solution:

```
        ** INFORMATION ENTERED **

        NUMBER OF NODES   6
        NUMBER OF LINKS   10

LINK      START    END     DISTANCE      REVERSE
          NODE     NODE                  DISTANCE

1         1        2       200           200
2         1        3       500           500
3         2        3       250           250
4         2        4       300           300
5         2        6       725           725
6         3        4       280           280
7         3        5       290           290
8         3        6       640           640
9         4        6       260           260
10        5        6       330           330


        ** RESULTS **


START              END           DISTANCE
NODE               NODE

1                  2             200
2                  4             300
4                  6             260

        TOTAL DISTANCE  760
```

Interpret this solution for management. What flight route should the travel staff recommend to management? How much will it cost to fly the candidate in for interviews?

9. In Example 11.2, Prestige provides tram service from the park entrance to each site in the Sunrise equestrian and jogging park. Moreover, a different tram is sent from the entrance to each station. Suppose that management labels this original service as the blue line.

   Now the company wants to offer an additional green line to the residents. This line will start at the park entrance, visit each site only once, and then return to the origin. Since tram expenses still will be paid by a distance-related fare, the residents want such a line to follow a route that is the fewest total miles from the park entrance. What route do you recommend for the green line? Explain.

10. Refer back to Example 11.4. Let X_{ij} represent the flow of natural gas over the pipeline joining facility i with facility j. For instance, X_{12} would denote the quantity of natural gas flowing from the exploration site (node 1) to facility 1 (node 2). Similarly, X_{67} would give the flow between facility 5 (node 6) and facility 6 (node 7). Also, suppose that F identifies the total flow through Atlantic's pipeline network. Develop the linear program that corresponds to the company's maximal flow problem. Then formulate and interpret its dual.

11. The Serpentine Corridor is represented by the following network of trails in the mountainous western region separating the warring nations of Northern and Southern Yetmite:

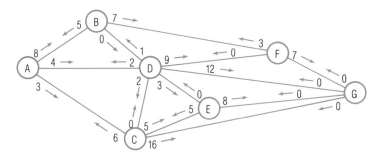

In the diagram, the nodes represent junction points (villages, cities, and towns), while the branches denote trails joining the nodes. Branch values give the number of troops (in thousands) that can be infiltrated each week along the trails. The corresponding arrows identify the infiltration direction.

General Swaggert, the commanding officer of the Northern Yetmite forces, wants to determine the maximal flow of troops that can be infiltrated between Serpentine Corridor points D and G. In this regard, his staff has provided the following MAXF1 solution of the maximal flow problem:

```
        ** INFORMATION ENTERED **

     NUMBER OF NODES: 7
     NUMBER OF LINKS: 17

LINK     START    END      FLOW
         NODE     NODE

1        1        2        2
2        2        1        4
3        1        3        1
4        1        4        2
5        1        5        3
6        1        6        9
7        1        7        12
8        2        3        8
9        3        2        5
10       2        4        3
11       4        2        6
12       4        5        5
13       5        4        5
14       3        6        7
15       6        3        3
16       5        7        8
17       6        7        7


             ** RESULTS **

OPTIMAL FLOW OVER ALL PATHS FROM

NODE 1 TO NODE 7 :

FLOW    NODES THAT DEFINE EACH PATH

12       1   7
3        1   5   7
2        1   4   5   7
2        1   2   4   5   7
1        1   3   2   4   5   7
7        1   6   7


OPTIMAL FLOW OVER EACH LINK:

START    END      FLOW
NODE     NODE

1        2        2
1        3        1
1        4        2
1        5        3
1        6        7
1        7        12
2        4        3
3        2        1
4        5        5
5        7        8
6        7        7


MAXIMUM TOTAL NETWORK FLOW: 27

        ** END OF ANALYSIS **
```

Interpret this solution for General Swaggert. What is the maximal total flow of troops through the Serpentine Corridor? How should troops be infiltrated every week along each trail in the Corridor?

12. Refer back to Example 11.5. Draw the transshipment network that corresponds to JBT's transportation table (Table 11.22). Interpret the nodes, branches, and flows in this network. Explain how the diagram differs from a transportation network.

13. In Example 11.5, suppose that the demand for corn at the Portland warehouse during the upcoming season becomes 2200 rather than 1200 truckloads. How will this change affect JBT's optimal distribution pattern? Explain.

14. Do you agree or disagree with each of the following statements? Explain.

   a. A minimal spanning tree will form a single series of connections between nodes.
   b. We are not always interested in the shortest route when using the shortest route procedure.
   c. If the decision maker wants to reduce travel or operating (instead of construction or setup) costs, he or she is better off using the shortest route (instead of the minimal spanning tree) procedure.
   d. Most network solution procedures assume that there is a conservation of flow, namely, that the flow in must equal the flow out of a node.
   e. The optimal tour in a traveling salesperson problem gives the minimal cost of achieving the required network flow.
   f. If the decision maker wants to reduce flow costs, he or she may be better off using the maximal flow solution procedure.
   g. Assignment and transportation problems can be viewed as special cases of a network flow problem.
   h. The transshipment problem is to find the least-cost path from each source to every sink in a network.

Technique Exercises

1. In Example 11.1, start with node C and show that the procedure outlined in Table 11.3 results in the minimal spanning tree shown in Figure 11.5.

2. Figure 11.4 gives Prestige's third connection. Use the procedure outlined in Table 11.3 to complete the remainder of the connections required for the minimal spanning tree (Figure 11.5).

3. The following diagram shows the physical layout and distances (in hundreds of feet) for forklift routes between work centers in a large manufacturing plant. Determine the minimal spanning tree for the network.

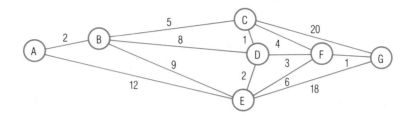

4. Consider the computer system design situation depicted in the following network:

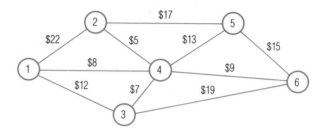

Each node represents the location of a computer terminal, while each branch identifies a potential hookup line between the terminals. Branch values give the costs (in thousands of dollars) for connecting each pair of terminals. The main computer facility is located at site 4.

What is the least costly way to join the main computer with every other terminal in the network? How much will this optimal design cost?

5. Refer back to Example 11.2. Figure 11.9 gives Prestige's third tram line route. Use the procedure outlined in Table 11.8 to complete the remainder of the connections required for the shortest tram route network (Figure 11.10).

6. The following network shows the costs (in hundreds of thousands of dollars) of distributing electricity from the production facility A through various transmission points to a large industrial customer H. Find the least costly routes from A to every other node.

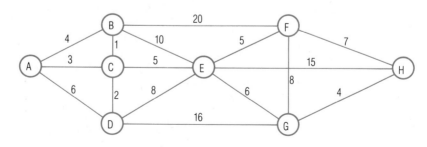

7. Refer back to thought exercise 7. Solve the linear program that corresponds to Prestige's shortest route problem. How does the recommended linear programming solution compare with the answer given in the text for Example 11.2? Explain.

8. In the following network, node A is the base center for a delivery service. Arc values represent driving time in hours to various cities within its service area. Find the shortest route from E to every other node.

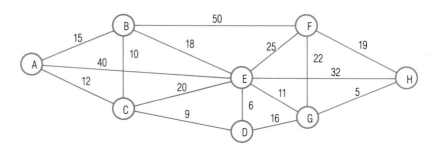

9. Refer back to Example 11.3. Show how Table 11.13 and Figures 11.14, 11.15, and 11.16 were developed.

10. An independent salesperson has customers in six locations throughout the county. The distance in miles between the locations is summarized in the following table:

From	To					
	A	B	C	D	E	F
A	—	11	23	19	13	25
B	13	—	49	7	46	39
C	11	44	—	12	55	70
D	15	5	13	—	55	57
E	16	51	59	60	—	12
F	28	42	82	62	13	—

The salesperson must start at location A, visit each customer only once, and then return to the origin. Which tour will minimize the total distance traveled? Show all your work.

11. A postal delivery person starts at the main office, delivers mail, makes pickups at various mail boxes around the city, and then returns to the origin. Her delivery system is depicted in the following network:

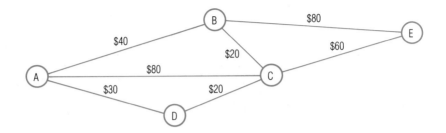

The nodes denote delivery and pickup points, while the branches identify the existing links between these points. The main office is located at node A. Branch values give the daily delivery cost over each link. Find the postal person's least costly delivery tour. What is the corresponding total delivery cost?

12. Figure 11.20 gives the maximal flow over Atlantic's exploration site/facility 1/facility 4/facility 6 path. Use the procedure outlined in Table 11.17 to find the maximal total flow through the pipeline network (Figure 11.21). Show all your work.

13. Refer back to thought exercise 10. Solve the linear program that corresponds to Altantic's maximal flow problem. How does the recommended linear programming solution compare with the answer given in the text for Example 11.4? Explain.

14. The following network depicts the flow of messages in a telecommunications system:

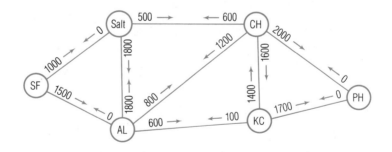

Nodes identify major switching stations, and the branches represent the available links between these stations. Branch values give the number of simultaneous messages each station can handle per hour. The arrows denote the flow directions.

What is the maximum number of simultaneous messages that this system can handle each hour between the San Francisco (SF) and Philadelphia (PH) locations? How many messages will flow over each link in the network? Show all your work.

15. Refer back to Example 11.5. Show how Table 11.23 was derived from Table 11.22.

16. Consider the following transshipment network:

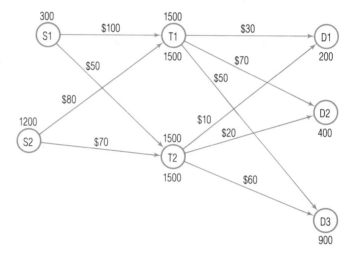

The S1 and S2 nodes identify supply sources, T1 and T2 are transshipment points, and D1 through D3 denote demand destinations. The branches represent the available routes between the nodes, and link values give the unit costs of transporting merchandise over these routes. Supply capacities are listed above the nodes, and the demand requirements appear below the nodes.
  What is the optimal distribution pattern for the merchandise? How much will it cost to follow this plan? Show all your work.

Applications Exercises

1. The Universal Outdoor Theater, Inc., holds concerts and plays in the fall, summer, and spring of each year. A renovation program was started last winter and is now complete except for rewiring the facility for sound. Distances between various loudspeakers and other sound equipment are shown in the following table:

		To								
From	Stage	Speaker 1	Speaker 2	Speaker 3	Speaker 4	Speaker 5	Speaker 6	Speaker 7	Speaker 8	Control Center
Stage	—	10	15	20	M	M	M	M	M	50
Speaker 1	10	—	15	5	25	M	M	M	30	M
Speaker 2	15	15	—	10	15	20	M	M	M	M
Speaker 3	20	5	10	—	M	M	15	30	M	M
Speaker 4	M	25	15	M	—	25	10	5	M	M
Speaker 5	M	M	20	M	25	—	15	20	30	35
Speaker 6	M	M	M	15	10	15	—	5	25	40
Speaker 7	M	M	M	30	5	20	5	—	10	15
Speaker 8	M	30	M	M	M	30	25	10	—	10
Control Center	50	M	M	M	M	35	40	15	10	—

The symbol M indicates that the corresponding connection cannot be made because of the theater layout. All other distances are measured in feet.

It costs $2 per foot to wire the layout. Management wants to determine the least cost of wiring the theater. What series of connections do you recommend? What is the corresponding minimum cost?

2. A small Savannah-based transportation company must purchase a special machine for transferring cargo from ships to its dockyard facilities. The machine can be purchased now for $50,000. After two years, the purchase price is expected to be $60,000. The machine can be resold, but the resale price will decrease with age. On the other hand, older machines need more repairs, and thus operating costs will increase with age. The following table shows the effects of age on the resale price and operating costs of the machine for the next six years. Company financial procedures calculate a machine's total net cost as the purchase price minus the resale value plus operating costs.

Machine Age (Years)	Resale Price at Year's End (% of Purchase Price)	Annual Operating Costs ($)
1	90	1000
2	80	1800
3	60	2600
4	40	3500
5	30	4500
6	20	5000

Management wants to determine the machine replacement policy that will minimize total net cost over the next six years. What years (if any) should the machine be replaced?

3. Quality Products processes six types of operations on the same packaging equipment. In the process, the work crew must change some attachments on the equipment. As a result, there is a changeover, or setup, time required between operations. Moreover, the changeover times depend on the sequence in which the operations are assigned to the equipment. For example, the changeover time from operation A to operation B is 10 hours. Yet it takes only 5 hours to change over from job E to job B. In fact, production records indicate that the changeover times in hours for all operation sequences are as shown in the following table:

From	To					
	A	**B**	**C**	**D**	**E**	**F**
A	—	10	8	3	4	11
B	12	—	5	6	9	2
C	6	13	—	4	2	1
D	15	6	8	—	5	12
E	2	5	6	9	—	3
F	7	12	10	10	14	—

Policy dictates that the work crew set up the original operation after completing the other five activities in a sequence.

Management wants to determine the sequence of operations that will minimize the total changeover time. What sequence do you recommend? How much changeover time will the recommended sequence involve?

4. A new civic center is being planned for Allendale. As part of the planning process, the municipal engineer wants to determine if the streets between the center and a city expressway can accommodate the expected flow of 18,000 cars. Various entries are available, but the flow capacities differ because of variations in available lanes, street lights, and so on. Studies indicate that these capacities are as shown in the following table:

From	To						
	Civic Center	Junction Point 1	Junction Point 2	Junction Point 3	Junction Point 4	Junction Point 5	Expressway
Civic Center	—	8	6	9	NA	NA	NA
Junction Point 1	0	—	6	NA	5	NA	NA
Junction Point 2	0	7	—	NA	4	9	NA
Junction Point 3	0	NA	NA	—	NA	2	7
Junction Point 4	NA	2	5	NA	—	NA	6
Junction Point 5	NA	NA	3	8	NA	—	4
Expressway	NA	NA	NA	0	0	0	—

In this table, the capacities are measured in thousands of cars. Also, NA indicates that the corresponding link is not available.

What is the maximum traffic flow that the streets can accommodate? How many cars will move along each street? Will the streets be able to handle the expected flow after a civic center event?

5. The Ecological Protection Agency wants to build a series of dams on the Postigula River system for flood control purposes. As part of the evaluation process, the agency has developed the following map of the system:

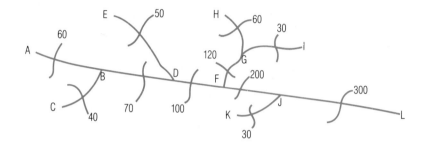

Possible dam locations are indicated on the map with wavy lines. The diagram also identifies the estimated costs (in millions of dollars) for building the dam, relocating displaced residents, and correcting any ecological damage to the environment. Water flows downstream from the highlands above site A to Clean Lake at location L.

Where should the dams be built to minimize the total costs of providing the flood control system? How much must the agency budget for this project?

6. A major household appliance company manufactures refrigerators at its two main production plants in Industry and Irving. The Industry plant is capable of producing 4000 refrigerators per month at an average cost of $300 per unit. Irving can manufacture 6000 refrigerators per month at an average cost of $320 per unit.

The finished products are then distributed through transfer points in Tulsa, Little Rock, Denver, Cheyenne, Columbus, and Grand Rapids on to final distribution centers at Milwaukee and Newark. Milwaukee's facility has a demand for at least 3000 refrigerators per month and the Newark center for another 7000 refrigerators per month. The costs associated with transporting a refrigerator between the various shipping points are given in the following table:

From	To							
	Tulsa	Little Rock	Denver	Cheyenne	Columbus	Grand Rapids	Milwaukee	Newark
Industry	NA	NA	$50	$75	NA	NA	NA	NA
Irving	$80	$30	NA	NA	NA	NA	NA	NA
Tulsa	$0	NA	NA	NA	$60	$70	NA	NA
Little Rock	NA	$0	NA	NA	$40	$50	NA	NA
Denver	NA	NA	$0	NA	$80	NA	NA	NA
Cheyenne	NA	NA	NA	$0	$75	$60	NA	NA
Columbus	NA	NA	NA	NA	$0	NA	NA	$20
Grand Rapids	NA	NA	NA	NA	NA	$0	$10	NA

As the cost data indicate, some routes are not available (NA) or involve a $0 actual expenditure.

Management wants to determine the production and distribution plan that will minimize total costs. What plan do you recommend? How much will it cost?

CASE: General Parcel Service

General Parcel Service (GPS) has been incorporated as a firm specializing in the national delivery of small packages. The service will link major cities with a variety of air and truck routes. Initially, the company will have to design appropriate delivery linkages and identify preferable routes within the design.

In this respect, management has identified the major cities GPS intends to service and the potential linkages that can be utilized between these locations. The results of the examination are summarized in Table 11.24. The table entries represent delivery time in hours between locations. The delivery cost is $10 plus $12 per hour.

The company intends to have two kinds of service. One type will start a courier from the headquarters in Atlanta, have the courier visit each GPS city only once, and then return the courier to the origin. The other service will send couriers between various sets of cities in GPS's delivery network.

To properly formulate corporate strategy, however, management needs the following information:

1. The delivery system layout that will minimize total travel time

2. The delivery system layout that will minimize total delivery cost

3. The least time-consuming routes from Atlanta to each other city in the selected layout

4. The least costly routes from Atlanta, New York, Chicago, and Los Angeles to each other city in the selected layout

5. The courier tour that minimizes total delivery time from Atlanta

6. The courier tour that minimizes total delivery cost from Atlanta

Prepare a report that provides the needed information in language that would be understandable to management.

Suppose that there are flow capacities in the selected layout. Explain how these constraints would affect the strategy.

Assume that some cities could serve as transfer points for the deliveries. Explain how such a possibility would affect the strategy.

Table 11.24 GPS Fact Sheet

From	To				
	Boston	New York	Philadelphia	Washington	Atlanta
Boston	—	10	15	20	25
New York	10	—	5	3	18
Philadelphia	15	5	—	6	12
Washington	20	3	6	—	10
Atlanta	25	18	12	10	—
Chicago	27	12	14	20	17
Denver	30	25	32	28	34
Dallas	24	20	27	18	12
Seattle	32	30	40	35	50
San Francisco	28	21	24	20	30
Los Angeles	26	21	24	22	20

From	To					
	Chicago	Denver	Dallas	Seattle	San Francisco	Los Angeles
Boston	27	30	24	32	28	26
New York	12	25	20	30	21	21
Philadelphia	14	32	27	40	24	24
Washington	20	28	18	35	20	22
Atlanta	17	34	12	50	30	20
Chicago	—	16	14	21	18	15
Denver	16	—	18	13	9	11
Dallas	14	18	—	25	14	10
Seattle	21	13	25	—	10	13
San Francisco	18	9	14	10	—	5
Los Angeles	15	11	10	13	5	—

Chapter 12
PERT/CPM

Large-scale projects consist of numerous specific jobs that must be completed, some in parallel and others in sequence, by various individuals and groups. The projects may be recurring programs, such as maintenance, or large, one-time efforts, like highway construction. In either case, the manager must plan, schedule, and control the jobs so that the entire project is completed on time. When there is a large number of interrelated tasks, timing and coordination become very complex. In these circumstances, network analysis can aid the decision maker in carrying out his or her project management responsibilities.

This chapter presents the most widely used project management tools. The first section introduces the Program Evaluation and Review Technique (PERT). We develop a PERT network, derive time estimates for the project tasks, estimate the project duration, and establish a complete activity schedule. Then, the data are used to find the probability of meeting a project deadline. Finally, we see how the information can be used to manage the time aspects of the project.

The last two sections focus on resource utilization and project costs. We discuss the time-resource trade-off and develop the Critical Path Method (CPM) for expediting a project. Then we see how an extension of PERT, called PERT/COST, can be used to control project costs.

PERT

There are many network approaches to project management, including Graphical Evaluation and Review Technique (GERT) [11, 13], Line of Balance (LOB) [1, 7], and others [8, 14]. However, the **Program Evaluation and Review Technique (PERT)** and Critical Path Method (CPM) have been the most prominent.

The Navy originated PERT in the late 1950s for planning, scheduling, and controlling the Polaris submarine project. CPM was developed concurrently by the DuPont Corporation to help schedule and control maintenance in chemical plants. Since then, the techniques have been applied to the preparation of bids and proposals [3], the design of

603

financial policy [6], systems analysis [15], and a wide variety of other business and economic projects [1, 9, 14].

Although PERT and CPM have the same general purpose and use similar procedures, the original versions differed in some important ways. PERT focused on novel, one-time projects that involved significant uncertainty in estimating task times. Consequently, in its evolution, PERT has emphasized time management and the role of uncertainty in this process. On the other hand, CPM has been applied primarily to industrial projects where task times can be predicted accurately. In its evolution, then, CPM has treated the job duration as a known value and instead has stressed the time-cost trade-off involved in project management. Also, different graphic devices evolved to depict the project. The CPM chart highlighted the tasks or jobs, while the PERT diagram was oriented toward the completion of various project phases.

Contemporary project directors recognize the importance of both time and cost management. As a result, the recent trend has been to merge the two techniques. In today's usage, then, a complete project analysis combines the essential features of both PERT and CPM. We present these features, starting with the PERT approach to project time management.

We begin by considering Example 12.1.

EXAMPLE 12.1 Office Construction

Olan Builders, Inc., will construct a new and unique office building in Springtown for the State Travelers Insurance Company. Olan knows that the project will involve several specific tasks or jobs. Some can be done concurrently, but several cannot be started until others are complete. Based on previous knowledge and experience, management has identified the jobs and the order in which they must be completed. The

Table 12.1 Olan's Construction Data

Task	Description	Immediately Preceding Tasks
A	Order structural materials	—
B	Obtain structural labor	—
C	Excavate	—
D	Pour foundation	C
E	Receive structural materials	A
F	Frame structure	B, D, E
G	Install plumbing	F
H	Install electrical facilities	F
I	Do interior finishing	G, H
J	Do exterior finishing	G
K	Do cleanup	I, J

relevant information is given in Table 12.1.

State Travelers wants to know how long it will take to construct the office building. Olan's subcontractors must also know when to schedule each task. In addition, Olan would like to know how long each job can be put off without delaying the entire project.

PROJECT NETWORK All PERT systems use a network to graphically portray the project interrelationships. The first step in developing the network is to determine all specific tasks that make up the project. Since poor planning and omission of activities will lead to inaccurate schedules, this listing process is a key step in the analysis. Let us assume that Olan has carefully planned its construction and that Table 12.1 lists all the tasks in the office project.

Typically, project elements are interrelated. Hence, the next step is to identify the relationships between jobs. One way to do this is to identify the tasks that must immediately precede each job. This additional information for Olan's problem is also listed in Table 12.1. It shows, for example, that the installation of plumbing (G) and electrical work (H) must be completed before the interior finishing (I) can be started.

Figure 12.1 depicts Olan's tasks and the order in which they must be performed. We refer to this diagram as a **PERT network**. As you can see, the network consists of numbered circles interconnected by several lines. In network terminology, the circles are called nodes and the lines are referred to as arcs. Each arc represents a specific task required by the project. The tasks, which are called **activities**, use financial and/or physical resources and require time to complete. Nodes mark points in time, called **events**, that signal the completion of all activities for a particular phase of the project. For example, node 1 refers to the event that the project has started, while node 2 indicates the event that Olan has completed ordering materials (activity A). Similarly, node 4 marks the event that activities E (receipt of materials), B (acquisition of labor), and D (pouring of the foundation) have all been completed.

Figure 12.1 Olan's Office Project Network

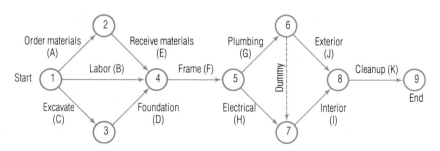

Figure 12.2 Incorrect PERT Network Segment

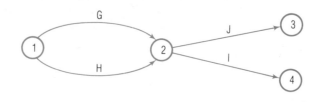

The arrowheads indicate the sequences in which the events must be achieved. Hence, event 1 (the start of the project) must precede event 2 (the completion of materials ordering, or activity A). In addition, event 2 must precede event 4. Furthermore, an event must precede the start of activities leading out of that node. For instance, event 4 (the completion of activities E, B, and D) must occur before Olan can start framing (activity F).

In Table 12.1, notice that plumbing must be installed (activity G) before exterior finishing (activity J). Also, interior finishing (activity I) cannot be started before Olan installs plumbing (G) and electrical facilities (H). Thus, activities I and J have an immediate predecessor in common—activity G. A graphic representation of this situation might appear as Figure 12.2.

Unfortunately, Figure 12.2 shows both activities G and H as immediate predecessors of J. In reality, activity G is the only predecessor of J. The problem arises because activities G and H appear to have the same starting and ending nodes. A project network avoids this difficulty by using dashed arrows, called **dummy activities**, to show the proper precedence. For example, there is a dummy branch from node 6 to node 7 in Figure 12.1. This dummy branch properly shows that only activity G must be completed before J can start. It also indicates that activity I cannot begin until G and H are complete.

ACTIVITY TIMES After establishing the project network, the decision maker must determine the time required to complete each activity. Since this information is used to schedule activities and events, accurate estimates are essential for successful project management. Inaccurate activity time estimates will cause errors in scheduling events and in forecasting the project completion date.

Many projects, like maintenance, repeat previous similar activity. In these cases, managers may have the experience necessary to make an accurate single estimate of the time required for each activity. Original versions of CPM were based on this assumption.

Figure 12.3 A Beta Distribution for an Activity's Duration

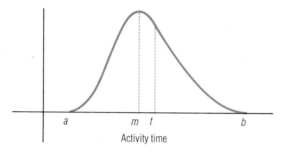

On the other hand, new or unique projects, by their nature, consist largely of novel component tasks. Under these circumstances, it is difficult to precisely estimate the duration of each task. Instead, an activity time is uncertain and perhaps best described by a range of values rather than a single estimate.

The developers of PERT recognized the task time uncertainty and studied methods of incorporating it into the analysis. In the process, they found that an activity's duration could be reasonably described by a form of the beta probability distribution. J. J. Moder and C. R. Phillips [10] and J. D. Weist and F. K. Levy [14] discuss in detail the nature of this distribution and its role in PERT. We can outline the concepts here with the aid of Figure 12.3.

Figure 12.3 presents a beta probability distribution of the activity times for a particular task. Project management defines the distribution by providing three time estimates. The **optimistic time** (denoted by a) is the time required to complete an activity when the work progresses exceptionally well. Since a is intended to be the shortest possible activity duration, it essentially sets the lower limit on the distribution. The maximum possible duration, or intended upper limit, is called the **pessimistic time** (denoted by b). It gives the time required to complete an activity when the work encounters significant delays or other adverse conditions. Both a and b are considered unlikely but possible times. In fact, the probability of completing the task in less than the optimistic time should not exceed 1%. Also, the project planner should be at least 99% confident of completing the activity within the pessimistic time. Hence, in about 98% of the cases, the activity's duration will be somewhere between the extremes (a and b). The **most likely time** (denoted by m) is intended to be the most realistic estimate. It represents the time most frequently required to complete an activity under normal conditions. Notice that m lies below the peak of the distribution.

Example 12.2 illustrates the three time estimation processes.

EXAMPLE 12.2 Activity Time Estimation

Although Olan has much construction experience, the new State Travelers office building will be unique in many ways. Consequently, Olan's project management is uncertain about the activity durations. However, T. K. Trueblood, the project manager, can make a best guess of the most likely time for each of the eleven activities. Also, T. K. will express her uncertainty by providing estimates ranging from the best to worst possible times for each activity. Table 12.2 presents these estimates. For instance, T. K. estimates that framing the office structure (activity F) will require anywhere from 22 to 50 days. But she also feels that this task most likely will take 30 days. Olan wants to incorporate this information into its planning, scheduling, and control process.

Table 12.2 Olan's Activity Time Estimates

	Time Estimates (Days)		
Activity	Optimistic a	Most Likely m	Pessimistic b
A	1	2	9
B	2.5	4.5	9.5
C	2	5	14
D	4	6.5	18
E	2	4	18
F	22	30	50
G	15	20	37
H	4.5	10	21.5
I	12	15	24
J	14	14.5	48
K	5	5	5

The three time estimates are used to determine the average or **expected activity time** (denoted by t in Figure 12.3). In PERT applications of the beta distributions, t is calculated with the following formula:

$$(12.1) \quad t = \frac{a + 4m + b}{6}$$

Notice that the formula weights the most likely time (m) four times as much as either extreme (a or b).

By substituting the data from Table 12.2 into equation (12.1), Olan finds that the expected time to frame the structure (activity F) is

$$t = \frac{a + 4m + b}{6} = \frac{22 + 4(30) + 50}{6} = 32 \text{ days}$$

Table 12.3 Olan's Expected Activity Times and Variances

Activity	Expected Time (Days) t	Variances VAR
A	3	1.78
B	5	1.36
C	6	4
D	8	5.44
E	6	7.11
F	32	21.78
G	22	13.44
H	11	8.03
I	16	4
J	20	32.11
K	5	0
Total	134	

Figure 12.4 Olan's PERT Network with Expected Activity Times

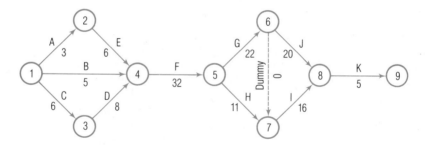

The project manager can compute the expected times for the other activities in a similar manner. Table 12.3 presents the results.

Recall that a dummy activity exists solely for the purpose of establishing proper precedence. It is a fictitious task and thus should be assigned a zero completion time. In effect, then, each dummy activity has an expected time of $t = 0$.

Figure 12.4 shows Olan's PERT network with the expected activity times written under the corresponding arcs. Project management typically plans and schedules activities on the basis of such a chart.

Variation, or dispersion, between the extreme time estimates (a and b in Figure 12.3) is usually described by the common statistical measure of variance. In PERT applications of the beta distribution, variance (denoted VAR) is computed as follows:

(12.2) $\text{VAR} = \left(\dfrac{b-a}{6}\right)^2$

Notice that the difference between the pessimistic and optimistic time estimates greatly affects the value of variance. When there are large differences between a and b, project management has a high degree of activity time uncertainty. Accordingly, the variance also will be large. For example, by referring to Table 12.2, Olan finds that the variance in framing the structure (activity F) is

$$\text{VAR} = \left(\frac{b-a}{6}\right)^2 = \left(\frac{50-22}{6}\right)^2 = 21.78$$

The project manager can compute the variance for the other activities in a similar manner. Table 12.3 presents these results. Management typically estimates the probability of completing the project within specified schedules on the basis of this information.

There are other methods to deal with uncertainty in project management, including those proposed by R. R. Britney [2] and P. Robillard and M. Trahan [12]. However, the beta distribution approach is still the most popular.

PROJECT COMPLETION DATE Table 12.3 suggests that Olan can expect to complete all construction within a total of 134 days. But this total does not account for the fact that several tasks can be done simultaneously. Figure 12.4, for example, shows that the company pours the foundation (activity D) while receiving materials (activity E). This characteristic will make the total expected completion time shorter than 134 days.

To determine the expected project duration, Olan must consider the activity time relationships. Figure 12.4 (the PERT network with expected activity times) provides the necessary information. Suppose that Olan starts construction (event 1 in Figure 12.4) at time zero. Then the earliest time that the company can begin ordering materials (activity A) is at zero days. (This is called the **earliest start time**.) Since this activity is expected to take 3 days, the **earliest finish time** will be

0 + 3 = 3 days

Event 2 denotes the completion of this task. Figure 12.5 illustrates the earliest start and finish times for activity A. Notice that the earliest finish time equals the earliest start time plus the expected activity duration. By letting

EF = the earliest finish time for an activity

ES = the earliest start time for the activity

Figure 12.5 Earliest Start and Finish Times for Olan's Activity A

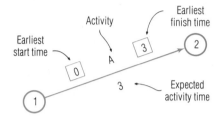

t = the expected activity time

the relationship can be expressed as

(12.3) $EF = ES + t$

Obtaining labor (activity B) and excavating (activity C) offer additional examples. Both of these activities start at event 1, and thus each has an *ES* of 0 days. Activity B is expected to take $t = 5$ days; so for activity B,

$EF = ES + t = 0 + 5 = 5$ days

Activity C has an expected duration of $t = 6$ days; so for activity C,

$EF = ES + t = 0 + 6 = 6$ days

If Olan knows each earliest start time, then equation (12.3) can be used to find the earliest finish time for all activities in the network. The *EF* value for the final activity (K in Figure 12.4) would then represent the expected project completion date. Unfortunately, the *ES* value for each activity is not obvious and must be derived from an additional analysis. We can illustrate the process with activity F.

Figure 12.4 shows that Olan cannot start framing (activity F) until the company has received materials (E), obtained labor (B), and finished the foundation (activity D). Furthermore, the company knows that each of these immediately preceding activities (E, B, and D) cannot be completed before its earliest finish time (*EF*). Hence, to determine the earliest start time (*ES*) for activity F, Olan must first find the *EF* value for each predecessor.

The company already knows that activity B has an $EF = 5$ days. Activities E and D require a little more thought. Figure 12.4 shows that activity D is immediately preceded by only one task, C. It indicates that Olan can start the foundation (activity D) as soon as excavation (activity C) is complete. When there is a single immediate predecessor, then, the earliest start time (*ES*) for an activity equals the earliest finish time (*EF*) of the immediately preceding task. In this case, Olan knows that the single predecessor (activity C) has an *EF* of 6 days. Hence, the earliest start time

Figure 12.6 The Earliest Start Time for Olan's Activity F

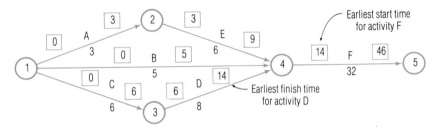

for activity D must be $ES = 6$ days. Since D has an expected activity time of $t = 8$ days, its earliest finish time is

$$EF = ES + t = 6 + 8 = 14 \text{ days}$$

Similarly, Figure 12.4 shows that activity A is the only immediate predecessor of E. Consequently, the already-available $EF = 3$ days for task A also represents the earliest start time for activity E. Since E has an expected duration of $t = 6$ days, its earliest finish time is

$$EF = ES + t = 3 + 6 = 9 \text{ days}$$

Olan now knows that the earliest finish time is

$$EF = 5 \text{ days for activity B}$$

$$EF = 14 \text{ days for activity D}$$

$$EF = 9 \text{ days for activity E}$$

Activity F cannot start until all three immediate predecessors (B, D, and E) have been completed. This event (node 4 in Figure 12.4) may not occur until the earliest finish time for activity D ($EF = 14$ days). Therefore, the earliest start time for activity F is $ES = 14$ days. Figure 12.6 illustrates the process for the portion of Olan's project network involving activity F. The analysis suggests that the earliest start time for any activity can be found with the following rule: The earliest start time (ES) for an activity leaving a project node equals the largest value of the earliest finish times for all activities entering the node.

In summary, Olan starts the search for the expected completion date with the initial node (event 1) in the network. Then the company works forward in time by successively establishing first the earliest start time (ES) and then the earliest finish time (EF) for each activity. This process, called a **forward pass**, ends with the final node in the network. Figure 12.7 shows the results of a forward pass through Olan's office project network.

Note that the earliest finish time for the last activity (K) is 93 days. This last EF represents the expected project completion date. It indicates that

Figure 12.7 Olan's Project Network with Earliest Start and Finish Times

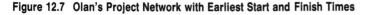

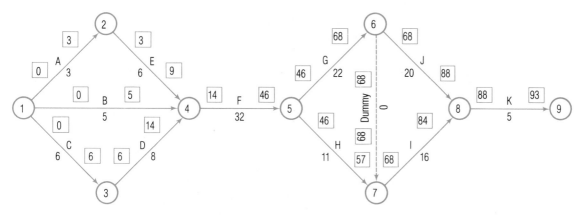

Olan may complete the entire office construction project in as short a time as 93 days. This estimate, however, assumes that each activity begins at its earliest start time (*ES*) and consumes only the expected activity duration (*t*).

ACTIVITY SCHEDULE At this stage, Olan knows the expected project completion date (93 days) if each activity begins and ends at the earliest times. Often, however, circumstances can delay the start or finish of an activity. Consequently, it would be useful to determine the latest time that each activity could begin and end without extending the project completion date. Figure 12.7 provides the necessary information.

Suppose that Olan wants to complete construction by the expected project completion date. This objective cannot be attained unless activity K is completed within 93 days. Therefore, the **latest finish time** for the final activity (K) in the network is the expected project completion time. Since this activity is expected to take $t = 5$ days, its **latest start time** must be $93 - 5 = 88$ days. That is, Olan can complete the building schedule if it starts activity K no later than 88 days into the project.

Note that the latest start time equals the latest finish time less the expected activity duration. By letting

LS = the latest start time for an activity

LF = the latest finish time for the activity

the following expression can be used to find the latest start time for a given activity:

(12.4) $LS = LF - t$

If management knows each *LF* value, then equation (12.4) can be used to find the *LS* value for each activity in the network. However, the *LF* values are not evident and must be deduced from an additional analysis. We can illustrate the process with activity G.

Figure 12.7 shows that Olan must complete plumbing (activity G) before it can start interior finishing (I) and exterior finishing (J). Remember, the dummy is a fictitious activity merely indicating that activity G is an immediate predecessor of I. Further, if the project is to be completed on schedule, each of the immediately following activities (I and J) must begin by its latest start time (*LS*). Thus, to determine the latest finish time (*LF*) for activity G, the company must first find the *LS* value for each follower.

In Figure 12.7, activities I and J are each followed by the same single task (K). Olan knows that the latest start time for activity K is $LS = 88$ days. Therefore, the schedule can be met only if the preceding activities (I and J) each finish no later than this time. That is, when we have a single follower, the latest finish time (*LF*) for an activity equals the latest start time (*LS*) of the immediately following task. In this case, then, activities I and J each have $LF = 88$ days.

Activity J has an expected activity duration of $t = 20$ days, so its latest start time is

$$LS = LF - t = 88 - 20 = 68 \text{ days}$$

Similarly, activity I has $t = 16$ days; thus,

$$LS = LF - t = 88 - 16 = 72 \text{ days}$$

Again, the dummy is a fictitious activity indicating the proper order of tasks G and I. As a result, the dummy will have the same *LS* and *LF* values, with both equal to the latest start time for activity I (72 days).

Olan now knows that the project may not be completed on schedule unless the latest start time is $LS = 68$ days for activity J and $LS = 72$ days for activity I (or the dummy). Furthermore, activity G must be complete (event 6 in Figure 12.7 must occur) before these two immediately following tasks (J and I or the dummy) can begin. Thus, the latest finish time for activity G is $LF = 68$ days. The analysis suggests the following rule for finding the latest finish time for any activity in a project network: The latest finish time (*LF*) for an activity entering a project node equals the smallest value of the latest start times for all activities leaving the node.

In summary, Olan starts the second search with the final node in the network. Then the company works backward in time by successively establishing first the latest finish time (*LF*) and then the latest start time (*LS*) for each activity. This process, called a **backward pass**, ends with the initial node in the network. Figure 12.8 shows the results of a backward pass through Olan's office project network. The latest start and latest finish times appear in boxes directly below the earliest start and earliest

Figure 12.8 Olan's Project Network with Latest Start and Finish Times

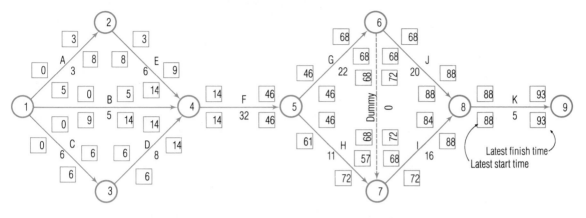

Table 12.4 Activity Schedule in Days for Olan's Project

Activity	Earliest Start ES	Latest Start LS	Earliest Finish EF	Latest Finish LF	Slack (LS − ES or LF − EF)	Critical Activity
A	0	5	3	8	5	No
B	0	9	5	14	9	No
C	0	0	6	6	0	Yes
D	6	6	14	14	0	Yes
E	3	8	9	14	5	No
F	14	14	46	46	0	Yes
G	46	46	68	68	0	Yes
H	46	61	57	72	15	No
I	68	72	84	88	4	No
J	68	68	88	88	0	Yes
K	88	88	93	93	0	Yes

finish times. Again, these latest time estimates assume that each activity begins at its latest start time (*LS*) and consumes only the expected activity duration (*t*).

The earliest and latest start and finish times depicted in Figure 12.8 provide a detailed schedule for all project activities. Table 12.4 presents the information in tabular form. For instance, the schedule indicates that Olan may start receiving materials (activity E) as early as *ES* = 3 days but no later than $LS = 8$ days into the project. This activity may be finished as early as $EF = 9$ days but no later than $LF = 14$ days into the project.

CRITICAL ACTIVITIES Recall that the project may not be completed on schedule unless each activity begins by its latest start time (LS). On the other hand, the ES value gives the earliest time that an activity may be started. The difference between LS and ES, then, tells management how long an activity may be delayed without extending the project completion date. By a similar reasoning, the difference between LF and EF provides exactly the same information. Either difference is referred to as the activity's free time or **activity slack**. Symbolically,

(12.5)   activity slack $= LS - ES = LF - EF$

For example, Olan knows that activity E has an LS value of 8 and an ES value of 3. Consequently, the slack for this activity is

activity slack $= LS - ES = 8 - 3 = 5$ days

This means that the company can delay receiving materials (E) for up to 5 days (start anytime between days 3 and 8) and yet construction can still be finished by the expected project completion date of 93 days. Table 12.4 presents the slack for each of Olan's activities.

When an activity has a positive slack, it is not critical for the task to start by its earliest start time or finish at its earliest finish time. Instead, such an activity can be delayed by an amount of time up to the slack without delaying the entire project. Table 12.4 shows that activities A, B, E, H, and I each have some slack and thus are noncritical tasks for Olan's project. On the other hand, there is no slack, or free time, associated with excavation (activity C). If the entire project is to be completed on schedule, this activity must be started at $LS = ES = 6$ days and finished at $LF = EF = 14$ days. Such a task, which must be started and finished without delay (has zero slack), is called a **critical activity**. Table 12.4 shows that Olan's critical activities are C, D, F, G, J, and K.

The sequence of critical activities that leads from the starting node to the ending node in the project network is referred to as the **critical path**. Olan's critical path, for instance, is C → D → F → G → J → K. In Figure 12.8, note that the expected times on this path have a sum of

$6 + 8 + 32 + 22 + 20 + 5 = 93$ days

In effect, then, the time it takes to traverse the critical path represents the estimated project duration. Consequently, tasks on this path deserve careful monitoring. Any delay in any one of these tasks may delay the completion of the entire project.

PROJECT DURATION So far, we have assumed that each activity takes its expected time t to
VARIABILITY complete. Now, let us examine the effects of activity time uncertainty on
the estimated project completion date.

Ordinarily, variation in noncritical activities (like A and B for Olan)
does not affect the project duration, because there is free time associated
with each of these activities. However, if a noncritical activity is delayed
long enough, eventually the task will expend all its slack and become
critical. Since critical activities govern the project duration, further delays
will therefore extend the expected completion date. Variation that leads to
longer-than-expected task times for the critical activities will also extend
the expected project duration. In other words, the variance in the critical
activities will effectively govern project duration variability.

Olan has assumed that the time required to complete a task does not
influence the duration of any other activity. As a result, the variance in the
project duration can be found by summing the variances of the times for
the critical (C, D, F, G, J, and K) activities. The data in Table 12.3 indicate
that

$$4 + 5.44 + 21.78 + 13.44 + 32.11 + 0 = 76.77$$

is the sum of the critical variances and therefore the variance in Olan's
project completion time.

The 76.77 value is expressed in terms of squared days. Such a measurement, however, could confuse Olan's management. After all, the original
data are expressed in days rather than squared days. To avoid the
confusion, management scientists usually measure variability with the
standard deviation σ instead of variance. By definition, the standard
deviation is the square root of variance, or in Olan's case,

$$\sigma = \sqrt{76.77} = 8.76 \text{ days}$$

This value indicates that there is likely to be an 8.76-day difference
between the actual and estimated project completion times.

The average project duration u is found in a similar manner. Since Olan
has independent task completion times, management can find u by
summing the expected durations of the critical activities. According to the
data in Table 12.3,

$$u = 6 + 8 + 32 + 22 + 20 + 5 = 93 \text{ days}$$

Moder and Phillips [10] and Weist and Levy [14] demonstrate that
under these circumstances the project duration can be assumed to follow a
normal probability distribution. In such a distribution, the project completion time has a mean of u with a standard deviation of σ. This
distribution can be used to find the probability of meeting a specified
completion deadline.

Figure 12.9 Normal Distribution for Olan's Project Duration

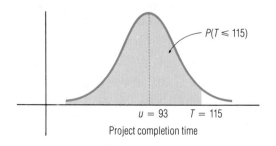

Figure 12.9 presents a normal probability distribution for Olan's project duration. Management defines the distribution by identifying the average duration u and the standard deviation σ of the completion time. In the diagram, Olan's $u = 93$ days appears below the peak of the distribution. Variation about this average is measured with the standard deviation of $\sigma = 8.76$ days.

Now, suppose that State Travelers has allotted 115 days for the construction project. Moreover, assume that Olan's management wants to know the probability of meeting the deadline. If T represents the desired completion date, then the problem is to find the likelihood that $T \le 115$ days. Such a likelihood corresponds to the shaded region in Figure 12.9.

There is a difference of $T - u = 115 - 93 = 22$ days between the allotted and expected project completion time. Furthermore, the standard score

$$(12.6) \quad Z = \frac{T - u}{\sigma}$$

expresses this difference in terms of standard deviations. Thus, the deadline T is

$$Z = \frac{T - u}{\sigma} = \frac{115 - 93}{8.76} = \frac{22}{8.76} = 2.51$$

standard deviations above the expected, or average, completion time.

Table 12.5 gives the cumulative probabilities of Z scores in the normal distribution. The table shows that a Z score of 2.51 corresponds to a probability of .9940. Therefore, even with the project duration variability, Olan has an excellent

$$P(T \le 115) = .9940$$

chance of meeting the 115-day deadline. Moreover, management can find the probability of attaining other company-imposed project deadlines with the same methodology.

Table 12.5 Probabilities for the Normal Distribution

Z	.09	.08	.07	.06	.05	.04	.03	.02	.01	.00	Z	Z	.00	.01	.02	.03	.04	.05	.06	.07	.08	.09	Z
-3.80	.0001	.0001	.0001	.0001	.0001	.0001	.0001	.0001	.0001	.0001	-3.80	.00	.5000	.5040	.5080	.5120	.5160	.5199	.5239	.5279	.5319	.5359	.00
-3.70	.0001	.0001	.0001	.0001	.0001	.0001	.0001	.0001	.0001	.0001	-3.70	.10	.5398	.5438	.5478	.5517	.5557	.5596	.5636	.5675	.5714	.5753	.10
-3.60	.0001	.0001	.0001	.0001	.0001	.0001	.0001	.0001	.0002	.0002	-3.60	.20	.5793	.5832	.5871	.5910	.5948	.5987	.6026	.6064	.6103	.6141	.20
-3.50	.0002	.0002	.0002	.0002	.0002	.0002	.0002	.0002	.0002	.0002	-3.50	.30	.6179	.6217	.6255	.6293	.6331	.6368	.6406	.6443	.6480	.6517	.30
-3.40	.0002	.0003	.0003	.0003	.0003	.0003	.0003	.0003	.0003	.0003	-3.40	.40	.6554	.6591	.6628	.6664	.6700	.6736	.6772	.6808	.6844	.6879	.40
-3.30	.0003	.0004	.0004	.0004	.0004	.0004	.0004	.0005	.0005	.0005	-3.30	.50	.6915	.6950	.6985	.7019	.7054	.7088	.7123	.7157	.7190	.7224	.50
-3.20	.0005	.0005	.0005	.0006	.0006	.0006	.0006	.0006	.0007	.0007	-3.20	.60	.7257	.7291	.7324	.7357	.7389	.7422	.7454	.7486	.7517	.7549	.60
-3.10	.0007	.0007	.0008	.0008	.0008	.0008	.0009	.0009	.0009	.0010	-3.10	.70	.7580	.7611	.7642	.7673	.7704	.7734	.7764	.7794	.7823	.7852	.70
-3.00	.0010	.0010	.0011	.0011	.0011	.0012	.0012	.0013	.0013	.0013	-3.00	.80	.7881	.7910	.7939	.7967	.7995	.8023	.8051	.8078	.8106	.8133	.80
-2.90	.0014	.0014	.0015	.0015	.0016	.0016	.0017	.0018	.0018	.0019	-2.90	.90	.8159	.8186	.8212	.8238	.8264	.8289	.8315	.8340	.8365	.8389	.90
-2.80	.0019	.0020	.0021	.0021	.0022	.0023	.0023	.0024	.0025	.0026	-2.80	1.00	.8413	.8438	.8461	.8485	.8508	.8531	.8554	.8577	.8599	.8621	1.00
-2.70	.0026	.0027	.0028	.0029	.0030	.0031	.0032	.0033	.0034	.0035	-2.70	1.10	.8643	.8665	.8686	.8708	.8729	.8749	.8770	.8790	.8810	.8830	1.10
-2.60	.0036	.0037	.0038	.0039	.0040	.0041	.0043	.0044	.0045	.0047	-2.60	1.20	.8849	.8869	.8888	.8907	.8925	.8944	.8962	.8980	.8997	.9015	1.20
-2.50	.0048	.0049	.0051	.0052	.0054	.0055	.0057	.0059	.0060	.0062	-2.50	1.30	.9032	.9049	.9066	.9082	.9099	.9115	.9131	.9147	.9162	.9177	1.30
-2.40	.0064	.0066	.0068	.0069	.0071	.0073	.0075	.0078	.0080	.0082	-2.40	1.40	.9192	.9207	.9222	.9236	.9251	.9265	.9279	.9292	.9306	.9319	1.40
-2.30	.0084	.0087	.0089	.0091	.0094	.0096	.0099	.0102	.0104	.0107	-2.30	1.50	.9332	.9345	.9357	.9370	.9382	.9394	.9406	.9418	.9429	.9441	1.50
-2.20	.0110	.0113	.0116	.0119	.0122	.0125	.0129	.0132	.0136	.0139	-2.20	1.60	.9452	.9463	.9474	.9484	.9495	.9505	.9515	.9525	.9535	.9545	1.60
-2.10	.0143	.0146	.0150	.0154	.0158	.0162	.0166	.0170	.0174	.0179	-2.10	1.70	.9554	.9564	.9573	.9582	.9591	.9599	.9608	.9616	.9625	.9633	1.70
-2.00	.0183	.0188	.0192	.0197	.0202	.0207	.0212	.0217	.0222	.0228	-2.00	1.80	.9641	.9649	.9656	.9664	.9671	.9678	.9686	.9693	.9699	.9706	1.80
-1.90	.0233	.0239	.0244	.0250	.0256	.0262	.0268	.0274	.0281	.0287	-1.90	1.90	.9713	.9719	.9726	.9732	.9738	.9744	.9750	.9756	.9761	.9767	1.90
-1.80	.0294	.0301	.0307	.0314	.0322	.0329	.0336	.0344	.0351	.0359	-1.80	2.00	.9772	.9778	.9783	.9788	.9793	.9798	.9803	.9808	.9812	.9817	2.00
-1.70	.0367	.0375	.0384	.0392	.0401	.0409	.0418	.0427	.0436	.0446	-1.70	2.10	.9821	.9826	.9830	.9834	.9838	.9842	.9846	.9850	.9854	.9857	2.10
-1.60	.0455	.0465	.0475	.0485	.0495	.0505	.0516	.0526	.0537	.0548	-1.60	2.20	.9861	.9864	.9868	.9871	.9875	.9878	.9881	.9884	.9887	.9890	2.20
-1.50	.0559	.0571	.0582	.0594	.0606	.0618	.0630	.0643	.0655	.0668	-1.50	2.30	.9893	.9896	.9898	.9901	.9904	.9906	.9909	.9911	.9913	.9916	2.30
-1.40	.0681	.0694	.0708	.0721	.0735	.0749	.0764	.0778	.0793	.0808	-1.40	2.40	.9918	.9920	.9922	.9925	.9927	.9929	.9931	.9932	.9934	.9936	2.40
-1.30	.0823	.0838	.0853	.0869	.0885	.0901	.0918	.0934	.0951	.0968	-1.30	2.50	.9938	.9940	.9941	.9943	.9945	.9946	.9948	.9949	.9951	.9952	2.50
-1.20	.0985	.1003	.1020	.1038	.1056	.1075	.1093	.1112	.1131	.1151	-1.20	2.60	.9953	.9955	.9956	.9957	.9959	.9960	.9961	.9962	.9963	.9964	2.60
-1.10	.1170	.1190	.1210	.1230	.1251	.1271	.1292	.1314	.1335	.1357	-1.10	2.70	.9965	.9966	.9967	.9968	.9969	.9970	.9971	.9972	.9973	.9974	2.70
-1.00	.1379	.1401	.1423	.1446	.1469	.1492	.1515	.1539	.1562	.1587	-1.00	2.80	.9974	.9975	.9976	.9977	.9977	.9978	.9979	.9979	.9980	.9981	2.80
-.90	.1611	.1635	.1660	.1685	.1711	.1736	.1762	.1788	.1814	.1841	-.90	2.90	.9981	.9982	.9982	.9983	.9984	.9984	.9985	.9985	.9986	.9986	2.90
-.80	.1867	.1894	.1922	.1949	.1977	.2005	.2033	.2061	.2090	.2119	-.80	3.00	.9987	.9987	.9987	.9988	.9988	.9989	.9989	.9989	.9990	.9990	3.00
-.70	.2148	.2177	.2206	.2236	.2266	.2296	.2327	.2358	.2389	.2420	-.70	3.10	.9990	.9991	.9991	.9991	.9992	.9992	.9992	.9992	.9993	.9993	3.10
-.60	.2451	.2483	.2514	.2546	.2578	.2611	.2643	.2676	.2709	.2743	-.60	3.20	.9993	.9993	.9994	.9994	.9994	.9994	.9994	.9995	.9995	.9995	3.20
-.50	.2776	.2810	.2843	.2877	.2912	.2946	.2981	.3015	.3050	.3085	-.50	3.30	.9995	.9995	.9995	.9996	.9996	.9996	.9996	.9996	.9996	.9997	3.30
-.40	.3121	.3156	.3192	.3228	.3264	.3300	.3336	.3372	.3409	.3446	-.40	3.40	.9997	.9997	.9997	.9997	.9997	.9997	.9997	.9997	.9997	.9998	3.40
-.30	.3483	.3520	.3557	.3594	.3632	.3669	.3707	.3745	.3783	.3821	-.30	3.50	.9998	.9998	.9998	.9998	.9998	.9998	.9998	.9998	.9998	.9998	3.50
-.20	.3859	.3897	.3936	.3974	.4013	.4052	.4090	.4129	.4168	.4207	-.20	3.60	.9998	.9998	.9999	.9999	.9999	.9999	.9999	.9999	.9999	.9999	3.60
-.10	.4247	.4286	.4325	.4364	.4404	.4443	.4483	.4522	.4562	.4602	-.10	3.70	.9999	.9999	.9999	.9999	.9999	.9999	.9999	.9999	.9999	.9999	3.70
-.00	.4641	.4681	.4721	.4761	.4801	.4840	.4880	.4920	.4960	.5000	-.00	3.80	.9999	.9999	.9999	.9999	.9999	.9999	.9999	.9999	.9999	.9999	3.80

COMPUTER ANALYSIS Table 12.6 summarizes the PERT procedure, including key assumptions and definitions and relevant project management information. As you can see, there are numerous calculations involved in performing a PERT analysis, and it is cumbersome and time-consuming to perform the computations by hand. Furthermore, the process is prone to error. Fortunately, management scientists have developed prewritten computer packages designed to solve large-scale PERT problems. One of these packages, itself called **PERT**, is available on the California State University and College System (CSUC) computer system. Figure 12.10 illustrates how this program can be used to solve Olan's construction problem.

The user executes the program with the LIB command. This command tells the computer that the program is contained in a library file. Next, the program asks for the name of the library program. The appropriate response is PERT.

At this point, the computer notes that PERT is available and asks if the data will be supplied from a file or the keyboard. In Figure 12.10, the data are provided at the keyboard with the KB: response. Then the program begins to request input data.

First, the decision maker must identify the number of time estimates that will be provided for each activity. In Olan's case, there is an optimistic, most likely, and pessimistic time estimate. Thus, 3 is the appropriate response to this first question (?) prompt.

The next group of data deals with the number of activities, the number of events, the project start date, and the completion date in the network. In Olan's case, there are twelve activities (the eleven regular tasks plus the dummy) and nine events, and the project starts at day zero. Also, it is assumed that management does not know the project completion date. Hence, the user should type the numbers 12, 9, 0, and 0 after the first four question prompts in this section.

Next, PERT asks for the code, preceding and succeeding event numbers, and the three time estimates associated with each activity in the network. Each activity must be coded with an integer, and the integers should be in consecutive order. Once more, the data are typed after the appropriate question prompts. Olan's first activity (A), for example, joins node 1 with node 2, has a 1-day optimistic time, a 2-day most likely time, and a 9-day pessimistic time. Thus, the values 1, 1, 2, 1, 2, and 9 are inputted after the first question prompt in this section.

The computer then requests corrections. If there are no errors, the user types NO after the question prompt. The program then prints the solution.

California State University's PERT output includes the earliest project completion date, the standard deviation associated with this date, and other relevant decision information. Figure 12.10, for instance, shows that Olan can expect to complete its construction project in 93 days. However, the standard deviation indicates that there is likely to be an 8.76229-day difference between the actual and expected completion dates. It also

Table 12.6 Summary of PERT

Procedure	Assumptions and Definitions	Decision Information
1. List all the activities that make up the project. 2. Identify the interrelationships between the tasks. 3. Draw the corresponding project network.		The network gives a clear, concise, detailed definition of the project.
4. Estimate the optimistic (*a*), most likely (*m*), and pessimistic (*b*) times for each activity.	An activity's duration is described by a beta probability distribution (Figure 12.3).	
5. Calculate the expected activity time (*t*) for each task.	$t = \dfrac{a + 4m + b}{6}$	The results measure activity time uncertainty.
6. Compute the variance (VAR) for each activity time.	$VAR = \left(\dfrac{b - a}{6}\right)^2$	
7. Using the expected activity times, determine the earliest start and finish times *ES* and *EF* for each task by making a forward pass through the network.	$EF = ES + t$ The *ES* value for each activity is given by the rule for finding the earliest start time. $ES = 0$ for each activity leaving the first node in the project network.	The earliest finish time for the last activity in the network is the expected project completion date.
8. Determine the latest start and finish times *LS* and *LF* for each activity by making a backward pass through the network.	$LS = LF - t$ The *LF* value for each activity is given by the rule for finding the latest finish time. LF = expected project completion time (*u*) for each activity entering the final project node.	The *ES*, *EF*, *LS*, and *LF* values give a detailed activity schedule for the entire project.
9. Compute the slack associated with each activity.	slack = $LS - ES = LF - EF$	The slack identifies how long an activity can be delayed without extending the entire project. The critical path identifies the activities that must be started and finished without delay in order to keep the project on schedule.
10. Identify the critical activities and the critical path.	Critical activities are the tasks with zero slack. The critical path is the sequence of critical activities that leads from the starting to the ending node in the project network.	
11. Use the variance (VAR) for each activity time to compute the variance (σ^2) for the project completion date.	Activity times are independent. σ^2 = the sum of the variances for the critical activity times.	
12. Identify the project completion deadline (*T*) and the expected project duration (*u*).	The project duration follows a normal probability distribution.	
13. Compute the corresponding standard score (*Z*).	$Z = \dfrac{T - u}{\sigma}$	The results identify the probability of completing the project by the specified deadline.
14. Use the normal distribution table to find the probability associated with the standard score.		

Figure 12.10 Olan's PERT Solution

```
   LIB

   Name of Library Program? PERT

   P E R T
   Input data from a file or KB: ? KB:

   TYPE NUMBER OF ACTIVITY TIME ESTIMATES (1 OR 3) ? 3

   TYPE DATA FOR:
        1. NUMBER OF ACTIVITIES
        2. NUMBER OF EVENTS
        3. PROJECT START DATE
        4. PROJECT COMPLETION DATE (IF UNKNOWN TYPE 0.0)
   ? 12
   ? 9
   ? 0
   ? 0

   TYPE ONE LINE OF DATA FOR EACH ACTIVITY.
   IF AN ERROR IS MADE, REPEAT THAT LINE.
   TYPE DATA IN THE ORDER:
        1. ACTIVITY NUMBER
        2. PRECEDING EVENT NUMBER
        3. SUCCEEDING EVENT NUMBER
        4. OPTIMISTIC TIME ESTIMATE
        5. MOST LIKELY TIME ESTIMATE
        6. PESSIMISTIC TIME ESTIMATE
   ? 1,1,2,1,2,9
   ? 2,1,4,2.5,4.5,9.5
   ? 3,1,3,2,5,14
   ? 4,3,4,4,6.5,18
   ? 5,2,4,2,4,18
   ? 6,4,5,22,30,50
   ? 7,5,6,15,20,37
   ? 8,5,7,4.5,10,21.5
   ? 9,6,7,0,0,0
   ? 10,7,8,12,15,24
   ? 11,6,8,14,14.5,48
   ? 12,8,9,5,5,5
```

provides the expected values and variances of completion times for each activity in the network. Activity 4 (task D), for example, has an 8-day expected completion time with a variance of 5.44 squared days.

In addition, the PERT output identifies the total slack associated with each activity in the network. Figure 12.10 shows that Olan can delay activity 8 (task H) for up to 15 days without delaying the completion of the entire project. On the other hand, there is zero activity slack associated

```
ARE THERE ANY CORRECTIONS (YES OR NO) ? NO

THE EARLIEST PROJECT COMPLETION DATE = 93

THE STANDARD DEVIATION =  8.76229
```

ACTIVITY NUMBER (J)	USERS EVENT NUMBERS (I) - (K)		EXPECTED COMPLETION TIME	VARIANCE OF COMPLETION TIME	ACTIVITY SLACK	FREE SLACK
1	1	2	3.00	1.78	5.00	0.00
2	1	4	5.00	1.36	9.00	9.00
3	1	3	6.00	4.00	0.00	0.00
4	3	4	8.00	5.44	0.00	0.00
5	2	4	6.00	7.11	5.00	5.00
6	4	5	32.00	21.78	0.00	0.00
7	5	6	22.00	13.44	0.00	0.00
8	5	7	11.00	8.03	15.00	11.00
9	6	7	0.00	0.00	4.00	0.00
10	7	8	16.00	4.00	4.00	4.00
11	6	8	20.00	32.11	0.00	0.00
12	8	9	5.00	0.00	0.00	0.00

NETWORK EVENT NUMBER	USERS EVENT NUMBER	EARLIEST DATE	VARIANCE OF EARLIEST DATE	LATEST DATE	EVENT SLACK
1	1	0.00	0.00	0.00	0.00
2	2	3.00	1.78	8.00	5.00
3	3	6.00	4.00	6.00	0.00
4	4	14.00	9.44	14.00	0.00
5	5	46.00	31.22	46.00	0.00
6	6	68.00	44.67	68.00	0.00
7	7	68.00	44.67	72.00	4.00
8	8	88.00	76.78	88.00	0.00
9	9	93.00	76.78	93.00	0.00

with tasks 3, 4, 6, 7, 11, and 12. Hence, the sequence of these tasks (C → D → F → G → J → K) forms the critical path for Olan's construction project.

The PERT output also lists the earliest and latest dates at which Olan's events can occur without delaying the completion of the entire project. Consider, for instance, event 7, which represents the completion of activities 8 and 9 as well as the start of task 10. According to the computer output in Figure 12.10, this event could happen as early as day 68, but must occur no later than day 72 of the project. Otherwise, the company will not complete construction within the 93-day schedule.

PERT also computes the variance associated with the earliest date for each event in the network. Figure 12.10, for example, indicates that event 7 has a variance of 44.67, or a standard deviation of

$$\sqrt{44.67} = 6.68 \text{ days}$$

This value indicates that there is likely to be a 6.68-day difference between the actual and estimated earliest occurrence dates for event 7.

The event data help to identify other types of slack as well, such as **event slack**, the difference between the event's latest and earliest dates. According to Figure 12.10, event 7 has $72 - 68 = 4$ days of free time or slack. Such slack tells management how long the event can be delayed without extending the project completion date.

Another type of slack deals with the amount of time an activity can be delayed without affecting the total slack available for other tasks in the network. Consider, for example, task H (activity 8), the dummy (activity 9), and task I (activity 10) in Olan's situation. According to Figure 12.10, the activity slack is 15 days for H, 4 days for the dummy, and 4 days for I. However, task I (activity 10) cannot begin until H (activity 8) and the dummy (activity 9) are completed at event 7. Thus, a 4-day delay in the dummy and/or a 15-day delay in task H will extend the earliest date for event 7. As a result, there will be no slack remaining for task I (activity 10).

In effect, then, Olan can delay the dummy for $4 - 4 = 0$ days and task H for $15 - 4 = 11$ days without affecting I's activity slack. Each of these differences is known as a **free slack**. That is,

$$(12.7) \quad \begin{array}{c} \text{free} \\ \text{slack} \end{array} = \left(\begin{array}{c} \text{activity} \\ \text{slack} \end{array} \right) - \left(\begin{array}{c} \text{ending node's} \\ \text{event slack} \end{array} \right)$$

As Figure 12.10 demonstrates, the PERT program computes and lists the free slack associated with each activity in the network.

CPM Recall that the time it takes to traverse the critical path represents the expected project completion date. Hence, if management can shorten a critical activity's duration, it can reduce the time needed to complete the entire project. For example, Olan can reduce the scheduled 93-day construction time by shortening activity C, D, F, G, J, or K. To do so, the company may have to add more workers, use overtime, and so on. In short, Olan would need more resources. Since additional resources are costly, project management must consider the trade-off between decreased

Figure 12.11 CPM Time-Cost Relationship

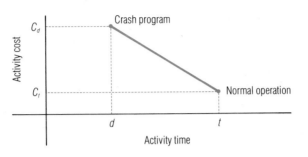

activity time and increased cost. The **Critical Path Method (CPM)** provides a method for accomplishing this purpose.

CRASHING ACTIVITY TIMES Suppose that unforeseen circumstances make it imperative for Olan to complete the State Travelers office building within three months (90 days). Recall, however, that this project normally has an expected duration of 93 days. Thus, Olan cannot meet the 90-day deadline unless it adds resources to shorten the duration of selected activities. In CPM, this extra effort is referred to as **crashing** the activity time.

There is a cost associated with the extra effort. The company has budgeted labor, material, and equipment costs for each activity on the basis of a normal effort. Crashing requires additional resources and thus involves increased expenses. Typically, CPM assumes that the increase in cost is proportional to the reduction in task duration. By letting

C_t = the normal activity cost

C_d = the cost when the activity is crashed as much as possible

t = the normal or expected activity time

d = the duration when the activity is crashed as much as possible

the time-cost relationship will be as shown in Figure 12.11. In this case, an activity's crash cost per time period (C) can be expressed as

$$(12.8) \quad C = \frac{C_d - C_t}{t - d}$$

For example, suppose that Olan normally can frame the office building (activity F) in its expected duration of $t = 32$ days at a cost of $C_t = \$200,000$. By using additional resources, the company could reduce the

Table 12.7 Olan's Normal and Crash Activity Data

Activity	Time (Days)			Cost ($)		
	Normal t	Crash d	Maximum Crash $t - d$	Crash C_d	Normal C_t	Crash per Day $C = \dfrac{C_d - C_t}{t - d}$
A	3	1	2	400	300	50
B	5	2	3	850	400	150
C	6	5	1	3,200	3,000	200
D	8	4	4	10,400	6,400	1000
E	6	6	0	900	900	—
F	32	28	4	214,400	208,000	1600
G	22	15	7	29,200	26,400	400
H	11	11	0	7,700	7,700	—
I	16	13	3	26,500	25,600	300
J	20	12	8	43,800	35,000	1100
K	5	5	0	300	300	—
					314,000	

completion time to $d = 28$ days at a cost of $C_d = \$206,400$. Then, activity F can be crashed for a maximum of

$$t - d = 32 - 28 = 4 \text{ days}$$

at a crashing cost of

$$C = \frac{C_d - C_t}{t - d} = \frac{\$206,400 - \$200,000}{32 - 28} = \$1600 \text{ per day}$$

Hence, if Olan wanted to reduce the duration by 2 (instead of the maximum 4) days, the added cost would be $\$1600 \times 2 = \$3200$. As a result, activity F would have a duration of $32 - 2 = 30$ days and cost $\$200,000 + \$3200 = \$203,200$.

CPM assumes that project management knows (or can find) the exact values for each activity's normal and crash times and costs. In fact, Olan reports the data shown in Table 12.7.

CRASHING DECISION According to Table 12.7, it will normally cost $314,000 to construct the office building. This cost is based on a normal, or expected, project time of 93 days. The table also shows that Olan can shorten this duration by crashing every task except E, H, and K. Activities E, H, and K simply cannot be crashed.

Unfortunately, Table 12.7 does not identify which activities to crash or how much they should be crashed. Since the project duration equals the length of the critical path, the natural tendency is to first crash those critical tasks capable of being crashed (C, D, F, G, and J). Table 12.7 shows that activity C has the smallest crashing cost per day ($200) of the critical activities. Olan can crash this activity by a maximum of 1 day and thus reduce the project duration (from 93) to 92 days. Activity G has the next smallest cost per day ($400), and it can be crashed by as much as 7 days. Thus, if Olan crashes G by 2 days, project completion time will be shortened (from 92) to the desired 90 days.

Crashing in this manner will reduce the time for activity C to $6 - 1 = 5$ days at an additional cost of $200. Activity G's duration will be shortened to $22 - 2 = 20$ days at an increased expense of $400 \times 2 = \$800$. The entire project will be completed in 90 days at a total (normal plus crashing) cost of $\$314{,}000 + \$200 + \$800 = \$315{,}000$.

LINEAR PROGRAMMING Crashing the current critical activities may affect other tasks. In many cases, noncritical tasks become critical and thus become additional candidates for crashing. Then it becomes necessary to check the critical path in the revised network and perhaps modify the initial crashing decision.

This trial and error approach may be sufficient for small networks. In large projects, however, a mathematical procedure is needed to determine the optimal crashing plan. Linear programming provides one such procedure. Again, we will illustrate with the office construction project.

Recall that activities, not events, generate project expenses. Furthermore, the total project expense will equal the normal cost plus the crash cost. As shown in Table 12.7, Olan's normal cost is fixed at $314,000 and thus will be unaffected by the crashing plan. Crash cost is another matter.

Each activity's crashing expense equals the crash cost per day multiplied by the number of days that are crashed. For instance, let $Y_A = $ the number of days that Olan crashes activity A. From Table 12.7, you can see that this activity has a crash cost of $50 per day. Hence, the crashing expense for activity A will be $50 times Y_A, or $\$50 Y_A$. Similarly, activity B will have a crashing expense of $150 multiplied by the amount of crashing time Y_B for this task, or $\$150 Y_B$.

By finding the crashing expense for the other activities in a comparable manner and then summing the results, Olan will get the following total crash cost (TC_d):

$$TC_d = \$50 Y_A + \$150 Y_B + \$200 Y_C + \$1000 Y_D$$
$$+ \$1600 Y_F + \$400 Y_G + \$300 Y_I + \$1100 Y_J$$

Notice that activities E, H, and K do not appear in the total cost expression, because these tasks cannot be crashed (have Y values equal to zero).

In CPM, the objective is to find the crashing plan that will meet the scheduled project completion time at least cost. Only crash (not normal) expenses are affected by the plan. Thus, Olan can achieve its objective by selecting the Y values that minimize total crash cost TC_d.

However, there are constraints on the objective. First, each activity cannot be crashed by more than its maximum crash time. For instance, Table 12.7 indicates that Olan can crash activity A by no more than 2 days. That is, $Y_A \leq 2$. Comparable crash time constraints for the other relevant activities are $Y_B \leq 3$, $Y_C \leq 1$, $Y_D \leq 4$, $Y_F \leq 4$, $Y_G \leq 7$, $Y_I \leq 3$, and $Y_J \leq 8$.

Another constraint is that the last event in the network must be finished no later than the project deadline. In Olan's case, Figure 12.8 indicates that node 9 is the last event in the office construction program. Also, there is a 90-day project deadline. By letting X_9 equal the time when event 9 occurs, the deadline restriction can then be expressed as $X_9 \leq 90$.

A final series of constraints describes the impact of the crash plan on the precedence in the network. The project events are key elements in this description. Recall that a project event marks the completion of all activities leading into that node. Consequently, the event will occur no sooner than the completion time for all the activities leading into that node. For example, in Figure 12.8, node 2 indicates when Olan has completed activity A. Hence, event 2 will not occur before this activity has been completed. You can also see that node 1 must occur before Olan can begin activity A. Furthermore, this activity will consume the normal time t less the time Y_A it is crashed. By letting X_1 equal the time when event 1 occurs and X_2 the time when event 2 occurs, Olan can describe the activity A portion of the network as follows:

$$X_2 \geq X_1 + \underbrace{t - Y_A}$$

Actual time for activity A

Time of occurrence for the immediately following event

Time of occurrence for the immediately preceding event

Since Olan knows that $t = 3$ days for activity A and event 1 occurs at a time of zero ($X_1 = 0$), this constraint can be rewritten as

$$X_2 + Y_A \geq 3$$

Precedence constraints for the remainder of Olan's activities can be developed in a similar way. Table 12.8 presents these additional constraints and the complete linear program for Olan's crashing decision. If

Table 12.8 Linear Program for Olan's Crashing Decision

Objective: minimize $TC_d = \$50\,Y_A + \$150\,Y_B + \$200\,Y_C + \$1000\,Y_D + \$1600\,Y_F + \$400\,Y_G + \$300\,Y_I + \$1100\,Y_J$, subject to:

Precedence Constraints	Crash Time Constraints	Nonnegativity Conditions	Schedule Constraint
$X_2 \quad + Y_A \geq \ 3$ days (activity A)	$Y_A \leq 2$	$Y_A \geq 0$	$X_9 \leq 90$
$X_4 \quad + Y_B \geq \ 5$ days (activity B)	$Y_B \leq 3$	$Y_B \geq 0$	
$X_3 \quad + Y_C \geq \ 6$ days (activity C)	$Y_C \leq 1$	$Y_C \geq 0$	
$X_4 - X_3 + Y_D \geq \ 8$ days (activity D)	$Y_D \leq 4$	$Y_D \geq 0$	
$X_4 - X_2 \quad \geq \ 6$ days (activity E)	$Y_F \leq 4$	$Y_F \geq 0$	
$X_5 - X_4 + Y_F \geq 32$ days (activity F)	$Y_G \leq 7$	$Y_G \geq 0$	
$X_6 - X_5 + Y_G \geq 22$ days (activity G)	$Y_I \leq 3$	$Y_I \geq 0$	
$X_7 - X_5 \quad \geq 11$ days (activity H)	$Y_J \leq 8$	$Y_J \geq 0$	
$X_8 - X_7 + Y_I \geq 16$ days (activity I)			
$X_8 - X_6 + Y_J \geq 20$ days (activity J)			
$X_9 - X_8 \quad \geq \ 5$ days (activity K)			

Olan solves the linear program, the company will find that the minimum crashing cost of $TC_d = \$1000$ is achieved by setting $Y_C = 1$, $Y_G = 2$, and $Y_A = Y_B = Y_D = Y_F = Y_I = Y_J = 0$. This least-cost plan involves the crashing of activity C by 1 day and task G by 2 days. Total project expenses will then be the $314,000 normal cost plus the $1000 crashing cost, or $315,000. As you can see, the linear programming approach and the trial and error approach yield identical solutions.

Project management can find the least-cost crashing plan for alternative project completion dates by modifying the schedule constraint and resolving the resulting linear program. It is even possible to determine the project duration that will give the best trade-off between completion time and all costs (including contracted penalties, interest, and supervisor salaries). S. E. Elmaghraby [7], Moder and Phillips [10], and Weist and Levy [14] provide the details for the interested reader.

COMPUTER PACKAGES There are numerous calculations involved in planning, updating, and revising PERT/CPM networks. In practice, it could be difficult and time-consuming to perform the calculations by hand. Furthermore, the process is prone to error. Fortunately, management scientists have developed prewritten computer packages designed to generate a complete activity schedule, determine the project cost, and identify the critical path in a network.

One such package, called **CPM**, is available on the California State University and College (CSUC) computer system. Figure 12.12 shows

Figure 12.12 Olan's CPM Solution

```
/FIND,CPM
WANT INSTRUCTIONS (YES OR NO) ? NO

CRITICAL PATH METHOD PROGRAM
BEGINNING PHASE 1

INPUT DATA FILE NAME: ? TERMINAL
? 12
? 1,2,3,300,
? 1,4,5,400,
? 1,3,5,3200,
? 3,4,8,6400,
? 2,4,6,900,
? 4,5,32,208000,
? 5,6,20,27200,
? 5,7,11,7700,
? 6,7,0,0,
? 7,8,16,25600,
? 6,8,20,35000,
? 8,9,5,300


NO ERRORS.

NUMBER OF ACTIVITIES:      12
STARTING EVENT:      1
ENDING EVENT:        9




CRITICAL PATH METHOD PROGRAM
BEGINNING PHASE 2


WHAT COLUMN FOR SORT, AND HOW MANY ACTIVITIES ? 1,12
```

how Olan can use this package to generate the new activity schedule that would result from its least-cost crashing plan.

The user executes the program with the FIND,CPM command. The program then asks if the decision maker wants instructions. A NO response tells the machine to run the program. Then CPM requests the file name for the data. When the data are supplied at the keyboard, TERMINAL is the appropriate response to this request.

At this point, the network data must be entered after the question (?) prompts. First, the user enters the number of activities in the network. Then the user provides the starting and ending events, duration, and dollar cost for each activity.

In Olan's case, the network has eleven regular activities plus the dummy activity. Hence, management should type the number 12 after the first

```
PROJECT DURATION:   90          TOTAL COST: $ 315000

CRIT    I       J      DUR     ES      EF      LS      LF      TF     LEV     $


        1       2      3       0       3       4       7       4      1      300

        1       4      5       0       5       8       13      8      1      400
   *
        1       3      5       0       5       0       5       0      1      3200

        2       4      6       3       9       7       13      4      2      900
   *
        3       4      8       5       13      5       13      0      2      6400
   *
        4       5      32      13      45      13      45      0      3      208000
   *
        5       6      20      45      65      45      65      0      4      27200

        5       7      11      45      56      58      69      13     4      7700

        6       7      0       65      65      69      69      4      5      0
   *
        6       8      20      65      85      65      85      0      5      35000

        7       8      16      65      81      69      85      4      6      25600
   *
        8       9      5       85      90      85      90      0      7      300

SORT ON ANOTHER COLUMN?  NO


NETWORK COMPUTATION COMPLETE  --  END RUN
```

question prompt in the data section. It is followed by the activity information. Consider, for example, activity C in Olan's project network. This activity starts at event 1, ends at event 3, has an expected duration of 6 days, and generates a normal cost of $3000. The company also knows that the project completion date can be reduced to 90 days when activity C is crashed by 1 day. However, it costs $200 per day to crash C. Consequently, the user should enter the values 1, 3, 5, and 3200 after the third question prompt in the activity section of the data file.

Similarly, activity G starts at event 5, ends at event 6, has an expected duration of 22 days, and generates a normal cost of $26,400. In addition, Olan knows that the project completion date can be reduced to 90 days when this activity is crashed by 2 days. Yet it costs $400 per day to crash activity G. As a result, management should type the values 5, 6, 20, and

27200 after the seventh question prompt in the activity section of the data file.

After all the network information has been entered, the CPM program analyzes the data for multiple starts and ends, illogical loops, and other errors. If there are no errors, the computer requests a sort of the output. Output can be sorted by any of the following criteria:

1. Starting events (I)
2. Ending events (J)
3. Activity durations (DUR)
4. Earliest starts (ES)
5. Earliest finishes (EF)
6. Latest starts (LS)
7. Latest finishes (LF)
8. Total slack (TF)
9. Position in the network (LEV)
10. Cost ($)

The 1,12 response in Figure 12.12 indicates that Olan's twelve activities will be sorted by starting events.

California State University's CPM program then prints the output information. It includes the project duration and total cost, the activity schedule, and the resulting total slack and activity cost. Critical activities are denoted with an asterisk.

Consider, for instance, the output section of Figure 12.12. This output indicates that Olan can expect to complete its construction project in 90 days for a total cost of $315,000 by following the listed activity schedule. Furthermore, the printout demonstrates that $C \rightarrow D \rightarrow F \rightarrow G \rightarrow J \rightarrow K$ still is the only critical path in the crashed activity schedule.

The CSUC computer packages are not the only programs available. Indeed, E. W. Davis [4, 5] identifies several others. Some can even execute the full range of PERT/CPM options, including the crashing decision. However, to effectively utilize these computer aids, project management will need a firm understanding of the PERT and CPM concepts presented in this chapter.

PERT/COST Although CPM introduces some expenses into project analysis, the primary emphasis is still on time (rather than cost) management. Often, however, the program director wants to plan, schedule, and control project costs as well. Management usually establishes an initial budget that identifies all project costs and forecasts when expenses are expected to occur. At various stages of the project, the actual expenses can then be compared with the scheduled, or budgeted, costs. If there are discrepancies, corrective action may be taken to keep costs within the budget. **PERT/COST** is a system designed to assist project directors in this cost management process.

PLANNING AND SCHEDULING COSTS The first step in PERT/COST is to break the project into components that are convenient for cost measurement and control. In this process, related activities under the control of one individual or group are often clustered together to form what are referred to as **work packages**. Then management identifies the cost of each work package. Example 12.3 illustrates.

EXAMPLE 12.3 Estimating Work Package Costs

Suppose that Olan considers each of the eleven activities to be an acceptable work package. Budgeted, or normal, costs for the work packages (activities) are given in Table 12.7. To meet the State Travelers 90-day deadline, however, it was necessary to crash activity C by 1 day and task G by 2 days. This process resulted in the work package (activity) time and budgeted cost data presented in Table 12.9. The crashed activity schedule is as shown in Figure 12.12. Olan wants to use this information to plan, schedule, and control project costs.

Table 12.9 Olan's Work Package Crash Time and Cost Data

Work Package (Activity)	Expected Time (Days)	Budgeted Cost ($)	Budgeted Cost per Day ($)
A	3	300	100
B	5	400	80
C	5	3,200	640
D	8	6,400	800
E	6	900	150
F	32	208,000	6500
G	20	27,200	1360
H	11	7,700	700
I	16	25,600	1600
J	20	35,000	1750
K	5	300	60
	Total project cost = 315,000		

Table 12.10 Olan's Budgeted Costs ($) for an Earliest Start Schedule

Activity	Day													
	1	2	3	4	5	6	7	8	9	...	87	88	89	90
A	100	100	100											
B	80	80	80	80	80									
C	640	640	640	640	640									
D						800	800	800	800					
E				150	150	150	150	150	150					
⋮														
K											60	60	60	60
Daily Cost	820	820	820	870	870	950	950	950	950	...	60	60	60	60
Total Project Cost	820	1640	2460	3330	4200	5150	6100	7050	8000	...	314,820	314,880	314,940	315,000

At this stage, Olan is ready to develop a budget that will show when costs should occur during the 90-day project duration. First, let us assume that Olan begins each activity at its earliest start time (ES). Figure 12.12, for example, shows that activity A has an earliest start date of $ES = 0$ days and an expected duration of $t = 3$ days. As shown in Table 12.9, this activity has a budgeted cost of $300. Ordinarily, PERT/COST assumes that costs accrue at a constant rate over the task's duration. Hence, Olan should expect activity A to show a $300/3 = $100 cost in each of the first 3 days of the project. Similarly, activity E has $ES = 3$ days, $t = 6$ days, and a budgeted cost of $900. Consequently, this activity is expected to generate a $150 cost in days 4, 5, 6, 7, 8, and 9. By using the data from Figure 12.12 and Table 12.9 in a similar manner, Olan can develop the daily cost forecast for each activity. Table 12.10 gives a portion of this schedule. Notice that the sum of each column gives the projected daily cost. By accumulating the daily expense, Olan can find an up-to-date total project cost schedule.

Project management can also develop a schedule showing the budgeted cost when each activity begins at its latest start time (LS). For example, Figure 12.12 shows that activity A has $LS = 4$ days and $t = 3$ days. As shown in Table 12.9, the budgeted cost for this task is $300. Hence, activity A can be expected to show a $100 cost in days 5, 6, and 7 of the project. Table 12.11 presents a portion of the daily activity cost schedule that results from this type of analysis.

Table 12.11 Olan's Budgeted Costs ($) for a Latest Start Schedule

Activity	Day															
	1	2	3	4	5	6	7	8	9	10	...	86	87	88	89	90
A					100	100	100									
B									80	80						
C	640	640	640	640	640											
D						800	800	800	800	800						
E								150	150	150						
⋮																
K												60	60	60	60	60
Daily Cost	640	640	640	640	740	900	900	950	1030	1030	...	60	60	60	60	60
Total Project Cost	640	1280	1920	2560	3300	4200	5100	6050	7080	8110	...	314,760	314,820	314,880	314,940	315,000

Figure 12.13 Olan's Possible Budgets for Total Project Costs

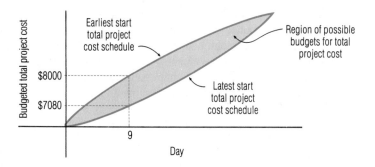

If the project progresses on its PERT or CPM schedule, each activity will be started somewhere between its earliest and latest start times. As a result, the total project costs should be between the earliest and latest start budget schedules. Figure 12.13 illustrates the possible budgets by depicting the schedules shown in Tables 12.10 and 12.11 for Olan's project. Note that the company's project budget must be in the shaded region between the two cost schedules. By the end of day 9, for instance, the earliest start schedule (Table 12.10) generates an accumulated project cost of $8000. At the same date, the latest start program (Table 12.11) results in a corresponding expense of $7080. Thus, at day 9, Olan should expect total

Table 12.12 Work Package Data at the End of Day 15 for Olan's Project

Work Package (Activity)	Actual Cost ($)	% Completion
A	350	100
B	400	100
C	3,000	100
D	6,000	90
E	600	80
F	22,000	10
G	0	0
H	0	0
I	0	0
J	0	0
K	0	0
Total actual cost = 32,350		

project costs to be between $7080 and $8000. Management can prepare an exact budget or forecast by committing activities to specific starting times.

CONTROLLING COSTS After establishing the budget cost schedules, project management next will want to record the actual expense as it occurs for each work package (activity). Then the decision maker can obtain an up-to-date status report by periodically comparing actual costs with the corresponding budgeted expenses. If actual costs exceed the budget, there has been a cost overrun. On the other hand, when actual expenses are below the budget, a cost underrun has occurred. By identifying the sources of cost overruns and underruns, the manager can take appropriate corrective action where necessary.

Suppose, for example, that Olan's project is at the end of its fifteenth day. The actual cost and percent completion for each activity are reported in Table 12.12. This information indicates that activities A, B, and C have been completed, tasks D, E, and F are currently in progress, and activities G, H, I, J, and K have not yet started.

Remember, Table 12.9 presents Olan's corresponding budgeted costs for each work package (activity) that has been 100% completed. However, some activities are still in progress or have not even begun at the end of day 15. Thus, before Olan can prepare a cost status report, management will have to compute the budgeted value for all currently completed work. By letting

p = the proportion of an activity that is completed

Table 12.13 Olan's Project Cost Status Report at Day 15

Work Package (Activity)	Actual Cost ($)	Budgeted Value ($) $V = pB$	Difference ($)
A	350	300	50
B	400	400	0
C	3,000	3,200	−200
D	6,000	5,760	240
E	600	720	−120
F	22,000	20,800	1200
G	0	0	0
H	0	0	0
I	0	0	0
J	0	0	0
K	0	0	0
Totals	32,350	31,180	1170

B = the budget for the activity

V = the budgeted value of the completed work for the activity

the value can be found as follows:

(12.9) $V = pB$

For example, Table 12.9 shows that activity D has a budgeted cost of $B = \$6400$. Table 12.12, meanwhile, indicates that this activity is 90% complete, or has $p = .9$, at the end of day 15. Consequently, the budgeted value of work completed for activity D is

$$V = pB = (.9)(\$6400) = \$5760$$

Table 12.13 computes budgeted values at the end of day 15 for all of Olan's work packages and compares them with actual costs. This table represents a cost status report at day 15 of Olan's project. It shows that actual expenses to date are $1170 over the budgeted costs. On a percentage basis, we would say that the project is experiencing a $1170/31,180 = .038$, or 3.8%, cost overrun. By checking each activity, Olan can see that activities A, D, and F are causing the problem. Since activity A has been completed, its cost overrun cannot be corrected. However, activities D and F are still in progress and thus should be reviewed immediately. By taking corrective action for these tasks now (at day 15), Olan can help bring actual costs closer to the budget. In addition, project management may want to consider the possibilities of reducing costs for yet-to-be-started activities (G, H, I, J, and K). Some hints may come from an examination of tasks (like C and E) that have been experiencing cost underruns, or savings.

LIMITATIONS   Although PERT/COST can be an effective cost control system, the technique involves potential difficulties. First, the work package cost-recording system may require significant clerical effort, especially for firms with large and numerous projects. Second, there may be problems in measuring some costs (like overhead) and then properly allocating them to work packages. Third, PERT/COST requires a recording and control system that differs substantially from most organizationally oriented cost accounting procedures. Hence, many firms will have to modify procedures or carry a dual accounting system to handle the PERT/COST activity-oriented approach.

SUMMARY   This chapter has introduced network-based procedures designed to aid decision makers in planning, scheduling, and controlling large-scale projects. The initial focus was on the Program Evaluation and Review Technique (PERT) for project time management. We saw how to develop a project network, derive activity time estimates, forecast the project duration, establish a complete activity schedule, and account for uncertainty. Table 12.6 summarized the PERT procedure, assumptions, and contributions to project management. PERT is particularly appropriate for new and unique programs, such as research and development.

In the second section, we examined the Critical Path Method (CPM), which was developed primarily for industrial-type projects. In these cases, task times and resource requirements are generally known or readily available. Consequently, this technique focuses on the project duration and appropriate ways to trade off activity time and cost. In particular, CPM provides the capability of shortening an activity's duration by adding additional resources (and thus cost). This process is called crashing. We considered all these concepts as well as the method of finding the crashing plan that would meet the scheduled project completion time at least cost.

The final section focused on the PERT/COST system for project cost management. We discussed the concept of work packages, developed a range for possible budgeted cost schedules, and established a procedure for measuring cost overruns and underruns. We saw how this kind of information can be used to plan, schedule, and control project costs.

Since there are numerous computations involved in planning, updating, and revising PERT and CPM networks, computer programs frequently have been used to implement these project management techniques. This chapter showed how to utilize two of the available packages.

Glossary

activities Specific tasks that use financial and/or physical resources and time and are required to complete a project.

activity slack The length of time an activity can be delayed without extending the project completion date.

backward pass A procedure that determines the latest finish and start times for each activity by successively moving backward through the project network.

CPM A prewritten computer package designed to generate a complete activity schedule, determine the project cost, and identify the critical path in a PERT/CPM network.

crashing The process of adding resources (and usually cost) to reduce an activity time.

critical activity A task that must be started and finished without delay (has zero activity slack).

critical path The sequence of critical activities that leads from the starting event to the ending event in a project network.

Critical Path Method (CPM) A network-based project management procedure that includes the capability of crashing.

dummy activities Fictitious activities used to indicate the proper precedence in a PERT network.

earliest finish time The earliest time when a project activity may be completed.

earliest start time The earliest time when a project activity may begin.

events Points in time that mark the completion of all activities for a particular phase of a project.

event slack The length of time an event can be delayed without extending the project completion date.

expected activity time The average time required to complete a PERT activity.

forward pass A procedure that determines the earliest start and finish times for each activity by successively moving forward through the project network.

free slack The length of time an activity can be delayed without affecting the activity slack available for other tasks in the network.

latest finish time The latest time when a project activity may be completed without delaying the entire project.

latest start time The latest time when a project activity may begin without delaying the entire project.

most likely time The most frequent time required to complete a PERT task under normal conditions.

optimistic time The time required to complete a PERT activity under ideal conditions.

PERT A prewritten computer package designed to solve PERT problems.

PERT/COST A variation of PERT designed to assist program directors in managing project costs.

PERT network A network in which the arcs represent project activities and the nodes represent project events.

pessimistic time The time required to complete a PERT task under adverse conditions.

Program Evaluation and Review Technique (PERT)   A network-based procedure for planning, scheduling, and controlling large-scale projects.

work package   A unit in PERT/COST formed by grouping naturally interrelated project activities for cost control purposes.

References

1. Baker, K. R. *Introduction to Sequencing and Scheduling.* New York: Wiley, 1974.

2. Britney, R. R. "Bayesian Point Estimation and the PERT Scheduling of Stochastic Activities." *Management Science* (May 1976): 938.

3. Dane, C. W., et al. "Factors Affecting the Successful Application of PERT/CPM Systems in a Government Organization." *Interfaces* (November 1979): 94.

4. Davis, E. W. "Network Resource Allocation." *Industrial Engineering* (April 1974): 22.

5. Davis, E. W. *Project Management: Techniques, Applications, and Managerial Issues.* Norcross, Ga.: American Institute of Industrial Engineers, 1976.

6. Doersch, R. H., and J. H. Patterson. "Scheduling a Project to Maximize Its Present Value: A Zero-One Programming Approach." *Management Science* (April 1977): 882.

7. Elmaghraby, S. E. *Activity Networks: Project Planning and Control by Network Models.* New York: Wiley, 1977.

8. Hoare, H. R. *Project Management Using Network Analysis.* New York: McGraw-Hill, 1973.

9. Koehler, A. B., and R. H. McClure. "The Use of Arcs and Nodes for the Determination of Critical Paths in PERT/CPM Networks." *Decision Sciences* (April 1979): 329.

10. Moder, J. J., and C. R. Phillips. *Project Management with CPM and PERT.* 2d ed. New York: Van Nostrand, 1970.

11. Moore, L. J., and E. R. Clayton. *GERT Modeling and Simulation.* New York: Petrocelli/Charter, 1976.

12. Robillard, P., and M. Trahan. "The Completion Time of PERT Networks." *Operations Research* (January–February 1977): 15.

13. Taylor, B. W., and L. J. Moore. "Analysis of a Ph.D. Program via GERT Modeling and Simulation." *Decision Sciences* (October 1978): 725.

14. Weist, J. D., and F. K. Levy. *A Management Guide to PERT/CPM.* 2d ed. Englewood Cliffs, N.J.: Prentice-Hall, 1977.

15. Whitehouse, G. E. *Systems Analysis and Design Using Network Techniques.* Englewood Cliffs, N.J.: Prentice-Hall, 1973.

Thought Exercises

1. In each of the following situations, explain whether the original version of PERT or CPM would be more appropriate:

   a. A training course for middle-level government officers
   b. An advertising campaign for a new and unique product
   c. An exploration of the planet Mars by a team of astronauts
   d. Airline maintenance

2. Jane Twine is a senior accounting major at the local college. She wants to become a certified public accountant (CPA) and knows that several tasks will be needed to complete her goal. They include:

   ◆ Passing her second-semester courses
   ◆ Graduating
   ◆ Taking a continuing education CPA preparation course
   ◆ Completing an internship
   ◆ Gaining some postgraduate practical experience
   ◆ Practicing on past CPA exams
   ◆ Getting counseling from professors and practicing CPAs
   ◆ Registering for the CPA exam
   ◆ Taking the CPA exam

   Jane is not sure how to plan and schedule this study project. Assist her by preparing an appropriate PERT network.

3. There is an alternative way to diagram project networks. Activities can be shown as nodes rather than arcs. The arcs, then, merely indicate precedence among activities. Events are not shown. For example, consider the following portion of a PERT network:

   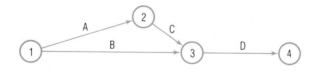

   The activity-on-node (AON) method would show this situation as follows:

   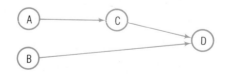

   Historically, the event-oriented (first) diagram evolved with PERT, while the AON method developed from CPM. Demonstrate that the two methods are interchangeable by developing the AON network for Olan's project (Table 12.1 and Figure 12.1).

4. Gigantic Enterprises's marketing manager has submitted her letter of resignation, to take effect in 60 days. The personnel manager must find a replacement by that time. He has prepared the following network for the replacement project:

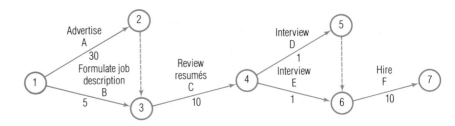

After completing a PERT analysis, the personnel manager states that none of the activities are critical to a successful completion of the project. How did he arrive at this conclusion? Do you agree? If not, what is the project's critical path?

5. Refer to the normal activity schedule for Olan's project (Table 12.4). According to this information, the company can delay installing electrical facilities (activity H) as much as 15 days and still complete the office in 93 days. Of course, this result assumes that each activity can be completed in its expected time (t). T. K. Trueblood, the project manager, is willing to accept this assumption. However, she does not think that the company should delay activity H by more than 11 days. Can you see how T. K. arrived at this conclusion? Do you agree with her reasoning? Explain.

6. Moonlight Zone Products, Inc., is planning an advertising campaign in support of its new toy, the Space Flyer. A PERT/CPM analysis indicates that the campaign will have an expected duration of 120 days. Twilight believes that the project completion time follows a normal distribution with a variance equal to 100. The Space Flyer will be marketed when the last advertising activity has been completed. If the company wants to be 98% confident in its timing decision, on what date should it plan on introducing the Flyer?

7. Refer to the linear program for Olan's crashing decision (Table 12.8) and the project network on which it is based (Figure 12.8).
   a. Relate each precedence constraint to the corresponding activity and events in the project network. Interpret these constraints in language understandable to Olan's project management.
   b. The complete solution to the linear program is $Y_A = 0$, $Y_B = 0$, $Y_C = 1$, $Y_D = 0$, $Y_F = 0$, $Y_G = 2$, $Y_I = 0$, $Y_J = 0$, $X_2 = 7$, $X_3 = 5$, $X_4 = 13$, $X_5 = 45$, $X_6 = 65$, $X_7 = 56$, $X_8 = 85$, and $X_9 = 90$. What is the interpretation for each X value?
   c. In the activity A precedence constraint ($X_2 + Y_A \geq 3$ days), the solution sum ($7 + 0 = 7$) exceeds the right-hand side (3). How

would you interpret the difference $(7 - 3 = 4)$? Interpret any similar differences for each of the other constraints.

8. Do you agree or disagree with each of the following statements? Explain.

a. Dummy activities are necessary in a PERT network in order to arrive at the correct activity schedule.

b. The PERT three-time approach cannot be used unless activity durations follow a beta probability distribution.

c. The expected project duration in a PERT or CPM network generally equals the latest finish time for the last activity.

d. The earliest time for a project event is always the latest finish time of the immediately preceding activities.

e. Project management cannot determine a feasible budget unless it establishes the earliest and latest start cost schedules.

Technique Exercises

1. Develop a PERT network for the following plant location project:

Activity	Immediately Preceding Activities
A	—
B	A
C	A
D	B
E	C
F	D, E
G	F, E

2. Develop a PERT network for the following plant location study:

Activity	Description	Immediate Predecessors
A	Prepare preliminary goals	—
B	Solicit proposals	A
C	Review proposals	B
D	Refine objectives	A, C
E	Identify appropriate sites	D
F	Gather financial data	E
G	Gather engineering data	E
H	Gather managerial inputs	E
I	Evaluate alternative sites	F, G, H
J	Select plant location	D, I

3. Suppose a project network involves the following activity time estimates:

	Time (Weeks)		
Activity	Optimistic	Most Likely	Pessimistic
A	2	5	9
B	6	12	15
C	4	6	7
D	8	8	12
E	12	20	40
F	10	12	19
G	20	25	28
H	5	5	5
I	16	32	90
J	7	14	23
K	2	2	2
L	1	8	18

Find the expected time and variance for each activity.

4. You are given the following project network for the production of a motion picture. The number below each arc represents the activity time in weeks.

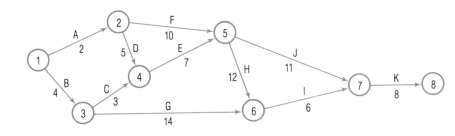

a. Develop a complete activity schedule.
b. Identify the critical path.
c. Determine how long it will take to complete the project.
d. Determine which activities can be delayed (and by how much time) without affecting the completion date.

5. The convention director of the Wellington Hotel has developed the following project network for the approaching National Union Meeting:

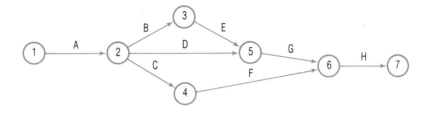

The corresponding activity time data (in days) are given in the following table:

Activity	Optimistic	Most Likely	Pessimistic
A	1	2	3
B	3	6	8
C	5	8	20
D	10	15	28
E	4	7	12
F	20	40	50
G	8	12	24
H	2	2	2

a. Compute the expected time and variance for each activity.
b. Develop a complete activity schedule.
c. Identify the critical path.
d. Determine the expected project duration and the corresponding variance.
e. What is the probability of completing the project within 1 month? 2 months? 80 days? 3 months?

6. Suppose a project has an expected duration of 4 months with a standard deviation of 30 days.

a. What is the chance of completing the project within 3 months?
b. What is the likelihood that the project will take 6 months or longer?
c. What is the probability of completing the project within the expected completion date?

7. Consider the following maintenance project.

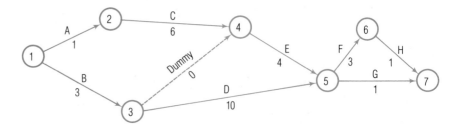

Time and cost data for this project are given in the following table.

	Time (Days)		Total Cost ($)	
Activity	Normal	Crash	Normal	Crash
A	1	—	200	200
B	3	2	1200	1600
C	6	4	3000	3100
D	10	6	2000	2400
E	4	—	1600	1600
F	3	1	600	650
G	1	—	200	200
H	1	—	300	300

a. Identify the critical path and the expected project duration.
b. What is the total normal project cost?
c. Suppose that the project must be crashed by 3 days. Use the trial and error approach to determine the optimal crashing plan.
d. Solve by linear programming.
e. What is the new activity schedule and the resulting additional project cost?

8. The following network describes a marketing research study:

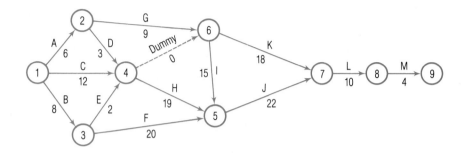

Relevant crash time and cost data appear in the following table:

Activity	Maximum Crash Time (Days)	Crash Cost per Day ($)
A	1	100
B	0	—
C	2	50
D	0	—
E	0	—
F	1	150
G	0	—
H	2	200
I	1	300
J	1	500
K	2	350
L	0	—
M	0	—

a. Identify the critical path and the expected project duration.
b. Suppose that the project must be crashed by 7 days. Use the trial and error approach to determine the optimal crashing plan. (*Note:* Your solution may create additional critical paths. If so, be sure to identify the new critical paths.)
c. Solve by linear programming.
d. What is the new activity schedule and resulting total additional project cost?

9. Table 12.10 in the text gives a portion of Olan's budgeted costs for an earliest start schedule. Table 12.11 gives a similar budget forecast for a latest start schedule.

   a. Use the information in Example 12.3 (and the referenced data: Table 12.9 and Figure 12.12) to complete Tables 12.10 and 12.11 for days 14 through 85.

   b. Suppose that Olan had the following work package (activity) data at the end of day 70:

Work Package (Activity)	Actual Cost ($)	% Completion
A	350	100
B	400	100
C	3,000	100
D	7,000	100
E	650	100
F	220,000	100
G	25,000	95
H	6,000	80
I	5,000	20
J	1,000	10
K	0	0

   Identify the cost overruns and underruns to date.

10. A bank branch expansion project has the following work package time schedule and corresponding cost budget:

Work Package	Budgeted Cost ($ Thousand)	Duration (Months)	Earliest Start	Earliest Finish	Latest Start	Latest Finish
A	100	1	0	1	0	1
B	500	2	0	2	1	3
C	1200	3	1	4	1	4
D	250	1	2	3	3	4
E	200	1	4	5	4	5
F	400	2	2	4	3	5
G	600	2	5	7	5	7
H	250	1	4	5	6	7

a. Prepare cost budgets for earliest and latest start schedules.
b. Determine the range for budgeted expenditures over the project duration. Graph your results.
c. Suppose that the bank had the following data at the end of month 3:

Work Package	Actual Cost ($ Thousand)	% Completion
A	120	100
B	200	70
C	600	50
D	250	100
E	0	0
F	300	90
G	0	0
H	0	0

Are the project costs in control? If not, identify the cost overruns and underruns.

Applications Exercises

1. A large defense contractor has an equipment division located in Southern California. Recently, this division received a $10 million contract to develop machinery for the space shuttle program. The project will last for approximately $1\frac{1}{2}$ years and employ 100 people.

Several tasks are necessary to complete the project. First, contract specifications must be developed by the company's personnel, materials, and engineering design departments. Estimates by department managers indicate that this task will take 2 weeks. Then the company needs 3 weeks to order raw materials, 14 weeks to hire required personnel, and 12 weeks to design engineering modifications for existing equipment. These three tasks can be done concurrently.

Raw materials will be received over a period of 20 weeks. According to the production managers, the facility modifications will require 19 weeks.

When the resources are on hand, it will take 2 weeks to train quality control personnel. At the same time, the company can train production people on the job in 3 weeks. Next, the equipment can be assembled in 18 weeks and then tested for quality in 5 more weeks. Final product preparations should take approximately 3 weeks.

a. How long will it take to fulfill the contract?
b. What activity schedule will be needed to meet this expectation?
c. What activities seem to be critical?
d. How long can each of the noncritical tasks be delayed without causing a change in expectations?

2. Jill Ward, a historian with the National Archives Association, is writing a book about political events in the United States during the 1970s. Based on previous experience, she knows that the first step is to prepare a prospectus/outline and a couple of sample chapters. Then the material must be sent to potential publishers. Jill estimates that these preliminary activities will each take 1 month. The publishers typically take about 3 months to review the material, gauge the potential market, and make a contract offer (or reject the project). In the interim, Jill will write additional chapters. Next, she plans to take 1 month to consider the offers and sign a contract. Meanwhile, the publishers usually assemble a project editing and production staff.

Jill thinks that after the negotiations she can finish the first draft in about 8 months. Then the publisher will subject the project to a complete professional and technical review. Typically, the process takes approximately 4 months. While the publisher is contacting prospective adopters, Jill will complete final revisions. Sales promotion and manuscript completion are each expected to take 3 months. Then the publisher will require another 10 months to produce and distribute the book. The expected sales life is 1 year.

All activity durations are considered to be the most likely times. However, since this project is new and unique, neither Jill nor any of the contacted publisher representatives is certain about these durations. In fact, they have jointly prepared the following additional estimates:

	Time Estimate (Months)	
Activity	Optimistic	Pessimistic
Prepare sample material	0.5	3.0
Send samples	0.2	2.0
Review prospectus	1.5	6.0
Write additional chapters	1.0	8.0
Select publisher	0.1	2.5
Assemble staff	0.5	1.5
Complete first draft	6.0	14.0
Review first draft	2.0	8.0
Promote sales	1.5	6.5
Produce book	8.0	15.5
Sell book	6.0	24.0

   a. If Jill and the publisher want to revise the current edition at the end of its sales life, when should they expect to start the new project?

   b. What activity schedule for the current project will be required to meet the deadline?

   c. What are the critical activities?

   d. If the publisher wants to be 95% confident in its revision decision, on what date should the publisher plan on starting the new project?

   e. What is the chance that the current project will take at least 3 months longer than expected? At least 4 months less?

3. Metropolistown's rapid transit department regularly performs maintenance service on a group of subway cars. The maintenance manual describes this project as follows:

Activity	Description	Immediate Predecessor	Expected Time (Days)	Cost ($)
A	Disassemble motors	—	5	2000
B	Disassemble transmissions	—	3	3000
C	Overhaul motors	A	10	5000
D	Overhaul transmissions	B	15	4000
E	Reassemble and clean cars	C, D	6	1500
F	Prepare maintenance report	E	1	200
G	Road-test cars	E	3	500
H	Issue certification	F	1	100

If necessary, the maintenance people can expedite transmission overhauling by 3 days at an additional expense of $1200. Also, cars can be reassembled and cleaned in 4 days for $2000. It will cost $1000 to road-test the cars in 2 days. No other activities can be expedited.

   Consumer pressure has forced the rapid transit department to institute a 3-week (21-day) maintenance policy. What activity schedule will be necessary to implement this policy? What will be the total maintenance cost?

4. Pills Mills, Inc., recently has experienced declining sales for its breakfast products. As a result, the marketing director has hired a consultant to develop a training program for the sales staff. The consultant has prepared a manual that describes the following training procedure:

Activity	Description	Immediate Predecessor	Time (Weeks)		
			Optimistic	Most Likely	Pessimistic
A	Plan curriculum	—	1.0	2.5	3.0
B	Inform sales staff	—	1.0	2.0	4.0
C	Obtain instructor/speakers	A	2.0	4.0	8.0
D	Prepare instructional supports	A	5.0	12.0	25.0
E	Conduct training sessions	B, C, D	6.0	10.0	16.0
F	Administer written test	E	0.5	1.0	1.5
G	Conduct sales practice sessions	E	1.0	3.0	6.0
H	Grade written test	F	0.1	0.5	1.0
I	Evaluate sales staff	G, H	1.5	2.0	4.0

The consultant estimates that activity A normally will cost $1600, task B about $400, and C another $1200. Other normal costs are expected to be: $25,000 for activity D, $50,000 for E, $200 for F, $1000 for G, $100 for H, and $500 for I.

After considering these data, the marketing director has allocated additional resources that could be used to expedite each activity. The allocation is described in the following table:

Activity	Maximum Reduction of Time (Weeks)	Additional Total Cost ($)
A	0.5	200
B	0.1	50
C	1.0	100
D	2.0	600
E	2.0	1000
F	0.1	20
G	0.2	25
H	0.1	10
I	1.0	250

a. When can Pills Mills normally expect the training to be complete?
b. What activity schedule must the company maintain to meet the expectation?
c. What activities are critical?
d. How long can each noncritical task be delayed without affecting the expected completion date?
e. What will be the total project cost?
f. Is it possible to shorten the completion time by 3 weeks? What is the least costly way of doing so?
g. What is the resulting total project cost and activity schedule?

h. What is the probability of meeting the new completion date without incurring the additional cost?

5. The Bridgeport Community Theater regularly sponsors a theme play each Easter. Thomas Todd, a theater patron and drama professor at the local university, annually donates his services to the project. Based on past experience, Thomas has prepared a manual describing the activities involved in the project. A portion of the document follows:

Activity	Description	Immediate Predecessor	Duration (Weeks)	Budgeted Cost ($)
A	Select play	—	3	2,100
B	Hire actors	A	4	10,000
C	Design costumes and set	A	10	26,000
D	Construct set	C	5	40,000
E	Conduct rehearsals	B	7	7,000
F	Publicize event	D, E	4	3,000
G	Print tickets	F	1	5,000
H	Conduct dress rehearsal	D, E	1	2,000
I	Sell tickets	G, H	2	8,000

a. How many weeks before Easter must the theater start the project?
b. If the theater is to meet the Easter deadline, what activity schedule must it follow?
c. According to this schedule, what will be the range of budgeted costs for each week during the project duration?

6. Annette Fonzarelli operates a small custom-order furniture upholstery business. She specializes in the Italian Provincial sofa. Operations for this product are described in the following table:

Activity	Description	Immediate Predecessor	Times (Hours)			Budgeted Cost ($)
			Optimistic	Most Likely	Pessimistic	
A	Contact customer	—	1.0	3.0	5.0	50
B	Define work	A	1.0	1.5	4.0	25
C	Perform credit check	A	2.0	4.0	8.0	30
D	Quote price	B	4.0	8.0	14.0	75
E	Contract order	D, C	1.0	2.0	3.0	20
F	Order fabric	E	3.0	5.0	9.0	600
G	Order trim	E	2.0	2.0	2.0	60
H	Pick up furniture	E	1.5	4.0	7.5	55
I	Receive materials	F, G	16.0	40.0	80.0	150
J	Upholster furniture	H, I	40.0	84.0	120.0	500
K	Deliver order	J	3.5	7.5	15.5	65

a. Annette has just received a new order. When can she expect to deliver the upholstered sofa?
b. What activity schedule must she follow to meet this expectation?
c. What activities are critical?
d. How long can each noncritical task be delayed without affecting the expected deadline?
e. What is the probability of completing the upholstery 1 working day (8 hours) ahead of schedule? 3 days later than expected?
f. According to the schedule, what will be the range of budgeted costs for each day during the project duration?
g. Suppose that Annette observes the following pattern of costs at the end of day 5:

Activity	Actual Cost ($)	% Completion
A	40	100
B	20	100
C	25	80
D	100	30
E	5	10

All other activities have not yet started. Are project costs in control? If not, what corrective actions might Annette employ?

CASE: Universal Research Corporation

The city of Falls Reach is concerned about the emigration of its population to neighboring towns. In an attempt to stem the flow, municipal government has decided to conduct an audit of community needs. Universal Research Corporation has been contracted to conduct the audit.

After considerable consultation with community groups, Universal's project manager has been able to identify the key tasks involved in the audit. First, Universal must define the community's objectives, needs, and problems. Next, Universal must recruit data collectors, design the sample, and prepare a questionnaire. These three tasks can be done concurrently. Questionnaire preparation is the basis for developing a survey procedure. Project management must establish this procedure and design the sample before it can document the study's methodology.

Universal will begin training data collectors after developing the procedure document and hiring survey personnel. Trained staff will then collect the data. At the same time, the company can contract data processing services and then process the collected information.

Universal will perform a demographic, statistical, and policy analysis on the processed data. The final report will contain the statistical summary and reports outlining the demographic and policy results. Finally, the document will be distributed to city officials.

Universal has presented the following time and cost information as part of its proposal:

Activity	Time (Weeks)				Total Cost ($)	
	Optimistic	Most Likely	Pessimistic	Expedited	Budgeted	Expedited
Objectives	3.0	6.0	12.0	4.0	2,600	4,000
Recruiting	4.0	7.0	11.0	6.0	20,000	32,000
Sample	2.0	3.0	5.0	2.0	1,400	1,800
Questionnaire	2.0	3.5	8.0	4.0	1,800	1,800
Mechanism	3.0	4.5	8.5	4.5	1,100	1,900
Document	3.0	4.0	5.0	3.5	2,300	2,500
Training	6.0	10.0	15.0	8.0	5,000	6,000
Contracting	2.0	6.0	10.0	6.0	700	700
Collection	8.0	15.0	45.0	18.0	55,000	70,000
Processing	3.0	4.0	7.0	3.5	900	1,000
Demo. analysis	1.5	3.5	7.5	2.0	1,300	1,500
Statistical	1.0	2.5	3.0	2.0	300	400
Policy analysis	2.0	4.0	7.0	3.0	2,100	2,500
Demo. report	2.0	3.0	6.0	3.0	200	250
Policy report	1.0	3.0	8.0	2.5	500	650
Final report	3.0	5.0	10.0	4.0	600	800
Distribution	1.0	1.5	2.0	1.5	100	100

City officials need answers to the following questions:

1. When can Falls Reach expect to receive the study report?

2. What activity schedules will Universal follow to meet the expected deadline?

3. What are the critical activities?

4. How long can each activity be delayed without affecting the expected completion date?

5. What is the probability that the project will be 2 weeks ahead of schedule? 6 weeks behind? Exactly on schedule?

6. According to the expected activity schedule, what will be the range of budgeted costs for each week during the study?

7. What will be the expected budgeted project cost?

8. Is it possible to shorten the project completion time by 4 weeks? 3 weeks? 2 weeks?

9. What is the least costly way of shortening the project duration by 4 weeks? 3 weeks? 2 weeks?

10. If the project can be expedited, what is the total project cost and activity schedule when the project is shortened by 3 weeks?

Prepare a report that addresses these questions in a form understandable to city officials.

Part V
Management
Science Topics

Frequently, decision makers must cope with a variety of planning and operations problems that cannot be strictly characterized as decision analysis, mathematical programming, or network situations. Instead, the problems involve unique features that require specialized treatments or tailored solution approaches. This part of the text examines such situations and presents some of the methodologies that are available to deal with these problems.

Chapter 13 explores how management science techniques can help decision makers manage and control inventories. The chapter begins with an examination of inventory types, costs, and objectives. Then it presents many of the popular inventory models, showing how to apply these models and evaluating their usefulness.

The next chapter examines the service system problem. Specifically, there are many circumstances in which a customer arrives at a facility for service. Since the facility usually has limited capacity, a waiting line eventually develops for service. Management's problem, then, is to design and operate the service system in a way that best achieves the organization's objectives. This chapter presents several models designed to predict the performance characteristics for a variety of specific systems. It also shows how such performance information can be used to select design configurations for these systems.

Chapter 15 focuses on sequential decision situations. Some processes start with a set of initial conditions, go through a number of changes, and eventually evolve into a stable system. This chapter describes the characteristics of such processes, presents a framework of analysis, and then shows how to predict the outcomes for the system. It also discusses a methodology for selecting the best strategy in a problem requiring a series of interrelated decisions.

After studying this part of the text, you will be able to:

♦ Identify the forms and characteristics of inventory and service systems

♦ Understand how models can be used to help manage and control inventories and assist in the design of service system configurations

- ◆ Recognize situations that involve evolutionary processes and a series of interrelated decisions
- ◆ Analyze these situations and develop a recommended decision strategy

These concepts and methodologies will also be utilized in the last part of the text.

Chapter 13
Inventory

CONCEPTS

♦ The rationale for carrying inventory

♦ Identifying the relevant inventory cost components

♦ Deciding how much inventory to order

♦ Deciding when to place the order

♦ Developing methods of inventory analysis for uncertain decision situations

♦ The nature of a material requirements planning (MRP) system

♦ Controlling inventory in an MRP system

APPLICATIONS

♦ Bookstore operations

♦ Fashion merchandising

♦ Manufacturing pens

♦ Automotive repair

♦ Data processing

♦ Agriculture

♦ Sanitation engineering

♦ Hospital administration

Enterprises transform resources (capital, labor, materials, and equipment) into finished products and services. At any given time, they may have idle stocks of the raw materials, capital, labor, equipment, partially completed goods (work in process), or finished products. These idle stocks are referred to as **inventory**.

Inventory serves several important business and economic functions. Some are related to product or service demand. For instance, idle stocks of finished goods make it possible to provide the product at the time and place desired by the consumer; often, such demand is unforeseeable or erratic. Other functions involve production considerations. An inventory of raw materials, for example, can help a company avoid the delays associated with searching for appropriate supply sources and then waiting for deliveries. Also, the outputs of some activities are partially completed goods that become inputs for subsequent tasks. In this case, a work stoppage in the preceding task may delay the next activity. Work-in-process inventory may prevent these delays. In addition, product or service demand often is seasonal or cyclical. If the production schedule followed such a demand pattern, there would be substantial expenses for transportation, hiring, firing, overtime, and idle facilities. By carrying an inventory of finished goods, a firm can maintain a fairly steady production rate and thus reduce these expenses. There are also supply considerations. Raw-materials inventory helps guard against inflation and irregularities of supply. In addition, it is often possible to obtain price discounts by buying in large volume. Unused materials are stored for future requirements. Also, work-in-process and finished-goods inventory protect against labor shortages resulting from strikes and market conditions.

An inventory generates certain expenses. First, there is the cost of the item. If it is manufactured by the firm, there will be labor, material, and overhead expenses. When the item is purchased, the company pays the purchase price plus taxes. These purchase and manufacturing expenses are collectively called **procurement costs**. Unless there are purchase or production cost discounts, these expenses typically remain the same regardless of the quantity ordered or manufactured.

The company incurs additional expenses when it places an order, including wages of the purchasing and inspection agents, postage, transportation, and bookkeeping charges. If the items are manufactured rather than purchased, management must physically prepare the production apparatus. In this situation, instead of order expenses, there will be costs associated with setting up the machines, scheduling work, and the like. The order or production preparation expenses are collectively referred to as **ordering (setup) costs**. Usually, these expenses remain the same regardless of the quantity ordered or produced.

The inventory itself creates other expenses. For one thing, there is the interest cost for the investment. If the company borrows money to finance inventory, it will have to pay an interest charge. Even when the firm uses its own capital, there is an opportunity cost involved in not being able to use the money for alternative investments. In addition, there are expenses associated with physically handling, storing, and maintaining the inventory. These expenses include wages, equipment-operating costs, insurance, taxes, breakage, pilferage, and depreciation. The finance, handling, storage, and maintenance expenses are collectively referred to as **carrying (holding) costs**. Such expenses increase with the size of inventory. That is, larger inventories involve larger holding costs.

Aside from these ordinary expenses, the company may incur a cost when available goods are insufficient to fully satisfy demand. If the customer is willing to wait, there may be expediting and notification expenses. If dissatisfied customers go elsewhere, the firm loses present (and perhaps future) sales and profits. Such expenses are collectively called **stockout (shortage) costs**. Typically, these expenses decrease with the size of inventory.

Inventory policy involves an organizational dilemma. Marketing wants large inventories to ensure the satisfaction of consumer demand. Production also wants large idle stocks in order to reduce ordering and setup costs, smooth operations, and minimize idle time. However, finance is interested in minimizing capital costs and thus prefers small inventories. Sound management should consider all viewpoints and then develop a policy that minimizes the total inventory-related costs. The basic issues are how much and when to order (or produce). Since inventory expenses are a substantial cost of doing business for most companies, these issues warrant serious consideration.

This chapter shows how quantitative methods can assist the manager in formulating a sound inventory policy. The first section introduces the problem and presents the most fundamental solution model. This approach is best suited for situations involving a single good or several independent products, each with a known and constant demand. Often, however, demand is erratic and uncertain. In addition, there may be other variations from the basic approach. The second section shows how to make inventory decisions under several of these conditions. Finally, some products are ordered or produced only once during a given time period.

Other situations, meanwhile, involve several items with interrelated demands. The last section discusses inventory systems designed for each of these circumstances.

CONTINUOUS AND INDEPENDENT DEMAND

Let us begin with a fundamental situation in which there is a continuous demand for a single finished good. Example 13.1 illustrates.

EXAMPLE 13.1 Stocking Office Supplies

Technical University's bookstore is in the process of establishing an inventory policy for notebook filler. Based on past experience, management knows that demand has been fairly constant at a rate of 6750 packages per month. Notebook filler can be purchased from a variety of suppliers for 50 cents a package. The price remains the same regardless of the quantity ordered. Jumbo Products, the most prompt and reliable supplier, needs 5 days' notice to ensure prompt service. Technical and Jumbo both work 250 days per year. Each supplier will deliver the entire order at one point in time.

Bookstore staff require 45 minutes to prepare and process a purchase order and another 15 minutes to set up the sales display after receiving the shipment. Staff earn $4 per hour. Paper, postage, telephone, and transportation cost an additional $1 per order. Annual pilferage, deterioration, interest, and storage expenses are estimated to be 18% of the value of average inventory.

Management policy is to fully satisfy customer demand. Management must determine the inventory actions necessary for implementing this policy at least cost.

In this case, there is a single product (notebook filler) with a known and constant demand (6750 packages per month). The purchase cost (50 cents) is known and remains the same regardless of the quantity ordered. All items are delivered and become inventory at one point in time. Also, management policy is to fully satisfy demand. Hence, the bookstore will order in time to allow for delivery by the inventory depletion point.

ECONOMIC ORDER QUANTITY

Technical's circumstances are characteristic of the so-called economic order quantity (EOQ) model. It is the best-known and most fundamental inventory decision tool. By letting Q = the quantity ordered or produced and T_0 = the time it takes to deplete an inventory of Q items, we can illustrate the situation with the aid of Figure 13.1.

Figure 13.1 Inventory Pattern for the Economic Order Quantity (EOQ) Model

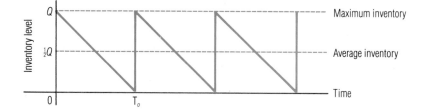

When the order arrives from a supplier at time 0, the bookstore will have its maximum inventory (the order quantity Q). Technical will then supply its customers at a constant rate from stock until the inventory is depleted at time T_0. In the process, the bookstore will have an average inventory of $\frac{1}{2}Q$ packages for the period. At time T_0, Technical will receive another supply of Q packages and immediately replenish its inventory to the maximum level. The pattern will repeat itself as time goes on. Consequently, the average inventory level over any time frame will still be $\frac{1}{2}Q$ packages.

The objective is to find the least costly order quantity. There are several expenses to consider. Since the bookstore plans to fully satisfy demand, there will be no shortage costs. However, Technical will incur procurement, ordering, and holding expenses.

Technical purchases each package of notebook filler for 50 cents. Furthermore, customers demand 6750 packages each month, or 81,000 per year. Thus, to fully satisfy this demand, the bookstore must incur an annual procurement expense of

$$\$.50 \times 81,000 = \$40,500$$

In effect, then, the procurement expense per period will equal the cost per item multiplied by the total demand. By letting $c =$ the purchase or manufacturing cost per item and $D =$ the total demand for the stated period, we can express the relationship as follows:

(13.1) $c \times D = cD$

In the EOQ model, the purchase or manufacturing cost per item (c) and total demand (D) are assumed to be known and constant. Consequently, the procurement expense per period (cD) will remain the same regardless of the quantity ordered or produced.

Technical's ordering expenses include the costs of placing an order and setting up a sales display. Preparing and processing an order involves

45 minutes ($\frac{3}{4}$ hour) of labor @ \$4/hour = \$3

plus

paper, postage, telephone, and transportation = $1

or a cost of $4. Setting up the display requires an additional expense of

15 minutes ($\frac{1}{4}$ hour) of labor @ $4/hour = $1

Therefore, it will cost the bookstore $4 + $1 = $5 for each order. The ordering expense per period will therefore depend on the number of orders.

The bookstore has a known and constant demand of $D = 81,000$ packages per year. Since the store orders a fixed amount Q, the number of orders will equal the demand divided by the order quantity. For example, if Technical ordered $Q = 8100$ packages at a time, it would need

$$\frac{D}{Q} = \frac{81,000}{8100} = 10 \text{ orders per year}$$

to satisfy customer demand. Since each order costs $5, this policy would involve an annual ordering expense of $5 × 10 = $50. On the other hand, an order quantity of $Q = 90$ packages would require $81,000/90 = 900$ orders per year and result in an ordering expense of $5 × 900 = $4500.

In general, then, the ordering expense per period will equal the cost per order multiplied by the number of orders. By letting c_o = the cost for one order or setup, we can write the relationship as

(13.2) $c_o \times \dfrac{D}{Q} = \dfrac{c_o D}{Q}$

In the EOQ model, the cost per order c_o is also assumed to be known and constant. Thus, as equation (13.2) indicates, the inventory ordering cost $c_o D/Q$ will decrease as the order quantity Q gets larger.

Pilferage, deterioration, interest, and storage expenses are holding costs. In this case, they are annually equal to 18% of the value for average inventory. Technical purchases each package of notebook filler for 50 cents. Hence, it will cost 18% of 50 cents, or 9 cents, to carry one package in inventory for a year. Since the average inventory is $\frac{1}{2}Q$ packages, the inventory holding expenses will be

$.09 \times \frac{1}{2}Q = $.045Q$ per year

In general, then, the holding expense per period will equal the carrying cost per item multiplied by the average inventory level. By letting c_H = the cost to carry one item for the stated period, the relationship becomes

(13.3) $c_H \times \frac{1}{2}Q = \frac{1}{2}c_H Q$

The carrying cost per item c_H is assumed to be known and constant in the EOQ model. Hence, inventory holding cost $\frac{1}{2}c_H Q$ will increase as the average inventory $\frac{1}{2}Q$ grows.

In the EOQ model, total inventory expenses per period, denoted TC, will equal the sum of procurement, ordering, and holding costs. That is,

(13.4) $\quad TC = cD + \dfrac{c_o D}{Q} + \frac{1}{2}c_H Q$

The relevant time period can be a day, week, month, year, or more. However, it is usually most convenient to measure demand and expenses on a yearly basis. Consequently, inventory models typically are expressed in terms of annual costs.

Technical's annual demand for notebook filler is $D = 81{,}000$ packages. Procurement cost per item is $c = \$.50$, the cost per order is $c_o = \$5$, and the yearly carrying cost per package is $c_H = \$.09$. Therefore, the bookstore's annual inventory cost will be

(13.5) $\quad TC = \$.50(81{,}000) + \dfrac{\$5(81{,}000)}{Q} + \dfrac{\$.09Q}{2}$

$$= \$40{,}500 + \dfrac{\$405{,}000}{Q} + \$.045Q$$

Equation (13.5) describes how total inventory costs TC are affected by the order quantity Q. Developing a realistic total cost model is the first (and perhaps most important) part of a quantitative inventory analysis.

Technical's problem now is to find the order quantity Q that minimizes the total inventory cost TC stated in equation (13.5). The problem can be solved in several ways. Using trial and error, the bookstore can select various possible order quantities and then compute the resulting total costs. For instance, suppose that the store orders $Q = 200$ packages. According to equation (13.5), the resulting total inventory cost will be

$$TC = \$40{,}500 + \dfrac{\$405{,}000}{Q} + \$.045Q$$

$$= \$40{,}000 + \dfrac{\$405{,}000}{200} + \$.045(200) = \$42{,}534$$

Similarly, a trial quantity of $Q = 5000$ packages gives a total inventory cost of

$$TC = \$40{,}500 + \dfrac{\$405{,}000}{5000} + \$.045(5000) = \$40{,}806$$

Table 13.1 presents the results for several other trial order quantities. The data show that Technical can minimize total annual inventory cost at $TC = \$40{,}770$ by ordering $Q = 3000$ packages each time it requests a shipment.

Although the trial and error approach is easy to understand and use, it does have disadvantages. For one thing, the method is cumbersome and

Table 13.1 Technical's Inventory Costs for Various Order Quantities

Order Quantity Q	Annual Costs ($)			
	Procurement	Ordering ($405,000/$Q$)	Holding ($.045$Q$)	Total
500	40,500	810.00	22.50	41,332.50
1000	40,500	405.00	45.00	40,950.00
1500	40,500	270.00	67.50	40,837.50
2000	40,500	202.50	90.00	40,792.50
2500	40,500	162.00	112.50	40,774.50
3000	40,500	135.00	135.00	40,770.00
3500	40,500	115.71	157.50	40,773.21
4000	40,500	101.25	180.00	40,781.25
4500	40,500	90.00	202.50	40,792.50
5000	40,500	81.00	225.00	40,806.00

Figure 13.2 Inventory Cost Behavior in the EOQ Model

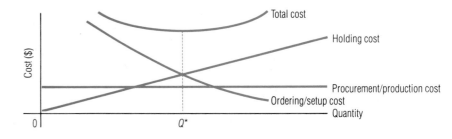

time-consuming, especially when there are many possible order quantities and products. In addition, the trial and error recommendation merely identifies the least-cost alternative among those examined. Since the approach does not test every possible order quantity, the recommended policy may not represent the optimal solution to the problem.

Fortunately, decision scientists have developed a formula that directly provides the least costly order quantity. J. H. Green [11], S. Larson [15], B. E. Lipman [18], and R. J. Tersine [27] discuss the mathematics. We can illustrate the concept with the aid of Figure 13.2.

Figure 13.2 shows the annual procurement, ordering, holding, and total costs resulting from an infinite number of possible order quantities. You can see that total expenses are at a minimum when the decision maker orders Q^* packages. The figure also indicates that this quantity balances ordering and holding costs. Up to that point, decreases in ordering costs outweigh the increases in carrying expenses. As a result, total costs are declining. Beyond that order size, increases in holding costs more than offset the decreases in ordering expenses. Consequently, total costs are rising.

In this model, then, management can determine how much to order directly from the available cost information. To do so, the decision maker must find the order quantity Q^* that equates inventory ordering cost $(c_o D/Q)$ and inventory holding cost $(c_H Q/2)$. Equations (13.2) and (13.3) indicate that this balance occurs when

$$\frac{c_o D}{Q} = \frac{c_H Q}{2}$$

or

$$(13.6) \quad Q^* = \sqrt{\frac{2c_o D}{c_H}}$$

The value Q^* is referred to as the **economic order quantity**.

In Technical's case, $c_o = \$5$, $D = 81{,}000$ packages, and $c_H = \$.09$. Therefore, the economic order quantity is

$$Q^* = \sqrt{\frac{2(\$5)(81{,}000)}{\$.09}} = 3000 \text{ packages}$$

This order size will balance ordering and holding expenses at

$$\frac{c_o D}{Q^*} = \frac{\$5(81{,}000)}{3000} = \frac{c_H Q^*}{2} = \frac{\$.09(3000)}{2} = \$135$$

each and minimize total inventory cost at

$$TC = \$40{,}500 + \frac{c_o D}{Q^*} + \frac{c_H Q^*}{2} = \$40{,}500 + \$135 + \$135 = \$40{,}770$$

These results confirm the bookstore's trial and error recommendation.

ORDER TIMING AND FREQUENCY Equation (13.6) gives the order quantity that minimizes total inventory costs. The equation, in effect, is a decision rule indicating how much to order. However, management must also know when and how frequently to place an order. Example 13.1 again will illustrate.

Since each source offers the notebook filler at the same price, Technical will probably want to order from the most prompt and reliable supplier (Jumbo Products). But even Jumbo needs 5 days' notice to ensure prompt service. Ordinarily, then, the bookstore will not receive the notebook filler until 5 days after placing an order. In inventory terminology, this 5-day delivery period is called **lead time**. During this period, consumers still will want the product. In fact, there will be a demand of 81,000 packages a year, or, since both Technical and Jumbo operate 250 days annually,

$$\frac{81{,}000}{250} = 324 \text{ packages per working day}$$

Hence, the bookstore can expect to sell $324 \times 5 = 1620$ packages during the lead time. Therefore, if management wants to fully satisfy demand, it will place an order when the inventory level reaches 1620 packages. In inventory terminology, this quantity is called the **reorder point**.

In general, then, the reorder point will equal the lead time multiplied by the rate of demand. By letting

$R = $ the reorder point

$d = $ the rate of demand (typically, items per day)

$L = $ the lead time (typically, number of days)

we can express the relationship

(13.7) $R = dL$

In the EOQ model, the lead time L and demand rate d are assumed to be known and constant. Consequently, in this system, the reorder point is the same as the demand during the lead time.

Equation (13.7) is a decision rule indicating when to place an order. Another question involves the frequency of ordering. To deal with this issue, we must again consider the economic order quantity Q^*.

Remember, Technical has decided to request $Q^* = 3000$ packages each time it orders. Since the annual demand is $D = 81{,}000$, this policy will require

$$\frac{D}{Q^*} = \frac{81{,}000}{3000} = 27 \text{ orders per year}$$

If the bookstore places these orders over the 250 working days, management will order approximately every $250/27 = 9.3$ working days. This 9.3-day period between orders is referred to as the **inventory cycle time**.

In general, a cycle time of T days will equal the working days per year N divided by the annual number of orders D/Q^*, or

(13.8) $T = \dfrac{N}{D/Q^*} = \dfrac{NQ^*}{D}$

Of course, in some cases, $N = 365$ days.

Figure 13.3 illustrates the order timing and frequency process for the EOQ model. When an order arrives from Jumbo at time 0, the bookstore will have an inventory equal to the economic order quantity Q^*. Technical will then supply consumers from stock until it reaches the reorder point R.

Figure 13.3 Order Timing and Frequency in the EOQ Model

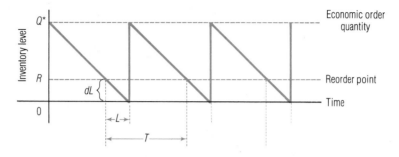

At that point, the bookstore will place another order for Q^* packages. The new order will be received just as demand during the lead time (dL) depletes inventories. Technical will immediately replenish inventory to the economic order quantity level. After a period of T days, the bookstore will place another order for Q^* packages. The pattern will repeat itself as time progresses.

DECISION CONSIDERATIONS The basic EOQ model has many limiting assumptions. It presumes the following conditions:

1. No discounts for large purchases
2. No inventory shortages
3. Instantaneous delivery
4. Constant unit costs
5. A constant demand and lead time
6. Continuous ordering or manufacturing
7. A single good or independent products

In many situations, however, these conditions are not met. In this section we will see how to make inventory decisions when there are quantity discounts, planned shortages, gradual inventory replenishment, and uncertain lead time demand. Later, we will discuss a single-order policy and a situation involving dependent items.

QUANTITY DISCOUNTS For various business and economic reasons, suppliers may want to sell large volumes of merchandise. As a result, they often provide an incentive to buyers by offering price discounts for larger purchases. Example 13.2 illustrates.

EXAMPLE 13.2 Discount Buying

To expand business, Jumbo Products quotes the discount schedule presented in Table 13.2. All other facts are the same as in Example 13.1. Once more, the management of Technical University's bookstore seeks the inventory policy that will fully satisfy consumer demand at least cost.

Table 13.2 Jumbo's Discount Schedule

Category	Order Size	Discount (% of Cost)	Cost per Item ($)
1	Less than 3100	0.0	.500
2	3100 to 3999	10.0	.450
3	4000 to 9999	24.0	.380
4	10,000 and over	24.2	.379

Except for the purchase cost discounts, Example 13.2 has all the characteristics of the EOQ model. As a result, total inventory-related costs will again take the general form of equation (13.4):

$$TC = cD + \frac{c_o D}{Q} + \frac{c_H Q}{2}$$

However, the discounts change the specific structure of this cost model.

In the basic EOQ model, the procurement cost per item c is constant and thus never affected by the inventory order policy decision. When there are quantity discounts, c varies with the order size Q. Each discount category, then, generates a different procurement expense. For example, if the bookstore orders up to 3100 packages (discount category 1), it will pay 50 cents per item. Since customers demand $D = 81,000$ packages per year, the corresponding annual procurement expense will be

$$c \times D = \$.50(81,000) = \$40,500$$

On the other hand, an order size of between 3100 and 3999 packages (discount category 2) results in an annual procurement expense of

$$c \times D = \$.45 \times 81,000 = \$36,450$$

Similarly, the annual procurement cost is $\$.38 \times 81,000 = \$30,780$ for discount category 3 (4000 to 9999 items) and $\$.379 \times 81,000 = \$30,699$ for the last category (10,000 items and over).

The discounts for large order sizes look tempting. However, the bookstore should realize that larger quantities result in higher inventory carrying expenses. Consequently, management must prepare a thorough cost analysis before making a final inventory policy decision. The next step, then, is to consider the effects of the discounts on other inventory expenses.

Within a given discount category, the procurement expense per item c is constant. Since the unit carrying cost is a percentage of this procurement expense, c_H will also remain the same within the category. The cost per order c_o and demand D are constant regardless of the discount structure. In effect, then, *within each purchase cost category*, the discount model has the same characteristics as the basic EOQ situation. Therefore, management can use equation (13.6)

$$Q^* = \sqrt{\frac{2c_o D}{c_H}}$$

to find the least costly order quantity for each discount category.

In this case, $c_o = \$5$ and $D = 81{,}000$. Since the first category involves a purchase expense of $c = \$.50$ per item, it will cost 18% of 50 cents, or $c_H = \$.09$, to carry a package in inventory for a year. Hence, the least costly order quantity for category 1, denoted by Q_1^*, is

$$Q_1^* = \sqrt{\frac{2(\$5)(81{,}000)}{\$.09}} = 3000 \text{ packages}$$

Similarly, category 2 has a c_H of $.18 \times \$.45 = \$.081$ and an economic order quantity of

$$Q_2^* = \sqrt{\frac{2(\$5)(81{,}000)}{\$.081}} = 3162.28 \text{ items}$$

Category 3 has a c_H of $.18 \times \$.38 = \$.0684$ and a least costly order quantity of $Q_3^* = 3441.24$ packages, while category 4 has a c_H of $.18 \times \$.379 = \$.06822$ and a Q_4^* of 3445.77 packages.

Since there are only slight differences in inventory holding costs, the resulting economic order quantities are approximately the same. However, some of these order sizes are insufficient in size to qualify for the discounts. For example, $Q_3^* = 3441.24$ is less than the 4000 minimum necessary to obtain a purchase cost of 38 cents per item. In such cases, management should select the minimum order size necessary to qualify for the discount. Thus, the bookstore should set $Q_3^* = 4000$ packages. Similarly, since a $Q_4^* = 3445.77$ is less than the 10,000 minimum necessary to obtain the $\$.379$ price, Technical should set $Q_4^* = 10{,}000$ items.

Each order quantity (Q_1^*, Q_2^*, Q_3^*, and Q_4^*) will generate a corresponding total inventory cost (TC). For instance, for discount category 1, $c = \$.50$,

Table 13.3 Technical's Costs for Each Discount Category

Category	Cost per Item ($) c	Order Quantity Q^*	Annual Inventory Costs ($)			
			Procurement ($c \times 81{,}000$)	Ordering ($\$405{,}000/Q^*$)	Holding ($\$.09cQ^*$)	Total
1	.500	3,000.00	40,500	135.00	135.00	40,770.00
2	.450	3,162.28	36,450	128.07	128.07	36,706.14
3	.380	4,000.00	30,780	101.25	136.80	31,018.05
4	.379	10,000.00	30,699	40.50	341.10	31,080.60

Table 13.4 Finding the Least Costly Order Quantity in the EOQ Model with Discounts

1. Identify the various discount categories for purchase cost.
2. Compute the economic order quantity $Q^* = \sqrt{2c_0 D/c_H}$ for each category. When the economic order quantity is insufficient to obtain the preferred purchase cost, set Q^* equal to the minimum size necessary for the discount.
3. Using the Q^* obtained in step 2, compute the total cost $TC = cD + c_0 D/Q^* + c_H Q^*/2$ for each discount category.
4. Select the order size that results in the smallest total cost.

$c_o = \$5$, $D = 81{,}000$, $c_H = \$.09$, and $Q_1^* = 3000$. Thus, the corresponding total cost is

$$TC = cD + \frac{c_o D}{Q_1^*} + \frac{c_H Q_1^*}{2}$$

$$= \$.50(81{,}000) + \frac{\$5(81{,}000)}{3000} + \frac{\$.09(3000)}{2} = \$40{,}770 \text{ per year}$$

Table 13.3 summarizes the total cost calculations for each discount category. As you can see, Technical can minimize total annual cost at $TC = \$31{,}018.05$ by purchasing $Q^* = 4000$ packages each time an order is placed. This recommendation involves a procurement cost of 38 cents per item (a 24% discount). Although the 10,000-package order size would result in a larger (24.2%) discount, its excessive holding cost ($341.10) makes this quantity the second-best solution.

The quantity discount policy recommendation also changes the order cycle time. In the basic EOQ situation, Technical was ordering 3000 items every 9.3 working days. Now the bookstore will place an order for $Q^* = 4000$ packages approximately every

$$T = \frac{NQ^*}{D} = \frac{250(4000)}{81{,}000} = 12.3 \text{ working days}$$

Table 13.4 summarizes the procedure for finding the order sizes and total costs in the EOQ model with quantity discounts.

PLANNED SHORTAGES In some cases, a firm can be short of inventory without losing sales during this period. By promising the customer top priority, a short waiting period, and immediate delivery when the goods become available, companies may convince consumers to wait for the order. When a customer's order is filled in this manner, the shortage is called a **backorder**. This situation is usually found where items are unique and expensive, in high demand, or adequately supplied by only one firm. Consider Example 13.3.

EXAMPLE 13.3 Managing Shortages

Suppose that experience now indicates that customers are willing to wait for their orders. As a result, the bookstore will no longer keep enough inventory on hand to fully satisfy demand. Instead, management will supply unsatisfied demand from future purchases as soon as the goods become available. Technical realizes that the new policy will necessitate additional labor expenses for record keeping and customer service. There may also be special delivery and handling expenses. These costs are estimated to annually total 22% of the value of the average shortage level. All other facts are the same as in Example 13.1. Management wants to determine the inventory actions that minimize costs.

There is only one difference between this situation and the basic EOQ model. Example 13.3 allows planned shortages. However, the backorder possibility changes the problem significantly. By letting

S = the amount of shortage or number of backorders

t_1 = the time when there is an inventory surplus (typically, the number of days)

t_2 = the time when there is an inventory shortage (typically, the number of days)

we can illustrate the situation with Figure 13.4.

Management will order Q packages. When the shipment arrives, S items will be used to satisfy previous backorders. The remainder $(Q - S)$ will immediately be put in inventory. Hence, the maximum inventory will be $Q - S$ packages. Technical will then supply its customers at a constant rate from stock until inventory is depleted. At a demand rate of d items per day, it will take

$$(13.9) \quad t_1 = \frac{Q - S}{d} \text{ days}$$

Figure 13.4 Inventory Pattern for the EOQ Model with Backorders

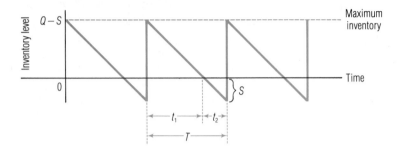

to deplete the maximum inventory. However, since Q packages are ordered every purchase cycle, it will be

$$(13.10) \quad T = \frac{Q}{d} \text{ days}$$

before another shipment arrives. Consequently, the bookstore will have no inventory for t_2 days. There will still be demand during this shortage period. Thus, backorders will grow to a maximum of S items before a new shipment arrives. The pattern repeats itself as time goes on.

In this model, the objective is to find the order quantity Q and shortage level S that minimize inventory-related expenses. Usually, backorders will not affect ordinary procurement and ordering activities. Thus, the procurement expense still takes the form of expression (13.1), cD, and expression (13.2), $c_o D/Q$, again gives the ordering cost. However, the possibility of shortages substantially changes the carrying cost expression.

Annual inventory holding expenses once more will equal the carrying cost per item c_H multiplied by the average inventory level. As shown in Figure 13.4, during the surplus period t_1, the maximum inventory will be $Q - S$ items. Customers will be supplied from this stock until inventory is depleted. In the process, there will be an average inventory of $\frac{1}{2}(Q - S)$ packages for t_1 days. During the shortage period t_2, the bookstore will have no inventory. Thus, over a purchase cycle of $T = t_1 + t_2$ days, inventory will average

$$(13.11) \quad \frac{\dfrac{Q - S}{2} t_1 + 0t_2}{T} = \frac{\dfrac{Q - S}{2} t_1}{T} \text{ items per day}$$

By substituting equations (13.9) and (13.10) into expression (13.11), we can write the average inventory in terms of the decision variables Q and S as follows:

$$(13.12) \quad \frac{\frac{Q-S}{2}t_1}{T} = \frac{\left(\frac{Q-S}{2}\right)\left(\frac{Q-S}{d}\right)}{Q/d} = \frac{(Q-S)^2}{2Q}$$

Annual inventory holding cost, then, will equal the cost per item c_H multiplied by this average inventory, or

$$(13.13) \quad c_H \times \frac{(Q-S)^2}{2Q} = \frac{c_H(Q-S)^2}{2Q}$$

in the backorder model.

In addition, unlike the basic EOQ model, the backorder situation involves a shortage expense. When Technical is out of stock, its customers will usually wait for the goods to become available. However, the bookstore will incur additional labor, delivery, and handling expenses by backordering. In Example 13.3, these shortage costs are annually equal to 22% of the value of the average backorder level. Since each package is purchased for 50 cents, it will cost 22% of $.50, or 11 cents, to have an item on backorder for a year. To determine the annual shortage expense, Technical must multiply this 11-cents-per-item cost by the average shortage level.

As shown in Figure 13.4, there will be no shortages during the inventory surplus period t_1. During the shortage period t_2, continued customer demand will create a maximum backorder of S items before the arrival of a new shipment. In the process, there will be an average backorder of $\frac{1}{2}S$ for t_2 days. Consequently, over a purchase cycle of $T = t_1 + t_2$ days, the shortage will average

$$(13.14) \quad \frac{0t_1 + (S/2)t_2}{T} = \frac{(S/2)t_2}{T} \quad \text{packages per day}$$

At a demand rate of d items per day, it will take

$$(13.15) \quad t_2 = \frac{S}{d} \text{ days}$$

to reach the maximum backorder level. By substituting equations (13.15) and (13.10) into expression (13.14), the average shortage level can be written as

$$(13.16) \quad \frac{(S/2)t_2}{T} = \frac{(S/2)(S/d)}{Q/d} = \frac{S^2}{2Q}$$

Annual inventory shortage cost will then equal the unit backorder cost, denoted c_B, multiplied by this average backorder level. That is,

$$(13.17) \quad c_B \times \frac{S^2}{2Q} = \frac{c_B S^2}{2Q}$$

gives the shortage expense in the backorder model.

Total cost TC is the sum of inventory procurement, ordering, holding, and shortage expenses, or

$$(13.18) \quad TC = cD + \frac{c_o D}{Q} + \frac{c_H(Q - S)^2}{2Q} + \frac{c_B S^2}{2Q}$$

Using calculus, decision scientists [14, 21] have established that an order quantity of

$$(13.19) \quad Q^* = \sqrt{\frac{2c_o D}{c_H}\left(\frac{c_H + c_B}{c_B}\right)}$$

with

$$(13.20) \quad S^* = Q^*\left(\frac{c_H}{c_H + c_B}\right)$$

backorders results in the minimum total cost.

Notice that there will be many backorders when the unit holding cost c_H is large relative to the unit shortage expense c_B. Otherwise, equation (13.19) and the basic EOQ formula (13.6) provide similar results.

In Example 13.3, $c_o = \$5$, $D = 81,000$, $c_H = \$.09$, and $c_B = \$.11$. Therefore, Technical should order approximately

$$Q^* = \sqrt{\frac{2(\$5)(81,000)}{\$.09}\left(\frac{\$.09 + \$.11}{\$.11}\right)} = 4045 \text{ packages}$$

at a time and plan for about

$$S^* = (4045)\left(\frac{\$.09}{\$.09 + \$.11}\right) = 1820 \text{ backorders}$$

If this solution is implemented, Technical will place an order approximately every

$$T = \frac{NQ^*}{D} = \frac{250(4045)}{81,000} = 12.5 \text{ working days}$$

and have a maximum inventory of

$$Q^* - S^* = 4045 - 1820 = 2225 \text{ items}$$

This policy will also involve the annual expenses shown in Table 13.5.

ECONOMIC PRODUCTION QUANTITY Many firms may want to manufacture, rather than purchase, items for inventory, as Example 13.4 illustrates.

Table 13.5 Technical's Annual Inventory-Related Expenses with Backorders

Type of Inventory Expense	Formula	Annual Cost ($)
Procurement	$cD = \$.50(81{,}000)$	40,500.00
Ordering	$c_0 D/Q^* = \$5(81{,}000)/4045$	100.12
Holding	$c_H(Q^* - S^*)^2/2Q^* = \dfrac{\$.09(4045 - 1820)^2}{2(4045)}$	55.07
Backordering	$c_B S^{*2}/2Q^* = \dfrac{\$.11(1820)^2}{2(4045)}$	45.04
Total		40,700.23

EXAMPLE 13.4 Producing Office Supplies

Suppose that Technical University can employ students in its print shop after normal business hours to manufacture the notebook filler. Such operations would have an annual capacity of 202,500 packages. Several trial runs indicate that the students can produce 810 packages each working day at a cost of 40 cents per item. Also, it will take 3 days and cost $5.40 to clean, prepare, and set up the printing equipment. Customers still demand 6750 packages each month, and carrying expenses remain 18% of the average inventory.

Management seeks the production and inventory policy that will fully satisfy consumer demand at least cost.

There is only one difference between this problem and the EOQ situation. The university can now produce, rather than purchase, the item. To do so, Technical will set up a manufacturing system (the student-operated print shop) and generate output at a constant rate (202,500/ 250 = 810 packages per working day). Since this output exceeds the rate of demand (324 packages per working day), inventory will gradually increase during the production period. Also, the manufacturing cost per item (40 cents) is known and constant.

Technical's manufacturing system is characteristic of the so-called economic production quantity (EPQ) model. By letting t = the time to complete one production run (typically, the number of days), we can illustrate the situation with Figure 13.5.

When the production run starts at time 0, the bookstore will have no inventory. Technical will then manufacture items at a constant rate during the production phase. Some of the output will be used to satisfy customer demand. The excess will be put in inventory. As a result, inventory will gradually increase during the manufacturing period to a maximum at time

Figure 13.5 Inventory Pattern for the Economic Production Quantity (EPQ) Model

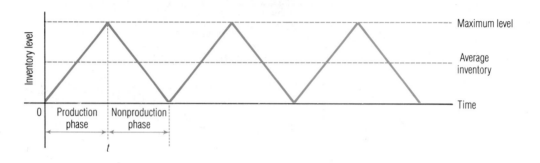

t. In the process, the bookstore will have an average inventory again equal to one-half the maximum level. At time *t*, Technical will complete the manufacturing run and begin the nonproduction phase. During this period, demand will be satisfied from stock until inventory is depleted. Then management will begin a new manufacturing run in time to allow for delivery by the inventory depletion point. The pattern will repeat itself as time progresses. Consequently, the average inventory over any time frame will still equal one-half the maximum level.

In this model, the objective is to find the production quantity Q that minimizes total inventory-related costs. Since demand once more will be fully satisfied, there is no shortage expense. However, there will be manufacturing, setup, and holding costs.

Technical manufactures each package of notebook filler for 40 cents. Since consumer demand must be fully satisfied, the annual production expense will equal the cost per item $c = \$.40$ multiplied by demand $D = 81,000$, or

$$cD = \$.40(81,000) = \$32,400$$

Notice that the manufacturing expense (cD) takes the same form as the procurement expression (13.1) in the basic EOQ model.

Setup expenses result from cleaning, preparing, and arranging the printing equipment. They total $5.40 for each production run. Since the bookstore produces a fixed output Q during the manufacturing period, management must schedule $81,000/Q$ production runs to satisfy annual demand. Therefore, the annual setup cost will equal the expense for one production setup $c_o = \$5.40$ multiplied by the number of runs ($81,000/Q$), or

$$\frac{c_o D}{Q} = \frac{\$5.40\,(81,000)}{Q} = \frac{\$437,400}{Q}$$

Note that the setup expense ($c_o D/Q$) takes the same form as the order cost expression (13.2) in the basic EOQ model.

Annual inventory holding expenses again will equal the carrying cost per item multiplied by the average inventory level. The bookstore knows that the average inventory will be one-half the maximum level. Unfortunately, this maximum is not evident but must be derived.

We assume that inventory is built up from excess production during the manufacturing period t. If p = the rate of production (typically, items per day) and d = the rate of demand, then the rate of excess production will be $p - d$. In Example 13.4, the students can produce $p = 810$ packages per working day. Since the consumer demand rate is only $d = 81{,}000/250 = 324$, the bookstore can add $p - d = 810 - 324 = 486$ packages to inventory each working day. Technical will accumulate a maximum inventory of

$$(p - d) \times t = (810 - 324) \times t = 486t$$

by the end of a production run.

Now, during the manufacturing period, the print shop will produce a total of Q packages at the rate of $p = 810$ per working day. As a result, it will take

$$t = Q/p = Q/810 \text{ days}$$

to complete a production run. Thus, the maximum inventory can be expressed in terms of the production quantity Q:

$$(p - d)t = (p - d)\frac{Q}{p} = \left(1 - \frac{d}{p}\right)Q = \left(1 - \frac{324}{810}\right)Q = .6Q$$

Average inventory will therefore equal one-half this maximum, or

$$\tfrac{1}{2}\left(1 - \frac{d}{p}\right)Q = \tfrac{1}{2}(.6)Q = .3Q$$

Notice that the average inventory in the EPQ model is a fraction $\left(1 - \dfrac{d}{p}\right)$ of the corresponding level ($Q/2$) in the basic EOQ formulation.

Technical's annual inventory holding costs equal 18% of the value of average inventory. The company manufactures each item for 40 cents. Hence, it will cost 18% of $.40, or 7.2 cents, to carry one package in inventory for a year. Since the average inventory is $.3Q$, the inventory holding expense will be

$$\$.072 (.3)Q = \$.0216Q \text{ per year}$$

In the EPQ model, then, inventory holding cost per period can be expressed generally as

$$(13.21) \quad \left(1 - \frac{d}{p}\right)\left(\frac{c_H Q}{2}\right)$$

The unit carrying cost per period (c_H), demand rate (d), and production rate (p) are all assumed to be known and constant.

It is usually more convenient to collect demand and production totals rather than rates. As a result, management may want to write inventory holding expenses in terms of these totals. The rate of demand, for instance, is

$$d = \frac{\text{total demand}}{\text{days of operation}} = \frac{D}{N}$$

Similarly, total output divided by the same number of days gives the rate of production p. If we let P denote the total production, then

$$\frac{d}{p} = \frac{D/N}{P/N} = \frac{D}{P}$$

and inventory holding expenses can be expressed as

$$(13.22) \quad \left(1 - \frac{D}{P}\right)\left(\frac{c_H Q}{2}\right)$$

Expressions (13.22) and (13.21) are alternative but equivalent forms.

Total inventory-related expenses per period will equal the sum of manufacturing, setup, and holding expenses. That is,

$$(13.23) \quad TC = cD + \frac{c_o D}{Q} + \left(1 - \frac{D}{P}\right)\frac{c_H Q}{2}$$

in the EPQ model.

Equation (13.23) is very similar to the total cost formulation (13.4) in the basic EOQ model. In fact, if manufacturing, setup, and holding costs for the EPQ model were plotted on a graph, the results would appear as in Figure 13.2. Furthermore, the diagram would again show that the least costly quantity involves a balance between setup and holding expenses. Equation (13.2) and expression (13.22) indicate that such a balance occurs when

$$\frac{c_o D}{Q} = \left(1 - \frac{D}{P}\right)\left(\frac{c_H Q}{2}\right)$$

or

$$(13.24) \quad Q^* = \sqrt{\frac{2 c_o D}{\left(1 - \dfrac{D}{P}\right) c_H}}$$

In the EPQ model, Q^* is called the **economic lot size** or economic production quantity.

The bookstore will have an economic lot size of

$$Q^* = \sqrt{\frac{2(\$5.40)(81,000)}{\left(1 - \dfrac{81,000}{202,500}\right)(\$.072)}} = 4500 \text{ packages}$$

Equation (13.23) indicates that this quantity will result in total inventory costs of

$$TC = \$.40(81,000) + \frac{\$5.40(81,000)}{4500} + \left(1 - \frac{81,000}{202,500}\right)\frac{(\$.072)(4500)}{2}$$

$$= \$32,594.40 \text{ per year}$$

Technical can also use the data for determining the production run timing and frequency. Example 13.4 tells us that it will take 3 days to set up the manufacturing mechanism. Hence, there is a lead time of $L = 3$ days. Since the demand rate is $d = 324$ packages per day, equation (13.7) indicates that the bookstore should begin a production run whenever the inventory level reaches a reorder point of

$$R = dL = 324 \times 3 = 972 \text{ packages}$$

Also, to fully satisfy demand, equation (13.8) indicates that Technical should plan a production run of $Q^* = 4500$ packages approximately every

$$T = \frac{NQ^*}{D} = \frac{250(4500)}{81,000} = 13.9 \text{ working days}$$

RISK AND UNCERTAINTY Each of the previous models assumes that unit costs and demand are known and constant. Although much time may be spent in deriving these numbers, management should realize that the values are, at best, good estimates. Fortunately, inexact unit costs do not present a serious problem. The total inventory cost curve is fairly flat over a considerable range, as Figure 13.2 illustrates. As L. A. Johnson and D. C. Montgomery [14], R. Peterson and E. A. Silver [21], and R. J. Tersine [27] demonstrate, this characteristic makes basic inventory models relatively insensitive to changes or errors in data values. Thus, with reasonable ("ballpark") unit cost estimates, management can use the basic formulas to obtain a good approximation for the least costly inventory policy.

Demand is another matter. In practice, the exact sales level is rarely known in advance. Instead, management may only be able to describe demand in probabilistic terms. Furthermore, lead time may not be constant as assumed. Rather, the company might experience unanticipated delivery delays. Either uncertainty may result in a larger-than-expected demand during the lead time and can create stockouts, or shortages.

There are several ways to deal with lead time demand uncertainty. A company can compute the average or expected demand. Then the average, along with other relevant data, can be used with the planned shortage or backorder model to develop a recommended inventory policy. Since the basic approaches are relatively insensitive to data inaccuracies, this procedure should provide a low-cost (though not necessarily optimal) inventory policy recommendation.

The planned shortage approach assumes that customers will wait for their order to arrive. It may even be appropriate when there are enough new customers to continually replace those permanently lost. However, since most firms face various degrees of competition, stockouts ordinarily result in some lost sales. In the extreme, continuous large shortages can force a company out of business. Consequently, management may want to consider an alternative approach.

SAFETY STOCKS   Stockouts can occur only during the lead time—after an order has been placed and until the shipment arrives. As protection against shortages, management can keep extra inventory on hand to absorb larger-than-expected demand during this period. The additional items are referred to as **buffer** or **safety stock**. In this case, management will want to place an order when inventory reaches a level sufficient to cover expected demand during lead time plus safety stock. The problem is to find the proper level for this buffer inventory.

As Tersine [27] and C. D. Lewis [16] illustrate, it is possible to develop inventory cost models that provide both the optimal order/production and safety stock levels. However, such formulations become quite complicated mathematically and are difficult to measure and implement. There is another, perhaps more practical, approach.

We can first ask management to specify the minimum percentage of customer demands that must be satisfied from inventory. This percentage is called the **service level**. It may be somewhat unrealistic to try for a 100% service level. Such a policy would completely prevent shortages but could create excessive safety stocks and very high inventory holding cost. Therefore, management ordinarily will define a service level percentage that allows some limited number of stockouts in a stated period. Then the problem is to determine the safety stock that provides the desired service level. Example 13.5 illustrates.

EXAMPLE 13.5 Maintaining a Proper Service Level

Recently, Technical has faced substantial sales competition from local stationery shops.

Now, when the bookstore is out of stock, customers are usually lost to the competition.

Stockouts also create ill will. Consequently, management will assess a 7-cent penalty cost for each package that is out of stock.

The competition has had other effects. Although the bookstore still averages 81,000 sales per year, there is a considerable daily variation in demand. In addition, the bookstore has recently experienced unexpected delivery delays. These factors have created a great deal of uncertainty about demand during the lead time. However, using historical data and some judgment, management has been able to describe sales in probabilistic terms. The findings suggest that lead time demand follows a normal probability distribution with an average $u = 1620$ packages and standard deviation $\sigma = 300$ packages. All other facts are the same as in Example 13.1.

In view of the lead time demand uncertainty and potential customer losses, management feels that the planned shortage or backorder model is no longer appropriate. Instead, the bookstore plans to keep a buffer inventory as a hedge against shortages. Management is willing to tolerate a stockout on an average of two orders per year.

Example 13.5 is very similar to Example 13.1. Unit costs are the same and demand still averages 81,000 items per year. Hence, the application of equation (13.6)

$$Q^* = \sqrt{\frac{2c_o D}{c_H}} = \sqrt{\frac{2(\$5)(81,000)}{\$.09}} = 3000 \text{ packages}$$

remains a good approximation for the economic order quantity. Using this quantity, Technical once more can anticipate placing an average of $D/Q^* = 81,000/3000 = 27$ orders per year with approximately $T = N/(D/Q^*) = 250/27 = 9.3$ working days between requests.

The reorder point is another matter. In Example 13.1, lead time is a constant $L = 5$ days. Since sales average $d = 81,000/250 = 324$ packages per working day, equation (13.7) suggests that Technical's reorder point should be $R = d \times L = 324 \times 5 = 1620$ packages. However, this policy does not consider the sales uncertainty inherent in Example 13.5.

Technical's lead time demand now follows a normal probability distribution with $u = 1620$ packages and $\sigma = 300$ packages. With such a distribution, there is exactly a 50% chance that sales will exceed the average. A reorder point of $R = 1620$, then, will satisfy only the average ($u = 1620$) rather than the actual demand during lead time. In effect, this strategy provides a 50% service level. It also means that on 50% of the occasions (13.5 out of 27 orders), the bookstore will be out of stock before the new supply arrives.

On the other hand, Technical's management is willing to tolerate a stockout on an average of only two orders per year. Since the bookstore places an annual average of twenty-seven orders, this strategy will result in a shortage approximately $2/27 = 7.41\%$ of the time. Consumer demand will be satisfied on the remaining $100 - 7.41 = 92.59\%$ of the occasions.

Figure 13.6 Relationship Between Technical's Service Level and the Reorder Point

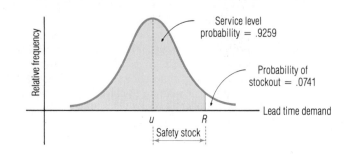

Management's problem, then, is to find the reorder point that provides a 92.59% service level. The situation is shown graphically in Figure 13.6.

Figure 13.6 gives a normal probability distribution for lead time demand. The shaded region to the left of the reorder point R gives the service level probability (.9259). By using mathematical analysis, management can find the value of R that corresponds to this service level. Most decision makers, however, are not likely to be familiar with the required analysis.

Fortunately, there is an alternative approach. In this regard, Table 13.6 gives the cumulative probabilities that correspond to standard

$$Z = \frac{X - u}{\sigma}$$

scores in a normal probability distribution. The Z score tells us how many standard deviations (σ values) a number X is from the average u value in the distribution. As Table 13.6 indicates, Technical can achieve a .9259 service level (cumulative probability) when the reorder point is approximately $Z = 1.45$ standard deviations above the mean $u = 1620$. Since lead time demand has a standard deviation $\sigma = 300$ packages, management should reorder when inventory reaches

$$R = 1620 + (1.45)(300) = 2055 \text{ items}$$

As shown in Figure 13.6, the difference between the reorder point and the average demand, $R - u = 2055 - 1620 = 435$ packages, represents safety stock.

In general, then, the reorder point equals the average lead time demand plus safety stock. By letting $B =$ the buffer, or safety stock, necessary to achieve the desired service level, we can express the relationship as

$$(13.25) \quad R = u + B$$

Table 13.6 Cumulative Probabilities for the Normal Distribution

Z	.09	.08	.07	.06	.05	.04	.03	.02	.01	.00
.00	.5359	.5319	.5279	.5239	.5199	.5160	.5120	.5080	.5040	.5000
.10	.5753	.5714	.5675	.5636	.5596	.5557	.5517	.5478	.5438	.5398
.20	.6141	.6103	.6064	.6026	.5987	.5948	.5910	.5871	.5832	.5793
.30	.6517	.6480	.6443	.6406	.6368	.6331	.6293	.6255	.6217	.6179
.40	.6879	.6844	.6808	.6772	.6736	.6700	.6664	.6628	.6591	.6554
.50	.7224	.7190	.7157	.7123	.7088	.7054	.7019	.6985	.6950	.6915
.60	.7549	.7517	.7486	.7454	.7422	.7389	.7357	.7324	.7291	.7257
.70	.7852	.7823	.7794	.7764	.7734	.7704	.7673	.7642	.7611	.7580
.80	.8133	.8106	.8078	.8051	.8023	.7995	.7967	.7939	.7910	.7881
.90	.8389	.8365	.8340	.8315	.8289	.8264	.8238	.8212	.8186	.8159
1.00	.8621	.8599	.8577	.8554	.8531	.8508	.8485	.8461	.8438	.8413
1.10	.8830	.8810	.8790	.8770	.8749	.8729	.8708	.8686	.8665	.8643
1.20	.9015	.8997	.8980	.8962	.8944	.8925	.8907	.8888	.8869	.8849
1.30	.9177	.9162	.9147	.9131	.9115	.9099	.9082	.9066	.9049	.9032
1.40	.9319	.9306	.9292	.9279	.9265	.9251	.9236	.9222	.9207	.9192
1.50	.9441	.9429	.9418	.9406	.9394	.9382	.9370	.9357	.9345	.9332
1.60	.9545	.9535	.9525	.9515	.9505	.9495	.9484	.9474	.9463	.9452
1.70	.9633	.9625	.9616	.9608	.9599	.9591	.9582	.9573	.9564	.9554
1.80	.9706	.9699	.9693	.9686	.9678	.9671	.9664	.9656	.9649	.9641
1.90	.9767	.9761	.9756	.9750	.9744	.9738	.9732	.9726	.9719	.9713
2.00	.9817	.9812	.9808	.9803	.9798	.9793	.9788	.9783	.9778	.9772
2.10	.9857	.9854	.9850	.9846	.9842	.9838	.9834	.9830	.9826	.9821
2.20	.9890	.9887	.9884	.9881	.9878	.9875	.9871	.9868	.9864	.9861
2.30	.9916	.9913	.9911	.9909	.9906	.9904	.9901	.9898	.9896	.9893
2.40	.9936	.9934	.9932	.9931	.9929	.9927	.9925	.9922	.9920	.9918
2.50	.9952	.9951	.9949	.9948	.9946	.9945	.9943	.9941	.9940	.9938
2.60	.9964	.9963	.9962	.9961	.9960	.9959	.9957	.9956	.9955	.9953
2.70	.9974	.9973	.9972	.9971	.9970	.9969	.9968	.9967	.9966	.9965
2.80	.9981	.9980	.9979	.9979	.9978	.9977	.9977	.9976	.9975	.9974
2.90	.9986	.9986	.9985	.9985	.9984	.9984	.9983	.9982	.9982	.9981
3.00	.9990	.9990	.9989	.9989	.9989	.9988	.9988	.9987	.9987	.9987
3.10	.9993	.9993	.9992	.9992	.9992	.9992	.9991	.9991	.9991	.9990
3.20	.9995	.9995	.9995	.9994	.9994	.9994	.9994	.9994	.9993	.9993
3.30	.9997	.9996	.9996	.9996	.9996	.9996	.9996	.9995	.9995	.9995
3.40	.9998	.9997	.9997	.9997	.9997	.9997	.9997	.9997	.9997	.9997
3.50	.9998	.9998	.9998	.9998	.9998	.9998	.9998	.9998	.9998	.9998
3.60	.9999	.9999	.9999	.9999	.9999	.9999	.9999	.9999	.9999	.9998
3.70	.9999	.9999	.9999	.9999	.9999	.9999	.9999	.9999	.9999	.9999
3.80	.9999	.9999	.9999	.9999	.9999	.9999	.9999	.9999	.9999	.9999

Z	-.09	-.08	-.07	-.06	-.05	-.04	-.03	-.02	-.01	.00
-3.80	.0001	.0001	.0001	.0001	.0001	.0001	.0001	.0001	.0001	.0001
-3.70	.0001	.0001	.0001	.0001	.0001	.0001	.0001	.0001	.0001	.0001
-3.60	.0001	.0001	.0001	.0001	.0001	.0001	.0001	.0001	.0002	.0002
-3.50	.0002	.0002	.0002	.0002	.0002	.0002	.0002	.0002	.0002	.0002
-3.40	.0002	.0003	.0003	.0003	.0003	.0003	.0003	.0003	.0003	.0003
-3.30	.0003	.0004	.0004	.0004	.0004	.0004	.0004	.0005	.0005	.0005
-3.20	.0005	.0005	.0005	.0006	.0006	.0006	.0006	.0006	.0007	.0007
-3.10	.0007	.0007	.0008	.0008	.0008	.0008	.0009	.0009	.0009	.0010
-3.00	.0010	.0010	.0011	.0011	.0011	.0012	.0012	.0013	.0013	.0013
-2.90	.0014	.0014	.0015	.0015	.0016	.0016	.0017	.0018	.0018	.0019
-2.80	.0019	.0020	.0021	.0021	.0022	.0023	.0023	.0024	.0025	.0026
-2.70	.0026	.0027	.0028	.0029	.0030	.0031	.0032	.0033	.0034	.0035
-2.60	.0036	.0037	.0038	.0039	.0040	.0041	.0043	.0044	.0045	.0047
-2.50	.0048	.0049	.0051	.0052	.0054	.0055	.0057	.0059	.0060	.0062
-2.40	.0064	.0066	.0068	.0069	.0071	.0073	.0075	.0078	.0080	.0082
-2.30	.0084	.0087	.0089	.0091	.0094	.0096	.0099	.0102	.0104	.0107
-2.20	.0110	.0113	.0116	.0119	.0122	.0125	.0129	.0132	.0136	.0139
-2.10	.0143	.0146	.0150	.0154	.0158	.0162	.0166	.0170	.0174	.0179
-2.00	.0183	.0188	.0192	.0197	.0202	.0207	.0212	.0217	.0222	.0228
-1.90	.0233	.0239	.0244	.0250	.0256	.0262	.0268	.0274	.0281	.0287
-1.80	.0294	.0301	.0307	.0314	.0322	.0329	.0336	.0344	.0351	.0359
-1.70	.0367	.0375	.0384	.0392	.0401	.0409	.0418	.0427	.0436	.0446
-1.60	.0455	.0465	.0475	.0485	.0495	.0505	.0516	.0526	.0537	.0548
-1.50	.0559	.0571	.0582	.0594	.0606	.0618	.0630	.0643	.0655	.0668
-1.40	.0681	.0694	.0708	.0721	.0735	.0749	.0764	.0778	.0793	.0808
-1.30	.0823	.0838	.0853	.0869	.0885	.0901	.0918	.0934	.0951	.0968
-1.20	.0985	.1003	.1020	.1038	.1056	.1075	.1093	.1112	.1131	.1151
-1.10	.1170	.1190	.1210	.1230	.1251	.1271	.1292	.1314	.1335	.1357
-1.00	.1379	.1401	.1423	.1446	.1469	.1492	.1515	.1539	.1562	.1587
-.90	.1611	.1635	.1660	.1685	.1711	.1736	.1762	.1788	.1814	.1841
-.80	.1867	.1894	.1922	.1949	.1977	.2005	.2033	.2061	.2090	.2119
-.70	.2148	.2177	.2206	.2236	.2266	.2296	.2327	.2358	.2389	.2420
-.60	.2451	.2483	.2514	.2546	.2578	.2611	.2643	.2676	.2709	.2743
-.50	.2776	.2810	.2843	.2877	.2912	.2946	.2981	.3015	.3050	.3085
-.40	.3121	.3156	.3192	.3228	.3264	.3300	.3336	.3372	.3409	.3446
-.30	.3483	.3520	.3557	.3594	.3632	.3669	.3707	.3745	.3783	.3821
-.20	.3859	.3897	.3936	.3974	.4013	.4052	.4090	.4129	.4168	.4207
-.10	.4247	.4286	.4325	.4364	.4404	.4443	.4483	.4522	.4562	.4602
.00	.4641	.4681	.4721	.4761	.4801	.4840	.4880	.4920	.4960	.5000

For a normal probability distribution, $B = Z\sigma$, with Z representing the number of standard deviations above the mean that is necessary to achieve the desired service level.

The anticipated annual cost for this system will still include the procurement (cD), ordering $(c_o D/Q)$, and holding $(c_H Q/2)$ expenses resulting from the economic order quantity. In addition, there will be an expense to carry the safety stock plus a shortage cost associated with the limited number of stockouts.

To ensure a 92.59% service level, Technical should order $Q^* = 3000$ packages whenever the stock level reaches a reorder point of $R = 2055$ items. This strategy involves a safety stock of $B = R - u = 2055 - 1620 = 435$ packages. Remember that it costs the bookstore $c_H = \$.09$ to carry an item for one year. Hence, Technical's annual holding cost for safety stock will be

$$c_H \times B = \$.09 \times 435 = \$39.15$$

Notice that this expense $(c_H B)$ increases with the size of the safety stock.

The shortage cost involves some other considerations. As shown in Figure 13.6, stockouts occur when lead time demand is greater than the reorder point R. Technical does not know the exact upper limit of this distribution. However, Table 13.6 indicates that most sales (99.99%) will be no more than $Z = 3.80$ standard deviations above the mean u value. With a reorder point of $R = 2055$ items, then, the bookstore could have a shortage of up to

$$S = u + Z\sigma - R = 1620 + 3.8(300) - 2055 = 705 \text{ packages}$$

each time there is a stockout. Furthermore, management will assess a $c_B = \$.07$ penalty cost for each item. Hence, each stockout could involve a cost of up to

$$c_B \times S = \$.07 \times 705 = \$49.35$$

Management also knows that a policy with $R = 2055$ items will satisfy lead time demand 92.59% of the time. With $D/Q = 81,000/3000 = 27$ annual requests, then, there will be a stockout on an average of $(1 - .9259) \times 27 = 2.0007$ orders per year. Since each stockout costs $49.35, the bookstore can expect a shortage expense of

$$c_B S(1 - \text{service level}) \frac{D}{Q} = \$49.35 \times 2.0007 = \$98.73$$

per year. Notice that this cost $[c_B S(1 - \text{service level})D/Q]$ decreases as the service level increases.

Total costs will equal the sum of the procurement, ordering, inventory holding, safety stock holding, and stockout expenses. If we let $P_S = $ the

Table 13.7 Technical's Expenses Associated with a 92.59% Service Level

Expense Category	Formula	Annual Cost ($)
Procurement	$cD = \$.50(81{,}000)$	40,500.00
Ordering	$c_oD/Q = \$5(81{,}000/3000)$	135.00
Holding of normal inventory	$c_HQ/2 = \$.09(3000/2)$	135.00
Holding of safety stock	$c_HB = \$.09(435)$	39.15
Stockout	$c_BSP_SD/Q = \$.07(705)(.0741)(81{,}000/3000)$	98.73
Total		40,907.88

probability of a stockout (1 − service level), the relationship can be expressed as follows:

$$(13.26) \quad TC = cD + \frac{c_oD}{Q} + \frac{c_HQ}{2} + c_HB + c_BSP_S\frac{D}{Q}$$

$$= cD + \frac{c_oD}{Q} + c_H\left(B + \frac{Q}{2}\right) + c_BSP_S\frac{D}{Q}$$

The probability of a stockout (P_S) is assumed to be known and constant.

In Example 13.5, $c = \$.50$, $c_o = \$5$, $D = 81{,}000$, $Q = 3000$, $c_H = \$.09$, $B = 435$, $c_B = \$.07$, $S = 705$, and $P_S = 1 - .9259 = .0741$. Hence, a 92.59% service level generates the annual expenses summarized in Table 13.7. Notice that the service level approach adds $\$39.15 + \$98.73 = \$137.88$ to the normal inventory-related expenses. The additional expenses for safety stock ($39.15) and stockouts ($98.73) in effect measure the cost of lead time demand uncertainty.

OPTIMAL SERVICE LEVEL The service level is usually determined by management policies. However, this approach cannot guarantee the lowest-cost solution for a given order quantity. To ensure the lowest-cost solution, we must compare the expense of carrying the safety stock with the cost of stocking out. Let us reconsider Example 13.5.

As shown in Figure 13.6, Technical increases the service level by adding safety stock to the inventory used to cover the expected demand. Each package of safety stock will increase holding cost by $c_H = \$.09$ per year. However, it will also reduce the chance of a stockout and hence save $c_BP_SD/Q = \$.07(81{,}000/3000)P_S = \$1.89P_S$ annually.

To determine whether or not an additional package of safety stock is

Table 13.8 Summary of Optimal Service Level Procedure

> 1. Find the economic order/production quantity Q^*.
> 2. Identify the probability distribution best describing lead time demand, and calculate the mean u.
> 3. Compute the lowest-cost service level for the given order quantity, $1 - (Qc_H/Dc_B)$.
> 4. Identify the demand level corresponding to the optimal service level. The result is the reorder point R.
> 5. Compute the optimal safety stock for the given order quantity, $B = R - u$.

necessary, Technical must compare the expected outcomes. As long as the expected stockout cost reduction $(c_B P_S D/Q)$ is greater than the increase in holding expense (c_H), the bookstore should safety-stock an additional package. Furthermore, buffer inventory should be added, one unit at a time, until the expected costs are equal. This balance occurs when

$$c_H = \frac{c_B P_S D}{Q} = \frac{c_B(1 - \text{service level})D}{Q}$$

or

$$(13.27) \quad \text{service level} = 1 - \frac{Qc_H}{Dc_B}$$

At this point, there is no incentive to safety-stock any additional packages.

In effect, then, equation (13.27) identifies the service level that minimizes the sum of safety stock holding cost plus stockout cost for a given order quantity. For Technical, this lowest-cost service level is

$$\text{service level} = 1 - \left(\frac{3000 \times \$.09}{81{,}000 \times \$.07} \right) \approx 95.24\%$$

According to Table 13.6, Technical can achieve this service level if the reorder point is about $Z = 1.67$ standard deviations above the mean.

In this situation, then, management should order $Q^* = 3000$ packages when inventory reaches a reorder point of

$$R = u + Z\sigma = 1620 + 1.67(300) = 2121 \text{ items}$$

and management should plan a safety stock of

$$B = R - u = 2121 - 1620 = 501 \text{ packages}$$

Table 13.8 summarizes this optimal service level procedure.

In Technical's situation, lead time demand follows a normal probability distribution. As Lewis [16] demonstrates, however, the procedure outlined in Table 13.8 can also be applied to service level problems that involve other probability distributions.

INVENTORY SYSTEMS   Table 13.9 summarizes the EOQ and EPQ models discussed so far. In these models, the company continually monitors inventory transactions. Items are either recorded manually, observed in marked storage compartments, punched on cards, or processed by a computer. Then management places an order of fixed size whenever the inventory level reaches its reorder point. Such an approach is referred to as the **fixed order quantity (Q) system** for inventory planning and control.

On the other hand, some suppliers take orders and make deliveries only at periodic intervals. For example, a dairy truck may stop at a grocery store every few days as it makes its rounds. Also, it may not be worthwhile for companies to continually review the available stock for items that are frequently issued but in small quantities, such as pencils, coffee, and bandages. In such cases, the inventory level is reviewed at equally spaced, predetermined points in time. As Larson [15] and Tersine [27] demonstrate, the optimal review period (which could be days, weeks, or some other period) is the time interval that minimizes total inventory costs. At each review, the company counts the available stock manually, by inspection of a marked storage bin, or with a computerized system. Then management orders the amount necessary to reach a target inventory level. The target provides enough items to satisfy demand during the delivery lead time plus the interval between orders. Such a periodic review approach is called the **fixed order interval (P) system** of inventory management.

The basic Q and P system models assume that there is a continuous demand for a single product. Yet most inventory situations involve many items. Ordinarily, however, it is possible to use the basic models as long as the items have independent demands and are purchased or produced separately. In this case, the optimal total inventory is simply the sum of the least costly order or production quantities for each item. H. G. Daellenbach [6], S. Larson [15], B. E. Lipman [18], and S. Senju and S. Fujita [23] extend the analysis to these and other multiple-product situations.

There are many other variations of the basic Q and P systems. For example, M. Rosenshine and D. Obee [22] present a model for emergency orders, and M. B. Dumas and M. Rabinowitz [8] discuss a situation where service level is more important than cost. In addition, H. Burman and J. Thomas [4] and G. M. Constantinides and S. F. Richard [5] incorporate financial considerations into inventory decision making. A complete research portfolio on the subject is presented by H. M. Wagner [28].

Each approach has its advantages, disadvantages, and areas of application. The Q system is well suited for high-cost items where constant review is desirable. Yet the resulting close control creates high clerical processing expenses. Since the periodic review involves scheduled replenishment and less record keeping, the P system results in low ordering expenses. On the other hand, the P system requires large inventories to satisfy demand

Table 13.9 Summary of the EOQ and EPQ Models

Model	Assumptions	Total Cost	Order/Production and Shortage Quantities	Reorder Point	Cycle Times
EOQ	Single product Constant demand Constant lead time Constant unit costs Instantaneous delivery No shortages No discounts	$TC = cD + \dfrac{c_o D}{Q} + \dfrac{c_H Q}{2}$	$Q^* = \sqrt{\dfrac{2c_o D}{c_H}}$	$R = dL$	$T = \dfrac{NQ^*}{D}$
EOQ with discounts	Same as EOQ model, except there are purchase discounts	Same as EOQ model	Least-cost feasible order size (see Table 13.4)	Same as EOQ model	Same as EOQ model
EOQ with backorders	Same as EOQ model, except there are planned shortages	$TC = cD + \dfrac{c_o D}{Q} + \dfrac{c_H(Q-S)^2}{2Q} + \dfrac{c_B S^2}{2Q}$	$Q^* = \sqrt{\dfrac{2c_o D}{c_H}\left(\dfrac{c_H + c_B}{c_B}\right)}$ $S^* = Q^*\left(\dfrac{c_H}{c_H + c_B}\right)$	$R = dL - S$	$T = \dfrac{NQ^*}{D}$ $t_1 = \dfrac{Q-S}{d}$ $t_2 = \dfrac{S}{d}$
EPQ	Same as EOQ model, except inventory is produced gradually over time	$TC = cD + \dfrac{c_o D}{Q} + \left(1 - \dfrac{D}{P}\right)\dfrac{c_H Q}{2}$	$Q^* = \sqrt{\dfrac{2c_o D}{\left(1 - \dfrac{D}{P}\right)c_H}}$	$R = dL$ when $T - L \geq t$ $R = (p - d)(T - L)$ when $T - L < t$	$T = \dfrac{NQ^*}{D}$ $t = \dfrac{Q}{P}$
EOQ with service level	Same as EOQ model, except there is variable lead time demand	$TC = cD + \dfrac{c_o D}{Q} + c_H\left(B + \dfrac{Q}{2}\right) + c_B SP_s \dfrac{D}{Q}$	Same as EOQ model	$R = u + B$ or procedure in Table 13.8	Same as EOQ model

during the review period and lead time and hence creates high holding expenses. As a result, the periodic review is best suited for situations in which a large number of items is regularly ordered from very few supply sources.

In practice, companies use Q, P, and hybrid systems. Tersine [27], for example, discusses an approach in which stock levels are reviewed at regular intervals, as in the P system. However, orders are not placed until the inventory level has fallen to a predetermined reorder point, as in the Q system. Such an approach provides the close control of the fixed order quantity method and the fewer item orders associated with the periodic review. Also, many organizations have access to computerized systems that will assimilate company records, forecast item sales, and generate ordering instructions for optimal inventory replenishment. Such systems can apply Q, P, or hybrid decision rules. One typical example is IBM's Inventory Forecasting and Replenishment Modules [13]. Other systems are discussed by J. H. Fuchs [10] and E. A. Stohr [24]. For smaller firms, there are less costly business machines that electronically adjust inventory levels at the transaction point. Management can plan and control inventory by using the information from these devices with appropriate decision models.

Finally, decision makers should realize that a sophisticated inventory analysis is neither necessary nor desirable in all circumstances. In a typical inventory, a small percentage of items accounts for most of the dollar value. Companies recognize this characteristic and usually divide inventories into various arbitrary classifications for planning and control purposes. One widely used approach is the **ABC (Pareto) system**. The A category typically contains about 20% of the items and 80% of the dollar value of inventory. Hence, most of the inventory value can be controlled by intensively managing these items. For these items, management might use a tight control system involving continuous review of stock levels and the use of sophisticated decision models. At the other extreme, class C usually contains 50% of the items and only 5% of the dollar value. For these items, management might use a looser control system involving periodic review and simple ordering rules. Class B, between the extremes, represents approximately 30% of the items and accounts for about 15% of the dollar value. These items require an intermediate level of management attention.

Of course, each organization should tailor the inventory system to its own peculiarities. Instead of using the ABC approach, some firms may prefer to group inventory into additional classifications based on relevant decision factors other than dollar value. However, the principle should be the same for any sensitive control system: high-value items receive the most attention and low-value items the least.

NONCONTINUOUS AND DEPENDENT DEMAND

Each of the previous approaches assumes that there is a continuous and independent demand for the product. Generally, this assumption is reasonable for most finished goods [1] and spare parts for replacement [9]. On the other hand, in many situations, the demand for an item may be noncontinuous or related to the demand for other goods. This section discusses inventory systems designed for such circumstances.

SINGLE-PERIOD INVENTORY

Until now, we have assumed that management continuously repeats the order or production cycle. Furthermore, it was possible to carry the resulting inventory for one or more periods. On the other hand, there are some products, like Christmas trees and bathing suits, that are highly seasonal. Others are either perishable (flowers, for example) or become obsolete very quickly (such as today's newspaper). These products cannot be carried in inventory and sold in future periods. In these situations, a buyer places a single preseason order for each item. Then, at the end of the season, either the product has sold out or there is a clearance sale on the surplus stock.

Under these circumstances, timing and frequency are already determined. There will be a single order placed at the start of the relevant period. Management must decide only how much to order. Obviously, if the exact sales level were known, the solution would be easy. The company would simply order the number of items necessary to fully satisfy demand. Unfortunately, these situations usually involve considerable demand uncertainty. As U. Dave and M. C. Jaiswal [7] and N. Nahmias [19] demonstrate, the uncertainty necessitates an analysis based on the demand probabilities. Example 13.6 illustrates.

EXAMPLE 13.6 Ordering Seasonal Merchandise

Each year, The Chic Shop buys the latest women's fashion spring suit for $70 apiece and sells it for $110. It also costs $5 to carry each suit in inventory for the season. Hence, each suit involves a total cost of $70 + $5 = $75. Stock must be requested in advance of the season, and it costs $6 to place an order.

Surplus suits are sold for $45 each during an end-of-the-season clearance sale. If Chic is out of stock, the customer will shop elsewhere and Chic will lose the sale. In addition, there may be lost profit from accessory items, such as shoes and purses, and customer ill will. Management estimates that such penalties amount to $15 per suit.

Distributor records indicate that past sales of comparable merchandise by similar shops have been as indicated in Table 13.10. Since the designer has maintained a solid reputation, Chic assumes that this sales pattern will continue.

Each season, management wants to order the number of suits that will maximize expected profit.

Table 13.10 Past Sales Data for Spring Suits

Suits Sold per Season	Number of Shops
45	5
46	25
47	40
48	20
49	10

Although Chic makes similar ordering decisions each season, the product rapidly becomes obsolete and thus cannot be carried in inventory from season to season. In effect, then, each order represents a separate decision.

Each season, the shop wants to order the number of suits demanded. Although the buyers do not know the exact demand ahead of time, Table 13.10 indicates that it could be between 45 and 49 suits. Thus, there is no sense in ordering fewer than 45 suits or more than 49. Indeed, Chic's alternatives are to stock either 45, 46, 47, 48, or 49 suits. Profit will depend on the resulting demand.

When the shop orders the exact number of suits demanded, it will earn a profit of $110 - $75 = 35 per suit. For example, if management stocks 46 suits and 46 are demanded, gross profit will be $46 \times \$35 = \$1610$. When the order quantity is less than sales, Chic will lose profit on accessories and invite customer ill will. The result is a $15 penalty for each stockout. Suppose, for instance, that the shop stocks 48 suits and has a demand for 49. Then profit will be

48 suits @ $35/suit = $1680

less

1 suit @ $15/suit = − $15

for a gross profit of $1665. On the other hand, if Chic orders more suits than the quantity demanded, it will salvage the surplus for $45 per suit. In this case, the revenue ($45) is less than the cost ($75), and there will be a $30 loss per surplus item. Hence, when 47 suits are ordered but 45 demanded, the profit will be

45 suits @ $35/suit = $1575

less

2 suits @ $30/suit = − $60

Table 13.11 Chic's Profits ($)

Order Quantity (Suits)	Demand (Suits)				
	45	46	47	48	49
45	1575	1560	1545	1530	1515
46	1545	1610	1595	1580	1565
47	1515	1580	1645	1630	1615
48	1485	1550	1615	1680	1665
49	1455	1520	1585	1650	1715

for a gross profit of $1515. Table 13.11 presents the profit data for each order quantity and demand combination.

Chic also knows the probabilities for each demand level. According to the available information, there is a

$5/100 = .05$ probability of selling 45 suits

$25/100 = .25$ probability of selling 46 suits

$40/100 = .40$ probability of selling 47 suits

$20/100 = .20$ probability of selling 48 suits

$10/100 = .10$ probability of selling 49 suits

Using these probabilities and the profit data in Table 13.11, the shop can compute the expected profit of each order quantity. For instance, when Chic orders 45 suits, management can expect a profit of $1575(.05) + $1560(.25) + $1545(.40) + $1530(.20) + $1515(.10) = $1544.25 less the $6 ordering expense, or a net profit of $1538.25. Similarly, when the shop stocks 46 suits, the expected profit is $1545(.05) + $1610(.25) + $1595(.40) + $1580(.20) + $1565(.10) = $1590.25 less the $6 ordering expense, or a net profit of $1584.25. An order of 47 suits yields a net profit of $1610.25, an order of 48 suits nets $1604.25, and an order of 49 suits results in an expected net profit of $1610.25.

Chic wants to select the inventory policy that maximizes expected profit. Thus, management should order 47 suits each season. Such a policy will result in an expected return of $1610.25 per order.

INCREMENTAL ANALYSIS Small inventory problems can be solved rather quickly by using the preceding expected value approach. However, the method becomes quite cumbersome when there are numerous alternatives. Also, decision makers may be able to identify only ranges of demand levels rather than exact

Table 13.12 Chic's Incremental Decision

	Demand Condition	
Inventory Action	No Additional Demand	Demand at Least One More Suit
Order no additional stock	$0	MU = $50
Stock one more suit	MO = $30	$0

Penalty for overordering   Penalty for underordering

values. In these situations, incremental, or marginal, analysis provides an efficient way to select a decision alternative.

The basic idea of incremental analysis is to compare the penalties associated with both ordering and not ordering each additional unit. We will again illustrate with Chic's situation (Example 13.6).

Assume that the shop wants to evaluate a previous order policy. Management must decide whether or not to order an additional suit. Suppose that Chic stocks no additional units. If there is demand for at least one more suit, the shop will have a shortage. This underordering will result in a $50 penalty ($35 in lost suit profit plus $15 for lost accessory profit and ill will). Of course, if the shop has no additional demand, there is no penalty. On the other hand, suppose that Chic stocks exactly one additional unit. When there is no corresponding demand, the shop will have a surplus. Such overordering will result in a $30 penalty (the $75 cost less a $45 salvage). But if there is additional demand, the shop avoids this penalty. By letting

MU = incremental loss from underordering ($50 in this example)

MO = incremental loss from overordering ($30 in this example)

we can summarize the situation as shown in Table 13.12.

Notice that the penalties again depend on the demand. Although the exact demand is unknown, Chic can identify the probabilities for the possible sales levels. These probability data and the information in Table 13.12 can be used to identify the optimal ordering policy. By letting

p = the probability of no additional demand

$1 - p$ = the probability of demand for at least one more suit

management can expect a penalty of

$$\$0p + \text{MU}(1 - p) = \text{MU}(1 - p)$$

when the shop orders no additional stock and

$$\text{MO}p + \$0(1 - p) = \text{MO}p$$

if the shop stocks one more suit.

To determine whether or not to order an additional suit, Chic must compare the expected penalties. As long as the expected penalty from ordering, $\text{MO}p$, is less than the loss from not stocking, $\text{MU}(1 - p)$, management should order an additional suit. Furthermore, suits should be added to the existing order quantity, one at a time, until the expected penalties are equal. This balance occurs when

$$\text{MU}(1 - p) = \text{MO}p$$

or

$$(13.28) \quad p = \frac{\text{MU}}{\text{MU} + \text{MO}}$$

At this point, there is no incentive to order an additional suit.

According to equation (13.28), management should stock whatever quantity the shop will have a p chance of selling. In Chic's case, since $\text{MU} = \$50$ and $\text{MO} = \$30$,

$$p = \frac{\$50}{\$50 + \$30} = \frac{5}{8} = .625$$

Hence, the shop must find the order quantity that will provide a 62.5% likelihood of selling as many suits as the shop stocks.

The value p is a cumulative probability. It gives the chance that sales will be less than or equal to a particular demand. For example, Chic knows that there is a .05 chance of selling 45 suits and a .25 probability of making 46 sales. Thus, there is a $.05 + .25 = .30$ likelihood that demand will be less than or equal to 46 suits. Chic's entire cumulative probability distribution is presented in Table 13.13. Recall that Chic will order the quantity corresponding to a cumulative probability of $p = .625$. As the table shows, this stock level is between 46 and 47 suits (but closer to 47). Unfortunately, management cannot order a fraction of a suit. Therefore, the shop must choose either 46 or 47 suits.

At 46 suits, the probability of no additional demand ($p = .30$) is less than the proportion ($p = .625$) given by equation (13.28). Consequently, the expected penalty from ordering an additional suit is less than the corresponding loss from not stocking. Chic should then stock $46 + 1 = 47$ suits. At 47 suits, the cumulative probability ($p = .70$) is more than .625. Thus, the shop should order no more than this amount.

Table 13.13 Chic's Cumulative Probability Distribution of Demand

Suits Demanded per Season	Probability of Demand	Cumulative Probability of Demand
45	.05	0.05
46	.25	0.30
47	.40	0.70
48	.20	0.90
49	.10	1.00

$$\leftarrow p = \frac{\text{MU}}{\text{MU} + \text{MO}} = .625$$

Table 13.14 Summary of Incremental Analysis

1. Identify the probabilities of each demand.
2. Compute the cumulative probability distribution of each demand.
3. Identify the penalties from underordering (MU) and overordering (MO) one additional unit.
4. Compute the proportion $p = \text{MU}/(\text{MU} + \text{MO})$.
5. The optimal course of action is to order the quantity corresponding to p in the cumulative probability distribution of demand. When demand can only be measured in whole units, p may correspond to a point between two demand levels. In this case, the optimal order quantity is the higher of the two demand levels.

Note that the incremental analysis leads to the same policy recommendation (stock 47 suits) as the expected profit method. Table 13.14 summarizes the incremental procedure. In Chic's example, the probability distribution of demand takes a specific form. On the other hand, the procedure outlined in Table 13.14 can be applied to single-period inventory problems involving any type of probability distribution for demand.

MATERIAL REQUIREMENTS PLANNING The demand for a finished good is influenced by market conditions that are, to a large degree, beyond the firm's control. Hence, this demand is essentially independent of company operations and must be estimated from product forecasts or company orders. Under these circumstances, it is not unreasonable to assume that each product has an independent, continuous demand.

On the other hand, the finished product is composed of raw materials and components. During production, the inputs are transformed into the desired end item. Therefore, when there is a demand for the end item, the production process will generate an accompanying demand for each input.

In effect, then, requirements for materials and components are derived from the demand for the finished product.

Production of the finished good cannot even begin until the required inputs are available. Thus, it is important to provide raw materials and work in process (components) in the correct amounts and at the right time during the manufacturing process. To do so, management must design an inventory system that accounts for the dependency between end item and raw material demand. Example 13.7 illustrates.

EXAMPLE 13.7 Manufacturing Ball-point Pens

Paper Symbol, Inc., is a major producer of ball-point pens. Each pen is composed of a shaft and top assembly. The company's engineering design department has identified each assembly's raw materials requirements and sources. Table 13.15 summarizes the data.

Based on product forecasts and customer orders, management estimates that approximately 5000 pens will be needed during week 4 of the current eight-week production schedule. Management also forecasts an additional

requirement for 7000 pens during week 7 of this schedule.

There is a one-week lead time for all manufactured raw materials, assemblies, and pens. The suppliers of the springs, refills, and pocket clasps each require a two-week lead time.

At the present time (week 1 of the current production schedule), Paper Symbol has 2000 pens, 1000 assemblies of each type, and 3000 units of each raw material in stock. Outstanding production orders will provide another 1600 pens and 250 assemblies of each type

during week 1 of the current production schedule. Similarly, outstanding purchase orders will supply 50 springs, refills, and pocket clasps during week 2 of the schedule.

Paper Symbol's management wants to determine the purchase/manufacturing plan that will satisfy finished product demand. The plan should identify the quantities of pens, assemblies, and raw materials of each type required each week of the production schedule.

Table 13.15 Raw Materials and Assemblies for Each Ball-point Pen

Requirements	Source
Shaft assembly	
1 four-inch plastic casing	Manufactured
2 two-inch springs	Purchased
1 four-inch ball-point ink refill	Purchased
Top assembly	
1 two-inch metal casing	Manufactured
2 one-and-one-half-inch metal pocket clasps	Purchased
1 two-and-one-quarter-inch metal shaft	Manufactured

Once more, there may be a continuous and independent demand by consumers for the finished product (pens). The demand for assemblies (shafts and tops) and raw materials (plastic and metal casings, springs, refills, and pocket clasps) is another matter.

Using customer orders and product forecasts, Paper Symbol has established that the end item (pen) demand can be met with the following production plan:

Week	1	2	3	4	5	6	7	8
Pens required	0	0	0	5000	0	0	7000	0

Such a time-phased plan, which lists how many finished items are needed and when, is called a **master production schedule (MPS)**. From the MPS, you can see that pens will be produced in intermittent "lumps" rather than on a continuous basis. Since requirements for assemblies and materials are derived from the output of the finished product (and hence the MPS), there will also be a "lumpy" demand for these components. For instance, in producing a batch of pens, management can expect a high rate of demand for plastic casings just before the company assembles shafts. Then there will be no demand for this component until Paper Symbol manufactures another batch of pens.

As R. G. Brown [3], J. Orlicky [20], and R. J. Tersine [27] have demonstrated, the EOQ/EPQ approaches are not effective inventory management devices for these situations. Such procedures constantly replenish inventory in anticipation of a continuous demand for the item. However, in the "lumpy" demand situation, this policy can create excessive inventory when it is not needed and shortages at other times. As a result, the company may have both an excessive inventory investment and customer service problems and costs. Also, the EOQ/EPQ approaches assume that each item has an independent demand. Hence, there is no assurance that materials and components will be available when required in the production process. To meet materials scheduling and delivery needs, then, the company may have to institute a support department with expediters.

Paper Symbol can avoid these operational problems and excessive inventory costs by scheduling components to arrive in inventory just before the items are needed. The appropriate schedule for the finished product (pens) can be derived from the MPS and inventory records. Table 13.16 illustrates the process.

According to the MPS, Paper Symbol can satisfy customer demand by manufacturing 5000 pens during week 4 and 7000 pens during week 7 of

Table 13.16 Paper Symbol's Planned Pen Transactions

Transaction Category	Week							
	1	2	3	4	5	6	7	8
Gross requirements				5000			7000	
Scheduled receipts	1600							
Stock on hand	2000	3600	3600					
Net requirements				1400			7000	
Planned order releases			1400			7000		

the current production schedule. In effect, this schedule establishes the gross requirements for the finished product (pens).

The company can use stock on hand and scheduled receipts from outstanding work and purchase orders to meet some or all of the gross requirements. To do so, however, management must maintain detailed records identifying the items on hand, the amounts previously committed to production, quantities on order with suppliers, and lead times. Such records are usually referred to as an **inventory master file (IMF)**.

From outstanding production orders, Paper Symbol is scheduled to receive 1600 pens during week 1 of the MPS. At day 1, the company also has 2000 pens in stock. Since none of these pens are required until week 4, Table 13.16 indicates that $1600 + 2000 = 3600$ items will be in stock during weeks 2 and 3.

During week 4, management can use the stock of 3600 pens to satisfy part of the 5000-item gross requirement. This action still leaves a net requirement for $5000 - 3600 = 1400$ pens. Assuming that Paper Symbol always requests the exact requirement, the company must plan work order receipts of 1400 pens during week 4. Furthermore, manufacturing involves a one-week lead time. Thus, to satisfy the net requirement during week 4, management must release the work order during week 3.

No additional finished products are required during the fifth and sixth weeks. During week 7, there is a gross requirement for 7000 pens. Since the company has no scheduled receipts or stock on hand, the net requirement is also 7000 items. As a result, with the one-week lead time, management must release a 7000-pen work order during week 6.

The planned work order releases for pens during weeks 3 and 6 will create requirements for the component materials and assemblies. To properly plan component work and purchase requirements, management will need a structured parts list that shows exactly how the finished

Figure 13.7 The Bill of Materials for a Paper Symbol Pen

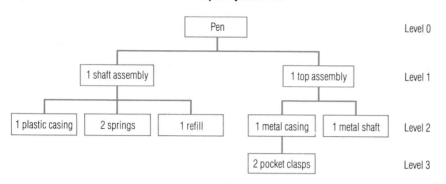

product is actually put together. Such a list is referred to as the **bill of materials (BOM)**.

Table 13.15 presents the BOM for a Paper Symbol pen. A representation of this product structure is shown in Figure 13.7. It shows that the company must have two pocket clasps available at level 3 before the metal casing can be completed at level 2. Also, both a metal casing and a shaft must be ready at level 2 before Paper Symbol can assemble the top at level 1. Similarly, the company cannot assemble the shaft at level 1 until a plastic casing, two springs, and a refill are available at level 2. Finally, both a shaft and top assembly must be complete at level 1 before Paper Symbol can produce the pen at level 0.

In effect, then, the BOM depicts how the finished product is exploded into its component parts and the hierarchy of steps involved in the manufacturing process. Paper Symbol can now use its BOM and IMF to plan component requirements. Figure 13.8 illustrates the process for a portion of the pen's top assembly. As Figure 13.8a and b indicate, the planned work order release for pens during week 3 creates a gross requirement of 1400 top assemblies in the same period. However, inventory records from Example 13.7 indicate that there will be stock on hand by that time. Outstanding production orders will provide 250 top assemblies and existing inventory will provide another 1000 top assemblies during week 1. Since none of the top asssemblies are required during the first two weeks, Paper Symbol will already have 250 + 1000 = 1250 in stock by week 3. Consequently, during week 3, there will be a net requirement for 1400 − 1250 = 150 items. With a one-week lead time, management should plan to release a work order for 150 top assemblies during week 2.

Similarly, the planned work order release for pens during week 6 creates a gross requirement of 7000 top assemblies in the same period. By that

Figure 13.8 Paper Symbol's BOM Explosion

Transaction	Week							
	1	2	3	4	5	6	7	8
Planned order releases			1400			7000		

(a) Level 0: Pens

Transaction	Week							
	1	2	3	4	5	6	7	8
Gross requirements			1400			7000		
Scheduled receipts	250							
Stock on hand	1000	1250						
Net requirements			150			7000		
Planned order releases		150			7000			

(b) Level 1: Top Assembly
     (one-week lead time)

Transaction	Week							
	1	2	3	4	5	6	7	8
Gross requirements		150			7000			
Scheduled receipts								
Stock on hand	3000	2850	2850	2850				
Net requirements					4150			
Planned order releases				4150				

(c) Level 2: Metal Casing
     (one-week lead time) 4150×2

Transaction	Week							
	1	2	3	4	5	6	7	8
Gross requirements				8300				
Scheduled receipts		50						
Stock on hand	3000	3000	3050					
Net requirements				5250				
Planned order releases		5250						

(d) Level 3: Pocket Clasps (two-week lead time)

time, there are no scheduled receipts or stock on hand and so the net requirement is also 7000 items. Considering the lead time, management must release a work order for 7000 top assemblies during week 5.

As shown in Figure 13.8c, the planned order releases for top assemblies create gross requirements of 150 metal casings in week 2 and another 7000 in week 5. Fortunately, there are 3000 metal casings already in inventory by week 2. Thus, management can use some to satisfy the entire gross requirement in week 2 and still have $3000 - 150 = 2850$ on hand by week 5. As a result, the company should release a work order for $7000 - 2850 = 4150$ metal casings during week 4.

Since two pocket clasps are used for each metal casing, the 4150-casing work order release will create a gross requirement for $4150 \times 2 = 8300$ clasps during week 4. As Figure 13.8d indicates, considering scheduled purchase receipts and stock on hand, this gross generates a net requirement of 5250 items in week 4. Now, Paper Symbol purchases the pocket clasps, and the supplier requires a two-week lead time. Therefore, the company must plan to release a 5250-clasp purchase order during week 2.

This system develops a work and purchase order plan that will provide necessary components at the times required to support the production schedule for the final product. Such a system is called **material requirements planning (MRP)**. The MRP process is summarized in Table 13.17.

Even in this simple illustration, you can see that the MRP process involves a large number of detailed calculations. In more complicated situations involving many products and parts, it is practically impossible to keep track manually of each item's production and inventory status. Until the development of large-scale computers, the sheer volume of calculations prohibited the effective implementation of MRP systems. Today, a number of firms, including IBM, Honeywell, and Burroughs, offer MRP computer software packages. Honeywell's IMS system [12] is a typical package. Companies can use these standard packages or develop their own computer programs.

OTHER CONSIDERATIONS In Example 13.7, Paper Symbol always planned work and purchase order releases for the exact net requirements. For example, Table 13.16 shows that there is a 1400-pen net requirement in week 4, and the corresponding planned order release (during week 3) is exactly the same quantity. Similarly, the 7000-pen net requirement in week 7 becomes a 7000-item planned release during week 6. This approach is called lot-for-lot ordering. As Figure 13.8 demonstrates, the company also uses lot-for-lot ordering of the pen components.

On the other hand, it may be economical or convenient to plan work and purchase order release quantities in excess of net requirements. For example, to avoid an extra order or setup charge, Paper Symbol might consider combining the 1400- and 7000-pen planned releases. This process

Table 13.17 Summary of the MRP Process

1. Using product forecasts and customer orders, develop a master production schedule (MPS). The MPS identifies the gross requirements for the finished product in each time period.
2. Using data from the inventory master file (IMF), identify the scheduled receipts and stock on hand for the finished product in each time period.
3. Compute the net requirement for the finished product in each time period. The net requirement = gross requirement − scheduled receipts − cumulative stock on hand. If receipts and/or stock exceeds the gross requirement, set the net requirement equal to zero.
4. Plan a work order for the finished product during each time period in which there is a positive net requirement. The quantity of the work order should be at least as large as the net requirement.
5. Plan the timing of the work order release for the finished product by subtracting the lead time from the time period in which the positive net requirement occurs.
6. Use the bill of materials (BOM) to identify the structured parts list for the finished product.
7. Using planned order releases for the finished good (level 0), the BOM, and the IMF, develop the work and purchase plan for each major (level 1) component assembly. Level 0 planned order releases identify the gross requirements for level 1 components in each time period. Level 1 net requirements and planned releases can be computed in a manner analogous to steps 3 through 5.
8. Using planned releases for level 1 components, the BOM, and the IMF, develop the work and purchase plan for each level 2 component in each time period.
9. Continue "cascading" through the BOM levels in a manner analogous to steps 7 and 8 until planned order releases have been issued for all component materials and assemblies.

of combining orders or setups, called lot sizing, should balance the costs of ordering and holding inventory. Many lot-sizing techniques are available. Tersine [27, ch. 3] discusses some, including the Wagner/Whitin, part period, and Silver/Meal algorithms and the EOQ and EPQ methods. J. R. Biggs [2] and Senju and Fujita [23] present others.

It is also important to recognize that the Q/P and MRP systems are complementary rather than competitive systems. As M. J. Liberatore [17] and J. M. A. Tanchoco and others [25] demonstrate, each approach has its own place in a firm's inventory management system. A company can use a Q or P system to manage end items and an MRP approach for components. In addition, as just noted, the firm may find it economical to use the EOQ/EPQ methods for lot sizing of planned order releases.

Another important aspect of MRP is the flexibility inherent in the system. The system maintains information on all items in production and inventory. Hence, when there are unexpected machine breakdowns or other delays, management can use this information to replan end item and component work and purchase schedules. It might also be possible to compress lead times by expediting items.

Finally, there are implementation considerations. An MRP system requires accurate MPS, IMF, and BOM data files, management participation and support, and user knowledge of the method's role and benefits. As C. J. Teplitz [26] discusses, it will be difficult to implement the system effectively unless these requirements are met. Even then, the development of an MRP system can be an expensive and time-consuming project. Thus, the firm must balance these considerations against the potential significant benefits before deciding whether or not to implement this approach.

SUMMARY In this chapter we have seen how quantitative methods can assist managers in formulating sound inventory policies. We began by defining the nature of inventory as an idle stock of raw materials, capital, labor, equipment, work in process, and/or finished goods. We also reviewed the business and economic functions performed by these idle stocks and identified the resulting procurement, ordering/setup, carrying/holding, and shortage expenses.

We considered a fundamental inventory situation and developed a method for determining the optimal order quantity, timing, and frequency. The basic analysis was then expanded to include the decision considerations of quantity discounts, planned shortages, production situations, and risk and uncertainty. These approaches were summarized in Table 13.9. It was noted that these approaches involve a fixed order quantity, or Q, system for inventory planning and control. In such a system, the company continually monitors inventory transactions and then places an order of fixed size whenever the stock level reaches its reorder point. We also discussed the fixed order interval, or P, system of inventory management. In this approach, the inventory level is reviewed at equally spaced, predetermined intervals. At each review, management counts the available stock and orders the amount necessary to reach a target inventory level. Each system (and its hybrids) has its own advantages, disadvantages, and areas of application. The ABC classification method is also an effective device for selective inventory planning and control in Q or P systems.

Basic Q and P systems assume that there is a continuous and independent demand for the item. The last section of the chapter presented inventory systems designed for situations in which these assumptions are not valid. Typical cases involve items that cannot be carried in inventory from period to period (like seasonal or perishable merchandise) or that have an uncertain demand. Under these circumstances, management places only a single order at the start of the relevant period; hence, the objective is to find the optimal order quantity. Table 13.14 summarized a procedure for doing so.

Another type of situation involves items that have related demands (like the components of a finished product). In this case, completion of the end item cannot even begin until the required inputs are available in the correct amounts at the right time. The objective is to develop a work and purchase order release plan that accounts for the demand dependency. This objective can be accomplished with material requirements planning (MRP). Table 13.17 summarized the process.

Inventory activities can be an extremely expensive phase of a firm's operation. Hence, it is important for managers to make correct inventory decisions. Since quantitative models can help decision makers develop sound inventory policies, these techniques offer a potential source for substantial cost savings.

Glossary

ABC (Pareto) system A selective control approach that classifies inventory into three groups: A, B, and C. Class A, which receives the most management attention, contains the few items with the largest value. Class C, which requires little control, contains the bulk of items with the smallest value. Class B, between the extremes, receives moderate management attention.

backorder A customer order that is filled from future purchases rather than from inventory on hand.

bill of materials (BOM) A structured parts list that shows exactly how the finished product is actually put together.

buffer (safety stock) Extra inventory held specifically to reduce shortages resulting from a larger-than-expected demand during lead time.

carrying (holding) costs The expenses associated with financing, physically handling, storing, and maintaining inventory.

economic lot size The production quantity that minimizes total inventory-related costs in the EPQ model.

economic order quantity The order size that minimizes total inventory costs in the EOQ model.

fixed order interval (P) system A planning and control approach in which management periodically reviews available stock and then orders the amount necessary to reach a target inventory level. The target provides enough items to satisfy demand during the delivery lead time plus the interval between orders.

fixed order quantity (Q) system A planning and control approach in which management continually reviews available stock and then places an order of fixed size whenever the inventory level reaches its reorder point.

inventory Idle stocks of raw materials, capital, labor, equipment, work in process, or finished goods and services.

inventory cycle time The period between the placing of two consecutive orders.

inventory master file (IMF) Detailed records identifying the stock on hand, amounts previously committed to production, quantities on order with suppliers, and lead times.

lead time The period between the placing of an order and its receipt.

master production schedule (MPS) A time-phased plan that identifies how many finished items are to be produced and when.

material requirements planning (MRP) A system that develops a work and purchase order plan providing necessary components at the times required to support a production schedule for a finished product.

ordering (setup) costs The expenses associated with placing

an order or physically preparing the production apparatus.

procurement costs The expenses associated with purchasing or manufacturing items for demand and inventory.

reorder point The inventory level at which a new order should be placed.

service level The percentage of customer demands that is satisfied from inventory.

stockout (shortage) costs The expenses incurred when available inventory is insufficient to fully satisfy demand.

References

1. Austin, L. M. "Project EOQ: A Success Story in Implementing Academic Research." *Interfaces* (August 1977): 1.

2. Biggs, J. R. "Heuristic Lot-Sizing and Sequencing Rules in a Multistage Production-Inventory System." *Decision Sciences* (January 1979): 96.

3. Brown, R. G. *Materials Management Systems—A Modular Library.* New York: Wiley, 1977.

4. Burman, H., and J. Thomas. "Inventory Decisions Under Inflationary Conditions." *Decision Sciences* (January 1977): 151.

5. Constantinides, G. M., and S. F. Richard. "Existence of Optimal Simple Policies for Discounted-Cost Inventory and Cash Management in Continuous Time." *Operations Research* (July–August 1978): 620.

6. Daellenbach, H. G. "A Model of a Multi-Product Two-Stage Inventory System with Limited Intermediate Bulk Storage Capacity." *Management Science* (August 1977): 1314.

7. Dave, U., and M. C. Jaiswal. "A Discrete-in-Time Probabilistic Inventory Model for Deteriorating Items." *Decision Sciences* (January 1980): 110.

8. Dumas, M. B., and M. Rabinowitz. "Policies for Reducing Blood Wastage in Hospital Blood Banks." *Management Science* (June 1977): 1124.

9. Flowers, A. D., and J. B. O'Neill. "An Application of Classical Inventory Analysis to a Spare Parts Inventory." *Interfaces* (February 1978): 76.

10. Fuchs, J. H. *Computerized Inventory Control Systems.*

Englewood Cliffs, N.J.: Prentice-Hall, 1978.

11. Green, J. H. *Production and Inventory Control Handbook.* New York: McGraw-Hill, 1970.

12. Honeywell, Inc. *Manufacturing IMS/66 (Extended) Systems Handbook.* DE 80, Rev. 1. Minneapolis: June 1977.

13. IBM Corporation. *INFOREM: Principles of Inventory Management: Application Description.* 2d ed. GE 20-0571-1. Armonk, N.Y.: May 1978.

14. Johnson, L. A., and D. C. Montgomery. *Operations Research in Production Planning, Scheduling, and Inventory Control.* New York: Wiley, 1974.

15. Larson, S. *Inventory Systems and Controls Handbook.* Englewood Cliffs, N.J.: Prentice-Hall, 1976.

16. Lewis, C. D. *Demand Analysis and Inventory Control.* Lexington, Mass.: Lexington Books, 1975.

17. Liberatore, M. J. "Using MRP and EOQ/Safety Stock for Raw Materials Inventory Control." *Interfaces* (February 1979): 1.

18. Lipman, B. E. *How to Control and Reduce Inventory.* Englewood Cliffs, N.J.: Prentice-Hall, 1975.

19. Nahmias, N. "On Ordering Perishable Inventory When Both Demand and Lifetime Are Random." *Management Science* (September 1977): 82.

20. Orlicky, J. *Materials Requirements Planning.* New York: McGraw-Hill, 1975.

21. Peterson, R., and E. A. Silver. *Decision Systems for Inventory Management and Production Planning.* New York: Wiley, 1979.

22. Rosenshine, M., and D. Obee. "Analysis of a Standing Order Inventory with Emergency Orders." *Operations Research* (November–December 1976): 1143.

23. Senju, S., and S. Fujita. "An Applied Procedure for Determining the Economic Lot Sizes of Multiple Products." *Decision Sciences* (July 1980): 503.

24. Stohr, E. A. "Information Systems for Observing Inventory Levels." *Operations Research* (March–April 1979): 242.

25. Tanchoco, J. M. A., et al. "Economic Order Quantities Based on Unit-Load and Material Handling Considerations." *Decision Sciences* (July 1980): 514.

26. Teplitz, C. J. "Is Your Organization Ready for MRP? A Case Study." *Interfaces* (June 1980): 103.

27. Tersine, R. J. *Material Management and Inventory Control.* New York: Elsevier-North Holland Publishing Company, 1976.

28. Wagner, H. M. "Research Portfolio for Inventory Management and Production Planning Systems." *Operations Research* (May–June 1980): 445.

Thought Exercises 1. Identify the nature and function of inventory in each of the following situations:
   a. A police department's officer roster at a given time of day
   b. A bank's monthly cash flow
   c. A newsstand's sales of a sports magazine
   d. Ships arriving at a seaport
   e. Consumer demand for electricity

2. Identify the appropriate inventory-related costs in each of the following situations:
   a. A U.S. wheat farmer selling in international markets
   b. A drugstore selling brand-name aspirin
   c. A professional football team's equipment manager stocking spare equipment
   d. Your decision to keep a supply of toothpaste on hand
   e. A military ordinance supply battalion servicing a domestic training division

3. Refer to Example 13.3. What is Technical's reorder point in this situation? Is this point higher or lower than the corresponding value in the basic EOQ situation (Example 13.1)? Explain. Develop a general expression for the reorder point in the EOQ model with backorders. Figure 13.4 may be helpful in your derivation.

4. The Broadmor Department Store operates an automotive repair shop. One of its most popular requests is the brake reline special. Service records indicate that the shop does an average of four relines on each of the 300 annual days of operation. Although Broadmor cannot stock the service, it is possible to inventory the parts necessary to perform the special. In this respect, each reline requires four packages of brake shoes (each package contains two brake shoes). It costs Broadmor $2 to stock each package of brake shoes for a year and $12 to place an order with its supplier.

   Top management believes that inventory systems are important decision-making aids and has frequently used an EOQ policy. However, shortages have always been considered "bad" policy, even though most Broadmor customers have demonstrated a willingness to wait for service. Recently, there has been increased pressure for cost reduction, and the shop manager has proposed a backordering policy for the brake special. He estimates that rescheduling of customers and other additional expenses will be $4 per backorder per year.

   a. Do you think that Broadmor should accept the proposal? Explain.
   b. Suppose that top management will tolerate no more than 20% of the order quantity on backorder. In addition, the company wants to make sure that no customer will wait more than 7 days for service. Will these constraints change your recommendation? Explain.

5. Science Associates (SA) has decided to begin processing its own data rather than contracting with an outside vendor. The company's projects create 1000 data processing jobs per month and involve a setup cost of $80 per job. Each completed job awaiting project usage is stored on a tape at an annual expense of $20. Once the system is operating, it can process 2500 jobs per month. The company normally operates approximately 300 working days per year. It takes 8 days to set up each data processing job.

   a. What is SA's reorder point? Is this point higher or lower than you would expect in the EOQ situation? Explain.

   b. Develop a general expression for the reorder point in the EPQ situation. Figure 13.5 may be helpful in your derivation.

6. Most of the basic EOQ/EPQ models presented in the chapter assumed that the lead time L was less than the cycle time T. This assumption may not be valid in practice. What would be the effect on the reorder point R if $L > T$? Explain. Develop general expressions for the reorder point in the EOQ, EOQ with backorders, and EPQ models when $L > T$. Figures 13.3, 13.4, and 13.5 may aid your derivation.

7. Each week, Market Fair buys bananas for $8.50 a crate and sells them for $12.50. The $8.50 cost includes inventory procurement and holding expenses. It costs $15 to place an order.

   Any surplus crates are sold at a discount price of $5.50 apiece at the end of the week. A customer will not come back if Market Fair is out of stock. Thus, a shortage results in lost profit (from the bananas and other items in the store). The market manager has assessed this penalty cost at $5 per crate. Of this penalty, $4 represents the banana profit and $1 results from ill will and lost income from other items.

   Observations show that sales over the past 50 weeks have been as follows:

Crates Sold	Number of Weeks
78	3
79	13
80	19
81	12
82	3

Since the market for bananas is relatively stable, the store assumes that this sales pattern will continue.

After analyzing the data, Zane Tirp, the assistant produce manager, recommends an order quantity of 81 crates. He feels that this policy will maximize expected profits at $301.14. Greta Smithfield, the accountant, has done an incremental analysis. According to her calculations, an order of 80 crates has a better

chance of balancing the penalties from over- and underordering.
  Can you explain how each person arrived at his or her
recommendation? There have been no errors in computing expected
profits. Is it possible to reconcile their differences? What order
quantity would you recommend? Explain. (*Hint:* Closely examine
the market manager's assessment of penalty costs.)

8. Explain why you agree or disagree with each of the following
   statements:

   a. In the EOQ model with quantity discounts, the optimal solution
      will never involve a purchase cost that leads to a Q^* larger than
      necessary to qualify for the discount.
   b. Since discounts encourage larger order sizes, management should
      expect a higher reorder point in the quantity discount EOQ
      model (as compared to the basic EOQ model).
   c. In the EPQ model, average inventory is a fraction of the
      corresponding level in the EOQ formulation because the
      production quantity does not go into inventory at one point in
      time.
   d. Safety stocks can be expected to increase inventory-related
      expenses.
   e. Safety stocks will decrease as the service level increases.
   f. Since the demand for components depends on the sales of the
      finished product, inventory levels for all items are generally higher
      in an MRP system.
   g. MRP is not really appropriate for service industries.

**Technique
Exercises**

1. A large business firm buys a machine component for $10 a box.
   Approximately two boxes are used every week. Machines are idle
   for maintenance 2 weeks of every year. The ordering cost is $1 and
   the company estimates annual carrying expenses at 20% of the
   purchase cost per box.

   a. Develop the procurement, ordering, carrying, and total
      inventory-related cost expressions for this situation.
   b. Determine the economic order quantity and the order timing and
      frequency.
   c. What are the resulting costs?

2. The Sharp Plume Men's Shop sells 1000 Supreme brand dress shirts
   a year. Order cost is $20 and inventory carrying expenses are 30%
   of the value of a shirt. Also, the supplier offers a generous discount.
   The price list is as follows:

Quantity	Purchase Price ($) per Shirt
0–99	9.00
100–199	8.00
200–499	7.50
500 and over	7.40

Find the economic order quantity that results in the smallest total cost. Then determine the order timing and frequency. Show all your calculations. Did you notice anything unusual in your EOQ calculations for the first purchase price category? Explain.

3. Flora Industries distributes large industrial cranes on the East Coast. Demand is known to be 100 units per year. The company can order cranes anytime and delivery from the plant is instantaneous. There is a fixed ordering expense of $1000, and each crane can be stored in the company warehouse for $200 per month. Although customers will wait for an order, the delay creates additional expenses of $400 per crane per month.
   a. Determine the economic order quantity, the order frequency, and the resulting minimum cost per cycle.
   b. Determine how many units will be supplied late each cycle.

4. The R&J Bottling Company has a forecasted annual demand of 50,000 cases for its specialty soft drink. R&J operates 250 days annually and can produce 400 cases daily. There is a $300 setup cost associated with each production run, and yearly holding costs are estimated at $12 per case.
   a. Compute the optimal production lot size and resulting time between runs.
   b. Determine the cost associated with the production plan.

5. Refer to Example 13.5. Demonstrate that the procedure outlined in Table 13.8 leads to fewer shortages and a lower cost than the 92.59% service level. Show all your calculations.

6. A large retail chain store sells its own brand of large-screen television systems. The M4-J system has a wholesale cost of $1200, an ordering expense of $40 per request, and annual carrying costs equal to 25% of the value of the average inventory.
   Demand is uncertain, but past sales show the following pattern:

Weekly Demand	Number of Weeks
5	10
10	25
15	40
20	15
25	10

The store operates 5 days per week and 50 weeks per year. There is a supply lead time of 2 days.
   a. Compute the average annual demand, the resulting economic order quantity, the average number of orders, and the cycle time.
   b. Determine the probability distribution for lead time demand.

    c. If management will tolerate no more than five stockouts per year, what is the reorder point and resulting safety stock?

    d. If there is a $150 penalty cost associated with each stockout, what is the optimal reorder point and resulting safety stock?

7. You are given the following profit data and corresponding demand probabilities:

	Demand				
	125	126	127	128	129
	Probability of Demand				
Order Quantity	.10	.30	.40	.15	.05
125	$1125	$1095	$1065	$1035	$1005
126	1085	1150	1120	1090	1060
127	1045	1110	1175	1145	1115
128	1005	1070	1135	1200	1170
129	965	1030	1095	1160	1225

    a. First use expected values and then incremental analysis to find the most profitable order quantity.

    b. Compare the results. Comment.

8. A retail outlet sells a seasonal product for $20 a unit. The product costs $15 a unit. All units not sold during the regular season are sold for one-quarter of the retail price at the end-of-season clearance sale. Assume that the demand for the product is normally distributed with $u = 300$ and $\sigma = 50$.

    a. What is the recommended order quantity? What is the probability of a stockout?

    b. Suppose that the owner wants to keep customers happy so that they will return to the store later. Hence, when there is a stockout, he believes there is a $2 ill will cost. Now what is the recommended order quantity? What is the corresponding probability of a stockout?

9. Refer to Example 13.7. Complete Paper Symbol's material requirements plan (MRP) by developing the BOM explosion for the entire shaft assembly and the metal shaft portion of the top assembly.

10. You are given the following master production schedule (MPS) for finished product A:

Week	1	2	3	4	5	6	7	8	9	10
Demand	0	0	2500	0	1000	0	0	0	3000	500

The corresponding bill of materials (BOM) is given in the following diagram:

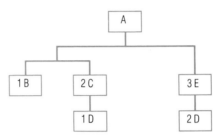

Data from the inventory master file is as follows:

			Scheduled Receipts in Week									
Item	Lead Time	Stock on Hand	1	2	3	4	5	6	7	8	9	10
A	1 week	1500	500									
B	1 week	1000				500				500		
C	2 weeks	3000	200									
D	2 weeks	0	100									100
E	1 week	500				200						

Assuming a lot-for-lot ordering policy, determine the planned work and purchase order MRP plan for the finished part and each component.

Applications Exercises

1. Big Z Discount House has experienced a relatively constant demand for 4000 Quick Start batteries each month. The store buys the Quick Start from a large national manufacturer for $10 each. It takes the manufacturer 3 days (1/2 week) to fill an order. Big Z can place an order for $10, and it costs 20% of the average inventory value to carry a battery for a month.

   a. How many Quick Starts should Big Z order at a time to minimize total inventory-related costs?
   b. What is the resulting ordering cost? Carrying cost? Total cost?
   c. What is the length of time between orders?
   d. How many batteries should be in inventory when Big Z places an order?
   e. Suppose that the cost of placing an order increases to $15 and that the price of the Quick Start rises by $10. How will these changes affect Big Z's inventory policy?

2. Talton Corporation is the manufacturer of an agricultural tractor that currently sells for $12,000. There is a relatively constant and continuous demand for 900 tractors per year. Until last year, the company had very little competition. Then several foreign firms entered the market and Talton's sales began to drop. In an effort to keep its market share, Talton did not increase prices even though inflation increased operating costs by 14%. Although the policy was successful in maintaining sales, the company's earnings decreased significantly. As a result, management is now considering proposals to reduce expenses.

   Talton has the capacity to manufacture 100 tractors per month at a unit cost of $9600. In addition, it costs $15,000 to set up the production apparatus. Merchandise awaiting distribution is stored at various places in the firm's warehousing system. Considering warehousing operating costs, obsolescence, theft, finance charges, and other factors, Talton's accounting department assigns 20% of the unit cost per tractor for annual storage expenses.

   At present, the company produces at a rate that exactly meets the demand. Management has commissioned a task force to study methods to reduce costs. After some deliberation, the group has identified two options for dealing with the problem:

   ♦ Change the frequency of production to produce the most economic lot sizes.

   ♦ Buy tractor components on the foreign market and assemble them at the plant.

   The most reliable and economical foreign supply source can ship the parts in lots of up to fifty tractors within 1 week. This shipment schedule is essentially the same as Talton's production lead time. Each set of foreign components will ordinarily cost $5000. However, the supplier will offer a 10% discount for orders of fifty or more tractors. Although the components do not create any setup expenses, it will cost Talton $5000 for assembly work. Also, the company will have to prepare design specifications, place the order, and inspect incoming components. These activities will involve a $1000 expense per order.

What option will lead to the smallest possible cost? What are the resulting expenses?

3. People's Credit Union receives cash deposits gradually over time during its "accumulation phase" and uses the money to make loans and other investments until the funds are depleted. The cycle is repeated continually over time. Historically, a typical branch has received $5000 in deposits per working day and made loans and investments at the rate of $4000 per day. People's Credit Union operates 200 days yearly.

People's Credit Union pays 6% annual interest on the average cash deposits and estimates that each accumulation phase involves $1200 in operating expenses. It takes 30 days for the finance committee to evaluate and act on the various investment options.

a. How many dollars in cash deposits should the Union receive each cycle to minimize costs?
b. What are the resulting costs?
c. How often should the Union repeat the cycle?
d. How long will the accumulation phase take?
e. When should People's Credit Union begin the accumulation phase?

4. The Cloverville Sanitation Department conducts a 6-week on-the-job training program for all its engineer trainees. Each session costs $30,000 for instructors, equipment, and materials, regardless of the class size. After completing the program, trainees are paid $1500 per month but do not work until a full-time position is open. Cloverville views this $1500 as an expense that is necessary to maintain a supply of qualified engineers available for immediate service.

Although the city needs an average of 120 newly trained sanitation engineers each year, the various needs of ongoing projects result in a fluctuating monthly demand. Past data indicate that the pattern follows a normal probability distribution with an average demand for 15 engineers during the training period. The standard deviation is 2.

When the program does not generate sufficient engineers, the city must contract with private firms for required services. It costs $2000 per month for each privately contracted engineer. Amy Cuter, the training program director, believes that the city should plan for the potential shortage by increasing the class size. Slide Rule, the chief engineer, thinks that a better approach would be to create a buffer stock of newly trained people by running more frequent training sessions.

a. What are the least costly class sizes under each person's proposal?
b. How many shortages can be expected under each plan?
c. What is the training session timing and frequency under each plan?
d. Which alternative would you recommend? Explain.

5. Jock's Sport Shop is a local newsstand dealing exclusively in sports magazines and newspapers. Based on past experience, Jock Hoop, the proprietor, knows that the weekly demand for *Sports Esquire* (his most popular magazine) is as follows:

Weekly Demand	Number of Weeks
20	5
40	15
60	10
80	20
100	30
120	10
140	10

Each *Sports Esquire* costs Jock 20 cents. If the magazine is not sold at the end of the week, he can return the issue and get 10 cents from the publisher. Jock sells the magazine for 50 cents. When he is out of stock, customers go elsewhere. Jock estimates this shortage cost at 50 cents per magazine. Lead time for ordering is 2 days, and the estimated carrying cost is 50% of the purchase expense. The stand is open 5 days a week.

a. How many magazines should Jock have in stock when he places an order?

b. What is the safety stock at that reorder point?

c. How many magazines should Jock order each week?

d. What is the expected shortage cost? Carrying cost? Order cost? Total cost?

6. Racine Corporation is a large producer of a commercial-sized pencil sharpener. Engineering and manufacturing specifications for its component assemblies and raw materials are summarized in the following table:

Component Requirements	Source	Lead Time
1 cutting instrument assembly	Manufactured	1 week
2 three-inch welded, grooved cutting panels	Manufactured	2 weeks
1 shavings container assembly	Manufactured	1 week
4 one-half-inch screws	Purchased	2 weeks
1 metal face	Purchased	3 weeks
2 welded metal sides	Manufactured	1 week

Based on product forecasts and customer orders, management estimates that approximately 8000 sharpeners will be needed during week 3 of the current twelve-week production schedule. Another 12,000 will be required during week 5, 7000 in week 9, and 3000 during week 11.

At the present time (week 1), Racine has 6000 sharpeners, 4000 instrument assemblies, and 1500 container assemblies in stock. Also, there is an inventory of 800 cutting panels, 12,000 screws, 6000 faces, and 900 sides. Outstanding production orders will provide another 5000 sharpeners, 1000 container assemblies, and 1200 sides during week 1. Similarly, outstanding purchase orders will supply 20,000 screws in week 5 and 500 faces during week 2 of the current production schedule.

Assuming that management will always request the exact component quantities required, what purchasing and manufacturing plan is necessary to support finished product demand? That is, how many sharpeners, assemblies, and raw materials of each type should Racine manufacture or purchase each week of the production schedule?

Racine can purchase a package of four screws for 10 cents and a metal face for 25 cents. A purchase order involves a $20 expense. Including the cost of materials, the company can manufacture a metal side for 50 cents and a grooved panel for 75 cents. It costs 30 cents to assemble a container, 40 cents for the cutting assembly work, and 15 cents to assemble the finished sharpener. Each manufacturing or assembly order involves an expense of $10. Annual inventory storage expenses are estimated at 10% of the manufactured value of the stock on hand. The company operates fifty weeks a year.

What is the total inventory-related cost of your recommended work and purchase plan?

CASE: Willington Hospital

The northeastern city of Willington has a relatively small hospital that provides essential medical services to the town and surrounding county. It is financed primarily through private funds. The organizational structure is shown in Figure 13.9.

Recently, the hospital has received a federal research grant to administer an experimental heart disease treatment program. As part of the program, Willington will use its outpatient and inpatient facilities to administer specified treatments on an experimental group of individuals in twelve-week intervals. Specifically, the program will send the hospital 50 outpatients during week 4, 100 during week 6, 150 during

week 7, 100 during week 10, and 50 during week 11 of each interval. In addition, there will be 150 inpatients during week 3, 200 during week 5, 350 during week 8, and 300 during week 12 of each interval.

The program specifies the medical and institutional support required for each type of patient. These requirements are summarized in Table 13.18. In anticipation of the start of the program, Willington Hospital has "stocked" 12,000 capsules and 200 beds. Also, the hospital manager has scheduled 50 administrative hours, 150 doctor hours, 200 nurse hours, and 50 orderly hours of effort during week 1 of the program. In addition, she has

scheduled the receipt of 5000 capsules, 100 beds, and 1000 special meals during that same week. People effort unused in one week will be rescheduled in the same amount for the subsequent week. All medical and administrative services can be provided with only one week's notice.

Federal policy restricts resource expenses as shown in Table 13.19. According to the regulations, the hospital also must order the exact people effort and corresponding services (X-rays, blood tests, and beds) required. On the other hand, Willington is directed to order the economic order quantities for the special meals and prescription capsules. However,

Figure 13.9 Organizational Structure of Willington Hospital

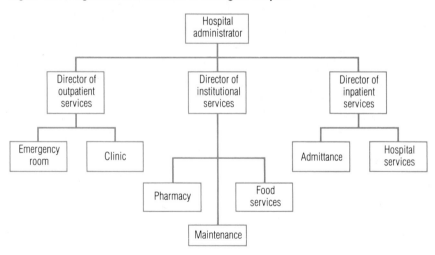

Table 13.18 Resource Requirements

Resources needed to support 1 outpatient for 1 week:

  2 hours of doctor effort
  3 X-rays
  10 prescription capsules
  1 blood test
  3 hours of nurse effort
  2 administrative hours

Resources needed to support 1 inpatient for 1 week:

  1 bed
  20 special diet meals
  7 hours of orderly effort
  6 hours of doctor effort
  9 X-rays
  30 prescription capsules
  3 blood tests
  12 hours of nurse effort
  6 administrative hours

Table 13.19 Federal Restrictions on Resource Expenses

Administrative effort	
Managerial	$30 per hour
Orderly	$7 per hour
Medical effort	
Doctor	$100 per hour
Nurse	$10 per hour
Physical facilities	
Bed	$560 per week
Services	
X-ray	$20
Blood test	$15
Special meal	$5
Prescription capsule	20 cents
Other expenses	
Ordering a service	$25 per order
Storing an item	15.6% of the item cost per year

shortages will not be permitted.

At times in the past, Willington Hospital has experienced significant patient service problems. It seems that medical staff, facilities, equipment, and support personnel were not always in the right place at the right time. As a result, operations did not run efficiently and an expediter often had to be called in. Although Willington was selected because of its technical expertise, the government would like to avoid the previous operational problems and potential expense for the experimental

program. Consequently, the hospital administrator has been asked to prepare a preliminary report outlining the following:

♦ The work order plan necessary to support the experimental program in the first twelve-week interval

♦ The corresponding cost for administering the plan

The plan will then be audited by the federal agency's operations analysis division.

1. If you were in charge of this audit, what plan would you expect from Willington?

2. How much should the hospital receive in funding for the experimental program?

Chapter 14
Queuing Theory

Most individuals in today's society must occasionally wait in line for some sort of service. It can occur at a bus stop, gas station, supermarket checkout counter, or at a variety of other locations. Most people will tolerate the inconvenience for a short while. Then the size of the line or the wait discourages them and they leave.

Managers realize that long lines mean that customers are not being serviced properly. More importantly, the decision maker recognizes that poor service creates consumer dissatisfaction and potential lost present and future sales. The company can reduce the waiting lines by adding more service facilities. However, the additional facilities will require more personnel, equipment, and space. Management, then, must balance the resulting additional expenses with the benefits from better customer service.

The problem of waiting lines, or queues, has received serious attention for a long time. As early as 1909, the Danish telephone engineer, A. K. Erlang, analyzed the queuing problems callers encountered at a telephone switchboard. Since then, many quantitative approaches have been developed to measure the operating characteristics and costs of waiting lines. These methods, often referred to as **queuing theory**, are designed to assist the manager in formulating an effective customer service system.

This chapter presents basic queuing theory and some useful extensions. In the first section, we discuss the nature and structure of a queuing system. The presentation identifies the diverse characteristics and behavior of customers and servers and shows how the differences affect the nature of the problems. The second section examines the elements of queuing analysis. A fundamental model is presented, its characteristics are identified, system performance measures are calculated and interpreted, and alternative service designs are evaluated. The final section extends the analysis to other decision situations, including systems with a limited number of customers, restricted service space, and multiple servers.

Figure 14.1 Typical Queuing Situation

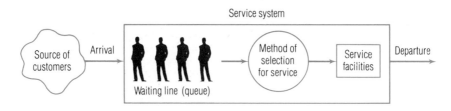

STRUCTURE OF A QUEUING SYSTEM

In a typical queuing situation, customers arrive at a service system, enter a waiting line, receive service, and then leave. As Figure 14.1 illustrates, the process involves several key elements, including source of customers, arrival process, waiting line (queue), method of selecting customers from the queue, service process, and departure process.

SOURCE POPULATION

A customer is any person or object in need of service. Depending on the nature of service, customers, or potential arrivals, can be generated from a variety of sources. Table 14.1 presents some typical examples. Where appropriate, references are identified in brackets.

Almost all sources involve a finite or limited number of customers. In some cases, like the maintenance of a few machines, the number is relatively small. Other circumstances, such as telephone calls in a telephone system, have very large source populations. When there are many (as a rule of thumb, more than 100) customers, the source can be treated as if it were infinite in size.

The number of potential customers will influence the arrival process for the service system. Hence, it is important to identify whether a source population is finite or infinite.

ARRIVAL PROCESS

The arrival process describes the manner in which customers reach the service system. There are several important characteristics involved in this process, including form and composition. In this respect, customers may arrive in batches (for instance, a family attending a sporting event) or individually (such as a ship docking at a port).

Another aspect involves the timing of arrivals. In some situations, customers arrive at a service facility on a scheduled basis. For example, dental clinics usually schedule nonemergency patients by appointment. In most situations, however, customers arrive haphazardly without prior notification.

Table 14.1 Typical Examples of Queuing Situations

Area of Application	Service Facility	Customer	Source Population
Production	Materials storeroom Shared equipment [23] Maintenance shop	Worker Mechanic Machine	Factory personnel Repair personnel Factory equipment
Marketing	Store clerk Car wash Sports stadium	Shopper Automobile Fan	People in service area "Dirty" cars Fans in area
Finance	Stockbroker Posting clerk [4] Bank teller	Investor Financial transaction Account holder	People with surplus funds All potential transactions Bank customers
Transportation	Hotel [19] Ship-loading dock Airport runway Subway train	Traveler Empty ship Airplane Commuter	Potential travelers Ship traffic Airline traffic City residents
Public Services	Library [16] Social worker Police unit [13] Courtroom	Reader Welfare recipient Crime Trial	Residents in area People on welfare Crimes in territory Potential cases
Private Services	Ambulance [22] Lawyer Tennis court [7] Telephone line [14]	Emergency patient Client Player Telephone call	Residents in area People with legal problems Potential players Potential telephone calls

Two measures can be used to describe the arrival process. One, referred to as the **arrival rate**, gives the number of arrivals per unit of time. Suppose, for example, that 960 automobiles reach a turnpike tollbooth in an 8-hour period. Then the arrival rate is $960/8 = 120$ per hour or 2 per minute. An alternative measure, called the **interarrival time**, gives the interval between two consecutive arrivals. For instance, since two automobiles reach the tollbooth in a minute, there is $1/2 = .5$ minute, or 30 seconds, between arrivals. Notice that the interarrival time $(1/2)$ is the reciprocal of the arrival rate (2).

When service is provided on a scheduled basis, the arrival rate and interarrival time is fixed. In unscheduled situations, however, customers typically arrive in a random pattern. That is, each arrival is not affected by preceding arrivals. Instead of being constant, then, there is a range of possible values for either the arrival rate or the interarrival time. Hence, in these cases, it is necessary to describe arrivals with a probability distribution. Example 14.1 illustrates.

EXAMPLE 14.1 Parts Storeroom Operations

Titan Industries has a central parts storeroom for its Mineola plant. Employees come to the storeroom to pick up needed supplies when necessary at various times during the working day. Management has observed the process and found that it is not possible to predict the exact time of arrival at the center. Furthermore, the time when an employee reaches the storeroom seems to be unaffected by preceding and future arrivals, the hour of the day, and the day of the week. A portion of the pattern is illustrated in Figure 14.2. By recording the employee arrival times at the storeroom over a period of 100 hours, the company obtained the data shown in Table 14.2.

Titan wants to describe the arrival process with some basic summary statistics.

Figure 14.2 Employee Arrivals at the Mineola Plant Storeroom

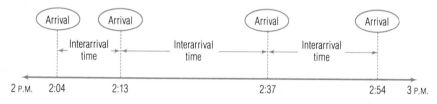

Table 14.2 Employee Arrival Data for the Mineola Storeroom

Employee Arrivals per Hour	Number of Hours	Probability
0	1	1/100 = .01
1	7	7/100 = .07
2	14	14/100 = .14
3	20	20/100 = .20
4	20	20/100 = .20
5	16	16/100 = .16
6	12	12/100 = .12
7	7	7/100 = .07
8	3	3/100 = .03
	100	

In Example 14.1, each employee reaches the parts storeroom in a completely independent manner. The number of arrivals in a specified time interval is unaffected by what happened in previous periods or when the event occurs. In addition, from Figure 14.2, you can see that customers arrive in a random fashion throughout the time period. Also, the number of arrivals increases as the length of the time interval grows. Hence, there is one arrival in the first 5 minutes, 2 during the initial 15 minutes, and so on. In effect, then, it will be extremely rare for more than one customer to arrive in a very small interval of time. Decision scientists have found that two related probability distributions are useful for describing this type of random arrival pattern.

Often, arrival rate probabilities can be accurately provided by the **Poisson distribution**. Let

X = the number of arrivals in a specified time interval

λ = the average, or expected, number of arrivals in the interval

T = the length of the time interval

Then, as R. B. Cooper [5] and G. F. Newell [17] demonstrate, the probability P of a specified arrival rate can be found from this distribution with the following equation:

$$(14.1) \quad P(X) = \frac{e^{-\lambda T}(\lambda T)^X}{X!}$$

The symbol ! represents a factorial, and $e = 2.71828$ (the base of natural logarithms).

Table 14.3 gives the values of e raised to the $-\Phi$ power, where values of Φ are provided between .05 and 10 in increments of .05. Moreover, Φ represents a number such as λT.

For Titan's situation, the length of the time interval is $T = 1$ hour. Management can calculate the average, or expected, arrival rate λ from the data in Table 14.2. Management simply multiplies the number of employee arrivals per hour by the corresponding probability and sums the results:

$$\lambda = 0(.01) + 1(.07) + 2(.14) + 3(.2) + 4(.2)$$
$$+ 5(.16) + 6(.12) + 7(.07) + 8(.03)$$

or

$$\lambda = 4 \text{ arrivals per hour}$$

Thus, if Titan's random arrival pattern follows a Poisson distribution, management can calculate the arrival rate probabilities with the following expression:

$$P(X) = \frac{e^{-4(1)}(4 \times 1)^X}{X!} = \frac{e^{-4}4^X}{X!}$$

For instance, there is a

$$P(X = 0) = \frac{e^{-4}4^0}{0!} = \frac{e^{-4}(1)}{1} = e^{-4}$$

Table 14.3 Values of $e^{-\Phi}$

Φ	$e^{-\Phi}$	Φ	$e^{-\Phi}$	Φ	$e^{-\Phi}$	Φ	$e^{-\Phi}$
0.05	.95123	2.55	.07808	5.05	.00641	7.55	.00053
0.10	.90484	2.60	.07427	5.10	.00610	7.60	.00050
0.15	.86071	2.65	.07065	5.15	.00580	7.65	.00048
0.20	.81873	2.70	.06721	5.20	.00552	7.70	.00045
0.25	.77880	2.75	.06393	5.25	.00525	7.75	.00043
0.30	.74082	2.80	.06081	5.30	.00499	7.80	.00041
0.35	.70469	2.85	.05784	5.35	.00475	7.85	.00039
0.40	.67032	2.90	.05502	5.40	.00452	7.90	.00037
0.45	.63763	2.95	.05234	5.45	.00430	7.95	.00035
0.50	.60653	3.00	.04979	5.50	.00409	8.00	.00034
0.55	.57695	3.05	.04736	5.55	.00389	8.05	.00032
0.60	.54881	3.10	.04505	5.60	.00370	8.10	.00030
0.65	.52205	3.15	.04285	5.65	.00352	8.15	.00029
0.70	.49659	3.20	.04076	5.70	.00335	8.20	.00027
0.75	.47237	3.25	.03877	5.75	.00318	8.25	.00026
0.80	.44933	3.30	.03688	5.80	.00303	8.30	.00025
0.85	.42741	3.35	.03508	5.85	.00288	8.35	.00024
0.90	.40657	3.40	.03337	5.90	.00274	8.40	.00022
0.95	.38674	3.45	.03175	5.95	.00261	8.45	.00021
1.00	.36788	3.50	.03020	6.00	.00248	8.50	.00020
1.05	.34994	3.55	.02872	6.05	.00236	8.55	.00019
1.10	.33287	3.60	.02732	6.10	.00224	8.60	.00018
1.15	.31664	3.65	.02599	6.15	.00213	8.65	.00018
1.20	.30119	3.70	.02472	6.20	.00203	8.70	.00017
1.25	.28650	3.75	.02352	6.25	.00193	8.75	.00016
1.30	.27253	3.80	.02237	6.30	.00184	8.80	.00015
1.35	.25924	3.85	.02128	6.35	.00175	8.85	.00014
1.40	.24660	3.90	.02024	6.40	.00166	8.90	.00014
1.45	.23457	3.95	.01925	6.45	.00158	8.95	.00013
1.50	.22313	4.00	.01832	6.50	.00150	9.00	.00012
1.55	.21225	4.05	.01742	6.55	.00143	9.05	.00012
1.60	.20190	4.10	.01657	6.60	.00136	9.10	.00011
1.65	.19205	4.15	.01576	6.65	.00129	9.15	.00011
1.70	.18268	4.20	.01500	6.70	.00123	9.20	.00010
1.75	.17377	4.25	.01426	6.75	.00117	9.25	.00010
1.80	.16530	4.30	.01357	6.80	.00111	9.30	.00009
1.85	.15724	4.35	.01291	6.85	.00106	9.35	.00009
1.90	.14957	4.40	.01228	6.90	.00101	9.40	.00008
1.95	.14227	4.45	.01168	6.95	.00096	9.45	.00008
2.00	.13534	4.50	.01111	7.00	.00091	9.50	.00007
2.05	.12873	4.55	.01057	7.05	.00087	9.55	.00007
2.10	.12246	4.60	.01005	7.10	.00083	9.60	.00007
2.15	.11648	4.65	.00956	7.15	.00078	9.65	.00006
2.20	.11080	4.70	.00910	7.20	.00075	9.70	.00006
2.25	.10540	4.75	.00865	7.25	.00071	9.75	.00006
2.30	.10026	4.80	.00823	7.30	.00068	9.80	.00006
2.35	.09537	4.85	.00783	7.35	.00064	9.85	.00005
2.40	.09072	4.90	.00745	7.40	.00061	9.90	.00005
2.45	.08629	4.95	.00708	7.45	.00058	9.95	.00005
2.50	.08208	5.00	.00674	7.50	.00055	10.00	.00005

Table 14.4 Poisson Probabilities for Titan's Employee Arrival Process

Employee Arrivals per Hour X	Probability $P(X) = (e^{-4}4^{X})/X!$
0	0.0183
1	0.0733
2	0.1465
3	0.1954
4	0.1953
5	0.1563
6	0.1042
7	0.0596
8	0.0297
9	0.0133
10	0.0053
11	0.0019
12	0.0006
13	0.0002
14	0.0001
	1.0000

chance, or, from Table 14.3, an

$$e^{-4} = .01832$$

chance of 0 employees arriving in an hour of storeroom operation. Similarly, the probability of 1 arrival in an hour is

$$P(X = 1) = \frac{e^{-4}4^{1}}{1!} = \frac{e^{-4}(4)}{1} = .0733$$

By continuing in this manner, the company will get the Poisson probabilities presented in Table 14.4. A comparison of Tables 14.2 and 14.4 shows that the Poisson probabilities (Table 14.4) are almost identical to the actual chances (Table 14.2) for the employee arrival rates. Although Titan may want to try some additional tests, this comparison suggests that the arrival rate at the storeroom can be reasonably described with the Poisson distribution.

There is another important property of the Poisson arrival pattern. Equation (14.1) indicates that there is a

$$P(X = 0) = \frac{e^{-\lambda T}(\lambda T)^{X}}{X!} = \frac{e^{-\lambda T}(\lambda T)^{0}}{0!} = e^{-\lambda T}$$

probability of zero arrivals within the time interval T. Put another way, $e^{-\lambda T}$ represents the chance that the time between arrivals (interarrival

Figure 14.3 Titan's Employee Interarrival Time Probabilities

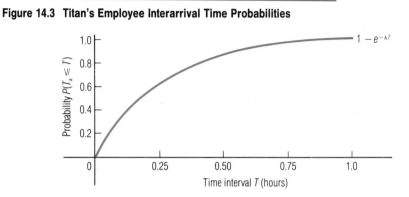

time) will be longer than the interval T. By letting T_a = interarrival time, we can express the relationship as follows:

$$P(X = 0) = P(T_a > T) = e^{-\lambda T}$$

Since all probabilities must sum to 1, there is then a

$$(14.2) \quad P(T_a \leq T) = 1 - e^{-\lambda T}$$

chance that the interarrival time T_a will be no greater than period T. Equation (14.2) provides the cumulative probabilities for the so-called **negative exponential** distribution.

In effect, then, when a queuing system involves a Poisson arrival pattern, the time between arrivals will follow a negative exponential probability distribution. Hence, in Titan's problem, interarrival times will follow a negative exponential distribution with a mean $= 1/\lambda = 1/4 = .25$ hour, or 15 minutes, between arrivals. As a result, there is a

$$P(T_a \leq 1) = 1 - e^{-4(1)} = 1 - .0183 = .9870$$

probability that the time between arrivals will be no more than $T = 1$ hour. Similarly, the probability that the interarrival time will not exceed 30 minutes ($T = .5$) is

$$P(T_a \leq .5) = 1 - e^{-4(.5)} = 1 - e^{-2}$$

or, since Table 14.3 indicates that $e^{-2} = .1353$,

$$P(T_a \leq .5) = 1 - .1353 = .8647$$

Figure 14.3 graphically shows the probability that each employee interarrival time T_a will be T hours or less.

QUEUE ACCOMMODATIONS AND BEHAVIOR Waiting lines may be accommodated in various ways. Usually, the queue is formed on the site of the company in some common area of the waiting facility. In some of these cases, as at an airport security station, actual lines may develop. For other circumstances, such as the waiting room in a clinic, customers do not physically form a queue. There are other situations, however, in which the waiting is not done at the place of business. For example, users of a central computer facility may spend most, if not all, of their waiting at the office doing normal daily tasks. Service systems can usually reduce queuing costs by shifting the wait from their site to off-premise facilities.

An important factor for on-site facilities is the size or capacity of the waiting area. Some systems, like a ticket window at a major stadium, are characterized by a (nearly) infinite queuing capacity. Others, such as a beauty shop or counselor's office, involve space limitations. In these limited- or finite-capacity situations, a customer may arrive and find the waiting area completely filled. Sometimes, the arrival does not return but instead seeks accommodations elsewhere. The company then loses any revenue or benefits that could have been gained from this customer. In other cases, the customer may return at a later time, hoping to find an available space. Although the revenue from such an arrival is not lost immediately, the resulting consumer frustration may have an impact on the arrival pattern and revenue in future periods.

Also, when the waiting area is filled to capacity, an arrival may block the operations of the service facility. Suppose, for instance, that new military inductees go through a sequence of orientation activities on the first day of service. Time breaks are scheduled between activities to allow for differences in the rates of processing inductees at each stage of the sequence. During a break, the inductee is assigned a waiting area adjacent to the appropriate orientation facility. Thus, when a specific activity's waiting area is filled to capacity, the inductee has no place to go. The resulting congestion may hamper or even halt preceding orientation activities.

It should be evident that finite-capacity systems have a definite effect on the arrival and output rates for a queuing system. When the waiting system is at capacity, potential arrivals are turned away and the effective arrival rate becomes zero. The resulting blockage may, in turn, reduce the output of the entire service system, particularly for situations involving a sequence of activities.

Another important characteristic is the organization of the waiting line. In some systems, regardless of the number of servers available, a single waiting line is used as a means of preserving the order of arrival. For other situations, a separate queue is allowed to develop for each server. Sometimes, as when automobiles reach the tollbooths at a multiple-lane turnpike, the customer is permitted to select the waiting line. In other cases, there may be differences in customer service needs or server skills.

Then, as when college students select advisors, the customer may be assigned to specific lines or wait for particular servers.

Consumer waiting behavior may also be a relevant factor. If a consumer feels that the queue is too long, he or she may **balk**, refusing to join the waiting line even though space is available. Similarly, customers actually in a queue may tire of waiting and **renege**, departing before being served. Balking and reneging affect the arrival pattern and can involve lost revenues and disgruntled customers. In addition, when there are multiple lines, customers often **jockey**, switching between queues in an attempt to reduce waiting time. A related phenomenon is the combining or dividing of queues, as often occurs in a bank or supermarket when a station is closed or opened. Jockeying, combining, and dividing may balance the length of the queues but may create wider deviations in waiting times. Also, there are situations, like the loading and unloading of ore cars at a mine, where the customer will cycle, or return to the queue, immediately after obtaining service. Among other things, cycling may affect the source population and the arrival process.

SELECTION PROCESS When designing the queuing system, management must prescribe the manner in which customers from the waiting area are selected for service. This prescription is referred to as the **queue discipline**.

In customer-oriented systems, the most frequently used approach is a first-in, first-served (FIFS) discipline. Sometimes, however, the number of waiting lines and customer waiting behavior (like jockeying) may disrupt the order. To avoid ill will in these and similar situations, companies often use a take-a-number system to accomplish the same thing. This second method can be seen at local Internal Revenue Service offices and butcher shops. Other firms, like restaurants, use a reservation system to schedule service. This approach maintains some elements of the FIFS procedure, reduces on-site waiting, and increases available space for service.

In other circumstances, it may be more desirable to serve the last arrivals first. As an example, for convenience and safety, the last people entering an elevator are usually the first to leave. Similarly, a company can often reduce material-handling activities and costs by first using the most recently delivered parts. These cases are illustrations of a last-in, first-served (LIFS) queue discipline.

When the quality of service will be affected by the amount of waiting time, management may prefer to use a priority scheme. For instance, supermarkets provide express lanes for customers with few items. Also, airlines first board the handicapped and passengers with reservations. Similarly, medical facilities typically treat emergency patients before nonemergency cases. In some cases, an important arrival not only has entrance priority but can even interrupt the service on other, less significant customers. An illustration of such a **preemptive priority system** is an emergency maintenance situation in a plant. The crew may interrupt its regular maintenance activities to repair a broken machine.

Sometimes it is difficult or even impossible to establish a waiting line. Then, selection may be done on a purely random basis. Examples include the signing of autographs by celebrities and service by a clerk during the peak hours of a department store sale.

In cases where the customers are objects rather than people, selection is often based on some measure of system performance. For instance, consulting companies usually give first attention to the products generating the most profit. Also, television stores typically repair sets with the shortest expected service time.

SERVICE PROCESS There are many ways to design a service system, some of which may be at least partly dictated by the nature of the process. Important options are the number and arrangement of the facilities.

The simplest case involves a single service facility, such as a traffic signal, a one-chair dentist's office, or a computer terminal. Other situations may have multiple facilities in parallel, each offering essentially the same service. Illustrations include the regular pumps at a gasoline station and the tellers in a bank. A variation exists where there are multiple and parallel but not identical facilities, such as turnpikes with both regular and exact-change tollbooths.

Service operations may also consist of a series, or sequence, of stages. The customer enters the first facility, gets a portion of the service, moves on to the second facility, and so on. In the simplest situation, the facilities are in tandem, one after the other, as in a car wash or cafeteria. Other circumstances involve more complex combinations of facilities, some in parallel, some in tandem, with a multiple of alternative routings. Examples are university registration, task routing in government agencies, restaurant operations, and assembly lines. Figure 14.4 illustrates the service facility design possibilities.

Regardless of the design configuration, it will take time to perform the service at each facility. There are two ways to describe this service process. First, the **service rate** measures the number of customers served per unit of time. Suppose, for instance, that a quality control device can calibrate 150 scientific instruments in a 3-hour period. Then the service rate is $150/3 = 50$ per hour. The **interservice time**, meanwhile, gives the interval between two consecutive service completions. For example, since 50 instruments are calibrated per hour, there will be $1/50 = .02$ hour, or 1.2 minutes, between service completions. Notice that the interservice time $(1/50)$ is the reciprocal of the service rate (50).

Some operations, particularly those that are machine paced, may have

Figure 14.4 Service Facility Design Possibilities

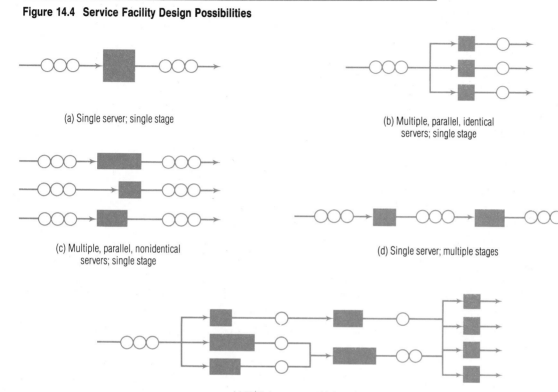

(a) Single server; single stage

(b) Multiple, parallel, identical servers; single stage

(c) Multiple, parallel, nonidentical servers; single stage

(d) Single server; multiple stages

(e) Multiple servers; multiple stages

constant service rates or interservice times. On the other hand, service time may fluctuate within some range of values. In such cases, the service process can be described with a probability distribution. Example 14.2 illustrates.

EXAMPLE 14.2 Storeroom Service

To ensure proper accounting control of requisitioned supplies, Titan employs a full-time clerk at the Mineola plant storeroom. The company has observed the clerk's activities but has found that it is im-

possible to predict the exact service completion time. Also, this time seems to be unaffected by how long the service has already taken, the identity of the customer, the hour of the day, or the day of the week. A

portion of the pattern is illustrated in Figure 14.5.

Management recorded the service completion times by the clerk over an extended period and found that the service rate probabilities could be reasonably described by the Poisson distribution. On average, the clerk was able to service 5 customers per hour. Titan wants to identify a probability distribution that will accurately provide service times.

Figure 14.5 Mineola Plant Storeroom Service

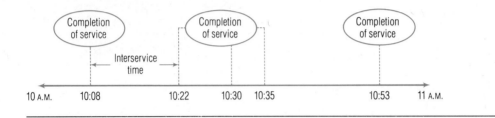

A comparison of Figures 14.2 and 14.5 shows that Titan's service process follows the same type of random pattern as its arrival process. Recall that the arrival rate probabilities were accurately provided by the Poisson distribution. Hence, it is not surprising to learn that the service rate probabilities also are described by a Poisson distribution. That is, if

Y = the number of customers that a single service facility can handle in a specified time interval

u = the average, or expected, service rate in the interval

then the expression

$$(14.3) \quad P(Y) = \frac{e^{-uT}(uT)^Y}{Y!}$$

will give the probability of the service rate Y.

In Example 14.2, the time interval is again $T = 1$ hour. The average, or expected, service rate is $u = 5$ customers per hour. Thus, there is a

$$P(Y = 0) = \frac{e^{-5(1)}(5 \times 1)^0}{0!} = e^{-5}$$

chance, or, from Table 14.3, an

$$e^{-5} = .00674$$

chance that 0 customers will be served by the clerk in an hour of storeroom operation. Similarly, the probability of 1 service completion in an hour is

$$P(Y = 1) = \frac{e^{-5}5^1}{1!} = e^{-5}5 = .0337$$

Figure 14.6 graphically shows the probability of each service rate in Titan's storeroom situation.

Figure 14.6 Titan's Service Rate Probabilities

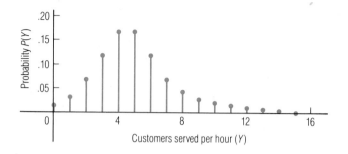

Now, recall that when there is a Poisson arrival pattern, the interarrival time will follow a negative exponential probability distribution. The same relationship exists for the service process. That is, when a queuing system involves a Poisson service pattern, the time between service completions will follow a negative exponential distribution. In particular, if $t =$ the interservice time, then the expression

(14.4) $P(t \leq T) = 1 - e^{-uT}$

gives the probability that service will be completed within a specific period of time T.

For Titan's situation, interservice times will follow a negative exponential distribution with an average of $1/u = 1/5 = .2$ hour, or 12 minutes, between service completions. Consequently, there is a

$P(t \leq 1) = 1 - e^{-5(1)} = 1 - .0067 = .9933$

chance that the clerk can complete service within $T = 1$ hour. Also, the probability that the interservice time will not exceed 30 minutes ($T = .5$) is

$P(t \leq .5) = 1 - e^{-5(.5)}$

or, since Table 14.3 indicates that $e^{-2.5} = .0821$,

$P(t \leq .5) = 1 - .0821 = .9179$

Figure 14.7 presents the probability that T hours or less will be required to service a Titan employee at the Mineola storeroom.

Although service times in Titan's situation follow the negative exponential distribution, other cases may be best described by different probability distributions. In fact, queuing pioneer A. K. Erlang developed a whole family of service distributions. Today, these distributions, which include the negative exponential as a special case, are called the Erlang distribu-

Figure 14.7 Titan's Interservice Probabilities

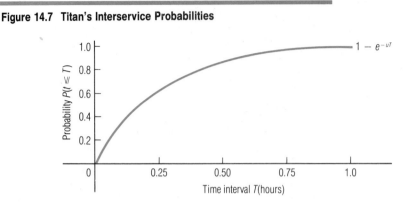

tions in honor of their originator. In practice, of course, the decision maker should use the distribution that best fits the actual data.

DEPARTURE In some situations, it is important to consider what happens to customers after they leave the queuing system. For most systems, departing customers return to the source population and become potential new arrivals. Most clients at a health club, for instance, will come back again and again for the same or similar treatment. On the other hand, some customers, like corpses entering a crematory, will not be reentries into the source population and will never again require service.

BASIC QUEUING ANALYSIS By now, it should be evident that there are many dimensions to consider when designing a queuing system. To evaluate the alternatives, management must develop some measures of system performance. There are several possibilities. One important measure is the proportion of time that the service facilities are in use, called the **utilization factor**. When utilization is low, server idle time will be high. Unless the idle service facilities can be used for other constructive purposes, the company may incur a substantial opportunity cost for the unused capacity. For instance, salaried personnel and public utility expenses still must be paid even when service facilities are idle and hence unproductive. Unfortunately, in some situations, management may have to design a system that automatically creates significant amounts of idle time during given periods. An electric utility, for example, must set its system capacity at a level sufficient to meet peak demands. But for this reason, the utility will have considerable idle capacity during nonpeak periods.

Other useful performance measures deal with the number of customers in the queuing system. First, management will want to know the average number of customers either in the waiting line or receiving service. A police station, for instance, might "book" 10 criminals in a given hour and have another 20 in jail cells. There would then be a total of 30 in the station. This characteristic can be used to find the average time a customer spends in the system waiting for service and being served. When a cost can be assigned to customer waiting, this average time will be helpful in making economic comparisons between alternative queuing system designs. A related factor is the average number of customers in the queue only (10 in the police station illustration). Knowing this value can help to establish the size of the waiting area. It can also be used to find the average customer waiting time in the queue. Companies often use this average to evaluate the quality of service.

When there is uncertainty concerning arrivals and service, some results will have to be stated in probabilistic terms. Some of these measures include the probabilities of an empty facility and finding a given number of customers in the system.

The specific values for these performance measures and the resulting costs will depend on the nature of the queuing system. Fortunately, decision scientists have developed quantitative models that provide such information for a variety of waiting line situations. This section shows how to calculate and interpret the measures for a basic system involving a single queue and only one server. It also illustrates how the results can be used to evaluate alternative system designs. The final section will extend the analysis to other circumstances.

ASSUMPTIONS Let us again consider Titan's storeroom situation. In this case, there will always be customers entering the queuing system (parts storeroom). For practical purposes, then, there is a very large or nearly infinite source population. Furthermore, the arrival process is best described by a Poisson distribution. The average arrival rate, $\lambda = 4$ per hour, remains constant throughout the entire working period. Titan's case does not describe the queue behavior or accommodations. However, in the plant situation, it is reasonable to assume that arrivals will form a single queue and wait in line until served. Also, adequate room will probably exist in the storeroom (or its immediate vicinity) to hold all customers waiting for service.

The Mineola parts storeroom has only one server. Since the supplies are ordinary items, chances are that customers will be handled on a first-in, first-served (FIFS) basis. Service time is random and best described by a negative exponential distribution. The average service rate, $u = 5$ per hour, remains constant throughout the period of operation. In addition, departing employees return to the plant (source population) and hence become potential new customers.

Another important consideration is the operating state of the queuing system. In Titan's situation, the working day begins with no customers in

Table 14.5 Summary of Titan's Queuing System

Assumption	System Element
Infinite source population	Employees in Mineola plant
Poisson arrival process	Employees entering parts storeroom
Infinite waiting room	Parts storeroom and vicinity
Single queue	Employees seeking supplies
No balking, reneging, or jockeying	Employees waiting for supplies
First in, first served (FIFS)	Employees receiving supplies
Single server	Storeroom clerk
Single-stage service	Clerk providing supplies
Negative exponential service process	Clerk dispensing supplies
Departures return to source population	Employees returning to plant
Steady-state conditions	Normal storeroom operations
Average arrivals less than average service rate ($\lambda < u$)	Clerk's efficiency

the parts storeroom. The initial start-up or transient period may involve unusual operating conditions. For instance, there could be a rush of employees entering the storeroom for parts. Eventually, the system will settle into a more "normal" flow of activity. In this equilibrium, or steady, state, storeroom performance characteristics will reach stable values that do not depend on time of day or day of week. Since Titan will be primarily interested in normal operating conditions, management should focus on the steady-state, rather than transient, characteristics of the queuing system.

Finally, notice that Titan's average arrival rate $\lambda = 4$ is less than the average service rate $u = 5$. Hence, the clerk is efficient enough to eventually process or service all arrivals. This type of system would not be feasible otherwise. For instance, if λ were greater than u, the average arrivals would outnumber the average number being served, and the waiting line would become infinitely large.

Titan's circumstances are summarized in Table 14.5. These characteristics are consistent with one of the most fundamental queuing models.

PERFORMANCE MEASURES In this basic model, customers arrive at the constant rate $\lambda = 4$ per hour and are served at the fixed rate $u = 5$ per hour. Consequently, the storeroom clerk will be busy

$$\frac{\lambda}{u} = \frac{4}{5} = .8$$

of the time or have an 80% utilization factor. This ratio

Figure 14.8 Steady-State Movements in Titan's Queuing System

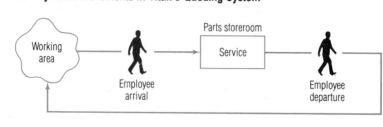

(14.5) $P_W = \dfrac{\lambda}{u}$

also represents the probability that an arriving customer will have to wait for service. Furthermore, there is a

$$1 - \frac{\lambda}{u} = 1 - .8 = .2$$

chance that the clerk will be idle. In other words,

(14.6) $P_0 = 1 - P_W = 1 - \dfrac{\lambda}{u}$

gives the probability of 0 customers in the queuing system.

In addition, management might be concerned with the number of customers passing through the parts storeroom. Excessive traffic, for instance, might encourage employees to socialize on company time or create unnecessary congestion. Information useful for this purpose would be the probability of finding a specified number of customers in the system. To see how such data can be derived, consider Figure 14.8.

Figure 14.8 illustrates how a Titan employee moves from the working area through the parts storeroom and back to the working area. When an employee arrives at the storeroom, the clerk will no longer be idle. That is, the number of customers in the system will change from 0 to 1. Since an average of $\lambda = 4$ employees arrives each hour and the clerk is free $P_0 = .2$ of the time, this change will occur at a rate of

$\lambda P_0 = 4(.2) = .8$ customers per hour

After the employee receives service and departs, there will be a change from 1 back to 0 customers in the system. The clerk can service an average of $u = 5$ employees per hour. If $P_1 = $ the probability of 1 customer in the system, the change from 1 to 0 will occur at the rate of

$uP_1 = 5P_1$ employees each hour

In the steady state, the rates of change from 0 to 1 and vice versa are equal. Such a balance occurs when

$$\lambda P_0 = u P_1$$

From this equation, you can see that the probability of finding 1 customer in Titan's queuing system is

$$P_1 = \frac{\lambda}{u} P_0 = \frac{4}{5}(.2) = .16$$

Similarly, the probability of finding 2 customers will be

$$P_2 = \frac{\lambda}{u} P_1 = \frac{\lambda}{u}\left(\frac{\lambda}{u} P_0\right) = \left(\frac{\lambda}{u}\right)^2 P_0$$

or

$$P_2 = \left(\frac{4}{5}\right)^2 (.2) = .128$$

In fact, as D. Gross and C. M. Harris [9] and L. Kleinrock [11] demonstrate, the probability of n customers in the system can be found with the following general equation:

$$(14.7) \quad P_n = \left(\frac{\lambda}{u}\right)^n P_0 = \left(\frac{\lambda}{u}\right)^n \left(1 - \frac{\lambda}{u}\right)$$

Titan, then, can use equation (14.7) to develop a complete probability distribution for the number of employees waiting or being served in the storeroom area. Table 14.6 presents a portion of the computed data.

Such probability information is also useful for computing other operating characteristics or performance measures. Using data from Table 14.6, Titan can compute the average, or expected, number of employees either waiting or being served in the parts storeroom. Management can compute this information by multiplying each specific number of customers n by the corresponding probability P_n and then summing the results:

$$0(.2) + 1(.16) + 2(.128) + 3(.1024) + \ldots$$

It is evident, however, that this procedure would be cumbersome and time-consuming for large-scale systems. Fortunately, as J. A. White and others [25] show, the following expression will give the same result:

$$(14.8) \quad L = \frac{\lambda}{u - \lambda}$$

where L represents the average number of customers in the system. Titan, then, will have an average of

$$L = \frac{4}{5 - 4} = 4 \text{ employees}$$

either waiting or being served in the storeroom.

Table 14.6 Partial Probability Distributions for the Number of Customers in Titan's System

Number of Customers n	Probability P_n	Cumulative Probability of n or Less	Probability of More Than n
0	.2000	.2000	.8000
1	.1600	.3600	.6400
2	.1280	.4880	.5120
3	.1024	.5904	.4096
4	.0819	.6723	.3277
5	.0655	.7378	.2622
6	.0524	.7902	.2098
7	.0419	.8321	.1679
8	.0336	.8657	.1343
⋮	⋮	⋮	⋮

Again, remember that an average of $\lambda = 4$ employees arrive at the storeroom per hour. Since Titan has an average of $L = 4$ customers in the system, an arrival will spend an average of

$$\frac{L}{\lambda} = \frac{4 \text{ customers}}{4 \text{ arrivals per hour}} = 1 \text{ hour}$$

either waiting or being served. In other words,

$$(14.9) \quad W = \frac{L}{\lambda} = \frac{1}{u - \lambda}$$

measures the average time that a customer will be in the queuing system.

The total period spent in the system (W) will include waiting and service time. Titan knows that it takes an average of $1/u = 1/5 = .2$ hour, or 12 minutes, between service completions. Consequently, a customer spends an average of

$$W - \frac{1}{u} = 1 - .2 = .8 \text{ hour}$$

or 48 minutes waiting in line. That is,

$$(14.10) \quad W_Q = W - \frac{1}{u} = \frac{\lambda}{u(u - \lambda)}$$

represents the average time that a customer must wait before being served.

Finally, an average of $\lambda = 4$ employees arrive per hour, and each spends an average of $W_Q = .8$ hour (48 minutes) waiting in line. Hence, there will be an average of

$$\lambda W_Q = 4(.8) = 3.2 \text{ employees}$$

Table 14.7 Summary of Performance Measures for the Basic Single-Server Model

Performance Measure	Formula	Titan's Value
Probability that an arriving customer has to wait for service	$P_W = \dfrac{\lambda}{u}$	$P_W = \dfrac{4}{5} = .8$
Probability that the service facility is idle	$P_0 = 1 - \dfrac{\lambda}{u}$	$P_0 = 1 - .8 = .2$
Probability of n customers in the system	$P_n = \left(\dfrac{\lambda}{u}\right)^n\left(1 - \dfrac{\lambda}{u}\right)$	See Table 14.6.
Average number of customers in the system	$L = \dfrac{\lambda}{u - \lambda}$	$L = \dfrac{4}{5 - 4} = 4$
Average time that a customer will be in the system	$W = \dfrac{1}{u - \lambda}$	$W = \dfrac{1}{5 - 4} = 1$ hour
Average time that a customer has to wait before being served	$W_Q = \dfrac{\lambda}{u(u - \lambda)}$	$W_Q = \dfrac{4}{5(5 - 4)} = .8$ hour
Average number of customers in the queue waiting for service	$L_Q = \dfrac{\lambda^2}{u(u - \lambda)}$	$L_Q = \dfrac{4^2}{5(5 - 4)} = 3.2$

waiting in the storeroom area for service. In effect, then, the expression

$$(14.11) \quad L_Q = \lambda W_Q = \lambda\left[\frac{\lambda}{u(u - \lambda)}\right] = \frac{\lambda^2}{u(u - \lambda)}$$

provides the average number of customers in the queue waiting for service. Table 14.7 summarizes these performance measures for the basic queuing model.

It is possible to calculate additional performance measures. Some possibilities include the probability of being in the system longer than a specified period, the average length of an occupied queue, and the probability of finding more than a desired number of customers in the system. Kleinrock [11] and White and others [25] provide a full discussion for the interested reader.

COMPARATIVE ANALYSIS The performance measures provide several useful insights concerning the storeroom operation. In particular, we know that an employee has to wait an average of $W_Q = .8$ hour, or 48 minutes, for service. Such a wait seems to be excessive and undesirable. The average queue ($L_Q = 3.2$) and high probability of waiting ($P_W = .8$) are additional indicators of a service deficiency.

Essentially, there are two ways to improve service. Management can either attempt to increase the speed of service or add more servers. Example 14.3 illustrates.

EXAMPLE 14.3 Increasing the Service Level

The employees who require parts from Titan's storeroom are paid $10 per hour. Hence, the production manager is concerned about the manufacturing time lost by the employees at the parts storeroom. Titan is considering two options for improving service. One alternative is to replace the existing clerk with a specially trained and certified parts processor. Under this plan, the service rate would double from 5 to 10 customers per hour. However, the parts processor will be paid $7 per hour as compared to the $5 hourly wage of the existing clerk. Amortization, insurance, and other fixed expenses for the storeroom facility would remain at $12,000 per year. The facility operates 8 hours a day, 250 days per year. In the second option, Titan would partially automate the current system. Purchase and installation of the required equipment would add $9000 to annual fixed expenses but provide a service rate of 12 customers per hour.

Titan's management must decide which option to select.

Under the existing system, the clerk can process $u = 5$ customers per hour, or one customer every $1/u = 1/5 = .2$ hour (12 minutes). Both options now being considered (the fast clerk and the partially automated system) improve the speed of service. The parts processor would service $u = 10$ per hour (one every 6 minutes), and the equipment-assisted clerk would process $u = 12$ an hour (one every 5 minutes). Employees would still arrive at the rate of $\lambda = 4$ customers per hour.

Titan can predict the effects of each plan on storeroom operations by using the data in equations (14.5)–(14.11). Table 14.8 summarizes the results. An examination of these results shows that each alternative substantially reduces the probability of waiting (P_W), the average waiting time (W_Q), and the average number of employees waiting for service (L_Q). Thus, Titan can improve service by using either a faster clerk or the partially automated system. Both options, however, also significantly increase the probability of an idle facility (P_0).

The operating characteristics will also affect the costs associated with the queuing system. Before reaching a final decision, then, Titan needs to estimate the economic impact of the alternative plans.

Table 14.8 Queuing System Characteristics for Titan's Service Plans

	Plan		
Performance Measure	Clerk	Processor	Automation
Probability of waiting P_W	0.8	.4	.333
Probability of an idle facility P_0	0.2	.6	.667
Average number of customers in system L	4	.667	.5
Average time in system (hours) W	1	.167	.125
Average time waiting (hours) W_0	0.8	.067	.042
Average number of customers in queue L_Q	3.2	.267	.167

COST CONSIDERATIONS When an employee goes to the parts storeroom, this worker is being diverted from his or her work on the production line. Yet, Titan pays this person $10 per hour whether the person is working or obtaining supplies. During any given hour, there are an average of L customers in the parts storeroom either waiting or being served. Therefore, it costs the company $10L per hour in lost manufacturing time to operate the queuing system.

With the existing clerk, $L = 4$, and the queuing system cost (cost in lost manufacturing time due to the queuing system) is

$10L = $10 \times 4 = 40 per hour

or

$40/hour $\times$ 8 hours/day $\times$ 250 days/year = $80,000 per year

Of this amount, $10L_Q = $10 \times 3.2 = 32 per hour, or $64,000 represents the annual cost of waiting for service. The faster clerk would substantially reduce these queuing expenses. For instance, the cost with the parts processor would be only $10L = $10(.667) = 6.67 per hour.

Titan must also consider the cost of providing the service facilities. Amortization, insurance, and other fixed expenses will be $12,000 per year under either of the manual approaches. The existing clerk is paid $5 per hour or

$5/hour $\times$ 8 hours/day $\times$ 250 days/year = $10,000 per year

Hence, it will cost $12,000 + $10,000 = $22,000 to operate the parts storeroom for one year. On the other hand, the faster clerk must be paid $7 per hour, or $14,000 a year. Consequently, the company will pay $12,000 + $14,000 = $26,000 per year for the improved service.

Titan must balance the cost savings from the improved service against the increased expenses. Table 14.9 computes the cost data relevant for this comparison. From this cost summary, you can see that the least costly

Table 14.9 Cost Summary for Titan's Service Plans

Plan	Queuing System Cost ($/Year) $10L \times 8 \times 250$	Service Facility Costs ($/Year) Fixed Expenses + Salary	Total Cost ($/Year)
Existing clerk	10(4)(8)(250) = 80,000	12,000 + 10,000 = 22,000	102,000
Parts processor	10(.667)(8)(250) = 13,340	12,000 + 14,000 = 26,000	39,340
Partial automation	10(.5)(8)(250) = 10,000	9000 + 12,000 + 10,000 = 31,000	41,000

Table 14.10 Summary of Queuing Methodology

1. Identify the structure of the queuing system, including the nature of the source population, arrival process, queue accommodations and behavior, selection process, service process, and departures.
2. Establish the appropriate operating characteristics or performance measures of the queuing system.
3. Compute the measures of performance, including the following:
   a. Probability of waiting P_W
   b. Probability of an idle facility P_0
   c. Probability of a specified number of customers P_n
   d. Average number of customers in the system L
   e. Average system time W
   f. Average waiting time W_Q
   g. Average number of customers in the queue L_Q
4. Compare the performance measures for each system design.
5. If possible, calculate the corresponding queuing and service facility costs.
6. Select the system design that leads to the most favorable performance characteristics and/or least total cost.

plan is to use the parts processor. Even though this person requires a ($14,000 − $10,000)/$10,000 = 40% higher salary than the existing clerk, the improved service will result in a reduction of total costs by ($102,000 − $39,340)/$102,000 = 61.4%. Although efficiency could be further improved with partial automation, the additional $9000 equipment expense would more than offset the cost savings from the faster service.

Note that in Titan's situation, the customers are themselves employees of the organization operating the service system. As a result, it is relatively easy to assess the customer waiting cost. However, when customers are external to the company or the firm is a nonprofit institution, it may be more difficult to determine this expense. Such things as ill will and social costs are very difficult to measure accurately.

Table 14.10 summarizes the methodology of queuing analysis.

PRACTICAL EXTENSIONS

As H. A. Taha [20] demonstrates, many practical situations do not conform to the assumptions of the basic queuing model. There may be a finite source population, arrivals in bulk quantities, limited waiting capacity, sequential waiting lines, or multiple servers. Also, the average arrival or service rate may vary with the number of customers waiting for service. In addition, the situation may involve something other than a Poisson arrival process, FIFS queue discipline, or negative exponential service times. This section presents queuing models applicable to some of these situations.

FINITE SOURCE POPULATION

In some situations, there is a small number of potential customers. As a result, the arrival rate will be affected by the number of customers already in the system. Example 14.4 illustrates.

EXAMPLE 14.4 Processing Office Work

Data Studies Associates, a small private research organization, employs three secretaries in its report preparation center. The nature of the work requires the staff to use the firm's single word processing machine.

Although the utilization rate varies, the pattern closely follows a Poisson distribution with an average usage of twice per 8-hour day. Word processing time also fluctuates but can be reasonably described

by a negative exponential distribution. The period on the machine is 80 minutes.

Data Studies wants to measure the word processing performance of its secretarial staff.

The circumstances for Data Studies are very similar to Titan's storeroom situation. There is a single service facility (the word processing machine) and hence a single waiting line. The arrival process of secretaries to the machine follows a Poisson distribution with an average of twice per 8-hour day, or $\lambda = 2/8 = .25$ per hour. It seems reasonable to assume that the machine will be used on a first-come, first-served basis. Also, service time (the period on the machine) follows a negative exponential distribution. Since the mean processing time is 80 minutes, or $1\frac{1}{3}$ hours, the average service rate will be $1/1\frac{1}{3} = .75$ secretary per hour.

There is one major distinction between the two situations. Titan has a very large number of potential customers (practically an infinite source population). On the other hand, the source population for Data Studies consists of only three secretaries and hence is finite.

The distinction is important because the probability of an arrival is affected by the number of customers already in the system. Suppose, for instance, that all three secretaries are currently at the word processing machine. Hence, there is no chance of an arrival during, say, the next minute. Yet, if only one secretary is at the machine, the probability of an

Table 14.11 Formulas for a Finite Source, Single-Server Queuing Model

Performance Measure	Formula
Probability that the service facility is idle	$P_0 = \dfrac{1}{\displaystyle\sum_{n=0}^{M}\left[\dfrac{M!}{(M-n)!}\left(\dfrac{\lambda}{u}\right)^n\right]}$
Probability of n customers in the system	$P_n = \dfrac{M!}{(M-n)!}\left(\dfrac{\lambda}{u}\right)^n P_0$
Average number of customers waiting in line	$L_Q = M - \left[\left(\dfrac{\lambda+u}{\lambda}\right)(1-P_0)\right]$
Average number of customers in the system	$L = L_Q + (1 - P_0)$
Average waiting time	$W_Q = \dfrac{L_Q}{\lambda(M-L)}$
Average time in the system	$W = W_Q + \dfrac{1}{u}$

arrival in the same time interval is much higher. Titan's situation is another matter. The Mineola plant has a relatively large source population. Consequently, the probability of an arrival does not change significantly if some of the employees are already in the storeroom area.

In effect, then, a finite population model involves substantially different probability calculations than the infinite population model. Formulas for the system performance measures must be modified to reflect these differences. As Kleinrock [11] and White and others [25] demonstrate, the relevant equations are as summarized in Table 14.11. In this table, M represents the number of customers in the source population. Also, λ gives the arrival rate for each individual rather than the group of M customers.

For Data Studies Associates, $M = 3$ secretaries, $\lambda = .25$ customer per hour and $u = .75$ customer per hour. Management can use this information and the appropriate formula in Table 14.11 to determine P_0. In this way, management will find that the word processing machine is idle

$$P_0 = \dfrac{1}{\displaystyle\sum_{n=0}^{M}\left[\dfrac{M!}{(M-n)!}\left(\dfrac{\lambda}{u}\right)^n\right]} = \dfrac{1}{\displaystyle\sum_{n=0}^{3}\left[\dfrac{3!}{(3-n)!}\left(\dfrac{.25}{.75}\right)^n\right]}$$

or

$$P_0 = \dfrac{1}{\dfrac{3!}{(3-0)!}\left(\dfrac{1}{3}\right)^0 + \dfrac{3!}{(3-1)!}\left(\dfrac{1}{3}\right)^1 + \dfrac{3!}{(3-2)!}\left(\dfrac{1}{3}\right)^2 + \dfrac{3!}{(3-3)!}\left(\dfrac{1}{3}\right)^3}$$

$$= .346$$

of the time.

Notice, however, that this formula requires extensive calculations. Fortunately, decision scientists have made the necessary computations for various values of the utilization ratio (λ/u) and population size (M). The results have been recorded in queuing tables and graphs. F. S. Hillier and O. S. Yu [10] provide such documents. When the actual numbers can be found in these documents, management can avoid the lengthy computations involved in using the formula for P_0.

Other operating characteristics can be found from P_0. The formula for P_n in Table 14.11, for example, indicates that there is

$$P_n = \frac{M!}{(M-n)!} \left(\frac{\lambda}{u}\right)^n P_0$$

or

$$P_1 = \frac{3!}{(3-1)!} \left(\frac{.25}{.75}\right)^1 (.346) = .346$$

chance of finding exactly one customer in the system and a

$$P_2 = \frac{3!}{(3-2)!} \left(\frac{1}{3}\right)^2 (.346) = .231$$

probability that two secretaries will be either waiting for the machine or using the machine.

Also, there will be an average of

$$L_Q = M - \left[\left(\frac{\lambda+u}{\lambda}\right)(1-P_0)\right]$$

$$= 3 - \left[\left(\frac{.25+.75}{.25}\right)(1-.346)\right] = .384 \text{ secretary}$$

waiting to use the word processor and an average of

$$L = L_Q + (1-P_0) = .384 + (1-.346) = 1.038 \text{ customers}$$

in the system waiting or being served. A secretary spends an average of

$$W_Q = \frac{L_Q}{\lambda(M-L)} = \frac{.384}{.25(3-1.038)} = .783 \text{ hour}$$

or 46.98 minutes waiting to use the word processor and

$$W = W_Q + \frac{1}{u} = .783 + \frac{1}{.75} = 2.116 \text{ hours}$$

or 126.98 minutes in the system.

In the future, Data Studies Associates might consider options for reducing the customer waiting time. One possibility is to increase word processing speed through a training program for the secretaries. As part of the planning process, the company can use the equations from Table 14.11 and appropriate cost data to evaluate the alternatives.

LIMITED WAITING CAPACITY Frequently, the waiting area for the queuing system has a limited capacity. Any customers that arrive while the waiting area is full must be turned away. Consider Example 14.5.

EXAMPLE 14.5 Furniture Refinishing

Elegant Woodworks, Inc., has for some time been experiencing rapid growth in its furniture-refinishing business. Current demand averages 30 jobs per week with interarrival times closely following a negative exponential distribution. The company can complete an average of 33 jobs a week.

Service times also appear to follow a negative exponential distribution. Jobs are processed on a first-come, first-served basis.

There is limited space available to store furniture awaiting refinishing. At the present time, Elegant storage capacity can accommodate only

6 jobs. Management is concerned about this limited capacity because Elegant may have to turn away customers and hence lose potential revenue. Management wants to evaluate the effects of this limitation on its operation.

Elegant's circumstances are very similar to Titan's storeroom situation. There is only one significant distinction. Titan has practically an unlimited waiting area and hence a potentially infinite queue length. In Elegant's case, however, the limited physical storage capacity restricts its queue to a finite length.

When the limited waiting area is filled to capacity, potential customers will be turned away and the effective arrival rate becomes zero. Formulas for the system performance measures must be modified to account for the finite queue length. Kleinrock [11] and White and others [25] show that the relevant equations are those presented in Table 14.12. In the table, K represents the maximum capacity of the system, or the largest number of customers both in the waiting line and being served.

For Elegant's situation, $K = 7$ (6 jobs that can be stored plus 1 in process), $\lambda = 30$ jobs per week, and $u = 33$ jobs per week. Hence, the furniture-refinishing operation will be idle

$$P_0 = \frac{1 - (\lambda/u)}{1 - (\lambda/u)^{K+1}} = \frac{1 - (30/33)}{1 - (30/33)^{7+1}} = .171$$

of the time. Also, the formula for P_n in Table 14.12 indicates that there will be 1 job in the shop

Table 14.12 Formulas for a Finite Queue Length, Single-Server Queuing Model

Performance Measure	Formula
Probability of an idle service facility	$P_0 = \dfrac{1 - (\lambda/u)}{1 - (\lambda/u)^{K+1}}$
Probability of n customers in the system	$P_n = \left(\dfrac{\lambda}{u}\right)^n P_0$
Proportion of arrivals that will be turned away	$P_K = \left(\dfrac{\lambda}{u}\right)^K P_0$
Average number of customers in the system	$L = \dfrac{\lambda/u}{1 - (\lambda/u)} - \dfrac{(K+1)(\lambda/u)^{K+1}}{1 - (\lambda/u)^{K+1}}$
Average number of customers waiting in line	$L_Q = L - \dfrac{\lambda(1 - P_K)}{u}$
Average waiting time	$W_Q = \dfrac{L_Q}{\lambda(1 - P_K)}$
Average time in the system	$W = W_Q + 1/u$

$$P_1 = \left(\frac{30}{33}\right)^1 (.171) = .155$$

of the time and 2 jobs

$$P_2 = \left(\frac{30}{33}\right)^2 (.171) = .141$$

of the time. The limited storage capacity forces the company to turn away

$$P_K = \left(\frac{\lambda}{u}\right)^K P_0 = \left(\frac{30}{33}\right)^7 (.171) = .088$$

or 8.8% of its potential customers.

In addition, there will be an average of

$$L = \frac{(\lambda/u)}{1 - (\lambda/u)} - \frac{(K+1)(\lambda/u)^{K+1}}{1 - (\lambda/u)^{K+1}}$$

$$= \frac{(30/33)}{1 - (30/33)} - \frac{(7+1)(30/33)^{7+1}}{1 - (30/33)^{7+1}} = 2.987$$

or about 3 jobs on the premises (waiting or being served). Of these jobs,

$$L_Q = L - \frac{\lambda(1 - P_K)}{u} = 2.987 - \frac{30(1 - .088)}{33} = 2.158$$

or an average of approximately 2 are waiting for refinishing. The average waiting time is

$$W_Q = \frac{L_Q}{\lambda(1 - P_K)} = \frac{2.158}{30(1 - .088)} = .079 \text{ week}$$

or, assuming a 5-day work week, .395 day. Each job will be in Elegant's refinishing system (waiting or being served) for an average of

$$W = W_Q + \frac{1}{u} = .079 + \frac{1}{33} = .109 \text{ week}$$

or .547 working day.

In the future, Elegant might want to consider the possibility of expanding its storage capacity. Perhaps the company could lease additional space or construct a larger waiting area. Such plans could reduce the number of lost customers and hence capture some additional revenue. Of course, the additional facilities would increase expenses. In any event, management can use the equations from Table 14.12 and appropriate revenue and cost data to evaluate the alternatives.

MULTIPLE SERVERS Many organizations can deliver service most efficiently with multiple servers. In one of the simplest cases, the system is composed of several identical and parallel service facilities. Arriving customers form a single queue and wait for a service channel to become available. Whenever a server is free, the customer at the head of the line goes to that facility. Example 14.6 illustrates.

EXAMPLE 14.6 Expanding Service Facilities

Titan Industries currently employs a single clerk in its parts storeroom. An analysis of other single-channel options indicated that the speed of service could be improved by using a parts processor rather than the existing clerk. The faster clerk would also reduce costs to an annual level of $39,340. Suppose that the production manager now wants to consider the desirability of hiring an additional clerk. The new person would have qualifications identical to those of the existing clerk. Hence, each clerk would receive a $5 hourly wage and would be capable of serving customers at the same rate of $u = 4$ per hour. Customers would still arrive at the rate of $\lambda = 4$ per hour. Arrivals would be instructed to form a single waiting line and then seek the first available clerk. Amortization, insurance, and fixed expenses would remain at $12,000 per year. Plant employees would still receive $10 per hour.

Management wants to compare the performance measures and costs of the two-clerk plan and parts processor plan.

Figure 14.9 Titan's Two-Clerk Queuing System

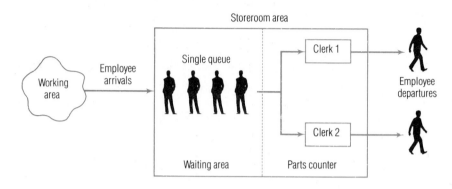

There is only one difference between Example 14.6 and Titan's previous circumstances (Examples 14.1 through 14.3). In the earlier examples, Titan had a single server (either the existing clerk, the parts processor, or the automated clerk). The new situation would involve two service channels (clerks) as shown in Figure 14.9.

When the quantity of customers in the system does not exceed the number of servers, all can receive immediate service. As a result, there is no waiting line. In this case, arrivals are processed at a factor equal to each facility service rate multiplied by the number of customers in the system. Suppose, for instance, that there is $n = 1$ employee in Titan's storeroom area. Then the combined service rate will be $nu = 1(4) = 4$ customers per hour. On the other hand, when the customer count exceeds the number of servers, a waiting line will form. Consequently, the combined service rate is equal to each facility's processing rate multiplied by the number of servers. For example, Titan has 2 servers. If 6 plant employees are in the storeroom area, then the system service rate is $2u = 2(4) = 8$ customers per hour.

In effect, then, the number of servers will influence the operating characteristics of the system. Queuing formulas should reflect this fact. As Kleinrock [11] and White and others [25] demonstrate, the equations given in Table 14.13 provide the relevant performance measures for the single-queue, multiple-server situation. In this table, S denotes the number of servers or service facilities. Also, notice that the system service rate (Su) must be greater than the arrival rate (λ). Otherwise, the waiting line and average waiting time may become infinitely large.

Example 14.6 involves $S = 2$ clerks, $u = 5$ customers per hour for each server, and $\lambda = 4$ employees per hour. Titan can use these data and the appropriate formula in Table 14.13 to calculate P_0. The computations will show that both clerks are idle

Table 14.13 Formulas for a Single-Queue, Multiple-Server Queuing Model

Performance Measure	Formula
Probability that all service facilities are idle	$P_0 = \dfrac{1}{\left[\sum\limits_{n=0}^{S-1} \dfrac{1}{n!}\left(\dfrac{\lambda}{u}\right)^n\right] + \dfrac{1}{S!}\left(\dfrac{\lambda}{u}\right)^S\left(\dfrac{Su}{Su-\lambda}\right)}$
Probability that an arriving customer has to wait for service	$P_W = \dfrac{1}{S!}\left(\dfrac{\lambda}{u}\right)^S\left(\dfrac{Su}{Su-\lambda}\right)P_0$
Probability of n customers in the system	$P_n = \dfrac{(\lambda/u)^n}{n!} P_0 \qquad \text{for } n \le S$
	$P_n = \dfrac{(\lambda/u)^n}{S!\,(S^{n-S})} P_0 \qquad \text{for } n > S$
Average number of customers waiting for service	$L_Q = \dfrac{\lambda u(\lambda/u)^S}{(S-1)!\,(Su-\lambda)^2} P_0$
Average number of customers in the system	$L = L_Q + \dfrac{\lambda}{u}$
Average time in the system	$W = \dfrac{L}{\lambda}$
Average waiting time	$W_Q = W - \dfrac{1}{u}$

$$P_0 = \frac{1}{\left[\sum\limits_{n=0}^{S-1} \dfrac{1}{n!}\left(\dfrac{\lambda}{u}\right)^n\right] + \dfrac{1}{S!}\left(\dfrac{\lambda}{u}\right)^S\left(\dfrac{Su}{Su-\lambda}\right)}$$

$$= \frac{1}{\left[\sum\limits_{n=0}^{2-1} \dfrac{1}{n!}\left(\dfrac{4}{5}\right)^n\right] + \dfrac{1}{2!}\left(\dfrac{4}{5}\right)^2\left[\dfrac{2(5)}{2(5)-4}\right]}$$

or

$$P_0 = \frac{1}{\left[\dfrac{1}{0!}\left(\dfrac{4}{5}\right)^0 + \dfrac{1}{1!}\left(\dfrac{4}{5}\right)^1\right] + \dfrac{1}{2}\left(\dfrac{16}{25}\right)\left(\dfrac{10}{10-4}\right)} = .429$$

of the time.

Note how tedious and time-consuming these calculations can become. Fortunately, decision scientists have performed the necessary mathematics for various values of the utilization ratio λ/u and for the number of servers S. The results have been recorded in queuing tables and graphs like those provided by Hillier and Yu [10]. When the actual λ/u and S values can be found in these documents, management can avoid using the cumbersome formula to find P_0.

Other operating characteristics can be determined from P_0. The formula in Table 14.13, for instance, indicates that

$$P_W = \frac{1}{S!}\left(\frac{\lambda}{u}\right)^S\left(\frac{Su}{Su - \lambda}\right)P_0 = \frac{1}{2!}\left(\frac{4}{5}\right)^2\left[\frac{2(5)}{2(5) - 4}\right](.429) = .229$$

or about 22.9% of arriving customers will have to wait for service. Also, suppose that Titan believes that the system currently has no more customers than servers. That is, $n \leq S$. In this case,

$$P_n = \frac{(\lambda/u)^n}{n!} P_0$$

and there will be a

$$P_1 = \frac{(4/5)^1}{1!}(.429) = .343$$

chance of finding exactly 1 customer in the system. On the other hand, when $n > S$,

$$P_n = \frac{(\lambda/u)^n}{S!(S^{n-S})} P_0$$

For example, there is a

$$P_3 = \frac{(\lambda/u)^n}{S!(S^{n-S})} P_0 = \frac{(4/5)^3}{2!(2^{3-2})}(.429) = .055$$

probability that 3 plant employees are waiting or being served in the parts storeroom.

In addition, there will be an average of

$$L_Q = \frac{\lambda u(\lambda/u)^S}{(S-1)!(Su - \lambda)^2} P_0 = \frac{4(5)(4/5)^2}{(2-1)![2(5) - 4]^2}(.429) = .153 \text{ employee}$$

waiting for service and an average of

$$L = L_Q + \frac{\lambda}{u} = .153 + \frac{4}{5} = .953 \text{ customer}$$

in the system. A customer will spend an average of

$$W = \frac{L}{\lambda} = \frac{.953}{4} = .238 \text{ hour}$$

or 14.28 minutes in the parts storeroom area and an average of

$$W_Q = W - \frac{1}{u} = .238 - \frac{1}{5} = .038 \text{ hour}$$

or 2.28 minutes waiting for service.

During any given hour, there are an average of L customers in the parts storeroom area (and hence not working). Since plant employees receive $10 per hour, the queuing system cost for lost production time is

$10L = 10(.953) = \$9.53$ per hour

or

$9.53/\text{hour} \times 8 \text{ hours/day} \times 250 \text{ days/year} = \$19,060$ per year

with the two clerk plan. Of this amount, $10L_Q = 10(.153) = \$1.53$ per hour, or $3060 represents the annual cost of waiting for service. Amortization, insurance, and other fixed expenses are $12,000 per year. The cost for the two clerks is an additional

2 clerks $\times$ \$5/hour $\times$ 8 hours/day $\times$ 250 days/year = \$20,000 per year

Thus, the two-clerk plan will involve an annual cost of $20,000 + \$12,000 + \$19,060 = \$51,060$.

Table 14.14 summarizes the operating characteristics and corresponding costs for all of Titan's system designs. Data from the three single-clerk plans are taken from Tables 14.8 and 14.9. The results show that the two-clerk plan involves a smaller probability of waiting P_W, less average waiting time W_Q, and a smaller average queue L_Q than any of the single-server options. However, customers spend a longer average time W in the two-clerk system than in the parts processor or partial automation system. On average, there are also more customers in the two-clerk plan than in either of these two single-clerk plans. Evidently, the two-clerk system has a slower average service time than either the parts processor or partial automation plan. As a result, the multiple-server plan is less economical than either of these single-server alternatives. In particular, the parts processor option is still the least costly plan.

OTHER MODELS All queuing models in this chapter assume that there is a Poisson arrival process and a negative exponential distribution of service times. In practice, arrivals and service completions may follow some other probability distribution. For example, service times may follow a normal distribution. Also, the waiting line situation may involve a constant arrival rate or constant service times. In fact, there is an infinite variety of probability distributions that may be appropriate in various situations.

To facilitate communication among researchers and practitioners, the British mathematician Maurice Kendall developed a shorthand notation

Table 14.14 Operating Characteristics and Costs for Titan's Service Plans

Performance Measure/Cost	Plan			
	Existing Clerk	Parts Processor	Partial Automation	Two Clerks
Probability of waiting P_W	0.8	0.40	0.333	0.229
Probability of idle facilities P_0	0.2	0.60	0.667	0.429
Average number in system L	4	0.667	0.50	0.953
Average time in system (hours) W	1	0.167	0.125	0.238
Average waiting time (hours) W_Q	0.8	0.067	0.042	0.038
Average number in queue L_Q	3.2	0.267	0.167	0.153
Queuing system cost ($/year)	80,000	13,340	10,000	19,060
Service facility cost ($/year)	22,000	26,000	31,000	32,000
Total cost ($/year)	102,000	39,340	41,000	51,060

that succinctly describes the possibilities. In Kendall notation, the first symbol describes the nature of the arrival process, the second gives the service process, and the third identifies the number of servers. An M/M/1 system, for instance, involves random arrivals and service times and 1 server. Similarly, M/M/S designates a system with random arrivals and service times but a multiple (S) number of servers. Since the Poisson and negative exponential distributions, among others, involve a random pattern of events, the models of this chapter represent M/M/1 and M/M/S systems.

Newell [17] and White and others [25] present situations with random arrivals, constant service times, and single servers. In Kendall notation, this situation is designated as an M/D/1 system. They also extend the analysis to multiple-server cases, or M/D/S systems. O. J. Boxma and others [3] and D. W. Matthews [15] discuss circumstances in which service times can follow any distribution. Assuming random arrivals, such events are designated as M/G/1 and M/G/S systems. C. Parkan and E. H. Warren [18] present a case in which arrivals can follow any probability distribution. Since their model has random service times and 1 server, it is designated as a G/M/1 system.

Other practical situations may not conform to the assumptions of the queuing models in this chapter. First, customers may arrive in bulk quantities rather than one at a time. Kleinrock [11] presents a queuing system designed for this situation. Second, the service process may be influenced by the arrival process. C. E. Bell [2], L. Green [8], and E. H. Warren [24] discuss models that allow varying degrees of interaction between these processes. Third, customers may not be serviced on a first-in, first-out basis. L. P. Bein [1] presents a model with a queue discipline based on customer preference. And E. Kofman and S. A. Lippman [12] discuss a priority system involving regular and "important" customers. Fourth, in addition to limited waiting capacity, there may be other restrictions on the nature of the queuing system. Y. Takahashi and others [21] discuss this situation in detail.

Finally, queuing theory basically describes the operating characteristics of a waiting line situation. Then the information is used to evaluate selected design configurations. Since management typically tests only a few alternatives, the approach cannot usually guarantee an optimal solution to the problem. However, there are queuing models that, under specific circumstances, can be used to determine the optimal speed of service or the best number of facilities. T. B. Crabill and others [6] present a bibliography of such methods.

SUMMARY

This chapter has presented the fundamental principles and concepts of queuing theory. The first section outlined the structure of a queuing system. A key element in the structure is the nature and size of the source population. In particular, the number of potential clients influences the arrival process, the manner in which customers reach the service system. This process is described by the arrival rate and interarrival time. In many cases, these measures must be expressed in probabilistic terms. The Poisson distribution often provides accurate arrival rate probabilities, but interarrival times frequently follow a negative exponential distribution.

Arrivals form queues that are accommodated on site in a common waiting area or off the premises. An important consideration is the size of the area. Limited, or finite, space often results in lost customers or blocked service facilities. Other important factors are the number of queues and the behavior of customers in the waiting lines.

Customers in the queue are selected for service in a variety of ways. Some systems use a first-in, first-served (FIFS) approach. Others use the last-in, first-served (LIFS) queue discipline. And a few select customers on a priority basis.

The chapter presented many different designs of the service facilities. Possibilities include a single channel, multiple parallel servers, and sequential systems. Regardless of the design, the service process is described by the service rate and the interservice time. In many cases, interservice times follow a negative exponential probability distribution.

Typically, departures from the queuing system return to the source population and become potential new arrivals. However, in some cases, departures permanently leave the queuing system and thus significantly reduce the source population.

After identifying the underlying queuing structure, management establishes appropriate measures for evaluating the performance of the system. Measures include the probability of waiting, the average number of customers in the queue, and the average waiting time. Table 14.7 presented formulas for computing such measures in a basic single server queuing model. These measures are then used to compare the operating characteristics and, where applicable, costs of alternative system designs. This comparative analysis is the basis for selecting a preferred design. Table 14.10 summarized the methodology.

The final section extended the basic analysis to other practical waiting line situations, including a finite source population with a single server (relevant performance measures were outlined in Table 14.11), a finite queue length with a single server (appropriate operating characteristics were summarized in Table 14.12), and a single waiting line with multiple servers (formulas for computing the performance measures in this system were provided in Table 14.13).

Glossary

arrival rate   The number of customer arrivals into a queuing system per unit of time.

balking   Refusing to join a waiting line even though space is available.

interarrival time   The time between two consecutive customer arrivals into a queuing system.

interservice time   The interval between two consecutive service completions at a facility in a queuing system.

jockeying   Switching between multiple queues in an attempt to reduce waiting time.

negative exponential distribution   A probability distribution used to describe the pattern of interarrival and/or service times for some queuing systems.

Poisson distribution   A probability distribution used to describe the random arrival rate for some queuing systems.

preemptive priority systems   A system in which an important arrival not only has entrance priority but can even interrupt the service on other, less significant customers.

queue discipline   The manner in which customers from the waiting area are selected for service.

queuing theory   Quantitative approaches that measure the operating characteristics and costs of waiting lines.

reneging   Departing from a queuing system before being served.

service rate   The number of customers served by a facility in a queuing system per unit of time.

utilization factor   The proportion of time that the service facilities are in use.

References

1. Bein, L. P. "An N-Server Stochastic Service System with Customer Preference." *Operations Research* (January–February 1976): 104.

2. Bell, C. E. "Optimal Operation of an M/M/2 Queue with Removable Servers." *Operations Research* (September–October 1980): 1189.

3. Boxma, O. J., et al. "Approximations of the Mean Waiting Time in an M/G/S Queueing System." *Operations Research* (November–December 1979): 1115.

4. Coffman, E. G., and M. Hofre. "A Class of FIFO Queues Arising in Computer Systems." *Operations Research* (September–October 1978): 864.

5. Cooper, R. B. *Introduction to Queueing Theory.* New York: Macmillan, 1972.

6. Crabill, T. B., et al. "A Classified Bibliography of Research on Optimal Design and Control of Queues." *Operations Research* (March–April 1977): 219.

7. Driscoll, M. F., and N. A. Weiss. "An Application of Queueing Theory to Reservation Networks." *Management Science* (January 1976): 540.

8. Green, L. "Comparing Operating Characteristics of Queues in Which Customers Require a Random Number of Servers." *Management Science* (January 1981): 65.

9. Gross, D., and C. M. Harris. *Fundamentals of Queueing Theory.* New York: Wiley, 1974.

10. Hillier, F. S., and O. S. Yu. *Queuing Tables and Graphs.* Amsterdam: Elsevier–North Holland, 1979.

11. Kleinrock, L. *Queuing Systems,* Vol. 1, *Theory.* New York: Wiley, 1975.

12. Kofman, E., and S. A. Lippman. "An M/M/1 Dynamic Priority Queue with Optimal Promotion." *Operations Research* (January–February 1981): 174.

13. Larson, R. C. "Approximating the Performance of Urban Emergency Service Systems." *Operations Research* (September–October 1975): 845.

14. McKeown, P. C. "An Application of Queueing Analysis to the New York State Child Abuse and Maltreatment Register Telephone Reporting System." *Interfaces* (May 1979): 20.

15. Matthews, D. W. "A Simple Method for Reducing Queueing Times in M/G/1." *Operations Research* (March–April 1979): 318.

16. Morse, P. M. "A Queueing Theory, Bayesian Model for the Circulation of Books in a Library." *Operations Research* (July–August 1979): 693.

17. Newell, G. F. *Applications of Queueing Theory.* London: Chapman and Hall, 1971.

18. Parkan, C., and E. H. Warren. "Optimal Reneging Decisions in a G/M/1 Queue." *Decision Sciences* (January 1978): 107.

19. Solberg, J. J. "A Tenancy Vacancy Model." *Decision Sciences* (April 1976): 202.

20. Taha, H. A. "Queueing Theory in Practice." *Interfaces* (February 1981): 43.

21. Takahashi, Y., et al. "An Approximation Method for Open Restricted Queueing Networks." *Operations Research* (May–June 1980): 594.

22. Taylor, I.D.S., and J.G.C. Templeton. "Waiting Time in a Multi-Server Cutoff-Priority Queue, and Its Application to an Urban Ambulance Service." *Operations Research* (September–October 1980): 1168.

23. Vogel, M. A. "Queueing Theory Applied to Machine Manning." *Interfaces* (August 1979): 1.

24. Warren, E. H. "Estimating Waiting Time in a Queueing System." *Decision Sciences* (January 1981): 112.

25. White, J. A., et al. *Analysis of Queuing Systems.* New York: Academic Press, 1975.

Thought Exercises

1. Identify the source population, customer, waiting area, and service facility in each of the following situations:
   a. A local dentist's office
   b. A laundromat
   c. The local Social Security office
   d. An orbiting space station
   e. An automobile inspection station

2. Jason Slick, the manager of the Limelight Movie Theater, has been using a Poisson distribution with $\lambda = 3$ customers per minute to predict arrival rates at the various shows. The predictions are then used to determine the number of ticket windows that should remain open for each show.

   Julie McKay works at the box office on a rotating schedule. Some days she works the day shift (10 A.M. to 6 P.M.), and other days she works from 6 P.M. to 2 A.M. Julie has noticed that Mr. Slick's system does not seem to work as well during the day shift as at night. To support her feelings, Julie collected some data over an extended period of time and found the following patterns:

Customer Arrivals per Minute	Number of Minutes	
	Day Shift	Night Shift
0	50	7
1	149	34
2	224	84
3	224	140
4	168	176
5	101	176
6	50	146
7	15	104
8	10	65
9	5	36
10	2	18
11	1	8
12	1	6
	1000	1000

After examining these data, Jason switched his forecasting strategy. He still employs his previous approach for the day shift, but now uses a Poisson distribution with $\lambda = 300$ customers per hour to predict arrivals for the night shows. How did Jason arrive at these conclusions? Do you see any potential problems in his forecasting approach?

3. The Centerville Information Center employs hosts and hostesses to answer tourists' questions on attractions in the immediate area. Previous studies reveal that the customer service times for each host or hostess follow a negative exponential distribution. The average service time has been 10 minutes per tourist.

Recently, management implemented a policy that requires each host or hostess to complete 95% of his or her service requests within 20 minutes. The limit applies only to service and does not include customer waiting time. Is this a realistic policy? If not, what do you recommend?

4. Determine the length of the waiting line and the service utilization factor for each of the following situations:

a. Customers arrive at a single-service facility every 30 minutes and are processed in exactly 30 minutes.

b. Ten customers arrive every hour at a single processing station capable of serving each arrival in exactly 12 minutes.

c. Every 45 minutes, an object arrives at a machine with a service capacity of 2 parts per hour.

5. The state highway system includes a short turnpike along the southeastern edge of Pikestown. It is controlled by a single tollbooth at the end of the road. Past data indicate that during the city's "rush" hours, cars enter the tollbooth in a random pattern with an average of 2 minutes between arrivals.

   College students and other part-time workers are employed at the booth to collect tolls. Collection times follow a random pattern with each worker capable of serving an average of 20 cars per hour.

   Ever since the state started using part-time employees, there have been "endless" traffic jams at the tollbooth during rush hours. Can you see why? Explain. What corrective action would you recommend?

6. Midtown Car Wash has a single machine capable of processing automobiles in an average of 6 minutes. Each hour, an average of 7 cars arrive at the facility. Service times and arrivals follow a random pattern.

   Management wants the car wash machine to be busy at least 70% of each working day. Another policy states that 50% of the time, there should be no more than 5 automobiles at the car wash. Are these objectives compatible under existing conditions? If not, what can be done to make them so?

7. A small fast-food restaurant currently has only one waiter. Although the service rate follows a random pattern, he is capable of serving an average of 9 customers an hour. Customers arrive randomly on the average of 1 every 10 minutes. It annually costs $36,000 to operate, finance, and maintain the restaurant. In addition, the waiter is paid $4 per hour. The restaurant is open 10 hours a day, 300 days a year.

   Advertisements state that a customer will wait, on average, no more than 3 minutes before being served. Can the restaurant keep this pledge with the existing service facility design? If not, is there an alternative system that will satisfy the advertised service policy and still not exceed the restaurant's annual $60,000 budget? Explain.

8. Explain why you agree or disagree with each of the following statements:
   a. Queuing theory is largely a descriptive rather than normative approach.
   b. There cannot be a waiting line and underutilization of service facilities in the same situation.
   c. Doubling the service rate will cut waiting time in half.
   d. The most efficient operation involves a service rate equal to the arrival rate.
   e. Two facilities, each serving customers at a standard rate, will yield results identical to a single server that is twice as fast as the standard.

Technique   1. The number of customers arriving at a clothing store was recorded
Exercises   over a period of 500 hours. The data are presented below:

Customer Arrivals per Hour	Number of Hours
0	70
1	140
2	150
3	90
4	40
5	10

    a. Compute the average arrival rate per hour.
    b. Compute the average interarrival time in minutes. Graph the
       distribution of arrivals. Do arrivals appear to follow a Poisson
       distribution? Explain.

2. Refer to Example 14.1. Demonstrate how the data in Table 14.4
   were derived. Show all your work. Calculate the cumulative
   probabilities for interarrival times of $T_a \le .8$, $T_a \le .75$, $T_a \le .4$, and
   $T_a \le .25$. Demonstrate how these values were used to develop
   Figure 14.3.

3. Following is the distribution of job processing times at a computer
   center, as recorded for a sample of 1000 requests:

Minutes per Job Request	Number of Requests
1	350
2	300
3	200
4	75
5	35
6	25
7	15

    a. Compute the average processing time in minutes.
    b. Compute the average number of jobs processed per hour.
    c. Graph the cumulative distribution of service times (values less
       than or equal to the given job processing times). Do processing
       times appear to follow a negative exponential distribution?
       Explain.

4. Refer to Example 14.2. Calculate the probabilities for each potential customer service rate. Demonstrate how these results were used to develop Figure 14.6. Compute the cumulative probabilities for service times $t \leq .8$, $t \leq .75$, $t \leq .4$, and $t \leq .25$. Show how these results were used to develop Figure 14.7.

5. Radio Station WBBB operates a popular sports talk show. Customer calls follow a Poisson distribution with $\lambda = 10$ per hour. It takes an average of 5 minutes for the single announcer to handle each call, and service time is assumed to have a negative exponential distribution. Callers are placed on hold until the announcer is free.

   a. What is the probability that the announcer will be available?
   b. What is the probability that a caller will have to wait?
   c. What is the probability that exactly 3 callers are waiting or being served? Less than 5? More than 2?
   d. What proportion of the time does the announcer actually spend handling these calls?
   e. How many callers, on average, are waiting for the announcer?
   f. What is the average waiting time for a caller?
   g. How many callers, on average, are being served or are waiting for service?
   h. How long, on average, will a caller be on the phone?

6. Again consider Titan's situation (Examples 14.1 and 14.2). Develop the entire probability distribution for the number of employees waiting or being served in the storeroom area. That is, complete Table 14.6.

   a. Using the data from your table, determine the probability that exactly 10 customers are in the system.
   b. Determine the probability that no more than 12 customers are in the system.
   c. Determine the probability that more than 9 customers are waiting or being served.
   d. Calculate the expected number of customers in the system. How does this result compare to the value L found from equation (14.8)?

7. A photocopying machine is shared by the 6 secretaries in a law office. On average, each secretary uses the machine twice an hour for an average of 1.2 minutes at a time. Both interarrival and service times appear to follow negative exponential distributions.

   a. What proportion of time is the machine actually in use?
   b. What is the probability that all 6 secretaries are using or waiting for the machine? Exactly 3? More than 4? No more than 2?
   c. On average, what proportion of a secretary's time is spent on tasks other than photocopying?
   d. How many secretaries, on average, are waiting to use the machine?
   e. What is the average waiting time?

    f. On average, how many secretaries are using or waiting for the machine?

    g. What is the average time spent for photocopying?

8. One attendant operates a gasoline station capable of serving an average of 20 customers per hour. Service times appear to follow a negative exponential distribution. There is a maximum space for 6 cars in the station (waiting and being served). Automobiles arrive at the station at an average rate of one every 4 minutes. The arrival rate appears to follow a Poisson distribution. Cars unable to find a space leave and do not return.

    a. Determine the proportion of arrivals that will leave.

    b. Determine the proportion of time the station will be empty.

    c. What is the probability of finding exactly 4 cars at the station? No more than 3? More than 5?

    d. Find the average number of cars at the station.

    e. Find the average time spent by a car at the station?

    f. Find the average number of cars waiting for gasoline.

    g. Determine the average waiting time.

    Suppose that a small adjacent lot can be rented for 80 cents per car space per hour. The lot can accommodate 4 additional cars. Also, each lost customer results in a loss of $1.50 profit. Should the gasoline station rent the lot?

9. Consider a two-channel queuing system with a mean arrival rate of $\lambda = 60$ per hour and an average service rate of $u = 100$ per hour for each facility. Both the arrival and service rates follow a Poisson distribution.

    a. What is the probability of an empty system?

    b. What is the probability that an arrival will have to wait?

    c. On average, how many customers will be in the system?

    d. How long, on average, will a customer spend in the system?

    e. On average, how many customers will be waiting for service?

    f. How long, on average, will a customer wait for service?

    Suppose that the system was expanded to three service facilities. What are the new values for the operating characteristics (a) through (f)? Which system exhibits the best performance? Explain.

10. Action Towing operates an emergency road service for disabled motor vehicles. Past data indicate that an average of 5 emergency calls are received per hour. It appears that these data follow a Poisson distribution. Each tow truck can handle an average of 8 calls per hour at an estimated hourly cost of $15 per truck. Service times are assumed to follow a negative exponential distribution. Customer waiting leads to ill will and other costs estimated at $20 per hour. The company is evaluating performance characteristics and costs of various plans. Management wants to determine the following values for a 1-, 2-, 3-, and 4-truck system:

    a. The probability that all trucks will be busy

    b. The probability that all trucks will be idle

c. The probability that exactly 2 disabled vehicles will be waiting or being served. More than 3. No more than 5.

d. The average number of emergency calls waiting or being served

e. The average time to complete emergency service

f. The average number of customers waiting for a tow truck

g. The average waiting time

h. The total (customer waiting plus service facility) costs

Calculate these operating characteristics and costs for each plan. Which alternative leads to the "best performance? To lowest total cost? Explain.

Applications Exercises

1. Geometric Field is a private airport for small commercial aircraft currently operating with one runway for landings. Airplanes arrive at the airport in a random pattern at an average rate of 12 per hour. Variations in weather and type of aircraft also result in fluctuating landing times that appear to follow a random pattern. On average, 1 airplane lands every 4 minutes. While waiting for a landing, each aircraft consumes an average of 11 gallons of fuel per minute. A gallon of fuel costs $2.50.

Management is in the process of evaluating airport-operating performance. Performance is measured by several factors:

◆ Runway utilization

◆ The average number of aircraft waiting for permission to land

◆ The average "circling" time

◆ The average fuel cost consumed by an aircraft waiting to land

In addition, airport officials would like to know the probability that an aircraft will have to wait to land. Moreover, they would like to know the probability of finding more than 5 aircraft in the airport vicinity ("circling" or landing). Prepare a brief report that addresses these issues in language understandable to management.

2. Passenger trains arrive at Midtown station in a random pattern on the average of 1 every 15 minutes. Although the actual time fluctuates in a random manner, each crew member can load and unload customer baggage in an average of 30 minutes. An increase in crew size will result in a proportional decrease in the average baggage service time. Baggage crew members are paid $7 per hour whether working or idle. The railroad owns the station as well as the trains using this facility. Operating expenses and other related charges cost the company an estimated $35 for each hour that a train spends at the station.

Company policy states that no train should wait more than 10 minutes for baggage service. In addition, 60% of the time, there should be no more than 3 trains at the station. What crew size will satisfy these policies at least cost?

3. The northeastern office of the Nuclear Regulatory Agency randomly inspects the three nuclear electric power plants in its region. A single commissioner issues a notice and then conducts the inspection an average of 8 times per year. The commissioner works 250 days a year and is paid an annual salary of $50,000. After receiving a notice, the plant is shut down and remains closed until it is inspected. In these instances, the utility must use more expensive energy sources. As a result, it costs the utility an estimated $240 in additional operating expenses for each day that the plant is inoperative. Inspection time fluctuates in a random fashion, but the average is 25 days per plant.

   The agency is currently evaluating the performance of its nuclear plant inspection process. The following data are relevant:

   1. The average number of inoperative nuclear plants
   2. The average time that a plant is inoperative
   3. The average number of plants waiting for inspection
   4. The average waiting time

   Other useful information includes the probability of an idle commissioner and the chance that more than one plant will be inoperative. Prepare a brief report to the agency that provides such data in a form understandable to agency officials.

4. In an effort to streamline its civil justice system, Mundane County has instituted a new small-claims program. Under this program, a conference center with a 10-seat capacity has been converted into a "nonscheduled" courtroom. Citizens, at their convenience, can bring small-claims actions before a single designated judge for adjudication. It costs the county an estimated $50 an hour to operate the nonscheduled courtroom. When the conference center has been filled to capacity, further arrivals are referred to the clerk of courts for conventional processing. Operations in the conventional program cost the county $75 per hour.

   In a preliminary experiment, citizens arrived randomly at the nonscheduled courtroom. There was an average of 30 minutes between arrivals. Although the actual time to hear a case fluctuated in a random fashion, the average was 20 minutes.

   County administrators have been pleased with the initial results of the streamlined program. In fact, they would like to expand capacity by converting an adjacent office. The conversion would add 5 seats to the nonscheduled facility at an amortized cost of $10 per hour of courtroom operation. Before reaching a decision, county officials want to evaluate the potential performance of both the unexpanded and expanded nonscheduled facilities. Relevant measures include:

   ◆ The average number of cases handled
   ◆ The average time to process a case
   ◆ The average number of citizens waiting for adjudication
   ◆ The average waiting time

Other useful data are the proportion of lost customers, the probability of an idle courtroom, and the chance of finding more than 8 cases in court. Prepare a brief report to the county that provides this information for both the original and expanded nonscheduled programs. Explain why the county should or should not expand the program capacity. What are the cost savings from each nonscheduled program over the conventional system?

5. Fresh Foods, Inc., operates a supermarket with 6 checkout stands in Hilltown. Past records indicate that customers arrive randomly throughout the day at an average rate of 9 per hour. Fresh Foods knows from past experience that long waiting lines create customer ill will and frustration. The company believes that these factors result in an estimated future lost profit of $80 per customer. Since orders vary in size and customers use different methods of payment, checkout times have fluctuated in a random fashion. However, each clerk has been able to check out a customer in an average of 6 minutes. Clerks receive an hourly salary of $8.

   a. How many checkout stands should the store keep staffed to minimize costs?
   b. What are the resulting costs?
   c. How many customers, on average, will be in the checkout area?
   d. On average, how long is a customer in the checkout area?
   e. How many customers, on average, are waiting for checkout?
   f. On average, how long does a customer have to wait for checkout?
   g. What is the probability that all checkout stands will be busy?
   h. What is the chance of finding no more than 3 customers in the checkout area? More than 10?

6. Crystal City's post office uses the window service system illustrated in the following diagram.

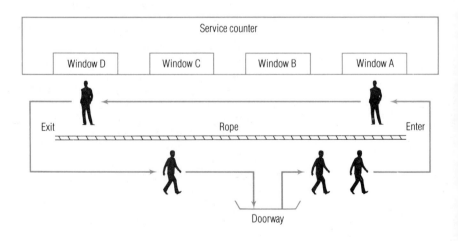

Customers arrive in a random pattern throughout the day, enter a single queue, and proceed to the first available service window. In midweek (Tuesday through Thursday), the arrival rate averages 18 customers per hour. On other days (Monday, Friday, and Saturday), the average is 30 customers per hour. As a result of differences in customer requests, service times also fluctuate in a random fashion. However, records indicate that each postal clerk completes service in an average of 3 minutes. Clerks work 8 hours a day and are paid $12 per hour.

Post office policy is to provide the best possible service for the available budget. Crystal City's post office, which operates 300 days a year, has an annual budget of $100,000 for clerks. Half of its operating days are in midweek. Reasonable service is defined as follows:

♦ There should be no more than a 50% probability of finding as many as 10 customers in the post office.

♦ There should never be more than an average of 8 customers waiting for service.

♦ The average waiting time should be no more than 7 minutes.

To comply with post office policy, how many service windows should the Crystal City branch keep staffed each day? Explain.

CASE: Sommerville Savings & Loan Association

Melissa Dinero has just been appointed Assistant Manager of Customer Services for the Sommerville Savings & Loan Association. Her first assignment is to investigate the potential effects of restructuring teller service facilities.

Under the current system, the savings and loan association has 5 tellers performing identical duties during peak periods. When customers arrive, they select what appears to be the shortest waiting line. The physical layout of the facility makes it difficult for customers to switch lines. As a result, each teller handles an average of one-fifth of all arrivals. The situation is illustrated in Figure 14.10.

Unfortunately, the system has not worked as well as planned. Typically, a customer will select the teller with the shortest waiting line. Yet, owing to differences in transaction times, some lines tend to move faster than others. Therefore, an arrival who picks a short line often waits an inordinate period of time if the preceding customer needs extended service.

Melissa has examined how banks and other savings and loan associations handle the problem. She has found two popular alternatives. One option is to designate one teller as the express window for customers with a single simple transaction (like a deposit or withdrawal). Other customers select one of the other four lines, as in the current system. A second plan is to have all customers form a single waiting line. As soon as any teller becomes available, the first customer in line proceeds to the free window. This second alternative is illustrated in Figure 14.11.

As part of her investigation, Melissa has also collected data on the customer arrival process, teller service patterns, and selected operating costs. Arrivals were recorded for a period of 100 hours during a representative sample of peak periods. The results appear in Table 14.15. In addition, observations of the time required to handle transactions for these arrivals provided the data given in Table 14.16. Each teller had this same distribution of service rates.

Figure 14.10 Current Queuing System at Sommerville Savings & Loan

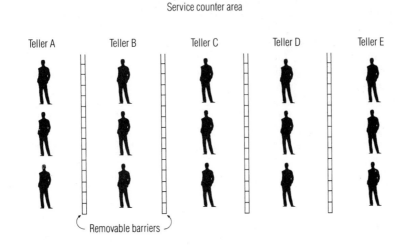

Figure 14.11 Alternative Queuing System for Sommerville Savings & Loan

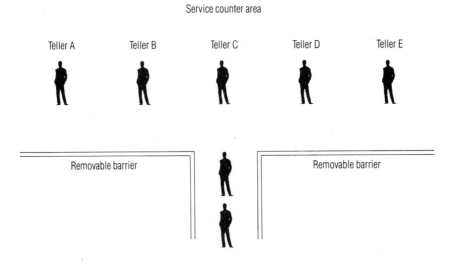

Previous industry experience indicates that arrival and service rates tend to be identical under the current system and the single-queue, multiple-server system. On the other hand, a preliminary survey has shown that the express system would reduce service time by an average of 3 minutes. The study also suggests that 30 % of all customers would use express service. However, service time for the remaining patrons is expected to increase by 4 minutes per customer.

Currently, tellers are paid $6 per hour. The savings and loan knows that

Table 14.15 Arrivals at Sommerville Savings & Loan

Customer Arrivals per Hour	Number of Hours	Customer Arrivals per Hour	Number of Hours	Customer Arrivals per Hour	Number of Hours
0	0	9	3	18	7
1	0	10	5	19	6
2	0	11	7	20	4
3	0	12	8	21	3
4	0	13	10	22	2
5	0	14	10	23	1
6	0	15	10	24	1
7	1	16	10	25	1
8	2	17	8	26	1

Table 14.16 Transaction Times at Sommerville Savings & Loan

Customers Served per Hour	Number of Hours	Customers Served per Hour	Number of Hours
0	0	6	15
1	3	7	10
2	8	8	7
3	14	9	4
4	18	10	2
5	18	11	1

waiting time creates customer frustration and eventually ill will. Management estimates that the association loses $10 of potential revenue for every hour a customer has to wait for service.

Melissa's boss has asked for her report comparing the current teller system with the two restructuring proposals. This report must include:

1. The nature of the arrival and service processes

2. The utilization factors under each system

3. The probability of idle service facilities under each system

4. The probability distribution for the number of customers in each system

5. The average number of customers in the service counter area under each system

6. The average time a customer spends in each system

7. The average number of customers waiting for service under each system

8. The average customer waiting time under each plan

9. The operating (customer waiting plus service facility) costs for each plan

10. The plan Melissa would adopt and why

Assume that you are Melissa and prepare such a report in a form understandable to Sommerville's board of directors.

Chapter 15
Sequential Problems

CHAPTER OUTLINE

CONCEPTS

♦ Recognizing situations that involve evolutionary processes

♦ Predicting, by hand and with the aid of a computer, the outcomes at various stages of an evolutionary process

♦ Utilizing the evolutionary outcome data to evaluate management policies

♦ Formulating and solving problems that involve a series of interrelated decisions

APPLICATIONS

♦ Brand switching
♦ Pricing
♦ Equipment repair
♦ Accounts receivable
♦ Food inspection
♦ Population mobility
♦ Antitrust action
♦ Telephone service
♦ Cosmetic surgery
♦ Labor productivity
♦ Tree farming
♦ Mortgage lending

The previous chapters have primarily dealt with static situations. That is, most of the problems involved circumstances in which the uncontrollable inputs remained at the same levels throughout the planning period. Distribution models, for example, assumed that all costs or returns, available supplies, and demand requirements continued unchanged for the entire period under consideration.

Yet, there are many situations in which the uncontrollable inputs change over time. For instance, distribution costs or returns, resource supplies, and consumer demands typically vary from one time period to another. Under these circumstances, the situation can be viewed as a problem involving a sequence of operations and decisions.

This chapter shows how to recognize and handle such sequential problems. The first section describes the characteristics of evolutionary processes. In particular, it develops the initial conditions, examines the pattern of change, and explores the behavior of these processes.

The second section presents a framework for analyzing evolutionary processes. First, a formal model is developed to describe the system's behavior. Then predictions are made from the model by hand and with the aid of a computer. In addition, some important extensions to the analysis are considered, as well as a sample of typical management applications.

The final section shows how to formulate a problem as a sequence of interrelated decisions and then develops an approach designed to generate the best solution to the problem. It also provides a sample of reported management applications and examines some important limitations to the analysis.

MARKOV SYSTEMS

Some situations involve an evolutionary process. The system starts with a set of initial conditions, such as the purchase behavior of a particular group of customers. Then certain changes develop in the conditions. For instance, customers may change their purchase patterns. Eventually, the system evolves into a stable pattern. Consider Example 15.1.

EXAMPLE 15.1 Brand Switching

A small, rural drugstore stocks two brands of paper towels: Absorber and Dainty. When a consumer shops for this product, he or she will select either Absorber or Dainty, but not both. The store knows that customers switch brands over time because of advertising, dissatisfaction with the product, and other reasons. Of course, the exact brand purchased at any particular time is not known with perfect certainty. However, store records do provide the following data:

1. Out of all the customers that bought Absorber in a given week, 80% purchased Absorber while 20% switched to Dainty the following week.

2. For the consumers that purchased Dainty in a given week, 70% bought Dainty and 30% switched to Absorber the following week.

No old customers leave and no new customers enter the market during this period. The store is making stock plans. As part of the planning, it must predict the proportions of consumers that will buy each brand in the future.

In Example 15.1, the drugstore is interested in describing consumers' brand-buying behavior. At the start of the process in week 1, customers have particular probabilities of purchasing the brands. Between weeks, some consumers switch brands. Consequently, the purchase probabilities in the future may differ from the current likelihoods. Store management, then, wants to determine the future outcomes from the evolutionary process.

Early in the twentieth century, the Russian mathematician Andrei A. Markov studied such a process. As a result of his study, Markov developed an approach that was designed to describe and predict the behavior of the evolutionary process. In honor of the originator, this approach is now known as **Markov analysis**.

The process analyzed by Markov had a set of well-defined characteristics. To properly use his approach, then, the decision maker must fully understand the nature of these characteristics.

CHARACTERISTICS In Example 15.1, the process involves consumer purchases of paper towels. The store monitors this process on a weekly basis by recording the proportion of customers that select each brand. In Markov terminology, each weekly observation is referred to as a **trial** or **stage** of the process. Week 1, for example, represents trial 1 of the towel purchase process.

The brand purchased in a particular week is known as the **state** of the system. In this regard, a drugstore customer can buy either Absorber or Dainty at each trial. Thus, there are only two possible states in Example 15.1. Moreover, since 2 is a finite number, management can list and identify each state in detail, as follows:

Figure 15.1 Drugstore Transition Patterns

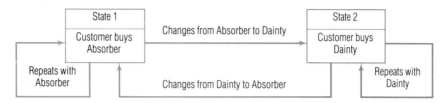

- State 1: The customer buys Absorber.
- State 2: The customer buys Dainty.

For example, the system will be in state 2 at trial 4, when the customer buys Dainty during the third week from the starting date (week 1) of the observations.

On the other hand, the store does not know exactly which brand will be purchased in a particular week. Instead, store records merely provide information on the customers' probabilities of buying the two brands. Hence, the purchase process is stochastic in nature.

Furthermore, consumer brand choices may change from week to week. In particular, each brand may retain, gain, or lose customers. Figure 15.1 illustrates the potential transitions. According to the diagram, one possibility is that consumers will switch from Dainty (state 2) to Absorber (state 1) in any particular week. Since store records show that towels are purchased weekly, there would be only one such change per trial (week).

Example 15.1 also indicates that the brand choice in any particular week is influenced only by the selection made in the immediately preceding week. Selections made two, three, or more weeks previously have no effect on the current brand choice. A stochastic system with this property is known as a memoryless or **first-order Markov process**.

In addition, the store records provide the probabilities that consumers will move from one state (brand) to another between trials (weeks) of the process. For instance, management knows that 80% of the customers who buy Absorber this week again will purchase Absorber next week. Similarly, Example 15.1 indicates that 30% of the consumers who buy Dainty in the current week will switch to Absorber next week. Such likelihoods are called **transition probabilities**.

Moreover, Example 15.1 suggests that these transition probabilities remain the same from week to week. Also, they do not seem to change for any customer. A Markov process with these properties is called a **homogeneous Markov chain**.

Table 15.1 summarizes these main characteristics of Markov situations. A situation that has all these characteristics can be referred to as a **Markov system**.

Table 15.1 Markov System Characteristics

1. The system involves a stochastic process that can be observed at numerous points. Typically, each point, which is known as a trial or stage of the process, represents a different time period.
2. All trials or stages are equal in length.
3. There is a finite number of outcomes, known as states of the system, that occur at each trial.
4. The state of the system can change from one stage to the next, but there will be only one such change per trial.
5. The system's condition at any particular trial depends only on the condition in the immediately preceding stage. In other words, the system involves a memoryless or first-order Markov process.
6. It is possible to determine the system's transition probabilities, that is, the likelihoods that the system will move from one state to another between trials.
7. The transition probabilities remain constant from trial to trial. Put another way, the process generates a homogeneous Markov chain.

TRANSITION PATTERN Practical problems can involve hundreds, even thousands, of transition probabilities. The decision maker therefore needs some device to conveniently record and keep track of such information. One device typically used for these purposes is a table with the general format shown in Figure 15.2. In this diagram, the letter m represents the finite number of states in the system.

Figure 15.2 shows that each row of the table depicts a state of the system in the current trial. Each column denotes a state in the next stage of the process. The corresponding transition probabilities are presented in the body of the table. Entries along the diagonal give the probabilities that the process will remain in the same state from the current trial to the next. Gains for the states are measured by the entries in the columns to the left of the diagonal. Losses from the states are provided by the entries in the rows to the right of the diagonal. Such a representation is known as a **transition table**.

Table 15.2 gives the drugstore's transition table. This table has several important characteristics. First, it is relevant to recognize that the entries represent conditional probabilities. That is, each entry measures the likelihood that the system will be in a particular state at the next trial if it is in a specified state during the current trial. In addition, the entries along the diagonal give the probabilities that the same brand will be purchased each week. They show, for instance, that Absorber will retain 80% and Dainty 70% of their customers. In effect, then, these diagonal values represent measures of brand loyalty or retention.

On the other hand, the off-diagonal entries in Table 15.2 measure the

Figure 15.2 Transition Table Format

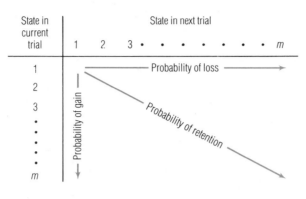

Table 15.2 Brand-Switching Transition Probabilities

Brand Purchased This Week	Brand Purchased Next Week	
	Absorber	Dainty
Absorber	.8	.2
Dainty	.3	.7

brand-switching propensities of the drugstore's customers. The row entry to the right of the diagonal, for example, indicates that there is a 20% likelihood that Absorber will lose customers to Dainty. Similarly, the column entry to the left of the diagonal shows that Absorber has a 30% chance of gaining consumers from Dainty.

Moreover, a customer who buys a particular brand one week must either repurchase the same brand or switch to the alternative in the next week. That is, these states are mutually exclusive and collectively exhaustive. As a result, the sum of the probabilities in each row of the transition table must equal 1. Consider, for example, the Absorber row in Table 15.2. It indicates that Absorber retains 80% and loses 20% of its customers. Therefore, there is a probability of .8 + .2 = 1, or 100% chance, that Absorber will either retain or lose customers next week. In essence, then, each row in Table 15.2 represents the probability distribution associated with the corresponding brand's transition pattern.

MARKOV ANALYSIS

Transition probabilities are used by management for the following tasks:

1. Predicting the condition of the system at each stage of the evolutionary process
2. Predicting the condition that the process will evolve into
3. Analyzing specified policies

This section shows how to make these predictions and perform the policy analysis.

STATE PROBABILITIES

Frequently, the decision maker must determine the probability that a Markov system is in a particular state at a specified trial. The drugstore in Example 15.1 may want to know the percentage of original Absorber customers that will remain loyal to the brand for the next two weeks. Put another way, management seeks the likelihood that the system is in state 1 during the first and second weeks (at trials 2 and 3) from the starting date (week 1) of the observation period. Such a likelihood is referred to as **state probability**.

By utilizing the information about the initial conditions and the transition pattern, management can find a state probability at any stage of the evolutionary process. The approach is based on the decision analysis concepts originally presented in Part II of the text. Figure 15.3 illustrates the calculations for the drugstore brand-switching problem.

Figure 15.3 is a probability tree in which the nodes, or circles, depict the states of the brand purchase system. Week 1 again is the starting date (current stage) of the observation period, while the broken lines denote future trials (subsequent weeks) of the towel purchase process. The transition probabilities are listed on the corresponding branches of the tree. As the figure demonstrates, the drugstore initially observes that a customer purchases Absorber during week 1 (trial 1) of the process. In addition, Table 15.2 indicates that Absorber will retain 80% of its current (week 1) consumers at the next stage (week 2) of the observation period. Therefore, there is a probability of .8 that the customer will remain loyal to Absorber (be in state 1) during week 2 (trial 2) of the process. In Figure 15.3, this likelihood appears as the transition probability on the branch joining the starting point with the week 2 Absorber node.

Recall that the transition pattern remains the same from week to week. That is, Absorber will retain 80% of its week 2 customers at the next trial (week 3) of the process. Consequently, there is a probability of

$$.8 \times .8 = .64$$

that the original Absorber customers will remain with the brand during both the second and third weeks of the observation period. In other words, the system has a .64 probability of being in state 1 at both trials 2 and 3 of

Figure 15.3 Drugstore Probability Tree

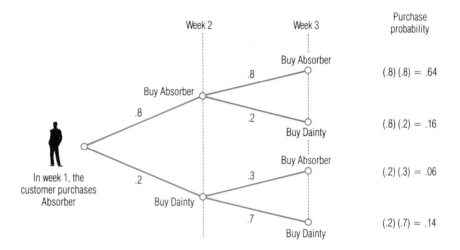

the process. This result is depicted as the purchase probability to the right of the top branch in Figure 15.3.

A purchase likelihood, then, is merely the joint probability associated with the corresponding system conditions. Furthermore, it can be found by multiplying the conditional likelihoods on the appropriate branches of the probability tree. In Figure 15.3, for instance, the lower branch emanating from week 1 shows that 20% of the customers switch from Absorber to Dainty during week 2 of the observation period. Also, the top branch emanating from the week 2 Dainty node shows that 30% of these same consumers switch back to Absorber in the third week. Thus, there is a joint

$$.2 \times .3 = .06$$

chance that the original Absorber customers will change brands during week 2 but return to Absorber in week 3 of the observation period. Put another way, the system has a .06 probability of being in state 2 at trial 2 but state 1 at trial 3.

Other joint purchase probabilities are calculated in a similar manner and recorded to the right of the corresponding branches in Figure 15.3. Moreover, these joint likelihoods can be used to determine additional state probabilities. The drugstore, for example, may want to know the percentage of original Absorber customers that will buy the brand during week 3 of the observation period. There are two ways that the system can be in state 1 (the customer purchases Absorber) at trial 3 (week 3) of the process. First, the original Absorber consumer may remain loyal to the brand during weeks 2 and 3 of the observation period. According to

Figure 15.3, this condition will occur $(.8)(.8) = .64$, or 64%, of the time. Second, the original Absorber customer might change brands in week 2 but return to Absorber during week 3 of the process. Figure 15.3 indicates that such a condition will occur $(.2)(.3) = .06$, or 6%, of the time. As a result, there is a $.64 + .06 = .70$ chance that a week 1 Absorber customer will buy Absorber in week 3 of the observation period.

The total likelihood that a specified state will occur at a particular trial is therefore the sum of the corresponding joint probabilities. According to Figure 15.3, for instance, there is a joint probability of

$$.2 \times .7 = .14$$

that the original Absorber customers will buy Dainty during weeks 2 and 3 of the observation period. In addition, there is a joint probability of

$$.8 \times .2 = .16$$

that the original Absorber customers will remain with the brand during week 2 but switch to Dainty in week 3 of the process. Therefore, the drugstore should expect $.16 + .14 = .30$, or 30%, of the week 1 Absorber consumers to purchase Dainty during week 3 of the observation period.

MATRIX APPROACH In practice, a Markov system can involve hundreds, even thousands, of states and trials. Under these circumstances, it will be very tedious and time-consuming to develop a probability tree and perform the corresponding likelihood computations. Fortunately, management scientists have developed a more efficient approach that utilizes matrix concepts to track the transition pattern and calculate the resulting state probabilities.

To see what is involved, let us reconsider the brand-switching situation depicted in Figure 15.3. According to the diagram, the drugstore observes that a customer purchases Absorber during week 1 of the observation period. That is, there is a probability of 1 that the system is in state 1 and a probability of 0 that it is in state 2 at trial 1 of the process.

These starting (week 1) conditions can be arranged in the following format:

$$P^1 = (1 \quad 0)$$

Such an arrangement of numbers is known as a **row vector of state probabilities**. The symbol P^1, then, denotes the row vector of purchase probabilities for week 1 of the drugstore's observation period. Notice that the number in the first column of this P^1 vector identifies the state 1 (Absorber purchase) probability, whereas the number in the second column identifies the state 2 (Dainty purchase) probability.

Table 15.2 describes the pattern of change in the purchase probabilities from one week to the next. These transition probabilities can be arranged in the following format:

$$T = \begin{pmatrix} .8 & .2 \\ .3 & .7 \end{pmatrix}$$

Such an arrangement of numbers is called a **transition matrix**. The symbol T, then, denotes the drugstore's transition matrix.

Note that the rows list the proportions of customers retained and lost by the brands during each week of the observation period. The first row of matrix T, for instance, shows that 80% of Absorber consumers remain loyal, but 20% switch to Dainty at each trial of the purchase process. On the other hand, the columns identify the percentage of consumers gained and retained at each trial. For example, the second column of matrix T indicates that Dainty gains 20% of Absorber's customers and retains 70% of its own customers during each week of the purchase process.

By multiplying the week 1 row vector P^1 by the transition matrix T, management can determine the system conditions during week 2 of the purchase process. That is, let the symbol P^2 denote the row vector of state probabilities in week 2 of the observation period. Then,

$$P^2 = P^1 \times T = (1 \quad 0)\begin{pmatrix} .8 & .2 \\ .3 & .7 \end{pmatrix}$$

Specifically, P^2 will list the proportions of customers that buy Absorber and Dainty during week 2 of the process.

As P^1 indicates, 100% of the customers purchase Absorber and 0% buy Dainty in week 1. In addition, the first column of T shows that 80% of Absorber consumers remain loyal and 30% of Dainty customers switch to Absorber each week in the process. Hence, the drugstore should expect

$$.8(1) + .3(0) = .8$$

or 80% of the paper towel consumers to buy Absorber during week 2 of the purchase process. Similarly, the second column of matrix T demonstrates that Dainty gains 20% of Absorber's customers and retains 70% of its own customers during each week in the observation period. Consequently, management can anticipate that

$$.2(1) + .7(0) = .2$$

or 20% of the customers will purchase Dainty in week 2 of the process.

These calculations indicate that the row vector of state probabilities in week 2 of the observation period is

$$P^2 = (.8 \quad .2)$$

In this P^2 vector, the number in the first column identifies the state 1

(Absorber purchase) probability. The number in the second column lists the state 2 (Dainty purchase) probability.

Equations (15.1) and (15.2) illustrate the computations needed to find the numbers in the P^2 row vector:

$$1 \times .8$$

$$(15.1) \quad P^2 = P^1 T = (1 \quad 0)\begin{pmatrix} .8 & .2 \\ .3 & .7 \end{pmatrix} = (.8 \quad .2)$$

$$+ (0 \times .3) \qquad 1(.8) + 0(.3) =$$

$$1 \times .2$$

$$(15.2) \quad P^2 = P^1 T = (1 \quad 0)\begin{pmatrix} .8 & .2 \\ .3 & .7 \end{pmatrix} = (.8 \quad .2)$$

$$+ 0(.7) \qquad 1(.2) + 0(.7) =$$

Each entry in the P^2 vector is found by multiplying the numbers in the P^1 vector by the values in the corresponding column of the T matrix and summing the results. Consider, for example, the .2 value in the second column of the P^2 vector. This value is the sum of the products obtained when the P^1 entries are multiplied by the numbers in the second column of the T matrix.

This same matrix approach can be used to determine the state probabilities for the third week in the observation period. In particular, the P^2 row vector gives the state probabilities in week 2 of the purchase process. Moreover, the transition matrix T identifies the pattern of change in the purchase probabilities from one week to the next. Thus, the system conditions in week 3, which can be denoted as the row vector P^3, will be

$$P^3 = P^2 \times T = (.8 \quad .2)\begin{pmatrix} .8 & .2 \\ .3 & .7 \end{pmatrix}$$

or

$$P^3 = .8(.8) + .2(.3) \qquad .8(.2) + .2(.7))$$

$$P^3 = (.7 \quad .3)$$

The number in the first column of P^3 indicates that 70% of the consumers will buy Absorber during week 3 of the process. The value in the second column shows that 30% of the week 3 customers will purchase Dainty.

These P^3 vector entries are the same values as the purchase likelihoods derived from the probability tree analysis. Such a result suggests that management can use the matrix approach summarized in Table 15.3 to predict the state probabilities at any specified trial of a first-order Markov

Table 15.3 Predicting State Probabilities

1. Formulate the matrix T of transition probabilities.
2. Identify the row vector P^n of state probabilities at trial n of the process.
3. Find the product of P^n and T. To determine the entry in each column of the product, multiply the entries in the P^n vector by the numbers in the corresponding column of the T matrix and sum the results.
4. The result $P^{n+1} = P^n T$ is the row vector of state probabilities at trial $n + 1$ of the process.

Table 15.4 Future State Probabilities for the Brand-Switching Problem When $P^1 = (1 \quad 0)$

State	\multicolumn{9}{c}{Probability for Trial}

State	1	2	3	4	5	6	7	8	→	Very large number
Absorber	1	.8	.7	.65	.625	.6125	.60625	.603125	→	.6
Dainty	0	.2	.3	.35	.375	.3875	.39375	.396875	→	.4

process. Table 15.3 demonstrates that a future stage's conditions can be predicted by multiplying the immediately preceding trial's state probability vector by the transition matrix. In other words,

$$P^4 = P^3 \times T$$
$$P^5 = P^4 \times T$$

and so on. Indeed, if the drugstore performs these matrix operations, they will obtain the results shown in Table 15.4.

STEADY STATE As Table 15.4 demonstrates, there are some relatively substantial adjustments in the purchase probabilities during the early trials (weeks 1 through 5) of the process. Eventually, however, these probabilities do not change much from one week to the next. After a very large number of trials, the purchase probabilities stabilize at equilibrium values of .6 for Absorber and .4 for Dainty.

Nevertheless, the results in Table 15.4 assume that a customer initially buys Absorber. On the other hand, suppose that a consumer purchased Dainty rather than Absorber in week 1. In this case,

$$P^1 = (0 \quad 1)$$

is the row vector of initial state probabilities. By utilizing P^1, the transition matrix

Table 15.5 Future State Probabilities for the Brand-Switching Problem When $P^1 = (0 \quad 1)$

State	Probability for Trial									
	1	2	3	4	5	6	7	8	→	Very large number
Absorber	0	.3	.45	.525	.5625	.58125	.590625	.5953125	→	.6
Dainty	1	.7	.55	.475	.4375	.41875	.409375	.4046875	→	.4

$$T = \begin{pmatrix} .8 & .2 \\ .3 & .7 \end{pmatrix}$$

and the procedure outlined in Table 15.3, management will obtain the likelihoods presented in Table 15.5.

You can see that the state probabilities in Table 15.5 are generally different from the purchase likelihoods in Table 15.4. Yet, after a very large number of trials, the state probabilities again approach .4 for Dainty and .6 for Absorber. In other words, the purchase probabilities eventually stabilize at the same equilibrium values regardless of the starting conditions in the system.

These equilibrium values of .6 for Absorber and .4 for Dainty are referred to as **steady-state probabilities**. They tell us that, in the long run, the drugstore can expect 60 out of every 100 customers to buy Absorber and 40 to buy Dainty. Consequently, these steady-state probabilities can be interpreted as each brand's eventual share of paper towel sales.

In practice, it may take a very large number of trials, or transitions, for the system to reach the steady state. Under these circumstances, the trial-by-trial transition approach will require many calculations to establish the steady-state probabilities. Fortunately, there is a more direct procedure.

As Tables 15.4 and 15.5 demonstrate, there are substantial adjustments in the week 1 through week 5 state probabilities. Such adjustments indicate that the gains and losses from brand to brand are quite large during the early trials of the process. Tables 15.4 and 15.5 also show that the gains and losses (changes in the purchase likelihoods) get smaller and smaller as the system approaches the steady state. That is, as the number of trials n increases, the difference between the row vector of state probabilities P^n at stage n and the corresponding vector P^{n-1} at stage $n-1$ becomes negligible.

After a very large number of trials, or transitions, each brand's gains will equal its losses, and the system will reach an equilibrium, or steady-state, condition. At this stage,

$$P^n = P^{n-1}$$

That is, the state probabilities will be essentially the same as the purchase likelihoods in the immediately preceding trial.

The drugstore can express these equilibrium conditions as the row vector

$$P = (p_1 \quad p_2)$$

In this vector, p_1 denotes the likelihood that a customer will buy the Absorber brand in the steady state. Similarly, p_2 represents the steady-state probability of a Dainty brand purchase.

Now, recall that the conditions at a specified trial n can be found by multiplying the immediately preceding stage's state probability vector by the transition matrix. That is,

$$P^n = P^{n-1} \times T$$

Furthermore, at the equilibrium stage,

$$P^n = P^{n-1} = P$$

or the purchase likelihoods in the current (n) and immediately preceding ($n-1$) trials will match the steady-state probabilities. As a result,

$$P = P \times T$$

in the steady state.

Management can use this matrix relationship to determine the steady-state probabilities directly. In particular,

$$P = (p_1 \quad p_2) \quad \text{and} \quad T = \begin{pmatrix} .8 & .2 \\ .3 & .7 \end{pmatrix}$$

for the drugstore. Thus,

$$P = P \times T$$

means that

$$(p_1 \quad p_1) = (p_1 \quad p_2)\begin{pmatrix} .8 & .2 \\ .3 & .7 \end{pmatrix}$$

at the equilibrium stage.

The row vector P shows that $p_1 \%$ of the customers purchase Absorber and $p_2 \%$ buy Dainty in the steady state. Furthermore, the first column of the transition matrix T indicates that 80% of Absorber consumers remain loyal and 30% of Dainty customers switch to Absorber during each week in the process. Therefore, at the equilibrium stage, management should expect

$$.8p_1 + .3p_2$$

of the paper towel consumers to buy Absorber. In other words,

(15.3) $p_1 = .8p_1 + .3p_2$

in the steady state.

    Similarly, the second column of matrix T demonstrates that Dainty gains 20% of Absorber's customers and retains 70% of its own customers during each week in the observation period. Consequently, the drugstore can anticipate that

    $.2p_1 + .7p_2$

of the consumers will purchase Dainty at the equilibrium stage of the process. That is,

(15.4) $p_2 = .2p_1 + .7p_2$

in the steady state.

    Equations (15.5) and (15.6) illustrate the matrix computations needed to identify these steady-state conditions:

$$p_1 \times .8$$

$$(15.5) \quad P = PT = (p_1 \quad p_2)\begin{pmatrix} .8 & .2 \\ .3 & .7 \end{pmatrix} = (\,p_1 = .8p_1 + .3p_2 \quad p_2)$$

$$+ (p_2 \times .3) \qquad .8p_1 + .3p_2 =$$

$$p_1 \times .2$$

$$(15.6) \quad P = PT = (p_1 \quad p_2)\begin{pmatrix} .8 & .2 \\ .3 & .7 \end{pmatrix} = (p_1 \quad p_2 = .2p_1 + .7p_2)$$

$$+ (p_2 \times .7) \qquad .2p_1 + .7p_2 =$$

    According to equation (15.3), the proportion of customers that will purchase Absorber in the steady state is

    $p_1 = .8p_1 + .3p_2$

Among this total proportion (p_1), $.8p_1$ is retained from previous Absorber consumers and $.3p_2$ is gained from the Dainty brand. Hence, the difference

    $p_1 - .8p_1 = .2p_1$

gives the percentage of customers that Absorber loses to Dainty.

    If we subtract $.8p_1$ from both sides of equation (15.3), we obtain the expression

    $p_1 - .8p_1 = .8p_1 - .8p_1 + .3p_2$

or

(15.7) $.2p_1 = .3p_2$

This expression shows that in the steady state, the proportion of customers lost from Absorber ($.2p_1$) must equal the percentage gained by the brand ($.3p_2$). Otherwise, the excess gains or losses will create instability in the market and thereby disrupt any equilibrium condition.

There is a similar relationship for the Dainty brand. According to equation (15.4), the proportion of customers that will purchase Dainty in the steady state is

$$p_2 = .2p_1 + .7p_2$$

Among the total proportion (p_2), $.7p_2$ is retained from previous Dainty consumers and $.2p_2$ is gained from the Absorber brand. Therefore, the difference

$$p_2 - .7p_2 = .3p_2$$

represents the percentage of customers that Dainty loses to Absorber.

When we subtract $.7p_2$ from both sides of equation (15.4), we get the expression

$$p_2 - .7p_2 = .2p_1 + .7p_2 - .7p_2$$

or

$$(15.8) \quad .3p_2 = .2p_1$$

This expression indicates that in the steady state, the proportion of customers lost from Dainty ($.3p_2$) must equal the percentage gained by the brand ($.2p_1$). Otherwise, the excess losses or gains would create instability in the market and disrupt any equilibrium condition.

Equation (15.8) provides the same information as equation (15.7). One of the equations is therefore redundant. Yet, neither equation contains enough data to compute the values of both steady-state probabilities (p_1 and p_2), because the drugstore still has not completely accounted for one other important equilibrium condition.

The purchase involves two mutually exclusive and collectively exhaustive states. A customer will buy either Absorber or Dainty during any particular week of the observation period. As a result,

$$(15.9) \quad p_1 + p_2 = 1$$

That is, the purchase likelihoods must sum to 1 in the steady state.

According to equation (15.9), the proportion of customers that will buy Dainty in the steady state is

$$(15.10) \quad p_2 = 1 - p_1$$

Furthermore, equation (15.8) indicates that

$$.3p_2 = .2p_1$$

Table 15.6 Finding the Steady-State Probabilities

1. Formulate the row vector P of unknown steady-state probabilities.
2. Identify the matrix T of transition probabilities.
3. Find the product of P and T. To determine the entry in each column of the product, multiply the entries in the P vector by the numbers in the corresponding column of the T matrix and sum the results.
4. Set the product PT equal to P.
5. Identify the simultaneous system of equations formed from the resulting row vector $P = PT$.
6. Discard any one of the equations identified in step 5.
7. Form an equation that sets the sum of the steady-state probabilities equal to 1.
8. Use the equations formed in steps 5 through 7 to find the unknown steady-state probabilities.

or

$$p_2 = \tfrac{2}{3} \times p_1$$

By substituting this result for p_2 in equation (15.10), we get

$$\tfrac{2}{3}p_1 = 1 - p_1$$

or

$$\tfrac{5}{3}p_1 = 1$$

and

$$p_1 = \tfrac{3}{5} = .6$$

In other words, at the steady state, the drugstore should expect 60% of the paper towel consumers to buy the Absorber brand. Thus,

$$p_2 = 1 - p_1 = 1 - .6 = .4$$

or 40% of the customers can be expected to purchase the Dainty brand.

Table 15.6 summarizes the direct approach for finding the steady-state probabilities. The direct method indicates that the steady-state probabilities are $p_1 = .6$ for Absorber and $p_2 = .4$ for Dainty. These likelihoods are exactly the same as the equilibrium values obtained in Tables 15.4 and 15.5 by the trial-to-trial transition approach. The direct method, however, will usually require far fewer computations than the transition approach.

COMPUTER ANALYSIS In practice, it may take a large number of complex computations to perform a Markov analysis by hand. Furthermore, the calculations can be time-consuming and prone to error. That is why management scientists

Figure 15.4 MRKV1 Analysis of Brand Switching

```
**   INFORMATION ENTERED   **

TOTAL NUMBER OF STATES      : 2
        TRANSITION TABLE

STATES

1    .8     .2
2    .3     .7

        MARKET SHARE

FUTURE PERIOD : 4

STATES          SHARE

1               1
2               0

** RESULTS  **

STEADY STATE PROBABILITIES

   .6     .4

       MARKET SHARE ANALYSIS

START PERIOD:   1
END PERIOD  :   5

TRANSITION MATRIX AFTER PERIOD 4

   .625    .375
   .563    .438

MARKET SHARE IN PERIOD 5

   .625    .375

** END OF ANALYSIS **
```

have developed prewritten computer packages to perform the analysis. One such package, called **MRKV1**, is available on the diskette provided with the W. J. Erikson and O. P. Hall book [8]. Figure 15.4 illustrates how this package can be utilized to calculate the drugstore's state probabilities.

As Figure 15.4 shows, the program requires the state and transition data to perform a Markov analysis. In this regard, the drugstore knows that a customer will purchase either Absorber or Dainty. Put another way, there are only two states in the purchase process. Thus, the user must enter the value 2 after the TOTAL NUMBER OF STATES prompt in MRKV1.

Moreover, the purchase process generates the transition probabilities shown in Table 15.2. Consequently, these probabilities should be entered into the computer one state at a time. Table 15.2, for instance, shows that the Absorber brand (state 1) retains .8 but loses .2 of its customers from one week to the next. Hence, the user must enter the values .8 and .2 alongside the state 1 prompt in the program. Similarly, Table 15.2 indicates that the Dainty brand (state 2) loses .3 but retains .7 of its customers. The decision maker, then, types the values .3 and .7 following the state 2 computer prompt.

At this point, MRKV1 begins to supply the relevant Markov results. First, the program gives the steady-state probabilities. In the RESULTS section of Figure 15.4, for example, the drugstore is given a

$p_1 = .6$ chance of selling Absorber

and a

$p_2 = .4$ chance of selling Dainty

at equilibrium. These probabilities, of course, are the same values obtained using hand computation.

The MRKV1 program can also be used to calculate the state probabilities in any specified future period. As Figure 15.4 demonstrates, the user executes such an analysis by selecting the MARKET SHARE option within the package. The computer then requests the number of periods that will elapse between the current and future period. In addition, MRKV1 asks for the current state conditions. For instance, suppose that the drugstore wants to determine the proportions of customers that will purchase each brand of paper towel four weeks from now. In this case, the decision maker must type the value 4 after the FUTURE PERIOD prompt in MRKV1. Moreover, let us assume that management observes that a customer buys the Absorber brand (state 1) during the current week. In other words,

$P^1 = (1 \quad 0)$

is the row vector of state probabilities in week 1 of the process. Under these circumstances, the user should input the value 1 after the state 1 prompt and 0 following the state 2 prompt. Such commands will generate the MARKET SHARE ANAYSIS reported in the RESULTS section of Figure 15.4. The analysis starts at the current week (period 1) and ends in week (period) 5.

According to the TRANSITION MATRIX AFTER PERIOD 4, 62.5% of Absorber customers remain loyal but 37.5% switch to Dainty at the end of week 4. Furthermore, only 43.8% of Dainty consumers remain loyal while 56.3% switch to Absorber during this period. Thus, the MARKET SHARE IN PERIOD 5 section shows that the drugstore can expect 62.5% of the customers to purchase Absorber and 37.5% to purchase Dainty in week 5. Once more, these probabilities are the same values obtained in Table 15.4 using hand calculation.

PASSAGE TIMES It is frequently desirable to identify the number of trials that will pass before a specified change occurs in the system conditions. For example, to help plan operations, the drugstore may want to know the average number of weeks that will elapse before an Absorber customer switches to Dainty for the first time. Such an average is known as a **mean first passage time**.

Since the consumer purchase decision is a stochastic process, there will be a probability distribution of first passage times. Moreover, this distribution depends on the transition pattern involved in the process. By finding the expected value for the distribution, then, management can obtain the mean first passage time. The required methodology, however, is beyond the scope of our discussion. D. Freedman [9] and J. G. Kemeny and J. L. Snell [17] present the details for the interested reader.

Nevertheless, several prewritten computer packages contain options that perform the calculations and generate the passage time data. Figure 15.5 illustrates how the MRKV1 program supplies the relevant information for the drugstore situation. Once more, the program requires the state and transition data to perform a Markov analysis. Next, the user executes the desired passage time analysis by selecting the appropriate output option within the package. In Figure 15.5, the drugstore utilizes all three passage time options contained in MRKV1.

At this point, the program begins to supply the relevant Markov results. Initially, MRKV1 gives the steady-state probabilities. Then it provides a table that lists the mean first passage times between each pair of states. Furthermore, this table will be arranged in a format similar to the transition matrix. Notice that the mean first passage times in Figure 15.5 are arranged in the following format:

$$M = \begin{pmatrix} 0 & 5 \\ 3.33 & 0 \end{pmatrix}$$

where the symbol M denotes the matrix of mean first passage times for the drugstore situation. In this matrix, the first row indicates that an average of 5 weeks will elapse before an Absorber customer (state 1) initially switches to the Dainty brand (state 2). The second row suggests that an average of 3.33 weeks will pass before a Dainty consumer (state 2) changes to Absorber (state 1) for the first time.

Another pertinent change deals with the number of trials that elapse before the system can make a transition from a specified state for the first time. The drugstore, for example, might want to know the average number of weeks that pass before an Absorber customer can initially consider a brand change. Such an average is referred to as an **equilibrium first passage time**.

Figure 15.5 MRKV1 Analysis of Passage Times

```
        **   INFORMATION ENTERED   **

        TOTAL NUMBER OF STATES      : 2
                TRANSITION TABLE

    STATES

    1     .8      .2
    2     .3      .7

        ** RESULTS   **

        STEADY STATE PROBABILITIES
            .6      .4

        MEAN FIRST PASSAGE TIMES
            0       5
            3.33    0

        EQUL FIRST PASSAGE TIMES
            1.33    3

        EXPECTED RECURRENCE TIMES
            1.66    2.5

        ** END OF ANALYSIS **
```

In Figure 15.5,

$$P = (.6 \quad .4)$$

is the row vector of steady-state probabilities. These probabilities represent the proportions of times that consumers purchase each brand at equilibrium. Furthermore, the matrix of mean first passage times

$$M = \begin{pmatrix} 0 & 5 \\ 3.33 & 0 \end{pmatrix}$$

gives the average number of weeks that elapse between initial brand shifts. By multiplying the row vector P by the matrix M, management can determine the equilibrium first passage times.

In particular, the row vector P indicates that Absorber is purchased 60% of the time and Dainty 40% of the time at the steady state. The first column of M suggests that it takes 0 weeks for an Absorber customer and

3.33 weeks for a Dainty customer to initially consider the Absorber brand. Therefore, the drugstore should expect

$$.6(0) + .4(3.33) = 1.33 \text{ weeks}$$

to elapse before an Absorber consumer can make a brand change for the first time. Similarly, the second column in M shows that it takes 5 weeks for an Absorber customer and 0 weeks for a Dainty customer to initially consider the Dainty brand. Consequently, management must anticipate that

$$.6(5) + .4(0) = 3 \text{ weeks}$$

will pass before a Dainty consumer can switch brands for the first time.

The calculations indicate that the equilibrium first passage time is 1.33 weeks for the Absorber brand and 3 weeks for the Dainty brand. The MRKV1 program contains an output option that performs the computations to generate these equilibrium times. Indeed, the EQUL FIRST PASSAGE TIMES data in Figure 15.5 shows that this option provides the same results as the hand calculation.

A third important passage time involves the number of periods that will pass between the repeat occurrences of a specified state in the system. To plan inventory, for example, the drugstore may need the average elapsed time between the repeat purchases of the Absorber towel brand. Such an average is called an **expected recurrence time**.

In this respect, the steady-state probabilities can be interpreted as the proportions of times that the process will enter each state in the long run. The .6 steady-state probability of Figure 15.5, for example, indicates that at equilibrium, a customer will purchase Absorber 6 out of every 10 weeks. As a result, the drugstore should expect

$$\frac{10 \text{ weeks}}{6 \text{ purchases}} = 1.66 \text{ weeks}$$

to elapse between repeat Absorber purchases.

In effect, then, the expected recurrence time will equal the reciprocal of the corresponding steady-state probability. That is,

$$(15.11) \quad \mu_i = \frac{1}{p_i}$$

where μ_i denotes the expected recurrence time and p_i the steady-state probability for state i. Hence, equation (15.11) and the steady-state data from Figure 15.5 suggest that an average of

$$\mu_2 = \frac{1}{p_2} = \frac{1}{.4} = 2.5 \text{ weeks}$$

will pass between repeat Dainty purchases (state 2).

The MRKV1 program contains an output option that performs the computations to generate these recurrence times. Indeed, the results in Figure 15.5 are the same as those obtained by hand computation.

ABSORBING STATES In the drugstore situation, customers may buy the same brand towel or switch to an alternative brand during each week of the observation period. That is, the system can change states between any two trials of the process. On the other hand, there are cases where a system enters one or more states from which, once there, it cannot exit to some other state. Example 15.2 provides a well-known accounting illustration of this situation.

EXAMPLE 15.2 Accounts Receivable Analysis

Master Bank has two aging categories for its credit card accounts receivable: 0 to 40 days old and 41 to 100 days old. Any portion of an account balance that is over 100 days old is written off as a bad debt. The bank ages the total balance in any customer's account according to the oldest unpaid bill. For example, suppose one customer's account balance on June 30 is as shown in Table 15.7. On June 30, the total $130 balance is assigned to the 41-to-100-day category because the oldest unpaid bill (April 10) is 82 days old. Assume that one week later, July 7, the customer pays the April 10 bill of $50.

The remaining total balance of $80 is now placed in the 0-to-40-day category. (The oldest unpaid amount, corresponding to the May 25 purchase, is less than 41 days old.) Since the total account balance is placed in the age category corresponding to the oldest unpaid amount, this approach is called the total balance method.

Under the total balance method, dollars appearing in a particular category at one point in time may be classified differently later. This was the case for $80 of May and June billings. After the April bill was paid, the $80 shifted from the 41-day-and-over category to the 40-day-and-under category. Past records provide the transition data shown in Table 15.8.

On December 31, Master Bank has a total of $500,000 in accounts receivable. Of this total, $200,000 is 0 to 40 days old and $300,000 is 41 to 100 days old. The bank's management would like an estimate of the amounts that eventually will be collected and uncollected. Any estimated amount of bad debts will appear as an allowance in the year-end financial statements.

Table 15.7 June 30 Account Balance

Purchase Date	Amount Charged
April 10	$50
May 25	20
June 12	60
Total	$130

Table 15.8 Transition Probabilities for the Accounts Receivable Problem

Previous Account Balance	Current Account Balance			
	Paid	Bad debt	0 to 40 days old	41 to 100 days old
Paid	1	0	0	0
Bad debt	0	1	0	0
0 to 40 days old	.5	0	.3	.2
41 to 100 days old	.4	.2	.3	.1

First let us concentrate on what happens to each dollar currently in accounts receivable. As the bank continues to extend credit, management can think of each week as a trial in a Markov process. Moreover, each dollar of accounts receivable may be classified in any of the following states for the system:

♦ State 1: paid
♦ State 2: bad debt
♦ State 3: 0 to 40 days old
♦ State 4: 41 to 100 days old

The decision maker can then track the week-to-week status of each dollar by determining the state of the system at the appropriate future period.

Using the data from Table 15.8, the bank will find that the matrix of transition probabilities is

$$T = \begin{pmatrix} 1 & 0 & 0 & 0 \\ 0 & 1 & 0 & 0 \\ .5 & 0 & .3 & .2 \\ .4 & .2 & .3 & .1 \end{pmatrix}$$

In this matrix, the rows list the proportions of accounts receivable that move from one state to another during each week of the observation period. The third row, for example, indicates that 50% of the 0-to-40-day dollars (state 3) will be paid (state 1) and none will become bad debts (state 2) in the next week. It also suggests that 30% of these accounts will remain 0 to 40 days old while 20% will become 41 to 100 days old during the next period.

Note that there is no chance that a paid account (state 1) will become a bad debt (state 2), 0 to 40 days old (state 3), or 41 to 100 days old (state 4). By definition, there is also no likelihood that a bad debt (state 2) can become paid (state 1), 0 to 40 days old (state 3), or 41 to 100 days old (state 4). In effect, then, an account that reaches either state 1 or state 2 will remain there indefinitely, becoming "absorbed" by the condition. For this reason, such conditions are known as **absorbing states**.

When a Markov process involves absorbing states, there is no need to calculate steady-state probabilities. After all, the process will eventually end up in one of the absorbing states. The bank's accounts receivable, for instance, ultimately will be paid or become bad debts. To help control the bad debts and properly manage cash flow, however, Master Bank should determine the total balance proportion that will end up in each absorbing state.

In this regard, it is useful to examine the lower left portion of the bank's transition matrix T:

$$A = \begin{pmatrix} .5 & 0 \\ .4 & .2 \end{pmatrix}$$

Specifically, the matrix A lists the likelihoods of moving from a nonabsorbing state (0 to 40 days old or 41 to 100 days old) to an absorbing state (paid account or bad debt) in each trial of the process. For example, the first column indicates that 50% of the 0-to-40-day accounts (state 3) and 40% of the 41-to-100-day accounts (state 4) become paid (state 1) every week during the observation period.

To compute the proportions that will eventually be paid or become bad debts, management still must determine how many weeks the accounts remain in the nonabsorbing states before being absorbed. Although such passage times can be found from the transitition matrix information, the required methodology is beyond the scope of this book. C. Derman [6] and D. L. Isaacson and R. W. Madsen [15] present the details for the interested reader.

Fortunately, several prewritten computer packages contain options that generate the passage time data. Figure 15.6 illustrates how the MRKV1 program supplies the relevant data for the accounts receivable situation.

Once more, the program requires the state and transition data. In Master Bank's case, there are four account categories (paid, bad debt, 0 to 40 days, and 41 to 100 days). Hence, the user must enter the value 4 after the TOTAL NUMBER OF STATES prompt. Furthermore, two of the four categories are absorbing states. Consequently, the decision maker should type the value 2 following NUMBER OF ABSORBING STATES. The transition probabilities from Table 15.8 are entered into the computer one state (row) at a time.

At this point, the computer begins to supply the relevant Markov results. As Figure 15.6 demonstrates, the first output is a table that lists the average passage times from the nonabsorbing states to the absorbing states. The table can be arranged in the following format:

Figure 15.6 MRKV1 Analysis of Absorbing States for Master Bank

```
        **   INFORMATION ENTERED   **


        TOTAL NUMBER OF STATES      :  4
        NUMBER OF ABSORBING STATES  :  2

             TRANSITION TABLE

    STATES

    1     1      0      0      0
    2     0      1      0      0
    3    .5      0     .3     .2
    4    .4     .2     .3     .1

        **  RESULTS   **



             FUNDAMENTAL MATRIX

      STATES

        3    1.57    .35
        4     .52   1.22


            TIME TO ABSORPTION

      STATES            TIME

        3                1.92
        4                1.75

        CONDITIONAL PROBABILITIES

      STATES

        3     .929    .07
        4     .754    .245

        **  END OF ANALYSIS  **
```

$$F = \begin{pmatrix} 1.57 & .35 \\ .52 & 1.22 \end{pmatrix}$$

Such an arrangement of numbers is called a **fundamental matrix**. The entries in the fundamental matrix F give the average number of periods that the system will be in each nonabsorbing state before it gets absorbed. For example, the first row indicates that a 0-to-40-day account (state 3) is expected to remain the same age (state 3) for 1.57 weeks and become 41 to

100 days old (state 4) for another .35 week before being absorbed as a paid bill (state 1) or bad debt (state 2). Similarly, the second row shows that a 41-to-100-day account (state 4) will remain the same age (state 4) for 1.22 weeks and become 0 to 40 days old (state 3) for another .52 week prior to absorption in state 1 or 2.

By adding the entries in the rows of the fundamental matrix, management can also determine the total number of periods that elapse prior to absorption. For instance, the first row of matrix F suggests that an average of $1.57 + .35 = 1.92$ weeks will pass before a 0-to-40-day account (state 3) is absorbed either as a paid bill or as a bad debt. The second row demonstrates that $.52 + 1.22 = 1.74$ weeks are expected to elapse before a 41-to-100-day account (state 4) becomes absorbed in state 1 or 2. Such averages are called the **times to absorption**.

These calculations demonstrate that the time to absorption is 1.92 weeks for state 3 and 1.74 weeks for state 4. Moreover, the MRKV1 program contains an output option that performs the computations that generate the absorption times. Indeed, the TIME TO ABSORPTION data in Figure 15.6 show that this option provides the same results obtained using hand calculation.

Note that the fundamental matrix F lists the average number of weeks that elapse before the aged accounts become absorbed as paid bills or bad debts. Furthermore, matrix A gives the likelihoods of moving from the nonabsorbing states to absorbing states during each week in the process. By multiplying matrix F by matrix A, management can determine the probabilities of moving from any nonabsorbing state to each absorbing state.

Specifically, matrix F's first row suggests that a 0-to-40-day account remains the same age for 1.57 weeks and becomes 41 to 100 days old for another .35 week before being absorbed. In addition, matrix A's first column indicates that 50% of the 0-to-40-day accounts and 40% of the 41-to-100-day accounts get paid each week of the observation period. As a result, the bank should anticipate that

$$1.57(.5) + .35(.4) = .93$$

or 93% of the 0-to-40-day accounts will eventually be paid.

Equations (15.12)–(15.15) illustrate the computations needed to find this .93 value and the other entries in the $F \times A$ matrix. (Values are rounded to the nearest hundredth.)

$$1.57 \times .5$$

$$(15.12) \quad FA = \begin{pmatrix} 1.57 & .35 \\ .52 & 1.22 \end{pmatrix} \begin{pmatrix} .5 & 0 \\ .4 & .2 \end{pmatrix} = \begin{pmatrix} .93 \\ \end{pmatrix}$$

$$+ (.35 \times .4) =$$

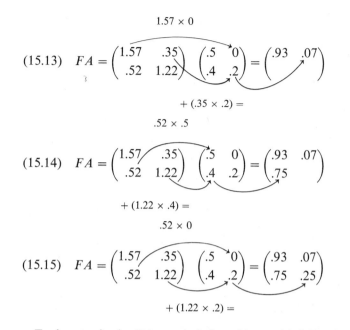

$$1.57 \times 0$$

$$(15.13) \quad FA = \begin{pmatrix} 1.57 & .35 \\ .52 & 1.22 \end{pmatrix} \begin{pmatrix} .5 & 0 \\ .4 & .2 \end{pmatrix} = \begin{pmatrix} .93 & .07 \\ & \end{pmatrix}$$

$$+ (.35 \times .2) =$$

$$.52 \times .5$$

$$(15.14) \quad FA = \begin{pmatrix} 1.57 & .35 \\ .52 & 1.22 \end{pmatrix} \begin{pmatrix} .5 & 0 \\ .4 & .2 \end{pmatrix} = \begin{pmatrix} .93 & .07 \\ .75 & \end{pmatrix}$$

$$+ (1.22 \times .4) =$$

$$.52 \times 0$$

$$(15.15) \quad FA = \begin{pmatrix} 1.57 & .35 \\ .52 & 1.22 \end{pmatrix} \begin{pmatrix} .5 & 0 \\ .4 & .2 \end{pmatrix} = \begin{pmatrix} .93 & .07 \\ .75 & .25 \end{pmatrix}$$

$$+ (1.22 \times .2) =$$

Each entry in the FA matrix is found by multiplying the numbers in the appropriate row of the F matrix by the values in the relevant column of the A matrix and summing the results. Consider, for example, the .75 value in the second row and first column of FA. This value is the sum of the products obtained when the entries in the second row of F are multiplied by the values in the first column of A.

The calculations, then, indicate that the matrix of probabilities for moving from any nonabsorbing state to each absorbing state is

$$FA = \begin{pmatrix} .93 & .07 \\ .75 & .25 \end{pmatrix}$$

The MRKV1 program contains an output option that generates these probabilities. In fact, the CONDITIONAL PROBABILITIES data in Figure 15.6 report the same results obtained using hand calculation.

Bank management can now use the probability information to predict the accounts receivable amounts that will either be paid or be lost as bad debts. Example 15.2 indicates that Master Bank has $200,000 in 0-to-40-day accounts and $300,000 in 41-to-100-day accounts on December 31. Moreover, the probability matrix FA's first column shows that 93% of the 0-to-40-day accounts and 75% of the 41-to-100-day accounts will be paid. Consequently, the decision maker should expect

$$\$200,000(.93) + \$300,000(.75) = \$411,000$$

of the $500,000 total balance to be eventually paid.

On the other hand, the second column of the FA matrix suggests that 7% of the 0-to-40-day accounts and 25% of the 41-to-100-day accounts will wind up as bad debts. Management, then, should expect

$$\$200,000(.07) + \$300,000(.25) = \$89,000$$

of the $500,000 total balance to be written off as bad debts. Thus, the bank's accounting department must set up an $89,000 allowance for doubtful accounts in the year-end financial statements.

POLICY DECISIONS Markov analysis provides information about the likelihood that a system will be in a particular state at any future trial of a process. It also generates data on the passage times that elapse before the system reaches specified states. Such knowledge can be used by the decision maker to evaluate the effectiveness of selected policies under various system conditions. Example 15.3 illustrates.

EXAMPLE 15.3 Evaluating Credit Policy

Suppose that Master Bank is unhappy with the $89,000 projected bad debt and is considering a new credit policy that involves increased financial charges to customers. Management believes that this policy will increase the probability of a transition from the 40-day-and-under category to the paid category. It should also decrease the likelihood that a 0-to-40-day account will become 41 to 100 days old.

In fact, a careful study reveals that the transition matrix

$$T = \begin{pmatrix} 1 & 0 & 0 & 0 \\ 0 & 1 & 0 & 0 \\ .65 & 0 & .30 & .05 \\ .40 & .20 & .30 & .10 \end{pmatrix}$$

will be applicable with the new credit policy. As the matrix demonstrates, the policy increases the probability from .5 to .65 that a 0-to-40-day account will get paid each week in the observation period. It also decreases the likelihood that a 0-to-40-day account becomes 41 to 100 days old from 20% to 5%.

Bank management wants to evaluate the effect of such a policy on bad debt expense.

According to the information given in Example 15.3, the new credit policy revises the bank's transition matrix. To evaluate the policy, management must determine the updated fundamental matrix, times to absorption, and conditional probabilities for being absorbed. A prewritten computer package, such as MRKV1, again can be used for these purposes. Indeed, if Master Bank enters the data from Example 15.3 into MRKV1, it will obtain the output shown in Figure 15.7.

By comparing Figures 15.6 and 15.7, you will find that the new credit policy decreases the times to absorption for each type of account. For example, Figure 15.6 suggests that a 0-to-40-day account is absorbed in an

Figure 15.7 MRKV1 Analysis of the New Credit Policy

```
    **   INFORMATION ENTERED   **


    TOTAL NUMBER OF STATES      : 4
    NUMBER OF ABSORBING STATES  : 2

         TRANSITION TABLE

STATES

 1    1      0      0      0
 2    0      1      0      0
 3    .65    0      .3     .05
 4    .4     .2     .3     .1

     ** RESULTS   **



         FUNDAMENTAL MATRIX

   STATES

    3    1.46    .08
    4    .48    1.13


         TIME TO ABSORPTION

   STATES          TIME

    3              1.54
    4              1.62

   CONDITIONAL PROBABILITIES

   STATES

    3    .983    .016
    4    .772    .227

     ** END OF ANALYSIS **
```

average of 1.92 weeks without the increased financial charges. The corresponding entry in Figure 15.7 shows that a 0-to-40-day account is absorbed in an average of 1.54 weeks with the increased financial charges. Under the new credit policy, then, such an account will be paid an average of

1.92 − 1.54 = .38 week

sooner than before.

The CONDITIONAL PROBABILITIES data in Figures 15.6 and 15.7 are also relevant. By comparing these data, you will find that the new credit policy increases the proportions of paid bills and decreases the shares of uncollectible accounts. For instance, the entries in Figure 15.6 indicate that without the increased financial charges 75.4% of the 41-to-100-day accounts get paid and 24.5% end up as bad debts. The corresponding values in Figure 15.7 show that with the new credit policy, 77.2% of the 41-to-100-day accounts get paid and only 22.7% end up as bad debts.

Once more, bank management can use the probability information to predict the accounts receivable amount that will be uncollectible. In particular, Master Bank has $200,000 in 0-to-40-day accounts and $300,000 in 41-to-100-day accounts. Moreover, the second column of CONDITIONAL PROBABILITIES in Figure 15.7 indicates that 1.6% of the 0-to-40-day accounts and 22.7% of the 41-to-100-day accounts will wind up as bad debts. Consequently, the decision maker should expect

$$\$200,000(.016) + \$300,000(.227) = \$71,300$$

of the $500,000 total year-end balance to be a bad debt expense with the new credit policy.

Under the previous policy, there is an $89,000 uncollectible balance. Thus, the increased financial charges can generate a savings of

$$\$89,000 - \$71,300 = \$17,700$$

These savings represent $17,700/$500,000 = .0354, or 3.54%, of the $500,000 total balance.

EXTENSIONS   The basic Markov model assumes that the underlying process can be observed at discrete points in time. While such an assumption is suitable for many problems, there are also cases in which the system will change continuously over time. Under these circumstances, the decision maker must use continuous time versions of the Markov model.

In addition, the basic Markov model presumes that the probability of the next event depends only on the outcome of the prior event. Yet, there are situations in which the system's condition is influenced by outcomes of the past two, three, or more periods. Management, then, must extend the basic analysis to incorporate the effects of all relevant past conditions.

The basic Markov model also assumes that the process generates probabilities that eventually stabilize at the same equilibrium values regardless of the starting conditions in the system. Nevertheless, some circumstances do not involve such steady-state probabilities. In these situations, the decision maker may be more interested in studying the short-run rather than long-run behavior of the system.

Table 15.9 Markov Model Applications

Area	Application	Reference
Air quality management	Analyzing the variation in air pollution levels	T. F. Anthony and B. W. Taylor [1]
Inventory control	Determining the best order quantity for a perishable product	D. Chazan and S. Gal [4]
Service system operations	Finding the queuing characteristics in a service system	B. Gavish and P. J. Schweitzer [10]
Marketing	Analyzing consumer response to selected marketing strategies	J. R. Hauser and K. J. Wisniewski [13]
Loan management	Determining the probabilities of repayment for loan portfolios	M. J. Karson [16]
Facility location	Finding the best plant and service facility locations	R. E. Rosenthal et al. [23]
Fire department management	Deciding how many resources to dispatch to a fire	A. J. Swersey [25]

There are methodologies available to deal with these and other important extensions of the basic Markov system. Derman [6], R. A. Howard [14], and Kemeny and Snell [17] present the details for the interested reader.

Finally, Examples 15.1 through 15.3 deal with situations in which the stages of the Markov process denote different time periods. Markov concepts are also applicable to cases where the trials of the system represent reference points (such as organizational levels or geographic areas) rather than time periods. In fact, Markov analysis has been applied to a wide variety of business and economic problems. Table 15.9 presents a small sample of the reported management applications. Additional illustrations are provided by Isaacson and Madsen [15] and W. F. Massy and others [20].

DYNAMIC PROGRAMMING

The primary purpose of Markov analysis is to predict the outcomes of an evolutionary process. In addition, such an analysis can be used to evaluate specified decision alternatives. However, it does not attempt to determine the optimal, or best, overall policy. In other words, Markov analysis is a descriptive rather than normative decision tool.

On the other hand, there are many cases in which a description of the process is not sufficient. Management may need to prescribe the sequence of actions that best meets some overall measure of performance. Example 15.4 illustrates.

EXAMPLE 15.4 Equipment Replacement

John's Neighborhood Grocery uses a small van to make home deliveries. Once a year, John decides whether or not to replace the present vehicle with a new van. His decision is based on the vehicle's current operating cost and resale value as well as the purchase price of a new van.

John always purchases the same type of van from the only dealer in town. According to the dealer's service records, the grocery store can expect the van to have a useful life of four years. These records also indicate that the vehicle's operating costs will be $2500 in the first year, $3000 in the second year, $4000 in the third year, and $5500 in the fourth year of its useful ife. In addition, the dealer's sales experience suggests that John should anticipate the resale values given in Table 15.10. A new van sells for $10,000. All the data are expressed in present-value terms. Moreover, the dealer believes that the values will remain stable for the next four years.

The grocery store has just purchased a new van, and John is eager to determine the replacement policy that will minimize total equipment costs. That is, he wants to know the best times to replace the vehicle over the next four years.

Table 15.10 Resale Values for John's Van

Van Age (Years)	Resale Value ($)
1	8000
2	6500
3	4500
4	2000

In Example 15.4, the grocery store is interested in describing the van's cost behavior. At the start of the process in year 1, John purchases a new van. Over the years, the operating costs change as the vehicle ages. Moreover, the store can replace an aging van with a new model in any year of the planning period. The substitution cost will depend on the age of the vehicle and the year of replacement. Total operating and replacement costs, then, can be expected to follow an evolutionary process.

FORMULATING THE PROBLEM Figure 15.8 depicts the nature of the grocery store's evolutionary process. As Figure 15.8 demonstrates, each year in the planning period can be thought of as a trial or stage of the process. The grocery store enters each stage with a vehicle that is purchased in a specified year of the planning period. Put another way, the year of purchase identifies the state of the system. In view of the state, John decides whether to replace or keep the present vehicle. The decision and state then determine the equipment

Figure 15.8 The Grocery Store's Evolutionary Process

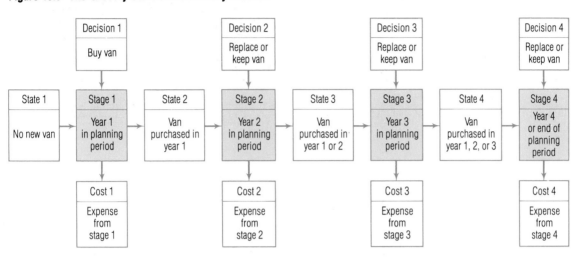

expenditure required during the corresponding stage of the process. Moreover, they fix the conditions for the next year in the planning period.

For example, Figure 15.8 shows that the grocery store enters stage 1 with no new van. In view of this state, John purchases a new vehicle at the start of year 1. By the end of stage 1, then, he will incur the replacement cost plus the first-year operating expenses for the new van. It also means that the store enters stage 2 with a vehicle purchased in year 1 of the planning period.

There is a similar pattern for each subsequent stage in the evolutionary process. The action in one trial influences the outcome during the trial and the state of the system at the next stage. The new state, in turn, affects the decision at this stage, and so forth. As a result, John's equipment replacement situation really involves the series of interrelated decisions illustrated by Figure 15.9. Every square shows a decision point in the process. The symbol R represents a decision to replace the present van, while K means that John will keep the current model. Every circle, or node, denotes a state of the system. Moreover, the number within the node identifies the year in which the grocery store purchases a van or replaces the present vehicle with a new model. The values above the branches give the total replacement and operating costs associated with the decisions and states.

At the start of the process, for instance, the grocery store purchases a new van for $10,000. This action is identified in Figure 15.9 with the decision square $\boxed{R}$ at the beginning of year 1. In addition, the data from Example 15.4 indicate that John must spend $2500 to operate the van during its first year of service. By purchasing the van, then, the grocery

Figure 15.9 John's Decision Tree

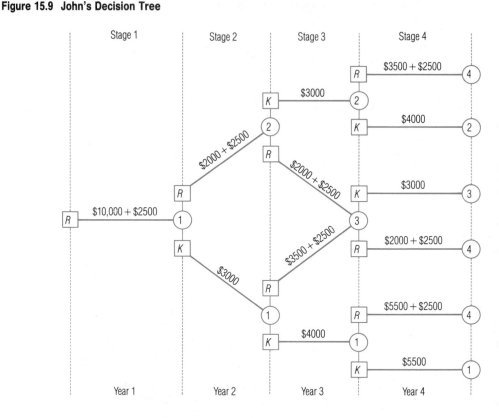

store will incur a $10,000 + $2500 equipment expense during year 1 of the planning period. Consequently, the label $10,000 + $2500 appears above the branch emanating from $\boxed{R}$ in year 1 of Figure 15.9.

John then enters the next year with a vehicle purchased in year 1 of the process. Hence state node ① appears at the start of year 2. At this point, the grocery store can replace ($\boxed{R}$) or keep ($\boxed{K}$) the present van.

According to the data in Example 15.4 and Table 15.10, each new van sells for $10,000 and has a $8000 resale value after one year of service. Therefore, it will cost $10,000 − $8000 = $2000 to replace the one-year-old vehicle at the start of year 2. In addition, the store must spend $2500 to operate the new van in its first year of service during year 2. By replacing the vehicle, then, John will incur a $2000 + $2500 equipment expense during year 2 of the planning period. Therefore, the label $2000 + $2500 appears above the branch emanating from $\boxed{R}$ in year 2 of Figure 15.9. Also, John enters the next year with a vehicle that is purchased in year 2 of the process (denoted as a ② state).

On the other hand, suppose that the grocery store keeps the original van at the start of year 2. In this case, the vehicle will be two years old by the end of year 2. Moreover, the data in Example 15.4 tell us that John must spend $3000 to operate the vehicle in its second year of service. Thus, the value $3000 is written above the branch emanating from $\boxed{K}$ in year 2 of Figure 15.9. Such an action also means that the store enters the next year with a vehicle purchased in year 1 of the process (depicted as a $\boxed{1}$ state).

Years 3 and 4 can be developed in the same evolutionary manner. John's problem is to determine the series of decisions that results in the minimum total equipment cost over the grocery store's four-year planning period. Such a series of decisions is referred to as the **optimal policy**.

To formulate the problem properly, John must specifiy the precise relationship between the expenses incurred at every stage of the sequential process. For example, an equipment decision generates an immediate cost during the specified year of the planning period. Such a cost, which depends on the van's year of purchase (state) S_n as well as the equipment decision D_n, can be denoted as $C_n(S_n, D_n)$ for stage n.

Moreover, the condition S_n and decision D_n fix the state S_{n+1} entering the next $(n + 1)$ stage of the process. The manner in which S_{n+1} will be determined by S_n and D_n is known as the **stage transformation** or **transfer function**. New state S_{n+1}, in turn, influences the decision D_{n+1} and expense $C_{n+1}(S_{n+1}, D_{n+1})$ incurred in year $n + 1$. The action D_{n+1} then affects the system conditions, decisions, and expenses at stages beyond $n + 1$ of the process. In short, John must utilize the S_{n+1} data to identify the best policy for all remaining years in the planning period.

This fact illustrates the following important property: *The current state provides all the information about the previous system behavior that is needed to determine the optimal policy for every subsequent stage in a sequential decision process.* Such a property is known as the **principle of optimality**.

Suppose that John uses the S_{n+1} knowledge to find the series of decisions that minimizes the total equipment expense from year $n + 1$ through the end of the planning period. The resulting expense, which depends on the van's year of purchase S_{n+1} at the start of stage $n + 1$, can be denoted as $F^*_{n+1}(S_{n+1})$. Under these circumstances, the grocery store knows that the total cost from stage n through the end of the process will be

$$F_n(S_n) = C_n(S_n, D_n) + F^*_{n+1}(S_{n+1})$$

In other words, the total cost equals the sum of the immediate $C_n(S_n, D_n)$ and resulting subsequent $F^*_{n+1}(S_{n+1})$ expenses.

At stage n, then, John should seek the equipment decision D_n that minimizes

$$F_n(S_n) = C_n(S_n, D_n) + F^*_{n+1}(S_{n+1})$$

The resulting minimum value, which depends on the system state S_n entering stage n, can be denoted as $F^*_n(S_n)$. That is,

Table 15.11 John's Stage 4 Computations

Stage 4 State S_4 Year Van Purchased	Stage 4 Decision Alternative D_4	Stage 4 Cost $C_4(S_4, D_4)$	Minimum Total Cost $F_4^*(S_4) = \min C_4(S_4, D_4)$	Best Stage 4 Decision D_4^*
1	Replace van Keep van	$5500 + $2500 $5500	$5500	Keep van
2	Replace van Keep van	$3500 + $2500 $4000	$4000	Keep van
3	Replace van Keep van	$2000 + $2500 $3000	$3000	Keep van

$$(15.16) \quad F_n^*(S_n) = \min[C_n(S_n, D_n) + F_{n+1}^*(S_{n+1})]$$

This equation ties together the outcomes obtained at all stages of the sequential decision process. It is called a **recursive relationship**.

In particular, the overall objective is to find the policy that minimizes the total equipment cost from year 1 through year 4 of the planning period. The resulting expense, which depends on the van's year of purchase S_1 at the start of stage 1, can be denoted as $F_1^*(S_1)$. However, such an expense has a recursive relationship to the corresponding outcomes in future years. Namely, $F_1^*(S_1)$ depends on the least-cost $F_2^*(S_2)$ from year 2 through year 4 of the process; $F_2^*(S_2)$ relies on the minimum expense $F_3^*(S_3)$ from stages 3 and 4; and so on. As a result, the grocery store must identify the series of interrelated decisions that generates these successive minimum total costs.

SOLVING THE PROBLEM Since the current actions will be influenced by future outcomes, John should begin the analysis at the final stage (year 4) of the process. The decision tree in Figure 15.9 again provides the relevant data. Table 15.11 presents the computations required for year 4 in the planning period. As the first column of the table shows, the grocery store will enter stage 4 with a van purchased in either year 1, 2, or 3 of the planning period. In view of this stage 4 state (S_4), John must identify each decision alternative D_4 and compute the resulting cost $C_4(S_4, D_4)$. These costs are reported in the third column of the table. For example, if the store replaces a year 2 van, it will incur a $3500 + $2500 = $6000 equipment expense during stage 4 of the process.

John should then select the decision (D_4^*) that leads to the minimum total cost $F_4^*(S_4)$ associated with the stage 4 state. The relevant analysis is given in the last two columns of Table 15.11. For instance, the grocery store can minimize the total cost associated with a year 1 van by keeping the vehicle during stage 4 of the planning period.

The stage 4 knowledge and the decision tree in Figure 15.9 in turn provide the information needed to make the year 3 decisions. Table 15.12 presents the required calculations. As the first column indicates, the grocery store will enter stage 3 with a van purchased in either year 1 or year 2 of the planning period. In view of this stage 3 state (S_3), John once more must identify each decision alternative (D_3) and compute the resulting cost $C_3(S_3, D_3)$. These costs again are reported in the third column of the table. For example, the data indicate that the store will incur a \$4000 equipment expense during year 3 by keeping a year 1 vehicle through stage 3 of the process.

Each stage 3 decision will also affect the costs incurred during year 4 in the planning period. To determine this effect, John must now identify the stage 4 state (S_4) and lowest remaining cost $F_4^*(S_4)$ resulting from the stage 3 conditions. Such knowledge is given in the fourth and fifth columns of Table 15.12. Consider, for instance, the decision to keep a year 2 van during stage 3 of the process. The fourth column shows that this decision leaves the grocery store with a year 2 vehicle entering stage 4 of the planning period. Under these $S_4 = 2$ circumstances, Table 15.11 suggests that the best stage 4 decision (D_4^*) is to keep the year 2 van and incur a minimum total cost of $F_4^*(S_4) = \$4000$. Hence, the fifth column in Table 15.12 has a \$4000 lowest-remaining-cost entry in the row where $S_4 = 2$ and $D_3 = $ keep van.

At this point, the decision maker can calculate the total cost $F_3(S_3)$ associated with the stage 3 state. The sixth column of Table 15.12 illustrates that such a cost is the sum of the stage 3 $C_3(S_3, D_3)$ and lowest remaining $F_4^*(S_4)$ expenses. For example, the data indicate that the store will incur a \$6000 + \$3000 = \$9000 total equipment cost during stages 3 and 4 by replacing a year 1 van at the start of year 3.

John should then select the decision D_3^* that leads to the minimum total cost $F_3^*(S_3)$ associated with the stage 3 state. The relevant data are given in columns 7 and 8 of Table 15.12. These data tell us that the grocery store can minimize the total cost associated with a year 2 van by keeping the vehicle during stage 3 of the planning period.

Figure 15.9's decision tree and the stage 3 knowledge in turn provide the information required to evaluate the year 2 alternative. Table 15.13 presents the necessary computations. The first column shows that the grocery store will enter stage 2 with a van purchased in year 1 of the planning period. In view of this stage 2 state (S_2), John again must identify each decision alternative (D_2) and calculate the resulting cost $C_2(S_2, D_2)$. These costs once more are reported in the third column of the table.

In addition, each stage 2 decision affects the costs incurred during subsequent years of the planning period. To determine these effects, John must identify the stage 3 state S_3 and lowest remaining cost $F_3^*(S_3)$ resulting from the stage 2 conditions. This knowledge is given in the fourth and fifth columns of Table 15.13.

Table 15.12 John's Stage 3 Computations

Stage 3 State S_3 Year Van Purchased	Stage 3 Decision Alternative D_3	Stage 3 Cost $C_3(S_3, D_3)$	Stage 4 State S_4	Lowest Remaining Cost $F_4^*(S_4)$	Total Cost $F_3(S_3)$ $= C_3(S_3, D_3) + F_4^*(S_4)$	Minimum Total Cost $F_3^*(S_3)$ $= \min F_3(S_3)$	Best Stage 3 Decision D_3^*
1	Replace van	$3500 + $2500	3	$3000	$6000 + $3000	$9000	Replace van
	Keep van	$4000	1	$5500	$4000 + $5500		
2	Replace van	$2000 + $2500	3	$3000	$4500 + $3000	$7000	Keep van
	Keep van	$3000	2	$4000	$3000 + $4000		

Table 15.13 John's Stage 2 Computations

Stage 2 State S_2 Year Van Purchased	Stage 2 Decision Alternative D_2	Stage 2 Cost $C_2(S_2, D_2)$	Stage 3 State S_3	Lowest Remaining Cost $F_3^*(S_3)$	Total Cost $F_2(S_2)$ $= C_2(S_2, D_2) + F_3^*(S_3)$	Minimum Total Cost $F_2^*(S_2)$ $= \min F_2(S_2)$	Best Stage 2 Decision D_2^*
1	Replace van	$2000 + $2500	2	$7000	$4500 + $7000 = $11,500	$11,500	Replace van
	Keep van	$3000	1	$9000	$3000 + $9000 = $12,000		

Consider, for instance, the decision to replace a year 1 van during stage 2 of the process. The fourth column of Table 15.13 shows that this decision provides the store with a year 2 vehicle entering stage 3 of the planning period. Under these $S_3 = 2$ circumstances, Table 15.12 suggests that the best stage 3 decision D_3^* is to keep the year 2 van and incur a minimum total cost of $F_3^*(S_3) = \$7000$. Therefore, the fifth column of Table 15.13 has a \$7000 lowest-remaining-cost entry in the row where $S_2 = 1$ and $D_2 =$ replace van.

John can now calculate the total cost $F_2(S_2)$ associated with the stage 2 state. As the sixth column of Table 15.13 illustrates, this cost is the sum of the stage 2 $C_2(S_2, D_2)$ and lowest remaining $F_3^*(S_3)$ expenses. For example, the data indicate that the store will incur a \$12,000 total equipment cost during stages 2 through 4 by keeping a year 1 van at the start of year 2.

John should then select the decision D_2^* that leads to the minimum total cost $F_2^*(S_2)$ associated with the stage 2 state. The relevant data appear in columns 7 and 8 of Table 15.13. As you can see, the grocery store can minimize the total cost associated with a year 1 van by replacing the vehicle at stage 2 of the planning period.

Finally, the stage 2 knowledge and the decision tree give the data needed to evaluate the year 1 decision. In this regard, Figure 15.9 shows that the grocery store enters the planning period with no new van. After considering the stage 1 state (S_1), John purchases a new vehicle at the start of the planning period. In other words, the only stage 1 decision (D_1) is to replace the van. As a result, the store incurs a $C_1(S_1, D_1) = \$12,500$ total equipment cost during stage 1 of the process.

These initial conditions also mean that the store enters stage 2 with a van purchased in year 1 of the planning period. That is, $S_2 = 1$ at the start of stage 2. According to Table 15.13, when $S_2 = 1$, the best stage 2 decision (D_2^*) is to replace the vehicle and obtain a minimum cost of $F_2^*(S_2) = \$11,500$. Put another way, the \$11,500 represents the lowest cost remaining after the stage 1 decision.

By reconstructing the sequence of decisions made in stages 1 through 4 of the process, John can identify the optimal equipment replacement policy. The analysis suggests that John should make the following decisions:

1. Replace the van in year 1 and enter stage 2 with a year 1 vehicle.
2. Replace the van in year 2 and enter stage 3 with a year 2 vehicle.
3. Keep the van in year 3 and enter stage 4 with a year 2 vehicle.
4. Keep the van in year 4 of the planning period.

Such a policy will generate a minimum total expense equal to

$$C_1(S_1, D_1) + F_2^*(S_2) = \$12,500 + \$11,500 = \$24,000$$

during years 1 through 4 of the four-year planning period.

Table 15.14 Summary of Dynamic Programming

1. Decompose the problem into a series of smaller segments, or stages.
2. Define the state S_n and decision D_n variables at each stage n of the problem.
3. Determine the transfer function, or the manner in which the stage n state S_n is linked with the state S_{n+1} at the next $(n + 1)$ stage of the problem.
4. Identify the outcome $O_n(S_n, D_n)$ associated with the state and decision at each stage of the process.
5. Formulate the recursive relationship $F_n^* = \min [O_n(S_n, D_n) + F_{n+1}^*(S_{n+1})]$ that ties together the outcomes obtained at all stages of the sequential process.
6. Use the recursive relationship to identify the decisions D_n^* that lead to the best outcomes at each stage of the problem.
7. Find the optimal policy by reconstructing the sequence of decisions made in stage 1 through the end of the process.

APPLICATIONS Table 15.14 summarizes the methodology for finding an optimal policy. This approach to decision making is known as **dynamic programming**.

Unlike most other management science techniques, dynamic programming does not involve a standard mathematical model. Indeed, the relevant recursive relationship must be tailored to the specific decision situation. As a result, the decision maker cannot normally use a general computational tool, such as the simplex method, to solve the overall problem.

Instead, dynamic programming reduces the complex situation into a series of simpler subproblems. The decision maker utilizes the most effective tool available to solve each subproblem. As S. E. Dreyfus and A. M. Law [7], R. E. Larson and J. L. Casti [18], and J. M. Norman [22] demonstrate, these tools can involve enumeration, decision analysis, mathematical programming procedures, and a variety of other specialized techniques.

Nevertheless, it is possible to classify dynamic programming into families, or prototypes. As D. P. Bertsekas [2], E. V. Denardo [5], and N. A. J. Hastings [12] illustrate, these families include allocation, multiple-period, network, multiple-stage production, feedback control, and Markov decision processes. The decision maker may then be able to develop a special computational procedure for each prototype.

Two factors, however, continue to limit the application of dynamic programming. For one thing, the approach must be tailored to the specific situation. Hence, the decision maker must design a new formulation, often at an unreasonable cost of effort and expense, every time there is a slight alteration in the problem. More importantly, the approach suffers from the "curse of dimensionality." Although a number of interesting and important situations can be formulated as dynamic programming problems, the resulting problem often involves too many computations to be

Table 15.15 Dynamic Programming Applications

Area	Application	Reference
Energy management	Finding the best economic policy to maximize energy benefits	H. Chao and A. S. Manne [3]
Markov decision systems	Determining the optimal policy to employ in a Markov decision system	J. Goldwerger [11]; E. J. Sondik [24]
Research and development	Finding the optimal search pattern for product/service research and development	T. K. Lee [19]
Public policy	Determining the optimal consumption policy for a consumer who faces an uncertain income stream	H. Mendelson and Y. Amihud [21]
Marketing	Finding the advertising policy that will best stimulate product/service purchases	C. S. Tapiero [26]
Operations management	Determining the optimal production and distribution schedule	J. F. Williams [27]

solved in a reasonable time at a moderate cost. In spite of these limitations, dynamic programming has been applied to a variety of business and economic problems as Table 15.15 indicates.

Example 15.4 involved a deterministic decision situation in which the years in the planning period formed natural stages for the problem. Moreover, there was a single state variable (the van's age) that could be measured in discrete units. But an examination of the prototypes and reported applications show that dynamic programming is also applicable to cases involving stochastic processes, stages other than time periods, multiple-state circumstances, continuous variables, and other decision situations.

SUMMARY This chapter has presented some methods for dealing with sequential problems, that is, situations involving a series of interrelated operations or decisions. The first section illustrated and described the nature of a basic Markov system, the characteristics of which were summarized in Table 15.1. Then we saw how to record and keep track of the changes that take place in the system from one trial to the next. Figure 15.2 outlined the relevant recording device.

The second section demonstrated how Markov analysis can be utilized in decision making. We saw how the model is used to predict the condition of a system at each stage of the evolutionary process. Table 15.3 summarized the procedure. Next, we considered ways to predict, by hand and with the aid of a computer, the eventual conditions in a Markov system. Table 15.6 outlined the manual method. There was also a discussion on absorbing states and about the approaches needed to determine the passage time between specified changes in the system conditions. The section then illustrated how the information can be employed to evaluate the effectiveness of selected policies under various system conditions. It concluded with some important extensions to and applications of Markov analysis. Table 15.9 listed some of the reported applications.

The final section introduced dynamic programming. In particular, this methodology can be used to find the optimal policy for a sequential decision problem. Table 15.14 summarized the approach. We also examined some important limitations of the analysis and presented a sample of reported applications. Table 15.15 listed the applications.

Glossary

absorbing state A state that cannot be left once it is entered.

dynamic programming A methodology designed to solve an optimization problem in a sequential manner.

equilibrium first passage time The average number of trials that elapse before the system can make a transition from a specified state for the first time.

expected recurrence time The average elapsed time between the repeat occurrences of a specified state in an evolutionary process.

first-order Markov process A stochastic process in which the current state of the system depends only on the immediately preceding state.

fundamental matrix A rectangular array of numbers indicating the average number of periods that a system will remain in nonabsorbing states before being absorbed.

homogeneous Markov chain A Markov process with constant, or stationary, transition probabilities.

Markov analysis An approach designed to describe and predict the behavior of an evolutionary process.

Markov system An evolutionary process that generates a homogeneous Markov chain.

mean first passage time The average number of trials that will elapse before the system changes from one state to another specified state for the first time.

MRKV1 A prewritten computer package designed to perform a Markov analysis.

optimal policy The series of decisions that will lead to the best outcome over all stages in an evolutionary process.

principle of optimality The principle whereby the current state provides all the information about the previous system behavior that is needed to determine the optimal policy for every subsequent stage in a sequential decision process.

recursive relationship An equation that ties together the outcomes obtained at all stages of a sequential decision process.

row vector of state probabilities A list of state probabilities arranged as a row of numbers.

stage transformation (transfer function) The manner in which a subsequent state is determined from the immediately preceding state and decision in a sequential process.

state The condition of the system at a particular trial of the evolutionary process.

state probability The likelihood that a system will be in a particular state at a specified trial of an evolutionary process.

steady-state probabilities The equilibrium values at which the state probabilities eventually stabilize after a very large number of trials for an evolutionary process.

time to absorption The average number of periods that elapse before a nonabsorbing state is absorbed.

transition matrix A list of transition probabilities arranged as a rectangular array of numbers.

transition probabilities The likelihood that a system will move from one state to another between trials of an evolutionary process.

transition table A table used to record and keep track of the transition probabilities involved in a Markov system.

trial (stage) A point at which the decision maker observes an evolutionary process.

References

1. Anthony, T. F., and B. W. Taylor. "A Stochastic Model for Analysis of Variations in Air Pollution Levels." *Decision Sciences* (April 1976): 305.

2. Bertsekas, D. P. *Dynamic Programming and Stochastic Control.* New York: Academic Press, 1976.

3. Chao, H., and A. S. Manne. "Oil Stockpiles and Import Reductions: A Dynamic Programming Approach." *Operations Research* (July–August 1983): 632.

4. Chazan, D., and S. Gal. "A Markovian Model for a Perishable Product Inventory." *Management Science* (January 1977): 512.

5. Denardo, E. V. *Dynamic Programming: Theory and Application.* Englewood Cliffs, N.J.: Prentice-Hall, 1975.

6. Derman, C. *Finite State Markov Decision Processes.* New York: Academic Press, 1970.

7. Dreyfus, S. E., and A. M. Law. *The Art and Theory of Dynamic Programming.* New York: Academic Press, 1977.

8. Erikson, W. J., and O. P. Hall. *Computer Models for Management Science.* Reading, Mass.: Addison-Wesley, 1983.

9. Freedman, D. *Markov Chains.* San Francisco: Holden-Day, 1971.

10. Gavish, B., and P. J. Schweitzer. "The Markovian Queue with Bounded Waiting Time." *Management Science* (August 1977): 1349.

11. Goldwerger, J. "Dynamic Programming for a Stochastic Markovian Process with an Application to the Mean Variance Models." *Management Science* (February 1977): 612.

12. Hastings, N.A.J. *Dynamic Programming with Managerial Applications.* New York: Crane, Russak and Company, 1973.

13. Hauser, J. R., and K. J. Wisniewski. "Dynamic Analysis of Consumer Response to Marketing Strategies." *Management Science* (May 1982): 455.

14. Howard, R. A. *Dynamic Probabilistic Systems.* Vols. 1 and 2. New York: Wiley, 1971.

15. Isaacson, D. L., and R. W. Madsen. *Markov Chains: Theory and Applications.* New York: Wiley, 1976.

16. Karson, M. J. "Confidence Intervals for Absorbing Markov Chain Probabilities Applied to Loan Portfolios." *Decision Sciences* (January 1976): 10.

17. Kemeny, J. G., and J. L. Snell. *Finite Markov Chains.* New York: Springer-Verlag, 1976.

18. Larson, R. E., and J. L. Casti. *Principles of Dynamic Programming.* New York: Marcel Dekker, 1978.

19. Lee, T. K. "A Nonsequential Research and Development Search Model. *Management Science* (August 1982): 900.

20. Massy, W. F., et al. *Stochastic Models of Buyer Behavior.* Cambridge, Mass.: MIT Press, 1970.

21. Mendelson, H., and Y. Amihud. "Optimal Consumption Policy Under Uncertain Income." *Management Science* (June 1982): 683.

22. Norman, J. M. *Elementary Dynamic Programming.* New York: Crane, Russak and Company, 1975.

23. Rosenthal, R. E., et al. "Stochastic Dynamic Location Analysis." *Management Science* (February 1978): 645.

24. Sondik, E. J. "The Optimal Control of Partially Observable Markov Processes Over the Infinite Horizon: Discounted Costs." *Operations Research* (March–April 1978): 282.

25. Swersey, A. J. "A Markovian Decision Model for Deciding How Many Fire Companies to Dispatch." *Management Science* (April 1982): 352.

26. Tapiero, C. S. "A Stochastic Model of Consumer Behavior and Optimal Advertising." *Management Science* (September 1982): 1054.

27. Williams, J. F. "A Hybrid Algorithm for Simultaneous Scheduling of Production and Distribution in Multi-Echelon Structures." *Management Science* (January 1983): 77.

1. For each of the following situations, explain whether it is appropriate to use the Markov model developed in this chapter:
   a. Three television stations compete for advertising shares of the market. Advertisers switch from station to station, depending on the previous time period's ratings. The pattern of switching changes from one time period to the next.
   b. A taxi company periodically inspects the bearings on its cabs and classifies them according to their condition. There are four possible categories. The bearing classification changes from one inspection to another, depending on conditions in several preceding time periods.
   c. A life insurance company wants to predict the percentage of a city's population that will be in various age brackets. People move from one category to another. The pattern of transaction is relatively stable from one period to the next.

2. Red Grape Company is one of the two largest wine growers in California. Their market analysts are currently investigating the brand loyalty to Red Grape. A questionnaire filled out by a group of wine drinkers led the analysts to construct the following tree diagram:

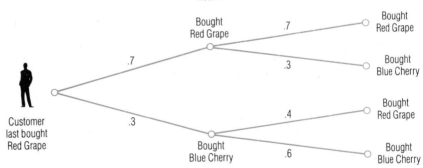

The company president, J. Foolhardy, has a set goal of a 70% market share for Red Grape. Elmer Studious, the market research director, informs Foolhardy that the goal cannot be met with existing market conditions. How did Studious arrive at this conclusion?

3. The data processing center at Campus Enterprises has been experiencing substantial periods of computer downtime. Operating conditions change from hour to hour. The transition pattern, however, is relatively stable. It can be summarized by the data in the following table:

Operating Condition Previous Hour	Operating Condition Next Hour	
	Running	Down
Running	.85	.15
Down	.25	.75

Currently, the system is running.

The company has an important project scheduled for the third hour from now. Campus will use the local university's computer for the project unless there is at least an 80% chance that the company's system will be running.

Based on the available information, the company decides to use the university computer for the project. Can you explain why?

4. There are three dairies that supply all the milk consumed in a community. The dairies have the pattern of retentions, gains, and losses given by the following table:

From Dairy	To Dairy		
	A	B	C
A	.8	.1	.1
B	0	.6	.4
C	0	.3	.7

According to an industry analyst, under current market conditions, dairies B and C will eventually capture all A's customers. How did the analyst arrive at this conclusion? What do you think dairy A will do about this situation?

5. Snap Shot, Inc., is a photographic studio in a small university community. Its main competition is Quality Photography. Reports from the local chamber of commerce indicate that Snap Shot has about 40% of the market of approximately $300,000 yearly sales. Last year, Snap Shot had a profit amounting to 10% of sales. As part of a project, a class in small business management at the local university has offered its advice. The class feels that a $5000 promotional campaign would create the following transition probabilities:

From	To	
	Snap Shot	Quality Photography
Snap Shot	.7	.3
Quality Photography	.3	.7

If Snap Shot wants to recoup the promotional investment within a year, should it take the student advice? Explain.

6. An inspector at a military surplus warehouse inspects food products each week and classifies them as "just delivered," "in good condition," or "uneatable." Uneatable foods are replaced the next week at an average cost of $30 per crate. Warehouse records show the following weekly transition pattern:

Food Condition This Week	Food Condition Next Week		
	Just delivered	Good	Uneatable
Just delivered	0	.9	.1
Good	0	.8	.2
Uneatable	1	0	0

If the food were discarded before it is uneatable, the average net replacement cost would be only $10 per crate.

The commanding officer believes that an expected savings of $5 per crate per week would be substantial. Based on the available information, do you think that the food should be replaced before it is uneatable? Explain.

7. A company's accounts receivable problem involves the following transition probabilities:

Previous Account Balance	Current Account Balance			
	Paid	Bad debt	0 to 30 days	31 to 90 days
Paid	1	0	0	0
Bad debt	0	1	0	0
0 to 30 days	0	0	.5	.5
31 to 90 days	0	0	.6	.4

The company notices that none of the account balances end up as either paid or bad debts. Can you explain why?

8. Refer back to Example 15.4. John's wife, Della, claims that the grocery store's equipment replacement situation can be formulated as a network problem. Explain how she arrived at this conclusion. Show the resulting network. Develop the recursive relationships involved in this network problem. Use dynamic programming to find the optimal route through the network.

9. A commodities broker buys a crop for her customers in a market that trades only once a week. Each week, there is a 25% chance that the crop will cost $200,000, a 50% likelihood that it will cost $300,000, and a 25% probability that it will cost $450,000. At the present time, the broker knows that the clients' investment plans cannot be satisfied unless the crop is bought within the next five trading weeks. The broker worries that unnecessary waiting may force her to buy at premium crop prices. On the other hand, if she buys early, future prices could be lower than anticipated. Under these circumstances, the broker would miss an opportunity to economize. Thus, the timing of the purchase poses a delicate management problem.

Formulate this commodity-trading problem in dynamic programming terms.

10. Explain why you agree or disagree with each each of the following statements:

   a. The only way to calculate the state probabilities at some future trial is to multiply the corresponding vector at the preceding trial by the transition matrix.
   b. After a large number of trials, the state probabilities are independent of the beginning state of the system.
   c. To calculate an expected value, the decision maker must use the steady-state probabilities.

d. Dynamic programming problems must be solved by working backward from the last to the first stage in the process.

e. The stages in a dynamic programming problem can be time periods, phases of a process, or artificially created segments.

f. The state variable at each stage of a dynamic programming problem is determined by the decision and state at the immediately preceding stage of the process.

Technique Exercises

1. You are given the following matrix of transition probabilities:

$$\begin{pmatrix} .6 & .4 \\ .5 & .5 \end{pmatrix}$$

Assuming that the system started in state 1, draw the tree diagram corresponding to three trials.

2. Suppose that a problem involves the following matrix of transition probabilities:

$$\begin{pmatrix} .7 & .2 & .1 \\ .1 & .8 & .1 \\ .2 & .2 & .6 \end{pmatrix}$$

Assume that the system started in state 3. Draw the tree diagram corresponding to two trials of the system. Show how the tree diagram would differ if we started in state 2.

3. The purchase patterns of two brands of shaving cream can be expressed as a Markov process with the following transition probabilities:

Brand Purchased Last Period	Brand Purchased This Period	
	A	B
A	.85	.15
B	.30	.70

Assume that the purchase probabilities are .5 for brand A and B at time period 0. What are the projected market shares for the two brands at time periods 1 and 2?

4. A machining operation can be expressed as a Markov process with the following transition probabilities:

Operating Condition Last Period	Operating Condition This Period		
	Normal	Variation	Abnormal
Normal	.9	.05	.05
Variation	0	.6	.4
Abnormal	1	0	0

Assume that machining is in state 3 at time period 0. What are the projected operating conditions at time periods 1 and 2?

5. Traffic delays across a major bridge in the San Francisco area can be described by a Markov process with the following transition probabilities:

Driving Conditions in the Last Half Hour	Driving Conditions This Half Hour	
	Delay	No delay
Delay	.6	.4
No delay	.2	.8

Assume that you are a motorist entering the traffic system and you hear a radio report of a traffic delay. What is the probability that there will be a delay for the next hour? What are the steady-state probabilities?

6. A new product was introduced on the market simultaneously by three companies: A, B, and C. Each firm launched its brand in January. At the start, each company had about one-third of the market. During the year, the following transition pattern took place:

Brand Purchased at Start	Brand Purchased Now		
	A	B	C
A	.6	.3	.1
B	.2	.5	.3
C	.1	.1	.8

Predict what the long-run market shares will be at the steady state if buying habits do not change.

7. An accounts receivable problem involves the following transition matrix:

$$T = \begin{pmatrix} 1 & 0 & 0 & 0 \\ 0 & 1 & 0 & 0 \\ .2 & 0 & .5 & .3 \\ .1 & .3 & .4 & .2 \end{pmatrix}$$

State (row) 1 is the paid category and state (row) 2 the bad-debt category. Currently, there is $500,000 in state 3 and $1,000,000 in state 4.

By utilizing the MRKV1 program, an analyst was able to develop the following fundamental matrix:

```
                    FUNDAMENTAL MATRIX

     STATES

        3            2.85               1.07
        4            1.42               1.78
```

a. Determine the times to absorption.
b. Find the probabilities that states 3 and 4 will end up in the absorbing states.
c. How much of the account balances will eventually be paid? How much will end up as bad debt?

8. You are given the following linear integer programming problem:

maximize $Z = 3X_1 + 2X_2 + X_3$

subject to $X_1 + X_2 + X_3 \leq 4$

$X_1, X_2, X_3 \geq 0$ and integers

Let X_1, X_2, and X_3 represent the stages, the amount allocated for the decision, and the amount available to the state variable in the problem. Use dynamic programming to solve this problem.

9. Refer to thought exercise 9. Use dynamic programming to solve the commodity broker's trading problem.

10. A consumer goods retailer sells a durable good with an estimated life of 5 years. The company must decide on an initial price, which, to be competitive, must be $400, $450, $500, or $550. Its policy is to change prices, if necessary, only once a year. Marketing research indicates that any price increase or decrease should be $50, and the resulting price must be within the competitive range of $400 to $550.

The anticipated yearly profit from the product is given in the following table where entries are in millions of dollars:

Price	Year				
	1	2	3	4	5
$400	0.5	1	0.75	1.25	2
$450	1	1.25	1.75	2	2.5
$500	1.5	1	0.5	3	2.4
$550	2	1.6	3.2	1	1.9

For example, if the price is $500 in the third year, the company will earn $500,000 profit.

In this problem, each year represents a stage of the process. The states are the existing prices, while the decisions are the new prices. Profits represent the outcomes. Use dynamic programming to find the optimal price policy. That is, determine the price that should be charged for the durable good in each year of its estimated life.

Applications Exercises

1. The population department of a government statistical agency has done a study of population mobility in the West. This study reveals several yearly trends among urban and suburban/rural families. It shows that 40% of the families in an urban location at the beginning of the year move to a suburban/rural location during the year. Also, 30% of the original suburban/rural families move to urban locations during the year. The population distribution is currently 30% urban and 70% suburban/rural. If the trends continue, what will the distribution look like in three years?

2. In January, Slick Petroleum, the nation's largest oil company, was issued a warning by the Federal Trade Commission (FTC). Slick was told that if its market share went above 60%, the FTC would initiate antitrust action. At that time, Slick had 40% of the market. Its chief competitor, Glide, had 20% of the market, and the rest of the market was divided among other companies. Slick's market analysts were able to develop the following data on consumer purchase behavior:

   ◆ Slick retains 90% of its customers from year to year. It loses 5% to Glide but gains 20% from Glide and 20% from others.
   ◆ Glide retains 70% of its customers from year to year. It loses 10% to Slick but gains 20% from others.

   Will Slick face antitrust action? If so, when?

3. Lake Telephone Company is a private system that services a small lakeside community. It is well known for the unreliable nature of its equipment on snowy days. This Christmas Eve began with a snowstorm in the area served by Lake. The company's engineering department quickly developed the following data on the likelihood of the trunk lines being in various states from one minute to the next:

◆ If the lines are currently open, there is a 50% chance that they will be open the next minute. In addition, the probability is .2 that the lines will be busy the next minute.

◆ When the lines are currently busy, the probability is .7 that they will be busy the next minute. Also, there is a 20% likelihood that they will be down the next minute.

◆ If the lines are currently down, there is a 10% chance that they will be down the next minute. In addition, the probability is .6 that they will be busy the next minute.

Of course, many calls are made on Christman Eve. Thus, if the phones are out of order on that day, the company will incur a large loss of customer good will. Lake's accounting department estimates that a busy line on Christmas Eve will eventually cost the company $10 per minute in lost revenue. A down line will involve a $50-per-minute loss.

How much lost revenue should Lake expect under these circumstances?

4. Parkview Hospital specializes in cosmetic surgery and serves an area where there is zero population growth. From past history, it is known that each month about .0005 of the 500,000 people in its service area are admitted for cosmetic surgery. By the end of the first month, a patient has an 80% probability of being released from the hospital. In addition, there is a 15% likelihood that he or she will stay another month and a 5% chance of death. For those who stay longer, 95% are released by the end of the second month and 5% die.

The administration is making long-range staff and facility plans. Thus, it would like to predict the eventual number of patients in the hospital who will have had cosmetic surgery within one month. Also, it wants to project the eventual number of patients in their second month of recovery and the number of surgical deaths each month. Find this information.

5. Building Blocks Industries, a manufacturer of prefabricated kitchen cabinets, employs three classes of machine operators, coded 1, 2, and 3. All new employees are hired as class 1 and, through a system of promotion, may work up to a higher classification. Promotions depend on employee productivity in the preceding quarter. Historically, class 1 has included 50% of Building's 500 operators and class 2 another 30%. Several months ago, the company adopted a union-sponsored system that groups operators into voluntary, self-supervised work groups. Production records kept since the reorganization have enabled the plant manager to compile some data on quarter-to-quarter changes in employee productivity. The data show the following:

◆ Forty percent of the class 1 operators remain in this category from quarter to quarter, while 50% move to class 2.

♦ Forty percent of the class 2 operators remain in this category from one period to the next, while 40% move to class 3.

♦ Eighty percent of the class 3 operators remain in this category from quarter to quarter, but 10% move back to class 2.

Operators earn an average of $1000 per month. Efficiency records indicate that there is a productivity loss of 30% associated with class 1 operators, 20% for class 2, and 10% for class 3.

How many employees will eventually be in each productivity classification? Can Building Blocks expect any monetary benefit from the reorganization? If so, how much?

6. Klamath Industries operates a tree farm with 10,000 spruces for experimental purposes. Each year Klamath allows nonprofit organizations to select and cut trees for transplanting. The farm protects small trees (usually less than 6 feet tall). Currently, 4000 spruces are classified as protected trees. However, even though a tree is available for cutting in a given year, it may not be selected until some future time. Some trees also die during the year. Of course, once a tree is cut or lost to disease, it will no longer be available in the future.

Based on past records, Klamath's management has found the following trends:

a. Of the spuces too small for cutting this year, 10% will be cut, 10% will die, and 70% will again be too small next year.

b. Of the available spruces not cut this year, 60% will be cut, 10% will die, and 30% will again be available next year.

A computer analysis also provides the following output:

```
        **   INFORMATION ENTERED   **


     TOTAL NUMBER OF STATES      : 4
     NUMBER OF ABSORBING STATES  : 2

             TRANSITION TABLE

   STATES

   1    1         0              0              0
   2    0         1              0              0
   3    .1        .1             .7             .1
   4    0         .1             .3             .6

     ** RESULTS  **



             FUNDAMENTAL MATRIX

     STATES

     3        4.44           1.11
     4        3.33           3.33


         TIME TO ABSORPTION

     STATES          TIME

     3               5.55
     4               6.66

     CONDITIONAL PROBABILITIES

     STATES

     3         .444           .555
     4         .333           .666

     ** END OF ANALYSIS **
```

In this output, the first row in the transition table denotes a cut tree and the second row depicts a dead tree. Moreover, the third row gives the protected state, while the fourth row identifies trees available to be cut.

How many of the farm's 10,000 trees will eventually be sold and how many will be lost?

7. A diplomat can carry an attaché case with no more than 10 pounds of government documents and supporting material. The weights of some potential contents and their diplomatic values (in points) are given in the following table:

Item	Weight (Pounds)	Diplomatic Value (Points)
Coding device	5	20
Trade book	2	10
Address list	1	30
Computer	8	15
Telephone	3	40

What should the diplomat carry to maximize total value?

8. Gemini Enterprises is making its annual allocation of salespersons to territories. A total of five salespeople are available for assignment to the three territories. The following table gives the sales revenues (in thousands of dollars) that correspond to each potential assignment. What assignment policy will maximize total revenue?

Salespersons	Territory		
	East	West	South
0	20	40	30
1	140	100	40
2	180	120	20
3	240	110	100
4	170	90	130
5	80	70	150

9. Giant Manufacturing Company (GMC) produces custom heating and air-conditioning equipment for large industrial organizations. After receiving a work request, GMC must retool the manufacturing apparatus, assign personnel, and schedule job activities. The equipment is then manufactured to the order specifications, delivered to the customer, and installed on the premises. Typically, the setup costs involve a $100,000 expense for every work request. In addition, it costs GMC $40,000 to manufacture, deliver, and install each piece of equipment.

   Currently, GMC has a contract to provide equipment for a national shoe distributor with new facilities in 6 different locations. The contract calls for the delivery of 2 units in each month from April through June. Any excess output can be stored at a monthly cost of $6000 per unit. However, GMC does not want any inventory at the end of the contract in June.

   Management wants to find the production schedule that will minimize the total cost of providing the contracted equipment. What schedule do you recommend? Explain.

CASE: The Federal Housing Agency

The Federal Housing Agency (FHA) guarantees mortgages or trust deeds for qualifying individuals purchasing residences. Although most insurees make their payments on time, a certain percentage are always overdue. Some debtors never pay, and their residences must be subjected to foreclosure proceedings. The FHA's experience has been that when a mortgage is two or more payments behind, the residence generally will have to be foreclosed. At the beginning of each month, the mortgage officer reviews each account and classifies it as paid, current, overdue, or a foreclosure. Current accounts are those being paid on time, while the overdue category refers to an account that is one payment behind. Agency records include the Mortgage Transition Report, shown in Table 15.16.

Table 15.16 FHA Mortgage Transition Report

Last Month's Account Status	This Month's Account Status			
	Paid	Current	Overdue	Foreclosure
Paid	1	0	0	0
Current	.2	.6	.2	0
Overdue	.1	.3	.4	.2
Foreclosure	0	0	0	1

Each entry represents the probability that an account dollar in a particular category last month will be in a particular category this month.

The loan officer also receives the FHA Mortgage Account Summary presented in Table 15.17. In addition, the agency's Information Systems Division provides the computer output shown in Figure 15.10. In this output, state 1 represents a paid account, state 3 a current account, state 4 an overdue account, and state 2 a foreclosure.

The loan officer has requested a report with the following information:

1. The probabilities that current and overdue accounts eventually end up paid or as foreclosures

2. The number of accounts that will eventually end up in each mortgage category

3. The dollar amount that will eventually be paid and the amount that will end up in the foreclosure category

Prepare this report.

Table 15.17 FHA Mortgage Account Summary

Account Status	Current Number of Accounts	Current Accounts Receivable Balance
Paid	20,000	$0
Current	500,000	$20 billion
Overdue	150,000	$200 million
Foreclosure	30,000	$100 million

Figure 15.10 Computer Analysis of Original FHA Credit Policy

```
         **  INFORMATION ENTERED  **


     TOTAL NUMBER OF STATES      : 4
     NUMBER OF ABSORBING STATES  : 2
           TRANSITION TABLE

  STATES

  1      1           0              0              0
  2      0           1              0              0
  3     .2           0             .6             .2
  4     .1          .2             .3             .4

     **  RESULTS  **



           FUNDAMENTAL MATRIX

     STATES

     3        3.33          1.11
     4        1.66          2.22


           TIME TO ABSORPTION

     STATES          TIME

     3                4.44
     4                3.88

     CONDITIONAL PROBABILITIES

     STATES

     3        .777          .222
     4        .555          .444

     **  END OF ANALYSIS  **
```

On the basis of the report, the FHA will consider instituting a new credit policy that involves a discount for prompt payment. The policy is expected to increase from .2 to .3 the chance of a current account becoming paid. It will have other effects as well. The probability of a current account becoming overdue will decrease from .2 to .1. Also, the new policy will increase from .3 to .4 the likelihood of an overdue account becoming current. The probability of an overdue account becoming a foreclosure will decrease from .2 to .1.

An additional computer analysis provides the output shown in Figure 15.11. The new credit policy will involve a cost, including discounts, of $50 million. Should the FHA implement the policy? Explain. Suppose the FHA could identify the relationship between the account states and credit policy. How could such information be used to determine the optimal credit policy?

Figure 15.11 Computer Analysis of New FHA Credit Policy

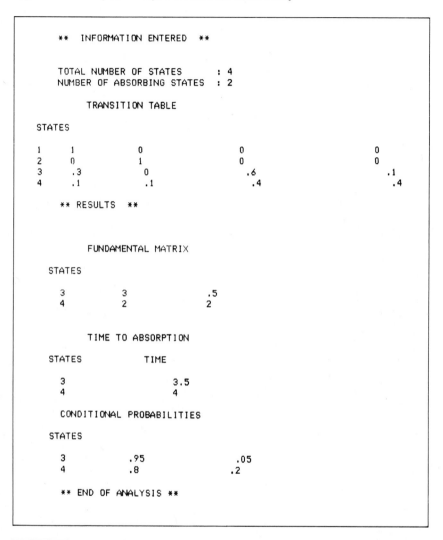

```
      **  INFORMATION ENTERED   **


      TOTAL NUMBER OF STATES        :  4
      NUMBER OF ABSORBING STATES    :  2

            TRANSITION TABLE

  STATES

  1     1            0                0                0
  2     0            1                0                0
  3     .3           0                .6               .1
  4     .1           .1               .4               .4

      **  RESULTS   **



            FUNDAMENTAL MATRIX

  STATES

      3            3                .5
      4            2               2

            TIME TO ABSORPTION

  STATES         TIME

      3                       3.5
      4                       4

      CONDITIONAL PROBABILITIES

  STATES

      3            .95              .05
      4            .8               .2

        **  END OF ANALYSIS  **
```

Part VI
Simulation

In previous parts of the text, the discussion has focused on the formulation and development of formal mathematical models. Such models were solved in an analytical or mathematical manner. Frequently, the analytical methods were in the form of algorithms that yielded best, or optimal, solutions to the problems.

On the other hand, there are many problems that become too complex and difficult to solve with existing analytical solution procedures. In these cases, the only viable means for analysis may be to experiment with the actual system or a model of the system. This next part presents a methodology for performing such experimentation.

Chapter 16 outlines the simulation approach. It describes the nature of the process and shows how to incorporate uncertainty and risk into the analysis. The chapter concludes with a presentation on the role of the computer in the experimentation process.

After reading this part of the text, you should be able to:

♦ Understand the nature of simulation
♦ Identify a simulation modeling framework
♦ Develop simulations by hand and with the aid of a computer
♦ Use simulation for decision making
♦ Recognize the advantages and limitations of the approach

The presentation will also prepare you for more advanced studies in management and corporate planning.

Chapter 16
Simulation

In past chapters, we have presented many techniques designed to aid decision making. Most of these techniques can be classified as analytical procedures. That is, a mathematical analysis is used to optimize some criterion (as in linear programming) or predict the behavior of a system (as in Markov analysis). However, many problems are too complex to solve using existing analytical solution procedures. In these situations, the only feasible method of analysis may be to experiment with the actual system or a model of the system. Such an approach is called **simulation**.

This chapter introduces the concepts and procedures of simulation. In the first section, we study the nature of the simulation process. We develop a model, perform a simulation, and interpret the results. The second section shows how to incorporate probabilistic inputs into the analysis. It describes the role of probability distributions and random selection in simulation. Finally, we present the computer simulation approach. We discuss the use of computer-generated random numbers, the role of the computer in the simulation process, and the advantages and limitations of the approach.

Simulation concepts are used in practice to analyze complex situations involving scheduling, inventory, queuing, and many other problems.

THE NATURE OF SIMULATION

Essentially, simulation is a technique for conducting experiments. In this approach, the decision maker first builds a device that imitates (acts like) the real situation. Then, by experimenting with the device, the decision maker can study the characteristics and behavior of the real situation.

Some simulations use physical devices. For example, an aircraft manufacturer can learn much about the aerodynamic properties of a new design by imitating (simulating) flight conditions in a wind tunnel. An analogy is another type of device. As an illustration, students can simulate the decision process of actual managers by analyzing the cases in a course on problem solving. Also, mathematical models can be used. Suppose, for instance, that government economists have developed an equation that relates gross national product (GNP) to various business indicators. They can then use the equation to simulate the economic effects of various changes in the indicators.

In this chapter, we concentrate on simulations that use tables, charts, and mathematical devices. Example 16.1 illustrates the nature of the simulation process.

EXAMPLE 16.1 Price Competition

Star Motors, Inc., will compete with Caste Cars Corporation in selling the Saver, a new energy-efficient automobile. Industry officials estimate that 1000 Savers will be sold in Star's area annually. The Saver has a suggested retail price of $5000 and a $4000 dealer cost.

Star's management wants to determine the price that will result in the largest profit from Saver sales. The decision is difficult because Star's market share depends on Caste's price.

If both dealers have the same price, Star will get 40% of the market. However, when Caste has the lower price, Star loses 4% of this share for every $100 price differential. On the other hand, when Caste has the higher price, Star gets 40% of the market plus 1% for every $100 price difference. A further complication is that Caste typically changes prices from week to week without notice.

During a strategy-planning meeting, Star's management

proposed that the company experiment with a variety of prices above the $4000 dealer cost. For example, Star might charge $4100 for a while, maybe 3 or 4 weeks, and then observe the resulting sales and profits. Next, the dealer could try $4200 for the same length of time, then perhaps $4300, and so on. Finally, management would select the price that resulted in the largest profit.

While Star's approach seems logical, it would be very time-consuming. It would take four or five months to collect profit data on only five trial price alternatives. Also, Star could experience several weeks of low profits or even losses if some of the trial prices were poor decisions. What the dealer needs is a way to carry out the trial and error procedure without actually setting the prices in practice. Simulation can be used to experiment with prices in just this manner.

DEVELOPING A MODEL In the simulation approach, management first develops a model that recreates, or imitates, Star's operation. We can begin by letting

P = Star's price for the Saver

C = Caste's price for the Saver

M = Star's market share

Q = Star's sales

Z = Star's weekly profit

There will be 1000 Savers sold in the area annually, or about

$$\frac{1000 \text{ units}}{50 \text{ weeks}} = 20 \text{ Savers per week}$$

Star's sales will equal its market share M times this amount, or $20M$.

Profit is the difference between price P and the \$4000 dealer cost multiplied by sales. We can express this relationship as follows:

(16.1) $Z = (P - \$4000)20M = 20(P - \$4000)M$

You can see that Star's profit from the Saver depends on its price P and market share M.

Market share depends on the competitive price structure. When both dealers have the same price, Star gets a 40% share. That is,

(16.2) $M = .4$ if $P = C$

When Caste's price is lower, Star's 40% share is reduced by 4% for every \$100 price difference. This can be expressed as follows:

(16.3) $M = .4 - .04\left(\dfrac{P - C}{\$100}\right)$ if $P > C$

| Share when prices are equal | Share lost for each \$100 price difference | Number of \$100 price differences |

On the other hand, Star gains 1% when it has the price advantage, or

(16.4) $M = .4 + .01\left(\dfrac{C - P}{\$100}\right)$ if $P < C$

| Share when prices are equal | Share gained for each \$100 price difference | Number of \$100 price differences |

Equations (16.1)–(16.4) form Star's profit model for Saver sales. A schematic representation is presented in Figure 16.1.

Star's objective is to maximize weekly profit from Saver sales. The controllable input is Star's price P, and the uncontrollable element is Caste's price C.

FLOWCHARTS As a next step, it is helpful to develop a diagram that shows the sequence of operations and computations required by the simulation model. Such a diagram is referred to as a **flowchart**. Typically, flowcharts use particular

Figure 16.1 Profit Model for Star Motors

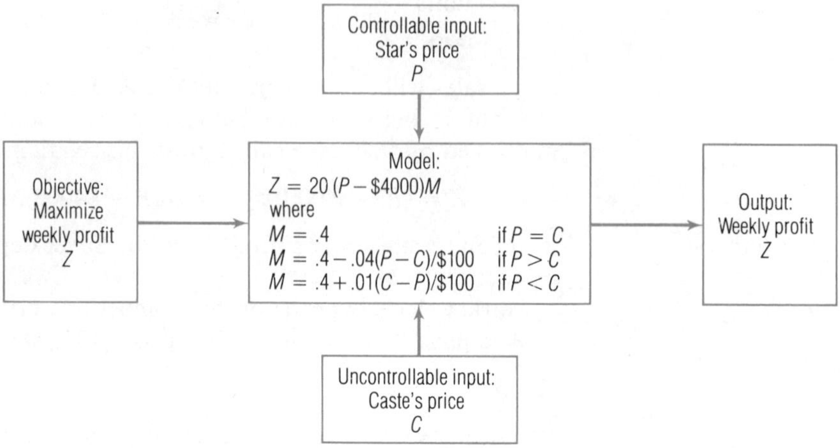

kinds of symbols to represent various types of computations and operations. Hence, before continuing with the Star Motors example, let us study Figure 16.2. This figure reviews standard flowcharting symbols that will be used in the text.

Figure 16.3 presents a flowchart for Star's price competition. The flowchart begins with the (Start) symbol. Next, inputs are obtained. Star specifies its price P and then generates Caste's price C. The symbol ⏢ is used to indicate these operations. Now Star must compare the two prices and select the appropriate computation. If $P = C$, then Star's market share $M = .4$. When $P > C$, $M = .4 - .04(P - C)/\$100$. Otherwise, P must be greater than C and $M = .4 + .01(C - P)/\$100$. The symbol ◇ is used to represent the selection process and □ to represent the computations. The resulting market share is reported with the symbol ⏢. Then, Star can compute profit as

$$Z = 20(P - \$4000)M$$

and report the result. Again, the symbol □ is used to indicate the computation and ⏢ to report the results.

At this point, Star has completed a simulation for one week of competition. Other selections may now be made. If Star does not want to simulate additional weeks, it can stop the process here. (Stop operations are indicated with the symbol (Stop).) To simulate another week at the same price P, Star must generate a new Caste price C. Then Star repeats the sequence of operations and computations required to calculate the new market share and profit.

Figure 16.2 Flowcharting Symbols

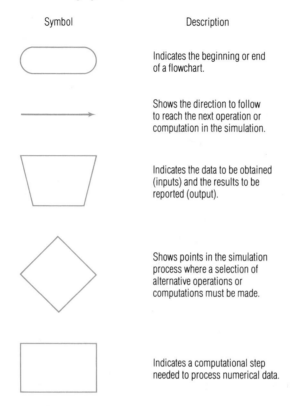

Symbol	Description
	Indicates the beginning or end of a flowchart.
	Shows the direction to follow to reach the next operation or computation in the simulation.
	Indicates the data to be obtained (inputs) and the results to be reported (output).
	Shows points in the simulation process where a selection of alternative operations or computations must be made.
	Indicates a computational step needed to process numerical data.

Suppose that Star has simulated several weeks of competition at a given price P. Now it must decide whether or not to try another price. If Star decides to continue, it will specify a new price P and then repeat the entire process. Otherwise, it will stop simulating.

PERFORMING A SIMULATION The next step is to develop some numerical simulations of the dealer competition. Star initiates the process by fixing its price at a trial value. Suppose, for instance, that Star sells the Saver for $P = \$4100$ this week. Now the company must generate a hypothetical competitor's price C.

If Star knew Caste's price C, it would have a deterministic model of the dealer competition. Then, Star could use the model (Figure 16.1) to project the exact profit that would result for a given price P. Such a recreation is referred to as a **deterministic simulation**.

Figure 16.3 Flowchart of Star's Price Competition

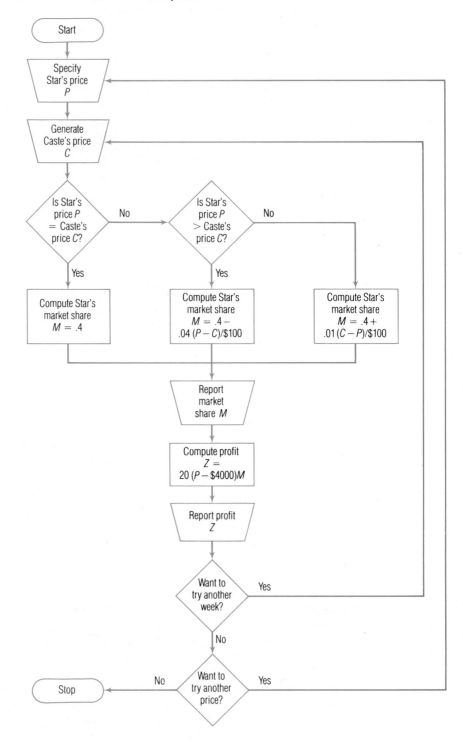

Unfortunately, Star does not know Caste's price in advance. However, Star does know Caste's potential price range. Assuming that the competitor will not sell at a loss, Caste's minimum price is the $4000 dealer cost. Also, if Star assumes that customers will not pay more than the suggested retail price, then there is a maximum $C = \$5000$. Thus, Caste's price will range from $4000 to $5000.

Now Star can find out what will happen if Caste's price is some value in this range. For example, what if Caste's price is $C = \$4000$ this week? Since $P = \$4100$, Star has the higher price. As shown in Figure 16.3, this means that Star's market share can be found with the expression

$$M = .4 - .04\left(\frac{P - C}{\$100}\right)$$

In this case

$$M = .4 - .04\left(\frac{\$4100 - \$4000}{\$100}\right) = .36$$

and Star's profit this week is

$$Z = 20(P - \$4000)M = 20(\$4100 - \$4000).36 = \$720$$

A simulation for one week of the dealer competition has now been completed. To simulate another week at the same price P, Star must generate a new Caste price C. In the second week of the competition, suppose that Caste's price is $C = \$4200$. Since Star's price is still $P = \$4100$, Caste has the higher price. As shown in Figure 16.3, this means that Star's market share can be found with the expression

$$M = .4 + .01\left(\frac{C - P}{\$100}\right)$$

In this case,

$$M = .4 + .01\left(\frac{\$4200 - \$4100}{\$100}\right) = .41$$

and Star's resulting profit is

$$Z = 20(P - \$4000)M = 20(\$4100 - \$4000).41 = \$820$$

Adding this $820 to the $720 profit from the first week results in a total of $1540 for two weeks of simulated competition.

Star continues this hand simulation process for eight more weeks of operation. Table 16.1 summarizes the results.

The $8660 is the projected, or simulated, total profit when Star sets a price of $P = \$4100$ on the Saver for each of the next ten weeks.

The same process can be used to perform similar simulations with other Star prices. For example, if the company uses the same set of hypothetical

Table 16.1 Simulation Results When Star's Price Is $P = \$4100$

Week	Caste's Price CP ($)	Star's Market Share M	Star's Profit Z ($)	Star's Total Profit ($)
1	4000	.36	720	720
2	4200	.41	820	1540
3	4100	.40	800	2340
4	4400	.43	860	3200
5	4300	.42	840	4040
6	4700	.46	920	4960
7	5000	.49	980	5940
8	4500	.44	880	6820
9	4600	.45	900	7720
10	4800	.47	940	8660

Table 16.2 Results from Simulating Ten Weeks Each of New Star Prices

Star's Price P ($)	Star's Total Profit ($)
4100	8,660
4300	23,880
4500	35,100
4700	40,880
5000	36,800

Caste prices ($C = \$4000, \$4200, \$4100, \$4400, \$4300, \$4700, \$5000, \$4500,$ $\$4600,$ and $\$4800$) to simulate ten weeks of competition for Star prices $P = \$4300$, $P = \$4500$, $P = \$4700$, and $P = \$5000$, then the projected total profit information will be as presented in Table 16.2.

Table 16.2 indicates that $P = \$4700$ is the price leading to the largest total profit ($\$40,880$). These data suggest that Star should set a weekly price of $\$4700$ for the Saver. However, the recommendation is based on only ten weeks of simulated competition. To reach a confident conclusion, Star must simulate the dealer competition for a much longer period.

It would be time-consuming and cumbersome to continue the simulation with this enumeration approach. Yet, the device does demonstrate the nature of simulation. Let us now review the process before proceeding further. Table 16.3. presents a summary.

Table 16.3 Summary of the Simulation Process

1. Develop a mathematical model that describes the decision situation. The model relates the decision objective to the controllable and uncontrollable inputs.
2. Develop a flowchart that shows the sequence of operations and computations required by the simulation model.
3. Specify a trial value for each controllable input.
4. Generate values for the uncontrollable inputs.
5. Use the flowchart and mathematical model to project the resulting value of the decision objective.
6. Repeat steps 3 through 5 as desired.
7. Identify the value of the controllable input that leads to the most preferred value of the decision objective.

MONTE CARLO METHOD

In Example 16.1, Star knew Caste's potential price range but was uncertain about the competitor's exact price. Since the uncontrollable input (Caste's price) was uncertain, Star's profit expression represented a stochastic model of the dealer competition. In that example, the stochastic inputs were generated by arbitrarily selecting values for Caste's price. This section presents a more systematic way to generate values of the stochastic inputs in a simulation problem. Example 16.2 illustrates the process.

EXAMPLE 16.2 Stochastic Price Competition

Star still does not know Caste's exact price in advance. However, Star's management assesses the probabilities for Caste's price range as presented in Table 16.4. In other words, Star's management believes that there is a 10% chance that Caste's price will be $4100, a 20% likelihood that it will be $4300, and so on. Furthermore, management does not think that any other price is possible. Also, it is believed that this price pattern will be representative of future competition. Star wants to use this information in its price-setting procedure.

Table 16.4 Probabilities for Caste's Price Range

Caste Price ($)	Probability
4100	.10
4300	.20
4500	.40
4700	.25
4900	.05

The model must be realistic. Thus, it is important to generate a hypothetical competitive price C that is a good representation of the actual pattern. That is, the method for generating stochastic inputs should generate the same Caste price pattern as shown in Table 16.4. Hence, 10% of the time Caste's price should be $4100, on 20% of the occasions it should be $4300, and so on. Since this representation is a critical part of any simulation study, it warrants serious consideration. In general, models based on inaccurate inputs will not provide useful results.

GENERATING INPUTS WITH A MECHANICAL DEVICE   There is a simple way to generate representative competitive prices. First, we take 100 equally sized index cards. Each card represents one week of dealer competition. Next, we write $4100 on 10 of the cards. We do this because Caste's price C is expected to be $4100 10% (10/100) of the time. Similarly, since C is expected to be $4300 20% of the time, we write $4300 on 20 (out of 100) cards. Also, $4500 should be written on 40 cards, $4700 on 25 cards, and $4900 on 5 cards. Note that 10% of the cards have $4100, 20% $4300, 40% $4500, 25% $4700, and 5% $4900 written on them. Thus, the "deck" of cards represents the probabilities for Caste's prices given in Table 16.4.

Since the cards are the same size, each has an equal (1/100) chance of being selected. We then shuffle the deck of 100 cards to thoroughly mix the prices. This step ensures that any two cards in a sequence will be independent. In such cases, picking a card is said to involve a **random selection**. By selecting a card at random from the deck, Star's management can generate a competitive price C that is representative of the actual situation. For example, suppose that the first card drawn has a $4300 written on it. Then Caste's price will be $C = \$4300$ for the first simulated week of competition.

Star can generate another competitive price by returning the selected card to the deck, reshuffling all 100 cards, and then drawing another card at random. For instance, on the second draw, suppose that the card has a $4700 written on it. Then Caste's price will be $C = \$4700$ for the second simulated week of competition. The process can be repeated for as many weeks as desired.

RANDOM-NUMBER TABLES   Although the index card procedure demonstrates the nature of stochastic simulation, it would be time-consuming and cumbersome to continue with that approach. Other mechanical devices, like spinning a roulette wheel, drawing markers from a bin, or rolling dice, can also be used to make a random selection. However, these devices have the same shortcomings as the index card procedure. It is more convenient to use random-number tables for generating the uncontrollable inputs in a stochastic simulation model.

Table 16.5 Table of Random Digits

341447	723998	905614	519309	926345	240082	395043
415603	129727	894956	780924	227496	134056	023014
014881	496311	750082	707823	738906	157591	072396
827235	783798	324650	485324	568156	098331	768720
261607	730824	341940	259028	253973	145183	658110
527920	834376	972906	627959	654790	342497	593779
356756	519371	679389	371912	502903	936741	636775
700770	781547	916968	136999	801855	605975	295802
279584	733750	487151	116069	274869	416181	610911
862434	481154	391464	021094	761599	474456	582253
199585	167701	170778	934765	761328	275799	323046
048736	514507	977406	158840	846761	198016	933522
815218	609732	629295	517386	824505	676788	304971
643021	527212	492869	261844	914505	354436	355772
164332	245407	517804	422658	751712	583087	286872
174303	085157	308590	535846	503131	266915	465641
136325	414066	452293	649359	844625	674828	953396
117780	407444	426115	108970	621527	601599	652376
435697	245510	946158	934221	824917	509832	362638
912252	579474	848845	824321	049853	151126	052643
754438	658573	717914	040054	630638	264060	594641
322053	924909	048177	957012	801464	833319	978384
897199	125506	708669	408374	737887	906201	599469
046637	642050	435779	502427	027842	515775	811203
721653	260190	842505	797017	157497	179041	979346
202312	011976	373248	374293	802292	646914	171322
354014	356787	511271	904434	068589	329862	829316
682909	809290	793392	098004	120575	469925	112743
897690	572456	871574	465543	486529	507767	608677
139029	160636	417690	191242	625269	104858	020808
345769	953810	627280	423578	353511	899906	827008
549075	004410	059309	271243	403382	248735	972383
423480	950812	197145	556566	655917	046169	363201
551518	514280	950974	482196	058868	474936	724289
797165	670995	791954	188521	950156	086813	033365
062730	163375	602168	908350	360861	152201	966097

Table 16.5 presents a random-number table. It contains the ten digits 0, 1, 2, 3, 4, 5, 6, 7, 8, and 9. Each digit appears with the same frequency and thereby has an equal chance of occurring. Also, any two numbers in a sequence are independent. That is, the digits appear in random order. Consequently, the analyst makes a random selection when he or she picks a digit from the table.

Now, let us see how Star can use this random-number table to generate Caste's prices. Note that the probabilities in Table 16.4 have up to two digits after the decimal point. Hence, our random numbers also should

Table 16.6 Random Numbers Associated with Caste's Prices

Caste's Price ($)	Probability of Caste's Price	Random Numbers	Probability of Random Numbers
4100	.10	00–09	$10/100 = .10$
4300	.20	10–29	$20/100 = .20$
4500	.40	30–69	$40/100 = .40$
4700	.25	70–94	$25/100 = .25$
4900	.05	95–99	$5/100 = .05$

have two digits. By selecting sets of two digits from the random-number table, Star can get two-digit random numbers from 00 to 99. The value 00 will be the first of 100 numbers in the sequence. Although it is possible to choose digits from any part of the table, for ease of reference, let us begin with the first row. Our two-digit random numbers then would be 34, 14, 47, 72, 39, 98, and so on.

According to Table 16.4, there is a 10% chance that Caste's price will be $4100. Thus, Star wants 10% of the 100 possible two-digit random numbers to correspond with $C = \$4100$. While any 10 numbers from 00 to 99 will do, for convenience, suppose that Star assigns $C = \$4100$ to the first 10 random numbers (00 through 09). Then, whenever any of these 10 random numbers is observed, Caste's simulated price will be $4100. Since the two-digit random numbers from 00 through 09 will occur 10% of the time, this method will generate $C = \$4100$ 10% of the time.

Similarly, Table 16.4 shows that there is a 20% chance that Caste's price will be $4300. By letting 20% (20 out of the 100) two-digit random numbers correspond to $C = \$4300$, Star will simulate this competitive price 20% of the time. The analyst can select any arbitrary set of 20 random numbers that have not been assigned to other Caste prices. However, for convenience, let us use successive random numbers. Thus, Star should assign $C = \$4300$ to the two-digit random numbers from 10 through 29. When management continues to assign competitive prices to random numbers in this fashion, it will get the results shown in Table 16.6.

Notice that there is an interval of random numbers associated with every Caste price. Further, each interval is such that the probability of the random number is the same as the probability of the associated competitive price. For instance, the probability of selecting a random number from 70 to 94 is exactly the same (.25) as the probability that Caste's price will be $4700.

It is now possible to simulate Caste's price by using Table 16.6 and two-digit random numbers drawn from Table 16.5. Recall that the first two-digit random number drawn from the first row of Table 16.5 was 34. From

Table 16.7 Results from Simulating Ten Weeks of Caste's Prices

Week	Random Number	Caste's Simulated Price ($)
1	34	4500
2	14	4300
3	47	4500
4	72	4700
5	39	4500
6	98	4900
7	90	4700
8	56	4500
9	14	4300
10	51	4500

Table 16.8 Monte Carlo Simulation Procedure

1. Develop the probability distribution for each uncontrollable input.
2. Assign an interval of numbers to each possible value of the uncontrollable input. The numbers must have as many digits as the probabilities for the stochastic input. For convenience, use successive numbers. Also, make sure that the chance of selecting a number from each interval is the same as the probability of the corresponding input value.
3. Use a mechanical device (like the index card technique) or a random-number table to generate a random number. The random number must have as many digits as the probabilities for the stochastic input.
4. Identify the interval that contains the random number generated in step 3. The uncontrollable input value that corresponds to the interval represents the simulated outcome.
5. Repeat steps 3 and 4 as desired.

Table 16.6, we see that this random number is in the interval 30 to 69, and this corresponds to a Caste price of $C = \$4500$. The second two-digit random number that appears in the first row of Table 16.5 is 14. This value is in the interval from 10 to 29 in Table 16.6. Hence, Caste's simulated price in the second week of competition is $C = \$4300$. By continuing in this manner for eight more weeks of operation, Star will get the results shown in Table 16.7.

The index card and random-number table approaches are both methods of randomly selecting stochastic inputs for a simulation model. Further, these approaches generate inputs that are from the same probability distributions as the actual values. Such a procedure is referred to as a **Monte Carlo simulation** named after Monaco's famous gambling casino. Table 16.8 summarizes the method.

Once the stochastic inputs have been generated, the decision maker can continue with the simulation process (Table 16.3).

COMPUTER SIMULATION

Clearly, it would require considerable time and effort to perform the calculations necessary for large, complex simulations. Hence, it should not be surprising to learn that simulation did not become a practical problem-solving tool until the advent of electronic computers. The computer can be used to carry out the well-defined operations and calculations that make up the simulation process. This capability makes it possible to perform large simulations in reasonable amounts of time. Indeed, the word *computer* so often precedes the word *simulation* because a computer is so frequently used in performing simulation calculations.

Practitioners and computer manufacturers have recognized that most simulations involve certain features. Values of various inputs must be generated from probability distributions, tables must be developed to keep track of the results, and so on. Thus, special computer programs and languages have been developed for simulation. Sometimes, there are "canned" programs that can be applied to particular applications such as inventory control and waiting lines. Quite often, however, the situation will not fit an existing program. Then the analyst can use languages like **SIMSCRIPT**, **GASP** (General Activity Simulation Package), **SLAM** (Simulation Language for Alternative Modeling), and **GPSS** (General Purpose Simulation Systems), which have been designed specifically for simulation studies. K. A. Dunning [7] discusses GPSS, P. J. Kiviat and others [16] SIMSCRIPT, and A. A. Pritsker [23, 24] the GASP and SLAM languages in detail. In addition, many analysts use general-purpose computer programming languages, like FORTRAN and COBOL, to develop the simulation "from scratch." The specific computer program that performs the simulation operations and computations is referred to as the **simulator**.

PSEUDORANDOM NUMBERS

To perform stochastic simulations with a computer, it is necessary to generate random numbers and values for the probabilistic components of the model. The computer can be programmed to store random-number tables (like the one in Table 16.5) and then follow the Monte Carlo procedure (Table 16.8). However, random-number tables require substantial computer memory. Consequently, the procedure usually involves an inefficient use of the computer.

Computer simulations use mathematical formulas that generate numbers that, for all practical purposes, have the same properties as the numbers selected from random-number tables. W. Graybeal and U. W.

Table 16.9 Pseudorandom Numbers Associated with Caste's Prices

Caste's Price ($)	Probability of Caste's Price	Pseudorandom Numbers	Probability of Pseudorandom Numbers
4100	.10	0 to .09999	.09999/.99999 = .10
4300	.20	.10 to .29999	.19999/.99999 = .20
4500	.40	.30 to .69999	.39999/.99999 = .40
4700	.25	.70 to .94999	.24999/.99999 = .25
4900	.05	.95 to .99999	.04999/.99999 = .05

Pooch [9] describe these formulas in detail. Since the computer-generated random numbers are based on mathematical formulas, they do not represent "pure" random numbers. Instead, the computer values are referred to as **pseudorandom numbers**. Nonetheless, in computer simulations, the pseudorandom numbers are used in exactly the same way as the random numbers selected from random-number tables.

Most mathematical formulas for generating pseudorandom numbers are designed to provide a value from 0 up to but not including 1, or 0 to .99999. In computer simulations, an interval of pseudorandom numbers is assigned to each value of the stochastic input. Further, the probability of generating a pseudorandom number must be exactly the same as the probability for the corresponding input value.

Table 16.4, for example, shows a .1 probability for a Caste price of $C = \$4100$. Thus, 10% of all possible pseudorandom numbers must correspond to $C = \$4100$. Since the values in the interval 0 to .09999 represent .09999/.99999 or about 10% of all possible pseudorandom numbers, this interval can be used to represent a Caste price of $4100. Similarly, Table 16.4 shows a .2 probability for a Caste price of $4300. By letting the values in the interval .1 to .29999 correspond to $C = \$4300$, the analyst will simulate this price $(.29999 - .1)/.99999 = .19999/.99999$ or approximately 20% of the time.

If Star continues to assign Caste's prices to pseudorandom numbers in this manner, it will get the results shown in Table 16.9. Notice that there is an interval of pseudorandom numbers associated with every Caste price. Further, each interval is such that the probability of generating a pseudorandom number in that interval is the same as the probability of the corresponding Caste price. For example, the probability of selecting a pseudorandom number in the interval .7 to .94999 is exactly the same (.25) as the likelihood of observing a Caste price of $4700.

It is now possible to simulate Caste's price by using Table 16.9 and computer-generated pseudorandom numbers. For instance, suppose that a computer is used to generate pseudorandom numbers between 0 and

.99999. Assume that the first pseudorandom number generated is .13351. Table 16.9 shows that .13351 corresponds to a Caste price of $4300. Similarly, suppose that the second computer-generated pseudorandom number is .85216. Table 16.9 shows that this number corresponds to a Caste price of $4700. By continuing in this manner, Star can simulate many weeks of Caste's price behavior.

DECISION MAKING By now you have a basic understanding of simulation and the role of the computer in the process. Now let us examine how computer simulation can help make decisions. Consider Example 16.3.

EXAMPLE 16.3 Investment Financing

Regional Power, Inc., is a publicly owned utility that supplies water and electricity to the northeastern states. The company must build a new generating plant to meet the growing demand for energy. It is difficult to determine the exact construction costs because of potential building delays and inflation. However, Regional's financial department has developed the expense data shown in Table 16.10.

The company plans to finance the investment by issuing bonds and borrowing from an insurance company. Bonds will yield 10% per annum to investors, while the interest rate on the loan will be 12% a year. As a lending condition, the insurance company insists that the bond

Table 16.10 Regional's Construction Cost Data

Construction Cost ($ Million)	Probability
100	.05
200	.35
300	.50
400	.10

Table 16.11 Bank Prime Lending Rate

Annual Interest Rate (% of Loan Amount)	Probability
8	.05
10	.15
12	.20
14	.30
16	.25
18	.05

flotation be no more than $1\frac{1}{2}$ times the loan amount. If Regional does not obtain enough funds from these sources, it will have to finance the residual with a bank loan at the prevailing prime interest rate. The future prime rate is not known exactly, but Regional's finance department has compiled the data shown in Table 16.11.

Regional's management wants to determine the pattern of financing (the bond and loan amounts) that will minimize the costs of obtaining the required funds. It does not want to use any currently available funds to pay for the plant's construction cost.

As before, the analysis begins with the development of a model. In this case, let

I = the total annual interest expense ($ million)

B = the bond issue ($ million)

L = the insurance loan ($ million)

C = the plant construction cost ($ million)

R = the bank loan ($ million)

r = the annual interest rate on the bank loan

Regional finances construction by issuing bonds and borrowing. Annual interest charges I will be 10% of the bond issue B plus 12% of the insurance loan plus an uncertain rate r on the bank loan. That is,

$$(16.5) \quad I = .10B + .12L + rR$$

The bank loan will be necessary only if the bond and insurance loan funds are not sufficient to cover the construction cost. Then, the bank loan will equal the difference, or

$$R = C - B - L \quad \text{if } B + L < C$$

On the other hand, if the bonds and insurance loan provide sufficient funds, there will be no need for a bank loan. Hence, in this case,

$$R = 0 \quad \text{if } B + L \geq C$$

and the annual interest charge will be

$$I = .10B + .12L + r(0) = .10B + .12L$$

The company wants to choose the values of B and L that will minimize total interest expense I.

Regional must meet two constraints. The total investment must be sufficient to cover the total cost of constructing the new generating plant, or

$$(16.6) \quad B + L + R \geq C$$

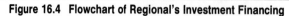

Figure 16.4   Flowchart of Regional's Investment Financing

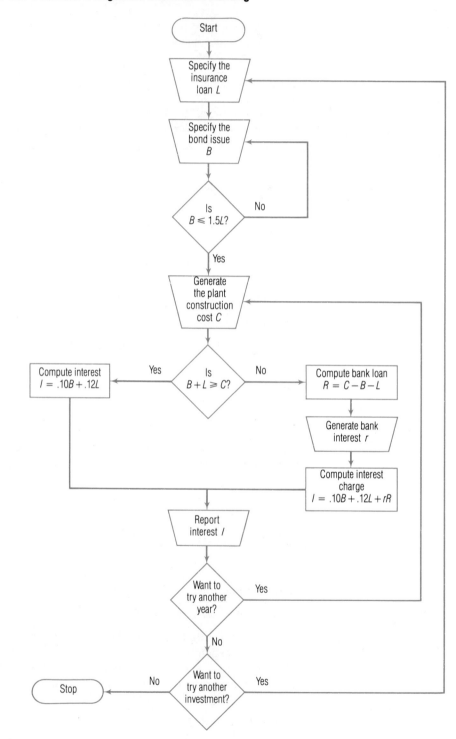

Also, insurance company policy requires the bond issue to be no more than $1\frac{1}{2}$ times the loan amount, or

(16.7) $B \leq 1.5L$

Expressions (16.5)–(16.7) form a model of Regional's investment situation. Figure 16.4 presents a flowchart of the problem.

This problem is more complex than the dealer competition problem because it involves two decision variables (B and L) and two stochastic inputs (r and C). Also, there are two constraints on the investment process, expressions (16.6) and (16.7).

THE SIMULATOR In computer simulation, the next step is to develop a computer program that will perform the simulation operations and computations specified by the flowchart. You are not expected to develop such a program. However, you will better understand computer decision making by examining the relationship between the flowchart and the computer simulation program.

Figure 16.5 presents a FORTRAN-language computer program that will perform the simulation operations and computations specified by Regional's flowchart (Figure 16.4). The program is a simulator that can be used by company management to evaluate various investment policies.

The flowchart (Figure 16.4) again begins with the symbol $\overbrace{\text{Start}}$. Then trial values are specified for the insurance loan L and bond issue B. The symbol $\boxed{}$ indicates these operations. Suppose that a group of Regional executives is polled to establish the values and the consensus is that Regional should issue between $80 million and $140 million in bonds and borrow between $80 million and $140 million from the insurance company. Management wants to evaluate the loan/bond combinations in $10 million increments within these ranges. The trial values are specified in statements 3 through 6 of the simulator (Figure 16.5). For instance, statements 3 and 4 tell the computer to try loan values of $L = 80$ through $L = 140$ in increments of 10. Also, the analyst must make sure that the bond issue is no more than $1\frac{1}{2}$ times the loan amount, or

$B \leq 1.5L$

The symbol $\diamondsuit$ indicates this operation in the flowchart (Figure 16.4). In the simulator (Figure 16.5), statements 7 and 8 instruct the computer to select only those B and L values that satisfy this condition.

Once the policy constraint is met, Regional must generate the plant construction cost C. In the flowchart, we use the symbol $\boxed{}$ to indicate this operation. To execute the operation, it is first necessary to assign an interval of pseudorandom numbers to each potential cost. Further, the probability of generating a pseudorandom number in an interval must be exactly the same as the probability of the corresponding cost. Table 16.10 gives the probabilities associated with the plant construction costs. It

Figure 16.5   Computer Simulation Program for Regional's Investment Problem

```
1.              PROGRAM SIMUIN (INPUT, OUTPUT, OUT, TAPE 5=INPUT, TAPE 6=OUTPUT,
                    TAPE 7=OUT)
2.              REAL I, ITOT, L, M.
3.              DO 500 K=80, 140, 10
4.              L=K
5.              DO 500 N=80, 140, 10
6.              B=N
7.              TEMP=1.5*L
8.              IF (B.GT.TEMP) GO TO 500
9.              ITOT=0
10.             AVE=0
11.             WRITE (7, 30) B, L
12.     30      FORMAT ("1", 10X, "YEAR INTEREST", 5X,"B=",F7.2," L=",F7.2)
13.             DO 300 J=1, 1000
14.             Y=RANF(A)
15.             IF (Y.LT..05) C=100
16.             IF (Y.GE..05.AND.Y.LT..4) C=200`
17.             IF (Y.GE..40.AND.Y.LT..9) C=300
18.             IF (Y.GE..90) C=400
19.             BL=B+L
20.             IF (BL.GE.C) GO TO 100
21.             GO TO 200
22.     100     I=.10*B + .12*L
23.             GO TO 220
24.     200     R=C-BL
25.             M=RANF(A)
26.             IF (M.LT..05) r=.08
27.             IF (M.GE..05.AND.M.LT..2) r=.10
28.             IF (M.GE..20.AND.M.LT..4) r=.12
29.             IF (M.GE..40.AND.M.LT..7) r=.14
30.             IF (M.GE..70.AND.M.LT..95) r=.16
31.             IF (M.GE..95) r=.18
32.             I=.10*B + .12*L + r*R
33.     220     WRITE (7,250) J.I
34.     250     FORMAT (12,X, I2, 4X, F5.2)
35.             ITOT=ITOT + I
36.             AVE=ITOT/1000
37.     300     CONTINUE
38.             WRITE (7,350) ITOT, AVE
39.     350     FORMAT (8X, "TOTAL = ", F7.2/, 10X, "AVE = ",F7.2)
40.     500     CONTINUE
41.             STOP
                END
```

Table 16.12 Pseudorandom Numbers Associated with Regional's Plant Costs

Construction Cost C ($ Million)	Probability	Pseudorandom Numbers
100	.05	0 to .04999
200	.35	.05 to .39999
300	.50	.40 to .89999
400	.10	.90 to .99999

shows that there is a 5% chance of incurring a $100 million cost. Since values in the interval 0 to .04999 represent about 5% of all pseudorandom numbers, this arrival can be used to represent $C = 100$. When Regional continues to assign pseudorandom numbers to costs in this manner, it will get the results shown in Table 16.12. Statements 14 through 18 in the simulator (Figure 16.5) assign pseudorandom numbers in accordance with Table 16.12 and randomly generate the corresponding plant construction costs.

At this point, the analyst must compare the amount of funds obtained from the investment $(B + L)$ with the construction cost C. Statements 19 and 20 in the simulator (Figure 16.5) make this comparison. In the flowchart (Figure 16.4), the symbol $\diamondsuit$ indicates the selection of alternative computations. If

$$B + L \geq C$$

then Regional can compute the interest expense I as

$$I = .10B + .12L$$

This calculation is indicated with the symbol ▢ in the flowchart and made by statement 22 in the simulator.

If there are insufficent bond and insurance funds, Regional must make up the difference with a bank loan R. The amount is computed as

$$R = C - B - L$$

in statement 24 in the simulator and again represented by the symbol ▢ in the flowchart. To compute the resulting interest expense, the analyst must generate the bank prime rate r. The symbol ▱ in the flowchart indicates this operation. Again, it is necessary to assign an interval of pseudorandom numbers to each possible interest rate. When Regional makes the assignment in accordance with the probabilities given in Table 16.11, it will get the results shown in Table 16.13. Statements 25 through 31 in the simulator assign pseudorandom numbers in accordance with Table 16.13 and randomly generate the corresponding bank interest rates.

Table 16.13 Pseudorandom Numbers Associated with the Prime Rate

Annual Interest Rate r (% of Loan Amount)	Probability	Pseudorandom Numbers
8	.05	0 to .04999
10	.15	.05 to .19999
12	.20	.20 to .39999
14	.30	.40 to .69999
16	.25	.70 to .94999
18	.05	.95 to .99999

Table 16.14 Simulated Average Annual Interest Expense for 1000 Years of Regional's Investment Financing

Bond Issue B ($ Million)	Insurance Loan L ($ Million)						
	80	90	100	110	120	130	140
80	30.77	30.90	30.40	31.08	23.98	22.54	22.58
90	31.31	30.67	30.38	22.31	22.20	22.11	22.58
100	29.95	30.28	22.67	22.62	21.91	22.61	22.07
110	29.95	23.41	22.28	21.88	22.54	21.87	23.25
120	22.39	22.72	22.05	22.23	22.40	21.84	21.88
130	*	21.11	21.09	21.43	21.44	22.11	21.84
140	*	*	22.51	22.13	21.43	22.75	20.40

* Indicates that this investment combination ($B + L$) does not satisfy the policy constraint $B \leq 1.5L$ and thus is not feasible.

Then, the interest expense I is computed as

$$I = 10B + .12L + rR$$

as indicated by the symbol ▭ in the flowchart. Simulator statement 32 makes this calculation.

When the interest expense has been recorded, the analyst has completed a simulation for one year of Regional's investment situation. Simulator statement 35 keeps a running total of the accumulated interest expense, and statement 36 computes an average. In the flowchart (Figure 16.4), the symbol ▱ reports the results and the symbol ◇ indicates that other selections are now necessary. If the company does not want to simulate additional years, it will stop the process at this point. Stop operations are represented by the symbol (Stop).

To simulate additional years with the same investment combination, the analyst must generate a new construction cost C. Then the entire sequence of operations is repeated to calculate the new interest expense. Simulator statements 37 and 13 instruct the computer to simulate 1000 years of financing with a given investment combination. Statement 40 repeats the entire simulation for each investment specified in statements 3 through 6 of the simulator. Finally, statement 41 tells the computer to stop simulating.

Table 16.14 presents the computer simulation results. It shows that an investment combination of $B = 140$ ($ million) in bonds and $L = 140$ ($ million) in insurance loans results in the smallest average annual interest expense ($20.4 million).

After studying the results, Regional's analyst might wish to consider other investment combinations near the apparent "best" solution. An additional analysis can be easily accomplished by changing statements 4 and 6 in the simulator (Figure 16.5) to the desired values and then executing the computer program. Otherwise, the simulation indicates that Regional can obtain low-cost financing by issuing $140 million in bonds and borrowing $140 million from the insurance company.

LIMITATIONS AND ADVANTAGES

Simulation is a trial and error approach. It tells what will happen if selected trial actions are implemented under given conditions. For example, in Regional's financing problem, the company does not examine every possible investment combination under all financial conditions. Instead, it simulates interest costs for selected bond and loan values. In effect, then, the simulation solution represents the best action among those specified for evaluation. However, simulation does not search out and find the best policy to implement. Although decision makers are usually able to identify reasonable policies for evaluation, better actions might exist but remain unrecognized by management. Therefore, the simulation solution may not give the optimal solution to the problem.

Simulation has other limitations. The approach is more time-consuming and costly to use than analytical devices. Someone must develop the computer programs or simulators. In large-scale projects, this step is usually a substantial undertaking. The user must have access to computer facilities and personnel. Also, the development of the simulator typically requires significant interaction between the manager and the computer staff and considerable experimentation. In addition, there are technical problems in the design, validation, and estimation of simulation models. Consequently, estimates from Monte Carlo simulations are imprecise and subject to statistical error. Although a complete discussion of these technical statistical issues is beyond the scope of the text, the reader should be aware of the potential difficulties. A. M. Law [17] and H. J. Watson [26] discuss these issues in detail.

Table 16.15   Simulation Applications

Form	Description	Area	Reference
Artificial intelligence	Programming a computer to imitate human thought	Financial analysis Management behavior	M. J. Bouwman [3] N. Findler and B. Meltzer [8]
Business operations	Simulating business operations for planning and control purposes	Product marketing Production management Inventory management Service systems	M. R. Crask [6] P. Y. Huang et al. [12]; C. Leggett [18] A. P. Johnson and V. M. Fernandes [14]; A. Kaplan and S. Frazza [15] J. M. Mellinchamp and C. P. Weaver [20]
Corporate planning models	Models that link decision making within an organization to conditions in the firm's environment	Fire department policy Strategic planning	D. E. Monarchi et al. [21] T. H. Naylor [22]
Heuristic programming	Using step-by-step procedures to arrive at feasible and satisfactory, though not necessarily optimal, solutions for complex problems	Land-use planning Mental health Alloy processing	E. D. Brill et al. [4] K. Heiner et al. [10] J. P. Hernandez and J. M. Proth [11]
Management games	A contrived situation that imbeds participants in a simulated environment, where they make decisions and analyze the results	Marketing Training Leadership	I. Ayal and J. Zif [1] S. Belardo et al. [2] M. W. McCall and M. M. Lombardo [19]
System simulation	Modeling the dynamics of very large business or economic systems	University retirement Regulatory performance Tar sands mining	F. A. Jacobs and F. E. Watkins [13] W. A. Thompson et al. [25] F. P. Wyman [27]

In spite of the limitations, D. P. Christy and H. J. Watson [5] have found that simulation is applied by many firms to a variety of decision problems. Table 16.15 outlines various forms of simulation applications.

There are reasons for simulation's popularity. For one thing, the approach does not require a great deal of mathematical sophistication. A business person who understands the sequence of activities and operations can, with practice, help develop a flowchart of the problem. Then the flowchart can be converted into a computer model that replicates the sequence. The model should be easy for the decision maker to comprehend because it simply describes the problem as seen by management. Also, the decision maker is usually instrumental in developing the simulation. These factors will facilitate the implementation of the simulation model.

Simulation also provides a useful and convenient management laboratory. The simulation model explicitly identifies the important relationships involved in the actual problem. Managers can therefore use the model to systematically and consistently evaluate proposed policies under a variety of simulated conditions. Also, the model can be used to isolate the effects of key elements on the simulated system. Furthermore, such experiments can be carried out without disturbing the actual system. This capability reduces the chance of implementing a poorly designed policy that could lead to economic, political, or social catastrophe. In addition, simulation makes it possible to compress time. An experiment that ordinarily would require months or years to perform on the actual system can be accomplished in seconds or minutes with computer simulation.

Problems that involve sequences of interrelated elements, several stochastic components, or unusual mathematical operations are often too difficult or complex to be solved by analytical models. Simulation is perhaps most appropriate in such circumstances. Also, it may be possible to solve an oversimplified version of a problem with an analytical solution procedure. Yet, the decision maker may want to incorporate additional realism into the analysis and thus may favor a simulation approach.

SUMMARY This chapter has presented the essential concepts of simulation and has shown simulation as a technique for conducting trial and error experiments. The decision maker first builds a physical, analog, or mathematical model that imitates (acts like) the real situation. In this respect, it is helpful to develop a diagram, called a flowchart, that shows the sequence of operations and computations required by the simulation model. Then, by experimenting with the model, the manager is able to study the characteristics and behavior of the actual system. Table 16.3 summarized the simulation process.

Simulation models often involve stochastic inputs. This chapter presented a systematic procedure, called the Monte Carlo method, to generate these inputs. We saw how mechanical devices (such as a deck of cards) and random-number tables are used to carry out the procedure. Table 16.8 summarized the approach.

In practice, most simulations deal with large and complex problems. Ordinarily, a computer must be used to perform the required operations and calculations in a reasonable time frame. Consequently, practitioners and computer manufacturers have developed computer programs, called simulators, to perform the required tasks. The simulators typically use general-purpose programming languages (like FORTRAN and COBOL) or special simulation languages (such as SIMSCRIPT and GPSS).

The chapter concluded with the limitations and advantages of simulation. The major limitations are:

♦ The inability of simulation to search out and find the best policy to implement
♦ The time-consuming and costly nature of simulation as compared to analytical devices
♦ The technical problems involved in the design, validation, and estimation of simulation models

Nevertheless, as illustrated by Table 16.15, the approach is popular for the following reasons:

♦ The ability of decision makers to easily comprehend and use the technique
♦ The usefulness and convenience of simulation as a management laboratory
♦ The capability of simulation to cope with problems that are too difficult and complex for solution by other quantitative approaches

In effect, then, simulation is an effective adjunct to, not substitute for, analytical solution procedures.

Glossary

deterministic simulation   A simulation in which the decision maker knows the values of the uncontrollable inputs.

flowchart   A diagram that shows the sequence of operations and computations required by the simulation model.

Monte Carlo simulation   An approach that uses a random selection procedure (such as a deck of index cards or a random-number table) to generate the stochastic inputs for a simulation model.

pseudorandom numbers Computer-generated numbers, developed from mathematical formulas, that have the properties of random numbers.

random selection   A method of selecting an input in a way that each value in a sequence is independent and has an equal chance of being selected.

SIMSCRIPT, GASP, SLAM, and GPSS   Popular computer languages used for simulation studies.

simulation   A technique that uses a model to recreate an actual situation and then studies the system's characteristics and behavior by experimenting with the model.

simulator   The computer program that performs the simulation operations and computations.

References

1. Ayal, I., and J. Zif. "R & D Marketing: A Management Simulation." *Simulation and Games* (December 1978): 429.

2. Belardo, S., et al. "Simulation of a Crisis Management Information Network: A Serendipitous Evaluation." *Decision Sciences* (Fall 1983): 588.

3. Bouwman, M. J. "Human Diagnostic Reasoning by Computer: An Illustration from Financial Analysis." *Management Science* (June 1983): 653.

4. Brill, E. D., et al. "Modeling to Generate Alternatives: The HSJ Approach and an Illustration Using a Problem in Land Use Planning." *Management Science* (March 1982): 221.

5. Christy, D. P., and H. J. Watson. "The Application of Simulation: A Survey of Industry Practice." *Interfaces* (October 1983): 47.

6. Crask, M. R. "A Simulation Model of Patronage Behavior Within Shopping Centers." *Decision Sciences* (January 1979): 1.

7. Dunning, K. A. *Getting Started in GPSS*. San Jose: Engineering Press, 1981.

8. Findler, N., and B. Meltzer. *Artificial Intelligence and Heuristic Programming*. New York: American Elsevier, 1971.

9. Graybeal, W., and U. W. Pooch. *Simulation: Principles and Methods*. Cambridge: Winthrop, 1980.

10. Heiner, K., et al. "A Resource Allocation and Evaluation Model for Providing Services to the Mentally Retarded." *Management Science* (July 1981): 769.

11. Hernandez, J. P., and J. M. Proth. "A Good Solution Instead of an Optimal One." *Interfaces* (April 1982): 37.

12. Huang, P. Y., et al. "A Simulation Analysis of the Japanese Just-in-Time Technique (with Kanbans) for a Multiline, Multistage Production System." *Decision Sciences* (July 1983): 326.

13. Jacobs, F. A., and F. E. Watkins. "The Relevance of State-University Retirement Plans in Job Selection." *Decision Sciences* (Winter 1984): 119.

14. Johnson, A. P., and V. M. Fernandes. "Simulation of the Number of Spare Engines Required for an Aircraft Fleet." *Journal of the Operational Research Society* (January 1978): 33

15. Kaplan, A., and S. Frazza. "Empirical Inventory Simulation: A Case Study." *Decision Sciences* (January 1983): 62.

16. Kiviat, P. J., et al. *The SIMSCRIPT II Programming Language*. Englewood Cliffs, N.J.: Prentice-Hall, 1977.

17. Law, A. M. "Statistical Analysis of Simulation Output Data." *Operations Research* (November–December 1983): 983.

18. Leggett, C. "A Case Study of a Batch Manufacturing Plant Simulation." *European Journal of Operations Research* (January 1978): 1.

19. McCall, M. W., and M. M. Lombardo. "Using Simulation for Leadership and Management Research: Through the Looking Glass." *Management Science* (May 1982): 533.

20. Mellinchamp, J. M., and C. P. Weaver. "Simulation and Sewage." *Decision Sciences* (July 1977): 584.

21. Monarchi, D. E., et al. "Simulation for Fire Department Deployment Policy Analysis." *Decision Sciences* (January 1977): 211.

22. Naylor, T. H. *Simulation Models in Corporate Planning.* New York: Praeger, 1979.

23. Pritsker, A. A. *The GASP IV Simulation Language.* New York: Wiley, 1974.

24. Pritsker, A. A., et al. *Introduction to Simulation and SLAM.* New York: Halsted Press, 1979.

25. Thompson, W. A., et al. "Performance of a Regulatory Agency as a Function of Its Structure and Client Environment: A Simulation Study." *Management Science* (January 1982): 57.

26. Watson, H. J. *Computer Simulation In Business.* New York: Wiley, 1981.

27. Wyman, F. P. "Simulation of Tar Sands Mining Operations." Part 2. *Interfaces* (November 1977): 6.

Thought Exercises

1. The following excerpts are taken from a panel discussion among business and government executives at a regional American Management Association conference:

   ♦ *Panelist 1:* I'm really excited about simulation! It clearly has revolutionized modern management. Now we can analyze *real* problems instead of these make-believe situations created by our operations research staffs to fit their mathematical models.

   ♦ *Panelist 2:* Yeah, I agree! For the first time since we started "getting sophisticated," I feel like I really have a grasp of what's going on! Before simulation, all I really understood was the results presented in the operations research summary report. Now I can see how the results are derived. It really makes me want to implement the recommendations.

   ♦ *Panelist 3:* Pretty soon, we won't even need the mathematical operations researcher. All that'll be necessary will be a computer programmer capable of communicating with us in our language. We can recreate the actual situation, get the programmer to develop a simulator, run a few simulations, and come up with a solution to the problem.

◆ *Moderator:* I think there are some basic misconceptions floating around the room. Apparently, we really don't understand the nature and purpose of simulation.

If you were a panelist, how would you comment?

2. In which of the following situations is simulation appropriate? Explain.

   a. The owner of a major-league baseball team is trying to decide whether she should move the team to another city. The decision depends on the legal implications of breaking the current stadium lease, uncertain future attendance, league approval, and player reaction.

   b. A private parcel post carrier wants to evaluate the profitability of several alternative routes. Profit depends on future demand, which is uncertain but follows a known probability distribution.

   c. The navy is deciding on how many drydocks to construct at its main eastern shipyard. Its decision depends on the number of arrivals and the service time. Although both factors are uncertain, there are some historical probability data available.

   d. An airline gives a periodic fitness test to its pilots. The rating is based on a weighted combination of performance attributes that are measured on various standard mechanical devices.

3. June Swoon, the production manager for Albright Glass Materials, has proposed the following quality control plan. A sample of glassware will be inspected from each lot produced, and June will set the maximum allowable proportion of defective glasses. If the actual proportion of defects in the sample is no more than the maximum, the entire lot will be considered of acceptable quality. Otherwise, the entire lot will be reworked.

   Since the sample represents only a part of the lot, June recognizes that the plan involves some uncertainty and potential error. On one hand, the lot may be deemed unacceptable (and rejected) when it is good. This error is referred to as producer's risk. In this case, Albright will be unnecessarily remaking good glasses at an expected cost equal to the rework expense times the probability of producer's risk. Alternatively, the lot may be accepted when it is bad. Since the customer unknowingly receives defective merchandise, this error is called consumer's risk. It has an expected cost equal to the ill-will expense times the probability of consumer's risk.

   June wants to determine the maximum allowable proportion of defective glasses in the sample that will minimize the total quality control costs. She has decided to simulate costs and has developed the following flowchart for the simulation:

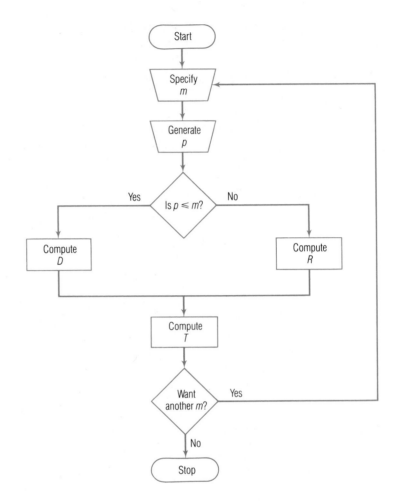

In this chart,

m = the maximum allowable proportion of defective glasses in the sample

p = the actual proportion of defective glasses in the sample

R = the cost of remaking good glasses

D = the ill-will cost of providing defective merchandise

$T = R + D$ = the total quality control cost

Unfortunately, Alex Hander, the firm's computer specialist, has been unable to develop an acceptable simulator from the flowchart.

a. Can you identify the shortcomings in June Swoon's flowchart? Explain.

b. Develop the appropriate flowchart for this problem.

4. Develop a flowchart for the Monte Carlo procedure that was used to generate Caste's prices in Example 16.2.

5. Felt Tip Enterprises manufactures the Elite Script pen with the new "magic eraser." The company is trying to decide whether to make or buy the eraser component. Quality Products, Inc., will sell the components on a monthly basis as follows:

$50 for the first thousand

$40 for every additional thousand

Felt Tip knows that the cost of making the component will depend on the uncertain demand for Elites. Corporate executives have developed the following demand, cost, and probability information:

Monthly Demand	Probability	Manufacturing Cost per Thousand Components ($)
250	.02	70
500	.08	66
750	.13	60
1000	.37	50
1250	.16	43
1500	.14	35

Felt Tip executives would like to simulate the costs of making and buying the eraser component, but they are having trouble doing so. Explain why. Develop a procedure for simulating the costs.

6. Figure 16.1 presents a schematic representation of the profit model for Star Motors (Example 16.1). Develop the same type of chart for Regional's investment model (Example 16.3).

7. A recent Nobel Prize winner in economics made the following remarks to his class:

"Economists realize that decision making is a dynamic and complex process involving sequences of interrelated elements. Furthermore, the exact values of several components are not known precisely. Yet, we know that successful managers process the information, analyze the alternatives, and make the correct decision. The challenge to managerial economics, then, is to accurately replicate the successful manager's thought process. Computer simulation provides the means to meet this challenge."

Why did the economist arrive at this conclusion? In general terms, briefly explain how computer simulation might be used to recreate a successful decision maker's thought process.

8. Explain why you agree or disagree with the following statements:

  a. The Monte Carlo procedure involves an arbitrary selection of the stochastic inputs in a simulation problem.

  b. Simulation is best used as a last resort substitute for an analytical solution procedure.

  c. Practical simulation users should have some knowledge of available computer software.

  d. Eventually, there will be "canned" computer programs for most simulation problems.

  e. Simulation can only be applied to those problems involving stochastic inputs.

Technique Exercises

1. A government economist has developed the following mathematical model of state business tax revenue:

$$B = tY$$

$$Y = 1 + .5R - .3D$$

$$D = (.2 + t)R$$

where B = the business tax revenue ($ million), t = the tax rate, Y = the business taxable income ($ million), R = the business revenue ($ million), and D = the business tax deductions ($ million). Assume that the state wants to maximize revenue from the business tax.

  a. Draw a chart like Figure 16.1 that gives a schematic representation of the problem.

  b. Develop a flowchart that can be used to simulate tax rate policy

2. The production cost for a major consumer goods manufacturer is given by the following mathematical expression:

$$C = 40 - 2Q + Q^2$$

where C = the annual production cost ($ million) and Q = the output of soap (millions of bars). The company wants to minimize the cost of production but must also satisfy an uncertain demand D.

  a. Draw a chart like Figure 16.1 that gives a schematic representation of the problem.

  b. Develop a flowchart that can be used to simulate production policy.

3. In one of its consumer booklets, the government gives the following flowchart to aid borrowers in computing annual mortgage payments:

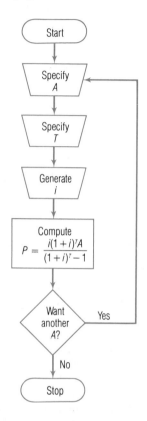

In this chart,

A = the amount borrowed

T = the term, or number of years for the mortgage

i = the interest rate

P = the annual mortgage payments

Use the flowchart to compute the annual mortgage payments for the following borrowers:

Borrower	Amount Borrowed ($)	Term (Years)	Interest Rate (%)
Johnson	80,000	20	10
Thomas	50,000	30	12
Indiri	100,000	30	11.75
Quanti	120,000	25	10.25
Smith	70,000	25	9.75
Jones	65,000	30	13
Olsen	75,000	30	12.50
Olanda	55,000	22	13.25
Ti	125,000	30	10.25
Wong	45,000	24	11.50

(*Note:* It will save time to look up the value of $(1 + i)^T$ in an annuity table. Such a table can be found in any basic finance text.)

4. The admissions officer of a major eastern public university has developed the following flowchart for selecting student applicants. In this flowchart,

> S = an acceptable score for admission
>
> GPA = the applicant's high school grade point average
>
> SAT = the applicant's Scholastic Aptitude Test score
>
> I = the applicant's interview rating
>
> A = the applicant's average admission score

The university accepts any student with $A \geq 2540$. Use the flowchart to simulate the admissions decision for the following students:

Student	GPA	SAT	I
Ann	3.5	400	80
Tom	2.8	600	90
Wally	4.0	600	50
Alaine	3.0	500	70
Phil	3.2	520	85
Jim	2.5	750	75
Judy	3.6	450	72
Nancy	3.8	400	65
Tina	2.7	650	100
Joe	3.9	800	55

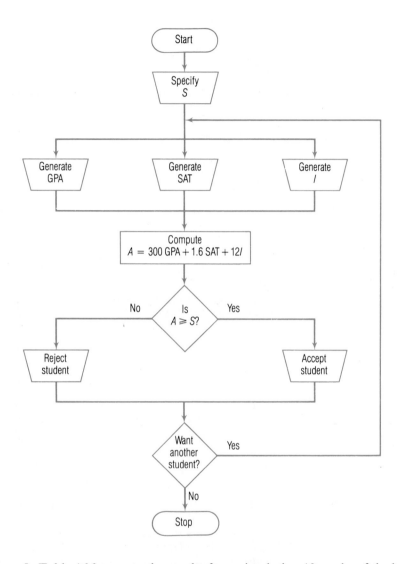

5. Table 16.2 reports the results from simulating 10 weeks of dealer competition in Example 16.1. Show how these results were obtained.

6. The following table reports data on employee absenteeism for a medium-sized brewery:

Days Absent per Year	Number of Employees
5	5
10	20
15	40
20	25
25	10
	100

Use the Monte Carlo procedure to simulate employee absenteeism for the next 20 years of brewery operations.

7. Store Surveys, Inc., uses the following procedure to determine the proportion of a territory that has "favorable market conditions." First, the decision maker superimposes a map of the territory on a graph that identifies market possibilities in the territories:

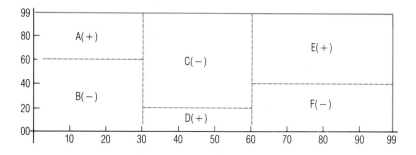

In this chart, there are 6 territories (A through F), with a plus (+) indicating favorable market conditions and a minus (−) unfavorable market conditions. Each axis has a scale of 100 integers numbered from 00 to 99. Next, a Monte Carlo procedure is used to generate coordinates on each axis of the map. The corresponding area of the map then identifies the likely market condition.
Use the Store Surveys procedure to simulate the likely market conditions for a sample of 30 areas within the territory. Estimate the proportion of these areas that are likely to have favorable market conditions.

8. In this chapter, we have seen three ways to generate random numbers for the Monte Carlo procedure: the index card approach, random-number tables, and pseudorandom numbers. Table 16.7 presented the results from simulating ten weeks of Caste's price behavior for Example 16.2 using the random-number table approach.

a. Use index cards and pseudorandom numbers to perform the same type of simulation shown in Table 16.7. Use one of the mathematical formulas in Graybeal and Pooch [9] to derive the pseudorandom numbers.

b. Tables 16.1 and 16.2 present the simulation results for the dealer competition problem (Example 16.1). Use the results from Table 16.7 and part (a) to derive similar simulations using index cards, a random-number table, and pseudorandom numbers.

Do the three approaches to Monte Carlo simulation lead to the same results? Explain.

9. Table 16.14 presents the simulated annual interest expense for Regional's investment financing situation (Example 16.3). It shows that an investment combination of $B = 140$ and $L = 140$ results in the smallest annual interest expense. Simulate additional investment combinations between $B = 140$ and $B = 145$ and between $L = 140$ and $L = 145$ in increments of 1. To use the simulator in Figure 16.5, input and run the program at your computer facility. In this problem, statement 3 becomes:

DO 500   K = 140, 145, 1

Statement 5 becomes:

DO 500   N = 140, 145, 1

If computer facilities are not available, simulate 20 years with the methods summarized in Tables 16.3 and 16.8. What do the results indicate?

10. Drill, Inc., knows that the chance of striking oil and the size of the strike depend on the presence of underground formations favorable for petroleum accumulation. When the formations exist, there is a 60% chance of striking oil. The following table gives the size of the strike and the corresponding probabilities:

Millions of barrels	40	80	120	160	200
Probability	.2	.3	.4	.05	.05

Even if the formations do not exist, there is still a 20% chance of striking oil. The size of the strike and the corresponding probabilities are as follows:

Millions of barrels	10	20	30	40	50
Probability	.1	.3	.4	.15	.05

Experience indicates that 50% of the sites explored have the underground formations.

a. Prepare a flowchart for this problem.
b. Use the Monte Carlo Method to simulate the results of exploring 20 sites. Show the computations in a table.
c. What is the total number of barrels projected from the 20-site exploration?
d. Based on the results from part (c), how many barrels should the company expect to strike if it explores 100 sites per year?

Applications Exercises

1. Fast Car Wash will buy a new waxing machine that is expected to have a useful life of 20 years. Even with good maintenance procedures, the machine will have periodic failures or breakdowns. Past records for similar machines indicate that the probabilities of failure during a year are as follows:

Number of Failures	Probability
0	.40
1	.20
2	.15
3	.10
4	.08
5	.07

Company management wants to simulate the number of breakdowns that will occur in the 20 years of operation.

You are asked to perform the simulation. According to the simulation, what will be the average number of breakdowns per year?

2. Gene Janen is the proprietor of Sweet Fragrance Floral Designs. He is trying to determine how many birthday bouquets to prepare each day. The objective is to maximize profits.

It costs $2 to prepare a birthday bouquet. Hence, with a $6 selling price, the floral shop realizes a $4 profit for each bouquet sold. However, if Gene overestimates demand, he must recycle the leftover bouquets at a salvage value of $.50.

Gene's decision is difficult because the daily demand is uncertain. He has experienced some days when there was no demand. Yet, one day last month there was a demand for 10 bouquets. The floral shop has the following data showing the daily demand during the past 100 days of operation:

Daily Demand	Number of Days Observed
0	5
1	8
2	12
3	20
4	30
5	15
6	5
7	5

If Gene continually fails to meet demand, he knows that the business will suffer a loss due to customer dissatisfaction. Gene estimates that the ill-will cost is $.60 per bouquet.

What quantity would give Gene the largest simulated profit over the next 30 days of operation?

3. The president of Western Telephone Company (WTC) has been informed that rank and file workers plan a strike action to protest working conditions. Unfortunately, the company's financial status makes it impossible to meet the workers' complete demands. Since the employees do not have substantial assets, the president is convinced that the strike will last no longer than one month.

   In consultation with WTC's personnel manager, the president has subjectively assessed the probabilities for the duration of the strike as follows:

Weeks on Strike	Probability
1	.20
2	.30
3	.40
4	.10

While the workers are on strike, the company must make alternative arrangements for phone service. Supervisory personnel can handle the work load on an interim basis. However, this arrangement will divert these people from their normal duties into unfamiliar activities. Company financial analysts estimate that the reassignment will involve an additional cost of $80,000 per week. There is an alternative. Universal Services, Inc., employs a variety of skilled personnel to continue service while the phone workers are on strike. Universal has proposed the following contract terms:

Weeks Contracted	Cost
1	$100,000
2	$180,000
3	$210,000
4	$240,000

Contracts can be renewed, or, for a $10,000 premium, a new agreement can be selected whenever an old pact expires.

What alternative will minimize Western's additional operating costs for a simulated 6 months of strike activity?

4. The Eastern Water Control Project (EWCP) wants to install a water recapture system at Portsmell along the banks of the Kihoshi River. In such a system, water from the Kihoshi would be diverted and stored for future agricultural and commercial needs. The system's ability to provide water is determined by its design configuration and demand. Future demand depends on temperature and the amount of rainfall. County records show that a normal year (of average temperature and rainfall) involves a demand for 200 million gallons of water. Demand increases by 1 million gallons for each degree increase in temperature above the norm. In addition, demand decreases by 2 million gallons for each additional inch of rainfall above the average. These relationships are symmetrical. Also, EWCP has the following meteorological data:

Temperature (°F)	Proportion of Days	Average Annual Rainfall (Inches)	Probability
20	.05	10	.10
40	.25	30	.30
60	.40	50	.50
80	.20	70	.10
100	.10		

Project management is considering two design configurations. Design A would involve a system of dams and pipelines. Design B would create a large single dam and an elaborate distribution system of pumping stations and storage areas. Each system has different annual amortized and operating costs. Relevant cost data are as follows:

Design	Annual Amortized Cost ($ Million)	Operating Cost ($1 per gallon)
A	6	.01
B	4	.02

EWCP wants to select the design configuration that will minimize total amortized plus operating costs over the next 20 years of operation. Which system should EWCP choose?

5. Tinseltown city management will add an airport route to its current public bus operations. Shown here are the alternatives being considered:

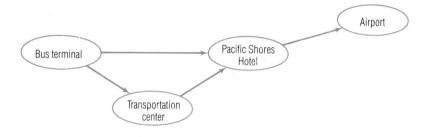

One route would start from the municipal bus station, go to a transportation center, move on to the Pacific Shores Hotel, and then proceed to the airport. The transportation center is a combination railway and intercity bus station located in the heart of town. Many airiline personnel and air travelers stay at the Pacific Shores Hotel because "it is close to everything." The other route would bypass the transportation center.

Bus service will be scheduled to complete each route once every hour. Each bus can carry 50 passengers at a cost of 20 cents per passenger mile. It is 15 miles from the bus terminal to the Pacific Shores Hotel and 5 more miles from there to the airport. The transportation center is 10 miles from both the hotel and the bus terminal. Fares will be collected at each stop according to the following fee schedule:

Route	Fare per Passenger ($)
Bus terminal to transportation center	1.50
Transportation center to Pacific Shores Hotel	1.50
Bus terminal to Pacific Shores Hotel	2.00
Pacific Shores Hotel to airport	0.50

Survey data indicate that hourly customer demand will be as follows:

Bus Terminal to Transportation Center		Transportation Center to Pacific Shores Hotel		Bus Terminal to Pacific Shores Hotel		Pacific Shores Hotel to Airport	
Number of Passengers	Probability	Number of Passengers	Probability	Number of Passengers	Probability	Number of Passengers	Probability
10	.20	10	.15	10	.05	10	.10
20	.50	20	.40	20	.25	20	.15
30	.25	30	.35	30	.45	30	.25
40	.05	40	.05	40	.15	40	.45
		50	.05	50	.10	50	.05

There are 5 buses available for the service. How many buses should city management schedule over each route to maximize simulated profits for the first 30 days of operation?

6. Bank of North America (BNA) issues a credit card. By law, the bank earns $1\frac{1}{2}\%$ interest per month on any unpaid credit balance of $500 or less. The bank charges 1% for any unpaid balance above $500. It costs BNA $.5\%$ to administer and finance balances of $1000 or less. Because of the increased likelihood for potential defaults and resulting legal expenses, larger balances involve an additional cost of $.75\%$.

A customer's current credit balance equals the unpaid amounts from previous months plus new purchases less payments. New purchases must not exceed the card holder's credit limit less any unpaid amounts from previous months. BNA sets the credit limit as a fixed proportion of the customer's recorded monthly income. Experience indicates that the bank is exposed to unacceptable risks when the proportion exceeds 40%.

Management wants to establish the proportion that will maximize profits from credit card operations. The decision is difficult because profits depend on the card holder's income, the amount owed, and monthly payments. Unfortunately, these amounts vary from customer to customer and month to month. The bank's accounting department has compiled the following data from credit records:

Reported Monthly Income ($)	Proportion of Customers	Monthly Payments ($)	Proportion of Customers	Amount Owed ($)	Proportion of Customers
1500	.05	50	.30	200	.50
2000	.10	100	.25	300	.35
2500	.15	150	.20	400	.10
3000	.40	200	.15	500	.05
3500	.25	250	.10		
4000	.05				

You are hired as a consultant.

a. Develop a model that recreates the credit card operation.
b. Simulate the next $2\frac{1}{2}$ years of operations for those customers that make new purchases equal to their available credit.
c. Recommend a credit limit policy.

CASE: Holiday Confections, Inc.

Holiday Confections, Inc., manufactures assorted candy products. The company's product line includes many stable items that sell at fairly uniform rates throughout the year. However, most of their revenue comes from gift-wrapped candy assortments for sale on special occasions, such as Valentine's Day, Easter, Thanksgiving, and Christmas. Consequently, Holiday's sales show pronounced seasonal variations. Expenses also fluctuate from month to month, and both sales and expenses are uncertain. Company records and recent experience provide the data shown in the following table:

The difference between sales and expenses gives Holiday's cash balance in any given month.

The company anticipates a net cash drain during the forthcoming year. Hence, management is searching for the pattern of financing that will minimize Holiday's total interest cost. The firm can borrow a maximum of $100,000 per month from a bank at an annual interest rate of 12%. The amount borrowed at the beginning of any month must be repaid with interest at the beginning of the following month. In addition, Holiday can issue up to $300,000 worth of 90-day commercial

paper bearing an annual interest rate of 9.6%. Interest charges on this paper are payable monthly. However, the amount borrowed at the beginning of each month cannot be repaid until the beginning of the third succeeding month. Also, the paper must be issued in $10,000 denominations. Any surplus funds are invested in government securities yielding 6% per annum.

Holiday's management has unsuccessfully tried to develop a financial plan. You are commissioned to develop a model that simulates this situation and to recommend a low-cost financial plan.

Quarter	Sales	Probability	Expenses	Probability
First	$200,000	.1	$400,000	.2
	300,000	.2	500,000	.4
	400,000	.5	600,000	.4
	500,000	.2		
Second	$400,000	.25	$300,000	.10
	600,000	.50	400,000	.15
	800,000	.25	500,000	.40
			600,000	.25
			700,000	.10
Third	$100,000	.2	$500,000	.4
	300,000	.4	700,000	.5
	500,000	.4	900,000	.1
Fourth	$ 500,000	.05	$400,000	.1
	700,000	.25	600,000	.7
	900,000	.60	800,000	.2
	1,100,000	.10		

Glossary

ABC (Pareto) system A selective control approach that classifies inventory into three groups: A, B, and C. Class A, which receives the most management attention, contains the few items with the largest value. Class C, which requires little control, contains the bulk of items with the smallest value. Class B, between the extremes, receives moderate management attention.

absorbing state A state that cannot be left once it is entered.

activities Specific tasks that use financial and/or physical resources and time and are required to complete a project.

activity slack The length of time an activity can be delayed without extending the project completion date.

ALP A prewritten computer package designed to solve large-scale assignment problems.

analog model A physical form that does not look like the real object or situation.

arcs (branches, links, edges) The lines connecting the nodes in a network.

arrival rate The number of customer arrivals into a queuing system per unit of time.

artificial variables Fictitious variables that enable the decision maker to develop an appropriate standard form and an initial basic feasible solution in the simplex method.

assignment problem A problem whose objective is to find the most effective way of assigning a group of indivisible resources to a set of indivisible tasks.

assignment table A standard tabular format used to conveniently record the data and keep track of the calculations in an assignment problem analysis.

asymmetric network A network in which the link between at least one pair of nodes is restricted to one-way traffic and/or has a different length in each flow.

backorder A customer order that is filled from future purchases rather than from inventory on hand.

backward induction The process of evaluating alternatives by successively working from right to left through the decision tree.

backward pass A procedure that determines the latest finish and start times for each activity by successively moving backward through the project network.

balking   Refusing to join a waiting line even though space is available.

basic feasible solution   A combination of decision and nondecision (slack, surplus, and artificial) variables that simultaneously satisfies all system constraints and the nonnegativity conditions in the standard form of a linear program.

basic solution   A combination of decision and nondecision (slack, surplus, or artificial) variables that simultaneously satisfies all system constraints in the standard form of a linear program.

basic variable   A variable that has a nonzero value in the basic solution of a linear program.

basis   The combination of basic variables in a solution for a linear program.

Bayesian analysis   The process of using additional information to revise and update the initial assessments of the event probabilities.

Bayes's formula (Bayes's theorem)   The relationship that states that a conditional probability is the ratio of a joint probability to a marginal probability. In decision analysis, it is used primarily to find the updated, or posterior, probabilities for the states of nature.

big M method   Assigning the artificial variables very large per-unit contributions to the criterion value.

bill of materials (BOM)   A structured parts list that shows exactly how the finished product is actually put together.

branch and bound method   An approach that develops an optimal solution by successively partitioning a problem into progressively smaller segments.

buffer (safety stock)   Extra inventory held specifically to reduce shortages resulting from a larger-than-expected demand during lead time.

canonical (standard) form   The form in which each nondecision variable (slack, surplus, or artificial variable) and decision variable is accounted for in the objective function, system constraints, and nonnegativity conditions of a linear program.

carrying (holding) costs   The expenses associated with financing, physically handling, storing, and maintaining inventory.

certainty   A situation where the decision maker knows exactly which state of nature will occur.

certainty equivalent   The sure outcome that the decision maker considers equivalent to a lottery providing a p chance for the best and a $(1 - p)$ likelihood of the worst outcomes in a decision problem.

chance-constrained programming   A methodology that accounts for parameter uncertainty by reformulating each original system constraint in a way that ensures that a mathematical programming solution provides a high probability of meeting the restriction.

closed path (loop)   The series of horizontal and vertical lines that trace the pattern of changes required by a reallocation in the transportation problem.

coefficient of optimism A value between 0 and 1 that measures the decision maker's degree of optimism concerning the attainment of the most favorable outcomes in a decision problem.

collectively exhaustive events A group of events that includes all possible future situations.

complementary slackness The relationships between the optimal values of the primal and dual variables.

conditional probability The probability of one event, given the condition that some other event has occurred.

constant sum game A game in which the outcomes to each participant sum to a constant value.

constraint A mathematical expression that describes restrictions or limitations involved in the problem.

controllable inputs (decision variables) Factors that influence the model's outcome and are controlled or determined by the decision maker.

courses of action (decision alternatives) The controllable inputs, or the options available to and controlled by the decision maker.

CPM A prewritten computer package designed to generate a complete activity schedule, determine the project cost, and identify the critical path in a PERT/CPM network.

crashing The process of adding resources (and usually cost) to reduce an activity time.

critical activity A task that must be started and finished without delay (has zero activity slack).

critical path The sequence of critical activities that leads from the starting event to the ending event in a project network.

critical path method (CPM) A network-based project management procedure that includes the capability of crashing.

cut A break that separates the source from the sink and thereby eliminates any flow through a network.

cutting plane method A procedure that obtains an optimal integer solution by successively adding constraints that eliminate fractional answers from a linear programming formulation of the problem.

data base An organized collection of data, usually in an MIS and frequently dealing with a firm's past and present operations.

DECIDE A computer program designed to solve sequential decision problems.

decision analysis (decision theory) A rational way to conceptualize, analyze, and solve problems in situations involving limited, or partial, information about the decision environment.

decision criteria Logical, or rational, methods for choosing the alternative that best meets the decision objectives.

decision point A square on a graph indicating that a choice must be made between two or more alternatives.

decision support system (DSS) An MIS that transforms "what if" questions into recommended decisions.

decision tree A graphic representation of the courses of

action, states of nature, and outcomes involved in a decision problem.

decision variables The controllable inputs in a linear programming problem.

degeneracy A condition in which the number of standard form variables with nonzero values is less than the number of system constraint equations.

deterministic model A model in which the values of the uncontrollable inputs are known exactly.

deterministic simulation A simulation in which the decision maker knows the values of the uncontrollable inputs.

deviational variables Variables that measure the amounts by which the target in a goal constraint will be exceeded or underachieved.

directed network A network in which flows can occur in only one direction.

dominance The situation where one alternative provides outcomes that are, for some events, equal to and, in one or more states, better than the payoffs from another action.

dual A linear programming problem that provides an alternative and complementary way of looking at the original (primal) program.

dummy activities Fictitious activities used to indicate the proper precedence in a PERT network.

dummy demand point A fictitious destination created to account for any excess supply in a transportation problem.

dummy resource A fictitious resource created to account for an excess task in an assignment problem.

dummy supply point A fictitious source created to account for any excess demand in a transportation problem.

dummy task A fictitious task created to account for an excess resource in an assignment problem.

dynamic programming A methodology designed to solve an optimization problem in a sequential manner.

earliest finish time The earliest time when a project activity may be completed.

earliest start time The earliest time when a project activity may begin.

Eastman/Shapiro algorithm A branch and bound methodology designed to solve traveling salesperson problems.

economic lot size (economic production quantity) The production quantity that minimizes total inventory-related costs in the EPQ model.

economic order quantity The order size that minimizes total inventory costs in the EOQ model.

efficiency rating The ratio of EVSI to EVPI multiplied by 100. It measures the ability of the sample, or indicator, information to accurately predict the states of nature.

entering variable The variable that is bought into the basis in the simplex method.

equilibrium first passage time The average number of trials that elapse before the system can make a transition from a specified state for the first time.

event (chance) point A circle on a graph indicating that two or more states of nature will follow.

events Points in time that mark the completion of all activities for a particular phase of a project.

events, possible futures, or states of nature The uncontrollable inputs or future events that affect the outcome of a decision.

event slack The length of time an event can be delayed without extending the project completion date.

exiting (departing) variable The variable that is taken out of the basis in the simplex method.

expected activity time The average time required to complete a PERT activity.

expected monetary value (EMV) criterion An expected value criterion in which the outcomes are measured in monetary terms.

expected net gain from sampling (ENGS) The difference between the EVSI and the cost of the sample or indicator information.

expected opportunity loss (EOL) criterion Selecting the decision alternative that leads to the smallest expected opportunity loss.

expected recurrence time The average elapsed time between the repeat occurrences of a specified state in an evolutionary process.

expected value An average found by multiplying each outcome by its probability of occurrence and then summing the results.

expected value criterion Selecting the decision alternative that leads to the best expected value.

expected value of perfect information (EVPI) The difference between the expected value under certainty (EVC) and the best expected value with only prior knowledge. It measures the expected value of information that would tell the decision maker exactly which state of nature will occur.

expected value of sample information (EVSI) The difference between the best expected value with the indicator information and the best expected value with only prior knowledge. It is a measure of the economic benefit that can be obtained from the specified sample, or indicator, information.

expected value under certainty (EVC) The best possible expected value of the objective if the decision maker knows exactly when each state of nature will occur.

extreme point A vertex, or intersection point, on the graph of the feasible solution area for a linear program. The intersection can occur between two restriction lines, between a restriction line and one of the axes, or at the origin.

feasible solution A combination of values for the decision variables that simultaneously satisfies all the restrictions in a linear program.

feasible solution area The region of a graph that contains the feasible solution points for a linear programming problem.

first-order Markov process A stochastic process in which the current state of the system depends only on the immediately preceding state.

fixed-order interval (P) system   A planning and control approach in which management periodically reviews available stock and then orders the amount necessary to reach a target inventory level. The target provides enough items to satisfy demand during the delivery lead time plus the interval between orders.

fixed order quantity (Q) system   A planning and control approach in which management continually reviews available stock and then places an order of fixed size whenever the inventory level reaches its reorder point.

flowchart   A diagram that shows the sequence of operations and computations required by the simulation model.

forward pass   A procedure that determines the earliest start and finish times for each activity by successively moving forward through the project network.

free slack   The length of time an activity can be delayed without affecting the activity slack available for other tasks in the network.

fundamental matrix   A rectangular array of numbers indicating the average number of periods that a system will remain in nonabsorbing states before being absorbed.

games   Problems that involve a conflict situation between two or more competing parties, each of whom knows the decision outcomes but is uncertain about the opponent's actions and reactions.

game strategy   A complete, predetermined plan for selecting a decision alternative for every possible circumstance. This plan should lead to the best expected outcome for the decision maker, regardless of the opponent's actions.

game table   A table showing the outcomes associated with each combination of decision alternatives in a conflict situation.

game theory   A framework for analyzing conflict situations.

GOAL   A prewritten computer package that can be used to solve relatively large-scale goal programming problems.

goal programming   A methodology designed to incorporate multiple criteria within the mathematical programming framework.

Gomory cut   A new constraint that eliminates some fractional decision variable combinations from a linear programming solution.

greedy algorithm   A procedure that can be used to find the minimal spanning tree.

homogeneous Markov chain   A Markov process with constant, or stationary, transition probabilities.

Hungarian method (Flood's technique, matrix reduction)   The standard procedure used to find an optimal solution to an assignment problem.

Hurwicz (coefficient of optimism) criterion   Weighting each best outcome by α and the corresponding worst payoff by $(1 - \alpha)$, summing the result, and then selecting the decision alternative that leads to the best weighted sum.

iconic model A physical replica of the real situation or object.

improvement index A value that measures the net effect on the objective of shipping one unit over a currently unused route in the transportation network.

indifference probability The event probability that equates the expected outcomes of the decision alternatives.

infeasible problem A linear program in which there is no combination of decision variables that simultaneously satisfies all restrictions.

inquiry-processing MIS An MIS that inputs "what if" questions into the data base and creates reports summarizing the projected consequences of possible conditions and decisions.

integer programming A methodology designed to deal with mathematical programming problems in which some or all of the decision variables must have whole-unit values.

interarrival time The time between two consecutive customer arrivals into a queuing system.

interservice time The interval between two consecutive service completions at a facility in a queuing system.

inventory Idle stocks of raw materials, capital, labor, equipment, work in process, or finished goods and services.

inventory cycle time The period between the placing of two consecutive orders.

inventory master file (IMF) Detailed records identifying the stock on hand, amounts previously committed to

production, quantities on order with suppliers, and lead times.

isocost line An isovalue line when the criterion is cost.

isoprofit line An isovalue line when the criterion is profit.

isovalue line The line on a graph that depicts all combinations of the decision variables yielding the same specific amount of the criterion variable.

iteration (pivoting) The process of moving from one basis to another in the simplex method.

jockeying Switching between multiple queues in an attempt to reduce waiting time.

joint probability The probability that two or more events will jointly occur.

labeling technique A procedure that can be used to find the shortest route through a network.

Laplace (rationality) criterion Selecting the decision alternative that leads to the best simple average outcome.

latest finish time The latest time when a project activity may be completed without delaying the entire project.

latest start time The latest time when a project activity may begin without delaying the entire project.

lead time The period between the placing of an order and its receipt.

linear program The complete formulation of a linear programming problem that includes the objective function, system constraints, and nonnegativity conditions.

linear programming A methodology for selecting the

combination of activities that most effectively uses an organizational unit's resources and meets specified restrictive guidelines.

linear programming sensitivity analysis A methodology for investigating the impact of parameter changes on the optimal primal and dual solutions to a linear program.

linear relationship A relationship in which each variable appears in a separate term and is raised to the first power (has an exponent of one). In a linear program, such a relationship indicates that each decision variable has an independent effect on the objective and the constraints and contributes a constant, proportional amount to the objective and each system constraint.

loop A sequence of branches that leads from a node back to itself through other nodes.

lottery indifference probability The probability that will make the decision maker indifferent to receiving a specified sure outcome or a risky lottery ticket. The lottery provides a p chance of earning the best possible outcome but a $(1 - p)$ likelihood of obtaining the worst payoff in a decision problem.

management information system (MIS) A system designed to collect, analyze, and report relevant and timely information needed by management to make effective decisions.

management science All systematic and rational approaches to decision making that are based on information and scientific analysis.

marginal probability The cumulative probability that an event will occur.

Markov analysis An approach designed to describe and predict the behavior of an evolutionary process.

Markov system An evolutionary process that generates a homogeneous Markov chain.

master production schedule (MPS) A time-phased plan that identifies how many finished items are to be produced and when.

material requirements planning (MRP) A system that develops a work and purchase order plan providing necessary components at the times required to support a production schedule for a finished product.

mathematical model A system of symbols and mathematical expressions that represent the real situation.

MAXF1 A prewritten computer package designed to find the maximal flow through a network.

maximal flow The largest quantity that can be sent through a network with branch flow capacities.

maximax criterion An optimistic criterion in which the objective is to find the largest outcome.

maximin criterion A pessimistic criterion in which the objective is to find the largest outcome.

maximum likelihood (ML) criterion Selecting the decision alternative that leads to the best outcome associated with the most probable state of nature.

mean first passage time The average number of trials that will elapse before the system changes from one state to another specified state for the first time.

minimal cut The network cut with the smallest total capacity.

minimal spanning tree A series of links that will minimize the total length of the branches required to connect all the nodes in a network.

minimax criterion A pessimistic criterion in which the objective is to find the smallest outcome.

minimin criterion An optimistic criterion in which the objective is to find the smallest outcome.

mixed integer programming problem An integer programming problem in which some, but not all, decision variables must have integer solution values.

mixed strategy The strategy whereby a participant in a game randomly shifts from one decision alternative to another.

model A simplified representation of a real object or situation.

modified distribution (MODI) method A procedure that evaluates a transportation solution by comparing direct expenses to the cost savings associated with each unused route in the network.

Monte Carlo simulation An approach that uses a random selection procedure (such as a deck of index cards or a random-number table) to generate the stochastic inputs for a simulation model.

most likely time The most frequent time required to complete a PERT task under normal conditions.

MRKV1 A prewritten computer package designed to perform a Markov analysis.

multiperiod decision A sequential decision in which the alternatives are selected at several points in time.

multiobjective programming A methodology designed to solve mathematical programming problems that involve separate objective functions for each relevant combination of decision variables.

multiple (alternative) optima The existence of more than one optimal solution to a linear program.

Multi Purpose Optimization System (MPOS) A prewritten computer package that can be used to solve relatively large-scale integer programming problems.

multistage decision A sequential decision in which tasks are arranged in a natural order.

mutually exclusive events Events that cannot occur simultaneously.

negative exponential distribution A probability distribution used to describe the pattern of interarrival and/or service times for some queuing systems.

network A diagram consisting of junction points interconnected by a series of lines that carry a flow through the system.

nodes The junction points (circles) of a network.

nonbasic variable A variable that is set equal to zero in the basic solution of a linear program.

nonlinear program A mathematical program that

consists of a nonlinear objective function and/or at least one nonlinear system constraint.

nonlinear programming　Any methodology designed to solve a nonlinear program.

nonlinear relationship　A relationship in which a decision variable has an exponent different than 1 and/or more than one activity appears in a single term of the relevant mathematical expression.

nonnegativity conditions Constraints requiring the decision variables to have values greater than or equal to zero.

northwest corner method　A procedure that finds an initial feasible solution to a transportation problem by making allocations by moving down and to the right through the transportation table.

objective function　A mathematical expression that describes the objective of a problem.

objective probability　The proportion of times that an event was actually observed in the past or in an experiment.

on line　Interacting directly with a computer system.

optimal policy　The series of decisions that will lead to the best outcome over all stages in an evolutionary process.

optimistic criterion　Selecting the decision alternative that leads to the best of the most favorable outcomes.

optimistic time　The time required to complete a PERT activity under ideal conditions.

ordering (setup) costs　The expenses associated with placing an order or physically preparing the production apparatus.

parametric programming　A form of postoptimality analysis in which the decision maker examines how specified continuous variations in the uncontrollable inputs influence the optimal linear programming solution.

path　The series of links that leads from the source to the sink of a network.

payoff (decision outcome)　The outcome that will result from the combination of a decision alternative and a state of nature.

payoff table (decision table)　A tabular representation of the elements (courses of action, states of nature, and outcomes) in a decision-making problem.

PERT　A prewritten computer package designed to solve PERT problems.

PERT/COST　A variation of PERT designed to assist program directors in managing project costs.

PERT network　A network in which the arcs represent project activities and the nodes represent project events.

pessimistic time　The time required to complete a PERT task under adverse conditions.

pivot column　The column in the simplex table that corresponds to the entering variable.

pivot element　The entry in a simplex table that is at the intersection of the pivot row and pivot column. It identifies the quantity of the exiting variable that must be given up to obtain one unit of the entering variable.

pivot row   The row in the simplex table that corresponds to the exiting, or departing, variable.

Poisson distribution   A probability distribution used to describe the random arrival rate for some queuing systems.

posterior analysis   The process of using sample, or indicator, information to develop a decision strategy.

posterior probability   The revised or updated probability of a state of nature, given the condition that a particular indicator has occurred.

postoptimality analysis   The examination of the optimal solution to an original linear program to identify the economic values of scarce resources and restrictive guidelines and to determine the effect of parameter changes on the problem.

preemptive priority system   A system in which an important arrival not only has entrance priority but can even interrupt the service on other, less significant, customers.

preemptive weight   A symbol indicating the priority assigned by the decision maker to the corresponding deviational variable.

preposterior analysis   The process of evaluating sample, or indicator, information.

primal   The original linear programming problem.

principle of insufficient reason   The principle that says if there is no basis for claiming that one event has a higher probability than another, each should be assigned an equal likelihood.

principle of optimality   The principle whereby the current state provides all the information about the previous system behavior that is needed to determine the optimal policy for every subsequent stage in a sequential decision process.

prior decision   A decision based on the prior probabilities.

prior probabilities   Preliminary, or initial, assessments of the probabilities for the states of nature.

probability tree   A diagram that organizes the prior and conditional indicator probabilities in a convenient format.

procurement costs   The expenses associated with purchasing or manufacturing items for demand and inventory.

program evaluation ahd review technique (PERT)   A network-based procedure for planning, scheduling, and controlling large-scale projects.

pseudorandom numbers   Computer-generated numbers, developed from mathematical formulas, that have the properties of random numbers.

pure integer programming   A situation in which all the decision variables in the mathematical program must have integer solutions.

pure strategy   The strategy whereby each party repeatedly selects only one decision alternative, regardless of the competitor's strategy.

queue discipline   The manner in which customers from the waiting area are selected for service.

queuing theory Quantitative approaches that measure the operating characteristics and costs of waiting lines.

random selection A method of selecting an input in a way that each value in a sequence is independent and has an equal chance of being selected.

range of feasibility The range of values over which a constraint amount can fluctuate without altering the optimal basis in a linear program.

range of optimality The range of values over which an objective function coefficient can fluctuate without altering the optimal basis and basic variable amounts in a linear program.

real time A computer system that can immediately provide processing results to the user.

recursive relationship An equation that ties together the outcomes obtained at all stages of a sequential decision process.

redundant restriction A system constraint that does not affect the feasible solution area and thus is irrelevant to the solution of a linear programming problem.

regret (opportunity loss) The difference between the best possible payoff for a state of nature and the outcome actually received from selecting a decision alternative.

regret table (opportunity loss table) A tabular representation of the decision alternatives, states of nature, and opportunity losses associated with a decision problem.

reneging Departing from the queuing system before being served.

reorder point The inventory level at which a new order should be placed.

report-generating MIS An MIS that creates historical and current status reports on business activities.

result variables Measures used to evaluate the performance or effectiveness of a system.

risk A situation in which the decision maker can assess only the probability of occurrence for each state of nature.

risk averse Willing to sacrifice some monetary value in order to avoid risk.

risk complex Displaying a combination of risk-averse, risk-neutral, and risk-seeking attitudes toward a range of monetary values.

risk neutral Neither seeking nor avoiding risk, but instead prizing money at its face value.

risk seeking Willing to take a high risk of a large loss in order to have an opportunity for a substantial gain.

row vector of state probabilities A list of state probabilities arranged as a row of numbers.

saddle point The equilibrium solution formed when each participant in a game adopts a pure strategy.

sample (indicator) information The new or additional knowledge provided through surveys, experiments, or simulations.

Savage (regret) criterion Selecting the decision alternative that leads to the smallest of the largest possible regrets.

scientific method The process of observing the situation, defining the problem, postulating a hypothesis, experimenting, and verifying the hypothesis.

sensitivity analysis Measuring the sensitivity of a prior decision to changes in the uncontrollable inputs.

sequential decision A problem that involves a series of interrelated decisions.

service level The percentage of customer demands that is satisfied from inventory.

service rate The number of customers served by a facility in a queuing system per unit of time.

shadow price The change in the criterion value that results from a one-unit change in the amount of a constraint.

SHARE A library of computer programs for management science commercially available on a national basis at a nominal cost to users.

SHORI A prewritten computer package designed to find the shortest route through a network.

shortest route A series of links that will minimize the total length of the branches required to connect a specified origin with a particular destination in a network.

simplex method A methodology designed to systematically solve large-scale linear programming problems.

simplex table A tabular format that conveniently organizes, keeps track of, and helps perform the calculations involved in the simplex method.

SIMSCRIPT, GASP, SLAM, and GPSS Popular computer languages used for simulation studies.

simulation A technique that uses a model to recreate an actual situation and then studies the system's characteristics and behavior by experimenting with the model.

simulator The computer program that performs the simulation operations and computations.

sink node The specified destination node for the flow over the branches in a network.

slack variable A variable that accounts for any unused, or idle, amounts of a resource.

solution point A point on a graph that identifies a particular value of each decision variable in a linear programming solution.

source node The specified origin node of the flow over the branches in a network.

spanning The process of connecting all nodes in a network.

SPNT1 A prewritten computer package designed to find the minimal spanning tree in a network.

stage transformation (transfer function) The manner in which a subsequent state is determined from the immediately preceding state and decision in a sequential process.

state The condition of the system at a particular trial of the evolutionary process.

state probability The likelihood that a system will be in a particular state at a specified trial of an evolutionary process.

steady-state probabilities The equilibrium values at which the state probabilities eventually stabilize after a very large number of trials for an evolutionary process.

stepping stone method A procedure that evaluates a transportation solution by tracing the pattern of changes required with each reallocation.

stochastic model A model in which the values of the uncontrollable inputs are uncertain and subject to variation.

stochastic programming A methodology that accounts for parameter uncertainty by incorporating stochastic elements into an expanded version of the original mathematical program.

stockout (shortage) costs The expenses incurred when available inventory is insufficient to fully satisfy demand.

subjective probability The decision maker's personal belief or judgment about the likelihood of a future event.

subtour A sequence of links that starts at the source, visits some (but not all) nodes in the network only once, and then returns to the origin.

surplus variable A variable that accounts for any excess, or extra, amount beyond some specified minimum requirement.

symmetric network A network in which the link between any pair of nodes has an identical length in either flow direction.

system A collection of interrelated parts intended to accomplish specific objectives.

system constraint A constraint on the linear programming solution that arises from limited resources, policy requirements, and the like.

systems approach Method of examining a problem from a systems perspective.

team (multidisciplinary) approach Approach in which a group of people from several disciplines analyze a problem.

technological (structural) constraint A restriction that deals with a resource capacity or other nongoal-oriented limitation.

time sharing The utilization of a computer system by many different users, typically through a series of remote terminals.

time to absorption The average number of periods that elapse before a nonabsorbing state is absorbed.

tour A sequence of links that starts at the source, visits each node in the network only once, and then returns to the origin.

trade ratio A ratio that identifies the maximum amount of the entering variable that can be obtained for the entire amount of a basic variable.

TRANLP A prewritten computer package designed to solve large-scale transportation problems.

transition matrix A list of transition probabilities arranged as a rectangular array of numbers.

transition probability The likelihood that a system will move from one state to another between trials of an evolutionary process.

transition table A table used to record and keep track of the transition probabilities involved in a Markov system.

transportation problem Problem whose objective is to find the most effective way of distributing a commodity from a group of supply sources to a set of demand destinations.

transportation table A standard tabular format used to conveniently record the data and keep track of the calculations in a transportation problem analysis.

transshipment point A location in a distribution network that can receive merchandise from one shipping point and then reship it to another destination.

transshipment problem A problem in which the objective is to find the most effective way of distributing merchandise from a group of supply sources, through transshipment points, and on to a set of demand destinations.

traveling salesperson problem A problem whose objective is to find the minimal-length tour through a network.

trial (stage) A point at which the decision maker observes an evolutionary process.

unbounded problem A linear program in which the constraints do not put an effective limit on the values of the decision variables.

uncertainty A situation in which the decision maker can identify the states of nature but is unable to assess their likelihood of occurrence.

uncontrollable inputs (environmental variables) Factors that must be considered but are beyond the decision maker's control.

utility A comprehensive criterion that incorporates absolute numerical measures (like monetary value) and intangible factors (such as attitudes and perceptions). It measures the true worth of the outcomes to the decision maker.

utility curve A graph that shows the relationship between monetary value and utility.

utility table A table that identifies the utility to management of each decision outcome.

utilization factor The proportion of time that the service facilities are in use.

value of the game The expected outcome of the conflict when each opponent repeatedly selects its optimal strategy.

variable sum game A game in which each combination of the opponents' decision alternatives typically will yield a different outcome sum to the participants.

Vogel's approximation method (VAM) A procedure that utilizes the opportunity loss concept to find an initial feasible solution to a transportation problem.

Wald (pessimistic) criterion Selecting the decision alternative that leads to the best of the worst possible outcomes.

work package A unit in PERT/COST formed by grouping naturally interrelated project activities for cost control purposes.

zero/one (binary integer) programming problem An integer programming problem in which each decision variable must have a solution of one or zero.

zero sum game A game in which the gains of one participant are necessarily the equivalent losses to the opponent. It represents a special type of constant sum game in which the sum of the outcomes is always zero.

Author Index

Subject Index